MW00577881

WHITE
SPOTS

. . . .

BLACK
SPOTS

PITT SERIES IN RUSSIAN AND EAST EUROPEAN STUDIES

Jonathan Harris, Editor

WHITE SPOTS

· ·

BLACK SPOTS

DIFFICULT MATTERS IN POLISH-RUSSIAN RELATIONS, 1918–2008

EDITED BY

ADAM DANIEL ROTFELD

&

ANATOLY V. TORKUNOV

UNIVERSITY OF PITTSBURGH PRESS

Published by the University of Pittsburgh Press, Pittsburgh, Pa., 15260
Copyright © 2015, University of Pittsburgh Press
All rights reserved
Manufactured in the United States of America
Printed on acid-free paper
10 9 8 7 6 5 4 3 2 1

ISBN 10: 0-8229-4440-5
ISBN 13: 978-0-8229-4440-9

Cataloging-in-Publication data is available from the Library of Congress.

Originally published in Polish as *Białe plamy—Czarne plamy: Sprawy trudne w relacjach polsko-rosyjskich (1918–2008)*
© 2010 Polski Instytut Spraw Międzynarodowych and Autorzy, Warsaw

Originally published in Russian as *Belye piatna—chernye piatna: Slozhnye voprosy v rosskiisko-polskikh otnosheniyakh*
© 2010 Aspekt Press, Moscow

In memory of contributors
Andrzej Przewoźnik
and
Nikolai I. Bukharin

CONTENTS

PREFACE

We offer our American readers a unique volume. It is the result of the collaboration of thirty-one Polish and Russian scholars—historians, political scientists, and economists. The work came into being at the initiative of the Polish-Russian Group for Difficult Matters, which was revived in 2008 by a decision of the governments of Poland and Russia (an earlier group had previously suspended its activity). In essence, the book is an attempt to present relations between Poland and Russia over the last ninety years, with particular reference to the most complex and controversial issues. A distinctive feature of the methodology incorporated herein consists in presenting the same problems from the viewpoints of the Polish and Russian researchers. The authors did not seek to uncover new, unknown facts and documents pertaining to the latest history of Polish-Russian relations but rather to achieve—from two different perspectives—a synthesis and assessment of facts, events, and processes that were known and unquestioned. Thus, the Polish and Russian scholars describe in fifteen parts the place in the memory of the two nations occupied by issues that often evoke emotional disputes and hinder the development of normal, future-oriented relations between Poland and Russia.

Disputes and divergent interpretations of the same facts and processes are natural and normal among academics. They occur not only due to different national memories and the different mentalities and cultures of the respective societies but also because of different schools of methodology in historical research. Thus, opinions depend not so much on the nationality of their authors as on their professional training and competence, though also on the time factor—generational change and access to new archival resources. Importantly, these opinions are the function of changes in the systems of values that guide societies in their mutual relations at different stages of the historical process.

In our work on this collection we did not strive to gloss over differences—and neither were we guided by any "political correctness." On the contrary: the authors had full freedom to present their points of view; at times the positions of the Polish and Russian scientists were convergent and their assessment of historical facts almost identical. The book also addresses issues where differences dominated. The editors fully and unconditionally respected the authors' right to free choice of methodology and presentation of independent judgments.

In effect, certain chapters (mainly by Polish authors) have the character of a synthesis, while others (mostly by Russian authors) are analytical and descriptive. Some are succinct and refer to common knowledge, while others minutely recall events and extensively recount various documents such as diplomatic cables, reports, and the relevant literature. Yet, all the authors, both Polish and Russian, have demonstrated integrity in presenting the historical truth—to the degree allowed by their knowledge of the source materials available at the time of writing.

This publication constitutes a first attempt to compile an "inventory" of issues demanding further research. Some of these problems—to specifically mention the Katyn crime—were the subject of lies over many years and required restoration and the manifestation of the full truth. The authors of the section on this subject, Andrzej Przewoźnik (Poland) and Natalia S. Lebedeva (Russia), differed over certain details and the motives behind the crime. However, their ruminations complement one another and are convergent in essence, particularly as regards the facts and moral qualification of the perpetrators of the crime. Many other chapters evoke similar observations and reflections.

This book is a recapitulation of the knowledge to date. It also constitutes a point of departure for further studies, with the purpose of filling in the remaining "white spots" with new findings of historians and eradicating the "black spots" by purging history of past lies and rejecting falsehoods, half-truths, myths, legends, and stereotypes accumulated over the years. They were a product of times when pseudohistorians were in the service of propaganda, while the freedom of research and access to archives were hindered and restricted by ideological and political considerations. The cooperation of Polish and Russian academics on this volume has demonstrated that, in Polish-Russian relations, it is possible in the sphere of history to jointly seek the full truth.

This abridged English edition contains mainly the summaries of the original Polish and Russian studies. Therefore, as a rule, the texts are not accompanied by references. Source citations are limited to direct quotations from documents. It is done with an understanding that the professional readers—scholars, researchers, and specialists—will consult, if needed, the original Polish- and Russian-language editions for all notes and source information, including the chapter on bibliography that is omitted in the English edition.

We express our appreciation to the translators (Polish contributions translated by Andrzej Więcko; Russian contributions translated by Andrei Vechyor-Scherbovich, Andrei Yegorov, Yekaterina Presniakova, Anastasia Popova, and Nina Dymshits), editors (including Masha Ogneva, Sergei Ognev, Craig Markham, John Lambert, Vladislav Vorotnikov, Marina Vasilevskaya, Katarzyna Rawska-Górecka, and Maureen Creamer Bemko), and all others without whose involvement the English edition of the joint publication would not have been possible in such fine editorial form and layout. We extend particular thanks to Peter Kracht, director of the University of Pittsburgh Press.

Grants by the Ministry of Foreign Affairs of the Republic of Poland and the Moscow High School Economic Development Foundation permitted successful implementation of the whole project, of which the English edition of this book is a key part.

WHITE
SPOTS
....
BLACK
SPOTS

ADAM DANIEL ROTFELD AND ANATOLY V. TORKUNOV

. . . .

INTRODUCTION

. . . .

IN SEARCH OF THE TRUTH

A BRIEF HISTORY OF THE POLISH-RUSSIAN GROUP ON DIFFICULT MATTERS

I

Times are changing. The same is true of people, countries, and the value systems guiding politicians in their endeavors at home and in relations with neighboring states. Twenty years after the start of the Great Transition and demise of the division of Europe into East and West, Poland and Russia have made a joint effort to clear their relations of the lies and deceit that have accumulated over the years. Our countries are trying to build a relationship based on partnerlike respect for national interests and on recognizing what is distinct and specific to each partner.

The current state of Polish-Russian relations carries the burden of history. Our memory of historical events significantly contributes to how we look at the world and how we perceive ourselves in the world around us. It is important to ensure that memory is not subject to manipulation and deliberate falsification of the past, that it resists attempts to obliterate the traces of what was shameful and deserves to be condemned.

Historical facts are indisputable. However, their interpretation may vary. Different nations have different assessments of the same events. Moreover, the passage of time makes new generations evaluate historical facts and events in a different way than their ancestors did. This is because the new generations are aware of the consequences of decisions made by their forebears.

Those who believe that it was not the Katyn massacre but the lie about the crime that put a divide between the Poles and Russians are right. Meanwhile, truth purifies, as Russian prime minister Vladimir V. Putin said on 7 April 2010 in Smolensk. Polish prime minister Donald Tusk added, "Truth not only purifies, but also illuminates." These words were uttered after the close of joint Polish-Russian commemorations in the Katyn Forest, organized to mark the passage of seventy years since the crime.

After the end of the mourning ceremonies, the two prime ministers met with the co-chairs of the Polish-Russian Group on Difficult Matters. During the meeting, they voiced appreciation for the work of our group, without which the joint commemoration to remember the Polish officers shot and killed in the Katyn Forest probably would not have taken place.

Established by the governments of both countries, the group has played the role of a catalyst in Polish-Russian bilateral relations. One of the results of the work of the Polish-Russian Group on Difficult Matters is the joint volume titled *White Spots—Black Spots: Difficult Matters in Polish-Russian Relations, 1918–2008,* published both in Warsaw and Moscow (in Polish and Russian, respectively). This book is based on the expertise of Polish and Russian scholars who, over fifteen pairs of chapters, assess the most difficult problems in bilateral relations over ninety years, from 1918 to 2008, in a "mirror" approach incorporating both the Polish and Russian perspectives. This book is about our common history in the twentieth century—a history that the two countries were largely destined to share. Polish and Russian authors wrote this book together, with readers in both Poland and Russia in mind. They tried to do this in a way so as to distance themselves from the difficult but, we repeat, shared past of the two countries. They were doing so with the future in mind—so that it is based on truth and mutual understanding.

II

The road to publishing this volume was not an easy one. It all began in 2002, when the leaders of our countries decided to create a mechanism unusual in the practice of international relations—the Group on Difficult Matters in light of Polish-Russian history. The group in its original makeup (which was entirely different from the current composition, as appointed in 2008) first met in 2005 and later held another meeting. These sessions, however, did not produce the expected results. This was in part due to political tension in Polish-Russian relations at the time.

A fundamental change in the lineup of the group took place in December 2007, when it acquired what in fact was a new status. Without going into the reasons behind that, we should note that in the early years of the twenty-first century, the concept of "historical policy" gained popularity, and that approach is not easy to assess. Problems arising from historical events affected interstate relations across Europe. The leaders of both our countries came to the conclusion that historical issues had in fact become an obstacle to the development of present-day relations between Poland and Russia, as well as between the Polish and Russian people. The focus was on the need to understand and explain how joint efforts can help deal with problems arising from historical events.

Such an effort can be successful only if both parties pay the utmost attention to each other's arguments, are ready to seek a compromise, and express a sincere desire to bring about a situation in which history is dealt with by historians and the truth is restored to the people.

Was this a difficult task? Not in strategic terms. We understood our goal in the same way: we wanted good relations and to relieve them of the burden of mutual historical grievances. But from a tactical point of view, this was not a simple task. We had to find a way of doing this.

The idea of giving the group a new status gained acceptance among political leaders and foreign ministry officials in both countries several months before the first meeting of the co-chairs, who at that time did not yet realize that such a role would be assigned to them. As a result, a decision was made to appoint new members and co-chairs of the group and to define a new mandate for the Group on Difficult Matters.

With relief, we welcomed the news about the names of the new members of the group. First, we knew each other, though not very well. Second, we had extensive experience under our belts and highly respected each other's research achievements. Third, as the co-chairs, we enjoyed considerable autonomy and freedom in making decisions. Fourth, senior officials and diplomats from both Poland and Russia demonstrated a willingness to help and showed great confidence in us.

The first meeting of the co-chairs was held on "neutral" ground, in Brussels (1–2 February 2008). We exchanged proposals we had prepared beforehand. They concerned the composition of the group, the range of issues requiring discussion, the procedures and frequency of meetings, and opinions on the desired and possible results of our activities. We then realized that the conditions had been created for us to go ahead with our work.

The composition of the Polish and Russian parts of the group was decided according to a rather complicated, but—as it turned out later—quite reasonable rule of thumb. It was obvious that historians familiar with the history of our two countries and aware of the European historical context of the last century should be present in both parts. However, the group was not intended to be a commission on history. It was important that those taking part in the group's work be experts who deal with contemporary affairs and realize how historical problems affect the present-day policies of our countries and how societies react to various historical issues taken up by the other party.

It was only natural that those who were responsible for solving the problems of history professionally—either as members of the legal profession or in their work as civil servants—had to be included in the group. This explains why lawyers and investigators, especially those focusing on the Katyn massacre, were invited to join our group. State archives employees also became members of the group. To work efficiently, the group needed people representing both countries' foreign ministries. Diplomats helped adapt our work schedule to the state of official relations between our countries, and they sometimes made it easier to find tactical ways of reaching compromise and achieving success together.

At a fairly early stage, we clarified what range of problems the group should deal with. We decided against discussing issues in which we had no authority or authorization—such as the still-unresolved ownership issues left behind after a period of legal "nihilism." This prohibition also applied to other economic and financial matters.

The group did not aspire to replace anyone or anything. To the best of our abilities, we filled those gaps in bilateral relations involving difficult historical matters that objectively existed and required resolution.

Neither did we aspire to formulate any new hypotheses or to make discoveries about history or a legal assessment of our past. To use official language, we took stock and systematized what other researchers before us had already found. This approach produced surprising results: it turned out that, in reality, there were not so many contradictions or major differences over facts. There was more emotion, which stemmed from a lack of desire or willingness to listen to or to hear what the other party had to say.

In this way the group embarked upon a historical retrospective covering almost a century—from the emergence of Soviet Russia and an independent Poland on the rubble of empires during and after World War I to the new breakup of the world order in the late 1980s and early 1990s, which marked another change of trajectory in the history of our countries.

III

The first session of the group in its new composition took place in Warsaw on 12–14 June 2008. This meeting was preceded by a separate meeting of Polish and Russian members of the group, organized among themselves, during which both sides set out their expectations about the program and what course the work should take. A few weeks earlier, the co-chairs had preliminarily agreed on the schedule of work.

We admit we were rather nervous ahead of that first meeting. This apprehensiveness was due to public expectations and reports in the press, especially as some of the assessments and views presented in them introduced an additional feeling of nervousness and irritability. We note with satisfaction that the Polish and Russian participants of the group distanced themselves from the pressure and talk surrounding the event.

To begin with, the group adopted a "zero option"—no mutual prejudices and complexes. The start of the group's meeting was not very formal in nature: most of its members met on 12 June 2008 at a reception celebrating a Russian national holiday and organized by the embassy of the Russian Federation in Warsaw.

The proper, active portion of the group's meeting took place in a palace owned by the Ministry of Foreign Affairs. In the courtyard of Przeździecki Palace, a building that has witnessed many international meetings and events, a group of journalists gathered. We were greeted by Radosław Sikorski, the Polish foreign minister, and Vladimir M. Grinin, the Russian ambassador to Poland. As the co-chairs of the group, we presented the positions of both parties, our visions, and the preliminary agreements we had made earlier. Then, with all members of the group taking part, a debate began with the aim of agreeing on a plan of work. This procedure later became routine in the work of the group.

When discussing our mandate and new tasks, we noted that neither the political aspect nor other aspects of relations between our two countries had met the expectations of the public in Poland and Russia in recent years. Members of the group said they were pleased to welcome an improvement in the political atmosphere, which is conducive to resolving the difficult and sensitive questions that history has left behind. They voiced the view that difficult problems of history should not be subject to political games; they require courage and responsibility from politicians and researchers in seeking solutions. In particular, this call for fortitude applies to the need to clearly explain all the circumstances and various aspects of the Katyn massacre, as well as to making the necessary political decisions in this area.

The members of the group unanimously and clearly stated that one of the key objectives of their work was to remove obstacles to the adoption, at the highest level, of solutions that would become a solid foundation for partnerlike relations based on truth and mutual respect. The group once again confirmed that its aim is not to replace other state institutions and structures established with a view to developing mutual relations between Poland and the Russian Federation. The group's work is instead designed to support state institutions in addressing those problems from the past that hinder mutual relations and inhibit their development.

At the very beginning, during the first meeting, it was decided that the group and its co-chairs would be guided in their activities by two complementary principles. First, our task would be to draw up recommendations—which should be both principled and realistic—for the authorities of both countries on how to better and more quickly remove historical obstacles from the agenda of current politics. Another purpose of our work would be to prepare a joint historical/documentary publication that would reach the widest possible audience.

Our common concern was to make sure that the publication presented both the Polish and Russian points of view on key contentious issues from the twentieth century in relations between our countries and peoples. Some of these problems were preliminarily defined during the Warsaw meeting. It was only natural that priority was given to issues related to the Katyn massacre and the war of 1920, as well as to the origins of World War II and to the development of the postwar world order.

Participants in the group proceeded from an assumption that including problematic and sensitive issues in a single publication would make it possible for those who revisit the political aspects of history in order to weigh their meaning to refer to this study in a formal way and with confidence.

To make the group's work as transparent, open, and interesting to the public and the media as possible, members decided that each meeting would end with a press conference. It was also decided that seminars involving experts focusing on current topics would be organized to accompany the meetings and that support would be given to organizing—under the auspices of the group and with the participation of its members—academic conferences and roundtable talks, as well as the preparation of joint publications.

Members of the group welcomed information from the co-chairs about their contacts with officials from the Roman Catholic Church in Poland and the Russian Orthodox Church. On this occasion it was noted that signals of readiness from both churches to actively join in social dialogue and ongoing efforts to bring about rapprochement between the Polish and Russian peoples would help add a spiritual dimension to relations between our two countries. The cooperation between the group and its co-chairs and church authorities continued, contributing significantly to the success of our work in the later stages.

An important event during the first meeting of the group was undoubtedly the participation of Prime Minister Tusk, who also provided a statement. That same day (13 June 2008), both co-chairs also were received by Lech Kaczyński, the Polish president. The presence of these high officials lent status to the meetings and was of significance because it encouraged the group's participants to continue constructively and productively working together.

One could be tempted to cite what the late president Kaczyński said at some length, but his approach was best reflected by one remark he made to us. Half jokingly, half seriously, he said, "It's often said that I'm supposedly a russophobe. That's not the case. Russian is the foreign language I know. Besides, both my great-grandfathers served in the Russian army."

The next day, 14 June, an open meeting of the group was held, and it was attended by the heads of the Federation of Katyn Families and other nongovernmental organizations and the media. It is worth noting that Andrzej Sariusz-Skąpski, president of the Federation of Katyn Families, and Bożena Łojek, president of the Polish Katyn Foundation, while calling for rehabilitation of the murdered Polish officers' good names, clearly stressed that they were interested in the moral, ethical, and political—and not the financial—aspects of the issue.

Between the group's meetings, active work continued on the blueprint of the joint publication. In collaboration with historians and lawyers, group members worked out the details of decisions on its concept and shape. Members of the group engaged in direct talks with the co-chairs. Contacts also were maintained as part of the Polish-Russian Civic Forum, which was chaired on the Polish side by Krzysztof Zanussi, the famous film director, and, on the Russian side, by Leonid V. Drachevsky, former ambassador to Poland. This structure was a convenient channel through which to inform the general public about the work of the group.

IV

The second session of our group was held in Moscow on 27–28 October 2008. This meeting was slightly less formal, because we already knew each other, had told each other about our expectations, and had a sense of working on a joint project. The group's meeting was held at the Reception House of the Russian Ministry of Foreign Affairs, a villa on Spiridonovka Street. Sergey V. Lavrov, the Russian foreign minister, opened the meeting.

It is important to abandon a selective approach to historical discourse, the minister said. "Talks about history require a comprehensive approach, according to the principle: the whole truth and nothing but the truth," he added. "Selective truth is always dangerous, primarily for those who are willing to accept it as the ultimate truth. History does not begin with a specific date; it is a process that consists entirely of cause-and-effect relationships. The course of historical development teaches us that, if the past is treated superficially and—even worse—in a way that is openly speculative, it becomes the basis for new political myths that poison the atmosphere in relations between states and peoples."

In keeping with the previously adopted practice, Jerzy Bahr, the Polish ambassador to Russia, took the floor during the session. On the Russian side, Deputy Foreign Minister Vladimir G. Titov also attended the meeting of the group. Along with his Polish counterpart, Deputy Foreign Minister Andrzej Kremer, he showed support for our work at all stages. The opening part of the group's Moscow meeting, with the foreign minister in attendance, was open to the press. As a result, the Russian media received more extensive information about the group's work.

During the Moscow meeting, the specific nature of the group's activities—based on almost continuous consultations during the group's stay in the host country—was finally approved. It was important to collect and take into account the views of all individuals who could contribute to the work of the group, thus making each other aware of the approach of both parties and settling emerging problems as a routine procedure.

A significant part of the Moscow session was spent discussing the concept of the joint publication. Participants formulated goals about the content specific chapters and those issues that should absolutely be reflected in the joint collective work. We agreed that members of the group would come up with the first, preliminary versions of their texts by the spring of 2009.

The group welcomed a plan to prepare a separate publication focusing on the seventieth anniversary of the outbreak of World War II. The institutions responsible for preparing the book were the Polish Institute of International Affairs (PISM, in Polish) and the Moscow State Institute of International Relations (MGIMO, in Russian). The coeditors of this publication were Sławomir Dębski, PhD, on the Polish side, and Prof. Mikhail M. Narinsky, on the Russian side. Among the contributors were many members of the group, who in this somewhat smaller circle managed to work out the practical aspects of cooperation on a joint text. Much like the "big" book now being presented to the reader, the publication on the origins and outbreak of World War II featured a "mirror" approach whereby two separate texts were prepared on the same topic, by Polish and Russian authors, accompanied by a joint introduction by the editors.

During the meeting in Moscow, members of the group pointed to the need for wider access to archival materials, which would help speed up work on the aforementioned publications. Participants welcomed Foreign Minister Lavrov's readiness to take action to facilitate access to the Foreign Policy Archive of the Russian Federation. The archive's resources were used during the preparation of the book about the outbreak of the war.

During the debate and in its final statement, the group noted that many issues related to archival resources could be solved in a routine manner, in accordance with established interstate procedures.

The group's participants once again highlighted the need to step up efforts to properly explain all the circumstances of the Katyn massacre, which was carried out by the Stalin regime, and they asked the authorities of both countries to somehow remove this matter from the agenda of present-day relations between our societies and states. The group discussed possible concrete steps to achieve this goal.

The next day, after the official meeting, a seminar focusing on Poland and the European Union's eastern policy was held at the MGIMO Rector's Auditorium. From the Russian perspective, this policy is often seen as a set of difficult issues related to the relationship between Russia and its neighbors in the Commonwealth of Independent States (CIS). Foreign ministry officials from both countries took an active part in the seminar. Of special note was detailed information from the director of the Eastern Department of the Polish Ministry of Foreign Affairs, Jarosław Bratkiewicz.

An important event that preceded the third session of the Group on

Difficult Matters was the co-chairs' meeting with Archbishop Hilarion of Volokolamsk and the heads of synodical sections of the Moscow patriarchate (Moscow, 24 April 2009). The church officials expressed their support for the work of the group and said they were ready to support social dialogue on historical topics.

V

The third plenary session of the Polish-Russian Group on Difficult Matters was held 28–29 May 2009, in Kraków. Members of the group ultimately agreed on the content and editorial details of the joint publication. The authors exchanged the prepared texts. They discussed these materials in considerable detail, and an agreement was reached on informing the public and the press about the mutually approved structure and subject matter of the upcoming publication. At a press conference at the end of the meeting, these materials were made available to the public.

One of the most important and undeniably most memorable moments of the third session was when members of the group met with Cardinal Stanisław Dziwisz, archbishop of Kraków.

Members of the group welcomed with satisfaction the constructive nature and results of an international conference on the origins of World War II. This conference was held in Warsaw 26–27 May 2009, on the eve of the meeting of the Group on Difficult Matters. Members of the group took an active part in the Warsaw conference. The work of academics from Poland, Russia, Germany, and other countries was a concrete example of productive academic dialogue and efforts to prevent attempts to falsify history.

The spring and summer of 2009 in Polish-Russian relations were marked by an expected meeting of both countries' prime ministers during commemorations of the seventieth anniversary of the outbreak of World War II. This created a unique opportunity for the constructive cooperation of academics in solving historical problems.

The co-chairs, in line with decisions made by the group, prepared a joint letter to the foreign ministers of both countries. The letter contained specific recommendations on some rather delicate matters. For this reason, we felt it appropriate that these specifically targeted suggestions should not be presented to the press. The leaders of both countries were expected to decide which of our proposals deserved their support and which should be adopted.

We notified the leaders of our countries that "the group's work on the issue of the Katyn massacre has reached the limits of what is possible in terms of the group's powers, and the group cannot guarantee further progress without proper support from the foreign ministers and leaders of both countries." As the co-chairs, we noted that "the upcoming seventieth anniversaries of the outbreak of World War II and the Katyn tragedy may become an additional factor stimulating negative sentiment around historical issues and hinder the development of relations between our countries." Therefore, we proposed that the efforts of the parties be "given a lasting and institutional dimension and that the Katyn issue should be jointly and finally taken off the agenda in bilateral relations."

This letter marked the first appearance of the idea to create two shared-history centers in Poland and Russia that would deal with issues such as "the maintenance of burial sites in a proper condition, both those related to the Katyn massacre and other Polish and Russian cemeteries [for] those killed on the territory of both countries." These centers "would counter attempts to falsify history by supporting research into history" and would deal with "educational activities, primarily those aimed at the young generation."

On 1 September 2009, a historic (for many reasons) meeting between Prime Minister Tusk and his Russian counterpart, Vladimir Putin, took place in Sopot. Everything that was said and done by both leaders meant that a fundamental breakthrough had occurred in the assessment of our common history. For us, this encounter was a signal that we, the group, would find it easier to reach agreement and that, in a way, we were entering the homestretch leading to the finish line.

VI

On 9 November 2009, the fourth session of the Polish-Russian Group on Difficult Matters was held in Moscow in an atmosphere of hope. On behalf of the Russian foreign minister, Deputy Minister Aleksandr V. Grushko welcomed the participants of the meeting.

Both co-chairs, in accordance with the established practice, presented a brief overview of the group's activities in the interval between the meetings and noted positive changes in the dialogue about history between the Polish and Russian peoples. In particular, they drew attention to the results of Prime Minister Putin's visit to Poland (on 1 September 2009) and to a video statement by Russian president Dmitry A. Medvedev (on 30 October 2009), in which he explicitly stressed the need to "examine the past, overcome indifference, and strive to move beyond the tragic chapters" of history.

The co-chairs also pointed to the importance of the social dimension of the group's work and its openness, including the publication by the Polish Institute of International Affairs and the Moscow State Institute of International Relations of a bilingual volume titled *The Crisis of 1939 as Interpreted by Polish and Russian Historians,* focusing on the origins of World War II. At the same time, a special edition of *Vestnik MGIMO,* marking the seventieth anniversary of the outbreak of the war, was presented. Many of the articles were authored by researchers from the Group on Difficult Matters.

The participants of the group focused on reaching final agreement on the text of the joint publication. In the debate, a lot of attention was paid to detailed consultations on issues of historiography, relations between our countries during World War II and immediately after its end, and "historical policy." Group members also discussed concrete steps to implement the decisions contained in the statements of the prime ministers of both countries, which concerned the establishment of centers dedicated to common history.

The most important issue was discussing specific aspects of organizing ceremonies in April 2010 marking the seventieth anniversary of the Katyn massacre. On the basis of this discussion, the co-chairs submitted their proposals to the leaders of both countries.

We also decided that it would be appropriate to notify the leaders of the Roman Catholic Church in Poland and the Russian Orthodox Church about the ceremonies being prepared and the possibility of jointly commemorating the victims of the Katyn massacre and other victims of the Stalin regime buried at Katyn.

During the meeting of the group, participants emphasized the necessity of paying special attention to the ninetieth anniversary of the Polish-Soviet war of 1920 and the need to organize ceremonies to honor the burial sites of those who were killed or died in captivity. Group members also decided that it was necessary to present a collection of documents dedicated to Russian prisoners of war and to consider organizing a conference focusing on historical issues.

During the Moscow meeting, we agreed that, in April 2010, a special meeting of the group would be held in Smolensk, combined with memorial ceremonies at Katyn. Some participants of the group and its co-chairs also were actively involved in the preparation of a historical meeting of the two prime ministers at Katyn on 7 April 2010.

In the run-up to this meeting, and also later in Smolensk, the co-chairs had an opportunity to communicate the position of the group to the prime ministers on matters concerning our activities, as well as to express their views on the need to establish "Centers of Dialogue and Understanding" in both countries.

The statements of the prime ministers at the graves of the victims of Stalinism in Katyn were extensively reported in the media. For the first time, the leaders of the new Poland and new Russia were together at a site that had divided our countries for many years. A process of historical reconciliation started.

We thought that this would be a clear landmark crowning the work of our group. The working meeting in Smolensk proceeded in this mood, continuing late into the evening. We agreed on details of the joint publication and discussed concrete steps related to the creation of historical-memorial Centers of Dialogue and Understanding, which the prime ministers had decided to establish. We also discussed some technical aspects of our work. We left a few matters unfinished. We planned to finalize them a few days later, when some of the Polish participants of the group would come to Russia again.

Then, on 10 April, disaster struck.

Two members of the group—Andrzej Kremer and Andrzej Przewoźnik, the author of one of the chapters of this publication—lost their lives in a plane crash along with the president of Poland, his wife, and many well-known people who were close to us.

VII

The events of 7–10 April became a turning point in relations between our countries. This shift occurred not only because a web of lies that had been woven for nearly seventy years was torn down but also, and more importantly, because these events made millions of Poles and Russians realize that thousands of other, nameless victims of Stalinist atrocities are buried in the mass graves in the forest near Smolensk alongside the Polish officers. Innocent people of different nationalities and ethnicities—Russians, Ukrainians, Belarusians, Jews, and representatives of many other nations of the former Soviet Union who suffered from repression and terror during the period of Stalinist purges—were killed there by NKVD executioners. Poles and Russians believed that a common plight and truth are together the cornerstone of a new type of relations between our nations.

The work of our group and the decisions of the leaders of both countries caused the truth about the Katyn massacre to reach millions of Russians. Andrzej Wajda's film *Katyn,* shown on the main channel of Russian public television, made the multimillion-member audience in the Russian Federation aware of why the truth about this crime is so important to Poles: it removes one of the main stumbling blocks on the road to reconciliation.

Prime Minister Tusk referred in his statement to the words of Aleksandr Solzhenitsyn: "One word of truth shall outweigh the whole world."

"Today I want to believe that one word of truth can pull together two great nations so painfully divided by history," the Polish prime minister said, "nations that today are looking for this simple and short road to reconciliation." On this road, two signposts were erected on 7 April at Katyn: memory and truth.

The airliner tragedy near Smolensk triggered a wave of empathy among millions of Russians, who spontaneously expressed goodwill and a readiness to break the ice that had cooled relations between our countries for years. During the meetings at the highest level, at Wawel Hill, Kraków, in the Royal Castle (on 18 April) and at the Kremlin (on 8 May), President Medvedev responded with understanding and sympathy to Polish requests to declassify the Katyn files and rehabilitate the victims of this crime. He stated that he would instruct his people to gradually declassify these files and work out an appropriate means of rehabilitating the victims to meet the expectations of the families of those killed in Katyn. Certified copies of sixty-seven volumes of files were handed to the Polish side when Bronisław Komorowski, who was Speaker of the Polish Sejm, the lower house of the Polish parliament, as well as acting president, paid his first visit to the Kremlin, at the invitation of Medvedev.

Official statements, meetings of leaders, and gestures pointing to a willingness to reach agreement—until recently treated as unusual events—are now becoming commonplace. But it would be naïve to believe that all the main obstacles to Polish-Russian reconciliation have been removed. A mindset steeped in stereotypes, conservatism, and the inertia of some administrative authorities, deeply rooted in both societies, along with the need to preserve an "external enemy," do not help the leaders of either country to achieve their objectives. It is important that the chosen direction of the march has met with the approval of millions of Poles and Russians.

What happened in the spring of 2010 presents an opportunity, but this opportunity can be taken advantage of only by reaching out to each other in a permanent and institutional manner. The culture ministers of both our countries have made steps toward creating Centers of Polish-Russian Dialogue and Understanding, the establishment of which has been announced by the two prime ministers. These centers will be a platform for efforts to build multifaceted contacts between Poles and Russians. Unprecedented, intense dialogue is in progress between the Russian Orthodox Church and Poland's Roman Catholic Church. It is difficult to overestimate the spiritual dimension that the two churches—which represent Eastern and Western Christianity—can give to the nascent process of reconciliation. In one of his essays, Kirill, the patriarch of Moscow and All Russia, referred to the holy martyr Ignatius of Antioch, who said, "Consider the conditions of the times." This is as profound and important an idea in our era as it was in his.

What was unthinkable twenty years ago is now becoming the new mindset of society before our very eyes, and this in turn determines the new political reality in relations between Poland and Russia.

1

THE BEGINNINGS

POLISH-SOVIET RELATIONS, 1917–1921

Daria Nałęcz (Poland)

Professor, undersecretary of state at the Ministry of Science and Higher Education, former director of the Head Office of State Archives, member of the Polish-Russian Group on Difficult Matters, 2008–12.

Tomasz Nałęcz (Poland)

Professor, History Department of Warsaw University and Political Sciences Department, Aleksander Gieysztor Humanities Academy in Pułtusk, advisor to the president of the Republic of Poland.

Gennady F. Matveyev (Russia)

Professor and chair of the Department of History of Southern and Western Slavs, Lomonosov Moscow State University.

DARIA NAŁĘCZ AND TOMASZ NAŁĘCZ

· ·

POLISH-SOVIET RELATIONS, 1917–1921

· ·

THE UPHEAVAL THAT transformed Russia in 1917 marked a watershed in Polish-Russian relations. Earlier, the tsarist authorities had totally disregarded the Poles' national aspirations. That policy line was maintained even after the outbreak of World War I. It changed only after the declaration of 5 November 1916, which presaged the restoration of the Kingdom of Poland aligned with Berlin and Vienna. Seeking to undercut that promise and prevent the Germans' formation of a Polish army that could be a significant factor in the war, Tsar Nicholas II announced in a New Year message to the troops that "the restoration of a free Poland, composed of the three parts hitherto separated," would constitute one of the primary goals of the war. That signaled a readiness to wrest the Polish provinces away from the rival powers and expand Russia's own zone of influence westward.

The Polish question gained prominence only after the tsarist regime was toppled. The new authorities set about rebuilding the crumbling state of the tsars and pledged to abandon the policy of subjugating the nations inhabiting it. In fact, there appeared to be a race of sorts between the competing power centers. The Petrograd Soviet of Workers' and Soldiers' Deputies was the first to speak out: on 27 March 1917, it declared that "democratic forces in Russia recognize the political self-determination of nations and state that Poland has the right to full independence as a state under international law."

The provisional government was more sparing in its promises. Its power base was more moderate, and, furthermore, as the official authority, it tended to weigh its pronouncements. In a manifesto to the Poles adopted on 29 March 1917, it declared that "the Russian people, which has cast off its yoke, grants the fraternal Polish people the right to full self-determination, in accordance with its own will." It promised to "assist with the establishment of an independent Polish state comprising all the territories in which Poles constitute a majority, as a guarantee of lasting peace in a future, newly organized

Europe." However, it made that promise contingent on a "free military alliance" between Poland and Russia and the endorsement of those concessions by the future Russian Constituent Assembly.

A completely new situation arose after the Bolsheviks assumed power. They cooperated only with extreme leftist parties among the Polish political groupings: Social Democracy of the Kingdom of Poland and Lithuania and the Polish Socialist Party—the Left. Both these parties were firmly opposed to the restoration of an independent Polish state, considering it an instrument of rule by the propertied classes.

The official declarations of Soviet Russia were quite different. The Decree of Peace, adopted on 8 November 1917 and just a day after the coup, contained the principle of immediate peace without annexation, that is, without the seizure of foreign territories or the forcible incorporation of other nations. On 15 November 1917, the Council of People's Commissars published its Declaration on the Rights of the Peoples of Russia, which sharply denounced both the national oppression of the tsarist regime and the imperial policies pursued by the provisional government. The document guaranteed equality and sovereignty to peoples wishing to remain within the borders of Russia, while those seeking independence were granted the right to self-determination—even to the point of separation and formation of an independent state.

At that point, declarations had to suffice since the Russian partition of Poland was occupied by Germany and Austria-Hungary. That state of affairs was consolidated in March 1918, following the peace imposed on Russia by the Central powers at Brest. The dictate led the Council of People's Commissars to issue a decree on 29 August 1918 that invalidated the partition treaties and recognized Berlin's right to determine the future of Central and Eastern Europe.

The declarations of the Bolsheviks made it easier for the Entente powers to act in favor of Polish independence. The first move was made by US president Woodrow Wilson in his Fourteen Points, unveiled in January 1918, wherein he supported the establishment of a Polish state inhabited by a Polish population, with access to the sea. France, which prized Poland as an ally in the war against Germany, went further. But in order to keep Germany in check and stabilize the new international order, Russia was needed to an even greater extent—naturally, on condition that its future system of government would be acceptable to the West. It was hard to imagine the Bolsheviks delivering on that.

Thus, the Entente's commitment to the Polish cause depended on the course of the civil war that was gaining momentum in Russia. The closer the Bolsheviks appeared to victory, the greater importance the West attached to Poland. In the event of a Bolshevik victory, Poland would be needed not only as an ally against the Germans but also as a crucial component of a *cordon sanitaire*, separating communist Russia from Europe.

Developments on the ground favored the Poles. Setbacks suffered on the battlefield by the three partitioning powers and revolutions that paralyzed them led to the collapse of the European order that, for more than a century, had made the partitions seem irrevocable.

Józef Piłsudski, who took the helm as chief of state, played a pivotal role in resurrecting Poland. He brokered a political compromise between the two camps that were scrambling for power: the left-leaning pro-independence movement and the right-wing National Democracy. That defused the threat of civil war and enhanced Poland's position in the run-up to the Paris Peace Conference, scheduled for 18 January 1919. Piłsudski left the day-to-day running of domestic affairs to the cabinet, headed by Ignacy Paderewski, while personally focusing on building the army, of which he was commander in chief.

Paderewski, assisted by Roman Dmowski, was also responsible for Polish interests at the Paris Peace Conference, with particular focus on obtaining an advantageous border with Germany. Piłsudski retained eastern policy for himself. Initially, he displayed little activity in this area, as he waited for the situation in the West to crystallize. Here, everything depended on the victorious Entente powers, since the young Polish state lacked clout to extract anything from Germany, which—while severely weakened by the disastrous war—was still incomparably stronger than Poland. In early February 1919, Piłsudski commented, "Everything that Poland gets in the West in terms of borders will be a gift from the Coalition, because in the West we do not owe anything to our own strength. In the East, on the other hand, we shall owe everything exclusively to our own endeavors." That strategy stayed in place until 28 June 1919, when the Entente powers and Germany signed the peace treaty at Versailles.

The territories of the former Romanov Empire to the east of reborn Poland were occupied under the Brest Treaty by German forces. In November 1918, they were eager to return home, but the Entente, wishing to prevent Soviet Russia from occupying the area, banned Berlin from evacuating the so called Ober-Ost. Gen. Max Hoffmann's half-million-strong army, holding positions that spanned fifteen hundred kilometers, was meant to stop the Bolsheviks from marching on Europe.

On 13 November 1918, Soviet Russia invalidated the humiliating Brest Treaty. Trotsky declared on 18 November 1918, "Through Kiev runs a line leading straight to a junction with the Austro-Hungarian revolution, just as through Pskov and Vilnius runs a line leading straight to a junction with the revolution in Germany . . . into the offensive on all fronts!" That meant war with Poland and a mortal threat to its independence. The Bolsheviks had no qualms about reneging on their earlier promises, which now were incongruent with the strategy of carrying the revolution into areas controlled by the

Germans and Austrians and, subsequently, deeper into Europe. They were motivated by Marx's theory of universal revolution and encouraged by events across the continent. All of Europe was at the boiling point. That was particularly true of defeated Germany and Austria-Hungary, where it seemed that a single spark would be enough to set off a communist revolt. The Bolsheviks dreamed of backing it, and doing so required eradicating the Polish barrier.

But Piłsudski, too, had a grand plan, which he could not implement without bringing Russia to its knees. He believed that Russia's extreme exhaustion resulting from the lost world war, the revolution, and bloody domestic conflict offered a unique opportunity to deprive it of its big-power status. He wanted to achieve that by supporting the independence strivings of nations oppressed by the tsars. He believed that nations that obtained statehood in the war against Russia would align themselves with Poland because that would be the only way of guaranteeing their own security. He thought that a planned East European union should be centered on a Polish-Lithuanian-Belarusian state rooted in the tradition of the Grand Duchy of Lithuania. He was also counting on an alliance with Ukraine. His broadest-ranging plans included Finland, Estonia, Latvia, and the states of the Caucasus. Poland, due to its human, economic, military, and cultural potential, was to play the role of hegemon in such a union.

The East European union was intended to hinder the reconstruction of Russia's might, to push it back from Europe, and to convince Russia that it should be content with its acquisitions in Asia. That, however, meant war to the death with Russia, regardless of its political system. Piłsudski believed that the Bolsheviks—also opposed by the Entente—constituted a lesser threat. However, he realized that if a showdown against "White" Russia occurred, Poland would antagonize the West, which could not imagine a postwar order in Europe without rebuilding the strength of its much-needed Russian ally.

The plan to push Russia away from Europe was flatly rejected by Piłsudski's rivals, the National Democrats, headed by Dmowski. They had remained convinced from the beginning of the twentieth century that Germany was Poland's greatest enemy, and the war only reinforced that belief. They were seeking guarantees of Polish security in an alliance with France, but also with Russia, where they were hoping for a speedy collapse of the Bolsheviks. They hoped that Moscow, its strength sapped by the revolution and civil war, would agree to a border advantageous to Poland.

The diametrically different perception of Russia caused friction between Piłsudski and Dmowski. For the time being, they managed to conceal their differences because they jointly faced the task of addressing the Soviet threat. With the Germans' tacit acquiescence, the Red Army was taking possession of ever more territory from them and systematically moving west. It was not until 5 February 1919 that a new agreement was signed, one allowing Poles to take over areas vacated by the Germans. Berlin was hoping for a Polish-Soviet war that would restrict Warsaw's ability to support the uprising in Greater Poland.

Polish units marched east, and, on 14 February, the first clashes with Red Army forces took place at the town of Mosty on the Niemen River. On the same day, other Polish units recaptured the town of Bereza Kartuska from the Soviets. A rapidly expanding Polish-Soviet front was thus born, though true war was still distant. Neither side as yet attached top importance to the conflict. The Poles were much more preoccupied with the fight against the Ukrainians for eastern Galicia and with maintaining military preparedness along the western border, threatened by German aggression. Meanwhile, the Soviets concentrated on dealing with the "Whites," particularly Adm. Aleksandr Kolchak, who had been making advances since March 1919. In mid-April, his forces, attacking in the direction of Samara and Kazan, were within one hundred kilometers of the Volga. To avert disaster, the Soviet command moved troops from the west to the east. That was done without much regret since, after the suppression of the communist revolt in Berlin in January 1919, there was little hope for revolution in Germany.

In April 1919, Piłsudski captured Vilnius in a bold maneuver. He did not intend to incorporate it into Poland but to make it the capital of a joint state of Poles, Lithuanians, and Belarusians, aligned with Poland. Alas, he found little support for his plans. The local Poles wanted to be reunited with their homeland. The Lithuanians, on the other hand, firmly insisted on independence and saw Poland as their main foe. For the first time, it was demonstrated forcefully that the reconstruction of Eastern Europe could be stymied by the indifference or even resistance of the nations that Piłsudski wanted to liberate.

The Poles fared much better in combat. They were gaining the upper hand while the activity of the Red Army ebbed as it focused on fighting Kolchak's army. That confrontation had now become the key theater of the war. The Soviets went on the counterattack in May 1919, recaptured Ufa in June, and began driving Kolchak east. In July, the Red Army—led by Mikhail Tukhachevsky, who proved himself a gifted commander—defeated the enemy at Chelyabinsk. Kolchak beat a hasty retreat and in the process lost the aura of "conqueror of the Reds."

But that did not spell the end of problems for Soviet Russia. Other "White" generals had been making effective attacks since May 1919. In the north, the forces of Gen. Nikolai Yudenich reached the approaches to Petrograd. In the south, Gen. Anton Denikin turned out to be an even more formidable adversary: in June 1919, he took Kharkov and Tsaritsin and, in early July, made his move on Moscow. By August, units of the Volunteer Army were in control of all of southern and central Ukraine, including Odessa and Kiev. The Soviet government found itself in mortal danger.

Meanwhile, the Polish army was successfully pushing east. A major offensive was launched on 1 July 1919, with the goal of forcing the Red Army back beyond the middle reaches of the Dnieper. It took just three days to capture Molodechno. In pursuit of the enemy, Polish forces marched on Minsk, which was taken on 8 August. In late August 1919, the front pushed up to the Berezina River, famous from Napoleonic times. Polish acquisitions here included the mighty fortress of Bobruisk. In the north, the enemy was beaten back to the line of the Dvina and Drissa Rivers. The Bolsheviks had also lost Polesie and Volhynia.

Unexpectedly, the fighting ground to a halt at the beginning of September 1919. Piłsudski became concerned by the successes of the Volunteer Army and decided to hold back his forces. In mid-October 1919, the Volunteer Army took Orel and found itself just a little more than three hundred kilometers from Moscow. Piłsudski was perfectly aware that now the defeat of the "Reds" depended on his actions. He also realized that it was the perfect moment to extract concessions from Denikin.

The problem was that "White" Russia was not prepared to make concessions. In the east, it wanted to restrict Poland within the borders of the former Kingdom of Poland, that is, roughly along the Bug River. That considered, Piłsudski decided not to support Denikin's offensive. He wanted the two foes to wear each other down so that he could impose conditions on them from a position of strength. He discreetly advised Lenin that Polish forces would not take any offensive actions for the time being. Lenin, his back against the wall, stripped the Polish front bare of his troops and committed more than forty thousand of them to the campaign against Denikin. Those reinforcements were instrumental in pushing the Volunteer Army away from Moscow and then driving it far south. On 12 December 1919, it lost Kharkov, on 16 December, Kiev, then the entire Donetsk Basin in January 1920. Now, the specter of disaster stared Denikin in the face as Soviet Russia coasted to a victorious conclusion of the civil war.

Piłsudski had correctly predicted that, once the Soviets had dealt with their internal enemies, they would commit all their forces against Poland, reviving the grand plan of bringing the revolution to the West. He did not intend to wait for that with folded arms. He knew that time was not working in his favor, since Soviet Russia—now in control of vast territories and resources—would be well positioned to beef up its forces. Meanwhile, the young Polish state made enormous efforts to boost its own military potential. By the end of 1919, its armed forces numbered six hundred thousand men and Piłsudski was planning further, intensive development. On 22 December 1919, he ordered the Ministry of Military Affairs to attain top combat readiness by April 1920. After Polish intelligence intercepted a dispatch from the Red Army command, dated March 1920, that spoke of preparations for a great offensive against Poland, Piłsudski knew he had to strike quickly.

Piłsudski expected the Red Army to attack from the north but decided to launch his own strike in the south. He wanted to drive the enemy out of Ukraine and to rebuild the Ukrainian People's Republic, with Symon Petliura as its leader. The Polish-Ukrainian alliance was to constitute the backbone of a future East European union, efforts for the establishment of which now entered a decisive phase. Earlier, in 1919, Petliura had been fighting against the Poles, but, after defeats at the hands of Denikin and the Red Army, he realized that Poland was the only potential backer of an independent Ukrainian state. On 21 April 1920, the parties signed an agreement under which Poland recognized the Ukrainian People's Republic and the Directorate, led by Petliura, as its legal government. Ukraine consented to a border between the two states along the Zbrucz River, leaving all of eastern Galicia on the Polish side. The agreement was supplemented by a secret convention on a military alliance and joint military struggle against Soviet Russia, under Piłsudski's command.

A great Polish-Ukrainian offensive, designed to restore Ukraine to Petliura, was launched on 25 April 1920. The Red Army suffered devastating losses and was driven beyond the Dnieper but was not vanquished. On 7 May, elements of Gen. Edward Rydz-Śmigły's Third Army entered Kiev, and soon afterward allied Ukrainian authorities also arrived in the city. Piłsudski, appointed marshal in March 1920, received a hero's welcome from the inhabitants of Warsaw upon his return from the front. Yet, contrary to popular conviction and propaganda claims, the Kiev campaign had not produced a strategic triumph, either in military or political terms: the Polish forces had not managed to effectively curtail the combat readiness of the Red Army, while the people of Ukraine had not given mass support to Petliura.

The threat that Ukraine could be lost helped the Soviet government mobilize society for the war against Poland. Thousands of former tsarist officers enrolled in the Red Army. Preparations for the big offensive in Belarus, planned since March, were now accelerated, and the operation was launched on 14 May 1920. It was commanded by Mikhail Tukhachevsky, still basking in the glory of his victorious campaign against Kolchak. He managed to push the Polish forces back 100 to 150 kilometers, but the Poles quickly brought in reinforcements—some from the Ukrainian front—and, after fierce fighting, they again drove the Red Army back, beyond the Berezina and the Auta Rivers. Meanwhile, a new crisis developed on the southern front. Polish troops, stretched thin between the Dnieper and the Boh, were attacked by fresh Soviet forces, battle-hardened in their victorious campaign against Denikin: it was the famous Konarmiya of Semyon Budyonny, which broke through to the Polish rear. The Poles hurriedly evacuated Kiev and had to withdraw farther and farther west to avoid total disorganization of the southern theater of the war.

Tukhachevsky exploited the situation and, on 4 July 1920, dealt the Polish forces in Belarus another numbing blow. His order to the troops made it plain that more was involved than just defeating the Poles. It sounded nothing short of a manifesto: "The time of reckoning has come. . . . Over the corpse of White Poland lies the road to worldwide conflagration. . . . To the West!"

Defeating the Polish army would create a chance for a revival of the revolution in Germany, where the struggle for power was not yet conclusively finished. That in turn offered hope for dismantling the order laid down at Versailles and for the victory of communism across Europe. Bringing those plans to fruition would have meant the end of independent Poland. An independent Polish state would be replaced by a Soviet republic.

That grim prospect loomed ever closer as the Red Army pressed its advantage, particularly on the northern front (referred to as the Western Front by the Russians). By late July 1920, Polish defenses were in a critical situation. Vilnius, Grodno, and Białystok all fell to the enemy. On 30 July, the Provisional Revolutionary Committee of Poland was installed in Białystok for the purpose of establishing communism in Poland according to the Bolshevik model.

Yet, the Soviet and Polish communists had failed to appreciate the determination of Polish society and its willingness to make the ultimate sacrifice in defense of the country's threatened independence. Earlier, the war in the east had had many critics, both among the independence-oriented left wing and the right-wing National Democrats. Now, they all came together to defend Poland's sovereignty. Workers, peasants, and members of the intelligentsia, including many students, enrolled en masse in the army. Between 1 July and 20 August 1920, its ranks swelled by a quarter of a million men.

Prior disputes, including those over the shape of eastern policy, were laid to rest. The day of 24 July 1920 saw the establishment of the Government of National Defense, composed of all the parliamentary factions. It was headed by a consummate politician, the peasant leader Wincenty Witos, who was assisted by Deputy Premier Ignacy Daszyński, a socialist and veteran of the struggle for the workers' cause.

Poland received material aid from the Entente, though it was hindered when dock workers in England and Gdańsk protested in support of Soviet Russia. Western governments attempted to broker a peace deal. In mid-July 1920, Lord Curzon, the British foreign secretary, proposed to the Soviet government a ceasefire along the line of the districts of Suwałki and Białystok and the Bug River, which the Supreme Council of the Entente had recognized as the border of indisputable Polish interests in the east. Moscow rejected the proposal and offered to begin bilateral negotiations with Warsaw, though on terms that amounted to Poland's surrender and that would have meant loss of independence and the communization of the country.

By August 1920, Polish defenses appeared on the verge of disintegration.

Early in the month, the Red Army broke through Polish positions along the Bug and captured Brest, from which Piłsudski had intended to launch his counteroffensive against Tukhachevsky's armies, which were rapidly pressing west. Now the only chance was to pull back beyond the Wisła and stage a counteroffensive from the region of the Wieprz River. That is what the commander in chief decided: the main thrust from the region of the Wieprz was to be executed by five divisions that would attack the exposed left wing of Tukhachevsky's forces advancing from the north. The risk was enormous, since the concentration of forces needed for the counteroffensive had weakened two key sections of the front: the Warsaw bridgehead and the northern flank, where the Soviet threat was particularly high. The fiercest fighting took place at Radzymin, where volunteer units, formed at the last moment, paid dearly for their lack of training. Yet, the enemy was halted.

As planned, the decisive blow was struck by the Wieprz group, personally commanded by Marshal Piłsudski. The Red Army, which was rushing west and had already started crossing the Wisła at Włocławek, suffered defeat and had to retreat. Many units were cut off by the victorious Polish divisions pushing forward from the region of the Wieprz. Thousands of soldiers were captured, while some units avoided disaster only by seeking refuge in German East Prussia.

Moreover, at the beginning of July 1920, Budyonny was finally defeated at Zamość, Hrubieszów, and Komarów. Some time prior, Tukhachevsky had demanded that Lev Kamenev, the Soviet commander in chief, withdraw the Konarmiya from the siege of Lvóv and use it against Piłsudski's forces gathering at Wieprz. In all likelihood, that would have decided the outcome of the war, because the Polish divisions attacked by Budyonny would not have been in a position to challenge Tukhachevsky's army in the north. Luckily, the order dispatching Budyonny to the region of Lublin was delayed, and, furthermore, he was in no hurry to carry it out. He shared the opinion of the all-powerful commissar of the southern front, Joseph Stalin, that the defeat of the Poles in both the north and south was inevitable, so Budyonny could better be used to revive the recently vanquished Hungarian Soviet Republic. In effect, the Konarmiya set out for the region of Lublin after some delay and was routed by the Poles, who, by that time, were in full control of the situation.

In September 1920, the Red Army lost a bloody battle along the Niemen. In terms of size, it exceeded the battle of Warsaw, but the victory received less publicity because it was achieved in incomparably less dramatic circumstances. Polish forces also advanced in eastern Little Poland and expelled Soviet troops beyond the old Austrian-Russian border. In Belarus and Volhynia, the front stabilized along the line of the old German trenches from the years 1915–16. Both sides were exhausted and incapable of continuing major combat operations. It was a situation conducive to the opening of peace talks.

The Polish government had already committed to peace talks in early August 1920, intending to use them to save the country from what seemed an impending catastrophe. The Soviets joined the talks on 17 August. Confident of victory, they attempted to impose a dictate that would have deprived Poland of independence. They abandoned that approach only after a series of battlefield setbacks. In the new situation, the two delegations decided on 2 September 1920 to move the talks from Soviet Minsk to Riga, capital of independent Latvia.

The talks resumed in Riga on 21 September, with the parties focusing on the terms of a ceasefire. The Polish delegation included proponents of both an incorporative and a federalist solution. Those favoring the latter did not rigidly cling to their positions, realizing that the extent of the Polish victory did not justify that. In historical terms, the victory was hard to overestimate: it had preserved the independence of Poland and saved Europe from the threat of communist revolution. However, the superiority gained in battle was not great enough for the Soviets to be pushed far to the east, allowing the Poles to provide support for the independence strivings of the local peoples. That forced Piłsudski, ever respectful of hard realities, to abandon his federalist plans.

On the first day of the negotiations, the Polish side recognized the representatives of Soviet Ukraine as partners in the talks, which meant that no attempts would be made to push for the independence of the Ukrainian People's Republic. That removed a problem that had had Warsaw and Moscow at loggerheads. Compromise was now easier to attain. It so happened that compromise was also on the agenda of Lenin and the Soviet leadership, who recognized that the defeats suffered by the Red Army made further hostilities a risky proposition. Accordingly, the new chair of the Soviet delegation, Adolf Joffe, was instructed not to overplay his hand and to work for a solution acceptable to both parties. A ceasefire agreement was signed on 12 October 1920, and it went into effect on 18 October at midnight.

The talks on a peace treaty were resumed in Riga on 17 November 1920. There was tough bargaining over a number of issues: the border, which the Poles wanted to run to the east of the ceasefire line in several spots; the recovery of property removed from Poland to Russia; the return of cultural goods plundered by Russia since the eighteenth century; and the repatriation of prisoners, hostages, and civilians who had found themselves deep in Russia as a result of various war-related developments, beginning with the great Russian evacuation in 1915. The negotiations dragged on and, in early 1921, reached a deadlock that threatened their collapse.

The crisis, brought about by the brinkmanship of the negotiators, was broken by the two governments, which were not interested in its perpetuation. Poland needed peace so as to enhance its position before a plebiscite in

Upper Silesia, scheduled for 20 March 1921. But Soviet Russia was in an even tighter spot: it had been shaken by internal convulsions, most spectacularly including the revolt of sailors at Kronstad, previously loyal to the Bolsheviks. In this situation, the parties toned down their demands, and the Polish-Soviet peace treaty was signed in Riga on 18 March 1921.

The border between the two states was established along a line connecting Dzisna, Dokszyce, Słucz, Korzec, Ostrów, and Zbrucz. This boundary approximated proposals made earlier by the National Democrats, and it sealed the final defeat of Piłsudski's federalist plans. This outcome was further affirmed by the recognition of Soviet Ukraine as the only form of Ukrainian statehood, which was tantamount to an abrogation of the 21 April alliance with Petliura. Simultaneously, Poland and Soviet Russia undertook not to interfere in each other's domestic affairs. National minorities on both sides of the border received guarantees of cultural, language, and religious rights.

Poland was to get back from Russia all war trophies, museum collections, libraries, book collections, archives, and other cultural goods removed from its territory after 1772, that is, the first partition. The Soviets were also obligated to pay 30 million rubles in gold as compensation for Polish shares in Russian companies across the old tsarist empire that had been confiscated by the Soviets. A further sum of 29 million rubles was to compensate for property removed by the Russians after the outbreak of World War I. Moreover, the parties agreed on terms of prisoner exchanges, repatriation of displaced civilians, and amnesty for political crimes committed during the hostilities. After ratification of the peace treaty, the parties would establish diplomatic relations and conclude a trade agreement.

The Riga Treaty was of crucial importance—and not only to Poland and Soviet Russia. It created a foundation of stability across all of Eastern Europe, which had not been covered by the Paris Peace Conference treaties. Alas, much would depend on its implementation.

Prisoner exchanges and the repatriation of civilians were among the most urgent challenges. A joint commission tasked with these matters was quickly formed and set to work in April 1921. Its reports testified to the horrific conditions in both Polish and Soviet camps, where people perished of exhaustion and disease. There was no shortage of mutual accusations and friction, though till the last days of the Second Republic there was not a single charge of intentional mass extermination of prisoners. That accusation was advanced in Russia only in 1990—for the most part by journalists and politicians—and it peaked in 1994–95, apparently to diminish the tragic impact of Katyn.

In an effort to determine the true course of events, Polish and Russian historians and archivists conducted meticulous document searches and published two extensive volumes of documents comprehensively presenting the fates of Red Army soldiers in Polish captivity and the fates of Polish prisoners in Soviet captivity. Historians working on both publications were given access to all documents preserved in Poland that had been produced by Polish army units and commands, including the Head Command, the Ministries of Military Affairs and Internal Affairs, the Sejm, and the presidium of the Council of Ministers, and also to files of local administration authorities, including prisoner of war (POW) camp records.

According to that documentation, the number of Bolshevik POWs held in Polish camps in late 1920, when the hostilities ended, can be estimated at between 80,000 and 85,000. They started trickling into the camps in February 1919, immediately after the fighting started. According to data provided by section 4 of the Head Command and testimony given by the Ministry of Military Affairs to a Sejm committee on 6 November 1919, there were 7,096 Bolshevik POWs in Polish captivity at that time.

Reports of bad conditions in the POW camps, including epidemics, prompted the Sejm to convene a five-member committee tasked with drafting a detailed report on the situation and proposing ways of addressing it. The report was submitted to the Sejm on 5 March 1920. It brought to light the scale of the problem, led to the launching of social humanitarian initiatives, and motivated the authorities to boost their efforts in dealing with the epidemics.

As the fighting intensified, the number of POWs increased. According to military data, Polish troops captured thirty thousand POWs during the Kiev offensive, including eighteen thousand Bolsheviks. The rest, that is, twelve thousand Ukrainians, were released. As for the Red Army prisoners, few of them were in fact transported to camps deep inside Poland because the Russian counteroffensive resulted in most of them being liberated.

Detailed reports by the respective Polish armies indicate that 41,161 POWs were captured between 14 August and 10 September 1920. Equally precise data are lacking for the subsequent period up to the ceasefire on 18 October 1920. However, press releases issued by the Polish general staff suggest that another 40,000 POWs had been captured.

Accordingly, about 110,000 Bolshevik POWs found themselves in Polish captivity. Some of them (between 20,000 and 25,000) defected to the Polish side immediately after being captured and joined the military formations established by Stanislav Bulak-Balakhovich, Boris Peremykin, Alexandr Silnikov, Vadim Yakovlev, and the army of the Ukrainian People's Republic.

Thus, 80,000 to 85,000 POWs remained in Polish captivity in late autumn of 1920, with half of them held in POW camps and the other half doing work for Polish state institutions, including the military, and for private persons, often as farm hands. Their lot was much better: they received better food and were accommodated in more sanitary conditions. Statistically, they still figured in the camp records, and that is why the data were subject to frequent changes, even though no new prisoners reached the camps. The changes were caused by transfers between the work details and the camps. According to data from the Ministry of Military Affairs in late 1920, of the total number of 76,842 POWs at that time, some 43,000 were working outside the camps.

An important issue often raised in the debate about the fate of the POWs is the high mortality rate within that group. According to Polish scholars, sixteen thousand to seventeen thousand Soviet POWs died during the entire period of the operation of the camps. Russian historians estimate the number at eighteen thousand to twenty thousand. Research has shown that the deaths were mainly caused by disease, prominently including epidemics of flu, typhus, cholera, and dysentery, which in the war-ravaged country claimed many lives in the POW camps, among the combatants, and in the civilian population. There were no executions of POWs in the camps, as occasionally happened on both sides during combat.

A repatriation agreement was signed on 24 February 1921, and the first groups of POWs were released in mid-March 1921. "Mixed Commissions" were formed to oversee the transfers. A Soviet delegation arrived in Poland and stayed at Strzałkowo, among other places, from 30 April to 4 May. By the end of April, 21,000 Bolshevik POWs had left Poland, and, in late May, 40,984 were still in the camps, with the number decreasing to 18,155 by 23 August. The operation was concluded in October. According to Monitor Polski No. 247, containing information supplied by the Ministry of Military Affairs, a total of 65,797 POWs had been transferred to Russia. A thousand more decided to stay in Poland, and another thousand asked to be released to Latvia, Germany, Hungary, or Austria.

The fate of Poles captured by the Bolsheviks is another aspect of the POW problem. No precise data are available on the number of Polish POWs. Documents of the Central Evacuation Board speak of 60,000 persons. Similar numbers are mentioned in correspondence of the Communist Party in each country. According to military sources, the number of POWs exceeded 44,000. They lived in conditions that were as harsh as those experienced by Soviet POWs in Poland. Epidemics also took their toll, though no precise data are available on the number of deaths. Members of the Polish delegation to the Mixed Commission, who visited Russia, estimated that 35 percent of the Polish POWs died in Soviet camps. According to the same calculations, that put the number of released Soviet POWs at 65,797, while the number of POWs who returned to Poland came to 26,440. NKVD sources speak of 35,000 repatriated Poles. Some of the Polish POWs voluntarily remained in Soviet Russia, though today it would be hard to accurately determine their number. Thus, the number of POWs who died in captivity constitutes part of the difference between the number of POWs captured and the number who managed to return home.

GENNADY F. MATVEYEV

· ·

POLISH-SOVIET RELATIONS, 1917–1921

· ·

FOR A LONG time, before the collapse of the tsarist regime, the "Polish issue" in Russian politics was the only question in Russia that could undoubtedly be referred to as a national one, that is, a question that could be resolved only by fundamentally changing the nation's status within the empire. Moreover, before the 1890s, the idea of a Polish national identity occupied mostly the Polish gentry, clergy, and intellectuals, whereas since the end of the nineteenth century, nationalist ideas have occupied the "lower" classes—workers, peasants, and the lower middle class.

None of Petersburg's projects for transforming the Poles of the Kingdom of Poland into loyal subjects of the Romanovs achieved unconditional success, unlike the case of the Baltic Germans. It is true that a large number of Poles did business and took jobs in the non-Polish regions of the empire, joined the army or civil service, entered into "mixed" marriages, and assimilated. However, the majority of the population went on living in the Kingdom of Poland and cultivated their Polish identity, protecting their language, culture, and faith. The results of military conscription into the Russian army at the beginning of World War I exceeded all expectations. This influx, combined with a complete lack of popular support for the rebellious project initiated by Józef Piłsudski, revealed the effectiveness of anti-German propaganda by those who had spent many years convincing the Poles that the Germans were their most bitter enemy, as opposed to demonstrating the loyalty of the Polish population to the Romanovs. This effect was also reinforced in August 1914, when German artillery destroyed the peaceful Polish town of Kalisz and killed eighty innocent civilians, thereby undermining the position of Germany's potential allies in the Kingdom of Poland.

Even before the war, the authorities in Petersburg had been well aware that there was no better way to solve the so-called Polish issue than by initiating a controlled process of restoring national statehood. Some advisors suggested granting complete independence to the Kingdom of Poland, though there were concerns that this move could provoke Germany to war with Russia. It could also set a precedent for other nations within the empire, the Finns primarily, who already enjoyed a high degree of autonomy. Neither domestic nor international political conditions were appropriate for such radical reform. However, the authorities did not consider the situation to be hopeless and thus were not ready to risk such potentially self-destructive steps.

The war that broke out, which would later be called World War I, was fundamentally different from all previous wars, primarily because the front and rear, army and civilians, were united as never before. The acting army's morale and fighting spirit could easily be influenced by those not on the front lines.

According to the original Russian warfare plan, once the mobilization of reserves was completed, the army should have withdrawn from the left-bank part of Poland and consolidated on the right bank of the Wisła. The plan became irrelevant almost immediately. To help France, which was suffering from a powerful assault by the German army, Russia decided to mount an offensive in East Prussia and Galicia. Poland was to become a base for offensive operations. Abandoning Poland was out of the question. It was important to establish with whom the Polish citizens would sympathize.

The Polish population came to understand the attitudes of both warring parties toward the Polish issue in August 1914. The Austro-Hungarian and German Eastern Front Command addressed the Poles on 9 August with a proclamation inspired primarily by Piłsudski's ideas—we are Europeans, we will liberate you from the Asians, and so forth—but it did not refer to other parts of the divided Poland.

The Russian supreme commander in chief, Grand Prince Nikolai Nikolayevich, addressed Poland on 14 August. His proclamation was composed with due consideration of Polish expectations as voiced by National Democrats. It contained a promise to reunite all parts of the divided Poland "under the scepter of the Russian Tsar" and to grant liberty of faith, language, and self-administration. However, it did not elaborate on the scope of self-administration, and the attitude toward the future Polish border was plainly equivocal. The words "one-hundred and fifty years ago the living body of Poland was torn to pieces" could have been interpreted as a promise to restore Poland within the Rzeczpospolita borders of 1772. But the condition that "Russia would only expect that you will show similar respect for the rights of those nationalities which were historically associated with you" threatened to nullify the promise, since it might mean that the Ukrainians and Belorussians would be permitted to remain beyond the self-administered Polish province. It is important to note that there were never comparable proclamations by the state authorities to any other nation of Russia, either in 1914 or in the years to follow, until the breakdown of the empire.

Historians have more than once thoroughly examined the context and circumstances under which the document (the proclamation "To the Poles") was prepared and adopted. The authors of the document were well known (among them was Minister of Foreign Affairs Sergey Sazonov). Roman Dmowski, the leader of the Polish National Democrats, became acquainted with the draft document when he arrived in Petersburg from Switzerland on 12 August. The draft was discussed at the Council of Ministers meeting and was shown to Nikolai II. For the next few years, until the end of 1916, when the Poles raised the issue of the postwar structure, the authorities in Petersburg referred them to the document. For many years thereafter, Nikolai II was criticized for not being specific and clear about the Russian position on the Polish issue. Many have voiced the fair criticism that his indecision was often attributed to weak character and his respect for principles of international law, which forbade changing state borders except at a peace conference. Also, the influential party advocating for a separate peace with the Central states opposed Nikolai II and thus limited his options. The fact that it was not critically important at the time is rarely taken into account. Polish soldiers in the Russian army never broke their military oath. When the Russian army occupied Czerniowce, the Russian commander in chief issued a declaration to warn all Russian subjects against joining paramilitary forces under the Austro-Hungarian command, threatening to treat them as wartime traitors. Indeed, the threat had an impact. However, the propaganda by the supporters of independence, led by Piłsudski, met a very weak response within Russian society, as previously mentioned. Thus, these factors fully justified the strategy adopted to address the Polish issue in August 1914. Any premature step that did not serve the immediate needs of the Russian Empire was fraught with disastrous and unpredictable possibilities.

The comparatively stable situation in Poland was shaken on 5 November 1916. In Warsaw and Lublin, two governors-general of the German and Austro-Hungarian occupation zones (the Russian army had withdrawn from the Kingdom of Poland during August and September 1916) issued a common declaration on behalf of their emperors. It declared the foundation of the Kingdom of Poland to be in the form of a hereditary constitutional monarchy and to be linked closely with the Central states. The Royal Polish Army would be formed with the direct participation of the Austrians and Germans. The declaration said nothing about the status of the Polish territories incorporated within the German and Austro-Hungarian Empires or about the future borders of the new state. However, Piłsudski's supporters viewed the document as a triumph of his plan for solving the Polish issue and reviving the Polish national identity. Whatever the real motives of the German and Austro-Hungarian authorities were, their declaration obviously caused very serious consequences with regard to the Polish issue.

Naturally, Russia immediately denounced such an overt violation of international law by its counterparts, though such a denunciation was insufficient to neutralize their disastrous plans. It was high time for Nikolai II to clarify the Russian point of view on the Polish issue without fearing accusations about disregarding international rules and regulations.

The emperor (who had also assumed commander-in-chief responsibilities), spelled out the Russian Empire's goals for the war in his Christmas Army Order of 25 December 1916. These goals included uniting the Polish territories "under the scepter" of the Romanovs and granting broad autonomy, similar to the conditions chartered by Alexander I to the Kingdom of Poland in 1815. The future Polish state was promised not only legislative and executive powers but also its own army.

It should be noted that these intentions would not have violated international rules. They were based on the nineteenth-century principle of nationalist law, whereby a divided nation was entitled to reunite, but not necessarily in the form of an independent state. In due course, the principle was successfully implemented in uniting Italy and Germany, demonstrating the feasibility of employing nationalist law widely acknowledged by the international community.

Russia's position was perceived positively by its allies and Washington. Since the beginning of 1916, US president Woodrow Wilson had shown growing interest in the Polish issue. In February 1917, a special council commenced its work on the Polish issue in Petrograd. It was called on to prepare practical solutions for implementing the monarch's will. The council had been working at a leisurely pace, which could be attributed to the following: Russia had won another battle for Poland against the partners on the division of Rzeczpospolita; the Kingdom of Poland was occupied and the end of the war was not expected anytime soon; National Democrats had taken another step toward their goal by receiving approval from Nikolai II for their plan to resolve the Polish issue; the recruitment of volunteers to the Polish military was hopelessly stalling; the Poles in the Russian army did not become poor fighters; and an Austro-German propaganda attack, carried out to arouse national contradictions within Russia, had failed.

The Polish Issue and the Petrograd Soviet, Provisional Government, and Council of People's Commissars

A distinctive feature of the second Russian revolution lay in the fact that power was divided between two political groups: the provisional government, organized on the basis of the Permanent Committee of the State Duma, and the spontaneously organized Petrograd Soviet of Workers' and Soldiers' Deputies.

Former members of the Duma, who were included in the provisional government, were experienced in management activities (for example, within their own enterprises, in local governments called *zemstvo*s, in the Duma, and on military-industrial committees) and in predicting the possible consequences of decisions. Since the provisional government did not resolve to keep its constituting body a temporary parliament, these functions were essentially undertaken by the Petrograd soviet. This fact became particularly evident after similar regional bodies had admitted metropolitan soviets as central players and the provisional government had declared the soviets' right to appoint and remove ministers. The Petrograd soviet was created by journalists, lawyers, and other "truth seekers" who were ever dissatisfied with the current state of affairs. They dedicated their lives not to the struggle against government (as is the case with Western-style democracies) but against the state, which encouraged its destruction. It is no wonder that the first act issued by the Petrograd soviet was Order 1, "On Democratization of the Army," which nearly resulted in disbanding this state institution, one of the most important and the country's mainstay in times of war.

While competing with each other over the degree of democracy, the Petrograd soviet and the provisional government could not ignore the Polish issue, which, in the context of the political coup and ongoing war, was hardly the country's most pressing problem. Representatives of the Polish settlement in Petrograd had access to authorities in both governing groups and therefore played a significant role in this issue. The Petrograd soviet was the first to announce its position. As early as 27 March 1917, in its appeal "To the Polish Nation," the Petrograd Soviet of Workers' and Soldiers' Deputies stated in its populist manner that "Russian democracy stands on the grounds of recognizing the national and political self-determination of people and declares the right of Poland to be completely independent in terms of state and international relations." Furthermore, "we send our respects to the Polish nation and wish it every success in the upcoming struggle to establish a democratic republican system within the territory of an independent Poland."

Based on this appeal, it is impossible to understand whether the Petrograd soviet deputies spoke about all parts of Poland or just the Kingdom of Poland. However, it is obvious that reconstituting the state of Poland per the spirit of the appeal would have unavoidably caused multiple conflicts in relations between Russia and Poland, including the most threatening territorial issue. Conflict would have been unavoidable because the Petrograd soviet did not make similar declarations regarding Ukraine, Belorussia, and Lithuania before the October coup. In other words, the soviet regarded these territories as integral parts of Russia, consequently making Russia a direct neighbor of Poland. And although the idea of reconstituting Poland within the 1772 borders of Rzeczpospolita met with a lively response from the Polish nation, it was impossible to avoid a territorial conflict.

GENNADY F. MATVEYEV

The appeal had also overlooked the problem of the foreign political orientation of an independent Poland. Given the unavoidable territorial conflict, it was hard to expect that Poland, even a democratic Poland, would become an ally of democratic Russia. Moreover, Petrograd soviet deputies actually refused to participate on behalf of Russia in the decision-making process for the future of its Polish province and declared the Polish issue to be opened.

On 29 March, the provisional government issued its own "To the Poles" proclamation. At the beginning of the document, the authors, as well as those who had developed the appeal by the Petrograd soviet, referred to the will of revolutionary Russia and recognized the right of the Polish nation "to define its own future at its own discretion." However, differences emerged at this point. First, the right of independent existence was given to Poles by *countries that were primarily inhabited by the Polish nation.* In other words, this right was also given to Poles living in Austria-Hungary and Germany. By this proclamation, the provisional government followed Nikolai II and declared the intent to annul all agreements on the division of Rzeczpospolita.

In full compliance with all the norms of a modern state's functioning, the provisional government, which was established to govern Russia only until the institutionalization of its new system, left the final decision on altering "the state territory of Russia, necessary to create an independent Poland from three separate segments," to the discretion of the Constituent Assembly.

It was highly likely that future relations between Russia and Poland would be peaceful under this solution to the Polish issue, which was understood as recognition of the right for the three parts of the divided Polish nation to reunite and create an independent state within ethnic borders. Many will recall that this approach by the provisional government was in full accord with the position of the United States and the Entente countries toward the issue of territorial reorganization of central and southeastern Europe.

The authors of the proclamation understood that, if reconstituted under ethnic principles, Poland would be small (only 120,000 to 150,000 square kilometers). Left with no strategic space, Poland would not be able to stand alone against Germany and Austria-Hungary (whose future had not yet been resolved by the allies) and would need a powerful protector from among its bordering neighbors. It would be strange if the provisional government, which cared for Russia's security, gave the future Poland a chance to choose its protector at its own discretion. That is why the provisional government openly declared a union of Poland with Russia by means of a "free military alliance" to be the main requirement for providing independence to Poland in order to convert the state of Poland into a "secure bastion against the pressure of Central states on Slavdom." Therefore, the final decision on the Polish issue was declared to be the prerogative of Russia. In general, the plan proposed by the provisional government through the proclamation took national interests fully into account.

The creation of the Liquidation Commission on the Kingdom of Poland under the direction of the provisional government, which was granted the necessary authority to settle all issues concerning the separation of Russia and Poland, indicates how serious the provisional government's plans were.

The provisional government's position on the Polish issue turned the tide toward the National Democrats in the philosophical dispute with Piłsudski's followers. Furthermore, it gave the Entente countries and the United States an opportunity to enact their Polish policies and make the country less dependent on Russia. In June 1917, France consented to form an allied Polish army on its territory. From August to December of the same year, the allies recognized the Polish national committee in Paris, headed by Dmowski, as an official Polish organization. Simultaneously, independent Polish military units began to be formed inside Russia. One can only guess how the Polish issue might have further developed, but it is obvious that Russia would definitely have taken part in resolving the Polish issue at the end of the war. It is unlikely that Western countries would not have considered its position on the border between Russia and Poland during peace conferences. However, other political groups were forced to decide the Polish issue on behalf of Russia.

As early as the day after taking control of Petrograd, the Bolsheviks, in their famous "Decree on Peace," proposed to annul "any joining of a small and weak ethnic group to a large and powerful state without accurately, clearly, and voluntarily expressing the consent and will of a given ethnic group, irrespective of the time when such a hostile takeover occurred, and irrespective of the level of development of the nation, which was annexed or is kept within the boundaries of a certain state by force, and, finally, irrespective of whether this nation resides within Europe or other countries overseas." There is no denying that such an approach to Poland equaled the recognition of a right to reunion and independence for each of its three parts. But on a global scale, a tough fate might have awaited humanity if this decree had been realized. The tragedy in Yugoslavia at the turn of the twentieth century provides a general idea of the potential cataclysm that threatened the world in that case.

The documents later issued by the Soviet government reveal that it was an "export-type" option for solving the national issue, that the Bolshevik leaders understood the degree of threat to Russia arising from their plans to rearrange the world. A week after the Decree on Peace, they also announced the "Declaration on the Rights of the Peoples of Russia," which, at first sight, seemed as radical as the Decree on Peace. It consisted of a detailed preamble and four clearly stated fundamental principles for the Council of People's Commissars' activities, all targeted toward solving the national issue in

Russia: equality and sovereignty of the nations within the country; the right of national self-determination, even to the extent of separating and establishing an independent state; cancellation of all national and national-religious privileges and limitations; and unrestricted development of ethnic minorities and ethnographical groups. Research is mostly confined to reviewing just this part of the document.

However, the preamble of the declaration is just as important as its recital. The usual condemnation of the national politics practiced under tsarism and by the provisional government was followed by a definition of the essence of the activities of the Council of People's Commissars in the sphere of national relations and the conduct of a "transparent and honest policy, leading to the absolute trust of the people of Russia." The purpose of the declaration was the creation of an "honest and lasting union of the people of Russia," because "workers and peasants from among the peoples of Russia can be united into a single revolutionary force, capable of resisting all attacks by the imperialistic-annexationist bourgeoisie, only as a result of such a union." Thus, Vladimir Lenin and Joseph Stalin, who signed this declaration, did not guide the new administration toward separating Russia along national seams. Relying on their prewar approaches to the range of national problems, they declared the unity of workers and peasants from among all nations of Russia to be a necessary condition for successfully protecting the social achievements of the upheaval performed by the Bolsheviks. They thereby declared themselves in support of maintaining Russia as a multinational country.

Since it was hard to understand from the declaration which Russian territories were intended, a question arises as to whether the declaration was ever addressed to the population of the Kingdom of Poland. The proclamation, issued by the executive committee and the administration of the Petrograd division of the Social Democracy of the Kingdom of Poland and Lithuania in Russia on 25 November 1917, can be regarded as an indirect response to this question. In particular, this proclamation stated, "The Bolshevik party is the only one to honestly and clearly raise the question of the national liberation of Poland, and the Council of People's Commissars is the only one to declare the provision of all possible rights to the nations which inhabit Russia, the only one to guarantee a wide range of rights to ethnic minorities, including the Poles, living in eastern border regions. The Council of People's Commissars honestly and clearly raised the question to the democratic world, thanks to which Poland ceased to be the subject of diplomatic bargaining." This proclamation proves that the Bolsheviks did not regard the Kingdom of Poland as an integral part of the new Russia. But it did not mean their refusal to take part in the decision-making process once the global revolution they anticipated had begun.

It is worth mentioning a circumstance overlooked by researchers studying this problem. Notwithstanding their radicalism in all foreign and domestic issues, the Bolsheviks did not settle for unilateral termination of the agreements on separating Rzeczpospolita and other agreements on which Russia had based its annexation of remote territories.

The Bolsheviks could not have done so before the opening of the Brest-Litovsk peace conference in December 1917 because, among other reasons, the future of the Kingdom of Poland could not help but become a subject of bargaining. Indeed, during the Brest-Litovsk conference, this issue was given much attention. According to the definition of Foreign Commissar Georgy Chicherin, the agreement concluded there in March 1918 separated Poland from Russia. Moreover, the Central states insisted on Soviet termination of all agreements on the division of Poland. On 6 April 1918, the Regency Council of the Kingdom of Poland appointed Aleksander Lednicki (the former chair of the Polish Liquidation Commission, which was dissolved in December 1917) as commissioner for the guardianship of Polish citizens within the Russian Soviet Federative Socialist Republic (RSFSR). His responsibilities included reevacuation of refugees and negotiations concerning property, funds, contributions, and deposits, Polish state possessions, *gminas* (municipalities), and public corporations. However, the Soviet government did not hurry to acknowledge the authority of Lednicki, because management of all Polish affairs was transferred to the commissariat on Polish issues (established in December 1917) under the People's Commissariat of Nationalities, which was granted a wide range of powers for organizing all aspects of Polish life within Soviet Russia.

Further developments revealed that the decisions on the Polish issue, which had been imposed on the RSFSR in the Brest-Litovsk deal, were extremely unfavorable, especially given that the West had not determined the location of Poland's eastern border until the end of 1919. Russia's termination of agreements on separating Poland gave Polish politicians an opportunity to demand the reconstitution of their state within the borders effective in 1772, in other words, to demand the inclusion of territories that were regarded by the Bolsheviks as integral parts of Russia according to the "Declaration on the Rights of the Peoples of Russia." This opportunity was one of the reasons for the Polish-Russian war that started in February 1919. In modern Poland, this war is still called the Polish-Bolshevik War, as it was defined by prewar propagandists.

In summary, the provisional government proposed the most balanced and conflict-free decision on the Polish issue, as if to choose among the three power centers operating in Russia during the revolutionary events of 1917. The plans of the Petrograd soviet and the Bolsheviks had some differences but were nevertheless quite similar to each other. Neither plan took into account the potential threats imposed by the long-term inclusion into Rzeczpospolita of what had been the western part of the Russian Empire.

GENNADY F. MATVEYEV

The End of World War I and the Establishment of the Versailles System

The prewar European order was based on a balance of power between five major European countries: Russia, Germany, Austria-Hungary, France, and Great Britain. From 1915 to the beginning of 1917, the agreements concluded between these countries and other countries involved in the war, such as Italy, Romania, and Bulgaria, showed that the leaders of these states were not going to abandon time-tested doctrine in favor of another doctrine that respected the interests of major countries as well as all other members of the global political scene. A different position was supported by the United States, in particular by President Wilson, who insisted on establishing a new basis for the postwar world order. Special attention should be given to the role of the United States in generalizing the principle of a nation's right to self-determination. In 1916, the question of US participation in the European war was actively discussed in Washington. It contradicted all prior policy of this country that had just started to gather its authority. Trenchant and lofty arguments were needed to persuade the American people to abandon the Monroe Doctrine.

Washington was not bound by alliances to any warring coalitions, was free from the threat of internal separatism, and possessed large discretion in developing any trailblazing projects to arrange the future world without wars. Wilson's speech before the American League to Enforce Peace on 27 May 1916 may be regarded as the first demonstrative step in this direction. For the first time, he referred to the right of any nation "to choose which supreme power to live with" as one of the principles of international relations. That choice can be regarded as one of the options within a nation's right to self-determination, down to separation as proposed by liberals, pacifists, and revolutionists.

The determination of possible conditions for future peace made by the warring parties at the beginning of 1916 was a particular achievement in the construction of a new world order, which was later called the Versailles system. Once more, the Americans declared the right to self-determination for minor nations and states (but they did so in a form that lacked concreteness). The allied states named the following among their requirements for a peaceful settlement: the reorganization of Europe supported by strict agreement, based on national principle, on each nation's right (whether the nation was major or minor) to enjoy absolute safety and freedom of economic growth; the liberation of the Italians, the Slavs, the Romanians, the Czechoslovaks, and the non-Turkish nations of the Ottoman Empire from alien domination; the absolute expulsion of Turkey from Europe; and implementation of the tsar's manifest on the liberation of Poland. These conditions were selective in nature and concerned only the Central states.

The attitude toward the principal issues of the future peace, as determined by the Entente, gave Wilson an opportunity to formulate the American vision of the problem. On 22 January 1917, in an appeal to the US Senate, Wilson proposed a basis for a strong, peaceful settlement of the Monroe Doctrine, namely, "that no nation should seek to extend its polity over any other nation or people, but that every people should be left free to determine its own polity, its own way of development, unhindered, unthreatened, unafraid, the little along with the great and powerful." At first glance, Wilson's position seemed to conform to a nation's right for self-determination. But the main idea of the appeal indicated that, at that moment, he had abandoned himself to the idea that any territorial changes in Europe based on the prewar period were undesirable. He made an exception only for Poland, because Austria-Hungary, Germany, and Russia gave their consent (although under different terms) to grant Poland independence.

Therefore, by January 1917, the Entente powers and the United States were close to recognizing the principle of national self-determination in very general terms, at least judging by their declaration. In practical terms, national self-determination referred wholly to solving the Polish issue, enclosed in the Russian territory.

The position taken by the Russian provisional government, which took an open international approach on the Polish issue, was widely approved by the allies. During the summer and autumn of 1917, the Western governments took practical steps toward creating conditions for reviving the Polish state: they began to form Polish military units in Russia and France, and the Polish National Committee in Paris, headed by Dmowski, was recognized as representative of the Polish people. In 1918, well after the October Revolution in Russia, the Western allies started to define the future borders of Poland.

On 8 January 1918, the American president formulated his appeal to Congress and defined his understanding of the issue in the thirteenth point of the "Fourteen Points" peace program as the following: "An independent Polish state should be erected which should include the territories inhabited by indisputably Polish populations, which should be assured a free and secure access to the sea, and whose political and economic independence and territorial integrity should be guaranteed by international covenant."

Six months later, on 3 June, the French, British, and Italian leaders— Georges Clemenceau, David Lloyd George, and Vittorio Orlando—declared that "the foundation of a united and independent Poland with access to sea is one of the conditions for establishing an enduring and just peace and restoring international law in Europe." Thus, there was no consensus of opinion among the allies in their approach to the question of future Polish borders. Wilson commented on establishing borders according to ethnographic principles, while his European partners remained silent. The French were particularly reticent; they generally supported the idea of establishing the postwar peace based on a strategic balance of powers. Therefore, the Poles gained an opportunity to participate in establishing their own borders, even though the Great Powers had undoubtedly reserved that right.

The Revival of the Polish State and Problems with Establishing Borders

The revival of the Polish state could not occur in a single step. It was a continuous process that started toward the end of 1916 with the recognition by the Great Powers of the right to self-administration of public life for all Poles (or just the Russian Poles), and it ended in March 1923 with international recognition of the borders of the Republic of Poland. The process could be easily divided into several steps. One of the milestones was the formation of a central government in Warsaw in November 1918, instead of the several regional administrations that, from January to February 1919, had managed to gain the recognition of the victorious powers. Piłsudski played a major role at this stage. Due to a number of objective and subjective reasons, he managed to become the consolidating center of all major political forces who considered the formation and establishing of the basis of an independent state as the highest national goal.

Piłsudski also played the leading part in accomplishing the most difficult task of establishing state borders for the newly independent Poland. The issue was that, since Poland had been erased from the political map of the world at the end of the eighteenth century, it was the core part of Rzeczpospolita, and its borders included ethnically Polish territories as well as historically East Slavic territories. At the same time, Poland did not exist as an independent state. But in the Polish public conscience, "Poland" and "Rzeczpospolita" were indistinguishable. Also ignored was the obvious fact that, during the previous 123 years, the mentality of the non-Polish population in the former outskirts of Rzeczpospolita had undergone significant changes. The nationalist identities of Ukrainians, Belorussians, and Lithuanians were steadily growing, particularly in eastern provinces where the majority of the population well remembered and steadily associated Poland and the Rzeczpospolita with the absolute power of the landowning Polish gentry. Those nations demonstrated growing ambition for forming national states, while the Jewish population, slowly migrating out of Qahals, leaned mostly toward Russian culture, rather than Polish. That was why the decision to restore Poland within the Rzeczpospolita borders was bound to cause cross-national clashes in the provinces.

The process of liberating Polish territories from foreign administration started in October 1918. It quickly showed that the problem of Polish borders would not be easy to solve. Western states reserved the right to establish a border between Poland and neighboring states, provided that the demarcation line would be defined during the course of a peace conference, which they were not in a hurry to call. Before the conference, the Polish territory was limited to the former Kingdom of Poland and the western part of the Austrian crown lands of Galicia. As for any other territories considered Polish, the Poles were to procure them with deadly force.

The eastern part of Galicia was first to be occupied by local Ukrainians, when they established their control over the city of Lvov on the night of 1 November 1918, thus proclaiming the Western Ukraine National Republic. This move started the Polish-Ukrainian war, which ended by the middle of 1919 with a Polish army victory, largely due to Piłsudski's efforts in forming a Polish regular army and his decision, despite direct prohibition by the Western allies, to transfer the Blue Army from France. Even after that, the Polish right to eastern Galicia was not recognized by the Entente states until March 1923.

The attempt to peacefully split Austrian Silesia from Czechoslovakia failed and ignited a short war between the newly founded states in January 1919; it ended in a Polish defeat. Similarly difficult was the process of demarcation with the former Prussian territories of Germany. Warsaw did not have a chance to take obvious initiatives there, as Germany was not dissociated, unlike Austria, and its government continued to keep the whole territory under its control. The Poles had to await the decision from peacemakers, which proved to be unhurried and was made only in June 1919. The alternative for the Poles was to secretly promote the irredentist movement within disputed territories, while widely demonstrating complete compliance with the allies' will. For that purpose, Warsaw sponsored the formation there of underground Polish military groups, supplying arms and smuggling instructors and experts specializing in sabotage and clandestine warfare from the Polish army's general headquarters. As a result of these rebellion activities, organized with direct but covert support from Warsaw, Poland acquired Great Poland at the beginning of 1919 and the majority of the industrial areas in Upper Silesia in 1921.

It seemed that the most painless example of border revision was the Danzig Corridor, cut along the lower reaches of the Wisła and providing free access to the Baltic Sea. But that misleading illusion of painless revision was engendered by the temporary weakness of Germany after losing the war.

Inevitability of the Dispute over Poland's Eastern Border

As far as the eastern border is concerned, if Russia had not fallen into chaos after the 1917 revolution, Poland would not have had the opportunity to receive territory to the east of the former border of the Kingdom of Poland. It seemed that the civil war in Russia gave Poland a unique opportunity to solve a couple of vital issues without any risk. First, the main political forces within Russia had no opportunity to manage the developing situation in the outskirts of the former Romanov Empire while they were involved in a struggle for control over Moscow and Petrograd. Within this power vacuum, the national frontiers were transformed into a peculiar "gray zone." Here, the evident social and national contradictions split local political elites into antagonistic groups. Each group, being incapable of holding tightly onto power, looked to external forces for help. The supporters of Bolshevism looked to Soviet Russia, while their opponents asked for help from the Entente, the United States, and Germany; some decided on Poland, which managed to achieve a certain level of domestic stability and acknowledgment from the Great Powers. As a result, Poland had a real opportunity to be involved in the creation of ally regimes in Lithuania, Belorussia, and Ukraine, simultaneously ensuring the most important condition of strategic security.

The latter instance is extremely important to understanding the inevitability of the armed conflict between Russia and Poland in 1919 and 1920. By 1918, European experience had proven that smaller states had little to no opportunity to carry on any kind of independent foreign policy and were able to ensure their safety only with the help of the Great Powers, paying for that with part of their sovereignty. The United States and the Entente announced the recording of the ethnic composition of the population to be the main principle for reorganizing the eastern part of Central Europe and the Balkans. This announcement indicated that Warsaw could extend its sovereignty to a relatively small territory, which was less than 150,000 square kilometers and had fewer than twenty million people. These territorial and demographic parameters would not allow Poland to fully ensure its security, because it was bordered by major European countries: Russia and Germany. Since the likelihood of acquiring territory at Germany's expense was low, only the eastern direction remained. This decision was also encouraged by the refusal of governments in England, France, Italy, and the United States to decide where to place the eastern border of Poland with a view toward favoring the anti-Bolshevik forces in the civil war.

In theory, Warsaw could pursue two strategic options under the circumstances. It could join the Western states and wait and assist the White Army in its fight against the Bolsheviks. In that scenario, they did not have much hope, since the leaders of the White movement were ready to accept the solution to the Polish issue suggested by the provisional government; Poland would thus be confined by the eastern border of December 1919 (the Curzon Line). Poland had better chances by exploiting another scenario: implementing a self-determined solution to the eastern border question and not waiting for the Russian riot to end, while at the same time assisting efforts to organize independent Lithuanian, Belorussian, and Ukrainian buffer states in the east. That was the strategy adopted by Piłsudski as head of state and commander in chief at the end of 1918, even before he received any support from influential Ukrainian, Lithuanian, and Belorussian politicians.

Obviously, that lack of support was a serious drawback to his plan, since the occupation of eastern territories by the Polish army could be viewed by the public as aggression, violating the principle of self-determination for the resident nationalities. If Piłsudski had intended to help form friendly national states to the east of ethnically Polish territories, then his steps would have seemed aggressive only to Bolsheviks and the White force supporters. But then he would have failed to provide security for Poland as it was understood then.

The date he decided to start a war on the eastern border was very important for understanding the developing relations between the new Russian state and the resurrected Poland. It was widely known that, since coming to power, the Bolshevik government had developed a goal of bringing the proletarian revolution to the states of Western Europe, even at the point of Red Army bayonets.

But plans were one thing, particularly for a group that had just gained political power, and implementation was another. Before starting on a foreign campaign, the Red Army had to win the civil war. During 1918 and 1919, the Kremlin government's attention was fully focused on the civil war's front lines. Until 1920, the RSFSR did not recognize the right of self-determination of the provinces, with the exception of Poland. The leadership considered establishing Soviet power, not undertaking a foreign military campaign, to be the primary objective of the civil war. Naturally, spreading the revolution by military means was pure aggression, especially considering the slogan of national self-determination up to and including dissociation, which the Bolsheviks had actively promoted before coming to power. No doubt the Bolsheviks were aware of that. To avoid the accusation of having a Russian imperialistic mentality, they agreed, with the help of their resident associates, to the formation of national states along the Russian perimeter, including the Baltic States, Belorussia, Ukraine, the Transcaucasia republics, and Turkestan. Hence, any military activities in those regions were attributed to social rather than national clashes, and the Kremlin even verbally agreed to organize referendums there. As far as ethnic Poland was concerned, the Bolsheviks did not have a detailed plan for invading Polish territory, either in 1918 or in 1919.

Therefore, the territories between Russia and Poland were considered by the politicians in both countries as an important objective for their politics, as an integral part of their plans to reinforce their countries' statuses. The attitude toward the resident nationalities was mainly pragmatic. Neither Moscow nor Warsaw was deeply concerned about the national idea of their future fate.

Piłsudski's decision to start a territorial war with the RSFSR armies and the Western Ukrainian and Ukrainian republics led to the failure of Soviet attempts to establish diplomatic relations with Poland from November to December 1918.

When the Soviet government learned about the formation of the left-wing nationalist government headed by Ignacy Daszyński, the Polish socialist leader from Galicia, in Lublin on 7 November 1918, it was considered a socialist revolution victory in Poland. Consequently, the Soviet government broadcast an appeal to Poland to establish diplomatic relations and to appoint a well-known Polish social-democrat, Julian Marchlewski, as the Russian diplomatic representative to Poland. The Soviet suggestion was not accepted.

The obvious reason for Warsaw's reluctance to establish diplomatic relations with Moscow, expressed even before Piłsudski came to power, was uncertainty about the international status of the Polish government. The Entente did not recognize either the Regency with its cabinets or the government in Lublin, just as it did not recognize the Russian Soviet government, which by then had been in place for more than a year. For Poland to recognize the RSFSR against the Entente would have enrolled Poland in the ranks of the enemies of the Great Powers, and Poland depended on them for international recognition of Poland itself, as well as for providing essential funding for the war in the east.

Military Actions in Wołyń and Belorussia in 1919

Until the latter half of February 1919, several rather weak Soviet armies were concentrated in the western theater of military operations (from Estonia on the right flank to Belorussia on the left flank). On 12 December 1918, the Soviet Western Army received an order to occupy territories up to the Poniewież-Vilnius-Lida-Baranowicze-Pińsk line. It was not difficult to execute the order, since the army had just been following the evacuating German forces, which had temporarily departed per the decision of the winners. On 5 January 1919, units of the Western Army occupied Vilnius, which the local Polish self-defense forces had taken control of after the Germans left. By 15 February, the Western Army had reached the desired line, and Chief of Staff of the Military Revolutionary Council Fyodor V. Kostyaev addressed Chicherin with a request, which is rather unexpected for those historians who believe that the Soviets had a specific plan for the "sovietization" of Poland: "The military situation allows further advance, especially in the direction of Brześć Litewski and Równe, but the political situation remains uncertain, chiefly on the part of Poland, so please indicate the line or the points up to which we may advance without disturbing the political balance, and also please define the eastern borders of Poland, which are still absolutely unknown to the military command."

Therefore, if Piłsudski had defined the war aims in the east as early as 1918, the Soviet command did not develop any guidelines concerning Poland

and did not convey them to the troops until the middle of February 1919. The directive by the chief command of the Workers' and Peasants' Red Army on creating a united front in the western theater of military operations was issued only on 12 February 1919. The directive's rather moderate objects were formulated even later, on 22 February. As far as Piłsudski is concerned, as early as 8 February, he concluded an agreement with the German command in Belorussia (with support from France) on unobstructed passage through the territories occupied by German forces, in order to give the Polish forces the ability to enter into battle with the Red Army. On 13 February 1919, fighting between Polish and Soviet forces occurred near Baranowicze. The Poles took eighty Red Army prisoners. This moment can be regarded as the beginning of the undeclared Polish-Soviet war, which lasted for twenty months and was primarily conducted on territories that were neither Russian nor Polish.

The course of military events from spring to early fall of 1919 has been reconstructed in sufficient detail by Polish and Russian historians. The survey of the military and political aspects of the Polish-Soviet war was started soon after the end of the war and continues to this day.

In this regard, it is possible to confine ourselves to the interpretation of certain moments of the Soviet-Polish conflict that are most important for understanding the complex future relations between Poland and its eastern neighbors, as well as its unusual nature in contrast with the "classic" wars of the twentieth century.

There is no doubt that the occupation of Vilnius by Polish forces on 19 April 1919 was the first key moment. Three nations had put a claim on the city: the Lithuanians, the Belorussians, and the Poles. Each claimant had its own arguments, and Piłsudski also had personal motives—it was his native town. The solution of the Vilnius question by force closed the door on cooperation with the political elites of Lithuania and Belorussia for Warsaw. Without this cooperation, creating a future Lithuanian-Belorussian state allied with Poland was problematic. Moreover, it stimulated Lithuania's rapprochement with the RSFSR, which ended in July 1920 with the conclusion of the Moscow Treaty, which recognized Lithuania's right to Vilnius.

At the same time, the perspective of cooperation with Symon Petliura started to take shape. The *ataman* (chieftain) had to fight the Ukrainian Soviet Socialistic Republic and the Volunteer Army of Anton Denikin. In the absence of worldwide recognition of the Ukrainian People's Republic, Poland was at that moment his critical need, as it was the main power in the eastern part of Central Europe. But in January 1919, the Ukrainian People's Republic joined the Western Ukrainian People's Republic, which automatically involved the Ukrainian People's Republic in a furious quarrel with Poland. The opportunity for rapprochement emerged during the second half of 1919, after the Polish army had occupied eastern Galicia with sanction by the Entente

Supreme Council (yet for the limited period of twenty-five years). The negotiations between Poland and Ukraine held in Warsaw in August 1919 ended with a verbal agreement under which the Ukrainian People's Republic should have transferred eastern Galicia and western Wołyń (in other words, those territories that, according to Piłsudski's plan, were to be integrated into Poland) to Poland. In return, Poland undertook to help the Ukrainian People's Republic in its struggle against the Ukrainian Soviet Socialist Republic. This was the second key moment in the development of Polish-Soviet relations in 1919. In Ukraine, unlike in Lithuania and Belorussia, Piłsudski managed to secure the environment for implementing his project. Yet, it could not be done all at once. In the summer of 1919, the Volunteer Army started a march on Moscow, and Ukraine lay within the zone of advance. Petliura did not have enough military units to fight Denikin, and Poland could not help him because doing so would engender conflict with the Entente.

In August 1919, the Polish army occupied Minsk and reached the Berezina line. Taking into account the agreements with Petliura, it should seem that Piłsudski had taken possession of all the eastern territories without which he thought it was impossible to ensure Poland's security. In other words, he successfully implemented his eastern plan. However, the question about the Polish-Russian buffer zone remained open, which implied that, in reality, Piłsudski's plan was only half complete.

For exactly this reason, he did not need peace with the RSFSR, but at the same time it was senseless to move farther toward Moscow, although he had enough forces at that moment.

White Russia in Piłsudski's Eastern Politics

Piłsudski could not make peace with the RSFSR for one more reason: in the summer of 1919, the Western states looked optimistically on the prospects of victory by the White forces. Piłsudski could not be satisfied with such an outcome of the Russian civil war since, unlike the Bolsheviks, neither Aleksandr Kolchak nor Anton Denikin had ever promised any territorial increments beyond the ethnically Polish territories. In the event of victory by the White Army, all of his achievements, with the probable exception of eastern Galicia, would come to nothing. To implement his eastern project, Piłsudski needed the Red Army to win, not lose.

The year 1919 was the most difficult for the Soviet government during the civil war. At times, it seemed that it needed a miracle to survive. The Bolsheviks were ready to make any territorial concessions at the expense of non-Russian regions in order to settle the conflict on the western border and to release forces for the eastern and southern fronts. And Piłsudski showed full understanding of the situation. During the summer and autumn of 1919, the third important period occurred in the development of relations between

Poland and the RSFSR. Earlier in 1919, after the outbreak of the unannounced war in Belorussia and Wołyń, Moscow undertook several attempts to start political negotiations with Warsaw in order to put an end to the conflict on very beneficial terms. In March 1919, Moscow readily accepted the diplomatic mission led by Aleksander Więckowski, though the Polish envoy did not have the power to conduct political negotiations and was interested only in the fate of the Lednicki mission and of the other Polish hostages in Russia. In the summer of 1919, talks between the Russian and Polish Red Cross delegations took place, but again the discussion focused on humanitarian rather than political issues. In early September 1919, Piłsudski sent an order to the Polish army, as well as to the covert Polish military organization that was active in Ukraine and Belorussia, to stop military actions against the Red Army. Moscow was informed that the Polish side was ready to reopen negotiations between the Red Cross delegations. The talks started in October 1919 at the small Mikaszewicze railway station in Polesie on the Polish side of the front line, under conditions of total secrecy, and continued until December 1919. The talks included political dialogue.

This time the talks yielded results. After securing a number of tough, war-related conditions for the agreement, Piłsudski promised the leader of the Soviet delegation, Julian Marchlewski, that he would not carry out any offensive actions against the Red Army along the Lithuanian-Belorussian front, provided the Soviets observed the conditions he had placed in the agreement. The Polish delegation, though, ignored the Soviet suggestion to start full-fledged peace talks.

Military, Diplomatic, and Propaganda Preparations before the Clash in 1920

The secret armistice met the interests of both parties. Winter had started a month earlier, and there was no harvest in Poland. Ill-equipped and suffering food shortages, the Polish army would be unable to undertake any active military actions. Older soldiers, who had taken part in World War I, were reluctant to fight. Hence, it was necessary to enlist as many young people as possible, and they needed time to be drilled. It was important to build up military strength, as Piłsudski was planning to undertake a major attack in Ukraine during the spring, when the snow melted and the unpaved roads dried. His plan was to transfer Petliura to Ukraine, with the help of the Polish army, to establish a Ukrainian state, independent from Russia and friendly to Poland, on the Dnieper's right bank within the territories not yielded to Poland. Petliura, who sheltered himself and his remaining army in Wołyń under the protection of Poland, was not able to do that without Polish support. His army was small. After the resurrection of the Ukrainian national republic and strengthening of Petliura's position in Ukraine, Piłsudski could consider the epochal project he had started in 1918—protecting Poland from the eastern danger—completed. It is no wonder that in Mikaszewicze he demanded that the Soviet government abandon all military actions against Petliura.

By the end of 1919, Soviet Russia could take a breath at last. Denikin's armies were destroyed, Ukraine was cleared of enemies, and Soviet power was once again resurrected in Kiev. Two forces still posed a real threat, however. First, there were the remains of the Volunteer Army in southern Russia. Significant forces were needed to overthrow that last serious center of the White movement in the European part of Russia. Second, there was the Polish alignment of forces in Belorussia, in proximity to the RSFSR, which then included the Mogilev and Witebsk regions. The Soviet command expected that, in the absence of a peace treaty with Poland, Piłsudski could restart offensive actions at any moment. Therefore, in 1920, effective military units released from other fronts were transferred to the Polish border and to the southern front line to provide protection along the Smolensk route.

The Kremlin feared not only new aggression from the Polish army but also its coordination with the White movement. Moreover, by the middle of December, a new cabinet of ministers had been formed in Poland, led by Leopold Skulski. In Moscow, the new cabinet was seen as evidence of Piłsudski's weakening position and the growing danger of Poland turning toward "killing the Bolsheviks, supporting Denikin." The objective was to get Poland out of play, using peaceful rather than military means. Soviet diplomats were entrusted with the task and were to persuade Poland toward peace. By the last week of December 1919, the decision was made in Moscow to present Warsaw with a peace proposal. The proposal had to be public, which would activate the left-wing forces in Poland in their activities against war, and would also "impede the activities of those who actively politic against us, and of the agreement with Denikin."

The diplomatic note to the Polish government was broadcast on 22 December, though it naturally did not contain any specific peace initiatives. That was the beginning of the Soviet "peace attack" of early 1920. It coincided with the Entente reconsidering its former policy on the Russian question. Instead of continuing to supply further financial support to the White movement, the Great Powers were inclined to support the idea of organizing a so-called sanitary cordon of neighboring states around Soviet Russia (the "barbed wire," as Clemenceau put it). That policy would also disturb the convergence and cooperation between the RSFSR and Germany, the two outcasts on the international political scene.

Warsaw found itself in a difficult situation. The Soviet note contained well-grounded accusations against the Polish government's reluctance to make peace. Accepting the talks would mean the end of Piłsudski's ambitious eastern project. He was not ready to take such a step, as the previous year had been a glorious one for the Polish army on the Soviet front. Instead, he took the tactic of delaying the response. In the draft reply to the Soviet note, the Polish government suggested that a specific response could not be given without consultations with the allies.

The Soviet government soon realized that the comparatively quiet situation on the Soviet-Polish front did not really offer an opportunity to confirm or deny propaganda statements by Poland. What they needed was the Soviet peace initiatives to be demonstrated in practice at the highest level, much higher than that of the Commission of Foreign Affairs. A special commission was established on 27 January, with the participation of Lenin, Trotsky, and Chicherin in order to work out an appeal to the Polish government. The text of the appeal was also sent to the VTsIK (All-Russian Central Executive Committee). On the following day, the appeal by the Soviet government to the government and people of Poland outlining the fundamental principles of the Soviet political stance toward Poland was conveyed to Warsaw. The appeal consisted of four principal issues: unconditional recognition of the independence and sovereignty of Poland; observation of the integrity of the current front line in Belorussia and Ukraine; refusal to enter into any treaties with Germany or with other countries aligned against Poland, either expressly or implicitly; and willingness to solve all bilateral relational issues, including territorial and economic questions, by way of peaceful negotiations, mutual compromises, and agreements. On 2 February, the Central Committee confirmed the terms of the appeal. The government of the Ukrainian SSR also expressed the desire to start peaceful negotiations on the principles outlined in the Soviet government appeal. Without a doubt, the Soviet party made a strong move when it publicly gave up territories that had historically belonged to Russia. But that move produced no changes. Piłsudski was waiting for the warmth of spring to arrive so that he could continue implementing his eastern project.

From February to March 1920, Warsaw slowly worked on the draft reply to the peace proposal. At last, on 8 March, a closed meeting of the Polish cabinet took place in order to work out a list of demands for the peace negotiations with the Soviet government. The ultimate program (allowing some room for compromise during negotiations) suggested reestablishing the borders of 1772; the minimum program was to guarantee a so-called line of security drawn between the 1772 border and the actual front line. The draft included a military coalition with Petliura to assist in recovering the Ukrainian national state on the lands to the east of the Zbruch, Stryi, and Horyn Rivers. The eastern border of the Ukrainian state was the Ukrainians' concern, and they would have to conquer it from Russia. As was agreed with Piłsudski, the government declined its plans to establish an independent Belorussian state. The

Grodno and Vilnius regions were to be included within Poland unconditionally, while, in the Minsk region and in "other acquired territories to the east of it," the Belorussians would enjoy "compromises in self-administration and culture." In fact, this was the idea of granting a certain form of cultural and administrative autonomy to the regions between the Lithuanian and Belorussian lands, incorporated within Polish territory and Soviet Russia. Thus, the government was adopting Piłsudski's project with modifications to account for the impossibility of forming an allied Lithuanian-Belorussian state.

As late as 27 March, two months after the Soviet initiative, Poland agreed to start peace negotiations in the front-line area at the town of Borisov, without putting a stop to "offensive actions" on other parts of the front. A slow dialogue regarding the place and conditions for negotiations continued until 25 April, when the Polish army started attacks in Ukraine.

It would be wrong to think that the Soviet army did not take advantage of the months-long respite and was not preparing to resume military action along the Polish front. By the beginning of 1920, the success achieved against the White Army had enabled the western front to be strengthened substantially. Mikhail Tukhachevsky was appointed commander of the western front in April. After fighting with Kolchak's army, he had proven himself to be a professional officer and deserving of complete political trust. He was determined to bring discipline to the troops, and he also recruited deserters and the local population. He made the western front a strong military force, capable of carrying out both defensive and offensive actions.

The Soviet forces along the Ukrainian sector of the Polish front (the Twelfth and Fourteenth Armies) were considerably weaker, as before, both in numbers and in firepower, than the opposing force of three Polish armies together with the Ukrainian divisions under Polish command.

The Course of Military Actions

The Polish onslaught in Ukraine, which was prepared in perfect secrecy, began on 25 April. It had developed so rapidly that, on 7 May, the leading Polish military patrols from Edward Rydz-Śmigły's group of forces rode a tram into Kiev, from which the Red Army had departed without resistance. However, the success, which originally seemed to be unqualified, was in reality only partial. The majority of the enemy's force managed to retreat across the Dnieper and southward.

From the very beginning of the April campaign in Ukraine, the Soviets tried to present their actions as a defense of Russian national territory against foreign invasion. On 29 April, the All-Russian Central Executive Committee and the Council of People's Commissars approved an appeal "to all workers and peasants and honest citizens of Russia" (the addressee itself was unusual for the Soviet power), and, as of 4 May, the decisions by the Politburo of the

Central Committee of the Russian Communist Party (Bolsheviks) included patriotic elements that sounded unusual for the Bolsheviks, although it was not so obvious as it was later, in 1941. There is no doubt that the letter from Aleksei Brusilov to N. I. Rattel of 1 May 1920 became widely recognized as a result of extensive propaganda by the Soviet media per the Politburo's order. In this letter, Brusilov spoke of the urgent need to "stimulate national patriotism, without which a strong and efficient army cannot exist," with regard to the foreign invasion.

A well-executed offensive operation conducted by the Polish army on the right bank of Ukraine had not only military but also mostly political aims. Polish military units reached the Dnieper in Ukraine and stopped. No offensive was planned in Belorussia. The Poles did not pose any direct threat to the Soviet government. Their actions were not coordinated with those of the White general Pyotr Nikolayevich Vrangel. The Ukrainian campaign was to ensure Petliura's ability to create sufficiently strong Ukrainian state institutions that would have no connection to Russia in the part of Ukraine occupied by the Poles. But for this purpose, Petliura lacked popularity, power, and time. Moreover, the Polish army, which was certainly stronger than in 1919, suddenly faced another significantly different enemy from the one it had once so easily defeated.

In May, the Polish troops barely withstood the pressure from Soviet units in Belorussia. At the end of May, the Red Army in Ukraine went on the offensive, which resulted in frontal penetration and a breakthrough by Semyon Budyonny's First Mounted Army behind the Polish-Ukrainian forces. The Polish retreat began and later transformed into a wild flight. This situation very closely resembled the April–May retreat of the Red Army in Ukraine. Although retreating violently, the Polish army preserved both its numbers and the ability to launch a counterattack after reforming and replenishment.

In July 1920, a range of events occurred that greatly influenced the subsequent development of relations between the warring parties. The Polish army's defeat in Ukraine alarmed Polish political parties and caused them to change their approach toward the eastern policy that had been under the absolute jurisdiction of Piłsudski since the moment of Poland's restoration. In light of the approaching disaster, the major Polish political parties assumed responsibility for the eastern policy. For this purpose, an extraordinary collegial body, the State Defense Council, was organized on 1 July 1920. As a matter of fact, it was led by Piłsudski, though not on his authority but rather according to formal criteria.

On 4 July, Soviet units went on the offensive in Belorussia. On the following day, the enemy's front was broken and a rapid retreat began.

Gathered in conference at the Belgian town of Spa, the Entente leaders were addressed by the State Defense Council via telegram on 6 July and by

Polish prime minister Władysław Grabski in person on 9 July. They were asked to mediate the cessation of any military actions with the Soviet republics. Grabski had to listen to many frank opinions regarding the eastern politics of Poland. But Poland was promised assistance. On 11 July, British foreign secretary George Curzon sent a note to the Council of People's Commissars of the RSFSR containing territorial offers with respect to future delimitation, which were rather favorable for the Soviets. The Entente Supreme Council's line, which was formulated in December 1919, was used as the basis. Poland was unexpectedly denied the ownership of eastern Galicia, which, in December 1919, had been transferred by the Entente to Polish control for a period of twenty-five years. Moreover, it was explained to Warsaw that the creation of Ukraine, independent from Russia, was absolutely out of the question. Ukraine was not mentioned among members of the planned peace negotiations in London.

Success at the fronts and the Curzon note required the Kremlin to answer a range of important questions: what would be the final frontier of the offensive, and what would be the Polish status after its army was defeated? The documents show that, as of the beginning of July, there was no consensus in the Soviet administration on these issues. But the party members could freely voice different opinions only before the adoption of a corresponding decision by one of the supreme party organizations. Afterward, they were presupposed to follow the decision strictly. On 17 July, the plenary session of the Central Committee of the Russian Communist Party (of the Bolsheviks, the Areopagus Party being second in order of importance), in a secret thesis not subject to public disclosure, recorded the following: "To help liberate the Polish proletariat and working masses from landlords and capitalists." This statement indicated a victory by the supporters of the "sovietization" of Poland with help from the Red Army. Moreover, they were trying to pretend that Poland would be a full-scale state within better boundaries compared to those guaranteed by Curzon on behalf of the Entente. The plenary session also refused the mediation of the League of Nations and Great Britain and declared a cessation of military actions with Vrangel to be impossible. The thesis indicated the Soviet administration's determination to continue the battle within the territory of ethnic Poland.

On 23 July, a temporary Polish revolutionary committee was established by the Politburo of the Central Committee of the Russian Communist Party (Bolsheviks). At the same time, the Red Army entered the territory of ethnic Poland. It seemed that the finale of the long-lasting Polish-Soviet tournament was approaching and that the Soviet republics would win. In the summer of 1920, the two sides reversed roles. If, in 1919, Piłsudski had dictated terms, then the Soviets now assumed this position. At the end of July, concurrent with continuous battles, the diplomatic activity of both parties increased, stimulated by Curzon's note. On 23 July, Chicherin sent a note to the Polish minister of foreign affairs, Eustachy Sapieha. This note instructed the Chief Command of the Red Army "*to immediately start negotiations with the Polish military Command to cease hostilities and to prepare for peace between both parties*" (emphasis by author). On the same day, the Soviet Chief Command informed the Polish Chief Command of the receipt of the order to start negotiations "*on the cessation of hostilities and peace*" (emphasis by author). It might seem paradoxical, but the differences noted in the texts served the interests of both parties. The Soviets, who planned to conduct negotiations on the cessation of hostilities without actually suspending military operations, preferred to commit the task to the military forces, without participation by "prominent politicians," and thought that peace negotiations should be conducted by a different commission in a different place. On 31 July, the Politburo of the Central Committee of the Russian Communist Party (Bolsheviks) approved preliminary terms for peace that resembled more of an ultimatum to the prostrate enemy. The military forces were better suited for imposing the terms.

In parliamentary states, military forces are not entitled to conduct negotiations on the preliminary terms of peace. This is a prerogative of political institutions. That is why the Polish party had an opportunity to deny the military forces a mandate to conduct negotiations on preliminary peace terms, without actually refusing the peace negotiations. The prolonging of talks gave the Polish army time to reform, reprovision, and supplement its armaments. They could have then tried to turn the tide at the front toward its own advantage. The Poles used these tactics until 17 August 1920.

Meanwhile, the situation at the front started to change in favor of Poland. In early August, the Polish-French military command performed a successful maneuver that gave the Polish army a chance to disengage from the enemy, rearrange its forces, and, by 12 August, to start the battle of Warsaw, which lasted almost two weeks. Its fate was actually sealed on 16 August, when, according to the plan approved by Piłsudski, special attack troops cut behind the Soviet armies approaching Warsaw. The western front was the first to retreat, and then, in September, the southwestern front also retreated. In October, the line came back to the frontiers that had been occupied by the warring parties on 25 April 1920.

The only significantly new point was that Piłsudski was no longer free to make his own decisions at that moment. The peace negotiations that began in Minsk in August 1920 were not interrupted, but the negotiations were transferred to Riga by mutual consent of the parties. On 12 October, the hostilities were suspended. After six days, the cessation of hostilities and preliminary terms of peace were signed.

The Riga Peace Treaty and Its Consequences
for Bilateral Relations

The Soviet delegation in Riga was headed by the best foreign commission negotiator, Adolf Joffe. The Polish delegation was headed by Jan Dąbski, the vice-minister of foreign affairs and member of the Polskie Stronnictwo Ludowe ("Piast"), or Polish People's Party. These two leaders were tasked with solving all major questions that had not been agreed upon by the specialized commissions. It should be noted that the situation in the Latvian capital differed from what might have been had negotiations taken place under Polish or Soviet dictates. It was a diplomatic battle of two equal partners.

The compromise on territorial issues was the easiest to achieve. Without long arguments, the Soviets agreed to yield prominent territories in Belorussia and in Wołyń. That important aspect proved that the demarcation line between Poland and the Soviet republics was a genuine proposal offered by the Soviets back on 28 January 1920. Further still, Chicherin did not rule out the possibility that the Poles might demand broader territories than those suggested by the Soviet delegation. Offering compensation to Poland in return for renouncing the Brasław corridor, separating Lithuania from the RSFSR, was seriously considered.

Major difficulties arose in determining the amount of compensation to Poland for "active use of Polish Republic lands for economic activities by the former Russian empire" and in determining the size of the rolling stock to be transferred. The Polish delegation originally insisted on 300 million rubles in gold and 509 steam locomotives. Dragging out negotiations due to financial issues was bound to influence decisions on other aspects of the peace treaty. The question of repatriating hostages, citizens, prisoners, the interned, refugees, and emigrants was under discussion, at a slow pace. The relevant draft agreement was ready at the beginning of January 1920. But Joffe connected the signing of the agreement with the Polish consent to prolong the notification period for cease-fire. According to the Soviet delegation's leader, "The Poles reasonably replied that their current agreement on prolonging the notification period would effectively mean their agreement to sign our version of the peace treaty's main provisions." The Poles associated the question of prolonging the notification period for cease-fire with the agreement regarding the amount of compensation and the rolling stock transferred by the Soviet republics to Poland. Only in February 1921 did the parties agree on 30 million rubles in gold and 300 steam locomotives (it was agreed that Russia and Ukraine should pay 27 million rubles in gold as a substitute for steam locomotives).

On 23 February 1921, Joffe informed Moscow that, considering there were no "drastic discrepancies in resolving the major gold and rail stock issues," he and Dąbski had agreed to immediately sign "a treaty on repatriation with all corresponding protocols (including the protocol on prolonging the notification period for waiving the armistice) and frontier commission instructions." The repatriation treaty was signed on 24 February 1921, and it went into effect in March of the same year.

The Riga Treaty, signed on 18 March 1921, put a final end to Piłsudski's eastern project. Although, from a military point of view, it created a sufficient "strategic region" in the east, Poland had acquired a joint border not with the allied Lithuanian-Belorussian and Ukrainian republics but with the Soviet republics of Belorussia and Ukraine, as well as Lithuania, which all had serious claims on Polish territories. The result was that, until 1939, Poland had joint borders with Germany and the Soviet republics, which the Poles considered offensive. However, millions of Ukrainians and Belorussians found themselves incorporated into Poland, though they did not demonstrate any wish to undergo any ethnic or administrative assimilation. This forced inclusion significantly weakened the inner unity and integrity of Poland.

The Fate of Soviet and Polish Prisoners of War

The Polish-Soviet war lasted twenty months and became a hardship for both sides. During the war, the conversion from military production was delayed. Since 1914, the economy had mainly supplied the army's needs. The territory involved in military actions suffered. The destruction across the territories occupied by the Poles was extremely noticeable. The war affected them at least three times. But the war's most painful impact was the death of people. According to official data, the irrecoverable losses of the Polish army in 1918–21 amounted to fifty thousand persons. The majority of them were killed during the war against the Soviet republics. Civilians also died. The level of irrecoverable losses by the Red Army cannot be precisely determined due to the absence of reliable sources.

The war also caused another problem, which still remains unsolved: the fate of Soviet and Polish prisoners of war. According to data from the Operations Division of the Polish Chief Command, the Poles captured 206,877 Red Army soldiers during battle. About 157,000 prisoners were sent to stationary prison camps. This variation in figures has many causes. For example, during the Kiev operation in April and May 1920, some of the prisoners were released (local inhabitants were sent home, the release of other persons was used as propaganda to prove that the Poles did not shoot prisoners). The Red Army managed to liberate about 7,000 prisoners during the counterattack in Ukraine. During the successful advance from August to October 1920, the Poles often left wounded and common soldiers of the Red Army on the battlefield. Their further fate is uncertain: some rejoined friendly forces, some died of injuries, but most of them were killed by local citizens.

According to Soviet data, as of November 1922, when the official repatriation was complete, 75,699 Red Army soldiers and officers had returned to their native land. The fate of the remaining 80,000 prisoners of war was different. Many of them died of injuries, lack of medical help, exhaustion, frostbite, epidemics of infectious diseases, and so forth. Unfortunately, the records of the Central Bureau of Prisoner of War Registration of the Polish Ministry of Military Affairs have still not been found. That is why any calculations of the number of Red Army soldiers who died in captivity cannot be regarded as precise. If the number of those who died is calculated based on the average death rate, which amounted to 7 percent of the prisoners and was documented in a letter from the sanitary department of the military ministry on 18 February 1920, we could account for 11,000 deaths. However, it is a well-known fact that more than 11,500 Red Army prisoners died just in the Strzałkowo and Tuchola camps. Consequently, the total number of those who died had to be significantly higher. It is known that, in the context of epidemics, the death rate quadrupled or even quintupled, reaching 30 percent and more. From 1919 to 1921, there were at least three epidemics. Each epidemic lasted for three to four months. Based on simple arithmetic, we can approximate that between 25,000 and 28,000 prisoners could have died (in other words, about 18 percent of all Red Army prisoners).

No fewer than thirty thousand captured Red Army troops decided, for various reasons, to serve in anti-Soviet formations. Some of them were killed, while some surrendered as prisoners or went over to the Red Army in the autumn of 1920 during the attempted breakthrough into Soviet territory. A portion of those who had retreated into Poland, as well as internees, came home after the November amnesty of 1921.

The majority of those interned from territories yielded to Poland under the Riga Treaty did not wish to return to the Soviet republics. That included about one thousand international prisoners (Hungarians, Greeks, Italians, Czechs, Slovaks, Romanians, Balts, and Finns) who were liberated from camps during the military actions. About seven thousand war prisoners escaped from the camps and labor gangs. Another thousand did not wish to return to the Motherland.

The number of Polish prisoners of war in the Soviet republics was between thirty-four thousand and forty-two thousand. Their fate from the moment of capture was not much different from the fate of Red Army prisoners. The attitude toward privates in permanent camps was perhaps slightly better. The Soviet administration and the Polish communists who were entitled to carry out political propaganda in camps considered them to be potential fighters for a Soviet Poland. But food, living conditions, and medical care were far from satisfactory. No fewer than two thousand persons died from 1919 to 1921.

From 1921 to 1922, about thirty-five thousand prisoners of war returned to Poland. About three thousand voluntarily resided in the Soviet republics. The fate of about two thousand former Polish prisoners of war remains unknown.

It should be mentioned that, until September 1920, neither the Soviet nor the Polish forces expressed sufficient interest in the fate of their prisoners of war. In June 1919, Julian Marchlewski discussed the issue with representatives of the Polish government. They agreed to permit a Russian Red Cross representative to visit Poland, but only if he would be under intensive supervision and would refrain from spreading any propaganda. But when the talks in Mikaszewicze started in the autumn, the issue was not raised again. For the Poles in 1919, the problem was a secondary priority, because at that moment there were fewer than fifteen hundred Polish prisoners of war in Russian camps in comparison with twenty-nine thousand Red Army prisoners in Poland. That was why the fate of prisoners of war was not discussed in Mikaszewicze; the main issue for the participants was the fate of refugees and the desire to "get our guys back" as quickly as possible.

It was in September 1920, during the talks on the cessation of hostilities and preliminary peace terms, when the representatives of the Russian and Polish Red Cross societies met in Berlin. The decision was made to organize mutual custody over the war prisoners. A well-known Polish human rights activist, Stefania Sempołowska, was appointed the representative of the Russian Red Cross in Poland. In Russia, the Polish Red Cross was represented by an equally well known person: Ekaterina Peshkova, wife of Maxim Gorky. Both parties quickly came to mutual agreement regarding their credentials and financing. Those representatives arranged for the first trains with prisoners of war to be sent to Moscow in March 1921. In April 1921, Moscow, Warsaw, and Kharkov were visited by the Polish and Russian-Ukrainian delegations of the joint commission on repatriation that had been set up in accordance with the Treaty on Repatriation of 24 February 1921. The delegations completed the repatriation and, until August 1921, also carried out some diplomatic functions. In August 1921, the bona fide diplomatic representatives and supporting staff arrived in Warsaw and Moscow—Lev Karakhan and Tytus Filipowicz, respectively. That was the beginning of a new and peaceful, though complicated, period in Soviet-Polish relations.

2

THE INTERWAR PERIOD

POLAND AND THE SOVIET UNION IN THE LATE 1920s AND EARLY 1930s

Wojciech Materski (Poland)

Professor, Institute of Political Studies, PAS, member of the Polish-Russian Group on Difficult Matters since 2008.

Aleksandr V. Revyakin (Russia)

Professor at the Department of International Relations and Foreign Policy of Russia at the Moscow State Institute of International Relations (MGIMO University).

WOJCIECH MATERSKI

· ·

POLAND AND THE SOVIET UNION IN THE LATE 1920s AND EARLY 1930s

· ·

AFTER THE CONCLUSION of the Riga Treaty, Polish-Soviet relations focused on the implementation of its provisions, with particular reference to the financial-economic sphere. The practically incessant conflicts between the parties were caused by Moscow's foot-dragging in this regard. Meanwhile, Poland treated the Riga commitments literally and linked progress in other spheres to their fulfilment—something that was understandable but which did not augur well for the future improvement of mutual relations. This outlook arose because, although the treaty reflected the balance of forces at the time of its signing, thereafter the balance had been shifting steadily against Poland. The last, failed attempt to exact the implementation of the Riga undertakings by way of political pressure was made in the latter half of 1923 by the center-right cabinet of Premier Wincenty Witos. His successor, Władysław Grabski, decided that the country's current economic interests were hobbled by the low level of mutual relations, and, in 1924, he moved to change that state of affairs, acquiescing to the suspension by the Soviet Union of the fulfillment of its treaty commitments. That policy enhanced the normalization of mutual relations, which, however, remained at an insufficient level.

The attitude of both states to the impending changes concerning the German question dominated their bilateral political relations. It was connected with the adoption by the Entente powers of the Dawes Plan concerning the payment by Germany of war reparations and their moves to relieve Germany of the status of a defeated state. A diplomatic campaign initiated by Britain led to the convening of the Locarno conference and, subsequently, to the admission of the Weimar Republic into the League of Nations.

The gradual alteration of the status of Germany alarmed the Polish government. The Soviet Union was also concerned, though for other reasons; it wanted to continue the cooperation outlined in the Rapallo Treaty between Germany and the Soviets. In this situation, the two foreign ministers,

Aleksander Skrzyński and Georgy Chicherin, even attempted to coordinate positions regarding the new approach in European politics to the German question. At a meeting in Warsaw in late September 1925, they exchanged opinions in connection with the forthcoming conference in Locarno but failed to reach any binding decisions or to formulate a common stance.

The Rhine Pact and the package of agreements concluded at Locarno would inevitably channel future German expansion eastward. That was a blow to the security of the Second Republic and, in the longer term, a threat to the security of the Soviet Union.

Poland and the Soviet Union after Locarno

In essence, the defeat suffered by Polish diplomacy at Locarno consisted of the weakening of the Polish-French alliance and the withdrawal of Entente guarantees concerning Germany's eastern frontier, which thus left the issue open.

The Rhine Pact also clearly undercut the Soviet Union's European policy, which was based on the Rapallo Treaty and the assumption of a permanent conflict between Germany and the Versailles system. That raised the question of whether the continuation of Soviet-German cooperation, which was particularly advanced in the military sphere, would at all be possible under the new conditions.

The Soviet-German talks launched after Locarno were meant to determine whether the countries' previous cooperation, with its anti-Versailles slant, would be continued. The talks resulted in the signing in April 1926 of a pact on nonaggression and neutrality (Berlin Treaty). Its conclusion was a serious blow to Poland. The Rapallo noose was not getting looser, as had appeared certain after Locarno, but in fact was tightening.

The coup of May 1926 and assumption of full power by Józef Piłsudski had a beneficial impact on Poland's eastern policy. The weakening of the Polish-French alliance after Locarno and France's clearly diminishing role in European affairs unavoidably forced the Polish leadership to seek another alternative for ensuring the country's security. That was probably one of the reasons for the conviction that Poland's relations with Germany and the Soviet Union needed to be at least as good as the relations between those two countries. Achieving that was quite another thing, especially in view of the progressing rapprochement of the Soviet Union and Germany.

However, the efforts of the new Polish government, primarily involving Foreign Minister August Zaleski, to invigorate political dialogue received a cool reception in the Soviet Union. That may have been connected with the setting of overly ambitious goals, including the concept of signing a bilateral nonaggression treaty within just a few weeks. Still, the talks were initiated.

Soviet consent to accredit a new Polish envoy, Stanisław Patek, in Moscow signaled that relations had entered a new, better phase. Patek was known to many top Soviet officials as a defense counsel in political trials in tsarist Russia. The arrival in Moscow of a new ambassador who enjoyed Piłsudski's confidence was seen as a chance for progress in negotiations on the nonaggression pact.

However, Patek's talks on the subject progressed slowly, with long interruptions. Both sides were very cautious, and tactics dominated over substance. The very formula of the pact turned out to be a major problem: Poland wanted it to have a multilateral character, or to consist of a series of agreements signed by the Soviet Union with states of the so-called Intermarum, comprising countries of Eastern Europe threatened, like Poland, by the Soviets.

Poland was extremely interested in improving relations with both the Soviet Union and Germany. The pact of nonaggression with Moscow was seen as an instrument for enhancing the country's security, which had been eroded by Locarno and the German-Soviet treaty of 1926. At the same time, however, Poland distrusted the Soviet leadership and sought to provide cover for its negotiations with the Soviet Union by incorporating them into a broad international context of similar nonaggression accords that the Soviet Union was to conclude with the Baltic States and Romania. That approach, however, did not enhance progress in the negotiations.

Therefore, it could be said that Poland was extremely interested in talks with the Soviet Union about a nonaggression treaty but less interested in actually concluding such an accord. Warsaw realized that its main ally, France, was seriously weighing the possibility of emancipation from the British policy line through political rapprochement with the Soviet Union. The signing of a Polish-Soviet nonaggression pact would have stimulated that tendency, and the Polish Foreign Ministry did not find that entirely congruent with the Polish *raison d'état*.

The Positions of Poland and the Soviet Union on Collective Security Initiatives

After Locarno, a tendency to reinforce the system of the League of Nations became increasingly evident. Poland was also involved in the related international dialogue, though Marshal Piłsudski was highly skeptical about multilateral mechanisms and preferred to strengthen the country's security through initiatives on the basis of bilateral relations.

The conclusion in Paris in August 1928 of the Kellogg-Briand Pact—a multilateral treaty whose signatories renounced war as an instrument of national policy—probably had the greatest impact on Polish-Soviet bilateral relations at the time. Since the ratification process was very slow, the Soviet Union proposed to Poland that the provisions of the pact become binding for both states from the moment they ratified it, without waiting for the completion of the whole complicated, multilateral procedure. Foreign Minister Zaleski immediately welcomed that initiative on behalf of the Polish government.

The proposal was open to other states in the region. It led to the signing in Moscow, on 9 February 1919, of a protocol by representatives of five states (Estonia, Latvia, Poland, Romania, and the Soviet Union). Those countries were shortly joined by Latvia, Persia, and Turkey. A regional accord on the renunciation of war as an instrument of national policy thus became a reality, unquestionably enhancing the security of the protocol signatories in terms of treaty diplomacy and the principle of *pacta sunt servanda*.

The Nonaggression Pact

The diplomatic campaign connected with the Moscow protocol and its ultimate success led to the suspension of the talks on the Polish-Soviet nonaggression pact. The talks were revived, though in a less binding format, in the autumn of 1930. At that time, the Polish Ministry of Foreign Affairs began drafting an updated version of the agreement that provided for the simultaneous signing by Moscow of similar documents with the Baltic States and Romania.

By then, the Polish-Soviet pact had a strong French context, since efforts were under way at the time for a comprehensive improvement of relations between Moscow and Paris. In April 1931, France presented to the Soviet Union proposals for a general upgrade of bilateral relations that included a nonaggression pact, a consular convention, and a trade treaty, as well as a number of further, minor accords. Soon afterward, the French government informed Moscow that it was making the conclusion of a bilateral nonaggression pact contingent on the signing by the Soviet Union of similar political agreements with Poland and Romania.

The Soviet-French negotiations made rapid advances, but the Polish government was not advised on their progress, hence its surprise at the information conveyed to the Polish embassy in Paris on 8 August that the pact would be initialed within two days.

On 23 September, the French Foreign Ministry officially informed the Soviet Union that the signing of the initialed pact would depend on the conclusion by Moscow of a similar accord with Poland: "The signing of the French-Soviet pact should be accompanied or preceded by the conclusion of a Polish-Soviet pact." This statement confirmed that the condition stipulated by French foreign minister Aristide Briand in his conversation on the subject with Soviet commissar for foreign affairs Maxim Litvinov was non-negotiable. That provided crucial stimulus for breaking the deadlock in Polish-Soviet negotiations, this time leading to their successful conclusion.

On 14 October 1931, Commissar Litvinov conveyed to the Polish embassy in Moscow a statement about Moscow's readiness to resume Polish-Soviet negotiations on the nonaggression pact. He indicated Moscow's willingness to sign it in the version initialed by France and the Soviet Union.

For Poland, the essence of the political accord with Moscow lay in the consolidation of security for all the western neighbors of the Soviet Union situated within the Intermarum. Poland's consistency on that point was rooted in the conviction that every effort should be made to counter Soviet attempts to differentiate the security of the countries in the region and whenever possible to turn them against each other. This time, however, Warsaw decided to be more flexible. It decided that the most important thing was for Moscow to begin working toward a system of such agreements, while the time and form of their conclusion was less pivotal.

Official talks with the aim of hammering out the final text of the Polish-Soviet nonaggression pact started in Moscow on 23 November 1931.

By that time, the final phase of the negotiations on the nonaggression pact and, indeed, eastern policy in general, was no longer supervised by Foreign Minister Zaleski; Marshal Piłsudski had assigned the task to Deputy Foreign Minister Józef Beck. The latter was very serious about coordinating policy with the Soviet Union's other western neighbors regarding the conclusion of nonaggression pacts with Moscow. Tallinn responded favorably to the Polish overtures, though the Estonian government indicated that it wanted to move hand in hand on the issue with Riga. Both the Latvian and Finnish governments were receptive to the Polish arguments and consented to open negotiations with the Soviet Union.

The initiation of contacts between Bucharest and Moscow proved to be more challenging. The Polish offer to facilitate the arrangement of the Romania-Soviet negotiations and, indeed, the prospect of the talks themselves evoked little enthusiasm among Romanian politicians. They feared that Romania's alliance with Poland would be weakened as a result and were skeptical about the possibility of finding an acceptable formula concerning Bessarabia in the talks with the Soviets. After repeated prompting by Warsaw and Paris, the Romanian authorities finally agreed to the talks, which were to begin on neutral ground—in the Latvian capital—in early January.

Meanwhile, the Polish-Soviet talks, conducted in late November and early December, revealed a convergence of positions on such concepts as "neutrality" and "aggression." Agreement was also quickly reached on the wording of articles dealing with the conduct of the parties in the event of aggression against one of them by a third state. However, it proved to be more difficult to make headway on the non-involvement of either party in international agreements ("combinations") directed against the other party.

Concerning arbitration, Patek indicated that the Polish side would be willing to abandon its demands on the issue if the Soviets accepted the Polish draft of Article 2 (conduct in the event of one party in conflict with a third state). It turned out to be impossible to bridge the gap concerning Article 3. Its Polish version affirmed that commitments stemming from previous treaties were binding on the parties as long as they did not contain elements of aggression; the Soviet version contained an additional passage obligating the parties to refrain from participation in accords manifestly hostile to the other side.

The parties managed to hammer out almost the entire text. A protocol was signed specifying the extent of the agreement reached, including a joint draft of the text, with two versions of Article 3. The negotiations were then suspended so decision makers in the two countries could determine the amount of room for possible compromise regarding the provisions that remained to be worked out. The talks resumed on 13 January 1932.

Progress in Soviet-Romanian negotiations and the signing of the Soviet-Finnish pact (21 January) induced Poland to relax its position concerning Article 3. Patek agreed to the addition of the controversial passage on non-involvement in agreements openly hostile to the other party. The full text of the document was nailed down by 23 January 1932.

The approved text consisted of a preamble and eight articles. It was to be complemented by an agreement on the amicable resolution of disputes (conciliation convention), treated as an integral part of the pact.

The parties renounced war as a method of settling conflicts between them, undertook to refrain from any agreements directed against the other party, and pledged that they were not currently participating in any such agreement. In the event of aggression against one of the parties by a third state, the other party would not support the aggressor. If one of the parties committed aggression against a third state, the other party would be entitled to denounce the pact without notice. All contentious issues that could be resolved through diplomatic channels would be subject to conciliatory proceedings laid down in the conciliation convention.

The text did not refer to the League of Nations, though it did affirm that the undertakings made by the signatories "shall in no case limit or modify the international rights and obligations of each Contracting Party under agreements concluded by it before the coming into force of the present Pact." Also, the parties deleted an article that had contained an invitation to the other signatories of the Moscow protocol to conclude similar political accords with the Soviet Union.

The pact was to remain in force for three years and automatically renewed for a further period of two years unless renounced by one of the parties not less than six months before its expiration.

On 25 July 1932 in Moscow, the Polish envoy to the Soviet Union, Stanisław Patek, and Nikolai Krestinsky, deputy commissar for foreign affairs, signed the text of the Polish-Soviet nonaggression pact. Also signed were two additional "protocols of signature." In the first, the parties declared that Article

7 of the pact could not be interpreted as meaning that the expiration of the time limit or renunciation of the pact could have as a result the limitation or cancellation of the obligations arising for the parties from the Pact of Paris of 1928 (Kellogg-Briand Pact). In the other protocol, the parties stated that they had exchanged views on the conciliation convention—a draft of which had been presented by Krestinsky—and that there was "no essential difference of opinion between them."

The signing of the pact was of pivotal importance to the Polish state, not so much with regard to bilateral relations with the Soviet Union as in the overall context of Poland's international position. The pact strengthened Poland vis-à-vis Paris and Berlin. It constituted a victory of the policy of solidarity with the region of Central and Eastern Europe, with the exception of relations with Romania, which became weakened. The pacts the Soviet Union concluded with Poland and the Baltic States enhanced security in the region.

The inclusion in the text of the assertion that any violation of Polish territory would constitute an "act of violence" was seen as an indisputable achievement of the Polish negotiators. It could be interpreted as recognition of the integrity of the entire Polish territory, including the border with Germany.

The signing of a political agreement of such stature created a favorable basis for rapprochement between Poland and the Soviet Union—with important economic and political connotations, especially in view of the mounting tendency to base security on regional treaties and Poland's German policy.

The Soviet Union mainly valued the pact as an instrument of leverage with Germany. Another key aspect was its pacifying effect on political tensions along the western rim of the Soviet Union at a time when the situation in the Far East appeared to be heading for war. After the Japanese aggression against Manchuria and the proclamation in March 1932 of the Manchukuo state, major armed conflict between Japan and China seemed imminent.

Thus began a period of several months of rapprochement between the Soviet Union and its western neighbors, including the improvement of both political and economic links, and—most prominently—the development of cultural and scientific contacts.

That vigorous advancement of relations in diverse spheres quickly waned after January 1934. Its complete dependence on political factors was thus emphatically confirmed.

Problems with the Policy of "Even Distance"

Analytical works conducted under Marshal Piłsudski's authority and coordinated by the National Defense Committee established in October 1926 indicated that Poland would not face the threat of war with one of its dangerous neighbors before the latter half of the 1930s. In order to reduce the likelihood of that happening, it was necessary to uphold the military alliances with

France and Romania while conducting a diplomatic campaign to persuade Berlin and Moscow of Poland's neutrality in the event of any conflict. Those political concepts had to be confronted with initiatives concerning new regional systems of European security.

The concept of the "Four-Power Pact" appeared in the early 1930s. Benito Mussolini unveiled the idea of creating a directorate of four powers, intended to be more effective than the League of Nations in guaranteeing peace and security on the European continent. In March 1933, his idea assumed the form of a concrete offer addressed to France and, subsequently, to Great Britain and Germany. Mussolini used persuasive phraseology, rooted in the spirit of the Kellogg-Briand Pact, to promote his concept. It appeared to build on the pact and implement its intent through the cooperation of the powers in revising peace treaties deemed likely to lead to conflict.

Germany, a prospective member of the directorate, was enthusiastic, particularly in view of the envisaged revision of the peace treaties. The French and British governments endorsed such a regional system, and soon (15 July 1933) the relevant document was signed (though never ratified), despite the resistance of other states, including the members of the Little Entente.

The controversies over the Four-Power Pact, which threatened Polish borders and presaged a return to the policy of isolating the Soviet Union, constituted a powerful stimulus for Polish-Soviet political collaboration. Yet, Polish diplomacy did not commit itself in that direction, restricting its response to a joint ascertainment of the threat. The reserve demonstrated by Poland reflected a strategic tenet of Polish foreign policy: the necessity of maintaining an even distance from both Berlin and Moscow. In fact, the situation seemed more conducive to an offer of improvement of relations addressed to Germany than to any actions that would further upset the rule of even distance, already eroded by the signing of the Polish-Soviet nonaggression pact.

While Warsaw and Moscow were unanimous in their extremely critical assessment of the Four-Power Pact, the two capitals adopted quite different positions concerning yet another international initiative of that period—the idea of the Eastern Pact. It surfaced in the autumn of 1933 in connection with work on the Soviet-French nonaggression pact, as a complementary regional security system encompassing, in its original version, Belgium, France, Czechoslovakia, Poland, the Soviet Union, Lithuania, Latvia, Estonia, and Finland. That configuration would have meant a definite end to the Rapallo cooperation. However, the original concept underwent major modifications in April 1934, when France presented a new version of the pact, which affiliated Germany, Czechoslovakia, Poland, the Soviet Union, and the Baltic States. France was to be included with the system through a corollary French-Soviet treaty on mutual assistance.

Warsaw flatly rejected the idea of the Eastern Pact, finding that it drastically limited Poland's role in the French system of alliances and undermined the détente achieved with such difficulty in relations with the Soviet Union and Germany. The proposed pact would have provided grounds for interference in Poland's internal affairs and would have allowed intervening foreign troops (e.g., Soviet or German armies) to cross Polish territory—with the threat of them remaining permanently.

The Polish stance was solitary, but, ultimately, Polish diplomats were not forced to defend it because the idea of the Eastern Pact was firmly rebuked by Germany. Moscow and Paris were convinced that Poland was colluding with Hitler to sink the idea of the Eastern Pact, even though the Polish Ministry of Foreign Affairs had provided no grounds for such speculation.

The Polish-German Declaration

The diplomatic campaign over the proposed Eastern Pact resulted in a significant improvement in Polish-German relations—something that alarmed Moscow. Efforts were launched to clarify Polish intentions and explain that Poland's negotiations with Berlin did not mean that the policy of rapprochement with Moscow had been abandoned. Foreign Minister Beck and Juliusz Łukasiewicz, an envoy, assured the Soviets that "Poland's talks with Germany in no way contradict the policy of rapprochement with the Soviet Union" and that "no special significance should be attached to them." They argued that the talks concerned routine matters between neighbors, though they might lead to the conclusion of a nonaggression pact. The Soviets were probably skeptical about such assurances, but, nevertheless, they invited the Polish foreign minister to pay an official visit to Moscow to review relations at a high level.

Meanwhile, the Polish-German talks were nearing their conclusion—something Poland was eager to see in view of the policy of even distance. Warsaw believed that the signing of a nonaggression accord with Berlin would reverse the erosion of security along its border with Germany, the result of Germany's exit from the League of Nations. Furthermore, the balance in relations between the Soviet Union and Germany would now be restored.

On 26 January 1934, the Polish envoy to Berlin, Józef Lipski, and the German foreign minister, Konstantin von Neurath, signed a bilateral declaration, valid for ten years, on the renunciation of the use of force in mutual relations.

The declaration affirmed the independence of Poland's foreign policy. It constituted a demonstration against such patronizing ideas as the Four-Power Pact. It also reflected Piłsudski's skepticism toward the League of Nations and of concepts of universal or regional collective security.

The declaration presaged a period of détente in relations with Berlin, which did materialize, though briefly. However, it did not incorporate something that was of the utmost importance from the point of view of Poland's western policy: a recognition of durable borders. In the final account, it was a document essential in the context of overall security policy, though the formula used—a declaration instead of a pact and imposed by the Germans—was clearly less advantageous to Warsaw. On the other hand, that diminished the odium of Poland contravening the policy of isolating Hitler.

On 25 January 1934, the Polish mission in Moscow advised the Soviet authorities that the signing of a Polish-German agreement on the non-use of force could be expected "in the nearest future" and that it did not have "any anti-Soviet content or implications."

Almost immediately after the signing of the agreement, the leading Soviet newspapers gave prominent coverage to the Polish-German declaration. The editorial comments were guarded, which was understandable in view of the forthcoming visit to Moscow by Foreign Minister Beck. The formally independent Comintern press, however, suggested that the declaration was clearly directed against the Soviet Union and that it incorporated secret military clauses.

At this point it would be useful to quote an incisive internal analysis formulated in November 1933 by the Soviet envoy to Warsaw, Vladimir Antonov-Ovseenko, in a memo to the head of the Polish desk at the Soviet Foreign Ministry, Boris Stomanyakov: "The struggle against German revisionism is being played out at the expense of Poland, in the bilateral talks the powers are conducting with Germany, and that has induced Poland to preemptively regulate its relations with Germany. . . . It is Poland, rather than Germany, that is threatened with isolation. . . . Rapprochement with us, following the actual scrapping of Rapallo, has allowed Poland to come out of isolation."

The Soviet leadership apparently shared the conviction that Poland was using the accord with Germany to defend itself against potentially dangerous solutions that could be elaborated in Paris or London. Thus, the occasional later comments by Moscow ascribing an offensive, anti-Soviet character to the agreement were probably made out of tactical considerations.

In an address to the Seventeenth Congress of the All-Union Communist Party (Bolsheviks), Joseph Stalin described Polish foreign policy as being marked by "surprises and zigzags." However, he ascertained that "a change for the better" had taken place, which constituted "a factor for the advancement of the cause of peace." It would be hard to assume that the signing of the Polish-German political accord, known to Moscow a day in advance, was not taken into account when Stalin's speech to the Congress was drafted. Thus, it was not seen as a threat.

The first commentaries that appeared in the Soviet Union immediately after the declaration was published were not directly critical of the document. At most, they identified the aspects that seemed doubtful from the Soviet point of view. These included the supposedly imprecise language of the declaration and the very purpose of its signing. It was admitted that the declaration should be seen as one of the documents likely to remove the prospect of war, particularly in Eastern Europe, though, at the same time, it was suggested that its opaque language weakened that potential role.

The visit to Moscow by Polish foreign minister Beck, which took place in mid-February 1934, no doubt had a restraining effect on press comments. The hosts obviously wanted to avoid anything that could adversely affect the attitude of the Polish side in the run-up to the imminent high-level talks.

The visit went well. Its most spectacular result was the extension by ten years of the nonaggression pact and the elevation of the diplomatic missions in Warsaw and Moscow to the status of embassies. Beck returned from Moscow clearly pleased. He believed that he had consolidated a positive atmosphere in bilateral relations without detriment to Poland's western policy.

Critics have charged that Beck—seeking a tactical success in the form of attaining balance in Poland's relations with the Soviet Union and Germany—lost the strategic opportunity for further rapprochement with the Soviet Union that might have led to a concerted stance against Germany. This view, however, is hard to accept because, at that time, many Polish military analysts convincingly argued that it was the Red Army that posed the greatest threat to the security of Poland and that this threat should determine the organization of the armed forces, the location of fortifications, and the development of military doctrine.

By extending the nonaggression pact with the Soviet Union for another ten years and signing the ratification documents of the Polish-German declaration of 26 January 1934, Beck attained in the realm of treaty diplomacy everything that he and Marshal Piłsudski considered of greatest importance to the country's security: a radical improvement of relations with Poland's two dangerous neighbors, based on the principle of even distance. Moreover, the pact with the Soviet Union and the declaration with Germany constituted a solid foundation for continuing the policy of resisting Poland's disempowerment by the European directorate.

Yet, Piłsudski feared that the successes scored in Poland's relations with both its dangerous neighbors could breed complacency and the notion that the country's security problems had been resolved once and for all. Accordingly, he insisted that the Foreign Ministry, the Military Affairs Ministry, and the General Staff of the Armed Forces treat both agreements as provisional and requiring further intensive work to lend their provisions permanence.

After Piłsudski

Marshal Józef Piłsudski died on 12 May 1935. The partly informal system of government in Poland, including the elaboration and execution of its foreign policy, was over. Despite his progressing illness, Piłsudski had tried, to the very end, to supervise both Eastern and Western policies. While their strategic goals remained consistent, he was preoccupied with the elaboration of current tactics. His towering authority and the mechanism of government after May 1926 gave him autonomy in these endeavors, and he had little use for consultations with the foreign relations committees of parliament. Foreign Minister August Zaleski acquiesced to that state of affairs. His successor, Col. Józef Beck, treated the marshal's every instruction or suggestion literally. He was an astute and intelligent executor. However, there existed the threat that, once he took the helm of foreign policy in his own hands, he would cling to Piłsudski's views and judgments, regardless of the changing circumstances.

Alas, the circumstances in the latter half of 1935 were disturbing. Significant changes were taking place in international politics. The World Disarmament Conference had ended in failure. War was under way in the Far East. The situation concerning Ethiopia was far from normal and threatened armed conflict at any moment. The mechanisms of the League of Nations turned out to be surprisingly ineffective in the face of such ominous developments. Poland was particularly sensitive to the situation in the Soviet Union and Germany, where power was being concentrated in the hands of Stalin and Hitler. Both were guided by ideological considerations in foreign policy that constituted a threat to the security of the Polish state. Simultaneously, both the Third Reich and the Soviet Union were rapidly boosting their military potentials. Poland's budget did not allow it to match their military spending, and, furthermore, it had a much smaller population base. All this meant that the Polish government faced increasingly daunting tasks.

In accordance with Marshal Piłsudski's unwritten "testament," the primary task of Polish foreign policy consisted of safeguarding the state from any threat in the east. Meanwhile, Moscow viewed Polish diplomacy as offensive and hostile. In their contacts with the leaders and diplomats of other states, Soviet leaders referred to Poland as a satellite of the Third Reich, claiming that a secret Polish-German accord had been concluded to destroy the Soviet Union, that plans had been made for a German-Polish-Romanian invasion, and so on. As a result, Polish-Soviet relations were at a very low ebb, putting in question the concept of even distance.

Moreover, their European context became still further complicated. In March 1936, Hitler renounced the Locarno treaties and ordered German forces into the demilitarized zone of the Rhineland. That was the most devastating blow yet to the Versailles peace order; that order threatened to precipitate a speedy collapse of the system but induced a temporary improvement in Polish-Soviet relations.

It is possible that the Soviet leadership realized only after the Rhineland crisis that, despite getting a permanent seat on the Council of the League of Nations and concluding a mutual assistance treaty with France, the Soviet

Union's influence on European politics was negligible. It remained sidelined and in danger of becoming completely isolated on such fundamental security issues as the German question. The commitment to relations with France had turned out to be a mistake, particularly considering the slowness of French responses to British policy moves. There remained the chance of Germany's diplomatic isolation in Central and Eastern Europe through a regional pact on mutual assistance. However, the involvement of Poland in it was crucial, and Poland was not interested in loosening its links with the Third Reich. This stance caused frustration in Moscow and led to charges that Poland was trying to weaken the Soviet Union's international position.

Beck would probably have welcomed limited cooperation with the Soviet Union as long as it did not undermine Poland's relations with Germany. However, any such cooperation—contrary to Moscow's wishes—would not be designed to counter the Soviet Union's isolation. In fact, that isolation was one of the secret priorities of Poland's eastern policy.

Thus, after a brief improvement in Polish-Soviet relations connected with the Rhineland crisis, links were again at a very low ebb in mid-1936. Deputy Commissar for Foreign Affairs Krestinsky made the following comments on 2 July, when receiving letters of credence from the new Polish ambassador to Moscow, Wacław Grzybowski: "Political relations between us could not be worse. We are working to strengthen the prestige of the League of Nations and advance collective security. We are combating all forms of aggression and all forms of fascism. We are currently pursuing an anti-German, anti-Italian, and anti-Japanese policy. Poland is pursuing a diametrically different policy, attempting to weaken the League of Nations, countering the attempts to create collective security, supporting Italy, and sympathizing with Japan. Poland is within the orbit of German policy." That was exceptionally undiplomatic language, considering the occasion.

Grzybowski refused to be drawn into polemics. He limited his response to the observation that political tensions could be defused through the development of trade. In any case, he would have found it hard to muster convincing arguments, since the Soviet Union truly had pursued an antifascist policy line since 1934, while Warsaw unquestionably had played a role in undercutting the Eastern Pact. Moreover, it did not seem sensible at the time to try and explain yet again to the Soviet side the principles of Polish security policy, including the role of good relations with both Moscow and Berlin.

Prometheism

The Soviet press increasingly accused Warsaw of riding on Berlin's coattails and, contrary to appearances, of conducting a policy directed against the Soviet Union. Those charges referred, among other things, to Prometheism (a political project aimed at the disintegration of the Soviet Union by supporting independence movements among the peoples subjugated by Moscow, also known since the mid-1920s as the Promethean movement). Soviet newspapers repeatedly quoted Polish journalists, writers, and politicians who advocated anti-Soviet cooperation with Germany. These views were then generalized and attributed to the Polish government. Alongside Poland, Soviet newspapers mentioned Germany and Japan as declared foes of the Soviet Union and insinuated a conspiracy against Moscow. Such media activity prevented the improvement of relations and hindered routine economic, cultural, and scientific contacts.

It is a fact that the concept of Prometheism was ever present in the thinking of Polish strategic planners. That was so because Marshal Piłsudski and Marshal Rydz-Śmigły, his successor as inspector-general of the armed forces, considered Prometheism to be a useful instrument for solving the problem of security on the eastern border. There are reasons to believe that efforts pushing Prometheism radically accelerated in the autumn of 1937.

Polish Prometheism in the latter half of the 1930s was of a defensive character. Undertakings within the framework of the so-called Promethean work were, as a rule, restricted to the enhancement of state security. A participant in the Prometheism project, Włodzimierz Bączkowski, recalled that, in 1937, Marshal Rydz-Śmigły did not respond to a Japanese proposal to organize a Promethean campaign in the Russian Far East. He explained that Polish Prometheism did not have the goal of conducting intelligence operations and subversion in Russia but was aimed exclusively at the "consolidation of our threatened security." It is noteworthy that Japan's overture was rejected at a time of exceptional rapprochement in the generally good Polish-Japanese relations, after the two countries' diplomatic missions had been elevated to the status of embassies and a Polish-Japanese society was launched in Warsaw.

No documentary references exist concerning the involvement, if any, of Polish missions in the Soviet Union on Promethean projects. However, that kind of activity would have been difficult to separate from routine information gathering, particularly since the missions were supervised by the Eastern Department of the Ministry of Foreign Affairs and Foreign Minister Beck was constantly updated on the progress of Prometheism.

It is hard to assess the impact of the Promethean campaign, particularly in the 1930s, when the Great Terror completely atomized a society that was already suppressed and incapable of political resistance. Internationally, Poland's importance as the leading Promethean state visibly flagged in the latter half of the 1930s—primarily in favor of Japan, followed by Italy and the Third Reich.

That regression was not only connected with the diminishing significance of the Polish segment of the international Promethean movement. Poland's international position was still unclear, despite promises made to

Beck concerning Polish participation in the Western Pact. Relations with Czechoslovakia remained bad, and relations with Lithuania were disastrous. The dispute over the Free City of Gdańsk was again heating up. Poland's relations with the Baltic States had cooled, and an unfavorable trend appeared in the attitude of traditionally friendly Romania. The Polish-French alliance increasingly seemed an illusion. Beck now faced Poland's two dangerous neighbors alone, having hitherto maintained a relative balance in relations with them. But the time was approaching when Hitler would embark on fulfilling the plans revealed in *Mein Kampf*: winning "living space" (*Lebensraum*) for the German people.

Beck has been accused of megalomania, of failing to understand that Poland had a back-row seat in the international concert, and of an inability to adjust tactics to international developments and the changing positions of Germany and the Soviet Union. Regardless of whether those charges are justified, it has to be admitted that it would have been difficult to propose a rational alternative to his foreign policy. This does not mean that Beck did not make any mistakes. However, his missteps did not relate to fundamental security issues but to secondary, tactical matters. But even his critics did not deny that Beck possessed an analytical talent and ability to forecast, several months into the future, political developments concerning Poland.

Poles in the Soviet Union

It is estimated that, after the mass repatriation envisaged by the Riga Treaty was completed in 1924, at least one and a half million Poles holding Soviet citizenship still remained in the Soviet Union. Probably only a small fraction of them did not relocate to Poland for ideological reasons; the majority were simply unprepared to make the trip. After 1924, Soviet Poles were able to apply for repatriation on an individual basis, under the repatriation accord, but had to make the arrangements through diplomatic channels. Even though this process was facilitated by a network of Polish consulates established in the mid-1920s, such repatriations were sporadic. Moreover, consular assistance for Poles in the peculiar Soviet conditions simply did not function.

In April 1937, the Soviet Ministry for Foreign Affairs unexpectedly demanded the closing of three of the five Polish consulates in the Soviet Union. At that time, Polish consulates were located in the capitals of three union republics—Minsk, Kharkov, and Tbilisi—and in two cities with sizable Polish minorities—Kiev and Leningrad. Soviet consulates operated in Lvóv and the Free City of Gdańsk. The Soviets, ignoring the huge disproportion between the number of Poles in the Soviet Union and the size of the Russian minority in Poland, threatened that, unless the Polish side acceded to their demands, they would renounce the consular convention of July 1924.

The Soviets put forward two arguments. First, they referred to the formal provision of the convention, under which Poland was entitled to have one consulate more than the Soviet Union had in Poland. Second, they claimed that all the Poles who felt an attachment to their country of origin had already left during the mass repatriation, and those who remained did so of their own free will.

In August 1937, a compromise hardly satisfying to Poland was reached by the parties. Poland would close two of its consulates (instead of three) and the closures would not take place "immediately" but within "a reasonable period of time." As a result, the Polish consulates in Kharkov and Tbilisi were not closed until 1 December 1937. By that time, the number of Poles in Ukraine had decreased so radically that the closing of the consulate in Kharkov was justified.

The crisis over the Polish consular network coincided with a general, drastic worsening of the situation of Poles with Soviet citizenship. Top-level decisions to change policy toward the Poles living in the Soviet Union—mainly in the Belorussian and Ukrainian Soviet Socialist Republics—were probably made in late 1935 or early 1936. Previously, these Poles seem to have been treated as potential officers and political commissars of a future Polish Red Army. However, during the period of collectivization, the authorities came to the conclusion that Soviet indoctrination of these Poles had brought negligible success, that the majority maintained a separate national, cultural, and religious identity, and that they were disdainful of the program of "socialist construction." Thus, instead of constituting a pool of cadres for a future revolution in Poland, they were a potential "fifth column" of an aristocratic, bourgeois, land-owning Poland.

A provocation—referred to as "the case of the Polish Military Organization"—was concocted to strike at the Polish communities in the Soviet Union. In 1933, under the pretext of foiling the activity of an imaginary Polish military organization, or PMO—which was allegedly seeking to separate Ukraine from the Soviet Union and bring about a confederation with Poland—the authorities began mass arrests. Those detained included leaders of the Polish Communist Party, who had arrived in the Soviet Union under an exchange of political prisoners, and more than one hundred Polish community leaders in the Ukrainian SSR. Practically the entire Polish intelligentsia was destroyed, along with political, local, and educational activists.

Soon afterward, Ukraine witnessed two rounds of mass repression (the second in the autumn of 1937) against the Polish population. Nikolai Ivanov, an expert on the subject, described the operation as genocide. Polish villages were surrounded by NKVD units. Next, three-member kangaroo courts tried men who were considered potential resisters. Other villagers were divided into groups according to who would be subjected to Soviet indoctrination and who would be deported. The number of those shot or otherwise murdered ran into the tens of thousands, while the mortality rate among those being transported to Kazakhstan and Siberia reached 20 percent to 25 percent.

An even greater tragedy befell the inhabitants of the Felix Dzerzhinsky Polish National Region, an autonomous territorial unit that had existed since March 1932 in the Minsk district of the Belorussian SSR. A mass repression launched in 1936 ended in the spring of 1938 with the formal dissolution of the region. Fourteen thousand people had been sentenced to death, and the remaining inhabitants were deported. So ended the Belorussian chapter of "the operation against Polish agents."

Poles from other Soviet republics, prominently including the inhabitants of Petrograd and Moscow, were also among those executed or deported. The campaign against the Polish minority was an integral part of the Great Terror that ravaged the entire Soviet Union. Tens of thousands were murdered, and tens of thousands were herded into prisons and camps or exiled to distant places where the harsh climate ensured their rapid demise. In the years 1937–38, at least 230,000 Poles with Soviet citizenship fell victim to repression.

Practically no information about these mass crimes reached Poland. Few people in the Soviet Union itself realized their scale, since the operation—despite its extent—was conducted with utmost secrecy. Grzybowski, the Polish ambassador to the Soviet Union, was unable to obtain any information about the repression of Soviet Poles. His extensive analyses of the internal situation in the Soviet Union make no mention of it whatsoever.

Poland obtained fragmentary information about the repression of Poles from intelligence sources. However, it was impossible to verify those sources through diplomatic channels. Any questions on the subject elicited answers such as "Deportations of Poles? Never heard about that. There is no decree to that effect. The Polish district still exists."

Poles with Soviet citizenship along the western reaches of the Soviet Union vanished in the waves of the Great Terror. The purge devoured party leaders, government officials, diplomats, and senior military officers, along with masses of unknown ordinary citizens.

Comintern and the Communist Party of Poland

The Polish communists' potential for antigovernment activity in Poland remained practically untapped due to the struggle within their ranks since the latter half of the 1920s. That situation was tolerated by both the Comintern and Stalin, who had long distrusted the Communist Party of Poland (Komunistyczna Partia Polski, or KPP) and suspected its members of being secret proponents of Trotskyism. The KPP's short-lived support for the coup of May 1926 was the beginning of persistent accusations that the party was susceptible to the influence of the Polish secret service and that the party leadership had been infiltrated by provocateurs. However, it was not until the second half of the 1930s that Stalin decided to solve the problem of the KPP in his characteristic way. The measures he took were closely connected with the campaign to extirpate Poles with Soviet citizenship, described previously.

The repression of Polish communists started long before the massive assault on the community of Poles in the Soviet Union. Its beginnings dated to 1931. At that time, a number of Polish communist leaders, as well as numerous lower-ranking activists who had been sentenced to long prison terms in Poland and went to the Soviet Union under a political-prisoner exchange scheme between the two countries, found themselves incarcerated by the Soviet government. The charges against them were typical: subversion within the KPP, cooperation with Polish police, spying for Poland, and "covert introduction of agents of the Polish Military Organization and the Polish Socialist Party into revolutionary organizations." Internally divided and intimidated, the KPP leadership did not even attempt to intercede on behalf of its prominent, imprisoned members.

In January 1936, the Comintern Secretariat, acting under Stalin's pressure, formally demanded that the KPP cleanse its ranks of "provocateurs and class enemies" who had proliferated within the party due to the ineptitude of the party's leadership. Among those targeted were Maria Koszutska-Kostrzewa, Edward Próchnik, Adolf Warski, and others. That led to a wave of mutual accusations and denunciations, as well as a hunt for "enemies of the people" and covert Trotskyists, resulting in the total disintegration of the party. The scene was set for the party's bloody dissolution.

In January 1938, a theoretical organ of the Comintern, *Kommunisticheskii Internatsional,* published an editorial headlined "Provocateurs at Work" and describing the KPP as a nest of traitors and spies controlled by the Polish secret service. That set in motion a process that several months later culminated in the dissolution of the KPP and its affiliates.

Stalin's annihilation of the leadership of the Polish communist movement instilled in Soviet society an extremely negative image of Poland as a country in which even communists were enemies of "the homeland of the world proletariat."

The resulting resentments fueled the tendency to restrict Polish-Soviet relations to an absolute minimum. The sporadic diplomatic contacts that did take place mainly focused on international issues, such as the problems and conflicts in Central Europe, and on developments at the League of Nations.

ALEKSANDR V. REVYAKIN

• •

POLAND AND THE SOVIET UNION IN THE LATE 1920S AND EARLY 1930S

• •

IT WAS EARLY spring 1936. The international crisis was in full swing due to the introduction of German troops in the Rhineland demilitarized zone and the denunciation of the Locarno agreements by Hitler's Germany. Jacques Chastenet, a former French diplomat and at that time the chief editor of the Paris newspaper *Le Temps,* had arrived in Moscow. He was reputedly tied closely to the French Ministry of Foreign Affairs. In the Soviet capital, the visitor was welcomed with heightened attention. On 16 March, he was received for a conversation by the Deputy People's Commissar for Foreign Affairs Nikolai Krestinsky (People's Commissar Maxim Litvinov was attending a session of the League of Nations Council in London at this time). On 19 March, Chastenet was received by Vyacheslav Molotov, chair of the Council of People's Commissars of the Soviet Union.

In addition to the vital international political issues, the French journalist was interested in the prospects for Soviet-Polish relations. Chastenet simply asked Krestinsky, "What can the Soviet side do to improve relations with Poland?" If the record of this conversation made by Soviet diplomats is true, Chastenet then pointedly remarked that, "in Poland itself, the difficulties in improving Soviet-Polish relations lay primarily in the area of sentimental and historical moments."

We have purposely decided to draw attention to these statements by the former French diplomat and journalist. It seems that Chastenet noticed one of the "pain spots" not just in Soviet-Polish relations at that particular point in time but also more generally in the relations between historical Russia and historical Poland.

It seems that even the "sentimental and historical" difficulties have been a constant stumbling block in the recently rejuvenated discussion between Russian and Polish historians on controversial issues of the countries' common history.

Our Polish colleagues have a good opportunity before them, if they wish to critically examine the conclusions and arguments of Russian historians. There can be no doubt that much of what we have done in studying international relations, as well as how it has been done, deserves to be criticized. If only the criticism would be of benefit. As for us, we cannot ignore some of the provisions in certain papers by Polish authors published in a joint Russian-Polish collection of articles.

In fact, an article by Stanisław Gregorowicz, "The Place and Role of the USSR in Polish Policy during the '30s," describes Soviet policy toward Poland more than it does Polish policy toward the Soviet Union. In addition, the author clearly defines Soviet policy as "anti-Polish," which is not quite consistent with the known facts, even those presented in the article. But let it be so, especially because the Soviet policy really merits reproach, to put it mildly. But at least a word could be uttered by the author about the fact that Poland itself pursued a policy far from friendly to the Soviet Union.

Also puzzling are some of the provisions in the article by Wojciech Materski, "Polish-Soviet Relations (1932–1939): The Key Problems." The author laments that, in the second half of the 1920s, Poland allegedly "found itself in the background" of Soviet foreign policy, behind Germany, France, and the United Kingdom. But, as is clear from the article itself, during the interwar period Poland also preferred relations with these same powers. And there were objective grounds thereto that are not even necessary to specify. If the case in question should be bilateral Soviet-Polish relations, then another regrettable thing would be that, in the 1920s and 1930s, the Soviet Union and Poland could not fully leverage the available potential in their relations (proximity, an extended common boundary, a certain cultural affinity, etc.) to their mutual advantage. Materski has not found any explanation of the fact that the thaw in Soviet-Polish relations that emerged after the 1932 nonaggression pact had, by 1934, already been replaced by a new cooling. He cannot see any connection therein with a sharp turn by Poland to rapprochement with Hitler's Germany, whose revanchist and expansionist aspirations at that time did not seem to inspire any fear among the Polish leadership.

However, the "sentimental and historical" difficulties are our common heritage with the Poles. One can hardly argue that this heritage is evenly distributed between the two nations; rather, it is asymmetrical: what one nation considers valor and merit, another often tends to view with a critical eye. To some extent, this is a result of the complicated history of the coexistence of these two states over a wide area of Eastern Europe in the past. It should be remembered that, over the past two centuries, Russia and the Soviet Union played an immeasurably greater and more tragic role in the fate of Poland than vice versa. But, though the days when Warsaw was perceived by Moscow or Saint Petersburg as a rival or a partner equal to Russia's potential are long gone, the Russian (and Soviet) capitals have always very much taken into account the danger that any third party would try to exploit Russian-Polish antagonism. Not in the least degree denying the legitimate right of the Polish nation to decide what is good and bad for itself, we must note that in the past (and not just in the past) Poland itself gave rise to such opinions and sentiments.

Fully aware of the fact that the documentation and publications we have used were affected not only by an inevitable incompleteness but also by a certain bias in delivery, nevertheless they have given us a basis for trying to establish particularities about the manner in which Polish foreign policy was perceived by Soviet diplomacy.

First of all, I would like to point out that the perception of Poland was influenced by some stable phobias of Soviet diplomacy in the 1920s and 1930s that were also reflected in these documentary publications. From the outset, Soviet diplomacy nurtured a deep distrust of most neighboring countries, and others as well. To understand this phenomenon, we should remember the constant anxiety of Soviet leaders over the "capitalist encirclement" and the danger of "counterrevolutionary intervention." At times, this anxiety took obsessive, paranoid forms. One example of this occurred during the second half of the 1920s, when diplomatic relations with Great Britain were broken and an armed conflict erupted in the Far East, near Soviet borders.

By the way, we have gotten the impression that Soviet diplomacy evidently paid more attention to Poland than to many other countries in Central and Eastern Europe. For example, while the Soviet Union did not have even normal diplomatic relations with Romania and the countries of the Little Entente for a long time, Poland was always the addressee of its diplomatic initiatives. I think that this was no accident. In comparison with other bordering countries, the Polish state possessed a feature to which the Soviet Union ascribed special significance: Poland's geographical position. It was not only because the shortest path between the Soviet Union and Western Europe passed through Poland; the main thing was that the border with Poland was the longest that the Soviet Union had in the West. So, for many evident reasons, this border caused increased anxiety for Soviet authorities.

Our sources provide evidence that, on entering the 1930s, Soviet-Polish relations by no means inspired optimism within Soviet diplomacy. The Soviet perception of Polish foreign policy had been largely formed under the influence of the 1920 war and the 1921 treaties of alliance among Poland, France, and Romania, which in varying degrees were directed against the Soviet state. In addition, Soviet diplomats could not let their Polish colleagues forget that, in 1922, Soviet Russia had proposed an arms limitation agreement with Poland and a number of other countries but was refused. Then, in 1926, after receiving a proposal to sign a nonaggression pact, Poland laid down conditions the Soviets considered to be deliberately unacceptable.

By the way, we have not noticed that Soviet diplomats held any special bias against the Poles as a nation, or against the Polish culture, state, and so forth. Whatever the subject of their speech or whatever tone, positive or negative, they used, never did they touch upon the ethnic, historical, or cultural heritage of their Polish counterparts. In principle, that should not be surprising. Soviet diplomats by their conviction and worldview were Marxists and communists. From a tender age, they were used to dividing people not on a national but rather a social basis (their tendency toward "class analysis," by the way, is strongly felt in the diplomatic correspondence).

We can even argue that Soviet diplomats, taking into account certain psychological complexes of their Polish colleagues, used to show some deference to them, sparing their self-esteem. For example, Józef Beck, Polish minister of foreign affairs, declared in a conversation with Litvinov that "Poland is not a small seasonal state, as it has been taken for." The people's commissar immediately agreed with him. According to some reports, Vladimir Antonov-Ovseenko, the plenipotentiary representative of the Soviet Union in Poland in the early 1930s, was able to speak with his Polish counterparts without an interpreter. It is rather interesting that, on one occasion, the leadership of the People's Commissariat for Foreign Affairs even accused him of exaggerating the seriousness of "Poland's peaceful intentions toward us." What a strange kind of bias.

The successor to Antonov-Ovseenko as plenipotentiary representative, Yakov Davtyan, as we shall see, very critically assessed Warsaw's official policy. But it could not prevent him from closely looking to the life of Polish society with sympathy and compassion. He was an ardent supporter of developing cultural exchanges with Poland. In 1935, he wrote with satisfaction, "No country has released so many Soviet films as Poland."

However, we can say with certainty that Soviet diplomats had difficulties getting along with Polish officials. In official correspondence, they often expressed taunts and other acrimony. The record of Davtyan's conversation with Polish foreign minister Beck on 24 April 1934 abounds with expressions like "he began to mumble something," "without any rhyme or reason he began to babble," "he plunged into philosophizing," he jabbered "rather vaguely and ambiguously," "once again he muttered something," and so on. Boris Stomonyakov, a member of the Board of the Soviet People's Commissariat for Foreign Affairs, resented the "tongue in cheek" manner that Polish diplomat Juliusz Łukasiewicz allowed himself while talking to him. However, Stomonyakov, as we shall see, was generally characterized by a certain harshness in his judgments. Even when considering such a polite and "politically correct" (as we would say today) person as Litvinov, his self-control sometimes failed him.

In part, these difficulties were due to the fact that the behavior of Polish diplomats was also far from friendly toward the Soviets. It is known, for example, that, until the 1930s, the Soviet Union was designated in Polish diplomatic correspondence as an "enemy."

However, as is evidenced by our documentation, the mutual coldness was based not only on an ethical misunderstanding but also on other, much more compelling reasons. It would be no exaggeration to say that relations between both countries were quite unhealthy due to an ample supply of diplomatic tensions and quarrels arising from border incidents to clearly hostile attacks by the official and semiofficial press in both countries, and from the working conditions of the diplomatic and consular offices to the hostile activities of White Guard organizations in Poland and the Comintern in the Soviet Union.

This revolutionary organization that existed under the wing of the Soviet authorities deserves a special elucidation of its role. It gave rise to particularly frequent complaints from Polish authorities during the second half of the 1930s after the successes of the "popular fronts" in Western Europe and the outbreak of the civil war in Spain. On 26 April 1937, Davtyan reported to Litvinov,

> Every day, all governmental organs of the press are printing bulky articles about an offensive by the Comintern in Poland, about new trends in the Comintern's policy directed toward unleashing the world revolution and the bolshevization of Poland, etc., with all sorts of "quotations" from resolutions of the Comintern, the All-Soviet Communist Party (Bolsheviks), etc. Of course, the Comintern is identified with the Soviet government, even with the People's Commissariat for Foreign Affairs, and the name of Comrade Stalin is very strenuously mentioned. All this has created the sense that the Soviet Union, under the lee of the Comintern, has begun active subversive activities in Poland with its bolshevization in mind.

However, Soviet diplomats would dissociate themselves from the Comintern, alleging that the Soviet government had no relation to it, but nothing could help.

But the most adverse influence on the character of relations between Soviet diplomats and their foreign colleagues was due to the Stalinist repressions that struck the People's Commissariat for Foreign Affairs during the second half of the 1930s. Many of the persons mentioned in this study, including the plenipotentiary representatives Antonov-Ovseenko and Davtyan, were victims of the terror. Not only were Soviet diplomats constantly living under the oppressive atmosphere of general suspicion and persecution of the "enemies of the people" that reigned in the Soviet Union and its foreign offices, but they were also powerless to resist the tremendous pressure of public opinion in foreign countries.

A large-scale campaign in the Polish press, which presented the repressions in the Soviet Union as a pretext, reached its culmination late in 1937. So, on 12 November, Boris Vinogradov reported to the People's Commissariat for Foreign Affairs, "The Poles took advantage of the departure of Davtyan and other comrades to organize a subversive attack against our embassy in the Polish and international press." On 1 December 1937, troubled by the aggressive press campaign, Litvinov asked Yakov Suritz, the Soviet ambassador to France, to notify the French minister of foreign affairs, who was about to pay a visit to Warsaw, that, "in Poland, the anti-Soviet campaign of every kind of absurd rumor about the Soviet Union had increased in recent days." Indeed, as Vinogradov wrote to the People's Commissariat for Foreign Affairs on 12 December 1937, during the French minister's visit, the Polish "press endlessly printed the most fantastic reports about the internal situation in the USSR, about the executions, etc. and as a result opined about the decreasing role of the Soviet Union in the international arena."

Of course, all of the aforementioned circumstances affected the perception of Polish politics by Soviet diplomats. But up to this point, we have discussed only the phenomena and factors that are collateral or external to diplomatic work. We have so far not touched on its substance, that is, the specific major problems that Soviet diplomats confronted and tried to settle in the Soviet Union's relations with Poland during the time frame of interest to us. Meanwhile, as we believe, their judgments and assessments first of all depended on their success or failure in solving these problems.

In 1931, when Poland expressed a willingness to resume negotiations on a nonaggression pact, the Foreign Ministry, in its offices at Kuznetskiy Most, was not too surprised. By this time, many European countries had shown an interest in developing similar agreements with the Soviet Union. But Soviet diplomats could not help feeling that the Polish were furthering some sort of political game. On 18 January 1932, Litvinov informed Valerian Dovgalevsky, the Soviet ambassador to France, "Disagreement with Poland has remained concerning only one point: it rejects our proposed article on the obligation of nonparticipation in the agreements, which are obviously hostile to the other side and contrary to the pact. Such a stubborn rejection of this obligation is not a sign of a genuine desire by Poland to establish peaceful and friendly relations."

In the context of this disagreement, Soviet suspicion regarding Poland was increasing. On 22 April 1932, in a letter to Antonov-Ovseenko during the visit of Marshal Józef Piłsudski to Japan, Stomonyakov wrote, "In all likelihood, he is holding specific military negotiations related to Far Eastern complications for the event of war with Poland and Romania against the USSR." In any case, this PCFA (People's Commissariat for Foreign Affairs) board member in charge of the Polish and Baltic regions advised the plenipotentiary not to have any illusions about Poland, which only "feigns quiet

ALEKSANDR V. REVYAKIN

yet keeps alert waiting for developments." Stomonyakov explained Poland's previously uncharacteristic "peacefulness" toward the Soviet Union by its current domestic and international challenges. So far, it is difficult to judge, he thought, in which "direction, depending on the international situation," the Polish government will steer its policy. But at the moment, "this peaceful wait-and-see position of Poland is consistent with our interests," and, therefore, "in resolving all current issues [we should] move as far as possible toward the Poles, while avoiding any exacerbation."

The Soviet-Polish Nonaggression Pact was signed in Moscow on 25 July 1932. On this occasion, the Soviets gently but clearly expressed their satisfaction. When a reporter from the French newspaper *Le Petit Parisien* asked Litvinov to comment on the signing of a similar treaty with France, the people's commissar for foreign affairs, at the risk of seeming tactless, opined at the beginning of his statement that he thought it possible "to mention another similar event of major international importance": the ratification of the Soviet-Polish pact. Litvinov said that the Soviet-Polish agreement "should be a turning point in relations between the USSR and Poland," that "its value is increasing many times over in terms of preserving world peace," and that "the hopes and plans" of anti-Soviet intervention partisans, of all those who hope for an armed clash between the Soviet Union and Poland, have "now suffered a big blow."

In our opinion, Soviet diplomats believed in the possibility of changing Soviet-Polish relations for the better in the spring of 1933, after the Nazis had come to power in Germany. They were convinced of it by the variety of favors Polish officials began to do for the Soviet Union. For example, at the end of March 1933, Beck said to plenipotentiary Antonov-Ovseenko that he "obligatorily wanted to speak on some specific issues" with Marshal Piłsudski. Antonov-Ovseenko met with Piłsudski on 1 May 1933.

At first, Soviet diplomatic leaders distrusted those signs of attention. On 4 April 1933, Stomonyakov wrote to Antonov-Ovseenko, "The triumph of Hitler in Germany and the progressive offensive of revisionist elements in Europe continue to strengthen the mood in Poland for a rapprochement with us, and allow the Polish government's desire to exaggerate the improvement of relations with the USSR to the outside world." He expressed concern at the "wrong messages" that appeared in the press of various countries, "on the conclusion of far-reaching agreements between Poland and the USSR, and on the establishment of a united front of Poland and the Soviet Union against Hitler."

Further, Soviet diplomats continued to have doubts about the sincerity of Poland's demonstrated desire to improve relations with the Soviet Union. Nevertheless, analysis of forces in Europe persuaded them of favorable conditions for cooperating with the country. On 19 April 1933, in a letter to

Antonov-Ovseenko, Stomonyakov argued that "putting the revisionist projects on the agenda of European policy" had diminished Poland's international standing by "increasing the chances of an armed clash between Poland and Germany." Thus, the "obvious desire of Poland, if not to improve, is at least to manifest improved relations with us." Stomonyakov found that "this desire of Poland wholly corresponds to our interests, as well." Therefore, he concluded, the leadership of the People's Commissariat had "decided to meet the Polish proposals on all current issues in our relations wherever it is permitted by our interests and to seek not only to strengthen our relations with Poland but also to manifest their improvement to the outside world." So, we can say that Soviet diplomacy was taking a course toward rapprochement with Poland.

However, the implementation of this course almost immediately ran into obstacles. On 12 June 1933, Stomonyakov noted "a certain slowdown in the tendency of the Polish government to move closer to us." He linked this fact directly with the outlined "prospect of Polish-German rapprochement," evidently at the expense of Polish neighbors to the east—Lithuania and the Soviet Union—which particularly bothered him.

Soviet diplomats were aware of the fact that the Polish government might be willing to make concessions to the Nazis regarding their claims on other countries if only they would leave Poland in peace, based on a conversation between Litvinov and the Polish envoy Łukasiewicz on 23 March 1933. Discussing the situation in Europe after the Nazis came to power in Germany, the people's commissar "suggested that Poland would probably not object to the annexation [of Austria], which for a time could distract Germany from the East." In response, he heard that "Poland really had no fundamental objections, though they were aware that it would substantially strengthen Germany."

The possibility of a Polish-German compromise on the basis of mutual territorial compensation at the expense of third countries concerned Soviet diplomats. In a letter to Antonov-Ovseenko dated 19 June 1933, Stomonyakov assumed such a scenario: "The occupation of Lithuania by Poland is only possible in the event of an armed conflict in the Far East and a subsequent attack on us by Poland." The PCFA board member noticed at the same time a number of "recent facts and circumstances that prove the determination of Piłsudski to outwardly manifest improving relations with us, while at the same time preventing the deepening of these relations, and in no way, to binding his hands with respect to us."

However, the détente in Soviet-Polish relations outlined in the spring of 1933 yielded tangible results, although not as significant as the Soviets had expected.

As far back as February 1933, the Soviet Union had introduced a draft of the declaration on the definition of an aggressor before the International Conference on Disarmament in Geneva. On 9 April of the same year, Litvinov handed a proposal to Polish ambassador Łukasiewicz in Moscow to conclude a regional convention on the definition of aggression. Although talks on this issue ended relatively quickly, Soviet diplomats were rather disappointed with the results.

In London, where leaders of the diplomatic offices of European countries gathered for the International Economic Conference, they signed not one but two general conventions on the definition of aggression. The comments by Stomonyakov on this event clearly betray his disappointment. On 19 July 1933, he wrote to Antonov-Ovseenko that, during the negotiations, Poland had sought in every way to "diminish" the value of the convention by "portraying it as a private and minor addition to the nonaggression pact." Poland wanted "to reduce the importance of the convention as an independent political act." This position taken by the Poles was explained by Stomonyakov as, "above all, a persistent unwillingness by Poland to allow the international influence and prestige of the USSR to increase." He saw therein some evidence of the "dual behavior of Poland toward the USSR." He wrote, "Poland is playing a very complicated diplomatic game, considering not only the possibility of further improvement in Soviet-Polish relations, but also the possibility of their deterioration." All this, according to Stomonyakov, "commits us to a very great caution regarding Poland and to a serious distrust of Polish policy."

Whatever it was, Soviet diplomats could congratulate themselves that the convention defining aggression, with all its shortcomings, was successfully signed and entered into force. According to the general opinion of historians, this event, along with the conclusion of a nonaggression pact, was the peak of the détente, the highest point in the development of Soviet-Polish relations, which was followed by a deep recession.

Could the 1932–33 agreements have, on the contrary, served as a basis for closer cooperation between both countries in international affairs? Although it cannot be proven, we can venture to answer positively. In the early 1930s, there were no insurmountable differences between the Soviet Union and Poland related to the security of both states.

Signs of a slowdown in Soviet-Polish relations had not gone unnoticed by Soviet diplomats. In the summer of 1933, they drew attention to the rumors circulating in the capitals of Europe about active contacts between Poland and Germany. On 6 July 1933, Litvinov, passing through Paris on his way from London, informed the People's Commissariat about his conversations with French minister of foreign affairs Joseph Paul-Boncour and Édouard Daladier, the prime minister, that "hinted at some Polish-German negotiations."

In the PCFA, these rumors were treated more than seriously. On 19 July 1933, in informing Antonov-Ovseenko, Stomonyakov compared them with "a number of other facts regarding Polish-German relations that very much concern us." In particular, he noted "the utmost restraint of the Polish press in relation to Germany" and the fact that "the German press is showing even more restraint in relation to Poland." Therefore, Stomonyakov could not exclude the possibility that "the Nazis[,] filled with bestial hatred for the USSR[,] seek a possible agreement with Poland against the USSR." It seemed very likely to him that "Piłsudski and Beck would agree to informal talks with Germany on this agreement," because "it is proved by nothing that Piłsudski forever refused his old conception of an agreement with Germany in order to free his hands for federalist plans at the expense of the USSR."

Therefore, to Kuznetskiy Most, a Polish-German agreement was believed to be possible. So, it would be an exaggeration to say that the news of Hitler's meeting in Berlin with Polish envoy Józef Lipski on 15 November 1933 was a complete surprise to the PCFA. Nevertheless, the meeting as such, and the significance attached to it in both Poland and Germany (an official communiqué published in the press about this meeting was often referred to as a "Declaration" in the Soviet sources), left a nasty impression on the PCFA. In addition, Soviet diplomats were further upset by the fact that Poland had arranged the Berlin meeting in secret and, even after its completion, was in no hurry to provide any necessary clarifications.

Only on 20 November 1933 did Beck provide an explanation to Antonov-Ovseenko. The latter listened to the arguments by the Polish minister, only occasionally interrupting him to make a remark. When Beck expressed his gladness that "the Polish-German agreement was quietly received in Moscow," Antonov-Ovseenko did not argue with him, confining his response to a single remark: "We welcome all that can promote the pacification of relations." However, the plenipotentiary expressed his perplexity: "Why was this démarche from Poland surrounded by such a mystery?" In the Soviet Union, he added, "we were just misinformed. We never acted in a similar manner with representatives from Poland."

To understand the nature of the Polish-German agreement, Antonov-Ovseenko conducted his own investigation. He spoke with Beck and with a number of informed Polish journalists, who tried to convince him that the agreement was not directed against the interests of third countries, including the Soviet Union. The plenipotentiary listened with disbelief to the arguments of his interlocutors. One of them, the editor of *Gazeta Polska*, Bogusław Miedziński, assured him that, "recently, Marshal Piłsudski reconfirmed the path toward further deepening relations" with the Soviet Union and that Beck would supposedly discuss the matter with him. On 23 November 1933, Antonov-Ovseenko was once again received by the Polish minister, but, according to the plenipotentiary, the conversation "did not meet my expectations based on Miedziński's hints."

As a result of his investigation, Antonov-Ovseenko did not settle on an unambiguous assessment of the 15 November Declaration. Allegedly, he noted, "in his interview with Lipski, Hitler sounded the possibility of an anti-Soviet collusion but did not meet with a favorable response." Therefore, continued the plenipotentiary, "with regards to us, this act makes no changes." However, Antonov-Ovseenko's overall impression from the Hitler-Lipski meeting as such, and from the political effect it had caused, was negative. He summed up his arguments thusly: "There are great forces working for the failure of our rapprochement [to Poland]," and these forces "are working with extreme energy."

Primarily, Antonov-Ovseenko did not attach importance to one episode from his conversation with Beck on 23 November. Only on 1 December 1933 did he report to the PCFA about Beck's wish to undertake some concerted action with the Soviet Union regarding the Baltic countries in order to "strengthen his soft point on the map of Europe." But at Kuznetskiy Most, Beck withdrew his attention, and they decided to use it as a touchstone for proving Poland's attitude toward the Soviet Union.

On 14 December 1933, in a conversation with Łukasiewicz, Litvinov raised the "Baltic theme." Referring to the fact that Beck, in conversation with Antonov-Ovseenko, "found it difficult to make any concrete proposal" on the issue, the people's commissar proposed a "joint declaration on the fate of the Baltic countries" and immediately handed over the draft to the Polish envoy. The document expressed the resolve of the Soviet Union and Poland to defend the "integrity and full economic and political independence" of the Baltic countries, as well as the obligation to "enter into immediate contact and discuss the situation" in the event of any threat to the independence of these countries.

What happened thereafter initially looked like a wonderful dream. It had never previously seemed possible to come to an agreement with Poland so easily and so quickly. By 19 December, Łukasiewicz had visited Litvinov to submit Beck's response. The people's commissar summarized it as follows: "The Declaration I have proposed corresponds to his own views and he considers it possible to make this declaration at an appropriate occasion." The people's commissar suggested that the most appropriate occasion for signing a joint declaration on the Baltic countries would be Beck's visit to Moscow.

On 22 December 1933, Antonov-Ovseenko and Beck exchanged pleasantries in Warsaw. The plenipotentiary said that Litvinov's proposal for a joint declaration was "the expression of a special confidence in the consistency of Polish policy toward the Soviet Union." In response, the minister assured him that he "does not intend to delay the elaboration of the declaration proposed by Litvinov." On 29 December, the Polish mission in Moscow announced that Beck had agreed to come to the Soviet Union and that, in his opinion, a joint declaration on the Baltic countries "could best be done during his visit to Moscow."

After another meeting with Łukasiewicz on 11 January 1934, Litvinov, quite satisfied with the course of events, said, "Beck has not changed his attitude toward our proposal for the declaration; he is ready to participate in it."

No other reason besides the complete confidence of Soviet diplomatic leaders in the favorable completion of the declaration can explain the fact that Stalin, speaking to the Seventeenth Party Congress on 26 January 1934, with the summary report of the Central Committee of the All-Union Communist Party (Bolsheviks), or AUCP (b), highly praised Soviet-Polish relations. In a series of international events that had, in the words of the speaker, "indisputably great importance," Stalin mentioned "a breakthrough for the better in relations between the USSR and Poland, and the USSR and France, which had recently occurred." The meaning of this breakthrough was defined by Stalin as follows: "It is not just that we have signed a nonaggression pact with these countries, though the pact as such is of the utmost importance. The main point is that the atmosphere infected by mutual mistrust is beginning to dissipate." However, Stalin managed to throw a fly in the ointment, quipping, "That does not mean, of course, that the incipient process of convergence can be regarded as sufficiently stable and assured of ultimate success. It is still far from impossible to preclude political surprises and zigzags, for example, in Poland, where anti-Soviet sentiments are still strong."

Ironically, the report was read at the party congress at a time when this assessment of Soviet-Polish relations was, in fact, already out of date. Only the remark about the "zigzags" of Polish politics was quite justified.

Apparently, neither the People's Commissariat nor the Soviet political leadership could adequately appreciate the value of the news that Łukasiewicz had confidentially communicated to Litvinov on 11 January 1934, namely, that Poland had received a formal proposal from Germany to sign a nonaggression pact. Judging by the conversation's record, Litvinov was satisfied with the assurance by the Polish envoy that the talks about this pact "will be held from the viewpoint of Polish-German relations and would not concern disarmament or third countries" and that Poland, by signing this pact, only sought to bring relations with Germany "in line with those of Germany's other neighbors" (an allusion to the 1925 Locarno Agreements, which guaranteed the inviolability of the borders between Germany and its western neighbors). Litvinov even asked Łukasiewicz to convey thanks to Beck for the message, obviously considering it a sign of trust in relations between the two countries.

On 26 January 1934, the Polish-German Declaration on Nonaggression and Understanding (often referred to as a "pact" in Soviet sources) was signed in Berlin and became a milestone in the history of relations between Poland and all of its neighbors.

The same day, the Polish Foreign Ministry notified the Soviet plenipotentiary about this event. Jan Szembek, the vice-minister of foreign affairs, even read him the preliminary text of the declaration, firmly stating that "behind this document there is nothing more, there are no other agreements."

However, Antonov-Ovseenko's claims were not related so much to the content of the Polish-German "pact" as to what generally constituted it. On 29 January 1934, in a conversation with Beck, he directly cast doubt on the relevance and timeliness of signing this document: "Everything that strengthens Germany is evil for the cause of peace; this pact unquestionably reinforces Hitler's regime, increases its solvency abroad," and so on. During the conversation, he again returned to this thought: "I repeat to Beck that I have no doubt, of course, that behind the Polish-German pact there is nothing else, but the objective significance of this act affects the interests of others."

As we see, the immediate reaction by Soviet diplomats to the reports on the preparation and signing of the 26 January Polish-German Declaration was relatively mild. They were more surprised that almost immediately after this event Polish diplomacy changed its tone in contacts with the Soviets, showing a harsh demeanor for the first time in several months. In the aforementioned conversation with the plenipotentiary on 29 January, Beck criticized Stalin's speech at the party congress, seeing therein "an expression of mistrust in the stability [per the source]" of Polish policy toward the Soviet Union. Moreover, referring to some remarks by Lithuanian minister of foreign affairs Dovas Zaunius, who tried to link the proposed declaration on the Baltic countries with the Vilnius issue, he expressed not only doubt about the possibility of signing the Polish-Soviet declaration on the Baltic countries but also mistrust in the head of the Soviet diplomatic mission: "Mr. Litvinov said that Lithuania fully supported our initiative, and now suddenly Lithuania will stipulate this support by the return of Wilno [Vilnius]!"

Soviet diplomats had not immediately grasped that the Poles were deliberately provoking a diplomatic dispute by their actions. But the facts were too eloquent. On 1 February 1934, Litvinov met with the Polish envoy in Moscow. According to the conversation record, "Łukasiewicz at once began to speak in an aggressive tone about the discontent in Poland caused by Comrade Stalin's statements concerning zigzags in Polish policy." He also again mentioned Zaunius, whose ill-fated speech was allegedly inspired by the Soviets. But more importantly, the Polish envoy disclosed goals set by the Polish Foreign Ministry for starting a conflict with the Soviet Union. In Litvinov's words, "[Łukasiewicz] is not authorized by Beck to tell me anything about Beck's planned visit to Moscow, but now he [Łukasiewicz] can personally doubt the likelihood of this trip, which was conceived under entirely different circumstances, in the situation of confidence. Expressing his personal opinion again, [Łukasiewicz] suggests that the declaration on the Baltic countries may now fade away." After such statements by the Polish envoy, Litvinov had no doubt that something more serious than a simple misunderstanding had occurred. His question, "Does Łukasiewicz think that if we mistrust each other, as he believes, that the best way to remove it would be to abandon Beck's trip?" remained unanswered.

The materials we researched, in our opinion, suggest with absolute clarity that the Soviet-Polish diplomatic incident actually took place, that it was inspired by the Poles, and that the latter played it well, without a hitch. It may even be said that the incident played out according to the laws of a classical drama: the first act (plot), Beck's conversation with Antonov-Ovseenko on 29 January; the second act (culmination), a statement by Łukasiewicz to Litvinov on 1 February; and the third act (dénouement), when, on 3 February 1934, the Polish envoy again appeared before Litvinov, this time with Beck's instructions.

Litvinov recounts how the meeting with the envoy began: "Reading from a note, [Łukasiewicz] said something like this (written almost word for word). Beck asked him to announce that[,] regardless of the nature of the issue, he believed that the Baltic declaration had tactically failed and caused a lot of complications." In support of his position on this matter, Beck referred primarily to the "harmful repercussions for Polish interests in Lithuania," that is, to similar statements by Zaunius. However, in conclusion, Beck still was willing to come to Moscow if the Soviets would confirm the desirability of his arrival. After listening to Łukasiewicz, Litvinov tried to explain to him the "absolute weakness of the Polish arguments" against the Baltic declaration: "Zaunius may talk as much as he likes about the Vilnius region, as he has talked until now," but "the declaration should only be made by Beck and me [Litvinov]." Poland's position was hardly understandable to Litvinov because "the idea of [Soviet-Polish] cooperation in the Baltic region was expressed by Mr. Beck for the first time." Litvinov lamented the "loss of such a good cause for truly strengthening mutual trust and creating fertile ground for further cooperation." Nevertheless, he concluded that "we will be happy to receive Mr. Beck in Moscow, regardless of the declaration."

Antonov-Ovseenko was the first person who realized that Soviet diplomacy had landed in a trap set by their Polish colleagues. In the autumn of 1933, comparing a number of events, he made note of a "parallelism" in Polish actions. Just a week before signing the Polish-German declaration on 15 November 1933, Warsaw organized a widely publicized trip to Moscow for a delegation of Polish pilots to be led by Col. Ludomił Rayski. This event attracted much attention in diplomatic circles and was accompanied by frenetic press coverage on both sides of the Polish-Soviet border. A few days after Rayski's delegation had visited, the "Polish maneuver in Berlin" took its turn.

Similarly, Polish diplomats played their Soviet colleagues from late 1933 to early 1934. Under the guise of negotiating on the Baltic issue, which played the role of a demonstration maneuver, they prepared and signed a "pact" in Berlin on 26 January. It is clear that the purpose of this diplomatic game in which Polish diplomacy managed to involve the Soviet Union was to create a kind of smokescreen around Poland's attempts to come to terms with the Nazi government of Germany.

It seems to us that the lessons of this "trick" were taken to heart by Soviet diplomats, who subsequently conveyed a much tougher tone with regard to Poland. In addition, shortly after this diplomatic scandal, Antonov-Ovseenko was recalled from the post of plenipotentiary of the Soviet Union in Poland. His place was taken by Yakov Davtyan, who presented his credentials to the president of the Republic of Poland on 13 April 1934.

The refusal of Poland to sign the Baltic declaration was not just a slap in the face to Soviet diplomacy. We should remind the reader that the Soviets considered this declaration to be a touchstone of the Polish attitude toward the Soviet Union. Now, all doubts had disappeared. As Stomonyakov stated in a letter to Antonov-Ovseenko on 4 February 1934, "The refusal of the Baltic act by Poland" indicated "the far-reaching nature of the Polish-German rapprochement."

Henceforth, Soviet diplomacy was mainly occupied with the issue of what threats to the Soviet Union might stem from Poland's course toward rapprochement with Germany. Alas, the forecasts were disappointing, especially for the security of the western borders of the Soviet Union. Soviet diplomats drew attention to the lack of a "normal clause" in the Polish-German "pact" of 26 January that would void the agreement in the event one side attacked a third state. "It is impossible to imagine," Stomonyakov wrote, "that the omission of this clause did not have special meaning. The absence of this clause in the Polish-German treaty actually ensures the neutrality of Poland toward Germany in the event of German aggression against countries with which Poland has no union treaties. This means that Poland will remain neutral, not only in the event of a German invasion of Austria but also in the event of German aggression against Lithuania and generally to the east."

Soviet diplomacy used Beck's visit to Moscow, 13–15 February 1934, not only to cover up the recent diplomatic conflict but also to possibly dampen the effect of the Polish-German "pact." Litvinov and Beck had long conversations, directly addressing the thorny issues. The most difficult among those was, of course, the question of relations between both countries and Germany. Litvinov did not agree with Beck's idea that it was getting "easier to come to terms" with Germany once it ceased to be ruled by the Prussians. On the contrary, he argued, "the Prussian spirit now dominates the whole of Germany" and finds "the most vivid expression in the teachings of the Nazis."

However, Litvinov did not directly criticize the Polish-German "pact." On the contrary, he even said something commendable about it: "Since the Polish-German agreement fosters the peaceful settlement of relations between the two countries, we welcome this agreement." However, as if to make a joke, he noted that this agreement had generated some "jealousy" in the Soviet government because Poland had signed it with Germany for ten years, whereas the nonaggression pact between Poland and the Soviet Union was for only three years. Litvinov's joke completely disarmed Beck, who was "obviously confused and even fidgeted in his seat." Litvinov took advantage of the interlocutor's confusion and obtained principal consent from him "to extend the Soviet-Polish Nonaggression Pact for ten years from now, without waiting for its expiration."

The negotiations succeeded in reducing tensions in Soviet-Polish relations and even created the appearance of an improvement. In particular, the parties consented to raise their diplomatic missions to the rank of embassies.

But Litvinov's overall impression from the Polish minister's visit remained extremely unfavorable: "Undoubtedly, a serious shift in the policy orientation of Poland has occurred." The conversations with Beck had the people's commissar convinced that "Poland found itself secured by Germany for the near future." Although Litvinov was far from thinking that "Poland had already entered into any secret agreement with Germany," nevertheless he fully admitted that "Poland was convinced from conversations with the Germans of the possibility of such an agreement at a time when Poland will want it." In any case, the people's commissar believed that "cooperation with Poland against Germany" was not an option for the Soviet Union in the near future and that "any joint action in the interest of security for the Baltic countries had definitively fallen away." However, Litvinov presumed that Soviet diplomacy would weigh heavily over the neighboring country's policy, as before. "Poland," he reasoned, "finds it useful to disguise its new orientation, moreover its new plans, by visibly putting on the mask of good relations with us, or even actually improving them. This masking is useful to us as well and we therefore should engage Poland" in order to "somewhat hamper the Polish government from switching onto a hostile path with us."

An occasion to apply this leverage presented itself to Soviet diplomacy almost immediately. Beck had barely left Moscow when the Poles tried to evade the agreements that had just been reached. On 20 February 1934, in a meeting with Litvinov, Polish envoy Łukasiewicz "expressed his personal views" that prolonging the Soviet-Polish Nonaggression Pact should be linked to the timing of similar pacts between the Soviet Union and the Baltic countries and even to the conclusion of a similar pact with Romania.

On 25 March 1934, Łukasiewicz presented Stomonyakov with Poland's official response to the Soviet proposal. The Polish envoy's main point was that the "prolongation of the Polish-Soviet Pact is impossible" without simultaneously "synchronizing" similar pacts between the Soviet Union and the Baltic countries. Łukasiewicz cited "Polish interest" in the security of these states as the motivation. Stomonyakov, describing the Polish response as a refusal of the Soviet proposal, did not fail to needle Łukasiewicz, saying that Poland, by signing the "10-year pact with Germany," had thus shown "no concern for the Baltics."

Meanwhile, Soviet diplomacy did not stand idly by. In turn, it prepared a surprise for Poland. On 28 March 1934, Stomonyakov told Łukasiewicz that, even before the arrival of Beck in Moscow, the Soviet Union had proposed that the Baltic countries extend their nonaggression pacts with the Soviet Union by ten years and that the governments of Estonia, Latvia, and Lithuania had adopted the Soviet proposal. This statement, according to Stomonyakov, made a stunning impression on the Polish envoy: "[Łukasiewicz] was apparently caught by surprise, he grew slightly pale, and then with great courtesy said that he would immediately convey my statement to Warsaw. Then, after a slight pause, clearly upset and not knowing what to say, he added with excessive politeness that he would send a telegram immediately upon his arrival at the mission. Then came a new awkward silence; [Łukasiewicz] did not look at me, and the movement of the muscles in his face betrayed his emotion."

Litvinov did not hide his satisfaction. On 4 April 1934, he wrote to Marcel I. Rosenberg, the chargé d'affaires of the Soviet Union in France, "Poland is evidently cornered by us." He explained that the Poles had truly put forward a new requirement for "any kind of cancellation of Chicherin's 1926 note about Lithuania," but they "were quickly convinced of the impossibility for us to meet this requirement." As a result, the people's commissar expressed his confidence that Poland, "in the end, cannot avoid prolonging the pact."

Litvinov's prediction was very accurate. On 5 May 1934, a protocol on prolonging the nonaggression pact between the Soviet Union and Poland was signed in Moscow. But that was little consolation amid the general cooling in Soviet-Polish relations.

However, despite the failure of bilateral rapprochement with Poland, Soviet diplomacy by this time had new expectations for entering into multilateral relations with Poland. As far back as October 1933, out of concern over the aggressive ambitions of Nazi Germany, France had proposed that the Soviet Union sign a treaty of mutual assistance. This proposal was fully consistent with both the Soviet Union's security interests and its new direction in foreign policy. The Soviet Union had long since abandoned its sweeping criticism of the existing international order and was increasingly speaking out for the defense thereof from encroachments by "aggressor states." While positively appreciating the initiative of France, the Soviet government for its part pushed for the involvement of Eastern European countries in the Soviet-French Pact. Louis Barthou, appointed minister of foreign affairs of France in February 1934, appeared to be a proponent of the regional pact in Eastern Europe. On April 20, he told Soviet diplomats in Paris about his willingness to start the negotiations. Barthou visited Warsaw 22–24 April 1934, in order to ascertain the position of the Polish government.

But Barthou returned from Warsaw virtually empty-handed. However, to the bewilderment of Soviet diplomats, this fact could not shake the confidence of their French counterparts in their policy toward Poland. On 7 May 1934, Charles Alphand, the French ambassador to the Soviet Union, mentioned that he could not share the Soviet "pessimism with regards to Poland," which evoked an angry retort from Litvinov:

> If we speak about our mistrust, it is thus based on facts. With Poland, we have held very serious talks about cooperation, but these talks were terminated by the Poles. Having accepted our proposed declaration in favor of independence for the Baltic countries, Poland refused the declaration after signing the pact with Germany. Our proposal to extend the pact was sabotaged by Poland more than two months ago. I will not even touch on the rumors and gossip about the secret Polish-German agreements. Finally, the results of Barthou's talks in Warsaw confirm rather than refute these rumors.

The question is: What did Soviet diplomacy rely on in feeding such a deep distrust of Poland's policy? According to our sources, it was based only on the fact that, as Litvinov wrote on 27 June 1934, "France has sufficient means at its disposal to pressure Poland into acceding to the pact."

The fact that the negotiations between the French ambassador to Poland, Jules Laroche, and Beck in Warsaw could not alter the position of the Polish government on the Eastern Pact draft was indirect proof to Soviet diplomats of secret agreements between Poland and Germany. On 4 July 1934, Alphand told Stomonyakov that the Polish minister held these talks "in an evasive manner and essentially said nothing."

On that same day, Stomonyakov wrote to Davtyan, "The main role in the failure of the pact is, of course, Poland's position, which, due to its geographic location, is undoubtedly the main obstacle to implementing this act."

Nevertheless, Soviet diplomacy was so interested in the agreement with Poland that Litvinov responded enthusiastically to the slightest signs of change in Warsaw's position. On 27 September 1934, he reported from Geneva about a note on the Eastern Pact draft containing a list of comments by Polish diplomats that Barthou had received from Beck. According to the people's commissar, who had read the note, the comments were shaped as "conditions" for Poland's accession to the pact. Litvinov was encouraged by the fact that the Poles were at least raising no objections to the pact. The Polish minister personally assured him that "he would by no means close the door to further negotiations." The people's commissar even had the impression that Beck had considered "an allusion to the possibility of releasing Poland from its obligations with respect to Lithuania," which had been made earlier. On 21 November 1934, Litvinov, speaking in Geneva with Pierre Laval, who had been appointed minister of foreign affairs of France after the tragic death of Barthou, proposed "to release Poland" from "aiding" not only Lithuania but also Czechoslovakia in the event of its participation in the Eastern Pact.

Meanwhile, Soviet diplomats noted a "significant deterioration in tone" in statements about the Soviet Union that appeared in the Polish press. As to Stomonyakov (in his letter to Davtyan dated 23 November 1934), there was no doubt that "the Polish government no longer attached such a value to maintaining illusions about good relations with the USSR as in the past; moreover, it was perhaps even preparing Polish public opinion for Polish policy to evolve in a more hostile direction toward the Soviet Union."

It appears to be no accident that, in the autumn of 1934, Poland was again mentioned in Soviet diplomatic correspondence in connection with military threats to the security of the Soviet Union. In one case, this warning was related to an informal proposal by Rudolph Nadolny, head of the German delegation at the Geneva Disarmament Conference, to conclude the Eastern Pact without the participation of France and Czechoslovakia, as presented to Yakov Suritz, the Soviet plenipotentiary representative in Berlin. Litvinov at once saw a trick in this proposal. On 4 November 1934, he wrote to Suritz, "In fact, what guarantee can his proposal give us against a German attack on the Baltic countries and the USSR? What if Germany and Poland were to attack us and the Baltic countries? Indeed, we may suspect the two states." In another case, Stomonyakov drew Davtyan's attention to the "information about the increasingly close relationship between Poland and Japan, namely about a treaty of alliance prepared [by them] for signing, which may already be signed."

Soviet-Polish relations reached a sort of moment of truth during Litvinov's conversation with Łukasiewicz on 10 February 1935. This encounter led to a serious quarrel between them, and the consequences, as we see it, were felt for a long time. According to the conversation record, the ambassador came to the people's commissar for an ostensibly innocent purpose: to complain about the poor state of relations between their two countries. But from complaints he quickly moved to charges against the Soviet Union, which, according to him, had allegedly "attached more importance to the alliance with France than to neighborly relations with Poland" and, even worse, was tending to sacrifice them to its "big policy aspirations." As Litvinov understood it, the ambassador tried to persuade him that "we should not see a threat in

Poland where Poland itself does not see it," because "it feels quite secured by Germany."

The people's commissar was particularly struck by Łukasiewicz's statement in that, since the Soviet Union had no common border with Germany, the Poles "must therefore suspect that its strong aspiration for the Eastern Pact has a completely different meaning."

In concluding the conversation, Litvinov clearly articulated the Soviet position on the issue of relations with Poland: "For the present time, these relations should be measured by Poland's response to the Eastern Pact proposal."

Even Germany's refusal to observe the military articles of the Versailles Treaty, to the disappointment of Soviet diplomats, did not cause any disturbance for Polish officials. On 17 March 1935, Davtyan was invited to a "tea party" by the wife of the Polish minister of foreign affairs. So, while "most of the conversations revolved around the announcement of conscription in Germany," as he had noted, "Beck himself was absent, evidently to avoid unwanted inquiries on this subject." On the other hand, the envoy managed to speak with Leon Kozłowski, the Polish prime minister. Not without irony, Davtyan asked, "To my direct question, what does Poland think about it?" With his usual military-style frankness, Kozłowski replied that he was calm and felt secure for Poland, having thirty "rather good divisions."

In April 1935, Poland rejected yet another compromise draft of the Eastern Pact, this time proposed by Great Britain. The following month, the Soviet Union signed treaties of mutual assistance with France and Czechoslovakia, on 2 May and 16 May, respectively. These developments terminated the active political dialogue between the Soviet Union and Poland that had lasted for several years.

Did this mean that Soviet diplomacy had finally put an end to plans for cooperating with Poland on European security issues or that it had just decided to demonstrate its firmness?

To us, Moscow seems to have continued attaching significance to relations with Warsaw. Therefore, Davtyan was quite excited by the obvious favor Polish officials began to show him for the first time after the long break. On 17 January 1936, he sent a telegram informing the People's Commissariat of overnight talks, held extempore during a dinner with Ignacy Mościcki, president of the Polish republic. First, Beck himself came to the ambassador and took him aside specifically to say that he "wanted to improve relations" with the Soviet Union. The minister persistently, "very pointedly (and repeatedly)," tried to convince Davtyan that "Poland would never participate in any coalition against the Soviet Union." The plenipotentiary representative had the impression that Beck, "in general, by his behavior[,] wanted to emphasize the desire of Poland to improve relations with us." Next, Davtyan had a "friendly and long talk" individually with Gen. Edward Rydz-Śmigły, then the actual second-in-command person among the ruling circles of Poland. This fact, according to observations by the plenipotentiary, has "even drawn the current attention of the public."

This "social graces" made such a great impression on the plenipotentiary representative that, on 10 January 1936, Poland's foreign policy was sharply criticized in public by Molotov, chair of the Council of People's Commissars, from the rostrum of the Second Session of the Central Executive Committee of the Soviet Union. In particular, he pointedly said that Hitler's Germany, carrying out aggressive plans against the Soviet Union but using the lack of a common border with the Soviet Union as a smokescreen, "entered into special relations with Poland, having a sufficiently long border with the Soviet Union." In a letter to Stomonyakov dated 24 January 1936, Davtyan noted with satisfaction that "Beck had consciously avoided any debates and had not responded to Comrade Molotov's report." He summarized his impressions of the contacts with Polish officials in the following way: "The Poles have now taken a certain path toward improving external relations with us."

Litvinov immediately reacted to the message from the plenipotentiary representative about the conversation with the head Polish diplomat. On 18 January, he telegraphed the PCFA that "Beck is clearly trying to pay court to us." Believing that such behavior by the Poles was not contrary to Soviet interests, the people's commissar decided, "It is possible for us to answer in the same manner."

After a couple of months, a new situation erupted. On 24 March 1936, Litvinov cabled from London (where he had participated in a League of Nations Council session), "Beck is ready, if we wish, to further exchange views on pressing issues[;] also, he is ready to talk on point about the issues and to give corresponding instructions to his Ambassador in Moscow." Although Litvinov accepted Beck's proposal with satisfaction, he continued to doubt the sincerity of the Polish minister. He openly said it in the telegram: "But I do not attribute serious value to Beck's statement."

Stomonyakov, whose letter to Davtyan allowed us to learn the details of this strange visit by Łukasiewicz to the people's commissar, saw the manifestation of a deeper pattern in this small diplomatic incident: "This fact, of course, surprises none of us. The anti-Soviet course of Polish policy is not only undiminished but perhaps even intensified in recent years. The Polish government, openly before the entire Polish society, has more and more been taking a course opposed to any rapprochement with the Soviet Union."

There is no doubt that Soviet diplomacy took into account not just incidents of this kind. It was much more concerned about the suspicions that Poland was either close to collusion with Germany or had already entered into such collusion at the expense of Soviet interests.

As we have seen, this topic was discussed in Soviet diplomatic circles for quite some time, since at least mid-1933. But, in 1936, the Soviets began to pay much more attention to it than ever before. As noted above, on 10 January 1936, Molotov for the first time publicly hinted at the possibility of collusion between the Poles and the Nazis. On 4 March, Stomonyakov drew the attention of B. G. Podolsky, chargé d'affaires of the Soviet Union in Poland, to no more or less than an attempt to "knock together the bloc of fascist states," including not only Italy, Germany, and Japan but also Poland. On 16 March 1936, Krestinsky, the deputy commissar for foreign affairs, in talking to French journalist Jacques Chastenet, described the Polish-German collusion as almost an immutable truth.

All of this information gives us reason to believe, paraphrasing Litvinov, that at this point the attitude of Poland toward Germany became the main "measure" for Soviet diplomats in Soviet-Polish relations.

For some time, Soviet diplomacy did not preclude the possibility of changes in Polish policy, namely, the weakening of Polish-German relations. After all, it was clear that Nazi Germany posed a threat to the security of not only the Soviet Union but also Poland. Therefore, Soviet diplomacy carefully monitored the situation for any signs of tension between Poland and Germany. On 28 August 1936, Suritz, the ambassador to Germany, noticed the volatility of the bases on which "German relations with its potential ally Poland are being built," and which were undermined by "a certain strengthening of Franco-Polish relations." In September 1936, Soviet diplomacy learned that Rydz-Śmigły had allegedly, "in written form," assured the French "of the absence of any agreement against the Soviet Union and Czechoslovakia between Poland and Germany."

Soviet diplomats tried to persuade the Polish government in manifold ways to abandon its focus on Germany. On 16 March 1936, Krestinsky directly warned the Poles about the rashness of such a policy. He argued that, whatever the motives behind the deal with Germany, which the Polish government entered into "in order to pay off German aggression, Poland can greatly miscalculate thereon, because if Germany is not strong enough to attack the Soviet Union and France, it will . . . start with Poland."

Davtyan resorted to historical analogies. In a conversation with Beck on 2 November 1936, he cited the example of Great Britain, whose "indecisive behavior before the war in 1914 accelerated the German attack." The plenipotentiary representative tried to suggest the idea to the Polish minister that "likewise now, a firmer and more definite policy would contribute to peace," thus hinting suggestively at "Poland's hesitation." As Beck, listening to Davtyan's arguments, plunged into extensive discussions about the general principles of Polish foreign policy, the plenipotentiary outflanked him: "When speaking of German aggression, we do not think only about the USSR, because Germany is first of all threatening others (I hinted at Poland as well)." However, once again, the Polish minister pretended not to have understood the allusion.

In the autumn of 1936, Soviet diplomacy toward Poland reached yet another important milestone. At this point, we see no evidence that Soviet diplomats still harbored any hope for changing the course of Polish policy or attempting to provoke Polish representatives to frank discussions of this issue. But it clearly stands out that their opinions about Poland's politics were becoming harder and more irreconcilable every day. Here are just a few typical examples.

On 18 October 1936, Davtyan wrote to Krestinsky, "Poland now has not only little desire to improve its relations with the Soviet Union, but on the contrary, it is strengthening its diplomatic campaign against us, almost believing it's no longer necessary to veil it." On 26 April 1937, glancing back at the recent past, Davtyan bitterly observed, "It is no exaggeration to say that [for] the last year, Polish foreign policy has been converging even more with German policy and has become more openly anti-Soviet."

On 19 September 1937, the deputy people's commissar for foreign affairs, in speaking with E. Ciuntu, Romanian ambassador to the Soviet Union, characterized Polish policy as such: "Contrary to the national interests of Poland, demanding loyal cooperation with the powers conducting a policy of peace, its current government allows itself to be led by Germany, pushing Poland toward the most dangerous of adventures. Sooner or later, Poland will have to pay for this policy." In response to the Romanian envoy's request for some clarification, Potemkin added, "Poland is led by its fascist government, which has cast its lot with Hitler."

By the end of 1937, Soviet diplomats had no doubt that Poland, together with Germany, sought to alter the boundaries of Eastern Europe in their favor.

Soviet diplomats thought about the consequences that could result from Poland's policy. In December 1937, in a conversation with French minister of foreign affairs Yvon Delbos, who was on a visit to Warsaw, Vinogradov sarcastically invited him to imagine the "interesting combinations" arising "in the event of an armed attack by Germany on Czechoslovakia." According to the Soviet diplomat, even the entry of France into the war on the side of Czechoslovakia would hardly encourage Poland to abandon "benevolent neutrality for Germany."

These judgments and assessments hardly permit multivalued conjectures. According to Soviet diplomacy, Poland had gone too far in its relations with Germany (whatever they might be called—convergence, balancing, etc.). As a result, the security interests of the Soviet Union came into conflict with the policy pursued by the Polish government. The implication was that the Soviet Union had no choice but to take care of its own safety, without regard for Poland.

The reader may ask: Was the perception of Polish foreign policy by Soviet diplomats accurate? Was it sufficiently consistent with reality? It is a large and complicated question that the present study does not presume to answer, as the question is so ample and laying out the answer would be labor intensive. In some regards, Soviet diplomacy was undoubtedly right, as it was, for example, concerning the fact that the ambitions of Poland and its territorial claims to neighboring territory could turn into big trouble for all. In some other regards, however, Soviet diplomacy was wrong. For example, it clearly overestimated the proximity between Poland and Germany, suspecting the existence of a secret, aggressive union between them. But the governments of other states also made mistakes in their assessments of the actual state of affairs. The policy of "appeasement" that Western countries pursued with regard to Germany proved to be built on sand. The Polish policy of "balancing" did not prove to be any better. But we have to say once more that evaluating the accuracy of Soviet perceptions of Polish policy was not part of our task. We have just tried to understand the motives that guided the Soviet Union in its relations with Poland. After all, for history, it is important to know not only the objective state of affairs but also the subjective perceptions of "earth-shaking" decision makers.

3

THE CAUSES OF WORLD WAR II

POLAND, THE SOVIET UNION, AND THE CRISIS OF THE VERSAILLES SYSTEM

Sławomir Dębski (Poland)

Historian and foreign policy analyst, PhD holder, director of the Center for Polish-Russian Dialogue and Understanding, former director of the Polish Institute of International Affairs (PISM), member of the Polish-Russian Group on Difficult Matters since 2008.

Mikhail M. Narinsky (Russia)

Professor, chair of the Department of International Relations and Foreign Policy of Russia at the Moscow State Institute of International Relations (MGIMO University).

SŁAWOMIR DĘBSKI

POLAND, THE SOVIET UNION, AND THE CRISIS OF THE VERSAILLES SYSTEM

MORE THAN SEVENTY years after the outbreak of World War II, it is extremely difficult to provide an original answer to the question about its causes. Germany—the state and the nation—bears primary responsibility for the outbreak of that war and its barbaric character contrary to all moral and legal norms. It is impossible to understand the war without ascertaining that it occurred as a result of the aggressive policies pursued by the chancellor of Germany, Adolf Hitler, who enjoyed broad support from the German people.

Poland, Soviet Russia, and the Versailles System

The outbreak of World War II brought to a definite end the twenty-year existence of the Versailles system. The positions of Poland and Russia in the system differed radically. The reborn Poland was one of its integral parts and chief beneficiaries. Aleksander Skrzyński, one of the outstanding Polish foreign ministers of the interwar period, commented, "The Treaty of Versailles means the existence of Poland," and "Poland holds the key to European security, so any combination that tries to ignore this will be doomed to complete failure." The reconstituted Polish state came into being in November 1918 as a result of synergistic diplomatic efforts in Paris, London, Washington, and Rome undertaken by national conservatives, as well as of takeovers of power in Polish territories by independence-oriented left-wing forces. The ethos of action and the tradition of struggle for one's own state influenced Polish thinking in the realm of international affairs. It was in line with the Polish *raison d'*état to collaborate with Paris and London for the stability of the new international system. With that goal in mind, in 1921 Poland concluded military alliances with France and Romania, strived for cooperation with Great Britain, and, during the first postwar decade, backed the institutions of the Versailles system, including the League of Nations. Warsaw assumed that it would be in France's national interest to defend the European order shaped after World War I. The Polish-French alliance established in the early 1920s was a natural consequence of the community of strategic interests of the two states, which, however, started eroding after the Locarno Treaty of 1925. It enhanced the security of countries situated along the Rhine, while making Central Europe a region of relatively diminished security. That differentiation drove a wedge into the Polish-French alliance and the strategic community of the two states.

Practically the day after the Treaty of Versailles was signed, some began to have the conviction that it would have to be modernized in the future. I use the term "modernized" rather than "reformed" because I feel it is closer to the intentions of the proponents of such changes. Warsaw suspected—usually with good reason—that the ideas for fixing the Versailles system, floated in London and Paris, were underpinned by concepts aimed at a reduction of Poland's territorial holdings and the instrumentalization of the issue of security in Central Europe. In December 1935, Ralf S. Stevenson, the deputy head of the League of Nations desk at the British Foreign Office, advised Polish diplomats in Geneva that,

> with regard to Germany, one has to choose between two methods: either to buy peace, or to wage war. England will, to the limit of what is possible, pursue the first course. . . . In Europe the Austrian question will end either with an Anschluss or with a "Gleichschaltung." This, however, will not stop [Germany's] expansion, which can unfold in the direction of Czechoslovakia, and maybe also Poland. England can intervene only in defence of the status quo in the West of Europe, but no Commons will acquiesce to an intervention in defence of the existing state of affairs in Central and Eastern Europe, such as in defence of the Corridor [i.e., Polish Pomerania].

The Polish political elite of the interwar period, conscious of France and Great Britain's stand on the issue of changes to the Versailles Treaty concerning Eastern Europe, always highlighted the importance of an independent foreign policy. That criterion determined the extent of Polish willingness to cooperate with the Western powers. It was a position frequently misunderstood in Paris and London.

The attitude of Soviet Russia to the Versailles order was different, because of the country's peripheral situation. In the interwar period, the Soviet Union remained outside international systems. The Bolshevik Revolution had pushed it to the margins of European politics. Although at the Versailles conference Russia was entitled to a seat among the victorious powers, no one in all of that country could be found to represent it. Emperor Nicholas and his family had been brutally slain, while the "Supreme Ruler of Russia," Adm. Alexander Kolchak, did not control the European part of Russia and thus could not make decisions concerning its western borders. Meanwhile, the adventurist intervention of the Entente powers eliminated the Bolsheviks from the conference. The loss of the empire was the price the Bolsheviks paid at that time for assuming power, but they never reconciled themselves to that reality. On 7 November 1937, at a dinner given by Kliment Voroshilov, Stalin shared the following observations with those present: "The Russian tsars perpetrated much evil. They robbed and oppressed the people. In the interest of the landowners, they conducted wars and conquered territories. But they did one good thing: they created a huge state, stretching as far as Kamchatka. We have received this state in legacy. And it is only we, the Bolsheviks, who have united and consolidated it, not in the interest of the landowners and capitalists, but for the benefit of the workers, of all the peoples comprising this state." A vision of seizing the world, as they had seized Russia, constituted another source of the Bolsheviks' foreign policy. It combined Russian tradition with Bolshevik innovation—their dream of turning Russia into the new center of the world. That idea would have never occurred to Russian tsars, even those most committed to Russia's modernization: Peter I, Alexander I, Alexander II, or any of the earlier Russian reformers.

That was the reason for the duality of Soviet foreign policy, conducted by both the Narkomindel and the Comintern. A revisionist Soviet Russia also supported the revisionist programs of other countries "wronged" in 1919: Germany (in the years 1919–32) and Hungary, which was seeking ways of regaining Transylvania (in 1939–40). In July 1940, during a conversation with the new British ambassador to Moscow, Stafford Cripps, Stalin confided, "We want to change the old balance of power in Europe, which has functioned against the USSR." It was Stalin's objective to overturn the Versailles order and then counter any efforts to restore it.

The two revisionisms, German and Russian, naturally attracted each other, as evidenced by the "Rapallo line" in their policies. The Locarno Treaty changed this relationship. Germany became a full-fledged participant in the Versailles system, while the Soviet Union remained on its periphery. Although both states still strove to enhance their positions, after 1925 Berlin was able to do that in the framework of the Versailles system. Henceforth, it was more difficult for the two countries to agree on a common course. From the beginning, Berlin perceived the Rapallo line as a mean of putting pressure on the Western powers, so, after Locarno, the political alliance with Moscow lost its earlier rationale. At the beginning of the 1930s, the international situation did not justify hopes that the Versailles system might collapse as a result of a new, general conflict in Europe. Thus, Moscow was left with the option of trying to change the order in Europe with the help of diplomatic instruments. The policy of collective security was designed to serve that goal.

At the same time, the general secretary of Comintern, Georgi Dimitrov, openly declared at its Seventh Congress, "Our struggle against barbaric fascism does not mean that we have become proponents of the facetious and corrupt bourgeois democracy. Indeed, we are not democrats! . . . Our struggle against fascism does not have the goal of installing a bourgeois democracy but of attaining rule of the soviets." Stalin, however, clearly implied that, if Hitler needed the support of the Soviet Union to overturn the Versailles system, he would be receptive: "Of course, we are far from being enthusiastic about the fascist regime in Germany. But it is not a question of fascism, if only for the reason that fascism in Italy, for example, has not prevented the USSR from establishing the best of relations with that country. Nor is it a question of any alleged change in our attitude toward the Versailles Treaty. It is not for us, who have experienced the shame of the Brest peace, to sing the praises of the Versailles Treaty."

The Munich Agreement or "Peace in Our Time"

In the latter half of the 1930s, the nations of Western Europe refused to acknowledge that German demands for a revision of the Versailles system could lead to a European war, particularly in defense of "*distant countries* of which we know *little.*" The policy of appeasement was thus considered politically correct and within the mainstream of thinking about European security. During his visit to Germany in November 1937, Lord Halifax proposed to Hitler a return to the concept of "rectifying the mistakes connected with the Versailles Treaty" by way of an accord between the four powers: Germany, Great Britain, France, and Italy. Lord Halifax was referring primarily to changes affecting Austria and Czechoslovakia, and he also expressed willingness to discuss a new division of the colonies in the framework of a "general settlement." Hitler, true to his policy, was not interested in multilateral deals; he intended to push through his plans concerning Austria and Czechoslovakia without making any commitments to the Western powers.

Both Poland and the Soviet Union were on the margins of the search for a general settlement conducted between Berlin, Paris, London, and Rome. There were different reasons for this situation. The normalization of Polish-German relations after 1934 meant that Poland could no longer be sacrificed by the Western powers in their haggling with Germany over a new order in Europe. Instead, Poland came to be regarded as a player favorably inclined toward Berlin's political moves.

Meanwhile, despite the efforts of Maxim Litvinov, Soviet commissar for foreign affairs, to conclude an alliance with France and gain accession to the League of Nations, the Soviet Union had not managed to attain the status of a full-fledged power. The French and British policy of appeasing Germany's growing aspirations by way of multilateral accords did not envision a place for the Soviet Union. The logic of the Versailles system—shaped without Russia—was dominant here. The Munich conference constituted the last successful attempt to modify the Versailles system. France and Great Britain hoped it would bring about the final eradication of the flaws of the Versailles Treaty and satisfy German revisionism. Warsaw tried to distance itself from the policy of appeasement pursued by the Western powers toward Germany. At the same time, it did not want to undermine its relations with the former, particularly in view of the French and British policy of acceding to German postulates. This stimulated Polish aspirations to obtain the status of a European power, something congruent with its striving for an independent foreign policy.

From Warsaw's point of view, the Munich conference amounted to a failure of the policy it had pursued for several years with the objective of preventing "the quarrels of the great powers (France, England, Germany, and Russia) from being played out at the expense of states devoid of imperialist interests" and countering the instrumental treatment of the smaller European states by the powers. Yet, things could have been even worse. That would have been the case if the Soviet Union had been given any say on the matter of Czechoslovakia in the event of Hitler backing down as a result of some French-British-Soviet action, or as a result of even a temporary dependence of western policy on the position of Moscow.

Warsaw felt that the predicament in which Czechoslovakia had found itself was a consequence of its excessively close relations with the Soviets. After all, Hitler had never concealed his hostility toward the Bolsheviks. He consistently opposed Soviet aspirations to gain the status of a full-fledged European power. It was no accident that, during the Munich crisis, German foreign minister Joachim von Ribbentrop probed Józef Lipski, the Polish ambassador to Berlin, about the possibility of Poland joining an anti-Comintern pact. Poland ignored that overture. At the same time, it felt that the French-Czechoslovak-Soviet combination put together in 1935 was detrimental to the position of its southern neighbor. The Soviets had pledged to aid Czechoslovakia if it first received assistance from France. Warsaw believed in neither the Soviets' good intentions nor their practical capacity to deliver on that promise.

In May 1938, the Polish ambassador to Moscow, Wacław Grzybowski, formulated the following assessment of Soviet intentions:

> The basic position of the USSR on Czechoslovakia was formulated in Litvinov's well-known declaration of 17 March. . . . Yet, in addition to moral support, the Soviet stance does not indicate a willingness to take an independent, active stand on the Czechoslovak matter. That position has depended from the beginning on the views of France and England on Central Europe. . . . The attitude of the Soviets in the Czechoslovak affair is very analogous to their stance in the Spanish question. Besides general assurances of allied solidarity and a supposed will to cooperate in the peaceful resolution of the Czechoslovak question, the Soviets' true efforts are consistently aimed at aggravat-

ing the situation in Central Europe, based on the political calculation that an armed conflict would result and the Soviets could then adopt a wait-and-see attitude.

It turned out to be an extremely insightful assessment of Soviet intentions. For all those reasons, during the Munich crisis Poland resolutely and actively countered all initiatives that would have involved the Soviet Union.

But Poland's opposition to the exclusive concept of the four powers shaping the European order and its striving to uphold an autonomous position on the Munich conference led Polish diplomacy into a trap. Shortly after it was announced that the four powers would be holding the conference in Munich, the Polish government decided to take independent action. Before midnight of 30 September 1938, the Polish envoy to Prague, Kazimierz Papée, presented an ultimatum to the Czechoslovak government, demanding that it cede the district of Teschen to Poland. In his special instructions for Papée, drafted in connection with the ultimatum, Foreign Minister Józef Beck spelled out his motives: "It is my understanding that the current Polish-Czechoslovak dispute has two fundamental aspects as regards the position of our State: (1) The first, a short-term one, concerns restoration of the lands to which we have a legitimate claim; (2) the second refers to the overall position of the Republic of Poland toward the new Europe and the way it is governed. At this profound juncture, I believed that only a bold decision can define the fundamental image of our state." The autonomous Polish move was conceived as a protest against the idea of a revived Concert of Europe and considered to be particularly dangerous to Poland. However, as Polish historians have rightly noted, that "act of sabotage against the spirit of Munich" played into Hitler's hands: "By challenging the rule, favored by Western politicians, that Central European disputes were to be settled exclusively by the Munich directorate, Poland made it easier for the chancellor to conclusively abandon the practice of consulting the Reich's demands with London and Paris, which had constrained the German freedom of movement." On the same day that Poland issued its ultimatum to Prague, Beck made one more mistake. In a conversation with Hans-Adolf von Moltke, the German ambassador to Warsaw, Beck, after thanking him for Germany's loyalty to Poland during the Sudetenland crisis, asked if Germany would adopt a favorable attitude toward Poland in the event of a Polish-Czechoslovak conflict. He also asked if Poland could expect a similar attitude on the part of Germany if the Soviet Union intervened, even though neither Beck nor Moltke believed that that was feasible. The next day Ribbentrop advised Lipski that in the first case the German attitude would be favorable and, in the second, "it would be much more than favorable toward Poland."

Polish historians have established that there existed a difference between Ribbentrop's answer to the question (which Lipski immediately conveyed to

Warsaw) and true German intentions. Ribbentrop's notes indicate that he believed "a new situation" would arise for Germany in the event of a Soviet intervention. Thus, it is highly probable that German support for Poland would not have been "absolute, but would have likely depended on the fulfillment by Poland of additional conditions."

Beck's two queries about the German position concerning two unlikely scenarios, made without duress, must be considered a serious mistake, discordant relative to his own policy. Its goal was to maintain an original and autonomous position in a rapidly deteriorating international situation. Meanwhile, on 30 September 1938, Beck adopted the role of a supplicant vis-à-vis the Third Reich. Berlin gladly availed itself of the opportunity. Ribbentrop gave Beck a positive response that cost the former nothing but enhanced his position in future talks with the Poles. Although one can appreciate the rationale of Polish resistance to the directorate of the big powers, as well as the fact that all European politicians made mistakes during the Munich crisis, there is no denying that Polish policy in September 1938 was misguided. Poland wavered between Berlin, which was seeking hegemony in Central Europe, and London and Paris, which were incapable of standing up to Hitler and were searching for some token in the region that could be exchanged for "peace in our time." Alas, Polish diplomacy failed to find the right balance.

There were certain similarities in the situation of Poland and the Soviet Union after the Munich conference, though they were limited and had different causes. Munich also turned out to be a spectacular disaster for Soviet policy. Litvinov's efforts to obtain for the Soviet Union the status of a full-fledged European power turned to be completely futile. London and Paris continued to perceive Soviet Russia as the *enfant terrible* of Europe. The achievements of the "Litvinov era"—support for the French concept of an "Eastern Locarno" and the conclusion of alliances with France and Czechoslovakia, designed to give the Soviet Union the role of a power that determined the fates of Central Europe—turned out in September 1938 to have been a delusion.

That may have been on Stalin's mind when, on 1 October 1938, he delivered a speech declaring that the Bolsheviks were not and had never been pacifists pining for peace and "taking up arms only when they were attacked." On the contrary, he explained, "Bolsheviks themselves will attack if the war is just, the situation conducive, and the circumstances favorable.... [Bolsheviks] in principle are not against going on the offensive, are not against war as such.... The fact that today we are shouting about peace is just a veil, a veil! All states conceal their intentions: when in Rome, do as the Romans do." In order for the situation to become conducive to Stalin's scenario, Hitler had to break the Munich accords.

The Soviet Union had no intention of intervening in defense of Czechoslovakia. In any case, it would have been unable to do that alone, and the attitude of London and Paris ruled out joint action. In a message to the Soviet plenipotentiary to France, Yakov Suritz, Litvinov predicted, "They will turn to us only if they can't dance their way to an accord with Berlin, and the latter makes demands they find unpleasant." At that point, Stalin was already pondering how to interest Hitler in collaboration with the Soviet Union. On 17 October, the Soviet leadership met at the Kremlin to consider the possibility of abrogating the Soviet-French treaty on mutual assistance. Litvinov managed to dissuade Stalin from taking that step. It would have been received across Europe as a vote of no confidence in the Western powers and a message that the Soviet Union no longer intended to participate in any undertakings to stop German expansion.

Had the Munich Agreement satisfied Hitler's expansionist aspirations, Stalin would have been forced to shore up his own position with methods developed by Litvinov over the previous several years. In any event, Stalin, seeking to bring down the Versailles system, had to root for Hitler.

The Great Tender

The structure of the Munich system was built on feeble foundations. Great Britain and France were becoming hostage to any future moves by the German chancellor, and Hitler considered the Munich accord a personal defeat. He reproached himself for not wanting or not being able to move from propaganda and diplomacy to military action. In later years, he would sometimes delay the date of an attack but would never change the decision to go through with it. In autumn 1939, Hitler called his ambassadors in Warsaw and London to Berlin and did not allow them to return to their posts. As he explained to his military commanders on 22 August 1939, he did that so no *Schweinehund* would plead for compromise at the last moment and try to fool him. The allusion to Neville Chamberlain and Munich was obvious.

The hopes of the Western powers connected with the Munich system were based on faith in the inviolability of political norms, prominently including the imperative of *pacta sunt servanda*. But Hitler considered himself a politician of a new type. He rejected traditional political conventions and "bourgeois morality." He insisted treaty obligations should not constrain a modern politician, and, for that reason, he had no intention of respecting the provisions of Munich. Preparing for the decisive showdown with France, he had to clarify his relations with Poland. On 24 October 1938, Ribbentrop met in Berlin with the Polish ambassador, Józef Lipski, and presented German conditions for a "comprehensive" settlement of Polish-German relations (*Gesamtlösung*). Ribbentrop demanded the incorporation of Gdańsk into the Reich, an exterritorial motorway through the "Polish corridor," and Poland's accession to the anti-Comintern pact, to be supplemented with a consultations clause. Thus, Poland would have to clear its foreign policy with Germany.

Ribbentrop sought to exploit Poland's isolation and bill Poland for the German support it had received in connection with the annexation of Teschen. Also, the German four-year armaments program was beginning to produce results, and, after it was completed in 1940, Hitler planned to wage war against France, the guardian of the Versailles system. But the prospect of a crisis was looming over the German economy, and one solution was to put it on a war footing. For that, Hitler needed a war. At first, he did not anticipate that it would be a war against Poland.

Preparing for confrontation with France, Germany had to break up the formal French-Polish alliance and establish a fully controlled buffer zone separating it from the Soviet Union. Yet, with regard to Poland, it was political postulates rather than territorial issues that were of pivotal importance to Hitler. The objective was to subordinate Poland to the goals of German foreign policy—something that was to be symbolized by Poland's accession to the anti-Comintern pact. Thus, Poland would have had to abandon a key principle of its foreign policy since 1919: abstaining from alliances with one of its big neighbors against the other. Accordingly, "as far as Hitler was concerned[,] . . . Poland's refusal thwarted his plans of eastward expansion against the Soviet Union and also posed the risk of a two-front war, in the event of armed conflict in the west. At that point, the German dictator did not appear to be planning war as soon as 1939."

On 5–6 January 1939, Beck held talks with Hitler and Ribbentrop at Berchtesgaden and Munich. Without as yet resorting to threats, the Germans repeated their earlier demands. Even though Polish-German relations were rapidly deteriorating and Berlin was gradually increasing its pressure on Warsaw, both sides concealed these matters. Hitler calculated that he could still force Poland into submission by increasing pressure. Warsaw, however, felt that, in the context of the policy of appeasement pursued by London and Paris, premature disclosure of German demands would not enhance Poland's situation. Polish politicians also deluded themselves by thinking the German proposal of Gesamtlösung was just a broadly drawn initial negotiating position and that compromise was still possible, though its likelihood was diminishing.

Meanwhile, Moscow worried that the improvement in Soviet-Polish relations after Munich could be used by Poland as a bargaining chip in negotiations with Germany. Polish ambassador Grzybowski reported to Warsaw after his talks in Moscow on 7 January 1939 with the deputy people's commissar for foreign affairs:

Potyomkin [Potemkin] . . . expressed concern that our joint declaration [of 26 November 1938] could be just a maneuver, something that could be bargained away. I stated very categorically that if the independence of our policy was not seen as a certainty, then indeed it would be very difficult to comprehend our policy. Then Potemkin said more clearly that if the Polish public opinion had the alternative of Hitlerism or Stalinism, it would be more likely to choose Hitlerism. I replied that the alternative did not exist but that we would consider the Bolshevization of Germany as undesirable as the Hitlerization of Russia.

In late February 1939, Moscow was still working on plans for an armed response in the event of a joint German-Polish military operation against the Soviet Union, which may indicate that the Soviet leadership was unaware of the rapid worsening of German-Polish relations. After Munich, the Soviets abandoned their previous calls for an antifascist front and instead implied that all options were now open. In a conversation with Jean Payart, the French chargé d'affaires to Moscow, in late January 1939, Litvinov's deputy, Vladimir Potemkin, affirmed that the French-Soviet treaty on mutual assistance "remains in force as far as we can see." But when asked by the French diplomat if the German-Russian talks on a trade agreement, scheduled to begin soon, would not be extended to political issues, he replied that, even though that did not seem very probable, "we have never excluded the possibility of normalizing our relations with any state." A few days later, Litvinov was equally enigmatic in a conversation with the new French ambassador, Paul-Émile Naggiar: "We are always ready for true cooperation if the other party finds it convenient, but we are capable of making do without it, so we will not go out of our way to get it."

The occupation of Prague by the Wehrmacht on 15 March 1939, in violation of the Munich Agreement, marked a turning point in European politics. Hitler no longer intended to consult with the Western powers on his actions in Eastern Europe, even though German diplomats were convinced that this time, too, he could have received the consent of the Western powers for revision of the Reich's eastern frontier. In February 1939, Ernst von Weizsäcker, a secretary of state at the Auswärtiges Amt, wrote in his diary that the incorporation of Gdańsk and Klaipėda into the Reich and the obtainment of a land connection with East Prussia would be "highly popular in our country and highly understandable abroad as the next act of German foreign policy." Germany could easily "reduce" an isolated and helpless Poland to the size of a mere "buffer" separating the Reich from Russia. Hitler could have conducted the annexation of Gdańsk and even the eradication of the "Polish corridor" in the framework of the Munich system. But in order to subordinate Poland to German policy goals in Europe, to deprive it of sovereignty, to destroy the Polish-French alliance and overturn the Versailles order—given the rejection of his demands by the Polish government—he was forced to break the Munich Agreement.

The liquidation of the remnants of Czechoslovakia was designed to flank Poland and exert the ultimate pressure on the Polish government. It is certain that Hitler did not envision war with Poland at that point. Otherwise, the occupation of Prague would have to be treated as the greatest mistake he made in his political career. The elimination of Czechoslovakia had to provoke a change in the policies of the Western powers. Thus, it allowed Poland to break out of its political and military isolation. Localizing a conflict with Poland now became more difficult, if at all possible. Władysław Kukulski, a former senior Polish diplomat and head of the legal department at the Ministry of Foreign Affairs, wrote in his memoirs, "If in March 1939, Hitler, instead of occupying Prague and ethnically pure Czech and Slovak territories, had demanded Poland's consent to incorporate Gdańsk and Pomerania, then he could have probably attacked Poland without worrying about the involvement of England and France in the war, whose public opinion would have believed that it was Poland's stubbornness that caused this local war."

Great Britain, in response to Hitler's violation of the Munich accord, made an unprecedented about-face in its foreign policy. It committed itself politically to defend the status quo in Eastern Europe. But that policy change had not been properly prepared in terms of conception and diplomatic methodology. As a consequence, the actions of the British Foreign Office in March 1939 were chaotic.

On 20 March, Lord Halifax proposed a joint declaration by Great Britain, France, the Soviet Union, and Poland (Romania was to join at a later date) providing for an immediate conference of the four in the event of any of the signatories being threatened with German aggression. The initiative, though poorly prepared, signaled a fundamental shift in British foreign policy. However, its potential for success equaled zero. Both Poland and Romania remained under German pressure and could not risk involvement in some symbolic undertaking without the prospect of practical backing by the Western powers. Poland was in fact interested in British support to supplement its alliance with France, but it wanted such support to take bilateral rather than multilateral form. Poland considered the multilateral format to be impractical and unlikely to shield Poland in the face of German demands. A format limited to Poland, Great Britain, and France would have ostentatiously excluded the Soviet Union: "As concerns France, the alliance of 1921 creates a situation wherein the new accord in the scope proposed does not seem to be needed, since on the basis of the existent legal relations with us France de facto finds itself within such a combination, while inviting it at present to a new consultative arrangement would highlight the circumstance that the USSR has been eliminated from it, and that is something we want to avoid."

Warsaw thought a combination involving the Soviet Union was risky and would potentially increase the threat of a German invasion. Beck explained this reasoning to British diplomats in the following words: "[T]he animosities that exist today between Berlin and Moscow are of the type that involving the Soviets in the agreement could, in a violent and unusually rapid manner, cause the outbreak of a general conflict. . . . Cooperation with the Soviets, however, could lead to a violent reaction on the part of Germany."

The Polish concerns worried Paris. The French were deeply impressed by the shift in British policy and wanted to encourage the British—at any cost—to uphold the new line. Mindful of the commitments stemming from the Polish-French alliance, Paris felt that Poland's attitude to the British proposals was of secondary importance. It was France's priority to engage the Soviet Union in cooperation, which would make it easier to fulfill the alliance commitments vis-à-vis Poland and stimulate fresh British engagement in Central Europe. For those reasons, Prime Minister Édouard Daladier of France was ready to conclude a French-British-Soviet agreement regardless of Poland's sentiments.

But the Soviet Union was playing for time. Soviet diplomats firmly denied rumors that, in the event of German aggression against Poland, the Soviet Union would automatically give the latter assistance. They indicated that Moscow had no intention of forcing its help on anyone and rather enjoyed the role of "uncommitted, watchful observer."

The British guarantees for Poland and Romania obviously protected the Soviet Union from Nazi aggression. In fact, Stalin had indirectly received a much more credible insurance policy than Poland. After all, it was impossible for Hitler to attack the Soviet Union without first conquering Poland, which was allied with France and enjoyed British support. At the time, it seemed that this plan of attack would have meant a military campaign lasting at least several years. That situation enhanced Moscow's role and its bargaining position. It raised its price. On 4 April, Litvinov wrote to Alexei Merkalov, Soviet ambassador to Berlin, "We know perfectly well that without us it is impossible to stop the aggression in Europe, so the later they ask us for help, the more they will have to pay us. That is why we are so calm about all the noise over the so-called change in British foreign policy."

For these reasons it is hard to escape the conclusion that, taking into account Great Britain's strategic goals and the tactical necessity of retaining room for maneuver vis-à-vis Moscow, the granting by Chamberlain of guarantees to Poland and Romania was premature and misguided. In effect, London had presented Stalin with trump cards that allowed him to decide the fate of Europe. Such were the consequences of the chaotic search for some salvation of the sinking empire.

The predictions made by Litvinov in October 1938 were coming true. Great Britain and France, seeking new ways to stop Hitler, asked the Soviet Union for help. But Stalin saw no advantage in salvaging the remnants of the Versailles order and the privileged positions it had provided to London and Paris. On 10 March, he made a speech at the Eighteenth Congress of the Communist Party in which he charged that Great Britain and France, by rejecting the principle of collective security, were in effect pursuing a disastrous policy of tolerating aggression. London and Paris wanted to sow discord between Germany and the Soviet Union and provoke conflict between them. Stalin went on to insist there were no grounds for such a conflict, which could be interpreted as a signal that he was receptive to talks with Hitler. The signal he had wanted to send as early as mid-October 1938 in response to the Munich conference had finally been dispatched. The Soviet Union would not "pull the chestnuts out of the fire" for the democratic powers; moreover, cooperation with the Third Reich was certainly possible.

On 15 April, Litvinov urged Stalin to take advantage of the current situation, which was favorable to the Soviet Union, "if we have any intention at all of taking up cooperation" with London and Paris. He believed the Soviet Union should propose the conclusion of a tripartite mutual assistance treaty between Great Britain, France, and the Soviet Union. The signatories would also undertake to "extend assistance to the European neighbors of the USSR." They would further pledge to "refrain from decisions and agreements with other states concerning the east of Europe without prior consultations between themselves. Simultaneously . . . they would not conclude a separatist peace with the aggressor." Litvinov was thus proposing that the collapse of the Munich deal be exploited to implement the Soviet Union's old aspiration of attaining the status of a full-fledged European power. The new status would manifest itself through the establishment of a directorate of the Soviet Union, Great Britain, and France—a kind of Three Nations Alliance—that would decide the fates of Eastern Europe. That was the price Litvinov wanted the Western powers to pay for Soviet cooperation in stopping Hitler.

However, Stalin and Vyacheslav Molotov had reservations. The chair of the Council of People's Commissars wanted the agreement and the tripartite guarantees to cover Turkey as well. Stalin, however, demanded that Great Britain make it clear that its guarantees for Poland and Romania did not apply to situations in which the Soviet Union would turn out to be the aggressor. Litvinov explained to Suritz, "Formally, it appears that England would also have to provide assistance against us. Though naturally we don't intend to invade Poland, we feel the existence of such an obligation on England's part would be incompatible with the spirit of relations we now intend to establish." In reality, Stalin's postulate amounted to questioning the status quo of the Soviet-Polish border. In the context of the rumors and speculations constantly circulating in Europe about the possible partition of Poland, it had to be received by Western diplomats as a warning sign that undermined Stalin's credibility as a potential ally against Hitler. By that time, European diplomats had acquired rich experience regarding the methodology of advancing territorial claims and were particularly sensitive to any false tones that could prognosticate new troubles of this kind. The very fact that the postulate had been formulated justifies the conclusion that, by April, Stalin was already investigating the possibility of revising the border with Poland and did not want any political-legal constructions tying his hands at the opening stage of his talks with the Western powers.

At about the same time, the Third Reich made its bid in the "tender" for an East European ally. On 17 April, Merkalov visited German secretary of state Ernst von Weizsäcker—the first such visit since he had presented his credentials to the chancellor on 5 June 1938. The German explained why the Skoda Works in Czechoslovakia had failed to fulfill a Soviet order: while German business circles were in favor of implementing Soviet contracts with the Czechoslovakian factory, the military was likely to ask "why should we supply anti-aircraft guns to the Soviet Union when the Soviet government is conducting talks on joining a pact . . . directed against Germany." Next, Weizsäcker declared, "Germany and the USSR differ with regard to political principles. At the same time, we want to develop economic relations with you." The suggestion that the two parties should try to clarify their positions was very clear.

In the latter half of April 1939, Stalin had two options: he could either cooperate with the Western powers to save the status quo in Eastern Europe or lean toward Hitler, who was trying to destroy it. The Soviet ambassadors in Paris, London, and Berlin were called to Moscow for consultations. Before leaving France, Suritz met at his residence with representatives of the French Left. After the official part of the function was over, Suritz had a long, private conversation with François de Tessan and André Liautey, deputies to the National Assembly of France, whom he described as "left-wing radical socialist candidates for leading positions at the Ministry of Foreign Affairs in case of a 'Popular Front restoration.'"

During the meeting, the Soviet ambassador presented Moscow's position on major international issues. He stated that the ongoing British-Soviet consultations concerning a mutual-assistance pact were not considered a priority by the Soviet Union, because such a pact would hardly advance Soviet interests. Suritz further confided that Stalin did not believe that "capitalist democratic" states were cable of revising their policy of "buying off" Hitler and were likely to continue it, trying to channel German "dynamism" eastward. According to Suritz, Stalin was particularly distrustful of the "Munich appeasers": Chamberlain and the pair of Daladier and Georges Bonnet, whom he considered proponents of the idea of "mutual embitterment of the USSR and Germany." Suritz explained that the Soviet Union was wary of the anti-German bloc promoted by the Western powers because joining it could mean "the Red Army would have to bear the brunt of the principal strike of the German armed forces as the USSR borders on those countries that are the object of German aggression." The Soviet diplomat further revealed that Moscow thought a German attack against the Soviet Union was unlikely and that was why "the USSR's assistance in Europe was considered 'unilateral,' one without equivalent from the other side"—the more so, since the Soviets believed that "France will be sitting behind the Maginot Line, making demonstrations of cautious proportion from time to time. . . . England can limit itself to defending the Netherlands, possibly Belgium, and to fighting in the air." Suritz also implied that the Soviet Union might weigh another option: "During the last meeting between Merkalov, the polpred in Berlin, and von Ribbentrop, Merkalov received far-reaching assurances from the German foreign minister that Germany considered the Soviet-German non-aggression agreement [a probable reference to the Berlin Treaty of 26 April 1926] as binding and was ready to confirm this point of view in a most formal manner, even in the form of a personal declaration by the Reichsführer. Von Ribbentrop then expressed the hope that the USSR would also treat this agreement as binding and would refrain from signing any obligation that would, formally, or in practice, annul its significance." Historiography does not record any conversation between Ribbentrop and Merkalov in which the content even faintly resembles Suritz's account. Was he perhaps referring to the Soviet ambassador's conversation with Weizsäcker? However, the crux of Suritz's account finds confirmation in other sources. Litvinov did in fact doubt the readiness and resolve of the Western powers to oppose Hitler, and Moscow did compare the competing "bids" of the Western powers and the Third Reich and analyzed their respective merits. And Suritz, indeed, was to be called to Moscow for consultations.

The Politburo—including Stalin, Molotov, Anastas Mikoyan, Lazar Kaganovich, and Voroshilov—met on 21 April. Also attending was the leadership of the foreign ministry: Litvinov and his deputy, Potemkin, as well as Merkalov, Ivan Maisky, and a counselor at the Soviet mission in Paris by the name of Krapiventsev. Apparently Suritz did not make it to Moscow after all. Perhaps the Soviet leadership wanted to avoid any speculation over the simultaneous absence from their posts of the ambassadors to London, Paris, and Berlin.

The meeting lasted from 1:15 p.m. to 4:50 p.m. The debate on the international situation and Soviet foreign policy must have been heated. Assessing Hitler's policies and international goals, Merkalov predicted that Germany would attack the Soviet Union within two or three years, so its "overtures" should be rejected. Litvinov came out for the establishment, on Soviet conditions, of an alliance of Moscow, Paris, and London, but he was opposed to the inclusion of Turkey in the proposed system of guarantees. Molotov, in turn, advocated the latter and also—in all probability—rejection of the offer made by the Western powers, in favor of collaboration with Hitler.

The meeting appears to have had a decisive impact on Soviet foreign policy in the summer of 1939. Litvinov was not received by Stalin again until 3 May, that is, the day when "the Politburo acquiesced to Litvinov's request and relieved him of his duties as People's Commissar for Foreign Affairs." He was replaced by Molotov. That same day, Stalin explained in a cable sent to Soviet ambassadors in major capitals that Litvinov had been dismissed because of a "serious conflict" between him and Molotov, caused by Litvinov's disloyalty to the Council of People's Commissars. Litvinov's fate was soon shared by Merkalov. After the 21 April meeting, he left for Berlin, was called back to Moscow on 5 May, and did not return to the German capital again. Soviet interests in Berlin during the last months of peace were represented by Chargé d'Affaires Georgy Astakhov, whom French historian Sabine Dullin believes to have been an NKVD officer. Thus, Stalin removed from the foreign ministry the main opponents of rapprochement with Germany.

Hitler became furious when he heard about the British guarantees for Poland and threatened to "prepare a devil's brew for them" (that is, the British). In a speech delivered in Wilhelmshaven, he attacked London for its policy of "encircling" Germany with the help of its "satellites." He warned that those who "pulled chestnuts out of the fire for the great powers could get their fingers burned," and he mocked British attempts to court "Stalin's Bolshevik Russia." One can detect in Hitler's Wilhelmshaven speech references to the address Stalin made on 10 March. Soon afterward, Hitler ordered his military planners to prepare for war with Poland.

Berlin quickly realized that the position of the Soviet Union could gain pivotal significance in the new situation on the continent. German diplomacy faced new challenges after the guarantees for Poland had been made and after the attempts of London and Paris to draw the Soviet Union into an anti-German coalition. Germany needed to knock the "Russian sword" out of the hands of Great Britain and France. The problem was that Hitler rejected all notions for rapprochement with the Soviets. Deceit may have been used to change the chancellor's mind. German diplomats, with Ribbentrop's blessing, started manipulating the transcripts of conversations with Soviet diplomats, putting their own proposals into the mouths of their Soviet interlocutors. Hitler was being told that Stalin was interested in rapprochement, while the Soviets were being informed that the Third Reich wanted a revival of political cooperation with the Soviet Union.

The German foreign ministry's campaign to neutralize any ideological resistance of the Nazi leadership to cooperation with the Bolsheviks was conducted on a massive scale. In early May 1939, the political department of the foreign ministry prepared an analysis of Soviet policy in the first months of 1939 and titled it "Russlands Neuorientierung." The authors argued that the opening of British-Soviet negotiations indicated that, in the event of an armed conflict in Europe, "intra-political and world-outlook differences would not prevent an alliance even if the ideological contradictions were as pronounced as in the case of the ultra capitalist, private, free-market English monarchy and the radically anti-capitalist, atheist, communist Bolshevism." The analysts insisted that that assumption placed the Third Reich in a much more advantageous situation than the "Western democracies." Ideological differences between the Soviets and the "German NSDAP" (Nationalsozialistische Deutsche Arbeiterpartei, or Nazi Party) were substantially smaller than those between "the state of the avant-garde of the proletariat" and "the capitalist English monarchy." In years prior, friction between Germany and Russia had been caused exclusively by ideological considerations. But now, in view of the new approach of the Soviet side to "ideological obstacles," they would no longer be a problem, particularly since, by joining the London-sponsored anti-German bloc, Moscow would have only strengthened its neighbors: Poland, Romania, and the British Empire (India). In the event of war, the engagement of the Soviet Union "together with Germany against Poland would be much less hazardous and could facilitate the regaining of ancient Belarusian and Ukrainian lands lost to Poland."

Thus, in May 1939, the Auswärtiges Amt accurately predicted the price that the Third Reich would have to pay Stalin for his cooperation in bringing down the remnants of the Versailles order. Ribbentrop probably used the same arguments when he persuaded Hitler to submit a German bid in the "tender" announced by the Kremlin. Traces of that reasoning are also evident in Ribbentrop's position, communicated to Molotov by the German ambassador to Moscow on 14 August 1939, containing an offer of the German-Soviet deal that would prejudge the future of peace in Europe. That was the turning point in the final phase of the Soviet-German talks that culminated in the Ribbentrop-Molotov Pact on 23 August 1939.

Hitler was pressing for a local war with Poland, and Stalin was well placed to help him keep that war localized by refusing to collaborate with the Western powers. In turn, Paris and London needed Stalin to keep Hitler at bay with diplomatic measures and political pressure. For his part, Stalin wanted to use the European crisis to change the status quo in Eastern Europe and bring to heel his country's western neighbors. In mid-April, Litvinov, when presenting his idea of the tripartite treaty to Stalin, extended the scope of the accord to "the European neighbors of the USSR." Meanwhile, the Western powers had given their guarantees only to Poland and Romania, the two Central European states under greatest threat of German aggression. Anyone who had the slightest understanding of European politics realized that there was practically no risk of a German attack against the Baltic States or Finland without the prior conquest of Poland. Aggression against the Soviet Union conducted in this way was even less likely. That is why, in autumn

1939, during the British-French-Soviet talks on an anti-German alliance, the Soviet side demanded the possibility of granting assistance to a victim of aggression without that country's consent. European diplomats had no doubt the Soviet Union was not trying to preserve peace but to carve out its own zone of influence in Eastern Europe.

A conversation symptomatic of the difficulties at hand took place in the latter half of June between Lord Halifax and Ivan Maisky. The British foreign secretary was trying to explain to the Soviet ambassador that London could not agree to the extension of the tripartite guarantees to Estonia, Latvia, and Lithuania since those countries did not want them and there was no precedent in history for granting guarantees to a country against its will. Maisky disagreed and, with frankness that was unusual for a diplomat, spelled out the Soviet intentions:

> As concerns your thesis about the absence of an appropriate precedent . . . first of all, no one is preventing anyone from setting new precedents. Secondly, . . . if the United States was able in 1823 to declare unilaterally (without asking the opinion of the South American republics) that any attempt by the powers of the Holy Alliance to extend "their system" onto South America would be considered a threat to its security . . . then why can't three great European powers do something similar in 1939 with regard to the three Baltic States? . . .
>
> —So you want us to initiate a Monroe Doctrine for Europe? [Halifax asked].
>
> —Not for Europe [Maisky replied] but, at least, for the Baltic States.

Maisky was extremely pleased with himself, but Halifax was in shock. In a Europe founded on Woodrow Wilson's vision, which rejected—albeit inconsistently—the "old diplomacy" of absolute rulers and was already considering the idea of a European Union (via Aristide Briand), the concept of delineating zones of influence, as had happened a hundred years prior, sounded anachronistic—particularly to the ears of a democratic politician. Alas, the time of the barbarians—Hitler and Stalin—was quickly coming.

The Soviet demands in effect forced London and Paris to choose between giving Eastern Europe to Hitler, who since Munich had been demanding a free hand in Eastern Europe, or putting the Baltic States and probably other countries in the region at Stalin's mercy. When, a few days after the Halifax-Maisky talks, the Soviet Union demanded that so-called indirect aggression also constitute a *casus foederis* of the future alliance, the negotiations reached a dead end. All the neighbors of the Soviet Union received that as a sign of resurgent Soviet revisionism. In fact, the possibility of receiving guarantees from Bolshevik Russia scared its western neighbors. For twenty years, all of Europe had viewed the Soviets with fear and suspicion and did not consider them a credible partner. So why now, in the midst of an all-

European credibility crisis, should the Soviet Union's western neighbors entrust their security to the revisionist power?

The opening of British-French-Soviet military talks, in the absence of a political agreement, amounted to make-believe on both sides. As early as July, German diplomats were certain that if, by the end of the month, the Western powers did not reach agreement with Moscow concerning the Baltic States, then the Third Reich and the Soviet Union would rapidly partition Eastern Europe.

Stalin was not interested in salvaging peace in Europe. He only stood to gain from the annihilation of the Versailles order. On its ruins he could build his own empire and zone of influence. As long as Hitler did not break the Munich Agreement, he could count on the revision of the Reich's eastern borders without resorting to war. For Stalin, that opportunity did not exist. He could only increase his holdings in the event of German aggression against Poland and the outbreak of war in Europe. On 7 September, Stalin revealed his reasoning: "I have nothing against them [the Third Reich, Poland, and the Western powers] having a good fight and weakening each other. It wouldn't be bad if the position of the wealthier capitalist states (particularly England) was shaken by German hands. Though he does not understand or want this, Hitler is undermining and weakening the capitalist system. . . . We can maneuver, pushing one side against the other, so they have a better fight." He further announced that the Soviet Union would collaborate with Germany to eradicate the Polish state: "The destruction of that state would mean one bourgeois, fascist state less! Would it be bad if by crushing Poland we extended the socialist system onto new territories and new population?"

The only thing that Stalin could potentially worry about was the resolution of the "Polish crisis" by way of some "new Munich"—again, without the participation of the Soviet Union. For that reason, beginning in April 1939, the Soviets campaigned to prevent the implementation of that scenario. It was crucial in their tactics, on the one hand, to assure Hitler that armed confrontation with Poland would not result in a conflict of interests with the Soviet Union and, on the other, to pretend that Moscow wanted to build some sort of opposition—together with France, Great Britain, Poland, and other Central European countries—against German aspirations in Central Europe.

Considering the evolution of the political situation in Europe in summer 1939, it was only possible to stop Hitler, who was pushing for war with Poland, through authentic British, French, Polish, and Soviet cooperation, based on unequivocal Soviet guarantees for the sovereignty and territorial integrity of all its neighbors. But Stalin had no interest in such cooperation. The conclusion of the nonaggression treaty with the Third Reich on 23 August 1939 marked the crowning of Soviet efforts to remove any obstacles that could dissuade Hitler from invading Poland. Although the outlook for an anti-German alliance of the Western powers and the Soviet Union was slim, Berlin worried that, if the alliance did materialize, it could thwart Hitler's plans. In order to avert that danger, Germany—for strictly tactical reasons—proposed the revival of German-Soviet cooperation, based on the community of interests connected with the program to liquidate the Polish state. On 22 August, Hitler explained his motives for concluding the agreement with Stalin: "Thus, I cut the ground from under their [British and French governments'] feet. Poland has been maneuvered into a situation we needed to achieve military success." Had Moscow rejected his proposal, Hitler intended to pull back and convene a Nazi Party congress in Munich "under peace slogans." But as far as Stalin was concerned, the Ribbentrop-Molotov Pact was of crucial importance. It pushed Hitler into war with Poland and consolidated the international position of the Soviet Union, which, by concluding the treaty, affirmed its aspirations to the status of a full-fledged European power. A Polish-German war, particularly if France and England remained passive, eliminated the influence of those powers from the Soviet Union's immediate neighborhood. The buffer zone was losing its protectors, which meant that the Soviet Union had prospects for the restoration of its prerevolutionary borders. However, the responsibility of the two signatories of the Ribbentrop-Molotov Pact for the outbreak of war in 1939 is by no means equal. Hitler wanted war and was striving for it, while Stalin had no intention of preserving the peace—but that is not the same thing. Poland could not back down before Hitler's demands, and the Western powers could not preserve the peace. It was too late.

MIKHAIL M. NARINSKY

POLAND, THE SOVIET UNION, AND THE CRISIS OF THE VERSAILLES SYSTEM

AN OVERWHELMING MAJORITY of Russian and foreign researchers agree that the aggressive policy of Nazi Germany and its allies became the main factor in escalating the prewar international political crisis. The rulers of the Third Reich put forward radical and far-reaching plans for territorial expansion and the creation of a "new European order" under the aegis of Germany. In March 1939, Maxim Litvinov, the Soviet people's commissar for foreign affairs, in the course of a conversation with Lord Privy Seal Anthony Eden of Britain, emphasized that the Soviet Union "does not have the slightest doubt in German aggression. German external policy is inspired by two main ideas[:] revenge and European domination."

The allies (or potential allies) of Germany were represented by fascist Italy and imperial Japan. The guarantors of the Versailles-Washington system of international relations—England and France—opposed the bloc of aggressors. But, amid escalating aggression, they chose a policy of "appeasement," a policy of concessions to fascist aggressors in an attempt to avoid a major new war. The Soviet Union, which tended to defend its own interests, played a special role in the alignment of forces in the international arena. The United States of America, which was inclined to support the Anglo-French bloc, adopted a wait-and-see attitude.

The established alignment of forces in the international arena caused an escalating crisis in the Versailles-Washington system.

In this situation, the Soviet leadership aimed to prevent the creation of an anti-Soviet coalition, avoid the threat of involving the Soviet Union in a great military conflict, achieve the creation of a collective security system in Europe that was favorable to itself, and consolidate the foreign policy positions of the Soviet Union, initiating contact with different potential partners. Moscow tended to provide itself with the maximum in opportunities for foreign policy maneuvers.

Strengthening the state's international position was the main objective of Polish foreign policy. In theory, Warsaw held a position midway between those of Berlin and Moscow, but nevertheless, the desire to solve its own problems urged Poland toward rapprochement with Germany. As Polish authors remark, "Minister Beck believed that, notwithstanding cooperation with the Third Reich (which occurred under certain frameworks), it was possible to maintain proper or even good relations with the USSR." In fact, relations between the Soviet Union and Poland during the second half of the 1930s steadily grew worse.

The Anschluss of Austria, which was carried out by Nazi Germany on 11–12 March 1938, was an important milestone in the development of the prewar international political crisis. The Soviet leadership evaluated all of the implications and risks resulting from this action. On 14 March, Litvinov sent a note to the Politburo of the Central Committee of the All-Union Communist Party (Bolsheviks) in which he remarked, "The acquisition of Austria represents the greatest event following the world war, fraught with the greatest risks and not in the last turn for our [Soviet] Union." The Anschluss of Austria signified an important stage in the collapse of the Versailles order, one occurring via military power.

The Soviet position was clearly articulated in an interview of Litvinov by representatives of the press on 17 March. It sounded like a passionate plea for collective action to repel the increased aggression, with the participation of the Soviet Union. "It may be late tomorrow," Litvinov emphasized, "but today the time has not yet passed for all of the countries, especially great countries, to take a strong, explicit line with respect to collectively rescuing the world." Litvinov offered to promptly organize a topical discussion of European issues by all interested states, but this offer received no response. The people's commissar himself gave a deep and somewhat prophetic assessment of his announcement in a letter to the plenipotentiary in Czechoslovakia, Sergey S. Aleksandrovskiy: "My declaration is possibly the final plea to Europe for cooperation, after which we will apparently take up a position of low interest in the further development of affairs in Europe, notwithstanding the further fate of Czechoslovakia."

In the opinion of the leadership of the People's Commissariat for Foreign Affairs, the Anschluss of Austria noticeably strengthened the position of Germany in Europe and worsened Czechoslovakia's situation. Litvinov remarked that he had always considered the Austrian and Czechoslovakian questions as the primary problem: "the rape of Czechoslovakia would be the beginning of Anschluss, in exactly the same way as the 'Hitlerization' of Austria decided the fate of Czechoslovakia." In his opinion, the Anschluss of Austria provided Hitler with hegemony in Europe, notwithstanding the further fate of Czechoslovakia.

MIKHAIL M. NARINSKY

The events of March 1938 revealed Poland's goal of using the crisis of the Versailles system for its own interests, especially in relation to the conflict with Lithuania because of Vilnius and the Vilnius region. On 17 March, Poland issued the Lithuanian government an ultimatum to immediately establish diplomatic relations, economic ties, and postal-telegraph communications between the two countries, as well as to repeal an article in its constitution stating that Vilnius was the capital of Lithuania. The Soviet leadership supported Lithuania in this conflict.

The Lithuanian leadership was obliged to meet the requirements of Poland, which used the increasing German expansion in Europe to further its interests. With respect to Moscow, through its démarche, it effectively emphasized the interests of the Soviet Union in Eastern Europe and ensured that no problems would be solved in that region without its participation.

In the meantime, the international situation became ever more complicated and strained. Having carried out the Anschluss of Austria, the Nazi Reich proceeded to prepare for aggression against Czechoslovakia. The Sudeten German party, active within the country and led by Konrad Henlein, became an instrument of Berlin; Germans accounted for about 20 percent of the population of the country. With German financing, Henlein's party launched a protest campaign against the alleged harassment of ethnic Germans and called for autonomy and then full self-determination of the Sudetenland. In a speech to his higher generals on 28 May 1938, Hitler said that Czechoslovakia should disappear from the map of Europe in order to "vacate the rear [of Germany] for the offensive against the West."

The Soviet leadership supported the swift decision of the president and government of Czechoslovakia to oppose the German pressure. The visit by army commander Grigory Kulik to Prague at the end of May 1938 should be evaluated specifically in the context of representing the Soviet Union's commitment "to decisively help the Czechs, if they will really fight for their independence."

In the middle of May, a disturbing situation emerged. On 19 May, the Czechoslovak intelligence service received information about a concentration of German troops along the border with Czechoslovakia.

But this time the affair did not lead to a military conflict. Mobilization took place in Czechoslovakia in an organized manner. On 21 May, a military emergency was proclaimed in Sudetenland and the border was fully blocked. The British and French ambassadors in Berlin warned German minister of foreign affairs Joachim von Ribbentrop that German action toward Czechoslovakia would mean a European war. Hitler was obliged to retreat temporarily.

Litvinov became the initiator of the Soviet diplomatic démarche in connection with the possibility that Poland would face off against Czechoslovakia. The telegram to the chargé d'affaires ad interim of the Soviet Union in

France on 5 June 1938 remarked, "Poland does not hide its intentions to use a possible offensive of Germany on Czechoslovakia for the divestiture of the part of Czechoslovakian territory in its favor. Such an intervention by Poland will be a direct help to Germany and their joint offensive on Czechoslovakia. We would like to know in advance, whether France will consider itself to be Poland's ally in the context of the Franco-Polish treaty of alliance in case we decide to interfere with Poland's intervention." Litvinov's reason for such an inquiry, which was intended to be leaked to the press, involved "really scaring Poland, making France determine its position on Poland, and really providing some help, at least diplomatically, to Czechoslovakia." Thus, the Soviet Union reiterated its own position.

In a few days, Georges Bonnet, minister of foreign affairs for France, replied that Poland had affirmed that France would maintain neutrality. In the event Poland attacked Czechoslovakia, the Franco-Polish agreement would cease to be in effect. At the same time, in the course of exchanging opinions in Paris, the Poles confirmed that Poland would not let Soviet troops pass through to help Czechoslovakia, and they would shoot down Soviet planes attempting to fly over Polish territory.

In this complicated international situation, Moscow did everything it could to avoid involvement in a serious international crisis. The telegram from Litvinov to the plenipotentiary of the Soviet Union in Czechoslovakia as of May 25 reported, in part, to the attention of Czech president Edvard Beneš, "Our contacts with France and Czechoslovakia, besides providing help in the event of war, also have the goal of preventing or reducing the risk of war itself in specific parts of Europe."

The Soviet position was clearly and distinctly articulated by Litvinov in his letter to Aleksandrovskiy, dated 11 August 1938. The people's commissar advanced the idea that opposition to the liquidation of the Versailles system should be the business of Western countries, primarily England and France. The Soviet Union was not a participant in these agreements, but "we are ready to provide our cooperation per the principle of fighting aggression, but we will not volunteer for that cooperation, let alone strive for it. I believe that we should proceed from it with respect to the Czech problem." Litvinov underlined the interests of the Soviet Union in preserving the independence of Czechoslovakia and in preventing the advance of Nazi Germany to the east and southeast. But the Soviet Union could not undertake any substantial actions without the Western states, "and the latter do not consider it necessary to seek our cooperation; [they] ignore us and decide everything by themselves concerning the German-Czechoslovakian conflict. We do not know of any case where Czechoslovakia itself would indicate to its western 'friends' the necessity of involving the USSR."

The leaders of England and France tended to search for a compromise with Hitler at the expense of Czechoslovakia. At the beginning of August 1938, the Soviet plenipotentiary, Ivan M. Maisky, assessed the position of British foreign secretary Lord (Edward) Halifax on the issue of Czechoslovakia in the following manner: "Czechoslovakia is an artificial state which is capable of neither protecting itself nor receiving help from the outside. England will not stay out of the Central European events, but France should press harder on Prague, demanding decisive concessions to Henlein. The Czechs should be made to reach an agreement with the Germans." That was the main objective of the mission by Britain's Lord (Walter) Runciman, who was present in Czechoslovakia as an intermediary between the Sudeten Germans and the Czechoslovakian government from 3 August to 16 September 1938.

Germany, using the Sudeten Germans, increased the pressure on Czechoslovakia. The draft directives for Operation Fall Grün, signed by Hitler on 18 June 1938, stated that "the solution of the Czech issue on its own discretion stands at the forefront of my political intentions and is my closest target. In order to implement this objective, I intend to use any political occasion starting from October 1, 1938."

Before September, the situation regarding Czechoslovakia became even more complicated. Nazi propaganda created the impression that war was imminent if Germany's demands were not carried out.

On 2 September, the French chargé d'affaires in Moscow, Jean Payart, officially posed a question to Litvinov concerning the kind of help that Czechoslovakia could count on from the Soviet Union, considering the difficulties created by Poland and Romania. Litvinov reminded him that Soviet assistance to Czechoslovakia was conditional, based on the provision of French assistance. The national commissar added that, "under the condition of France providing assistance, we are determined to discharge all of our obligations under the Soviet-Czechoslovakian pact, using all the means that are available to us." In order to determine the specific forms of assistance, Moscow deemed it necessary to convene a meeting of representatives of the Soviet, French, and Czechoslovakian armies.

German pressure on Prague was increasing. Hitler threatened, blackmailed, and provoked. England and France also pressured Czechoslovakian leaders to make concessions to Hitler. The leading role was played by British prime minister Neville Chamberlain. On 15 September, he met with Hitler face to face at the residence of the Reich chancellor. "Czechoslovakia will end its existence," the Nazi dictator claimed directly. On 19 September, the leadership of Czechoslovakia received the Anglo-French proposal for ceding to Germany all Sudetenland districts in which Germans amounted to more than 50 percent of the population. It was assumed that the new borders of Czechoslovakia would be determined by a special international committee. Czechoslovakia was to renounce its treaties of mutual assistance with France and the Soviet Union. In the course of fulfilling these requirements, England and France expressed their commitment to guarantee the new borders of Czechoslovakia against direct aggression.

President Beneš called the plenipotentiary of the Soviet Union and asked him to promptly state the position of the Soviet government. Moscow gave a clear answer on the following day that the Soviet Union was ready to provide "immediate and actual assistance to Czechoslovakia, if France remained loyal to it and provided assistance as well," pursuant to the agreement. The Soviet Union announced that it was ready to provide assistance to Czechoslovakia as a member of the League of Nations by virtue of Articles 16 and 17 of its statute. The content of this answer was communicated by the Soviet plenipotentiary to President Beneš by telephone on 20 September.

The Czechoslovakian leadership initially rejected the Anglo-French proposals. But representatives of the two countries increased pressure on Prague. In a conversation with Beneš on the night of 21 September, the diplomats from England and France insisted that the Anglo-French proposals were "the sole means of preventing war and acquisition of Czechoslovakia. If Czechoslovakia's answer is negative, it will bear responsibility for unleashing the war." In that case, England and France refused to come out in support of Czechoslovakia. The position was hopeless, and, early in the morning of 21 September, Prague accepted the Anglo-French ultimatum.

On 22 September, another meeting between Chamberlain and Hitler took place. Feeling in control of the situation, Hitler ratcheted up his demands on Czechoslovakia. He called for the establishment of a new border for Czechoslovakia without any international commission and insisted that the evacuation of the regions transferred to Germany would be finished by 8:00 a.m. on 28 September. By intimidating the interlocutor, the Reich chancellor threatened that, if the stated requirements were not met, "he will be obliged to seek a military solution to the issue."

On 24 September, the actual ultimatum of Hitler that bolstered the demands of Germany even further was communicated to Czechoslovakian representatives. These demands were rejected by Prague, and President Beneš declared a general mobilization.

On 25 September, in the course of the ensuing Anglo-French negotiations, French premier Édouard Daladier admitted that Hitler's ultimatum meant the "dismemberment of Czechoslovakia, and German domination in Europe." Most British ministers refused to accept Hitler's demands; the French government rejected them unanimously. The aggressive actions by Nazi Germany put Europe on the brink of war.

During the course of the crisis, the Soviet Union sequentially confirmed its commitment to discharge its obligations in the treaty of alliance with Czechoslovakia in the event of assistance by France or subject to a decision by the League of Nations, and it provided Prague with political and diplomatic support. At the same time, as many modern Russian historians remark, "there were grounds to believe that the Soviet leadership had precluded taking extreme military measures without the participation of France and recourse by Czechoslovakia itself, which capitulated under the conditions of dictate." It was necessary to take the negative position of Poland and Romania into account as well.

In truth, Litvinov, who was in Geneva at the League of Nations assembly, offered to undertake a more decisive démarche. On 23 September, he telegraphed Moscow, saying, "Considering that this European war in which we will be involved is not in our interests, and that everything must be done to prevent it, I put out the question as to whether we should declare at least a partial mobilization and hold such a campaign in the press to make Hitler and Beck believe in the possibility of a major war with our participation." But the Kremlin rejected Litvinov's proposal, believing the international situation to be insufficiently clear. Moscow subsequently proposed calling a conference with the Soviet Union, France, and England on the Czechoslovakian issue and for the participation of the Soviet Union in settling the international crisis.

In the course of the Czechoslovakian crisis, Poland actually identified itself with Nazi Germany. The Polish press launched a campaign for the autonomy of Poles in Cieszyn Silesia and then for transferring this region to Poland. The Polish diplomats announced that all decisions related to the position of Germans in Czechoslovakia should also refer to the Poles. On 20 September, Poland began to concentrate troops along the entire border with Czechoslovakia.

In this situation, Moscow supported Czechoslovakia. On 23 September, Deputy People's Commissar of Foreign Affairs Vladimir P. Potemkin communicated to the chargé d'affaires ad interim of Poland in the Soviet Union the hardline Soviet position regarding the concentration of Polish troops on the border with Czechoslovakia. It warned Warsaw of the Soviet intent to promptly denounce the nonaggression agreement between the two countries in the event of an act of aggression by Poland against Czechoslovakia. The French ambassador in Moscow, Robert Coulondre, announced to Potemkin that he gave Soviet political action "substantial international weight. Its positive effect should concern not only Czechoslovakia but France as well." Later, Polish Minister of Foreign Affairs Józef Beck remarked that during the days of crisis, "the Russians concentrated a few army corps on the Russian-Polish border, some of which deployed directly near the borderline." The Poles were even ready to launch an attack on the Red Army if Soviet forces advanced into Poland.

Nevertheless, the Soviet Union was eventually pushed aside from any role in regulating the Czechoslovakian crisis. The maneuvers by Western leaders led to the convening of a conference in Munich between government heads from Germany, Italy, Great Britain, and France on 29 September. That night, Hitler, Daladier, Mussolini, and Chamberlain signed the agreements that met virtually all of the demands of the Führer. During the period from 1 through 10 October, Czechoslovakia was to transfer all regions with a predominantly German population to Germany. This territory was transferred to Germany together with all facilities, including military installations and industrial enterprises. The final borders of Czechoslovakia had to be determined by international commission. The agreement also provided for settling the issue of Polish and Hungarian minorities in Czechoslovakia, that is, the satisfaction of territorial claims by Poland and Hungary. Such actions thus dismembered Czechoslovakia, which lost almost one-third of its territory and population and half of its heavy industry.

The Soviet position on the Munich decisions was reflected in messages from the Telegraph Agency of the Soviet Union on 2 and 4 October 1938, which declared the full non-involvement of the Soviet Union in the Munich conference.

As for the Polish leadership, it actively participated in implementing the actual measures for dismembering Czechoslovakia. On 30 September, the Polish government conveyed a letter to Czechoslovakia demanding the immediate transfer of a portion of the Cieszyn and Freistadt regions from Czechoslovakia to Poland. That was an ultimatum that went even further than the arrangements reached in Munich. The letter from Beck to the Polish ambassador in Czechoslovakia, Kazimierz Papée, on 30 September, stated that "the term . . . of the ultimatum . . . expires . . . on October 1, at 12 o'clock in the afternoon" and that "this requirement is unconditional." The Soviet plenipotentiary in Czechoslovakia, Aleksandrovskiy, in his telegram characterized this Polish action as "a Hitlerite provocation."

The governments of England and France, having indicated through their diplomatic representatives "the fatal consequences for Poland which an armed action against Czechoslovakia would have," in practice took no measures to oppose Poland. The government of Czechoslovakia was obliged to yield the Cieszyn region, which was transferred to Poland. The divestiture of this region from the Czechoslovakian republic substantially hampered the connections between the Czech Republic and Slovakia because the main railway line went directly through this territory, thus connecting the two parts of the country. The Polish historian Stanisław Żerko has remarked,

> The Polish-German rapprochement reached its peak during the Sudetenland crisis of 1938. The position of Poland suited the Reich[,] and the German party thanked the Poles many times for that. The Polish leaders would be madmen if during the period of pacification they had campaigned against

Germans or even protected the unpopular and ill-disposed Czechoslovakia. What is a totally different matter was the active participation in an anti-Czechoslovakian campaign. The insufficiently considered presentation of the ultimatum in Prague to award the Cieszyn region under threat of armed attack was perceived by public opinion as Poland copying German methods.

What were the results of Munich and their meaning?

The Polish historian Eugeniusz Duraczyński has remarked that "a practically unanimous opinion dominates among historians that the Munich agreement of 29 September 1938, entered into by Germany, Italy, France, and Great Britain to the prejudice of Czechoslovakian interests, attached a completely new quality to international relations. The process of destabilization in Europe, without a doubt, overcame its critical point. . . . In Munich, a decisive blow was struck against the Versailles system[,] which, notwithstanding its drawbacks, had stabilized the situation in Europe and provided a feeling of security for its central countries, albeit not without unrest." We can agree with this point of view.

Czechoslovakia became the victim of the Munich agreements. The decisions at Munich were made without Czechoslovakia and at its expense. They meant the actual dismemberment of the country and created a threat to its very existence. Along with almost half of its heavy industry, Czechoslovakia lost important defenses along the border.

The Soviet Union was failing at international relations as well. Munich became an example of states making important decisions on Eastern Europe without the input of the Soviet Union, and to some extent, against the Soviet Union itself. Munich increased Stalin's distrust of the policy of "Western democracies." An extremely unfavorable alignment of forces was forming against the Soviet Union, which found itself under threat of international isolation. Munich objectively pushed Moscow to search for rapprochement with Berlin. Pursuant to information from Coulondre, the French ambassador in Moscow, Potemkin said to him after Munich, "My poor friend, what have you done? I don't see any other way out for us than the fourth partition of Poland."

Munich also caused France to suffer an indisputable political defeat. The irreparable damage was inflicted on the entire system of French unions in Eastern Europe. On 12 October, the plenipotentiary of the Soviet Union in Paris, Yakov Suritz, reported to Moscow, "All Frenchmen are aware of the fact that France suffered its second Sedan and that a terrible defeat was inflicted on it in Munich." The ability of Paris to provide effective guarantees was placed in doubt. Munich fully revealed the movement of France in the waterway of British policy. The Soviet plenipotentiary in London, Maisky, reported to Moscow the opinion of MP David Lloyd George, "Western democracies suffered a cruel defeat. France eventually became a second-rate state."

Munich became the apogee of Anglo-French appeasement policy, in which England played the leading role. The main feature of this policy was the effort to avoid a major new war, which was believed would be meaningless, unnecessary, and dangerous. The proponents of pacification turned out to be susceptible to Hitler's demagogy on "the correction of Versailles errors."

There is an opinion among Russian historians that Munich became a peculiar "point of no return" that amounted to further progress toward the beginning of war. But the development of the international crisis after Munich demonstrated the presence of different alternatives; complicated political zigzags were to be found in the policies of all major players. It appears that we can agree with the conclusion of the Russian historian S. Z. Sluch: "The Munich agreement did not exclude the alternative development of international relations, and was not a turning point on the way to war; it should not be explained only by the anti-Sovietism of western leadership, since the main motive in their actions tended to be avoiding war at all costs."

Munich attempted to replace the Versailles system with a new international order, one based on the concept of the Four-Power Pact. In any case, this was the way London and Paris viewed the Munich accords. It is no mere chance that the Munich agreements were followed by the Anglo-German declaration, signed on 30 September 1938. Having underlined the importance of Anglo-German relations for the two countries and for Europe, Hitler and Chamberlain announced their decision to use consultations "to proceed . . . with efforts to remove possible sources of disagreements and thus to cooperate in securing peace in Europe." In essence, it was an agreement for nonaggression and mutual consultations. The British leaders sincerely hoped for a new stabilization of the European situation.

French politics fostered similar hopes. On 6 December 1938, the French and German ministers of foreign affairs signed a Franco-German declaration in Paris. It documented a commitment by both governments to develop peaceful and neighborly relationships between the two countries and to resolve any unsettled territorial issues between them. Both governments decided to communicate with each other over any issues of interest to both countries, as well as to mutually consult in cases in which the subsequent development of these issues could lead to international complications. The Franco-German agreement on consultations was perceived in Paris as contributing to the preservation of peace in Europe. The calculation was made with respect to pacifying Nazi Germany at the expense of concessions in Eastern Europe and in the colonial sphere.

The main miscalculation of the initiators and supporters of appeasement was in misunderstanding the essence of Hitler's regime and in underestimating its aggressiveness. For German leaders, all of the agreements they signed were only a tactical maneuver on the way to achieving German hegemony in Europe.

Munich meant an indisputable victory for Germany. The Nazi Reich notably strengthened its geopolitical positions and increased its war-industry potential. Munich also became a personal success for Hitler. The Führer managed to consolidate his position both inside the country and in the international arena. Munich encouraged Hitler to further German expansion in Europe.

As for Poland, it received additional territory in the form of Cieszyn Silesia. For a while, Poland believed that it was cooperating with Germany and its allies. At the same time, Warsaw notably improved its relations with London, Paris, and Moscow.

By tending to restore the lost balance between Berlin and Moscow, the Polish leadership took the initiative to improve relations with the Soviet Union. In his conversation with Potemkin on 21 October 1938, Polish ambassador Wacław Grzybowski raised a question as to whether Poland and the Soviet Union should "consider a substantial improvement in their relationship." Moscow made overtures to Warsaw and displayed interest in continuing the positive shift in bilateral relations by making mutual commitments. On 4 November, Litvinov offered the Poles the draft of a joint communiqué that confirmed the commitment of both parties to the Soviet-Polish nonaggression agreement of 1932. The draft of the communiqué stated that, "being interested in preserving peace and calm throughout Eastern Europe, both governments will consult each other in the event any danger threatens peace and calm."

In the course of subsequent negotiations, the Polish government attached a rather general tone to the communiqué, in part, excluding a clause of mutual consultations from it. On 26 November 1938, Litvinov remarked, "The Polish government emasculated our project, and we received a rather colorless document." Nevertheless, both governments confirmed that the existing bilateral agreements, including the nonaggression agreement of 1932, remained the basis for their relationship. It was noted that this agreement "has a sufficiently broad basis which guarantees the inviolability of peaceful relations between the two countries." Both governments expressed a positive attitude toward the expansion of mutual trade and agreed on the "necessity of positive solutions for a range of current issues." But the Polish Ministry of Foreign Affairs sought to downplay the meaning of the negotiation document. The notification from the press department of the Polish Ministry of Foreign Affairs remarked that the "just now-published Polish-Soviet declaration pursues only the aim of normalizing relations. Poland, in its foreign policy, has always adhered to the view that the participation of the Soviet Union in European politics is unnecessary." The Polish leadership held the political line on keeping equal distance in relation to the Soviet Union and Germany, with a noticeable slant in favor of Berlin.

After Munich, Nazi Germany enhanced its influence in eastern and southeastern Europe. On 24 February 1939, Hungary joined the Anti-Comintern Pact made between Germany and Japan in November 1936.

In its directive dating to 21 October 1938, Hitler had assigned the Wehrmacht to be permanently ready to settle the Czechoslovakia issue and to occupy the Klaipėda region. The Anglo-French guarantees of the new post-Munich borders of Czechoslovakia turned out to be a fiction that the Führer was not going to recognize. As a result of the German dictate of 15 March 1939, all Czech lands were declared the "protectorate Bohemia and Moravia" of the Reich and were occupied by German troops. Slovakia became an "independent state" but fully subordinate to Germany.

At the same time, Transcarpathian Ukraine was captured by Hungary. Such developments put an end to discussions and speculations concerning Hitler's intentions to include Transcarpathian Ukraine within the Reich so as to later carry out German expansion in the direction of Soviet Ukraine.

The Soviet government protested the full liquidation of independent Czechoslovakia. It announced that it "cannot acknowledge the inclusion of the Czech Republic within the German empire, nor in one form or another of Slovakia as well, as lawful and corresponding to the generally recognized rules of international law and justice or to the principle of self-determination of peoples." Subject to the opinion of the Soviet government, Germany's actions created and reinforced threats to global peace, "disrupted the political stability in Central Europe, and struck a new blow against the feeling of security among nations."

At the same time, in March, Hitler decided to annex the Lithuanian Klaipėda region (Memel region) to the Reich. Nazi groups were activated within the region, ready at any moment to raise a revolt on command. The Lithuanian government was prepared to receive a guarantee of the inviolability of its borders from Germany in exchange for domestic-policy concessions in the Klaipėda region. On 20 March, a meeting between Juozas Urbšys, the Lithuanian minister of foreign affairs, and Ribbentrop took place in Berlin. During the course of this conversation, as Urbšys remarked, "Germany presented Lithuania with an ultimatum: either the Klaipėda region, or the German army marches into Lithuania." On 21 March, the Lithuanian government decided to yield to force and agreed to cede Klaipėda to Germany.

After Munich, the Nazi Reich leadership began to put pressure on Romania and Poland, seeking economic and political concessions from them. On 17 March, the Romanian envoy in London, Viorel Virgil Tilea, even requested that the British government state its position on the alleged German ultimatum to Bucharest in the course of bilateral economic negotiations.

At the same time, Germany was also increasing pressure on Poland. As far back as October 1938, Ribbentrop had advanced proposals "of a general settlement of disputed issues between Poland and Germany." They included "the reunion of Danzig with the Reich" and the construction of an exterritorial highway and railroad line through Polish Pomerania (along the coastline). Germany also suggested that it might not guarantee Polish-German borders if the Poles failed to cooperate with the Reich's policies: "The German Minister of Foreign Affairs named joint actions on colonial issues and the questions of Jewish emigration from Poland as a possible sphere of future cooperation between the two countries, as well as the joint policy with respect to Russia on the basis of the Anti-Comintern Pact."

The Polish minister of foreign affairs, Józef Beck, believed that German claims might be bypassed by procrastinating on a solution or using other diplomatic maneuvers. The Polish historian Żerko gives the following assessment of Beck's position: "It is hard to give a better example of disorientation, nonchalance, and overestimation of the role of one's own country." The leaders of the country began to assess the seriousness of the immediate situation for Poland only as a result of Beck's talks with Hitler and Ribbentrop on 5–6 January 1939. Hitler assured Beck that, "under all circumstances, Germany will be interested in maintaining a strong national Poland, regardless of the state of affairs in Russia." At the same time, Hitler stressed the need to resolve the issue of Danzig and the Polish Corridor. The Führer claimed that "he is thinking of the formula, in accordance with which Danzig would become politically German, though would remain in Poland's possession in economic terms. Danzig remains and will always be German; sooner or later this city will go to Germany." As far as the Polish Corridor was concerned, Hitler admitted that a "connection with the sea is absolutely necessary for Poland . . . [but] Germany needs a connection with Eastern Prussia to the same extent." In exchange for the Polish concessions, Germany could guarantee Poland's borders, documented on a contractual basis. Beck took into account "the wishes, expressed by the Führer," but emphasized the complexity of settling the issues that had been raised. He assured Hitler that Poland would still be loyal to the political line arising out of its 1934 agreement with Germany.

The talks in Germany were a shock for Beck. He later admitted that it was precisely at that time that he first considered the possibility of war with Germany. The time for tough decisions soon came for Warsaw. On 8 January, a conference of the Polish leadership with the participation of the president and members of the government took place at the Royal Castle. The decision was made to refuse to meet the German demands.

Nevertheless, the German leadership continued increasing pressure on Poland. On 21 March, Ribbentrop invited the Polish ambassador and strongly pressed him to meet the demands of Berlin regarding Gdańsk (Danzig) and the exterritorial highway through the Polish Corridor. Ribbentrop's words sounded like an obvious threat. He stressed that Hitler had not received any positive response from Poland to German proposals. That is why Ribbentrop insisted on an urgent visit by Beck to Berlin to negotiate with Hitler. But the position of the Polish leadership precluded any concessions to the German dictate.

Could Warsaw have responded to the demands of Berlin any other way? Apparently not. The policy of concessions to Hitler meant Poland would lose its independent role in Central Europe. It meant Poland's transformation into a German vassal and the loss of independence.

At the same time, it was the firm Polish decision to reject Hitler's demands that changed the entire course of the international political crisis in 1939. After the Munich Agreement, the Führer was becoming more and more inclined toward war with the western European countries, and he needed time to prepare. In the case of a first strike in the West, Germany would assign Poland the role of an obedient satellite and reliable rear. On 22 August 1939, in his speech to the Wehrmacht leadership, Hitler explained that "at first I wanted to establish acceptable relations with Poland in order to lead the battle against the West." But the implementation of that objective did not succeed.

The events of March 1939, and primarily the increase in German aggression, led to the beginning of a major realignment of forces in the international arena. The failure of the pacification policy pursued by western European countries revealed itself. The attempt to reach a new stability in Europe by means of concessions to Germany did not succeed. Hitler violated all of his promises and agreements. On 17 March, the main diplomatic advisor to British foreign secretary Robert Vansittart told Soviet plenipotentiary Maisky that "the Prime Minister's foreign policy was an unqualified disaster," that the annexation of Czechoslovakia was the final blow, and that, therefore, the "appeasement policy is dead and there is no way back to it."

The leaders of England and France came to the conclusion that a barrier to Hitler's aggression was needed to prevent the establishment of German hegemony in Europe. The provision of British guarantees to Poland became a step in this direction. On 31 March, British prime minister Chamberlain stated in the House of Commons "that in case of any action obviously threatening the independence of Poland against which the Polish government will deem it necessary to maintain resistance with its national armed forces, His Majesty's government considers itself obliged to immediately provide the Polish government with all possible assistance." This declaration provided the Polish government with a critical assurance. The French government took a similar position. In spite of its lack of precision, Chamberlain's declaration represented an important transition in British policy, which became a "policy of guarantees." At the same time, the government of Great Britain proceeded from its own interests. When discussing the issue of guarantees at the meeting of the government foreign policy committee, Chamberlain remarked, "The main line of our policy with respect to Germany is determined not by protecting separate countries which might be under the German threat, but by striving to prevent the establishment of German domination over the continent, as a result of which Germany would become so powerful that it could endanger our safety. The domination of Germany over Poland and Romania would strengthen its military power, and that is why we have provided guarantees to these countries."

A commitment to enter into a permanent bilateral agreement that would guarantee "mutual support in case of any threat, direct or indirect, to the independence of any of the parties" was expressed as a result of Beck's visit to London of 4–6 April 1939.

Building up the political and diplomatic opposition to the further strengthening of Germany, on 13 April Chamberlain announced a declaration of British government guarantees for Greece and Romania. On the same day, the government of France issued a similar declaration. In addition, it confirmed its obligations under the Franco-Polish Union.

During the period of 23–27 March, Robert Hudson, the British secretary of overseas trade, visited Moscow. During breakfast in the British embassy, Hudson told Potemkin, the deputy people's commissar for foreign affairs, that "an armed conflict between European democracies and Germany seems inevitable. Public opinion in England is fully convinced that this confrontation is imminent. In order to oppose the aggressors, the cooperation of Great Britain, France, and the USSR is necessary." London and Paris faced the issue of involving Moscow in the implementation of the "policy of guarantees."

The key approaches by Soviet leadership to international policy issues were outlined by Stalin in the summary report of the Politburo of the Central Committee of the All-Union Communist Party (Bolsheviks) to the Eighteenth Party Congress on 10 March 1939. In that report he stated, "A new imperialistic war became a fact. . . . Wars are waged by aggressor states, discriminating against the interests of nonaggressive states in every possible way, first of all against England, France, [and] the United States[,] which are backing away and retreating, giving the aggressors one concession after another." At the same time, the main thrust of Stalin's report turned out to be directed against the policy of non-intervention, against the policy of plotting aggression, and against attempts to confront Germany. The Kremlin chief warned the Western leaders, "It is necessary, however, to note that the big and dangerous political game launched by the supporters of non-intervention may end with a serious failure for them."

Stalin formulated the main objectives for the party in the sphere of foreign policy:

1. To maintain the policy of peace and strengthen business connections with all countries henceforth;
2. To maintain caution and not allow the provocateurs of war, which are used

to somebody pulling the chestnuts out of the fire for them, to involve our country in conflicts.

Thereby, the Stalinist leadership placed priority on the battle for the national and state interests of the Soviet Union on its own terms. It declared its intention to carry out a cautious, pragmatic policy and to remain out of reach of the imperialistic war as much as possible, and to achieve favorable agreements with its potential partners to the extent possible.

A distinct clarification of the Soviet position was given by People's Commissar Litvinov in his conversation with British ambassador William Seeds on 1 April 1939. Speaking of the Soviet reaction to the British initiatives, Seeds asked, "Does this mean that henceforth you are not going to help a victim of aggression?" Litvinov answered that this "may be—we will help in certain cases, but we believe that we are not bound by anything and will act in conformity with our own interests."

Soviet leadership displayed a keen interest in preventing a new Munich and actively participated in the discussion of possibilities for repelling aggression. On 18 March, in connection with Germany's increasing pressure on Romania and Poland, the Soviet Union offered to "immediately convene a meeting of representatives from the USSR, England, France, Poland, and Romania." On the following day, Litvinov offered to add Turkey as a potential participant in the conference. The Soviet Union expressed a willingness to sign the draft declaration by Great Britain, the Soviet Union, France, and Poland stipulating the commitment of the relevant governments "to immediately hold a consultation on those steps which must be undertaken for the general opposition" to any actions that constituted a threat to the political independence of any European state. However, Litvinov imposed a condition: the Soviet Union would not sign that declaration unless Poland signed it as well.

The Soviet leadership was explicitly apprehensive about possible Polish-German agreements. Obviously, Moscow's striving to improve its relations with Warsaw was driven by these considerations. As early as 19 February 1939, the Soviet Union and Poland had signed a trade agreement that provided for growth in commodity sales between the two countries. On 10 March, Litvinov wrote, "New relations with Poland may be described in the following way: they have become less hostile, but by no means more friendly, whereas Polish-German relations have become less friendly and more hostile. Beck still continues to tack between the USSR and Germany, but now with slightly less of a tilt toward the German side."

At the end of March, the Kremlin provided additional evidence of its commitment to the Soviet-Polish rapprochement. On 28 March, during the course of his talk with Deputy People's Commissar Potemkin, Ambassador Grzybowski of Poland made a request to settle some issues of bilateral relations prior to his planned journey to Warsaw for consultations. The ambassador listed the most important issues: establishing an air connection between Moscow and Warsaw, transferring some archival documents to the Polish government, finding a Roman Catholic priest for the Polish Roman Catholic Church in Moscow, and releasing a number of Polish citizens who had been arrested. Having studied the record of this conversation, Stalin dictated to Potemkin by telephone his positive (or evasive) answers to the ambassador's questions.

Nevertheless, Poland refused to sign the Declaration of the Four Nations offered by England. The Polish government adhered to a firm position in which it would refrain from entering into any agreements either with Germany against the Soviet Union or with the Soviet Union against Germany. As the Soviet plenipotentiary, Maisky, reported from London, "The Poles have absolutely strictly, and the Romanians in less decisive form, claimed that they will not adjoin any combination (either in the form of declaration or otherwise), if the USSR is also a participant." According to Suritz, the Soviet plenipotentiary in Paris, Daladier had warned that the Polish policy would in the end lead to the division of Poland. The perilous position of Poland and the uncertainty and hesitations of England and France did not permit any actual result to be achieved.

As for Soviet leadership, it sought specific binding agreements and was reluctant to help Poland without all kinds of preliminary agreements in the event of German aggression. At the beginning of April, Litvinov initiated publication of a TASS (Telegraph Agency of the Soviet Union) announcement that denied the existence of any promises or commitments by the Soviet Union to provide assistance to Poland. On the same day, Litvinov detailed a conversation with Grzybowski: "But when necessary, Poland will request assistance from the USSR, Grzybowski edged in. To which I replied that it may turn to us when it's too late and that the position of a general automatic reserve is hardly acceptable for us." Litvinov's words turned out to be somewhat prophetic. The people's commissar assessed the Soviet position even more frankly in his letter to the Soviet plenipotentiary to Germany, A. F. Merkalov, on 4 April. Litvinov wrote, "We know perfectly well that it is impossible to hold or stop aggression in Europe without us, and the later they request our help, the heavier the price they will pay to us." The idea of payment for Soviet assistance became an important element of the Kremlin political course.

Nazi Germany, for its part, continued to increase pressure on Poland. As is now known, on 3 April 1939, the command of the German armed forces made a decision to prepare an attack on Poland (a strategic plan known as the Fall Weiss) by 1 September of the same year. On 11 April, the plan for a military campaign against Poland was approved. According to the document, "The political leadership considers it an objective to isolate Poland to the extent possible, i.e., to restrict the war to military operations against Poland." On 28 April, Hitler declared the termination of the 1934 nonaggression pact with Poland, thus making it clear from then on that Germany did not rule out the possibility of war against its eastern neighbor.

Litvinov was right when he maintained that it would be impossible to create a barrier against aggression in Europe without the Soviet Union. In connection with increasing German pressure on Poland and Romania, the question arose of involving the Soviet Union in the Anglo-French "guarantees policy." In the middle of April 1939, the Soviet Union received an official partnership proposal from England and France. London proposed to give a unilateral Soviet guarantee to Poland and Romania, and possibly to other bordering states. Paris came forward with an initiative to extend the Soviet-French pact of mutual assistance in the event one of the parties provided assistance to Poland or Romania. At the same time, France was prepared to support the English proposal as well.

Informing Stalin of these proposals, Litvinov added a specific reservation: "if we want to cooperate with England and France at all. . . ." This reservation by the people's commissar enables us to assume the presence of disagreements within the Soviet leadership on this matter. Litvinov formulated the minimum Soviet requirements in the following way:

1. Mutual assistance commitment among England, France, and the Soviet Union in the event of aggression against one of these states as a result of assistance provided to any European neighbor of the USSR, including the Baltic States and Finland.
2. England, France, and the USSR commit to one another to provide assistance to European neighbors of the USSR.
3. Representatives from the three states shall immediately enter into a discussion to establish the scope and the forms of assistance.
4. The USSR, England, and France shall not make decisions or enter into agreements with other states in relation to any issues which concern Eastern Europe without the mutual consent of the three states. In like manner, they shall not make peace with aggressors separately from one another.

On 17 April, the expanded and updated Soviet proposals aimed at uniting the English and French approaches were submitted to London and Paris for consideration. The following constituted the main points of the Soviet proposals: conclusion of an agreement for immediate mutual assistance, including military assistance, by England, France, and the Soviet Union in the event of aggression in Europe against any of the parties to the agreement; the commitment of the three states to provide all kinds of assistance, including military assistance, to the Eastern European neighbors of the Soviet Union, from the Baltic to the Black Sea, in the event of aggression against these states; and immediate preparation of a military convention to be signed together with a political agreement. Thus, the trilateral Anglo-French-Soviet negotiations went into effect.

The Soviet position was directed toward the formation of a military and political alliance among the three states, with strict commitments of mutual assistance and joint guarantees to the European neighbors of the Soviet Union. The implementation of this program would make the Soviet Union an equitable participant in decision making on the situation in Eastern Europe. The Soviet proposals meant guarantees for the European neighbors of the Soviet Union but said nothing of the western neighbors of Germany, except France.

The disparate positions of England, France, and the Soviet Union were conditioned by both objective and subjective factors. England and France had already expressed their interest in preventing further strengthening of the German positions in eastern and southeastern Europe. They had already bound themselves with commitments to Poland, Romania, and Greece. Litvinov stressed that "the Soviet leadership is free from any commitments with respect to helping Poland or Romania, and it has now offered to undertake one-sided commitments where . . . [they are] in its own interests. The Soviet government, of course, knows its own interests perfectly, and it also knows what it is going to undertake and do in accordance with these interests." In addition, Poland and Romania opposed the Soviet guarantees and were perceived in Moscow as unfriendly states. Nevertheless, the Soviet Union was consistently encouraging Poland to oppose German demands.

The British government was not ready to accept the Soviet proposal to create a broad military and political alliance capable of repulsing prospective allies and bringing together the members of the Anti-Comintern Pact. Thus, the Anglo-French duo was focused on impeding the negotiations, which might, in the opinion of London and Paris, "prevent Germany from beginning the war in 1939 and hamper the possible Soviet-German rapprochement."

The background for this situation was the deep suspicion and mutual distrust between London and Paris on one side and Moscow on the other. The effect of the "Great Purge" and massive repressions in the Soviet Union increased the traditional hostility of Western democracies to Stalin's regime. The traditional distrust behind English and French policy, increased by Munich, persisted in Moscow as well. Stalin did not believe that Western democracies would provide the Soviet Union with military assistance in certain circumstances.

Unfortunately, the chance to achieve an agreement by virtue of the Soviet proposals was lost by the leaders of the Western states. London delayed its reply, believing that "it is still not time for such a universal proposal." On 25 April, Paris presented new proposals, which, according to Litvinov, looked "almost mocking: we will receive assistance only if England and France find themselves in conflict with Germany, only by their own initiative, and they will be receiving our assistance." Nevertheless, Litvinov was doing his best in order to continue the negotiations on a positive note. He believed France's first proposal was "fundamentally acceptable"; he found changes of a "positive character" in the second proposal (originally there were talks only about assistance to Poland and Romania). The issue in the new proposal was about preventing all kinds of changes imposed by force in Central or Eastern Europe.

Litvinov's course toward achieving agreements (of course, agreements favorable to the Soviet Union) with England and France stirred up the discontent of Stalin and Molotov. On 21 April 1939, a meeting took place in Stalin's Kremlin office with the participation of some members of the Politburo, Litvinov, and Deputy Potemkin, as well as Maisky and Merkalov, summoned from London and Berlin, respectively. The cardinal question of the future foreign policy course was discussed. Litvinov's policy, oriented toward a union with England and France, was subjected to strong criticism. Molotov emphasized the need to search for alternative solutions to strengthen the foreign-policy position of the Soviet Union, as well as possibly improving relations with Nazi Germany.

In the opinion of some Russian researchers, this very meeting predetermined the retirement of Litvinov from the post of people's commissar for foreign affairs. On 3 May, Stalin sent a telegram to twenty leading officials of the People's Commissariat for Foreign Affairs. In it, he informed them,

> In view of the serious conflict between the chairman of the Soviet of People's Commissars comrade Molotov and People's Commissar for Foreign Affairs comrade Litvinov, arising based on the disloyal attitude of comrade Litvinov to the Council of People's Commissars of the USSR, comrade Litvinov filed a request to the Central Committee to relieve him of his duties as the People's Commissar for Foreign Affairs. The [Politburo] accepted the request of comrade Litvinov and relieved him of his duties. Chairman of the Council of People's Commissars of the USSR comrade Molotov received an additional appointment as People's Commissar for Foreign Affairs.

The dismissal of Litvinov meant that Soviet leadership was deviating from the policy of collective security—the course of tacking between opposing groups in the international arena and striving for the most favorable conditions of agreement. It is no wonder that most German newspapers assessed Litvinov's retirement as "the end of the Geneva policy and the policy of unions with western capitalist states, which was allegedly carried out by the previous People's Commissar."

But the leaders of England and France did not display a complete understanding of the seriousness of the international situation and the need to find a compromise with the Soviet Union. Their new proposals at the end of April and beginning of May consisted of either the Soviet Union providing assistance to England and France in connection with fulfilling their commitments or unilateral commitments of the Soviet Union in support of these guarantees. Molotov's assessment of the Anglo-French proposals was sharply negative: "The English and the French require unilateral and gratuitous assistance from us, without undertaking to provide equivalent assistance to us." This assessment also reflected the position of Stalin, who told Georgi Dimitrov, secretary general of the Executive Committee of the Comintern, on 7 September 1939, "But the English and the French wanted to have us as servants and pay nothing for that!" Therefore, the Soviet concept of negotiations with England and France underestimated the common threat and common interest in opposing the potential aggression. The Soviet Union expected to receive unconditional guarantees from London and Paris, as well as "additional payment" for the union of Moscow with them. The Soviet leadership insisted on the principle of reciprocity in the business of mutual assistance among England, France, and the Soviet Union and on extending the guarantees of these three countries to all countries of Eastern Europe bordering the Soviet Union.

However, the growing German pressure on Poland and the conclusion of the German-Italian alliance on 22 May urged the participants in the trilateral negotiations toward their activation. The experts at the British Foreign Office came to the conclusion that an Anglo-Franco-Soviet agreement was, possibly, "the sole means of preventing the war." On 27 May, the representatives of Great Britain and France in Moscow handed Molotov a draft trilateral agreement for mutual assistance against aggression.

Molotov publicly admitted that the Anglo-French proposals were a "step forward" since they "provided for the principle of mutual assistance between England, France, and the Soviet Union under reciprocity conditions in case of a direct attack by aggressors." At the same time, Molotov expressed his negative attitude toward the draft document in conversation with the representatives of England and France, bringing forward different remarks and reservations. The unsolved issue concerned guarantees to the Baltic States of Estonia and Latvia, as well as Finland (which was considered to be included in that grouping). "In order to avoid any misunderstandings, we see it fit to warn that the issue of the three Baltic States is the kind of issue which requires satisfactory settlement to complete the negotiations," wrote Molotov to Maisky on 10 June.

On 2 June, Molotov handed the Soviet draft of the trilateral agreement to the representatives of England and France. The draft provided for "immediate comprehensive effective assistance" to each other if any of the contracting parties turned out to be involved in military actions with a European state, either as a result of aggression on the part of this state against any of the three countries or as a result of aggression against Belgium, Romania, Poland, Latvia, Estonia, or Finland, which the parties of the agreement would be obliged to protect. The political agreement was to take effect simultaneously with the agreements on military affairs.

The political negotiations entered a crucial stage. The British government was not ready to accept the Soviet version. The British considered it to be inappropriate to directly name Latvia, Estonia, and Finland in the agreement. London also believed that Moscow's proposal for the political pact and the military agreement to take effect simultaneously could delay the completion of the talks. Finally, the British government had doubts concerning the principle proposed by Moscow for not concluding a separate peace.

At the same time, the British and French governments were interested in an agreement with Moscow in order to fulfill the guarantee commitments already given by them. On 8 June, the British government decided to send the head of the Central Europe Department of the Foreign Office, William Strang, to Moscow to speed up the course of the trilateral negotiations.

On 15 June, Molotov was handed the new Anglo-French formulations on the trilateral negotiation issues. They stipulated immediate mutual assistance among the three states in the event of aggression against one of them, as well as the immediate assistance of the Soviet Union to Poland, Romania, Belgium, Greece, and Turkey "in the event of an aggressor's attack on them and the involvement of England and France in the war in connection with that." In addition, the agreement stipulated immediate consultation by the participants in case of emergency.

The Soviet leadership analyzed the Anglo-French proposals and found them unacceptable. On 16 June, Molotov wrote to Maisky and Suritz, "The Anglo-French proposals received yesterday, for the most part, repeat their previous proposals. In particular, they demand from us immediate assistance to the well-known five countries but reject immediate assistance to the three Baltic countries in view of their alleged refusal to take such assistance. It means that the French and the English have put the USSR into a humiliating unequal position, and under no circumstance shall we accept this fact."

Henceforth, the trilateral negotiations focused on the list of guaranteed states, particularly on the issue of guarantees to the Baltic neighbors of the Soviet Union. By the end of June, the representatives of England and France agreed that those neighbors with guarantees of assistance included the Baltic States, Poland, and Romania; the inviolability of those countries represented one of the elements of the Soviet Union's security. For France and England, such neighboring states were represented by Belgium, the Netherlands, and Switzerland, on which the guarantees of the three countries were proposed to extend. At the same time, the French ambassador suggested that the countries provided with guarantees by the three states be listed in a separate document not subject to publication. The Soviet project dated 8 July 1939 was close to the Anglo-French proposals.

It appears that the Anglo-French and Soviet proposals created an acceptable basis for entering into the trilateral agreement of mutual assistance and guarantees. On 14 July, French premier Daladier stated to the Soviet pleni-potentiary, "It's time to finish, especially now when I don't see any serious discrepancies." With respect to Paris, French ambassador Paul-Émile Naggiar wrote from Moscow at the beginning of July, "The main target of the agree-ment from the very beginning consisted in integrating the USSR into our sys-tem and keeping it on our side as a base of supply and possible assistance to Poland and Romania. This target seems to be achieved at the current mo-ment, if we take into account the main provisions of the agreement, pursuant to which we already agree with the USSR." There was a lack of political will on both sides to enter into an agreement. Soviet leadership persistently argued for the equality of rights and some "bonuses" in Eastern Europe for itself.

The situation being what it was, the Soviet leadership chose to delay the negotiations, using the question of "indirect aggression" and the linking of the political agreement to the military convention. The trilateral agreement was to provide guarantees not only against direct attack but also against "in-direct aggression." This concept was disclosed by Molotov on 9 July. The So-viet version of the letter accompanying the trilateral agreement suggested, "The expression 'indirect aggression' refers to an action for which any of the aforementioned states agrees under the threat of using force on the part of the other state or without such threat but which entails the usage of terri-tories and forces of that state for aggression against it or against one of the contracting parties, and consequently, entails the loss of independence of that state or the violation of its neutrality." This definition of "indirect ag-gression" was extremely broad and actually provided the Soviet Union with certain freedoms of action in adjoining countries during crisis situations. The suggested Soviet formulation was completely unacceptable to the British, who were prepared to accept the breakdown of negotiations because of it. With the advancing threat of direct German aggression, the discussions of "indirect aggression" did not indicate the participants' interest in the quick-est conclusion of a trilateral pact. Molotov admitted that the sticking points on the political elements of the agreement were of secondary importance.

Under the circumstances, the Soviet leadership deemed it appropriate to proceed to discussion of specific military problems. Since April 1939, Mos-cow had been insisting on signing the military convention together with the political agreement. The British and French leadership at the end of July agreed to send a mission to Moscow for negotiations on military issues. At the same time, Lord Halifax was counting on Soviet concessions in relation to the definition of "indirect aggression." One way or another, the way to the trilateral military negotiations in Moscow was opened. Nevertheless, in the middle of July the negotiations became notably complicated.

The Anglo-French proposal to reach agreement on the political issues first and only then to proceed to the military agreement evoked Molotov's sharp criticism. On 17 July, he wrote to the Soviet plenipotentiaries in London and Paris, "Only the cons and swindlers, which resemble the negotiating gentlemen on the Anglo-French side all this time, may now pretend, shamming as if our requirement for simultaneously concluding a political and military agreement was something new in negotiations. . . . Apparently, there will be no use to all these negotiations and we will have to tell them to go to hell. Then let them have only themselves to blame!" The Soviet leadership persistently competed for a binding military-political agreement with certain advantages for the Soviet Union in Eastern Europe.

In addition, at this particular time, Soviet distrust of British motives and objectives increased. Both England and the Soviet Union led a peculiar "double game," conducting parallel contacts with Germany.

In general it is impossible to understand the course of the trilateral negotiations without an analysis of the developing relations between the Soviet Union and Germany. On December 1938, the Germans declared their readiness to resume trade and credit negotiations with the Soviet Union. These negotiations began in January 1939 and were progressing intensively and slowly. There is an impression that the Soviet leadership expected some political move on the part of Germany, but Berlin did not undertake it. In March 1939, Litvinov remarked, "Germany itself would like to use the Soviet trump in its game with England and France, but cannot decide to make the appropriate political gestures which it wants to replace with economical rapprochement if possible."

The turn toward Soviet-German rapprochement was outlined in April 1939. The careful mutual probing of possibilities for improving relations between Moscow and Berlin was carried out in the course of conversations between Merkalov, the Soviet plenipotentiary in Berlin, and Ernst von Weizsäcker, state secretary of the German Ministry of Foreign Affairs, on 17 April. According to the Soviet record of the conversation, the German diplomat, characterizing relations between the two countries, stated, "They cannot be better than now. . . . You know that we have some discrepancies in ideological character. But at the same time, we sincerely want to develop economic relations with you." According to the German version of the conversation, Merkalov emphasized that, "from the point of view of Russia, there are no reasons which should hinder normal relationships between us. And beginning with the normal ones, relations may become even better and better." This probing suited the policy initiatives of the Soviet Union and Germany. When it comes to Moscow, one should remember the conference with Stalin on 21 April 1939, in which Molotov raised the issue of considering the possibility of improving relations with Nazi Germany. And on 11 April, the German leadership had an approved plan for attacking Poland (the Fall Weis), which included its isolation. What is quite characteristic is the remark of Soviet representative Georgy A. Astakhov in his letter to Molotov dated 14 June: "That, of course, created an impression that the pro-Soviet . . . maneuver in German policy during the past two months had been conceived somewhat deeper than it seemed to many in the beginning." Therefore, this "pro-Soviet maneuver" commenced exactly in the middle of April 1939.

After the retirement of Litvinov, it was decided in Berlin to actively probe the Soviet Union, but, in the course of contacts during the first half of May, the Soviets replied that an improvement in bilateral relations depended on Germany.

Nevertheless, in May 1939, Molotov made a decisive step toward rapprochement with Germany. On 29 May, in the course of discussing the Soviet-German economic negotiations, he stated, "We came to the conclusion that the relevant political base should be created for the success of economic negotiations. Without such a political base, as the experience of negotiating with Germany showed, it is impossible to settle economic issues. . . . The economic negotiations should be preceded by the creation of a relevant political base." This approach turned out to be absolutely new to the German leadership. To his questions regarding how political relations between the two countries might be improved, the ambassador heard in reply that "both governments should think about it." The Soviet démarche met with a favorable response in Berlin. On 22 May, Ribbentrop, in his conversation with Ambassador Coulondre of France, frankly stated that the German-Soviet rapprochement was "inevitable and necessary[;] it corresponds to the nature of things and traditions." At the same time, he said that the Polish state would "have to disappear sooner or later, divided between Germany and Russia."

What is characteristic is that, on 23 May, Hitler, in determining military-political plans, outlined the "problem of Poland." He stated, "The 'problem of Poland' cannot be separated from the problem of confrontation with the West. . . . That is why it is impossible to bypass the Polish issue; only one solution remains[:] to attack Poland as soon as practicable." Nevertheless, the contacts between Germany and the Soviet Union remained very cautious; the main goal for Berlin consisted of preventing Moscow from engaging in rapprochement with England.

Without rejecting the possibility of improving German-Soviet relations, Berlin did not put forward any specific proposals. A pause occurred in the process of improving Soviet-German relations, although, on 21 July, the two countries resumed economic negotiations.

At the end of July, the Nazi leadership proceeded to the final stage of preparations for the attack on Poland. Warsaw did not make concessions, and, in case Germany attempted to capture Gdańsk (Danzig), it was ready to make war even without allies. At the same time, London did not guarantee Berlin that England would stay out of a future conflict. During the spring and summer of 1939, the objective growth of disagreements between Germany and England that took place made it practically impossible for the leaders of the two countries to reach a compromise. In addition, the trilateral negotiations in Moscow caused growing concerns in Berlin.

Under the circumstances, the Nazi government was determined to advance its contacts with Moscow. On 24 July, the energetic and charming counselor of the Economy Department of the German Foreign Ministry, Julius Schnurre, invited Soviet chargé d'affaires Georgy A. Astakhov for a conversation. According to Schnurre, the successful completion of trade and credit negotiations was to be just the first stage in improving bilateral relations. The second stage could consist of improving relations through media and cultural contacts and the like. "After that we can move on to the third stage and raise the question of political rapprochement. . . . There aren't any points of disagreement between the USSR and Germany," Schnurre emphasized. He developed the idea of improving Soviet-German relations during a dinner with Soviet diplomats at the elegant Evest restaurant in Berlin on 26 July. Schnurre brought up the question of prolonging or renovating the Soviet-German political treaty. In the next few days, the German ambassador in Moscow, Friedrich-Werner Graf von der Schulenburg, joined the negotiations. On 3 August, while talking to Molotov, the ambassador stressed that "the German Government has authorized him to state that in their opinion there are no political differences between the USSR and Germany."

Molotov's reply to Astakhov suggested "a desire to go on with their interchange of opinions on improving relations." As for the rest, much depended on the results of the trade and credit negotiations in Berlin. The Germans propelled the negotiations forward and very soon raised the question of working the goal of improving political relations into the trade treaty. According to Astakhov, the Germans would not mind "involving us in a more far-reaching discussion, including a review of any political and territorial issues that might arise between us and them. In that regard, the statement about there being no contradictions 'from the Black Sea to the Baltic Sea throughout' can be interpreted as a desire to settle all the issues related to the countries within that zone." Further, in dwelling on specific questions, Astakhov emphasized, "I just think that in the short run they consider it quite possible to enter into an agreement like the one mentioned above and thereby neutralize us in the event of war with Poland." That comment implied the absence of a military-political treaty between Britain, France, and the Soviet Union.

The Kremlin welcomed Germany's overtures. On 29 July, Molotov wrote to Astakhov, "As soon as economic relations between the USSR and Germany improve, their political relations can improve as well. . . . If the Germans are truly shifting milestones and they really want to improve their political relations with the USSR, they have to tell us how exactly they see that improvement."

On 3 August, Ribbentrop entered into the Soviet-German negotiations. While talking to Astakhov, the German foreign minister stressed that "we believe there are no political differences between our countries throughout the territory from the Black Sea to the Baltic Sea. All of the issues can be settled[,] and if the Soviet government agrees with these prerequisites, views can be exchanged in a more specific way."

On 10 August, Astakhov informed Moscow of the crucial question raised by the German government: "For their part, the German government is mainly interested in our attitude toward the Polish issue. If attempts to peacefully settle the Danzig issue fail, and the Polish provocations continue, war may break out. The German government would like to know what the Soviet Government's position will be in this case."

Therefore, the subject matter was not just improvement in Soviet-German relations but also the Soviet Union's position in the forthcoming military conflict caused by Germany's aggressive actions.

For the Kremlin, it was time to make fundamental decisions. It should be kept in mind that, on 5 August, the British and French military missions set off to the Soviet Union to conduct trilateral negotiations, which began in Moscow on 12 August.

The existing data prove that it was during those days in August when crucial decisions were made in Moscow. On 7 August, Kliment Voroshilov, the people's commissar for defense, recorded the instructions for negotiating with the British and French military missions. Presumably these instructions were dictated by Stalin. The document contained the following primary objectives: "The negotiations must be reduced to a discussion of certain fundamental issues, mainly the safe conduct of our army through the Vilno [Vilnius] corridor, Galicia[,] and Romania. . . . If it turns out that the safe conduct of our army through the territory of Poland and Romania is impossible, it must be declared that no agreement can otherwise be reached, since without the free passage of the Soviet army through the above territory any defense against any form of aggression is doomed to failure." Taking into account the negative attitude of Poland and Romania toward the passage of the Soviet army through their territory, the Kremlin's position condemned the trilateral military negotiations to failure.

After the mission's scope of authority had been clarified and general views had been exchanged, on 14 August the Soviet representatives posed a direct question: "Will the Soviet army be allowed to pass through the territory of Poland and Romania to come into direct contact with the enemy in case the aggressor attacks Britain and France, Poland, Romania, or Turkey?"

In response to the attempts by the British and French to evade that issue, the Soviets stated that Voroshilov "requires a definite answer as to whether the Soviet army will be allowed through the territory of Poland and Romania as a prerequisite for continuing the negotiations."

After the declaration of that stringent requirement by the Soviet marshal, the negotiations were adjourned. Going out into the garden, the head of the British delegation, Adm. Reginald Drax, said, "I believe our mission is over." Gen. Joseph Edouard Aimé Doumenc conceded that the questions brought up by Voroshilov were "absolutely legitimate."

The French military and political leaders were much more interested in an agreement with Moscow than were the British. They were aware of Warsaw's negative attitude toward allowing the Soviet army to enter and pass through Polish territory. Nevertheless, Paris made a desperate effort to save the trilateral negotiations in Moscow. On 17 August, one of Doumenc's assistants, Capt. André Beaufre, set out for Warsaw in an attempt to receive approval from the Polish government for the Soviet army's passage through Poland in case the need arose.

However, the Polish military leaders adopted an extremely negative position. The commander in chief of the Polish army, Marshal Rydz-Śmigły, and the chief of the general staff, Gen. Wacław Stachiewicz, stated that no Polish government would ever consider "any proposal involving occupation of any part of Poland by the Russian army, whatever the consequences." The problem was not so much the material issues as the sacramental principle that originated from Marshal Piłsudski's political testament: "With Germans, we risk losing our freedom, whereas with Russians we shall lose our soul." The Polish leaders believed neither in the goodwill of Soviet leadership nor in their desire to take an active part in war against Germany.

Only after the forthcoming visit of German minister Ribbentrop to Moscow was announced on 21 August did another push by the British and French military attachés make the Polish government give an evasive answer as to their possible cooperation with the Soviets. On 23 August, the French ambassador in Poland, Léon Noël, sent the following telegram to Moscow: "We are convinced that in the event of joint actions against German aggression, Poland may cooperate with the USSR on technical conditions which are to be agreed on. The French and British General Staffs believe that all possible forms of cooperation must be explored promptly."

According to Naggiar, the French ambassador in Moscow, "That concession has been made too late. Besides, it is insufficient as it does not make it possible to refer to the Polish Government's own decision." After the Soviet-German nonaggression pact was made, the trilateral negotiations became pointless and were terminated on 25 August.

The Polish government's position in August 1939 is hard to explain. Noël stressed that "the issue of responsibility for Poland, which was exposed to a greater threat than any other country and whose very sovereignty was endangered, will be raised determinedly if Poland persists in its totally negative position."

The position of Warsaw in the summer of 1939 was related to a number of mistakes and mistaken beliefs. Beck believed that Polish-Soviet cooperation could speed up the Third Reich's attack against Poland. The erroneous assumption that Stalin would fail to make a pact with Hitler was critical for the Polish politics of that period.

Looking back at the resolutions adopted in Moscow at the beginning of August 1939, it should be noted that, on 11 August, just before the start of the negotiations between the military missions, the Politburo adopted a resolution "to have an official discussion of the issues brought up by the Germans, of which Berlin is to be informed."

Based on mutual interest, the negotiations between Moscow and Berlin were developing quite fast. On 12 August, Astakhov reported from Berlin, "The events are developing fast and now the Germans are apparently reluctant to linger on the intermediate stages[,] like press talks and cultural exchange, but wish to immediately start a discussion on political and territorial subjects, in order to have a green light in the event of an armed conflict with Poland which is quickly brewing up." As early as 13 August, the German government agreed to negotiate in Moscow to improve relations between the two countries and, for that reason, to send a person who was close to the Führer. On 15 August, Schulenburg presented Molotov with a memorandum that stated, in part,

> There aren't any real differences in the interests of Germany and the Soviet Union. Our countries' living spaces are contiguous, but in terms of their bare necessities, they do not compete against each other. Therefore, there are no grounds for any aggressive tendencies between our countries. Germany has no aggressive intentions against the USSR. The German government is firm in its position that there isn't a single issue between the Baltic Sea and the Black Sea that couldn't be settled to the full satisfaction of both countries. This concerns the issues of the Baltic Sea, the Baltic countries, Poland, the South-East, etc. Besides, the political cooperation of our two countries can only be beneficial.

In response, Molotov raised the point of making a nonaggression pact and addressed a prior discussion of some specific issues.

During his conversation with Schulenburg on 17 August, Molotov presented the Soviet government's action plan for developing relations with Germany. The first step was to complete the trade and credit negotiations. The second step could be "drawing up a nonaggression pact or confirming the neutrality pact of 1926, and simultaneously signing a protocol specifically acknowledging the contracting parties' interest in certain matters of foreign affairs, so that the latter would constitute an integral part of the pact." For its part, the German government insisted on arranging Ribbentrop's visit to Moscow in the immediate future.

On 19 August, Molotov provided Schulenburg with a draft of the Soviet-German nonaggression pact, which included a clause on simultaneously signing a specific protocol without which the pact was null. The German government again insisted on an early visit to Moscow by Ribbentrop, alleging that "Berlin is concerned about the possible conflict between Poland and Germany."

The credit agreement between the Soviet Union and Germany was signed in Berlin on 19 August 1939, and, on 21 August, Hitler sent a letter to Stalin. As chancellor of the Reich, Hitler approved the Soviet draft of the nonaggression pact. He suggested agreeing upon the issues of the pact and the additional protocol immediately. Hitler insisted on sending Foreign Minister Ribbentrop to Moscow no later than 23 August, emphasizing the fact that the "tension between Poland and Germany has become unbearable." After two hours, Molotov handed Schulenburg Stalin's response to Hitler, in which the Soviet leader noted that the German government's consent to enter into a nonaggression pact "establishes a basis for eliminating political tension and stimulates peaceful cooperation between our countries." The Soviet government gave its consent to receive Foreign Minister Ribbentrop in Moscow on 23 August.

Ribbentrop did arrive in Moscow on 23 August, and that same evening his negotiations with Stalin and Molotov began. The subject under discussion was delineating the "sphere of influence" of the two states. The Germans suggested the Soviet sphere include Finland, Estonia, eastern Latvia (up to the Dvina River), and eastern Poland up to the border of the Narew, Wisła, Bug, and San Rivers. Stalin also claimed the Latvian ports of Liepaya and Ventspils, which were west of the designated border. Ribbentrop promptly got Hitler's consent thereto.

On the night of 23 August, the heads of the foreign ministries of the two countries, Molotov and Ribbentrop, signed the nonaggression pact between the Soviet Union and Germany, as well as a secret additional protocol.

The Soviet-German nonaggression pact of 23 August 1939 came into effect immediately after its signing and was valid for a period of ten years. Both parties promised to "refrain from any aggression and attacks against each other, either individually or together with other countries." In the event that one party was subject to military action by a third power, the other side undertook not to support this power in any form. It is worth noting that, at the insistence of the Germans, the reservation was withdrawn that made that obligation non-applicable in the event one of the parties initiated military action itself. It was not acceptable for Hitler, because the Soviet-German pact was entered into on the eve of the Nazi Reich's aggression against Poland.

The secret additional protocol that delineated the spheres of interest between the two powers was an integral part of the agreement. It was established that, "in the event of a territorial and political rearrangement of the areas belonging to the Baltic States," the delineation of the spheres of interests between Germany and the Soviet Union would be based on the northern border of Lithuania. "In the event of a territorial and political rearrangement of the areas belonging to the Polish state," the delineation of the spheres of interests between Germany and the Soviet Union would be along the course of the Narew, Wisła, Pisa, and San Rivers. The parties to the pact agreed to clarify in the course of further political development the following question: "Is retaining an independent Polish state desirable in the interests of both parties[,] and what would be the boundaries of such a state?" In addition, the interest of the Soviet Union in Bessarabia was emphasized in the secret protocol, and the German side expressed complete political disinterest in these areas.

Thus, according to the secret protocol, the sphere of interests of the Soviet Union included the eastern part of Poland, as well as Finland, Estonia, Latvia, and Bessarabia (Lithuania was added in September 1939 in exchange for some other parts of Poland).

The negotiators were very pleased with the agreements. The Soviet-German pact meant an agreement between the rulers of two totalitarian states bent on military and political transformation of Europe, as well as the division of spheres of influence in the eastern part of the continent.

Through the treaty with Moscow, which the Nazi leadership was so impatient to sign, the Germans partially solved the problem of Poland's isolation in Germany's coming war against that state. As early as 23 May 1939, Hitler had set the task "to attack Poland at the earliest opportunity. Repetition of the Czech Republic is out of the question. Military action is inevitable. The task is to isolate Poland. Successful isolation is crucial." By concluding the Soviet-German pact, Hitler made a treaty by which the Soviet Union was obliged not to support Poland in the event of war and not to assist England and France should the Western powers fulfill their obligations after the German attack on Poland. Hitler did not hide his satisfaction over the agreement reached by Ribbentrop in Moscow, since the treaty was executed exactly when it was most needed, thus putting Germany in a significantly more powerful position on the world stage. The Soviet-German cooperation on the basis of the nonaggression pact was desirable and advantageous for Hitler.

As to the meaning of the Soviet-German pact for the Soviet Union, long discussions between the supporters and opponents of this action continue in Russian historiography.

As I see it, some fundamentally incorrect assumptions made by the Stalin administration during its international activities on the eve of the war deserve discussion.

First of all is the Soviets' misunderstanding of the nature and extent of the threat posed by Nazi Germany, which sought the enslavement of Europe and world domination. Stalin and his associates underestimated the threat of Nazi Germany and did not see a significant difference between the two groups of capitalist countries. Moreover, the politics of Nazi Germany seemed more flexible and vibrant to them than those of the bourgeois democracies. Therefore, the Nazi leadership at some point began to be perceived as a more convenient and reliable partner in the international arena, so the potential for reaching agreements with Britain and France was not fully exploited. Stalin relied on the long-standing conflict in the West, which allowed him to play the role of *tertius gaudens.* In a talk with Dimitrov on 7 September 1939, Stalin declared that the war between the two groups of capitalist countries for domination of the world would be beneficial for the Soviet Union. "We do not mind them having a good fight and weakening each other," he said. The events of May–June 1940 showed this smug attitude to have been unwarranted.

Second, the Soviets had engaged in essentially geopolitical thinking with its desire to ensure the security of the country through territorial gains and an expanded sphere of influence. In fact, in the situation of acute international crisis during the summer of 1939, a better strategy for gaining real security would have been bringing together all potential opponents of the aggressors. Apparently, concessions and compromises were required to achieve this goal, but neither the Soviet leadership nor the ruling circles of Great Britain or France showed any consistent commitment to such a strategy.

The principal miscalculations of Stalin's leadership set the basis for the policy of Soviet-German rapprochement, which resulted in the conclusion of the nonaggression pact on 23 August 1939.

In light of new documents made available to researchers, the thesis promulgated by the Soviet Union for decades—that the agreement gave the Soviet Union a break that made it possible to delay the beginning of the war—turns out to be unjustified. This statement is repeated by some historians even today. But there is no evidence that the German leadership was planning a war against the Soviet Union in the autumn of 1939. The Nazi Reich at that time was not ready for such a war and did everything to avoid it. However, the well-known story of the development of Operation Barbarossa makes it possible to state with confidence that Hitler undertook aggression against the Soviet Union exactly when he had prepared for it and when, in his opinion, the most appropriate conditions existed.

By entering into the Soviet-German pact, Stalin won not time but territory. He found the agreement with Hitler more profitable and entered it. The Polish historian Eugeniusz Duraczyński reasonably argues, "Stalin could get much from the West, but immeasurably more from Germany. By signing the treaty with the Third Reich, he could count on real territorial gains on his western borders while staving off the threat of escalating conflicts and confrontation with Japan [turning] into a full-scale war."

There is no doubt that the Soviet-German nonaggression pact was a tactical win for Stalin. The Soviet Union became one of the major powers that influenced world politics. It managed to prevent a new Munich, and it achieved territorial gains. Based on the goals pursued by Soviet leadership, according to Mikhail I. Meltyukhov, "it was not a miscalculation, but rather a desirable result. Therefore[,] some authors regard the pact as a success of the Soviet leadership, which [had] been able to achieve its goals."

There are reasons to believe that, even if the Soviet-German pact was a tactical success for Stalin, the whole policy of cooperation with Berlin was a strategic miscalculation. It allowed Hitler to defeat Poland and get to the border of the Soviet Union. Subsequently, Germany was able to defeat France, which deprived the Soviet Union of a potential ally in Europe. Stalin's tactical win turned into his strategic loss by June 1941. Evaluating Stalin's course toward collaboration with Nazi Germany, the famous Russian historian Aleksandr Chubarian writes, "As subsequent events showed, tactical successes turned into strategic miscalculations."

Soviet historiography argued that, due to the conclusion of the Soviet-German pact, Stalin prevented the political isolation of the Soviet Union. But how can we speak of any threat of isolation with respect to the period when the Soviet leadership was negotiating with Britain and France on the one hand and Germany on the other? In fact, the Soviet Union occupied a favorable position during the summer of 1939, and Stalin's administration had plenty of room to maneuver.

Finally, it should be noted that the secret protocol signed by Molotov and Ribbentrop was contrary to the norms of morality and international law. Two states not only divided territory not belonging to them into spheres of influence but also challenged the very existence of an independent Poland, a recognized member of the international community. There is no doubt that this move violated a number of Soviet-Polish agreements, in particular the Riga Treaty of 1921, the 1932 bilateral agreement on nonaggression, and the protocol of 1934. A cynical grab for power was made, neglecting the interests of the smaller states.

Therefore, in December 1989, the Soviet Union's People's Deputies Congress stated that "the delineation of the spheres of interests" prescribed in the secret Soviet-German protocols of 1939–41 and other actions as well were illegal since they contradicted the sovereignty and independence of certain third countries. The congress condemned the signing of the secret additional protocol and declared the secret protocols "null and void from the very moment of their signing."

As mentioned above, the Soviet-German nonaggression pact was advantageous to Hitler. However, in our opinion, there are no grounds to believe that the pact became the critical factor for starting World War II. It is well known that the Nazi government had made the crucial decision to attack Poland no later than 1 September back in April 1939, that is, prior to any serious contacts with the Soviet Union.

The last days of August 1939 were filled with feverish diplomatic maneuvers. The British government resorted to political and diplomatic pressure in its effort to make Hitler give up his plans to start war and get him back to the negotiating table. That political direction went along with the mutual aid treaty concluded between Britain and Poland on 25 August. However, Britain succeeded only in postponing the German attack on Poland until 1 September. Meanwhile, Germany consistently exerted its efforts to neutralize Britain in the event of a German-Polish war. Nevertheless, Hitler's efforts failed.

On 1 September, Nazi Germany attacked Poland. On 3 September, Great Britain and France, fulfilling their obligations to Poland, declared war on Germany. World War II broke out.

It is beyond doubt that Nazi Germany and its allies were the principal warmongers. It was Hitler who staked Germany's domination on territorial expansion and aggression, first in Europe and then in the whole world.

Western countries, and first of all Britain, pursued the vicious policy of appeasement of the aggressor, hoping to establish a new world order together with Nazi Germany. In fact, their policy encouraged and enabled the aggressors to break the Versailles system without any resistance from the West.

The Soviet government sought to prevent another Munich and stop Britain and France from concluding a large-scale agreement with Germany without the participation of the Soviet Union. The underestimation of the Nazi German menace and the inability to make reasonable compromises resulted in the failure of the trilateral British-French-Soviet negotiations in the spring and summer of 1939.

In the complicated international situation of August 1939, Stalin's government preferred to make a nonaggression pact with Nazi Germany so that it could carve out "spheres of interests" in Eastern Europe with Berlin's participation. I believe the nonaggression pact and the secret additional protocol were Stalin's tactical successes and, at the same time, strategic miscalculations. The pact was advantageous for Hitler and let him start World War II under favorable conditions.

The prewar international political crisis provided vivid examples of a lack of foresight and political miscalculations, as well as an observance of outdated dogmas and an unwillingness to realize fundamentally new tendencies in the international situation.

4

POLAND BETWEEN THE SOVIET UNION AND GERMANY, 1939–1941

THE RED ARMY INVASION AND THE FOURTH PARTITION OF POLAND

Albin Głowacki (Poland)

Professor at the History Institute of the Philosophy and History Department, Łódź University.

Natalia S. Lebedeva (Russia)

Leading researcher, head of the Center for the Publication of Twentieth Century History Documents of the Institute of World History of the Russian Academy of Sciences.

ALBIN GŁOWACKI

THE RED ARMY INVASION AND THE FOURTH PARTITION OF POLAND

AT DAWN ON 1 September 1939, Germany—without a formal declaration of war—launched an armed invasion of Poland. The attacks came from four directions at once and involved more than 1.8 million troops, almost 2,800 tanks, more than 2,000 aircraft, and 10,000 artillery pieces and mortars. Despite the heroism of the Polish defenders, Hitler's armies, possessing overwhelming numerical and technical superiority, broke through the main defense lines and made rapid progress into the Polish heartland. The Poles hoped their Western allies—Great Britain and France—would help them turn back the tide by opening a second front against Germany. Instead, the first ten days of fighting brought a Polish retreat along the entire front and collapse of the concept of holding a second line of defense—something that augured even-tual disaster. Although from 9 to 18 September the Polish forces tried to regain the initiative in the battle on the Bzura River, that effort also ended in defeat. In two weeks of fighting, the Polish armies had lost half their combat forces.

On 12 September, motorized German units reached Lvov. Soon, the aggressors were in control of most of western and central Poland. The Polish army command ordered a further retreat and withdrawal to the so-called Romanian bridgehead. The plan was to organize a protracted defense in the vicinity of the Dniester and Stryi Rivers, until the Allies launched their offensive on the western front. However, despite declaring war against Germany on 3 September, Great Britain and France had no intention of fulfilling their commitments. At a conference in Abbeville (France), the Anglo-French Supreme War Council—its members already familiar with the secret protocol to the Ribbentrop-Molotov Pact—decided that Poland had already lost the war against Germany. Accordingly, it was agreed on 12 September that no offensive operations to relieve Poland would be conducted on the western front.

Meanwhile, the Red Army came to Germany's aid. It was a sign that there was no Soviet diplomatic reaction to Germany's invasion of Poland. However, the Soviet leadership did take measures of a military nature to fulfill the provisions of the secret protocol to the nonaggression treaty of 23 August 1939. So, on 1 September, the Politburo decided to increase the strength of the Red Army by almost 80 percent (to 173 divisions) and, on 3 September, to delay by one month the demobilization of privates and noncoms who were due to end their service. Simultaneously, on 1 September, the Supreme Soviet passed an act on obligatory military service, and a day later the Presidium of the Supreme Soviet ordered a general mobilization. On 3 September, the German ambassador to Moscow, Friedrich-Werner von der Schulenburg, met with Vyacheslav Molotov, the Soviet premier and people's commissar for foreign affairs, and demanded that the Soviets enter Poland and occupy their designated zone of interests. But the Soviets were in no hurry and waited to see how Poland's allies in the West would react. The Soviets also needed time to finish their mobilization and regrouping of forces and to prepare a propaganda campaign justifying the attack.

A secret mobilization of reservists in seven military districts of the European part of the Soviet Union was ordered on 6 September. The operation proceeded so chaotically that, by the time of the attack on Poland, not all the units had attained combat readiness and not all had reached their regions of concentration and deployment along the western frontier. There were shortages of personnel, arms, equipment, fuel, spare parts, and food.

On 8 September, the Soviet Ministry of Internal Affairs started establishing operational groups intended to work in Polish territories occupied by the army (to set up provisional authorities and NKVD cells, ensure order, suppress "counterrevolution," and take over communications, banks, printing plants, prisons, etc.).

In a conversation on 7 September with Georgi Dimitrov, general secretary of the Executive Committee of the Communist International (Comintern), Joseph Stalin remarked that the annihilation of Poland "would mean one fewer bourgeois fascist state to contend with!" Stalin added cynically, "What would be the harm if as a result of the rout of Poland we were to extend the socialist system onto new territories and populations?"

That "guideline" led the Comintern to issue a directive to the communist parties, with the following instructions: "The international working class can certainly not defend fascist Poland, which has rejected the help of the Soviet Union and suppressed other nationalities."

On 8 September, after inaccurate reports reached Moscow that the Germans had captured Warsaw, Molotov assured the ambassador of the Third Reich that Soviet military action would begin within the next few days. The pace at which Hitler's armies were advancing suggested that the Germans had already attained their military goals in Poland. Furthermore, the Kremlin was worried by the possibility of a ceasefire on the German-Polish front—and, for these reasons, the Soviet leadership set the date of the Red Army's invasion for the night of 12 September. In any event, logistical problems delayed the Soviet attack.

Launching a propaganda campaign to justify the aggression, the Soviet authorities prepared an article headlined "On the Internal Causes of Poland's Military Defeat" and published it in national newspapers. Later, it appeared in the local and army press and in leaflet form. Poland was portrayed as a country of social injustice, national subjugation, and class and national conflicts. The political message of the article amounted to a claim that only the Red Army could save "our Ukrainian and Belarusian brothers" suffering under the rule of "Poland of the lords."

Germany's assurances that it would respect the accord on the separation of interest zones and its urging of action by the Red Army led Molotov to inform Schulenburg on 16 September that the military intervention would take place any day and that the Soviets would justify it by the need "to protect our Ukrainian and Belarusian brothers."

At about that time, the Red Army troops deployed along the Polish border were given the order to begin their attack on 17 September (Sunday) at 5:00 a.m. Moscow time. Their task was to crush the Polish forces with a swift thrust and reach target positions on Poland's border with Latvia, Lithuania, and East Prussia, along the rivers Pisa, Narew, Wisła, and San, and on the border with Hungary and Romania. In other words, the Soviets were to occupy the interest zone agreed upon in the pact with Germany in August 1939. The battle orders contained propagandistic lies that the Soviet troops were coming to the aid of the workers and peasants of "Belarus, Ukraine, and Poland," who had supposedly risen up against landowners and capitalists. The troops were also told they were preventing the occupation of western Belarus and western Ukraine by Germany. The Red Army was not advancing to conquer but to "liberate our Belarusian and Ukrainian brothers and the working people of Poland."

Meanwhile, Polish troops were heroically resisting German forces along a line stretching from Augustów, Hajnówka, Brześć, Łęczna, Biłgoraj, Zamość, Tomaszów, Lubelski, Lvov, and Drohobycz to the Hungarian border.

On 17 September, at 2:00 a.m., Stalin received Schulenburg at the Kremlin and disclosed that the attack against Poland would begin in four hours. That same night, the Polish ambassador to Moscow, Wacław Grzybowski, was summoned to the Ministry of Foreign Affairs, where, at 3:00 a.m., Molotov's deputy, Vladimir Potemkin, read out an official note to him. In it, the Soviets claimed that, as a result of the war with Germany, Poland "has lost all her industrial regions and cultural centers," that "Warsaw, as the capital, no longer exists," and that "the Polish government has fallen to pieces and shows no signs of life." The conclusion was that "the Polish state and its government have virtually ceased to exist." This list belied reality (the nation was still fighting; the president, government, and the commander in chief were in eastern Lesser Poland) but was used to justify the Soviet position that the treaties between the two countries were no longer in force. In this situation, the Soviet government could not remain indifferent to the fate of its "blood brothers," who had been "abandoned to their fate and left without protection" and had ordered the Red Army to "take under its protection the lives and property of the population of Western Ukraine and Western Belarus."

Ambassador Grzybowski refused to accept the note and firmly rejected its content and form. Later that day, the Polish government issued a protest against the unilateral abrogation of the nonaggression treaty and invasion of Poland. But the aggression was a fact. The Polish embassy in Moscow had to end its mission.

On 17 September, the Soviet government—in violation of a number of bilateral and international treaties and conventions—sent its forces against Poland, as the latter struggled to hold back German armies. Thus, the Soviet Union had joined World War II on Hitler's side. Outposts of the Border Defense Corps were the first to be attacked. The main Soviet forces initiated armed hostilities along the entire Polish-Soviet border at 5:00 a.m. At the time of the invasion, the assault forces on the two fronts, Belarusian (commanded by Gen. Mikhail Kovalev) and Ukrainian (commanded by Gen. Semyon Timoshenko), numbered almost 470,000 troops, 4,850 tanks, 5,500 armored vehicles, and more than 2,000 aircraft. They were supported by NKVD Border Troops and sabotage groups. The invasion force grew in subsequent days as reinforcements arrived from the east.

Meanwhile, the Polish forces in the country's eastern territories numbered 350,000 to 450,000 men (including reservists and trainees) serving in different types of units. Most of them were unarmed and supported by relatively few field guns and tanks.

The Soviet attack came as a huge surprise to the Polish and international community. It signified a radical change in Poland's military situation, making further resistance futile. Yet, the fight against the German invasion continued. Warsaw and the Modlin fortress did not surrender until 28 September, the Hel Peninsula on 2 October, and the Independent Operational Group Polesie of Gen. Franciszek Kleeberg on 6 October, at Kock.

On 17 September, the Polish commander in chief, Marshal Edward Rydz-Śmigły, ordered the troops to make their way by the shortest possible route to Hungary and Romania. There was to be "no fighting with the Bolsheviks"—unless they attacked or tried to disarm Polish units. The Soviet aggression had disorganized the Polish defenses at the Romanian bridgehead and the struggle against German forces. It also threatened attempts to evacuate troops to neutral countries; the Polish authorities wanted to remove from the aggressors' reach as many soldiers as possible so that they could become the backbone of future Polish armed forces in the West. With that in mind, Polish troops crossed the borders into Latvia, Lithuania, Hungary, and Romania, thus avoiding Soviet capture.

These border crossings did not mean that there were no clashes of any kind with the Soviets. Border Defense Corps units fought heroically; both Vilnius and Pinsk defended themselves, albeit briefly. On 20–21 September, the town of Grodno bravely beat back the enemy; its inhabitants were later subjected to criminal punishment for their valor. On 22 September, the Lvov garrison surrendered to the Soviets. Despite the surrender terms, the officers were imprisoned (in Starobelsk), while many police officers were shot.

The Soviet invasion undermined the morale of the Polish army—and particularly Belarusian, Ukrainian, and Jewish soldiers. The new situation was the main reason for their desertions, especially from reserve units formed in Poland's eastern territories.

The top authorities of the Republic of Poland left the country before midnight of September 17, crossing into allied Romania—and thus avoiding Soviet capture. However, the Romanians—fearing a German reaction—interned the Poles. In these circumstances, President Ignacy Mościcki resigned his office in favor of Władysław Raczkiewicz. This move preserved the continuity of Poland's state authorities and made it possible to establish in France a legal cabinet in exile. On 30 September 1939, leadership of the cabinet was assumed by Gen. Władysław Sikorski, with the priority of fighting for the restoration of an independent Poland. That goal was to be attained through the reconstruction of the Polish armed forces in exile and organization in occupied Poland of clandestine armed resistance and an underground civilian administration. The international community largely recognized the new Polish authorities, which retained the status of an ally of Great Britain and France. Neither Germany nor the Soviet Union appeared to notice the existence of the Polish government in exile.

Despite the defeat of the Polish army in September 1939, the armed struggle against the Red Army and the civilian administration of the occupiers lasted several more weeks. It was conducted by isolated units and groups of Polish soldiers who had holed up in forests. Some members of the local population (Belarusians, Ukrainians, Jews) helped hunt them down.

It is estimated that the Red Army's losses in Poland totaled twenty-five hundred to three thousand killed and eight thousand to ten thousand wounded. The Polish losses were much higher, since they included not only combat casualties but also people murdered by the Red Army, the NKVD, terrorist-subversive groups, and nationalist militants. According to Polish sources, these losses included six thousand to seven thousand dead and about ten thousand wounded.

Soviet-German Treaty of Friendship, Cooperation, and Demarcation of 28 September 1939

On 21 September 1939, Germany and the Soviet Union signed a secret accord concerning the demarcation line between their forces. Under its provisions, German forces were to start pulling back on 22 September and reach the western banks of the rivers Pisa, Narew, Wisła, and San by the evening of 4 October. That meant they would return to the line specified in the protocol to the Soviet-German nonaggression treaty. It was also agreed that the Red Army would assist German forces—if requested to do so—in suppressing Polish units and "gangs" along the march route of small German units.

On 25 September 1939, Stalin and Molotov received Schulenburg at the Kremlin, and one of the topics discussed was the future of Poland. Stalin felt that "anything that in the future might create friction between Germany and the Soviet Union must be avoided." He believed it would be "wrong to leave an independent rump Polish state" and proposed that, if Germany waived its claim to Lithuania, it would receive the entire Lublin voivodeship and part of the Warsaw voivodeship. Those proposals were discussed with Ribbentrop during his next visit to Moscow (27–29 September), which led to the signing of the Soviet-German Boundary and Friendship Treaty (28 September). In it, the parties declared that they "consider it exclusively their task, after the collapse of the former Polish state, to reestablish peace and order in these territories and to assure the peoples living there a peaceful life in keeping with their national character." The Soviet Union and Germany also determined the definitive boundary of "their respective national interests in the territory of the former Polish state" and warned that they "shall reject any interference of third parties in this settlement." They further declared their boundary deal to be "a firm foundation for a progressive development of the friendly relations between their peoples."

The text of the treaty and a related map were published immediately, but two secret protocols and one confidential protocol attached to the document were not. The first secret protocol concerned modifications of the boundary line between the spheres of influence, determined on 23 August 1939; the territory of Lithuania was recognized as falling within the Soviet sphere of interests, while the Lublin voivodeship and part of the Warsaw voivodeship would be in the German zone. After the Soviet Union occupied Lithuania, the southwestern part of that country was to be transferred to the Third Reich.

The second secret protocol contained a provision that the parties "will tolerate in their territories no Polish agitation which affects the territories of the other party" (they would nip such agitation in the bud and inform each other of the measures taken). That, in effect, meant a commitment to suppress any independence-oriented clandestine resistance.

The confidential protocol guaranteed the possibility of voluntary resettlement of Reich nationals or persons of German origin from the sphere of Soviet interests to Germany or the sphere of German interests, and the same possibility for persons of Ukrainian and Belarusian origin wishing to move from the sphere of German interests to the Soviet Union.

On 30 September 1939, Polish diplomats officially protested the treaty, declaring that Poland would never recognize that act of violence or abandon its struggle to completely free itself of the invaders.

On 4 October 1939, the Soviet Union and Germany signed in Moscow a supplementary boundary protocol, detailing its course. The actual delineation of the Soviet-German border in the field was conducted by joint teams of specialists.

Even before the formal incorporation of Poland's eastern territories, the Soviet Union "gave" a small part of that area to Lithuania. This was done on the basis of a treaty on the transfer to the Republic of Lithuania of the town of Vilnius and the Vilnius region, as contained in the Soviet Union–Lithuania Mutual Assistance Pact (10 October 1939). Lithuania took possession of sixty-nine hundred square kilometers of territory, hitherto occupied by the Red Army, on 28 October 1939. Numerous arrests, as well as looting of property, took place prior to the Soviet withdrawal. But the Soviets were back in mid-June 1940, when they imposed Soviet rule on all of Lithuania and incorporated it into the Soviet Union on 3 August 1940 as the Lithuanian Soviet Socialist Republic.

Annexation of the Eastern Territories of the Second Republic

In September 1939, the aggressors wanted to rapidly dismantle the structures of the Polish state and install new authorities in the occupied territories. At the news that the Red Army had crossed the border with Poland, communists and their sympathizers started establishing self-styled organs of the Soviet system ("revolutionary committees," "peasant committees"). They sprang up in places where the Polish military and police presence was weak. It was these committees—with the assistance of the "militia" and "worker guards"—that began "keeping order" and protecting public buildings.

However, the main role in establishing the structures of the new system was played by the Red Army, strengthened with party activists and NKVD officers. On 8 September, NKVD chief Lavrentiy Beria ordered the creation of nine operational groups, which—proceeding in the footsteps of the lead units of the Red Army—were tasked with "taming" the captured territories (which included taking over communications, radio stations, banks, treasury offices, archives, printing plants, and prisons and arresting landowners, capitalists, civil servants and members of the uniformed services, and leaders of parties and social organizations).

Contrary to Soviet claims that, in 1939, the working masses spontaneously took part in a sociopolitical revolution in Poland's eastern territories, there is no doubt that the operation had been planned in Moscow and carried out by its military and security forces. An NKVD directive of 15 September and directives by Red Army war councils of 16 September contained a list of tasks to be undertaken in the occupied territories. After entering each town, the Soviet forces were supposed to establish ("in the name of the army, as the sole authority") a provisional management—rather than a revolutionary committee—composed of a political officer of the Red Army (as the chair), a member of an NKVD operational group, and one "representative" each from among the local workers and the leftist intelligentsia. In the countryside, peasants' committees were to be set up with members from among the poorer farmers. Moreover, assistance was to be provided with the organization of Worker Guard units, and measures were taken to prevent the new authorities from being infiltrated "by counterrevolutionary elements and *agents provocateurs* with hostile intentions."

The directives also spelled out procedures designed to "legitimize" the seizure of the occupied territories. In order to "settle" the issue of the character of the new authorities and the mode of their appointments, the order was given to hold ("after thorough preparations") general elections for three people's assemblies: Ukrainian ("in the Voivodeships of Western Ukraine"), Belarusian ("in the Voivodeships of Western Belarus"), and Polish ("in Voivodeships with a Polish majority"). They would have the task of approving the seizure of land estates by peasants' committees, resolving the issue of the character of the political system (whether Soviet or other), and deciding on accession into the Soviet Union (the Ukrainian voivodeships into the Ukrainian SSR, the Belarusian voivodeships into the Belarusian SSR, and the Polish ones into the Polish Soviet Union Republic).

In November 1939, NKVD, local militia, and railway militia were established in the occupied territories; between December 1939 and February 1940, judicial and prosecution organs were put in place, thanks to the arrival of personnel from the east.

The new reality in the occupied territories of the Second Republic was shaped strictly according to the Kremlin's plan. In essence, it provided for the annexation of the occupied territories and their rapid unification with the Soviet Union. The project was executed by the military, designated functionaries of the Communist Party, and the NKVD. They were implementing the relevant resolution of the Politburo of the Central Committee of the All-Union Communist Party (Bolsheviks), of 1 October 1939. Thus, on 22 October, "elections" were held for the People's Assembly of Western Ukraine and the People's Assembly of Western Belarus. In late October 1939, the two bodies adopted a number of declarations: the proclamation of the Soviet system of government and a request for admission into the Soviet Union; the confiscation of large land estates and the nationalization of land, forests, and bodies of water; and the nationalization of banks and major enterprises. Western Ukraine and Western Belarus were admitted into the Soviet Union at the Fifth Extraordinary Session of the Supreme Soviet of the USSR (31 October–2 November 1939).

"Passportization"

On 29 November 1939, the Presidium of the Supreme Soviet adopted a decree (unpublished): "On the acquisition of citizenship in the USSR by the inhabitants of the western districts of the Ukrainian and Belarusian SSRs." The decree imposed Soviet citizenship on the following categories of persons: (1) "former Polish citizens" who were in Soviet-occupied territories at the time of their incorporation into the Soviet Union (1 and 2 November 1939, respectively); (2) persons who had legally arrived in the Soviet occupation zone from the German occupation zone; and (3) persons (Polish citizens) who had moved to the Soviet-occupied territories in connection with the transfer of the Vilnius region to Lithuania.

On 30 December 1939, the Soviet government introduced an internal passport system in the occupied territories. It applied to the populations of district and regional centers, to worker-housing estates, state farms, the railways, new construction sites, and an area within seven and a half kilometers of the border. All persons aged sixteen or older had to register with the authorities. The "passportization" was implemented in the spring of 1940. Persons who were refused a passport or who—as political uncertainties—had a special annotation made on their identification papers, were forced to move to distant provincial localities. Usually, that meant the loss of one's job and home. Persons who refused to accept the new ID were in most cases arrested and deported. The "passportization" was used to purge the occupied territories of persons hostile to the Soviet system.

Nationalization of Assets

The appropriation by the Soviet state of Poland's economic assets in the occupied territories started even before the People's Assemblies passed the relevant "decisions." The process was implemented in stages and lasted until the spring of 1940. Abandoned plants and institutions were put at the disposal of the local provisional management, which had the job of restarting them. This process continued until the end of September 1939. Elsewhere, "worker control" was introduced. With time, the workers "learned to run the plants without the capitalists," then removed the latter from managerial positions and prepared the ground for formal nationalization.

On 1 October 1939, the Politburo decided to nationalize enterprises whose owners had fled or were "sabotaging" their operation. It also instructed the party authorities in Ukraine and Belarus to submit proposals concerning the nationalization of major enterprises and to compile a register of other plants that should also be taken over by the state.

In formal terms, the economic system in the occupied territories was determined by the People's Assemblies, which adopted (on 28 October in Lvov and 30 October in Białystok) declarations on the nationalization of banks and major industry. On 20 November 1939, the state took over the printing, metal, and chemical industries of Western Belarus and, in early December 1939, cinemas and light industry. The process of the nationalization of industrial plants was completed by the Presidium of the Supreme Soviet on 4 December 1939 with the adoption of decrees on the nationalization of those entities in Western Ukraine and Western Belarus. In the "substantiation" of the move, it was explained that the state was pushing ahead with the nationalizations as a result of the incorporation on 1–2 November 1939 of Poland's eastern territories into the Soviet Union. Nationalization applied to enterprises and institutions enumerated in unpublished registers, submitted by the governments of Ukraine and Belarus. Also subject to nationalization were railways, communications, the printing industry, power plants, hotels, swimming pools, bathhouses and other municipal establishments, fisheries, all schools and universities, hospitals, pharmacies, holiday resorts, retirement homes, the residences of wealthy company owners and others who had fled the Bolsheviks, theaters, cinemas, museums, stadiums, zoos, art galleries, public libraries, and large commercial enterprises.

A total of twenty-two hundred large- and medium-sized industrial enterprises were nationalized in Western Ukraine and seventeen hundred more in Western Belarus. The operation was able to move ahead quickly thanks to the appointment of "trusted managerial cadres."

By the time of the German invasion of the Soviet Union, only 13 percent of the private farms in the western districts of Ukraine and only 7 percent of those in the western districts of Belarus had joined collective farms.

To the former owners, mainly Poles and Jews, the new system meant an abrupt loss of the basis of their material existence, confiscation of their property, and marginalization—which led to a radical intensification of anti-Soviet sentiment. At the same time, however, the fundamental structural and ownership changes meant the beginning of modernization and an injection of capital into the industrial enterprises in the region, linking them with the vast market of the Soviet Union. But it also signified the onset of waste, low productivity, and poor on-the-job discipline.

ALBIN GŁOWACKI

The Forms, Scale, and Effects of Repression against Polish Nationals

Arrests

When NKVD officers entered the occupied territories of the Second Republic, they had fairly good knowledge of the communities they intended to neutralize and thus prevent from mounting a resistance movement. They had precise lists of "the most active enemies of the Soviet system," including not only Polish nationals but also Ukrainian, Belarusian, and White Russian émigrés. The lists provided the basis for the arrests of such persons, and the local population supplied other names, as did captured documents, particularly those belonging to the Polish special services. The Soviet authorities thought the greatest threat to their rule was posed by workers of the state and local administration, members of the uniformed services, officers of the intelligence and counterintelligence services, landowners, factory owners, merchants, and teachers, as well as leaders of political parties and social organizations.

According to incomplete data, by May 1941, the NKVD had arrested more than 110,000 people in Poland's eastern territories, of whom Poles constituted 40 percent; Ukrainians, 22.5 percent; Jews, 22 percent; and Belarusians, 7.5 percent. More than 1,100 of them were sentenced to death. A further 7,305 prisoners were murdered on the basis of a criminal decision made by the Politburo on 5 March 1940. After the German invasion of the Soviet Union, the NKVD and the NKGB shot 11,000 selected prisoners in late June 1941. In prisons or during the evacuation, the security forces murdered people charged with or convicted of "counterrevolutionary activity," "economic sabotage," "subversive activities," or "anti-Soviet actions." To the total number of prisoner deaths should be added an estimated several thousand persons who died in prisons and labor camps.

Prisoners of War

Archive materials indicate that the Red Army took several hundred thousand (possibly 450,000) Polish prisoners of war. However, such a high number may be the result of the same POWs being counted more than once. For example, it happened on occasion that, after being disarmed and interrogated, recruits (mainly Ukrainian and Belarusian peasants) were released, detained again by another Red Army unit, and again registered as POWs. Historians believe that, in fact, between 232,000 and 255,000 Polish troops were taken prisoner.

On 20 September 1939, the Red Army started conveying POWs to designated points along the Polish-Soviet border. Contrary to international law, they were then turned over to the political police, that is, the NKVD. From there, they were transported under guard in overcrowded freight trains deep into the Soviet Union. On 19 September 1939, the NKVD set up a Department for POWs and Internees in the Katyn Forest, headed by Pyotr Soprunenko. It was tasked with establishing and supervising eight POW camps: Ostashkov (Kalinin district, today Tver), Yukhnov (Smolensk district), Kozelsk (Smolensk district), Putivl (Sumsk district), Kozelshchany (Poltava district), Starobelsk (Voroshilovgrad district, today Lugansk), Yuzha (Ivanov district), and Oranky (Gorky district, today Nizhnyi Novgorod). The camps were designed to hold a total of 68,000 prisoners. Since the actual number of POWs was considerably higher, two more camps were established: at Gryazovets (Vologda district) and Zaonikiyevo, near Vologda. In all, the Red Army transferred to the NKVD some 125,000 Polish POWs. Soon, it became evident that the authorities were incapable of providing them with suitable accommodations, sanitary conditions, food, or adequate medical care. The camps in most cases were set up in dilapidated former monasteries or sanatoriums and holiday facilities. Some of the prisoners were "housed" in farm buildings (stables, pigpens, barns), cellars, crude dugouts, sheds, and barracks. Overcrowding was prevalent, and the quarters were cold, stuffy, humid, and filthy. The prisoners did not receive regular hot meals, and there were even shortages of water for drinking and washing. In order to gauge the political mood among the prisoners and ferret out those who belonged to "counterrevolutionary groupings" or were officers of uniformed services, intelligence agents, workers of the judiciary, political leaders, or activists of "nationalist" organizations, the camp authorities conducted "operational-reconnaissance" work and recruited informers.

Since the NKVD was unprepared to hold such a large number of POWs, the Politburo decided on 3 October 1939 to send home POW privates from Western Ukraine and Western Belarus (42,500 in total). Those from territories occupied at that time by the Third Reich were to remain in the camps until their future was settled. Army officers, intelligence and counterintelligence officers, police officers, gendarmes, and prison guards were to be grouped in special camps. There was also a decision to keep 25,000 privates and noncoms to serve as road workers until the end of December 1939.

All this resulted in major shifts in the distribution of POWs, with some of the old camps being closed down and new ones established. Having determined the ranks and professional affiliations of the POWs, the Soviets concentrated army and navy officers in the camps at Starobelsk and Kozelsk. The camp at Ostashkov held police officers, gendarmes, intelligence officers, prison guards, settlers, and persons connected with the judiciary and prosecution. More than 15,000 privates and noncoms were dispatched to build the Nowogród-Wołyński-Równe-Dubno-Lvov road (subsequently extended to Przemyśl). A POW labor camp was established at Równe. After that project was completed, the POWs were transferred at the start of 1940 to construct another road, from Płoskirów, Tarnopol, Lvov, and Jaworów to the border with the Third Reich (a camp was established at Lvov). In the autumn of 1939, another 10,000 POWs in this category were forced to start work in mines, steel mills, and quarries of southeastern Ukraine (in POW labor camps at Krivyi Rih, Zaporozhe, and Yelenovka-Karakub).

In October and November 1939, the Soviets transferred 42,500 Polish POWs, and later 600 more, to the German authorities and received 13,700 POWs from the territories occupied by the Third Reich (they were sent to their places of residence to be interrogated by local security officers, as was the case with persons released from NKVD camps). In late December 1939, the Lithuanian authorities handed over to the Soviets 1,700 interned Polish soldiers who had decided to return to their homes in territories occupied by the Soviets. They, too, had to undergo NKVD "filtration" designed to ferret out officers, policemen, gendarmes, prison guards, and civil servants.

By the end of 1939, the NKVD was still holding in its POW camps almost 39,000 Polish citizens, of whom more than 15,000 (39 percent) were incarcerated in special camps and some 24,000 in labor camps. The national composition of the prisoners was such that Poles constituted more than 98 percent of those held in the three special camps and 71.4 percent of those in the labor camps (Belarusians, 21.1 percent; Ukrainians, 3.8 percent; and Jews, 2.8 percent).

Following the Politburo decision of 5 March 1940, more than 14,500 thousand Polish POWs from the Kozelsk, Starobelsk, and Ostashkov camps were shot in April and May 1940 in the Katyn Forest and dungeons of the NKVD prisons in Kharkov and Kalinin (Tver). Only 395 selected prisoners were spared. They were transferred briefly to the Yukhnov camp and then to Gryazovets, where, in the summer of 1941, they were released under an "amnesty." By that time, the NKVD had managed to win over from among them a small number of officers who were willing to cooperate with the Soviet side in establishing a Polish unit within the Red Army. In October–November 1940, those considered most trustworthy (including Col. Zygmunt Berling) were taken in groups of a few persons each to Moscow prisons (Butyrka, Lubyanka) for political talks, and later to Malakhovka, outside Moscow, where they conducted secret staff work. These activities were capped on 4 June 1941 with the decision by Soviet authorities to establish in Central Asia an infantry division, within the Red Army, composed of Poles and other Polish-speaking soldiers.

Meanwhile, after the Red Army occupied Lithuania and Latvia in June 1940, the NKVD immediately took over camps with Polish internees, organized in those countries in 1939. In July–September 1940, they were moved to the camps in Kozelsk (officers, policemen, workers of the judiciary) and in Yukhnov (privates, noncoms, cadets). Poles constituted 98.2 percent of the fifty-two hundred internees. Following their interrogation, Soprunenko, the head of the NKVD Department for POWs and Internees, addressed a memo to Beria suggesting that the cases of fifteen hundred "active and implacable enemies of the Soviet system" be considered by the Special Panel of the NKVD (a repetition of the Katyn crime?). Alas, that did not happen. In May and June 1941, more than thirty-nine hundred prisoners from the camps in Yukhnov and Kozelsk were transported to a camp at Ponoi (Murmansk district), where the construction of a military airfield was planned. The outbreak of the German-Soviet war foiled those plans.

When the POW labor camps in southeastern Ukraine were closed down in spring 1940, two thousand of the Polish inmates were transferred to the Lvov camp and eight thousand of them to the construction site of the North Pechora Kotlas–Vorkuta railway line in the district of Arkhangelsk and the Komi autonomous republic. There they became charges of the Northern Railway Correctional Work Camp of the NKVD.

Relocations and Deportations

The progress of the war, coupled with the repressive policies of the occupiers, resulted in large-scale relocations of Polish citizens. In the territories annexed by the Soviet Union, this lasted from the autumn of 1939 until the summer of 1941.

On 16 November 1939, the Soviet Union and Germany signed an agreement in Moscow on the voluntary evacuation of ethnic Germans (Polish citizens) from the Soviet occupation zone and of Ukrainians, Russians, and Ruthenians from the German occupation zone. It was planned that the operation would be completed by 1 March 1940. Over its course, 128,000 persons were resettled westward. Those arriving from German-occupied territories (more than 13,000) were quartered in buildings vacated by departing Germans and deported settlers.

On 10 November 1939, the Soviet government established a commission tasked with estimating the number of refugees and suggesting ways of dealing with them. In December 1939, the Soviet Union and Germany reached agreement on their exchange. It envisaged the return eastward of Polish citizens of Ukrainian and Belarusian descent and the transfer westward of refugees from the German occupation zone. On 31 December 1939, the Soviet Union decided to admit fourteen thousand refugees from the German occupation zone and give them jobs. However, it appears that relatively few of them (perhaps some two thousand) decided to return.

According to NKVD data, some 150,000 persons (mostly Jews) were seeking refuge in Western Ukraine at that time, of whom more than 44,000 had returned to the German occupation zone by January 1940. In view of the dramatic plight of the refugees, the Ukrainian republican authorities adopted a resolution intended to deal with the problem. The respective ministries were instructed to provide the refugees with jobs concordant with their professions, end overcrowding in living quarters, provide fuel for winter heating, ensure meals in canteens, and provide vocational training and medical care. Children were to attend schools, and illiterate adults were to receive classes in reading and writing. Supplies of shoes, warm clothing, and underwear were to be increased in districts where the refugees were staying. However, considering the practical realities of the time, it is hard to imagine that the resolution was ever fully implemented.

In the period between 18 April and 4 June 1940, another fifty-two thousand refugees (two-thirds of them Poles and one-quarter Ukrainians) returned to the German occupation zone. Meanwhile, forty thousand persons were given jobs in Ukraine, though mainly in the eastern districts of the republic. However, the working and living conditions offered to them disgraced the Soviet authorities: the refugees considered them intolerable, which led to mass escapes, camping at railway stations, returns to the western districts of Ukraine (twenty-five thousand persons), and even demands for relocation to the German occupation zone.

The number of refugees in the new territory of the Belarusian SSR (western districts) was estimated to be more than 120,000 (more than 90 percent of them Jews) at the end of 1939. At the request of the republican authorities, on 16 October 1939, the Soviet government consented to the employment of 20,000 persons (in reality, almost 24,000 were involved) in factories and enterprises (peat digging, construction, lumberjacking) of eastern Belarus and, on 21 October, allowed the payment of 3 million rubles in cash aid to the refugees. As of 1 November, almost 45,000 refugees were registered in the towns of so-called Western Belarus, and, in February 1940, there were 73,000 such persons in the whole republic, two-thirds of them without jobs. On 13 November 1939, the Belarusian party leadership asked Moscow to resettle 50,000 persons from the western districts of the republic.

Since the moves to help the refugees did not produce the desired effects (the local authorities were unable to cope with the problem on their own), on 2 March 1940, the Politburo decided to deport into remote areas of the Soviet Union those who had refused Soviet citizenship and applied for relocation to the German zone. Single refugees were arrested.

Deportations into remote parts of the Soviet Union were the most prevalent form of repressions against Polish citizens. In the years 1940–41, they affected different social and professional groups whom the authorities believed to pose the greatest threat to the new "order." Polish settlers (described by the NKVD as "military-police agents of the Polish government" and "a base for counterrevolutionary activities") were designated on 4–5 December 1939 as the first group for deportation. On 22 December 1939, the Soviet government approved proposals by Ukrainian authorities concerning the utilization of the deported settlers' properties and decided to supplement that category of deportees with forestry workers (foresters, rangers, guards, inspectors). The settlers' land (except land already divided among peasants) was to be allocated to state and collective farms.

The deportations started at dawn on 10 February 1940, in extremely harsh winter conditions. Almost 52,000 Soviets (NKVD officers, militia members, soldiers, party officials, administration workers, and youth activists) were involved in its implementation. More than 140,000 innocent people were taken away in inhumane conditions, mostly in cattle cars. As "special refugees," they ended up in remote special NKVD settlements in seventeen districts, *krais* (territories), and republics of the Russian Soviet Federative Socialist Republic, as well as five districts of Kazakhstan. There, in extremely tough climatic and living conditions, they had to perform exhausting manual work in the forest industry, building industry, and mines. Poles constituted an overwhelming majority of the deportees (81.7 percent), with much smaller groups of Ukrainians (8.8 percent) and Belarusians (8.1 percent).

On 2 March 1940, the Politburo and Soviet government selected another group for deportation: families of people subjected to repression (they were to be deported by 15 April 1940 to Kazakhstan, for ten years) and war refugees. The operation began at dawn on 13 April 1940. More than sixty-one thousand people were affected. Among those deported, Poles constituted a clear majority (74.9 percent), with smaller groups of Ukrainians (19.5 percent), Jews (4.1 percent), and Russians (0.7 percent).

The deportation of refugees started only after the exchange of this group of people with the Germans. Those whom the Germans refused to admit and who had refused Soviet passports were deported on 29 June 1940, in a manner similar to the earlier deportations. They totaled about seventy-nine thousand persons, mostly city dwellers. Jews (84.1 percent) dominated in this group of deportees, which also included Poles (11.3 percent), Ukrainians (2.3 percent), and Belarusians (0.2 percent). Almost seventeen thousand "suspect" single refugees had been arrested earlier, on 25 June, and their cases were submitted for consideration by the Special Panel of the NKVD.

The next round of deportations was organized almost a year later. On 14 May, the Politburo and Soviet government adopted a resolution on "purging" the territories annexed in 1939–40 to remove "anti-Soviet, criminal, and socially undesirable elements." The following categories of persons were to be sent into twenty-year exile: former landowners, factory owners, major merchants, landlords, senior officials, officers, policemen, gendarmes, prison guards, members of families whose heads had been active in clandestine "counterrevolutionary organizations" and were on the run from the authorities or under the sentence of death, "criminal elements," and refugees from Poland who had refused Soviet citizenship. The property of all these was subject to confiscation. On 22 May 1941, more than eleven thousand were deported from the western districts of Ukraine, followed on 14 June by several thousand Polish nationals from Lithuania and, on 20 June, by more than twenty-two thousand people from the western districts of Belarus.

A total of 320,000 persons (more than 60 percent of them Polish) from Poland's annexed eastern territories were deported deep into the Soviet Union in 1940–41.

In order to protect the state border from violations by refugees and others, on 1 February 1940 the Soviet government strengthened its new sections in the western districts of Ukraine and Belarus by establishing border zones of 7.5 kilometers, 500 meters, and 4 meters in width. Entry into and residence in these zones was allowed only for local populations and persons holding passes issued by the militia. On 2 March 1940, the government ordered the relocation of all people living within 800 meters of the border and the dismantling of all buildings. Some 130,000 people were forced to leave the zone.

Conscription into the Red Army

The citizenship regulations also meant that inhabitants of the occupied territories were subject to mandatory service in the Red Army. By registering all men aged eighteen to fifty and women (medical and veterinary service workers, as well as persons with sanitary and nursing training), the authorities were able to estimate the number of able-bodied persons, the degree of their military preparedness, and their social background and nationality. The Polish government protested the registration to the Allies and neutral countries.

The first call-up took place in autumn of 1940. It applied to men born in 1918–19 and those born in 1917 who had not yet served in the Polish army. Conscripts from the "exploiter classes" were inducted into work battalions. The next call-up was conducted in the spring of 1941. After the German-Soviet war broke out on 22 June 1941, Poles from the occupied eastern territories of Poland serving in the Red Army were viewed as untrustworthy—some were arrested and others transferred from combat units to multinational construction battalions. They lived in extremely harsh conditions and were used to build defensive fortifications and transportation routes and to work in arms factories.

According to Polish estimates, between 100,000 and 230,000 persons from the annexed territories of the Second Republic were inducted into the Red Army. Conscription into the army of the occupiers, a military oath of loyalty to a foreign state, dispersal—without knowledge of the Russian language—in the multinational mass of recruits, service in extremely tough climatic and living conditions, and an aggressive "political education" were all treated by these recruits as yet another form of repression.

Indoctrination of the "New Citizens" of the Soviet Union

Educational, scientific, and cultural institutions, as well as the media, were to play a key role in in instilling communist values. Accordingly, these institutions underwent fundamental organizational, programming, and staffing changes.

Classes resumed in schools in late September 1939. At first, Polish teaching programs and textbooks were used, though classes in religion and the history and geography of Poland, as well as in Greek and Latin, were struck from the curricula. The symbols of "bourgeois" Poland were also removed and replaced with portraits of Lenin and Stalin and quotes from the "classics of Marxism-Leninism," the Soviet constitution, and Communist Party documents. Private and monastery schools were closed. Priests and nuns were banned from schools, which assumed a lay character and were separated from the church. Mixed-sex classes were introduced and pupils subjected to crude atheist propaganda. Banned youth organizations were replaced with the Young Pioneers and the Komsomol, tasked with communist indoctrination of youngsters. Collectivism was the rule. The didactic process was conducted under close political control. The new schools disgusted believers, who did not like the changes. However, most people—especially those of modest means—were glad that the schools were now financed out of the state budget. Education became more accessible to children from the countryside and workers' families.

At the beginning of October 1939, there were 6,199 schools in so-called Western Belarus. Of these, 95.7 percent were Polish, and not a single one was Belarusian. After reorganization (and three rounds of deportations), the number of schools was down to 5,643 in October 1940. Belarusian was the language of instruction in 4,278 schools (75.8 percent), Polish was used in 932 schools (16.5 percent), Russian in 173 (3.1 percent), Yiddish in 150 (2.6 percent), Lithuanian in 61 (1.1 percent), and Ukrainian in 49 (0.9 percent).

At about the same time (September 1940), in the western districts of the Ukrainian SSR, schools teaching in the Ukrainian language constituted 84.5 percent of all schools; Polish was the language of instruction in 12 percent of schools, and Yiddish in 2 percent.

All national minority schools either had Ukrainian, Belarusian, or Lithuanian language lessons as a mandatory subject, and Russian lessons were mandatory in all schools.

The need to turn working-class and peasant youth into intelligentsia with a Marxist-Leninist outlook necessitated a speedy reorganization of higher education in the occupied territories. For that reason, commissars and plenipotentiaries were immediately dispatched to Lvov to administer the local Jan Kazimierz University, the Lvov Technical University, the Foreign Trade Academy, and the Academy of Veterinary Medicine.

According to a commission from Moscow tasked with reorganizing the academic schools of Lvov, at the time of the invasion of Poland, there were 9,976 students, 77.9 percent of them Polish, 12.9 percent Ukrainian, 6.7 percent Jewish, and 2.5 percent other nationalities. The social background of the students was such that only 7.7 percent belonged to working-class families, 13.6 percent were from peasant families, 37.7 percent from the families of civil servants, 23.7 percent from bourgeois families, 8.3 percent from the families of merchants, 3.1 percent from landowning families, 3 percent from the families of police and military officers, and 2.9 percent from the families of clergy. The Soviet authorities considered 41 percent of the students to be from the exploiter class. The faculty was 100 percent Polish, and the language of instruction was Polish. The students had to pay tuition.

All of the Lvov academic schools were formally nationalized by decree of the Presidium of the Supreme Soviet of the Ukrainian SSR on 4 December 1939. Education was now free. Student organizations active in Polish times were disbanded and replaced by the Leninist Communist Youth League—the Komsomol.

In the process of sovietizing students, the Ukrainian language was assigned the role of "carrier of socialist values" and Marxist-Leninist ideology. However, Moscow was careful not to stimulate "Ukrainian nationalism." The new lecturers conducted classes in Ukrainian or Russian, which meant that Polish was being forced out. Polish faculty members had to learn Ukrainian.

The Lithuanian authorities closed the Stefan Batory University in Vilnius on 15 December 1939 and established in its place a Lithuanian academic school, treated as a branch of the Vytautas Magnus University in Kaunas. After the annexation of Lithuania by the Soviet Union in the summer of 1940, the school was reorganized and underwent sovietization. Lithuanian became the language of instruction, though Polish and Russian were also used. Lithuanians (51.1 percent) and Jews (29.9 percent) were the predominant groups among the students, with Poles comprising less than 15 percent of the student body.

The same ideological assertiveness spread to the media and the cultural sphere. The old newspapers and publishing houses, now considered "hostile" and "nationalistic," were closed down. The demand for information in the occupied territories led the political apparatus of the Red Army to start publishing local newspapers. National and republican newspapers were also distributed on a mass scale. Soon, the local party, administrative, and Komsomol authorities also launched new publications in Ukrainian, Belarusian, Lithuanian (from 1940), Polish, and Yiddish.

The censored press was used as a propaganda tool to promote communist values, exhort people to harder work and with greater discipline, present the revolutionary past of the nation and party history, and to extol Soviet "achievements."

"Creative space" became restricted—it was only possible to write about certain topics and only in the "correct" spirit. The party also sent a signal to those who refused to toe the line: a group of writers, including the "poet of the revolutionary proletariat," Władysław Broniewski, were arrested in Lvov in late January 1940 and accused of nationalism. But others who decided to collaborate with the regime were rewarded in the autumn of 1940 with admission into the Union of Soviet Writers.

"Bourgeois-nationalistic" publications were withdrawn from circulation and replaced with books on Marxism-Leninism as well as mass political and antireligious literature. New publishing houses (branches of state publishers) appeared; their publishing plans were determined by the party.

The pride of Lvov—the Ossolineum Library—fought hard to keep its Polish character, but it underwent "Ukrainization" in the spring of 1940. Its staff managed to save many priceless treasures of Polish culture, including items received from private collections and land-estate, monastery, and other libraries (almost half a million books). But as a result of the reorganization of the libraries and book trade, Polish culture suffered irrevocable moral and material losses.

The new authorities also seized and appropriated Polish archives.

During the first occupation of Vilnius, the Soviets removed (as war trophies) documents from the former Vilnius, Smolensk, and Vitebsk provincial archives, the collection of the Institute of East European Studies, and many other cultural treasures.

The holdings of the archives in Tarnopol, Sokołów, and Sokal were transferred to the State Archive in Lvov, which was renamed Central Archive of Historic Records. Also established in the same town was the District Historic Archive. It was tasked with appropriating the records of former Polish offices, institutions, enterprises, and organizations.

The network of archives was reorganized and their holdings redistributed, in line with Soviet requirements. Also appropriated were family archives from private collections. Birth registers were seized from parishes and transferred in April 1940 to Register Offices subordinated to the NKVD. The network of new archives was established with the help of experienced archivist-historians sent in from the east; they also replaced the Polish managerial staff of these institutions.

Perhaps the most important ideological confrontation took place between the Communist Party and religious groups. The Soviet authorities, experienced in suppressing religion in the Soviet Union, proceeded cautiously in this area, being well aware of the enormous social role and influence of the main denominations (Roman Catholic, Orthodox, Greek Catholic, and Jewish) and religious organizations. It is symptomatic that the security forces involved in the invasion of Poland were instructed to abstain—"for now"—

from arresting clergy members, particularly Catholic ones. Still, there were instances of the Red Army destroying, looting, and desecrating houses of worship and murdering members of the clergy.

In view of the situation that developed after the aggression of Germany in May 1940 against the Benelux states and France, the premier of the Polish government—despite the state of war with the Soviet Union—recognized the need for a more pragmatic approach to the issue of relations with the Soviet Union. The urgent need to restore the Polish army, lost as a result of the defeat of France, led him to assure London that he would not hinder any talks between the British and Soviet governments. He further suggested that Polish recruits from Poland's eastern territories could be formed into a three-hundred-thousand-strong Polish army to fight the Germans. However, he also emphasized that Poland would not give up its rights, which the Red Army invasion on 17 September 1939 had violated. The relevant memorandum conveyed to the British was quickly withdrawn and the Soviet side was probably never briefed about its content. However, the same issues appeared on the political agenda the very next year.

The process of unification and sovietization of the annexed eastern territories of Poland was disrupted by Germany's attack against the Soviet Union on 22 June 1941. Although less than two years had passed since the beginning of the occupation, it turned out that the Soviets—despite the general stance of society—had managed to install the structures of a foreign system founded on the monopolistic rule of the Communist Party, a pervasive ideology, and a powerful apparatus of repression.

In implementing their policy toward Poland and its population in the eastern territories, in the years 1939–41 the Soviet authorities committed crimes against peace, war crimes, and crimes against humanity.

NATALIA S. LEBEDEVA

THE RED ARMY INVASION AND THE FOURTH PARTITION OF POLAND

THE TOUGH AND dramatic start of World War II used to be on the margins of historical research in Soviet times. Until the middle of the 1980s, Soviet historians and writers simply regurgitated articles from the notorious communiqué "Falsifiers of History." They fully justified the Soviet-German treaties of 1939, denying the existence of secret protocols related to these treaties, and they also praised the Soviet Union's prewar policy, claiming that it was designed to ensure peace and security for the Soviet population. Alongside Germany, the governments of England, France, and the United States were alleged to be the main instigators of the war. It was claimed that Poland had ceased to exist as a state by 17 September 1939, and they called the Red Army's operations there "the liberation campaign in Western Belarus and Western Ukraine." Cooperation between the Soviet Union and Germany in the period dating from autumn 1939 to June 1941 was simply "forgotten," as was the fourth partition of Poland, sovietization, deportations, and mass repressions in those areas annexed in September 1939.

Significant changes did not occur until the late 1980s. At this time, historians and the general public alike began to revise their view of Soviet foreign policy from 1939 to 1941. The abolition of censorship opened up access after the collapse of the Soviet Union to many previously closed archives, while new funds allowed academic research to be intensified. Tens of thousands of documents were brought to light and published, indicating details of the activities of Stalin, Molotov, the Politburo of the All-Union Communist Party (Bolsheviks), the People's Commissariat for Foreign Affairs, the People's Commissariat for Internal Affairs, the People's Commissariat for State Security, and other authorities in the 1939–41 period. Volume XXII of *Foreign Policy Documents, 1939,* dealt with not only the Soviet-German treaties and secret protocols but also the abundance of material related to their preparation, as well as detailing other aspects of Soviet-German relations such as the sovietization of the territories annexed to the Soviet Union. Volume XXIII of *Foreign Policy Documents, 1939,* contained materials belonging to the period between 1940 and early 1941. These covered Soviet-German relations in detail. In 1992, Russian and Polish researchers and archivists started work on a four-volume edition of the Katyn documents. Russian-Polish volumes of materials on the Polish underground in the Soviet Union in 1939–41 and on deportations in 1940 were also published at that time.

Many works, published in the 1990s, detailed the fourth partition of Poland, the fate of Polish prisoners of war, and mass repressions. Nevertheless, recognition of the historical realities was quite complicated in the Soviet Union and post-Soviet Russia. Even today, there is no consensus in Russian society on the "Polish" policy of Stalin, as well as on many other issues. There is a fairly widely held view that, in August 1939, the Soviet authorities, not believing that Great Britain and France's appeasement policy would lead to any decisive steps in holding back the Nazis, agreed to sign a nonaggression pact with Germany, thus winning time to prepare for war.

On 11 April 1939, Hitler issued a directive, codenamed Fall Weiss (Case White, or the White Plan), to prepare for an attack on Poland; it was to be ready to implement by 1 September. On 23 May, at a meeting with the top military ranks, Hitler announced, "There is no room for mercy on Poland and there is only one solution left: to attack Poland as soon as possible. A replay of the Czech scenario is out of the question. It shall come to military action. Our goal is to isolate Poland. The success of this isolation is critical." Speaking on 22 August 1939 in front of the Wehrmacht's top commanders, Hitler clearly defined the goal as the destruction of Poland. "This is not about reaching a certain milestone or a new boundary, this is about the destruction of the enemy," he stressed.

As for Stalin, he had far-reaching ambitious plans of his own—collecting the territories of the former Russian Empire lost during revolution and the civil war and also a weakening of Western democracies and the Axis powers as a result of the war.

The actions of Hitler's Germany and Stalin's Soviet Union, which had concluded a nonaggression pact with a secret additional protocol attached to it on 23 August 1939, were aimed at eliminating the national sovereignty and territorial integrity of the aforementioned countries, and, as such, they harshly violated the generally accepted rules of international law.

It was at the end of August and September that relations between Moscow and Berlin were closest. It was at this point that Hitler was most willing to make concessions to the Kremlin. However, as the Third Reich was solving its problems, the role assigned to the Soviet Union was changing. The German authorities' interest in the Soviet Union began to weaken in October 1939, whereas the importance of Germany in the Soviet Union's foreign policy increased until the autumn of 1940.

At the fourth extraordinary session of the Supreme Council of the Soviet Union, Vyacheslav Molotov, chair of the Council of People's Commissars, stated in his speech on the ratification of the Soviet-German pact on 31 August that the Soviet Union and Germany "are no longer enemies" and that the treaty of nonaggression between them "is a turning point in the history not only of Europe but of other parts of the world." The next day Hitler told the Reichstag that he could "support every word delivered in the speech by the Russian People's Commissar of Foreign Affairs Molotov."

Around 5:00 a.m. on 1 September 1939, the Luftwaffe attacked Polish airfields, launching a massive military campaign against the Rzeczpospolita. Believing that Great Britain and France, who had provided guarantees for the independence of Poland, would not initiate active military operations, the German command left its western front vulnerable and sent most of its forces—nearly two million soldiers, accounting for two-thirds of all German forces—to Poland. The Wehrmacht was distinguished by its modern level of communications, high-tech equipment, and motorization, which, in comparison with the Polish army and its horse-drawn sweep, increased the rate of their advance by four to five times and made maneuver easier. Five German armies attacked Poland from the north and the south, with the aim of uniting their forces, which were greatly superior, especially in tanks and aircraft. The main attack was carried out by the Tenth Army, which had the task of swiftly taking over the middle course of the Wisła River and capturing Warsaw. The actions of the main southern division were covered by the Eighth Army from the north, which passed through Łódź to occupy Warsaw. The task of the nine hundred thousand Polish troops, as they covered a front more than fifteen hundred miles long, was to provide stiff resistance to the enemy and stave off defeat before the Allied states in the West took action. However, for the Polish side, the events of the first week of war developed extremely unfavorably. Armies and support units abandoned almost every point along the main line of defense, retreating across the whole front. Still, the Nazi forces did not destroy the Polish forces in the battles along the banks of the great Wisła River, as had been the original intention.

On 3 September, England and France declared war on Nazi Germany. The British Crown Dependencies—Canada, South Africa, Australia, and New Zealand—as well as French and British colonies, including India, all joined the war. However, England and France did not provide any real assistance to Poland, although they initially had a great superiority of forces on the western front.

Fascist Italy took the position of a "nonbelligerent ally"; Japan announced that it would not interfere with the war in Europe; the United States reported its neutrality. At this stage of the war, the Soviet Union evaded giving a clear definition of its position.

Nevertheless, on 1 September, the military and political cooperation between the Soviet Union and the Third Reich began. From this day, with the consent of Molotov, as head of the Soviet government, the Soviet radio station in Minsk was used as a radio beacon to guide German aircraft in combat operations with Poland. Germany received the consent of Moscow to use the port of Murmansk as a transit point for German goods and to use it to dock their cargo and passenger ships. Later, the Reich was provided with a repair facility for its submarines and auxiliary cruisers. All of these actions showed serious violations of Soviet neutrality in favor of Germany during the first days of World War II.

On 3 September, as he presented his credentials to Hitler, Aleksandr Shkvartsev, the new Soviet ambassador in Berlin, gave a speech composed in Moscow and approved by Molotov. It stated that the "peoples of the Soviet Union were very pleased to see an improvement in relations between the Soviet Union and Germany. The nonaggression pact between Germany and the Soviet Union lays a solid foundation for friendly and fruitful cooperation between these two great European states in economic and political areas, thereby narrowing the potential for possible military conflict in Europe and responding to everyone's interest to restore peace to the world." The Führer responded by saying that the German nation was happy that the nonaggression pact between Germany and the Soviet Union had been concluded. He assured the ambassador that the war would destroy Poland and eliminate the situation that had existed since 1920 under the Treaty of Versailles.

On 4 September, Friedrich-Werner Graf von der Schulenburg, the German ambassador in Moscow, related to Molotov the main contents of Foreign Minister Joachim von Ribbentrop's telegram, which indicated that the defeat of the Polish army would take a few weeks; as a result, areas within the sphere of German interests would be occupied. The Reich minister offered to find out "whether the Soviet Union would see it as profitable to attack the Polish armed forces at certain points within the sphere of Russian interests and to then occupy that territory." Ribbentrop wrote that this "will free us from the need to destroy the remnants of the Polish Army, chasing them up to Russian borders," something that would not only be a relief for the German side but "would also correspond to the spirit of the Moscow agreements and Soviet interests." Aleksandr Chubarian, the prominent Russian historian, notes that, "in Berlin, of course, they were aware of the worldwide effects that would be felt if there were a new partition of Poland." Realizing this potential impact, the Soviet authorities chose to delay bringing Soviet troops into Poland until there was evidence of its imminent defeat.

On 4 September, Molotov handed Schulenburg the answer: "We agree that at the appropriate time we will need to commence certain activities. But we believe that this time has not yet come."

Nevertheless, since the beginning of the war, the Soviet authorities had been taking military, economic, and ideological measures to prepare for the Red Army's invasion of Poland. On 1 September 1939, the Supreme Soviet implemented a law on military conscription while, at the same time, the Politburo decided to increase the number of rifle divisions in the Red Army from 51 to 173. On 3 September, the same authority prolonged military service in the Red Army by an extra month and ordered sergeants (in total, 310,632 soldiers) to be ready. They also ordered training sessions for designated personnel to be held in the Leningrad, Kalinin, Belorussian, and Ukrainian military districts, as well as for aerial surveillance, communications, and transport units, so they could alert air defense units and so on. On 6 September, the commissar of defense ordered large training sessions in the seven military districts; it was the start of a secret military mobilization.

On 8 September, the Politburo and the Soviet of People's Commissars approved a joint resolution to significantly decrease civilian cargo and passenger trains during the period of 10–20 September. Their aim was to free up the railroad for military purposes. On 10 September, the Politburo requested that the Economic Soviet provide the army and navy with a constant supply of foodstuffs, clothing, and other provisions and that the Defense Committee provide weapons, equipment, ammunition, and transport.

The party's highest body undertook other measures in order to prepare for the so-called liberation campaign in Western Belarus and Western Ukraine, which entailed the annexation of the eastern Kresy area of Poland. The People's Commissariats for Internal and Foreign Affairs were ordered to urgently systemize information about Poland and submit their notes to Andrei Zhdanov, the secretary of the Politburo. The note sent by Lavrentiy Beria, the people's commissar for internal affairs of the Soviet Union, described the state structure of the Rzeczpospolita, its ethnic composition, its economy, its military, and its transportation systems. It also pointed out that Poland's president had powers that went "far beyond the functions and rights of any president of a bourgeois-democratic state," stressing that "the Polish constitution does not promise any social security or guarantee of employment. It does not guarantee any freedoms, it does not prohibit the exploitation of children, and it does not provide any means for the protection of mothers and children." It was stated that the population of the country was 34.5 million people, that ethnic minorities, according to Beria's office, constituted 40 percent of the population. The largest ethnic minorities consisted of 7 million Ukrainians, 3 million Jews, 2 million Belorussians, 1 million Germans, and 100,000 Lithuanians living in Poland. It was also documented that in the Stanisławów, Tarnopol, Nowogródek, Brześć Litewski, and Wołyńskie voivodeships, Poles accounted for less than 25 percent of the population; in the Lwowskie and Wileńskie voivodeships, less than 50 percent; and in Białystok, more than 50 percent. This information was used to find a legal justification for "returning" these lands to Soviet Ukraine and Soviet Belorussia. Information was provided on all branches of the Polish Armed Forces and means of defense.

The board of the Comintern was assigned the task of preparing fact sheets about Western Ukraine, Western Belarus, and Polish government policy. At the beginning of the war, the Comintern authorities did not punish the communist parties of various countries for issuing statements that condemned German aggression, supported Polish sovereignty, and appealed to other countries to fight Nazism and fascism. However, on 7 September, Georgi Dimitrov, the secretary general of the board of the Comintern, was summoned to Stalin's office. The "Man of Steel" explained to him, "This current war is being fought by two groups of capitalist countries . . . to take over the world, for world domination! We do not mind them fighting away and weakening one another." Describing Poland as a fascist state that repressed Ukrainians, Belorussians, and other ethnicities, Stalin explained that destroying Poland would lead to expanding the socialist system into new territories and countries. On 8 September, a directive was sent out to the various communist parties emphasizing that the ongoing war was imperialistic and unjust and that all the belligerent, "bourgeois" nations were held equally responsible for the war: "The war cannot be supported in any country, by any working class[,] and let alone by the Communist Party. . . . This current war is being fought by two groups of capitalist countries for world domination. The international proletariat cannot in any way defend a fascist Poland, which rejected the help offered by the Soviet Union, and repressed other ethnic groups."

Along with political preparations for the invasion of Poland's eastern regions, military preparations intensified as well. On 7 September, Stalin and his generals met in the Kremlin. These generals were soon to play a key role in the Polish operation. During the period of 7–16 September, reserves were ordered to be drafted from five military districts, several military units were to be redeployed to the western frontier, and new divisions and corps were to be formed. Large and powerful task forces were formed, becoming part of the Kiev Special Military District and the Belorussian Special Military District, and later on becoming armies in themselves. Designated personnel (11,915 in total) assigned to ships from the Baltic, Black, Northern, and Far Eastern fleets were sent to training.

In connection with the previously unconfirmed information from the Third Reich concerning the Nazi occupation of Warsaw, Molotov sent congratulations and warm regards to the German government on 9 September.

He also told Schulenburg that "the Soviet military action is set to start in the next few days." That same day, Kliment Vorosilov, the defense commissar, and Boris Shaposhnikov, the Red Army's chief of staff, signed directives number 16633 to the Military Council of the Belorussian Special Military District and number 16634 to the Military Council of the Kiev Special Military District. The directives concerned the crossing of the Belorussian and Ukrainian fronts, to be attempted on the night of 12 September 1939. The Soviet-Polish border was also to be crossed, with the objective of defeating the Polish army. The directives contained tasks for each army division to complete, with the end result that the Belorussian and Ukrainian fronts were established on 11 September. On 10 September, Molotov informed Schulenburg that three million people had already been mobilized.

On 8 September, Beria signed orders for nine operational teams consisting of fifty to seventy security officers, to be attached to the army groups in the Kiev Special Military District and the Belorussian Special Military District. Each operational team of security officers kept an eye on three hundred soldiers. To carry out all the necessary activities, Vsevolod Merkulov, Beria's first deputy and head of security, was sent to Ukraine, and Viktor Bochkov, the chief of the Special Department of the People's Commissariat for Internal Affairs of the Soviet Union, was sent to Belarus. Traveling with the army groups, the security officers had to establish local authorities (temporary administrative bodies) and offices of the People's Commissariat for Internal Affairs in each populated area in order to establish order and to suppress subversion.

News about Warsaw still holding the field caused the Red Army to postpone the planned crossing of the Soviet-Polish border. On 10 September, Molotov told Schulenburg that the Soviet Union was going to declare that, as a result of the attack of the German troops, Poland had ceased to exist and therefore the Soviet Union was compelled to defend the Ukrainians and Belorussians from the German threat. "This pretext makes the intervention of the Soviet Union look plausible in the eyes of the masses and allows the Soviet Union to avoid looking like an aggressor," said the people's commissar.

The success of the German attack prompted Molotov to inform Schulenburg on 14 September that "the Red Army was ready sooner than expected. That is why Soviet action can start ahead of schedule. Taking into account the political motivation behind the Soviet actions (the fall of Poland and protection of Russian "minorities") it would be extremely important not to start activities before the fall of the administrative center of Poland, Warsaw." The next day, Ribbentrop replied that the fall of Warsaw would happen in a matter of days. At the same time, he rejected the Soviet thesis concerning the need to protect the Ukrainian and Belorussian peoples from Germany and sent a draft bilateral communiqué to Moscow that stated, "In view of the apparent division among ethnic groups in the former Polish state, the Government of the Reich and the Soviet Government consider it necessary to put an end to the intolerable political and economic situation which currently prevails in the Polish territories. They consider it their common task to restore peace and order in their natural spheres of influence and to reach this new order by creating natural boundaries and viable economic organizations." This text tended to equate the actions of Germany and the Soviet Union and, as such, was unacceptable to Moscow. Molotov told Schulenburg that the Soviet side doubted the need for communiqués. The best rationale for Soviet military action was considered to be the arguments regarding the termination of the Polish state and the need to protect the Ukrainian and Belorussian brothers. Understanding the concerns of Berlin, Molotov agreed to give up the argument of defense against the German threat.

On 14 September, Stalin decided to start the attack on Poland in three days' time. That same day, Voroshilov and Shaposhnikov sent directives to the Belorussian and Ukrainian fronts ordering the Soviet forces to attack at 5:00 a.m. on 17 September. At the Belorussian front, where the commanding general was Lt. Commander Mikhail Kovalev, four army divisions (Polotsk, Minsk, Dzerzhinsk, Bobruisk divisions) and one mechanized cavalry division were set to operate. Battle order number 01 for the Belorussian front was issued on the night of 15 September. It stated that "the immediate task of the front is *to destroy and capture the armed forces of Poland, operating to the east of the Lithuania boundary and Grodno-[Kobryń] line*" (emphasis by author). This goal could be achieved by delivering a strong blow to the Polish army at the center of the front in the general direction of Grodno-Wołkowysk. The plan was to completely cut off the "Vilnius Corridor" from the central regions of Poland. The specific operational tasks were received by each army group of the Belorussian Special Military District: the Polotsk division was to occupy the area of Święciany and Michaliszki by the end of 18 September and then move to Vilnius; the Minsk division, while breaking through the front, was to leave the area of Oszmiana Iwie, with some of its units to be sent to help the Polotsk division occupy Vilnius, and the rest to attack Grodno; the Dzerzhinsk division was to continue focusing on the border; the mechanized cavalry group "was to defeat the enemy with a powerful blow, advancing in the direction of Novogrudok Volkovysk, and by the evening of 18 September, it should be set to approach the [Mołczadź] river . . . and then move to [Baranowicze] and attack Volkovysk." The Bobruisk division needed to reach Baranowicze by the evening of 18 September. The Twenty-Third Rifle Corps and the Dnieper flotilla provided a junction with the Ukrainian front, and within two days they were expected to capture Łuniniec.

As part of the Ukrainian front commanded by Gen. Semyon Timoshenko, there were three army groups fighting. The right wing of the front included the Shepetovsky (northern) division (led by Col. Ivan Sovetnikov). It was deployed across the 250-kilometer front, and, by nighttime on 17 September, it was supposed to have occupied Równe and Dubno. By 18 September, it was supposed to have occupied the region of Lutsk, and it was then to move on to Włodzimierz Wołyński. It was this army that subsequently captured the largest number of Polish soldiers—more than 190,000. The Volochisk (later Eastern) division (led by Corps Commander Filipp Golikov) was located in the center of the Ukrainian front, across an area of around 90 kilometers. It was to deliver a powerful blow to the Polish troops on 17 September in the vicinity of Tarnopol, and the next day it reached Busko, Przemyślany, and Bóbrka, and then proceeded farther to attempt the occupation of Lvov. The Kamenetz-Podolsk (Southern) division (led by Lt. Commander Ivan Tulenev) was deployed over a radius of 70 kilometers in the direction of Stanisławów and Drohobycz. This division had the task of defeating enemy units, and, by 17 September, it was supposed to be approaching the Strypa River and, by 18 September, the areas of Halicz and Stanisławów, moving on to attack Stryj and Drohobycz in order to cut off the enemy's escape route to Romania and Hungary.

Thus, the documents show that a detailed campaign plan had been developed and specific orders were given to conduct an offensive against the neighboring sovereign state. The troops were sent not to free and protect the Ukrainian and Belorussian population (had they been doing so, they would have needed to push Polish units back only to Romania and Hungary) but to destroy and totally defeat the Polish army, in which Stalin's authorities had seen a potential enemy for years.

By 16 September, German forces occupied nearly half the territory of Poland. However, Warsaw and Modlin were still holding out, the battle on the Bzura River continued, and the coastal defense lines were still in place. Severe battles went on in the Lublin area, and Lvov was holding out. Measures were taken to strengthen the so-called Romanian bridgehead. In the ranks of the Polish army at that time there were around 600,000 soldiers, 250,000 of whom continued to fight the Germans.

On 17 September at 2:00 a.m., Stalin sent for Schulenburg and told him that the Red Army would cross the Polish border at 6:00. He read aloud the Soviet government's message to Poland and took the advice of the ambassador into account, readily accepting corrections to the text. The final version of the message stated that "the Polish-German war has revealed the internal inconsistencies which plague the Polish state. Warsaw no longer exists as the capital of Poland. The Polish government has collapsed and shows no signs of life. This means that the Polish state and government have effectively ceased to exist. Therefore, any treaties between the Soviet Union and Poland are no longer of legal consequence. Poland, left to itself and without leadership, has become a breeding ground for all kinds of contingencies and surprises which could pose a threat to the Soviet Union."

At 3:00 a.m. on 17 September, Vladimir Potemkin, the deputy foreign minister, tried to hand a note to Grzybowski, the Polish ambassador, who had been roused out of bed. Potemkin later told Stalin that, after reading the note,

> the ambassador, agitated, could hardly pronounce his words and told me that he could not approve the note handed to him. . . . He rejects the estimation of the military and political situation in Poland. The ambassador says that the Polish-German war has just begun and it is impossible to talk about the collapse of the Polish state. The main forces of the Polish Army are safe and are preparing for a resolute rebuff to German armies. Under these conditions, any crossing of the border by the Red Army is an unprovoked attack on the Republic. . . . If it happens, it will mean a fourth partition of Poland.

Interrupting the ambassador on the pretext that he needed to contact Molotov, Potemkin ordered a staff member of his secretariat to take the Soviet message to the Polish embassy.

Grzybowski was right—the text of the Soviet message did not match the real situation. The capitulation of Warsaw was signed only on 28 September, and the "Polesie" army group held the field until 5 October. The Polish president, government, and high command were at this time still in the country and even attempting to regroup the troops.

At dawn on 17 September, without a declaration of war, a section of the Red Army entered Poland, thereby authorizing military action against its army and violating the peace treaty with Poland signed on 18 March 1921, as well as Litvinov's protocol of 9 February 1929, prohibiting the use of war as an instrument of national policy. It also violated the 1933 convention defining aggression; the treaty of nonaggression between the Soviet Union and Poland of 25 July 1932, as well as the protocol renewing this treaty up to 1945; and the joint communiqué issued by the Polish and Soviet governments in Moscow on 26 November 1938 in order to reaffirm that the basis for peaceful relations between the two countries was the treaty of nonaggression of 1932. The absence of a formal declaration of war by the Soviet Union, as well as by Poland, did not change the fact that a massive incursion by the Red Army into the territory of a sovereign state meant a state of war existed between the countries.

On 17 September, the representatives of twenty-four states were given notes stating that the Soviet Union would be pursuing a policy of neutrality with respect to those states. The same day, Molotov made a radio announcement "to the citizens of the Soviet Union." Repeating once again the point about the "inconsistency" of the Polish state, he also added new arguments: the location of the Polish government was not known, the previous treaties had lost effect, and thus the Soviet Union had decided to lend "a willing hand to our brothers"—the Ukrainians and Belorussians living in the Polish territories. The propaganda in the Red Army had very distinctive features. It focused on the "revolutionary war offensive," the purpose of which was to abolish the capitalist oppression of fellow brothers, that is, Ukrainians and Belorussians who had been "under the yoke of the Polish gentry" for a long time.

From the first days of the Red Army's operations, there were twenty-eight rifle divisions, seven cavalry divisions, ten armored brigades, and seven artillery regiments. In total, there were more than 466,000 personnel, nearly 4,000 tanks, more than 5,500 guns, and 2,000 aircraft. These units alone could outweigh the whole Polish army in strength. Directly on the border, the troops of the Ukrainian front prevailed only on the Polish part of the Frontier Corps. The area of Sarny was reasonably well fortified, protected as it was by an interservices team of 10,000 troops. In Równe, the remaining units of the Seventh, Eighth, and Eleventh Polish divisions were being reformed. The staging area for those units unfit for action and those to be merged with new compounds were located at Kovel and Dubno. In the area of Tarnopol, there were six infantry divisions that had lost many of their soldiers in battles against the Wehrmacht. Gen. Władysław Langner led the division, which included 15,000 infantry and cavalry in charge of defending Lvov from the advancing German units. In total, by 15 September, across the eastern provinces there were about 340,000 Polish soldiers and officers, 540 guns, and more than 70 tanks.

The Soviet invasion of Poland shocked the West. The Soviet Union was accused of aggression, and its actions were associated with imperialistic ambitions. The head of the French government, Édouard Daladier, summoned the Soviet ambassador, Yakov Suritz, and told him that the "all-shocking" actions of the Soviet Union, in his opinion, were a glaring contradiction with the "previously declared neutrality." In his words, "For the French government there was a crucial issue: is there a single German-Soviet front, is this a joint action or not?" Following the publication of the Soviet-German communiqué, any last doubts vanished. However, the ruling circles of Britain and France had not issued a guarantee to Poland regarding a violation of its integrity by the Soviet Union and rejected attempts to induce them to break all relations with Moscow in order not to "throw the Soviet Union in the arms of Germany." At the same time, Paris and London put forward an argument that the border established by the Allies had always been the Curzon Line. As for the borders defined by the Riga Treaty, only many years later were they registered by the conference of ambassadors, and only under the "responsibility of signatories."

For the government and the supreme military command of Poland, the

Red Army invasion was a complete surprise. Assuming that the Soviet troops were brought in to prevent the Wehrmacht from occupying a significant part of their country, and based on the fact that a fight on two fronts was impossible, the Polish authorities decided to fight only against the Nazis. The army, as a rule, implemented the orders of its commander in chief, Edward Rydz-Śmigły, who ordered his soldiers not to fight the Soviets, except in cases where they were trying to disarm Polish units. Formations approached by Soviet troops had to negotiate with them in order to transfer the garrison to Romania or Hungary.

On 17 September, speaking on the radio, Molotov stressed that the Polish state was bankrupt and had in fact ceased to exist. The next day, the Soviet-German communiqué drawn up by Stalin was signed. This communiqué clearly defined the main intention of the Soviet Union and Germany in the war against Poland as the desire "to restore order and peace in Poland, currently disturbed by the collapse of the Polish state, and to help the people of Poland to rearrange the conditions of their existence as a state." In fact, Poland had been liquidated as an independent state.

As witnessed by Ernst Koestring, the military attaché of Germany in Moscow, military cooperation between the Soviet Union and Germany had been developing continuously and without any obstacle, especially during fighting by Soviet and German units in Poland from 17 September to 6 October 1939.

At 5:00 a.m. on 17 September, the Belorussian front forces crossed the border and were free to move west at nearly fifty to seventy kilometers per day. The Polotsk division, defeating the detachments of the Frontier Corps, took Święciany by the evening of the following day and went on to the area of Postawa. The Minsk group had captured Mołodeczno by 3:00 p.m. and by the end of the following day had captured the fortified area on the Oshmiany-Kurmielany-Holszany line. The Dzerzhinsk mechanized cavalry group captured the fortified area of Baranowicze without a fight, then occupied Novogrudok, and then reached the Vilnius-Baranowicze railway line by the end of the following evening. On 17 September, at 5:00 p.m., the Bobruisk group reached Baranowicze, then entered the area to the southwest from the town of Słonim the following day. On the night of 17 September until the next morning, troops from the Belorussian front were initiating the Vilnius operation. Capturing Vilnius with units from the Polotsk division in the north, and from the Minsk division in the south, a tank unit broke into the city on 18 September at 11:30 a.m. and ten thousand Polish soldiers were taken prisoner. By the morning of 19 September, the front troops had reached the Lithuanian border along the Vilnius-Lida-Wołkowysk-Różana-Iwacewicze line. After this, the command suspended the movement of the two army groups on the right, having ordered an infantry outpost to be put in place along the

Lithuanian and Latvian border. From the evening of 19 September, the Belorussian front units began establishing a connection with German troops on the Sopoćkinie-Białystok line and started their occupation of Kobryń. On 22 September, during the course of massive attacks, they broke the stubborn resistance of the defenders of Grodno, having repulsed several tank attacks. They fired machine guns and rifles from the attics of houses and threw incendiary bombs at tanks. From 21–22 September, Soviet troops began coming into contact with the German army, and the Wehrmacht units began to retreat to the west while the Red Army, keeping a distance of twenty-five kilometers, started moving toward the demarcation line. By 30 September, the Belorussian front forces had completed their assigned task.

At 5:00 a.m. on 17 September, army groups at the Ukrainian front also crossed the border and, meeting no considerable resistance, they began to move forward with speed. The most extensive front—230 kilometers—belonged to the Shepetovsky (Northern) division. By the end of the day, it had crossed the Horyń River and, by 18 September, had occupied Równe. The Eastern army division crossed the Zbrucz River at 5:00 a.m. and started "a decisive offensive on the whole front." On 18 September, Zolochev was occupied. The Southern group (later, the Twelfth Army), having crossed the Zbrucz and Seret Rivers, captured Czortków by the end of the day and approached the Strypa River. The left flank of the group moved toward the Dniester River. On 19 September, Soviet troops entered Sokal, Brody, Bóbrka, Rohatyn, and Dolina and approached the outskirts of Lvov. The commander of the front sent a battle report to Stalin, Molotov, Voroshilov, and Shaposhnikov. It stated that "at 12:00 on September 19th, the 36th Tank Brigade occupied Vladimir-Volynsky [Włodzimierz Wołyński]. Six thousand prisoners and many trophies were captured." According to the summary of the General Staff of the Red Army, 120,000 troops were taken prisoner from 17 to 21 September.

Two hours after the Red Army crossed the Polish border, the German troops were ordered to "stay on the Skole–Lvov–Vladimir Volynsky [Włodzimierz Wołyński]–Bialystok [Białystok] line." The next day, the command of the Ukrainian front provided a four-part summary to the staff of three army groups.

First, the high command of the German troops ordered that, in the event of approaching Soviet aircraft, its troops were to show the following signs: (1) a spread white cloth, possibly in the form of a swastika; and (2) green and red missiles, launched alternately.

Second, by the end of the day on 17 September 1939, the German troops occupied the following lines: (1) the Eighteenth Corps by the right flank to the southeast of Sambor, mostly by large units to the west of Lvov, which was surrounded by troops; (2) the Seventeenth Corps by the right flank to

NATALIA S. LEBEDEVA

the east of Jaworów and the left flank, Wiszenka; (3) the Twentieth Corps were moving along the Tomszów–Lubaczów–Rawa Ruska line, with a unit in Komarno; (4) the Seventh Corps was in Janów; (4) the Fourth Corps in Giełczew (thirty kilometers southeast of Lublin); (5) the Nineteenth Corps was in Sławatycze (forty kilometers south of Brześć Litewski), and there were large units in Brest; and (6) the Twenty-First Corps was in Zabłudów and Białystok.

Third, during the Soviet approach to the Germans, the German command asked Soviet troops not to attack at night so as to avoid all kinds of accidents.

Finally, the high command of the German troops issued an appeal that read (in essence, not verbatim), "The army of the Soviet Union has crossed the western border. The meeting between the two countries on the line where they stopped is expected soon. At the meeting of the units from both sides, each battalion of the German troops is to send one officer and say the following words: The German army welcomes the army of the Soviet Union. Both the officers and the soldiers of the German army would like to be on good terms with you. The Red Army is expected to maintain this friendliness in return."

It should be noted that Moscow was alarmed by the information received from Berlin. The chief of the Wehrmacht operational staff of Gen. Walter Warlimont showed a map to the Soviet military attaché on which the future border ran along the Wisła River through Warsaw, but then differed from the arrangements of the secret protocol and left Lvov on the German side. Molotov lodged a strong protest to Schulenburg. By order of Stalin, he once again appealed to the German ambassador, proposing a negotiation in Moscow concerning the fate of the Polish state and the final demarcation of the Soviet-German border along the Pisa-Narew-Wisła-San line. A few hours later, Molotov specified that neither he nor Stalin could agree to the demarcation line crossing the cities along the Przemyśl-Turka-Izotk-Uzhoksky line of passage. Molotov told Schulenburg that the Soviet government insisted on the line across the upper course of the San River, as it was Ukrainian territory. It was "ready to give up [Suwałki] and the surroundings of the railway, but not [Augustów]." As a result, the German leaders agreed to Moscow's demands.

On 20 September, a demarcation line was established along the Pisa, Narew, and Wisła Rivers, and it also spanned the railroad along the San River. The next day, the sides signed the protocol that fixed the order and timing of the withdrawal of German troops to the west all the way to the established line. The withdrawal was scheduled to be completed by 4 October.

By this time, Red Army units had occupied the Kowel–Włodzimierz Wołyński–Sokal line in the outskirts of Lvov. Characteristically, the German troops, who had been surrounding Lvov for ten days, could not get the city to surrender, even under threat of destruction by artillery and air strikes. In the battle for Lvov, German and Soviet troops fired at each other in a number of instances.

However, as Moscow insisted, in accordance with the agreement reached, the German troops began to withdraw to the west. The Eastern army division took over from them, with the order to capture Lvov by the evening of 19 September. In the area of Krasny, the advancing units met with strong Polish army opposition, led by Gen. Wilhelm Orlik-Ruckemann. As a result, by the evening of 19 September, Soviet units were able only to approach the outskirts of Lvov, not to capture the city itself. To help the Lvov garrison, Gen. Kazimierz Sosnkowski's group tried to break in; some units had been sent from the city to help it. However, the large grouping of Soviet forces approaching Lvov destroyed Poland's last hope of defending itself. What is more, on 20 September, it was announced that the German troops had defeated Sosnkowski's divisions. The withdrawing Polish troops in the area of Laszki Murowane were met by Red Army units. The latter completed the work begun by the Germans, having captured a large number of Polish soldiers. General Sosnowski himself escaped to Hungary with some of his troops. On 21 September, Generals Timoshenko and Nikita Khrushchev told Stalin, Molotov, Voroshilov, and Shaposhnikov, "As a result of new fighting in the city at 08:40 on September 22nd, the garrison commander of Lvov, General [Langner], appeared in person at the command post of the commander of the Eastern division, Golikov, and handed us the city of Lvov. There is no water or bread in the city. Measures were taken to provide people with food."

In accordance with the terms of surrender of the city, the Polish garrison was guaranteed escape to Romania or Hungary. However, these promises were not kept. Most of the officers, more than two thousand in total, soon found themselves in the prisoner-of-war camp in Starobelsk, and, between April and May 1940, they were executed, along with the other inmates, in accordance with the decision of the Politburo on 5 March 1940.

Any Polish crossover of the border was aggressively repelled during other operations as well. On 19 September, Timoshenko ordered that Divisional Commander Vasily Osokin, (commander of the Frontier Troops of the Kiev Special Military District) "immediately close the state border in the specified section [along the Zbrucz River and to the west]. Do not allow the Polish soldiers and officers to escape to Romania in any event." Voroshilov demanded explanations from the command of the Kiev Special Military District as to why the section of the border near the town of Kolomyia (Kuty) was not covered, thus allowing Polish troops to escape to Romania. In his report to Stalin, Molotov, and Voroshilov, Grigory Kulik, the deputy people's commissar of defense, also recommended the urgent dispatch to the active areas of the south of an extra strong operational team of the People's Commissariat for

Internal Affairs. He believed that the actions of "several gangs" in the area of the Romanian and Hungarian borders could grow into guerrilla warfare if these territories were not cleared.

As a consequence of the German troops meeting with the Soviet troops, considerable coordination between the Wehrmacht and the Red Army was needed. To such an end, negotiations were held in Moscow 20–21 September; the Soviet side was presented by Voroshilov and Shaposhnikov and the German side by Koestring, the military attaché, and his deputy, Hans Krebs, as well as the air attaché, Lt. Gen. Heinrich Aschenbrenner. As a result of negotiations, the Wehrmacht pledged to prevent "possible provocation and sabotage from Polish gangs and the like" in those towns and villages that were to be handed over to the Red Army; the Red Army commanders also pledged, if necessary, to provide "forces to destroy any units of Polish troops or gangs while the German troops withdrew to their area of occupation."

On 20 September, Defense Commissar Voroshilov informed the commanders of the Northern, Eastern, and Southern army divisions that they must reach the designated line by 8:00 p.m. that day in order to start moving forward again on the morning of 23 September. On 22 September, one brigade commander, Aleksandr Vasilevsky, was informed of this personally, by direct line, while Vatutin received the following directive from the commissar of defense:

(1). The units of the German army, under agreement with us, starting from September 22, are to withdraw to the demarcation line between the German Army and the Red Army, namely, the west bank of the Pisa river up to the mouth, the west bank of the Narew river to the mouth, the west bank of the Bug river to the mouth, the west bank of the Wisła river up to the mouth of the San river, and the west bank of the San river up to its head. (2) In order to avoid all possible provocation and diversion from Polish gangs, the German command shall take the necessary measures to preserve in those cities and towns which are to be transferred to the authority of the Red Army and to pay special attention to the fact that these cities, towns, and important defense and economic structures . . . should be kept from damage and destruction until they are transferred into the authority of the Red Army representatives. (3) I order the troops of the Belorussian and Kiev Special Military Districts to start moving to the established border line at the dawn of September 23, guided by the following: (a) the movement of the troops will be organized in such a way as to allow for an average distance of 25 km between the advance units of the columns of the Red Army and the tails of the columns of the German units. This will allow us to reach the east bank of the [Pisa] river by the evening of September 29 and the east bank of the Narew river by the evening of October 1; (b) in order to resolve issues that may arise while the troops are moving and the German units are transferring areas to the Red Army, special delegates are to be appointed to each of the main lines of movement of our troops. These delegates are to be taken from staff representatives of the division or political headquarters, or from the division or the tank brigade, and they are to contact the delegates of the German units in order to clarify and regulate all issues that might arise. These delegates are to be personally appointed and instructed by the Army's military council; their names shall be reported to the military council of the district as well as to me personally. (4) *Subject to the request by German representatives for the command of the Red Army to render assistance in the destruction of the Polish units or gangs who are standing in the way of small units of the German troops, the command of the Red Army, heads of the columns, if necessary, shall allocate forces to ensure the elimination of obstacles which lie in their way . . ."* [emphasis by author].

Thus, the commissar's order not only provided a basis for interaction between the armies of the two states but also arranged for the units of the Red Army to render tactical support to the Wehrmacht in its struggle against the Polish armed forces.

The strict execution of the order was observed with considerable attention, though incidents could not be completely avoided. On 20 September, to the east of Lvov, the German artillery hit a few Soviet tanks moving in a column. On 23 September, units of the Tenth Armored Division of Gen. Ferdinand Schaal ended up fighting a Soviet cavalry unit by mistake. On the Soviet side, troops fired at German soldiers during their departure from Lvov, in response to which the German high command filed a claim. Shaposhnikov demanded to know whether or not the commanders of the Belorussian and Kiev Special Military Districts had received Voroshilov's directive. Koestring and Vatutin went to the scene of the incident.

After a reprimand from the People's Commissariat, the command of the eastern army group tended to take more care when rendering tactical support to the Wehrmacht. The chief of staff, Savinov, and the military commissar, Detukhin, reported to Vatutin that their representatives, Shipov and Demianov, had agreed with the German command on the need for a liaison officer in order to facilitate the lines of movement and to prevent any more incidents. "The Germans have offered to enter into radio communication with them, for which purpose they have sent preliminary calls and waves. In general, their behavior is politely intrusive," the chief of staff and the commissar of the eastern army group wrote. But the "politely intrusive conduct" of the German high command did not stand in the way of it deceiving its newfound ally. From Stryj they took everything they could, even furniture. Hoping to send from Drohobycz to Germany as much oil as possible, the Germans had delayed the transfer of this area to the Red Army. The commander of the southern group was forced to send a protest against the violation of the troop withdrawal plan. It was pointed out that, on 24 September, according to the schedule, the German troops should have left Drohobycz, Borysław, and Sambor.

But the truth is that the demanding tone was more of an exception than the rule. A submissive attitude toward the Germans was starting to prevail, with all their wishes immediately satisfied. Dismissing Ribbentrop's claim to the oil-producing area of Drohobycz, Stalin still undertook to supply Germany with three hundred tons of oil each year. The following facts are also worth noting: the people's commissar of defense ordered the military councils of the northern, eastern, and southern groups entering Wołyń and Galicia to show a positive attitude toward any colonists of German origin. It was forbidden to carry out requisition, and food and supplies were to be purchased only for cash, at local market prices.

However, the extensive care for the colonists, religious workers, and concessionaires was not all that was on offer. On 23 September, a delegation of four German officers arrived in Lvov; they brought information indicating that, to the west of Hrubieszów, large forces of Poles were gathering (up to three infantry divisions, four cavalry divisions, and artillery divisions). It was said that the German high command was going to attack the flank from the northern direction, with tanks. Divisional Commander Ivanov pointed out in the report to the command of the Kiev Special Military District that, "at the same time[,] they suggest that we take part in joint destruction of the group. The staff of the German troops is in [Gródek Jagielloński], where we are asking to send our delegation." General Timoshenko wrote on the document, "This is not my call. This is a call that the central staff has to make!" Apparently, the "central staff" responded favorably to the German command's idea of a joint operation. In any case, the Eighth Rifle Corps was sent to the area of Hrubieszów, where it joined the battle with the Polish troops. On the morning of 24 September, the commander of the eastern army group gave the commanders of the Second Cavalry Corps, Tenth Tank Brigade, and Ninety-Ninth Rifle Corps the following order:

> According to German commanders, large forces of Poles are grouping in the region of [Zamość], [Tomaszów], and [Hrubieszów]. According to the General Staff, on September 9, in the area of [Tomaszów], the Poles carried out a counterattack against the German units. By the evening of September 23 the Eighth Rifle Corps of the Northern division, situated somewhere between [Hrubieszów] and Sokal, came into contact with the unknown enemy. I give the following orders: (1) the Second Cavalry Corps along with the Twenty-Fourth Tank Brigade are to occupy the districts of [Turynka], Dobrosin, and [Żółkiew] by 16:00 on September 24; they are to be assisted by the advance units of [Lipniki], [Magierów], [Wiszynka Wielka]. The reconnaissance shall be conducted in the direction of the towns of [Krystynopol], [Bełz], and

[Uhnów]. If large forces of the enemy are found in front of the Eighth Rifle Corps, they shall be attacked and captured. Do not allow any attempts by the enemy to break into Lvov.

The operational report for 24 September also noted that, after a day of rest, the Second Cavalry Corps, along with the Twenty-Fourth Brigade, had moved on to the areas of Turynka, Dobrosin, and Żółkiew in order to assist the Eighth Rifle Corps of the Northern division, which had crossed the Bug River and taken Hrubieszów on that very day.

Taking into account the relatively wide acceptance of the "Curzon Line" by the international community as the justified border between Poland and Russia, in addition to Stalin's interest in annexing the Baltic States to the Soviet Union, his conversation with Schulenberg on 25 September showed his willingness to give Germany the Lublin and Warsaw voivodeships in exchange for Lithuania. This information was also passed on to Ribbentrop, who arrived in Moscow on 27 September.

The Treaty on Alliance and Borders between the Soviet Union and Nazi Germany was signed on 28 September in Moscow by Ribbentrop and Molotov, and it established the final boundary of mutual national interests in the territory of the "former Polish state." The reconstruction of the state, to be carried out by Germany in the west and by the Soviet Union in the east, was considered "to be a solid foundation for further development of friendly relations between their peoples." A few secret protocols were added to the treaty to enable Germany and the Soviet Union to exchange their subjects in the new territories. It also stated that "neither side would allow any Polish agitation in their territories to affect the territory of the other side."

In their joint public statement, the Soviet and Nazi governments declared that, having settled "issues that arose as a result of the collapse of the Polish state," they had consequently "created a solid foundation for lasting peace in Eastern Europe." They declared their intention to bring an end to the war, and, in case of their failure, the responsibility for its continuation was assigned to England and France. In such a scenario, the sides were threatening to "consult each other on the necessary measures." Molotov, speaking on 31 October at the fifth session of the Supreme Soviet of the Soviet Union, stated that the concept of "aggressor" did not apply to Germany, adding, "It is not only pointless but even criminal to pursue such a war as that being fought 'to destroy Hitlerism' covered by the fake flag of a fight for 'democracy.'" After this, in an interview with the newspaper *Pravda*, Stalin said that "it was not Germany who attacked France and England; France and England attacked Germany, thus taking responsibility for this war."

Yet, the refusal to annex regions of central Poland to the Soviet Union was met with relief in the West. Paul-Émile Naggiar, the French ambassador in Moscow, remembered how the West paid tribute to the "wisdom of the Soviet government, which managed to find an invulnerable resolution of the issue of the Western Ukraine and Western Belorussia and to refrain from annexing territories inhabited mainly by the Poles." On more than one occasion, the politicians of Great Britain, including Winston Churchill, assured Soviet ambassador Ivan Maisky that there were no irresolvable issues between Great Britain and the Soviet Union as a result of the Polish conflict.

Despite the fact that, on 25 September, Stalin had offered Germany the Lublin voivodeship and the right bank of the Warsaw voivodeship, Red Army units continued to advance into these areas. The command also ordered its units to prevent the withdrawal of Polish units to the north and to eliminate any units of the Polish army it encountered, so as "to occupy [Lubartów] and Lublin through the moving units by the end of September 29." However, on 2 October, it was the Red Army's turn to withdraw its units to the new line of the state border. Voroshilov's directive to Soviet troops that were to be relocated to the Soviet-German border also mentioned the need to observe that, "in those cities and areas being passed over to the German forces, necessary measures are being taken to preserve them from danger and to pay special attention to the fact that cities, towns, and important military, economic, and defensive structures, as well as the roads leading to them, are preserved from damage and destruction before being transferred to representatives of the German Army."

As is known, during the meetings of the German and Soviet armies, joint military parades were held in a number of towns. In Grodno, these parades were hosted by Commander Vasily I. Chuikov in tandem with a German general; in Brześć, Heinz Guderian and Brigade Commander Semyon Krivoshein oversaw the parades.

Overall, during the twelve days of combat operations in Poland, the Red Army advanced 250 to 350 kilometers to the west and occupied a total area of 190 square kilometers (50.4 percent of the territory of Poland), which had a population of about thirteen million people.

During the Polish campaign, 3,500 soldiers and civilians died on the Polish side, and about 20,000 were wounded or went missing. The Soviet side officially announced that there were 737 killed and 1,862 wounded, but these figures seem understated in comparison with other estimates.

Thus, although the Soviet Union did not declare war on Poland, it waged war in close cooperation with Germany. The attack and the military operations were carefully planned, prepared, and implemented with the use of large numbers of troops and weapons. The enormous military might of the Red Army descended upon almost unarmed civilians, upon units that had been ravaged in battles with the Germans, and upon those who showed no resistance, all in concert with orders from their commander in chief. In December 1939, on his sixtieth birthday, Stalin, in response to Hitler's and Ribbentrop's well wishes, wrote an open letter to them: "The friendship between Germany and the Soviet Union, cemented by blood, has every reason to be long and strong." Germany was now bordered by a "friendly country" and would not fear a war on two fronts, as the Führer had said when discussing the issue with Wehrmacht authorities on 23 November 1939.

The battles with the Wehrmacht claimed the lives of 66,300 Polish soldiers and left 133,700 wounded. About 420,000 soldiers were taken prisoner. Hitler's decrees dating from 8–12 October 1939 declared the Polish state annihilated; the Poznań, Pomorze, Śląsk, and Łódź voivodeships, along with parts of the Kielce and Warsaw voivodeships, all together comprising 9.5 million people, were declared German land and annexed into Germany. In the remaining Polish territories, a governorate general of Polish regions was created; a year later this post became known as the Governorate General of the German Empire. The basis of the Nazis' policy was the systematic and merciless destruction of the Polish state, as well as mass murder of the Polish and Jewish ethnicities. Six million lives—this was the price of Hitler's "new order" in Poland. Hans Frank, the governor general of the occupied territory of Poland, wrote in his diary, "I have taken a position that involves managing the conquered eastern territories and carrying out the order to ruthlessly devastate this area as befits an area of war and a trophy country. It is my task to dismember the economic, social, cultural, and political structures of this country." On 3 October 1939, he said that "Poland should be regarded as a colony, the Poles will be slaves of the Great German World Empire."

On the basis of the evidence provided, the Nuremberg International Military Tribunal stated that "occupation policy was aimed at the complete destruction of Poland as an integral nation and at the ruthless exploitation of its human and economic resources for the German war effort. Any opposition was suppressed with extreme brutality. The regime of terror was established, supported by the police courts, which [were] ordered to conduct such activities as public executions of large groups consisting of anywhere [from] 20 to 200 Poles, and widespread executions of prisoners. The system of concentration camps was introduced by the Governorate General through the creation of the notorious Treblinka and Majdanek camps."

On 25 January 1940, Frank announced his intention to move one million workers to Germany, and, by August 1942, eight hundred thousand people had already been deported. By January 1944, of the three million Jews who had lived in Poland before the war, only one hundred thousand were left.

On 1 October 1939, upon completion of the "liberation campaign in the Western Ukraine and Western Belorussia," the Politburo made a detailed statement concerning the sovietization of the captured territories. It decided to convene a "Ukrainian People's Congress" in Lvov on 26 October; this congress was to consist of those who had been elected to represent the regions of

Western Ukraine. In Belarus, there would be a "Belorussian People's Congress" in Białystok consisting of those people who had been elected to represent the regions of Western Belorussia. These "people's congresses" were to be used to approve the transfer of private land to peasant committees, to decide on the nature of power, including the problem of entering the Soviet Union, and to approve the nationalization of banks and major industries. The right to nominate candidates for the "people's congresses" was given to the peasant committees, temporary local administrations, trade unions, and the Workers' Guard. Then, at the district meetings, the "delegates" were to agree on a common candidate for the district. Thus, there was only one person from which to "choose," as was often the case in the elections of the Soviet Union. The campaign was to be carried out under slogans designed to encourage the establishment of Soviet power in Western Ukraine and in Western Belorussia, and their entry into the union as the Ukrainian and Belorussian SSRs, and it came with approval to confiscate private land and to nationalize banks and major industries. On the agenda were "declarations" that had to be adopted; the text of these declarations was prepared by the Central Committees of the Communist Party (Bolsheviks) of Ukraine and the Communist Party (Bolsheviks) in Belorussia.

The Politburo needed to create communist organizations in these territories. To this end, the party admitted "advanced workers who have assisted the Red Army" and demobilized one thousand communists, leaving their fate in the hands of the Ukrainian party organization; a further eight hundred communists were demobilized and sent to the Belorussian party organization. Some two thousand Ukrainian and fifteen hundred Belorussian communists were mobilized to work in the western regions. Prior to the elections in these areas, four interim offices were to begin operations—two from the army authorities, one from the People's Commissariat for Internal Affairs, and one from the temporary administration of the regional city. Temporary regional administrations appointed commissars to the banks, and authorized officers of the State Bank of the Soviet Union were sent to Lvov and Białystok. Virtually every account was frozen. Foreign consulates in the western regions of Ukraine and Belorussia were shut down. Later on, in October, the Politburo adopted several resolutions concerning the organization of elections and other issues that had arisen.

The main methods of dominance in these areas were terror and mass deportations. Even before the end of military action, on 28 September, Lev Mehlis, the head of the political directorate of the Red Army, proposed to Stalin and Voroshilov the idea of granting the military councils of the Belorussian and Ukrainian fronts the right to enact the ultimate measure of punishment in cases of counterrevolutionary crimes by civilians and soldiers from the former Polish army in the newly annexed territories. In a note on the order of approval of sentences (addressed to Zhdanov), Mehlis clarified the situation: "There are a lot of cases and they need to be resolved as soon as possible." On 3 October, the Politburo made a corresponding decision. In addition to military tribunals, the executions were approved by the military collegium of the Supreme Court as well. They were considered by the Commission of the Politburo of the All-Union Communist Party (Bolsheviks) and approved by the supreme authority of the party.

On 4 October, the Politburo assigned the delegates of the Central Committees of Ukraine and Belorussia to work in the party in the voivodeships of Western Ukraine and Western Belorussia. These delegates soon became first secretaries of the corresponding regional committees and were in charge of organizing the sovietization of the territories under their control.

At the end of October 1939, the elections took place, and people's congresses were created in Białystok and Lvov, which proclaimed Soviet power and appealed to the Supreme Soviet of the Soviet Union to be admitted into the Soviet Union. On 1–2 November, the fifth session of the Supreme Soviet of the Soviet Union "reunited" Western Ukraine and Western Belorussia with the Ukrainian and Belorussian SSRs. After the "voluntary" unification of Western Ukraine and Western Belarus, over the next six months the Soviet Politburo made a multitude of decisions regarding the administrative, economic, financial, social, and ideological unification of this area with the rest of the Soviet Union. In addition, steps to eradicate even the lightest forms of resistance were taken.

On 29 November 1939, the Politburo approved the Decree of the Presidium of the Supreme Soviet of the Soviet Union concerning "the acquisition of Soviet citizenship by the people of the western areas of the Ukrainian and Belorussian SSRs." On 30 December, the Politburo also approved the Resolution of the Council of People's Commissars of the Soviet Union regarding the provision of Soviet passports, and, on 11 April 1940, a resolution was passed concerning the registration of acts of civil status.

One of the important features of unification was the introduction of the Ukrainian and Belorussian SSRs and of an administrative division in common with the Soviet Union, as well as the creation of party and soviet bodies. On 4 December, the Politburo approved the proposals of the Central Committees of Belarus and Ukraine concerning the formation of regions and personnel on regional committees of the party and executive committees. At the same time, the heads of regional divisions of the People's Commissariat for Internal Affairs (UNKVD) were included in the regional and executive committees, but in fact they reported to Lavrentiy Beria alone. On 5 January, the Politburo set a date (24 March 1940) for elections to the Supreme Soviets of the Ukrainian and Belorussian SSRs.

The Politburo took vigorous measures to nationalize not only large- and medium-sized industries but also small enterprises. First, it was decided to nationalize the oil industry (10 November), then the coal industry (1 December), and, finally, the remaining industries (3 December). On 8 December, a decision was made to stop exchanging złoty, and citizens and businesses could exchange a maximum of 300 złoty for 300 rubles, the monthly salary of a typist in the People's Commissariat and an amount that constituted an unfair exchange rate.

Special provisions were made for the establishment of collective farms and state farms. The Politburo decision on 2 December 1939 to carry out a mass deportation of 21,000 families of *osadniki* (interwar Polish army veterans who were living in the newly captured lands) to areas of the far north is closely associated with these farms. Deportation was to take place in early February so that the collective and state farms could be established on the land, with its movable and stationary property, in time to sow crops. On 21 December, the Politburo also added to the deportation list a number of foresters, also known as the Forest Guard. In addition, it approved a proposal by the Central Committee of Ukraine on the use of property of osadniki. On 29 December, it approved a resolution concerning methods to be used in the relocation of osadniki and refugees, as well as "regulations on the special settlements and labor of 'osadniki,' the deportees from the western Ukrainian and Belorussian SSR, as developed by the People's Commissariat for Internal Affairs." On 14 January, the number of deportees increased by 5,000 families. In accordance with these decisions, on 10 February 1940, the Politburo and the Council of People's Commissars held the first mass deportation of Poles—osadniki, foresters, and their families. In total, 139,590 people were deported. Of this number, there were 33,665 men, the rest being women and children. They were relocated across 115 villages and 21 regional areas and provinces. The living and working conditions in the relocation camps differed only slightly from those in Gulag prisons.

On 2 March 1940, the Politburo adopted a resolution "on border protection in the western regions of the Ukrainian and Belorussian SSR," which included a decision on conducting evictions by 15 April and sending to the northern regions of the Kazakh SSR for ten years the families of officers, police officers, and prisoners; three days later, however, these persons were executed. In total, 25,000 families were deported. Their deportation (about 60,000 persons) was carried out on 13 April. In late June, a forced eviction of refugees from the central Polish voivodeships was carried out. At the end of May 1941, shortly before the war began, the People's Commissariat for Internal Affairs conducted another mass deportation from the territories annexed in September 1939. About 40,000 Poles were deported. According to the prominent Russian diplomat Andrey Vyshinsky, 388,000 Poles were deported from the western Ukrainian and Belorussian SSRs in 1939–41.

On 12 December 1940, Beria, in a memo to Stalin and Molotov, resumed the work of "removing anti-Soviet and hostile elements" that the People's Commissariat for Internal Affairs had been conducting from September 1939 to 1 December 1940. During this period, "up to 407,000 people were arrested and 275,784 deported to Kazakhstan and the northern regions of the Soviet Union"; this number included 134,463 osadniki, 59,787 families of the repressed, and 80,397 refugees who had not been granted asylum in Germany. According to documentation from this time, the crimes of the Soviet authorities against Polish POWs and civilians were not individual or occasional episodes but instead were an integral part of the sovietization and depolonization of the population in those territories annexed to the Soviet Union in the autumn of 1939. These were the means for consolidating the results of aggression and preventing liberation movements from growing in these regions.

After the end of the September campaign, Germany and the Soviet Union continued their cooperation. Both were prepared to implement any immediate tasks: for Germany, the campaign in the West, and for the Soviet Union, annexing the Baltic countries and war with Finland, which still had refused to conclude a treaty of "mutual assistance" with Moscow. During this period, the Kremlin in fact supported the struggle of the Third Reich against the Western powers, especially Great Britain. At the request of the Navy Command of Germany, Soviet tankers and cargo ships provided bunkering missions, delivering fuel and supplies by sea to German cruisers and submarines and allowing them to stay longer in the combat zone.

In accordance with the agreements concluded with Berlin, the Soviet Union was one of the most important suppliers of strategically important raw materials and supplies for Hitler's Germany, thereby undermining the economic blockade of the Reich by its opponents. For example, in 1940 Germany received 52 percent of all Soviet exports. The Soviet Union supplied Germany with wheat, oil, petroleum, chrome and manganese ore, phosphates, and wood. The last train to carry goods over to the Third Reich crossed the border on the night of 22 June 1941.

Until the second half of 1940, Berlin had an official position of friendly neutrality toward the Soviet Union. Thus, during the Soviet-Finnish conflict, the Reich tried not to irritate the Kremlin, and it blamed the destructive influence of London on Helsinki for the outbreak of the "Winter War." The annexation of the Baltic States by the Soviet Union, carried out through a complex combination of events from October 1939 to August 1940, also did not prompt any reaction from Berlin.

Intensive Soviet-German contacts were carried out, particularly during an operation by the Central Mixed Border Commission of the two countries. The atmosphere in which the negotiations took place in Warsaw reflected the "spirit of cooperation for the benefit of German and Soviet nations." The parties made this statement on 27 October 1939 during a social gathering hosted by Governor General Hans Frank in honor of the Soviets. Frank told the commission's chair, Aleksandr M. Aleksandrov, "These cigarettes we are smoking symbolize what is left of Poland—just the wind."

Nevertheless, both parties were wary of one other. On 9 October 1939, in a memorandum addressed to the commander of the armed forces and chief of staff of the Oberkommando der Wehrmacht (OKW), Hitler pointed out that no treaty could ensure the neutrality of Soviet Russia. The only way to guarantee neutrality would be a demonstration of German superiority and power. At a meeting on 30 October in OKW, it was emphasized that "the focus on Russian support should not mean that we willfully ignore all other concerns." The prolonged inaction of the Wehrmacht in the West seriously concerned Stalin's authorities, who, through their ambassador in Berlin, had repeatedly tried to find out when the Germans were going to attack. However, Stalin's expectations of a protracted war in the West were not realized. After the surrender of France, Soviet-German relations became tenser, and their views grew more opposed.

Toward the end of June 1940, Germany opposed the annexation of Bukovina to the Soviet Union; this had not been mentioned in the protocol to the nonaggression pact, which had identified annexation of only the northern part. On 31 July, Hitler told his generals of his decision to start a war with the Soviet Union in the spring of 1941. On 30 August 1940, Germany and Italy acted as arbiters in a dispute between Romania and Hungary, leading to accusations that Moscow had violated paragraph 3 of the Soviet-German pact of 23 August 1939. On 27 September 1940, Germany, Italy, and Japan signed the Tripartite Agreement, thereby creating a military alliance. In November 1940, Hungary, Romania, and Slovakia joined the Tripartite Agreement. All these actions could not but increase anxiety in the Kremlin.

In an effort to seek new agreements with the German authorities regarding the further delineation of spheres of influence, Stalin agreed to Hitler's proposal to send Molotov to Berlin. This visit took place 12–14 November. The Soviet authorities showed a willingness to join the Tripartite Agreement and to cooperate with the Reich, provided that the Finland issue was resolved. Any resolution was to include the immediate withdrawal of German troops from Finland. There were other issues to be resolved, including those affecting the sphere of Soviet interests in Bulgaria and the area of the Straits (Bosphorus and Dardanelles). However, these proposals did not find any support in Berlin, which was no longer interested in cooperation with the Soviets.

On 18 December, Hitler approved a secret directive to attack the Soviet Union, the "Barbarossa" plan, according to which the Soviet Union was to be defeated using a blitzkrieg. Stalin's authorities were not aware of the real extent of the rapidly approaching Nazi threat and continued to send oil, food, and strategic raw materials to the Reich.

Despite the defeat of the Polish army and the occupation of the country, the Polish state did not cease to exist. On 30 September 1939 in Paris, Pres. Władysław Raczkiewicz and the government headed by Władysław Sikorski set to work. They were supported and recognized by France, Great Britain, the United States, and many other countries.

The partition of Rzeczpospolita, which resulted from the joint aggression of Germany and the Soviet Union, prepared the way for future difficulties in relations between Russia and Poland. From that moment on, the Soviet Union shared a border with Nazi Germany, which continued to grow in strength. At the same time, relations with England, France, and the United States deteriorated. In the fall of 1939, after the German attack on Poland, any chance for the Soviets to join an anti-Nazi coalition had been lost.

5

THE KATYN MASSACRE

THE PROCESS OF REVEALING THE TRUTH AND COMMEMORATING THE VICTIMS

Andrzej Przewoźnik (Poland)

Secretary of the Council for the Protection of Struggle and Martyrdom Sites (1992–2010), member of the Polish-Russian Group on Difficult Matters (2008–10 April 2010).

Natalia S. Lebedeva (Russia)

Leading researcher, head of the Center for the Publication of Twentieth Century History Documents of the Institute of World History of the Russian Academy of Sciences.

ANDRZEJ PRZEWOŹNIK

THE PROCESS OF REVEALING THE TRUTH AND COMMEMORATING THE VICTIMS

AFTER THE EVENTS at Katyn were brought to public attention in April 1943, the name of that small town became the symbol of one of the most revolting and brutal crimes committed by the Soviet regime against—as we know today—almost twenty-two thousand citizens of Poland. Obviously, it is just one of many places connected with crimes perpetrated by the NKVD on the basis of a decision made by the Politburo of the All-Union Communist Party (Bolsheviks), or AUCP (b), on 5 March 1940. The opening of Russian archives and investigations carried out by Russians, Poles, and Ukrainians revealed other crime sites: Mednoye, Kharkov, Kherson, Kiev, Bikovnya, and Minsk.

The decision by the top party and state authorities of the Soviet Union on 5 March 1940 to exterminate 25,700 Polish citizens decimated the elite of the Polish nation and the leadership stratum of the young Polish state, so laboriously reconstructed after 123 years of subjugation. The great majority of those murdered by the NKVD at Katyn and other execution sites were not professional soldiers. In civilian lives, they had been teachers, doctors, engineers, lawyers, entrepreneurs, landowners, artists, and civil servants or filled other roles. They were people known and respected not only in areas where they resided and worked but also across Poland and abroad. Many of the junior officers were young people, only beginning their adult lives. They belonged to the first generation of Poles brought up in an independent Poland. Others had fought for Poland's independence and later defended the threatened frontiers of a resurrected state that was building a new existence. They were the tutors of that first generation of independent Poland. In September 1939, they rallied in defense of their country, invaded by Nazi Germany, and mobilized as its citizens or reported for duty as volunteers. They became its defenders, with all the consequences of that act.

While defending itself against overwhelming enemy forces attacking from the west, the Polish state on 17 September 1939 was struck with a knife in the back—from the east. The Republic of Poland was invaded by the Red Army—the armed forces of the Soviet Union, with which Poland had signed a nonaggression treaty in 1932 that was binding until the end of 1945. Confused Polish units (their commander in chief, Marshal Edward Rydz-Śmigły, issued a directive in the evening of 17 September that there should be no fighting against the Soviets) in most cases were deceitfully disarmed and taken prisoner in their own state's territory. Despite the absence of a formal declaration of war, these soldiers were de facto prisoners of war (that is how they were described in Soviet documents), with their status regulated by the Geneva Conventions. Yet, all died at the order of the Soviet authorities. In the "substantiation" of his criminal motion, Lavrentiy P. Beria wrote that they were "hardened and implacable foes of Soviet rule."

To Poles, the document discovered in Soviet archives ordering the elimination of thousands of their compatriots, prisoners of war, and close relatives is and will surely forever remain an unequivocal, indisputable accusation against the communist system, which—in violation of international law—did not hesitate to commit even the gravest crime. The murder, perpetrated exclusively for political reasons, is one of the few World War II mass crimes that has yet to be denounced and adjudicated, either by Russia or by international tribunals.

The victims of Katyn were killed with gunshots to the back of the head; attempts were also made to kill the memory of them. It is symptomatic that even though the authorities accused the Germans of the crime, there was a ban in the Polish People's Republic on honoring the victims or even publicly mentioning them. Yet, the attempts to erase and eradicate the memory of Katyn proved ineffective and, paradoxically, contributed to its cultivation by Poles with greater determination and persistence.

From the very beginning, Katyn was shrouded in lies. Its initiators attempted to conceal the truth from the world. During the wartime hostilities and also later, for whole decades when the communist system functioned in this part of Europe, Soviet security services, in collaboration with the services of their European satellites, doggedly and consistently, using every possible method, suppressed or even liquidated witnesses of the crime and people propagating the truth about its circumstances. Every effort was made to erase Katyn forever from the historic consciousness of Poles and to remove it from the public domain and awareness of the free world. A good example is the draft note adopted by the Politburo of the Central Committee of the Communist Party of the Soviet Union (CPSU) on 2 March 1973, in which the Soviet ambassador was to convey to the British foreign secretary a protest of the erection in London of a monument to the victims of Katyn (ultimately, the monument was unveiled on 18 September 1976, at Gunnersbury Cemetery, a less prestigious location than originally planned). The note refers to the inscription on the monument as one that "crudely distorts historical facts about the true perpetrators of the Katyn tragedy and repeats the outrageous claims, already circulated by the Nazis during World War II, for the purpose of concealing the bloody crimes of Gestapo henchmen, known to the whole world."

In communist-ruled Poland, there was a ban on diverting from the official propaganda line or censorship rules when speaking publicly or writing about Katyn. In accordance with censorship guidelines, publications on or references to the fate of the Polish officers murdered in Katyn were possible exclusively in the context of German responsibility for the crime.

On 12 March 1952, the Polish Ministry of Public Security published Instruction No. 6/52. It stipulated that "persons, proven to have provocatively spread slanderous claims, distributed Nazi brochures and 'Katyn' documents forged by the German occupation authorities[;] persons, proven to have written anonymous signs and slogans in public places, published and distributed leaflets[;] and organizers of collective listening of the Katyn programs of the Voice of America should be arrested and tried."

The 1975 Guidelines of the Central Office for the Control of Press, Publications, and Performances (censorship office) read in part,

> When evaluating materials about the deaths of Polish officers in Katyn, the following criteria should be applied: (1) No attempts of any kind are permitted to blame the Soviet Union for the deaths of the Polish officers in the Katyn Forest. (2) In academic studies—clearance may be given to formulations such as "shot by the Nazis in Katyn," "died in Katyn," "perished in Katyn." When the date of death is provided in conjunction with the phrase "died in Katyn," the date must be later than July 1941. (3) The term "prisoners of war" should be eliminated from references to Polish soldiers and officers interned by the Red Army in September 1939. The correct term is "internees." Clearance may be given to the names of the camps in Kozelsk, Starobelsk, [and] Ostashkov, where Polish officers were interned prior to being shot by the Nazis in the Katyn Forest. (4) Obituaries and announcements about masses for Katyn victims, or other forms of their commemoration, may be cleared only with the consent of the leadership of the COCPPP.

The establishment in the 1980s of the trade union Solidarity and the relative freedom of public debate that resulted opened the way for a revival in different forms (masses for the victims, leaflets, publications) of that chapter of the wartime experiences of a large part of Polish society. The imposition of martial law on 13 December 1981, as well as the attendant dissolution of the legal structures of Solidarity, triggered a rapid and unprecedented development of publishing outside the control of the communist authorities. The case of Katyn became one of the main historical events taken up in independent publications. In addition to reprints of *Zbrodnia katyńska w świetle dokumentów* (The Katyn crime in the light of documents), published in London in 1948 with a foreword by Gen. Władysław Anders, and of books authored by Józef Czapski, Stanisław Swianiewicz, and Józef Mackiewicz, there also appeared numerous leaflets, short studies, stamps, posters, and other objects dedicated to Katyn.

As resistance to the authorities increased, people whose relatives had lost their lives as a result of the criminal decision of the Soviet authorities of 5 March 1940 were holding meetings, discussions, and otherwise attempting to establish mutual contacts. Independent historians were also getting in touch. A group of people came together in Kraków in 1978 and in April 1979 and established the public Katyn Institute (full name: Institute for the Documentation of the Katyn Crime). Its primary goal was to combat lies about Katyn. Later that year, the institute started publishing the clandestine *Biuletyn Katyński* (Katyn bulletin). Holy masses, organized across Poland on anniversaries of the crime, initiated an unprecedented movement by families of Katyn victims, completely beyond the control of official institutions. The need to articulate the grief, suppressed for decades, of having lost loved ones and, first and foremost, the wish to bring to light the circumstances of their deaths and commemorate in a worthy manner the victims of the NKVD crime led in 1988 to the emergence in Konin, Warsaw, and Kraków of an organization called the Katyn Families. It affiliated the relatives of Polish army officers and policemen murdered in Katyn and at other undetermined places in the Soviet Union.

Soon, other groups dedicated to revealing the truth about Katyn started organizing themselves around the country. The first meeting of the Katyn Families from across Poland took place on 17 September 1989 at the Saint Karol Boromeusz Church in Warsaw, where the Sanctuary to the Fallen and Murdered in the East had been previously established. The meeting led to the registration three years later of the Federation of Katyn Families (FKF). In addition to integrating the families of the victims of Katyn, the FKF exerted pressure on state authorities on issues of importance to its members. It was largely this grass-roots movement, independent of the communist authorities, that demanded the truth about the fates of their loved ones and caused the authorities to become active in matters relating to Katyn. The publicly expressed demands for the truth left the authorities little room for maneuver.

Breakthrough after Fifty Years

A long-awaited breakthrough concerning Katyn finally occurred in the spring of 1990. On 13 April 1990, precisely fifty years after the Polish officers and policemen detained in camps at Kozelsk, Starobelsk, and Ostashkov were murdered by the NKVD in the Katyn Forest, Kharkov, and Kalinin, and forty-seven years after the German radio announcement about the discovery in the Katyn Forest of mass graves of victims of Soviet crimes, TASS, the

Soviet press agency, issued the following statement, conveyed to the public by Moscow radio and television broadcasts: "The disclosed archive materials justify the conclusion that Beria, Merkulov, and their aides bear direct responsibility for the crimes in the Katyn Forest. The Soviet side, expressing deep regret in connection with the Katyn tragedy, declares that it constituted one of the gravest crimes of Stalinism."

That did not amount to a full confession that the state and party leadership of the Soviet Union was responsible for the murder of the Polish officers and policemen. Yet, Katyn had been committed on the basis of a decision by the Politburo of the AUCP (b), adopted at the motion of Beria, the people's commissar for internal affairs and alternate member of the Politburo. His note is marked with the signatures of top party and state officials: Vyacheslav M. Molotov, chair of the Council of People's Commissars (prime minister) and people's commissar of foreign affairs; Kliment J. Voroshilov, deputy premier and people's commissar for defense; Lazar M. Kaganovich, deputy premier and people's commissar for transport; Anastas I. Mikoyan, deputy premier; and Mikhail I. Kalinin, chair of the Presidium of the Supreme Soviet (parliament).

Furthermore, the Soviet reference to Katyn was restricted to the murder of the Polish prisoners in the Katyn Forest, and no disclosure was made of the burial sites of prisoners from the camps in Starobelsk and Ostashkov. Also, the authorities concealed the fact that the decision of 5 March 1940 had also applied to Polish citizens incarcerated in NKVD prisons in western districts of the Soviet republics of Ukraine and Belarus (that is, eastern territories of the Republic of Poland). Most important, the perpetrators of the crime were not denounced—the president of the Soviet Union, Mikhail S. Gorbachev, did not muster the courage to do that. Still, the TASS statement was unprecedented. Fifty years after the crime, and after repeatedly upholding the lies that were meant to conceal Soviet responsibility for the crime, the authorities of the Soviet Union officially affirmed something that all those interested had known for decades. For the first time, the "social memory" that had preserved the horrific truth about the fate of thousands of Polish citizens triumphed. Henceforth, Katyn was no longer off limits.

Only a few hours earlier, the president of the Republic of Poland, Gen. Wojciech Jaruzelski, paying an official visit to Moscow, received from Gorbachev, after a two-hour private meeting, two file holders of Katyn documents. They contained several hundred sheets of copied records concerning the NKVD camps at Kozelsk, Starobelsk, and Ostashkov and, most important, lists compiled in April and May 1940 of prisoners from the Kozelsk and Ostashkov camps who had been transported in groups to the NKVD District Directorates in Smolensk and Kalinin (Tver), as well as the names of prisoners who had "vacated" the NKVD camp at Starobelsk. The next day, 14

April 1990, General Jaruzelski and the rest of the Polish state delegation paid tribute to the Polish officers murdered by the NKVD in Katyn. For the first time ever, a roll of honor was called at the graves of the Katyn victims in the presence of Polish and Soviet honor guards, who fired salutes. However, the presence of President Gorbachev in "lie-free" Katyn would have been a natural gesture, very well received by Polish society and the international community. Alas, no leader of the Soviet Union or the Russian Federation dared attend. Also, the words that Poles considered the most important and were waiting to hear were not uttered.

Still, those developments marked a turning point and new chapter in the annals of the Katyn case. They also opened the way for moves designed to bring to light all the circumstances of the case and, first and foremost, to launch an investigation into the crime and a search for the graves of prisoners from the NKVD camps in Starobelsk and Ostashkov. Also, as a consequence of these undertakings, it would now be feasible to begin the extremely difficult process of commemorating the victims of Katyn. Now, Poles had Russians and Ukrainians as allies, and they too had suffered because of the criminal activities of the Stalinist system.

In this context, the search for the graves of prisoners from the two other special NKVD camps—of Polish army officers from Starobelsk and policemen from Ostashkov—assumed a different dimension. Poles had long searched for them, following up on the available documents (including survivor accounts) and all possible traces. Uncertain information about the supposed deportation of prisoners or the destruction of the remains of the officers murdered in the Katyn Forest was also recorded and analyzed. In particular, there were many theories about the murder of the prisoners from Ostashkov. It was rumored that those prisoners had been either on ships that were scuttled in the White Sea or the Arctic Ocean or on barges sunk in Lake Seliger. The town of Bologoye was also mentioned as one route or "trail" of the prisoners' journey, in the account of an Ostashkov survivor. It was at Bologoye railway station that a carriage filled with what would become Ostashkov survivors was unhooked from the train and rerouted to the Yukhnovsky camp.

Meanwhile, the Kharkov "trail" had already appeared in the accounts of prisoners transported from Starobelsk to the Yukhnovsky camp. Beginning in the mid-1980s, mention was being made (initially, in the West) of villages located near Kharkov: Bezludovka and Dergache. The ultimate discovery of the places where the bodies were concealed became possible thanks to the changes that occurred in the late 1980s, in both Poland and the Soviet Union. Henceforth, Russians were able to look for the graves along with Poles.

The discovery of the graves at Kharkov and Mednoye took place almost simultaneously. The first significant signal concerning the graves of the officers from Starobelsk came from the Kharkov youth newspaper *Nova Zmina*. On 3 March 1990, it published a letter from a driver for the Kharkov military district staff. He had heard from an NKVD driver that, before the German-Soviet war of 1941, the bodies of persons shot at the NKVD building in Kharkov had been taken to a wood at Pyatikhatki (he first recounted this in 1989). The information was conveyed to the *Gazeta Wyborcza* journalist Leon Bójko by Gennady N. Zhavoronkov of *Moskoskiye Novosti*. He also had in his possession a letter from a Leningrader; in the early 1950s, when this person was a young boy, he and his friends had occasionally dug up buttons, eagle emblems, and military markings from Polish uniforms along a forest road known as "the black road."

In early 1990, the Federation of Katyn Families circulated a questionnaire among its members asking for opinions on how to commemorate the victims at the town of Katyn, which at that time was the only known site of the mass execution of officers. On 24 March 1990, the first meeting on the matter took place between representatives of the FKF and officials of the relevant state institution—the Council for the Protection of Struggle and Martyrdom Sites (CPSMS). The Katyn Families wanted an exterritorial Polish military cemetery established at the site of the graves and a ceremonial funeral to be conducted, with full military honors and an ecumenical mass. After the places of concealment of the bodies of prisoners from Starobelsk and Ostashkov were discovered, the FKF decided that the cemeteries in all three locations should be of the same character.

In May 1990, two journalists, Bójko from Warsaw and Zhavoronkov from Moscow, traveled to section 6 of the forest park in Kharkov, which includes Pyatikhatki. Following the directions of a forest ranger, they reached the "black road," partly overgrown, leading into the forest beyond KGB facilities. In it, they found the remnants of collapsed pits.

On 13–14 June 1990, Polish newspapers reported that the deputy head of the KGB District Directorate in Kharkov, Col. Aleksandr Niessen, had sent a cable to *Moskovskiye Novosti* informing the editors that section 6 of the forest park was the burial site of more than 1,760 Soviet citizens and that Polish soldiers, whose number was being determined, had also been illegally executed there in 1940. On 15 June 1990, the head of the KGB Directorate in Kharkov, Gen. Nikolai G. Gibadulov, stated that it was 99 percent certain that Polish officers were buried in section 6 of the forest park. Furthermore, he handed over to the Polish side copies of some documents pertaining to the matter. On 23 June 1990, the head of the Ukrainian KGB, Gen. V. Galushko, and his deputy, Gen. Grigory Kovtun, conveyed to the Polish authorities a list of the names of 4,031 Polish officers who had been held at Starobelsk. It was then that wreaths and lights were first placed at the graves of the Polish officers.

In mid-May 1990, members of the Tver Memorial (Kalinin branch of the

International Human Rights Historical and Educational Charitable Society) published in *Kalininskaya Pravda* an article headlined, "Where are the bodies of repression victims?" which drew many letters from readers. In one, the author recounted a conversation with an NKVD officer, the now deceased Col. Andrei P. Leonov. Leonov reported that the Poles from Ostashkov had been taken to Kalinin (formerly Tver) in the winter of 1940 and detained in the basement and attic of the NKVD building on Sovietskaya Street. At night, they were taken in groups outside Kalinin, to the vicinity of NKVD dachas near the villages of Yamok and Mednoye, and shot there (or they were shot at the NKVD headquarters in Kalinin). Later, a wooden dacha was erected on the spot where they were buried.

On 6 June 1990, after publication of the *Kalininskaya Pravda* articles, the District Prosecutor's Office in Kalinin initiated proceedings to determine the burial place of the Polish officers from Ostashkov. In early July 1990, the head of the Kalinin KGB confirmed reports that graves of the Polish officers from Ostashkov had been discovered at the village of Mednoye. In mid-July 1990, the spokesman for the Soviet Ministry of Foreign Affairs, Gennady I. Gerasimov, officially announced that there were mass graves of Polish officers and policemen near Kharkov and Tver.

In July 1990, Stefan Śnieżko, the Polish deputy general prosecutor, was assigned to head a planned investigation into Katyn. Later that month, he twice requested that the Polish side be permitted to participate in the exhumations in Kharkov planned by Soviet prosecutors.

Issues relating to the investigation, exhumation of the victims' bodies, and establishment of Polish military cemeteries were on the agenda of talks conducted in Moscow in October 1990 by Krzysztof Skubiszewski, the Polish foreign minister. A meeting on 11 October was attended by Col. Ivan Abramov of the Soviet General Prosecutor's Office, who was instructed to open an investigation by 15 November 1990. Subsequently, the investigation was taken over by the General Military Prosecutor's Office of the Soviet Union as penal case number 159 against parties responsible for the Katyn crime.

The Soviet authorities set the exhumations in Kharkov and Mednoye for the period from 25 July to 30 August 1991 and refused to extend it. The exhumations were to be conducted with the participation of representatives of the Polish General Prosecutor's Office and Polish experts, whose goal was to obtain evidence for the Soviet investigation into the crime. Their primary task was to confirm that those buried there were in fact Polish prisoners from the special NKVD camps in Starobelsk and Ostashkov and to determine the precise location of the burial sites, their area, and the number of those buried there.

Parallel to preparations for the exhumation work, a Polish delegation composed of representatives of the Ministry of Foreign Affairs, the Ministry of National Defense, and the CPSMS conducted talks in Moscow, Kiev, and Kharkov on 22–27 July 1991 concerning the establishment of the cemeteries. While the work in Kharkov was in progress, on 30 July 1991 the Federation of Katyn Families addressed a letter to CPSMS chair Stanisław Broniewski in which the FKF defined its position concerning the cemeteries and commemoration of Katyn victims: Polish military cemeteries should be established in Katyn, Mednoye, and Kharkov, and the burials should be conducted in accordance with the relevant Geneva Conventions. The FKF further called for the Polish government—with the CPSMS acting on its behalf—to organize a competition for the design of the monument cemeteries, which were to be built and arranged in the spirit of the Geneva Conventions. Also, families of the victims were to have the opportunity to express their opinions and take part in the selection of the winning designs.

The Polish exhumation teams working in Kharkov and Mednoye were led by prosecutor Śnieżko. They included prosecutors from the Ministry of Justice and the Military Prosecutor's Office and experts: forensic doctors; anthropologists; archaeologists; representatives of the Executive Board of the Polish Red Cross; historians; specialists in faleristics, uniforms, and firearms; and documentalists. A Russian prosecutor, Col. Aleksandr V. Tretetsky, was in charge of the overall operation.

The exhumation work in Kharkov lasted from 15 July to 7 August 1991 and uncovered the remains of 167 Poles and 20 Soviet citizens. Three mass graves of Polish officers were discovered, along with related objects. The investigators also uncovered two mass graves of Soviet citizens. The effort confirmed that bodies of Polish officers from Starobelsk had been buried in the woods around Kharkov. The team also determined many facts concerning the murder methods and the circumstances of the crime and recovered material evidence.

It is noteworthy that, shortly after the exhumation began, a coup was attempted in the Soviet Union (the Yanayev Putsch), and the head of the District KGB Directorate demanded that the work be stopped and those involved vacate the area where the graves had been found. However, both the prosecutors from the Chief Military Prosecutor's Office of the Soviet Union and members of the Polish team ignored those demands and continued their work.

After the exhumation work in Kharkov was completed, members of the team placed the excavated remains of the Polish officers in nine coffins, each of which had a cross placed on the lid. These coffins were placed in one of the discovered graves, with the remains of Soviet citizens interred in another grave, dug nearby. A tenth casket, with the remains of one officer, was prepared for a ceremonial funeral. It was held on 10 August 1991, in the presence of an official Polish delegation and family members. The casket, covered with a white-and-red flag and the sash of the Cross of the Order of Virtuti Militari was lowered into the grave. A seven-meter oak cross was erected over the grave, and mounted beside it was a plaque with the following words: "In memory of the 3,921 generals and officers of the Polish Army, prisoners of Starobelsk, murdered in the spring of 1940 by the NKVD and buried here. Kharkov 10.08.1991 Compatriots." The Holy Mass was celebrated, with prayers by clergy of different denominations. Also taking part in the ceremony were representatives of the central and regional authorities of the Ukrainian Soviet Socialist Republic.

The exhumation work at Mednoye was conducted 15–30 August 1991. The Polish team was supervised by representatives of the Chief Military Prosecutor's Office and the General Staff of the Soviet Union. Colonel Tretetsky was also in charge here. The collective graves were located between the villages of Mednoye and Yamok, within a fenced-in recreational area of 700 by 400 meters that had earlier belonged to the NKVD and in 1991 was in possession of the Kalinin KGB. It included a hillside and ridge covered with pine and dotted with summer cottages overlooking the floodplain valley of the Tvertsa River. Before the arrival of the Polish team, an area of 120 by 80 meters, where the exhumation work was to be conducted, was fenced off. As it turned out, all the Polish graves were located within that rectangle. When another Polish team visited the location in 1994, it discovered the remnants of a barbed-wire fence around the burial site, ringing an area slightly smaller than that designated for the exhumation work in 1991.

The Polish experts located three mass graves, then another one and part of yet another. Because of the short period of time allocated for the exhumation, only one of the graves could be fully studied. It contained the bodies of at least 243 men, closely fused, bonded with adipocere, and saturated with water. Only the top layer of the bodies—lying in a disorderly manner—showed signs of skeletonization. However, it rarely proved possible to excavate whole bodies. Frequently, the heads of the victims were wrapped in police overcoats—which affirms the testimony of the Kalinin NKVD chief, Dmitry S. Tokarev. The bodies had been thrown into the graves haphazardly.

The exhumation work in Mednoye in August 1991 confirmed that the area contained mass graves of the Polish police officers from the camp in Ostashkov and also yielded information about the mode of their execution and burial. A funeral ceremony for the victims was held on 31 August 1991, with the participation of delegations of the Katyn Families and the Police Family 1939 Association, as well as members of parliament and representatives of the Polish government. A delegation of Russian authorities also attended. A casket covered with a white-and-red flag and the Cross of the Order of Virtuti Militari sash was the last to be lowered into the grave. After a Catholic mass, clergy of other denominations prayed. Mounted at the foot of a cross placed at the grave was a granite plaque with the Polish state emblem and the following words: "To the memory of the 6,295 policemen, soldiers of the Border Protection Corps and other units, Border Guard officers, workers of the state and justice administration of the Republic of Poland—prisoners of Ostashkov, murdered by the NKVD in the spring of 1940 and buried here. Mednoye—August 1991. Compatriots."

On 24 August 1991, Ukraine proclaimed independence. On 25 December 1991, the Soviet Union ceased to exist. After its disintegration, the independent Russian Federation was established. The complicated political situation both facilitated and hindered Katyn-related undertakings. In order to build Polish military cemeteries at the resting places of Polish officers and policemen, it became necessary to adopt legislation permitting such moves in the new reality.

In March 1992, Polish authorities established the Katyn Advisory Board, attached to the Ministry of Foreign Affairs. It consisted of representatives of the Ministry of Internal Affairs, the Ministry of National Defense, the General Staff of the Polish Armed Forces, the General Prosecutor's Office, the Executive Board of the Polish Red Cross, the CPSMS, the Polish Episcopate, the FKF, the Police Family 1939 Association, the Independent Historical Committee for the Investigation of the Katyn Crime (IHCIKC), the Polish Katyn Foundation (established in 1990), and the Association of Architects of the Republic of Poland. The chief objective of the board at that point was to prepare agreements with Russia and Ukraine on the protection of graves and remembrance sites. Drafts of such agreements, prepared by the Ministry of Foreign Affairs in collaboration with the board, and notes requesting consent for the resumption of exhumation work were conveyed to the authorities of the Russian Federation on 13 June 1992 and, after that, to those of Ukraine.

Overtures made by the Polish side led to the signing of declarations of intent on joint measures to build Polish cemeteries in Katyn, Mednoye, and Kharkov; in April and June 1992, such declarations were signed with the authorities of the Smolensk and Tver districts of the Russian Federation and, in mid-July, with the authorities of the Kharkov district in Ukraine.

On 18 May 1992, in Warsaw, Poland and Ukraine signed a treaty on good neighborliness, friendly relations, and cooperation.

In early July 1992, the CPSMS, in implementing the postulates of the Katyn Families, assumed coordination of all activities related to the location and construction of the military cemeteries. On 16 July 1992, the Katyn Advisory Board was transformed—though retaining its previous composition—into the Katyn Team attached to the CPSMS. Henceforth, all major undertakings relating to Katyn were handled by that organization. At its meetings, the Katyn Team addressed issues connected with exhumations and the cemetery design competition. A working group prepared a document titled "Organization of the Exhumation Works and Arrangement of the Katyn-Mednoye-Kharkov Cemeteries," which on 27 July 1992 was approved by the team for implementation.

On 22 September 1992, the Ukrainian authorities gave their consent to further exhumations in section 6 of the Kharkov forest park. It is noteworthy that, in all talks on the subject (July 1991 and August 1992), the Ukrainian side opted for the construction of a joint cemetery for victims of totalitarianism, while the Polish side underscored that it was essential to keep the two cemeteries separate.

On 19–25 September 1992, an eight-member delegation of the Federation of Katyn Families visited Moscow at the invitation of Dr. Sergey B. Stankevich, political advisor to the president of the Russian Federation, Boris N. Yeltsin. The Poles held a number of meetings (including some at the Chief Military Prosecutor's Office). On 23 September 1992, the delegation members were received by Vice President Aleksandr V. Rutskoi, and they presented him with a petition. Rutskoi declared that, in view of the difficulties that had been signaled to him related to the matter of Katyn, he would assume—with President Yeltsin's consent—personal oversight. Soon afterward, he established a working group on Katyn, headed by Gen. Leonid M. Zaika, with Dr. Pyotr Romanov as secretary. It was tasked with bringing the investigation to a speedy conclusion and providing assistance with the exhumations and conclusion of the arrangement of the cemeteries in 1994. Agreement was reached concerning visits to Katyn and Mednoye by Polish topographers.

In the autumn of 1992, the CPSMS, acting in concert with the head of the Topography Directorate of the Armed Forces and the Military Geodesy and Teledetection Center, arranged for army geodesists to visit Katyn (12–16 November) and Mednoye (19–21 November). They were tasked with preparing the basic map (scale 1:500) of the future cemeteries (for the needs of the competition), a raised-relief map (scale 1:1,000), and a terrain model (1:250). The maps were ready by the end of January 1993.

Archive Search

The opening of Russian archives made it possible to determine the mechanisms of the crime—something of crucial importance in bringing to light the fates of thousands of Polish citizens and in identifying places connected with the crime, including spots where the NKVD hid the victims' bodies. Most of the subsequent actions taken by state institutions and the numerous publications detailing hitherto unknown aspects of the Katyn case largely ensued from the work of Polish and Russian archivists.

In 1990, the representatives of Poland's Head Office of State Archives began talks with their Russian counterparts concerning the disclosure of documents relating to Katyn. A year later, the archive services of Poland and

Russia agreed that archivists and historians from both countries would prepare a source publication on the fates of Polish prisoners of war in Soviet captivity after 17 September 1939. An accord on archival cooperation was signed in Warsaw on 27 April 1992. An additional protocol, adopted on that occasion, stipulated the publication of source materials documenting the fates and annihilation of the Polish prisoners detained in the special NKVD camps in Kozelsk, Ostashkov, and Starobelsk. The historians and archivists were to focus on the fates of the prisoners, the mass murder perpetrated on a selected group of Polish citizens, and on repercussions of the Katyn case during the war and in the postwar period until the present time.

On 29 April 1992, Janusz Onyszkiewicz, the Polish defense minister, established the Military Archival Commission (MAC), which was tasked with copying Russian archive documents—previously inaccessible to Polish historians—pertaining to the fates of Polish soldiers in Soviet captivity after 17 September 1939. The commission, composed of researchers from the Central Military Archive and the Military Historical Institute, began copying selected source materials in Moscow archives in mid-September 1992. Precedence was given to sources connected with Katyn, personal files of the prisoners (Polish officers and enlisted men captured in September and October 1939), documents from the POW camps, and files related to the repatriation campaign.

On 14 October 1992, Prof. Rudolf G. Pikhoya, President Yeltsin's special envoy and chair of the State Archives Committee of the Council of Ministers of the Russian Federation, conveyed to Pres. Lech Wałęsa in Warsaw copies of documents constituting dossier number 1. Hitherto, it had been part of the most closely guarded collection of archival documents in the Soviet Union, with only general secretaries of the CPSU permitted access. The transfer of these documents was an unprecedented development. It meant that Poland had received documents of exceptional importance to Poles and especially to the families of the Katyn victims. Handing over the documents, Professor Pikhoya stated, "Conveying these documents to the Polish people and world opinion, the government of Russia and President Boris Yeltsin wish to exclude lies from relations between Russia and Poland. Honest relations between our nations need to be built on honest foundations."

Two days later, on 16 October 1992, the Polish Sejm—appreciating the weight and significance of the gesture made by President Yeltsin—passed by acclamation a statement in which it expressed the conviction that "the two states, building a new future, will—relying on the law and truth—cope with the burden of the past."

Dossier number 1, brought to Poland by Professor Pikhoya, contained a copy of a document that was of pivotal importance in determining the circumstances of the Katyn crime: Beria's motion of 5 March 1940, with the signatures of Stalin, Voroshilov, Molotov, and Mikoyan (with an annotation "for

M. I. Kalinin and L. M. Kaganovich"), recommending the murder of 25,700 Polish officers and policemen held in the special NKVD camps at Kozelsk, Ostashkov, and Starobelsk and Poles detained in NKVD prisons in so-called Western Ukraine and Western Belarus.

Other documents were also related to the Katyn case. An interesting part of the dossier consisted of materials connected with the "official line" of the Soviet authorities concerning Katyn, namely, attempts to cover tracks, promote lies and distortions, and divert public attention in Poland and other countries from the Katyn case. These documents exposed the actions Soviet authorities were taking until the very end of the Soviet Empire. And so, in 1990, after Gorbachev conveyed the Katyn documents to General Jaruzelski, the Soviet Politburo attempted to "balance" the Soviet crime against Poles with claims that Poles themselves had committed mass crimes against Soviet POWs. Numerous statements and publications compared the NKVD murder of Polish POWs to the deaths in captivity due to disease of Soviet POWs captured by Polish forces during the victorious war against the Bolsheviks in 1920. The idea of an "anti-Katyn," concocted by Valentin M. Falin at the Foreign Department of the Central Committee of the CPSU, assumed its own life and still keeps reappearing, invoked by Russian politicians and writers.

However, Poland did not receive the minutes of meetings held by the central "troika" (Vsevolod N. Merkulov, Bakhcho Z. Kobulov, Leonid F. Bashtakov) tasked with examining the cases of the Polish prisoners, adopting the relevant resolution on their fates, and confirming the implementation of its "sentences." We still do not know if the Katyn documentation (record files and other materials) was really destroyed, as proposed by KGB chief Aleksandr N. Shelepin in a memo of 9 March 1959 to Soviet Premier Nikita S. Khrushchev, who, however, suggested preserving the minutes of the troika meetings and the confirmation that the decision concerning the Poles had been implemented.

The materials handed over to Poland also did not contain the dispatching lists from Starobelsk, even though it is certain that they must have been stored together with the dispatching lists of prisoners detained in Kozelsk and Ostashkov—documents received by General Jaruzelski in April 1990. The personal files of the POWs are also of exceptional importance to the Katyn Families.

The joint efforts of Polish and Russian archivists produced results. Two editing committees were established: the Polish group was led by Prof. Aleksander Gieysztor and the Russian, by Professor Pikhoya. In November 1995, they unveiled the first volume of the Polish edition, titled *Katyń: Dokumenty zbrodni,* which initiated the publication of sources related to the Katyn case provided by Russian archives. Further volumes (a total of four) appeared in subsequent years thanks to the support of many institutions, including the

CPSMS. They constitute the fundamental source of knowledge about Katyn and, simultaneously, an example of substantive, highly fruitful cooperation of Polish and Russian archivists and historians.

The Russian Archive Service (Rosarkhiv) was instrumental in the publication of a portion of the Katyn documents in Russian. The original idea of publishing all the volumes of the documents in parallel Polish and Russian editions was only partly implemented. The whole four-volume edition appeared in Poland in the years 1995–2006, but just one volume was issued on the Russian side: *Katyn: Dokumenty; Plenniki neob'yavlennoi voiny,* brought out in Moscow in December 1997 in the Russia 20th Century series. A collective volume titled *Katyn: Mart 1940–sentyabr' 2000; Dokumenty,* containing a selection of documents from the whole edition, appeared in 2001. Other noteworthy Russian publications devoted to Katyn include the 1994 book by the eminent expert on Katyn and Polish-Soviet relations during World War II, Prof. Natalia S. Lebedeva, titled *Katin: Prestuplenye protiv chelovechestva,* and a work by other eminent experts on Katyn, Inessa S. Yazhborovskaya, Anatoly S. Yablokov, and Valentina S. Parasadanova, titled *Katynskii sindrom w sovetsko-pol'skikh otnosheniakh,* published in Moscow in 2001.

The disclosed archival sources significantly widened the knowledge about Katyn. The works written on their basis brought to light various hitherto unknown aspects of the Katyn case and made it possible to search for other places connected with the tragic fates of Polish citizens in the Soviet Union. Thanks to these publications, the case of Katyn gained a special presence in the collective consciousness of Poles.

The Road to the Katyn Cemeteries

Throughout 1993, difficult Polish-Russian negotiations were conducted on an agreement that was to open the way to fulfilling the most important postulate of the families of the Katyn victims: the construction of Polish military cemeteries at the resting places of Polish officers and policemen at Katyn, Mednoye, and Kharkov.

On 22 February 1994, the foreign ministers of the two countries, Andrzej Olechowski and Andrei V. Kozyrev, signed an agreement in Kraków between the government of the Republic of Poland and the government of the Russian Federation on graves and sites of remembrance of victims of wars and repression. A joint statement by the two foreign ministers constitutes an integral part of the accord. It reads, in part, "Guided by goodwill and humanitarian values, the Russian Party intends to begin in May 1994 the exhumation in Katyn and Mednoye of the remains of victims of totalitarianism, including Polish officers, and to participate in their fitting burial. The Russian Party declares that it is prepared to cover the related costs and to assist in the arrangement of the cemeteries-memorials at Katyn and Mednoye." That statement was the first in which mention was made of the construction of cemeteries at the resting places of the Katyn crime victims. Pursuant to Article 11 of the agreement, each party was supposed to designate "an authorized body, responsible for coordinating actions connected with the implementation of the provisions . . . of the agreement."

Poland had a similar accord with Ukraine. Signed in Warsaw on 21 March 1994, it was an intergovernmental agreement on the protection of remembrance sites and resting places of victims of war and political repression. Both agreements provided the legal basis for the exhumations and construction of the cemeteries.

The Polish government empowered the CPSMS to direct the preparations for the exhumation works, which it did with the assistance of the Executive Board of the Polish Red Cross, the General Staff of the Armed Forces, the Ministry of National Defense, and the Ministry of Internal Affairs.

The exhumation work in Kharkov was preceded by the work in Starobelsk. Some thirty officers (the exact number is unknown due to gaps and inaccuracies in the NKVD documents handed over to Poland) had died in the camp before the executions began. The KGB and residents of Starobelsk indicated the place of burial to the CPSMS at a municipal cemetery that was due to be removed. On 2 February 1994, the general secretary of the CPSMS, Andrzej Przewoźnik, signed an agreement with municipal and regional authorities in Starobelsk concerning the exhumation work and designation of a Polish section at the new municipal cemetery of Chimerovka. On 15–21 April 1994, the exhumations, commissioned by the CPSMS, were conducted by a team of specialists led by an archaeologist, Dr. Marian Głosek, with the participation of a prosecutor from the Polish Ministry of Justice and a representative of the Executive Board of the Polish Red Cross. Forty-eight of the excavated sets of remains were identified as those of Poles, who had probably died in the camps of Starobelsk 1 and Starobelsk 2 (yet another NKVD camp established in August 1940; its inmates were escapees who had been detained when they tried to cross the Soviet-German border). Determining their names proved impossible due to the absence of any identification documents. On 21 April 1994, caskets with their remains were placed in individual graves in the Polish section of the new cemetery, subsequently consecrated on 22 September 1995.

In the summer of 1994, Przewoźnik signed an agreement with the authorities of Kharkov, under which exhumation work in section 6 of the forest park in Kharkov was to start on 1 September that year. The works were conducted during three field seasons in the years 1994–96: 2–27 September 1994, 3 June–22 September 1995, and 27 May–14 September 1996. The works were supervised by Prof. Andrzej Kola, an archaeologist.

In September 1994, a team of army geodesists—on assignment from the

CPSMS—conducted geodesic field work in section 6 of the Kharkov forest park, preparing the basic map of the terrain of the future cemetery, at a scale of 1:500. Later, that research served as the basis for the preparation of altitude and relief maps and a terrain model of the area of the future cemetery. The terrain model and numerous objects discovered by CPSMS specialists during the exhumation work on the remains of the murdered officers and policemen were conveyed to the Katyn Museum in Warsaw. The museum, established in 1992 by a decision of the minister of national defense as a branch of the Museum of the Polish Armed Forces in Warsaw, collects memorabilia connected with the victims of the crime and materials documenting the Katyn case.

On 14 July 1994, a Polish government delegation led by Andrzej Zakrzewski, secretary of state at the Chancellery of the President, paid a visit to Moscow and was received by Deputy Premier Yuri F. Yarov. This was a critical period, as it concerned the matter of the exhumations. Contrary to the provisions of the agreement, the Russians insisted that the exhumations would be of little use since various remains were intermingled and included persons of other than Polish nationality, so Russian society might object if only Poles were exhumed. In this situation, the Russian side proposed the erection of a joint memorial to honor all those murdered. After difficult negotiations, it was agreed that within ten days the parties would designate their plenipotentiaries, who would address the issue in bilateral talks. Also, the Russian side pledged to set a date for the beginning of the exhumations before the end of 1994.

In a note dated 25 July 1994, the Russian Ministry of Foreign Affairs advised that, on 23 July, the Russian government had affirmed the composition of the new Coordinating Committee for the Commemoration of Victims of Totalitarian Repressions in Katyn and Mednoye. At the same time, the committee was assigned the functions of a coordinating body for the implementation of the agreement of 22 February 1994. The committee was further instructed to establish an operational group composed of representatives of the Smolensk and Tver districts, the Ministries of Foreign Affairs, Internal Affairs, Defense, Finance, and Culture, the Federal Security Service, the Russian Orthodox Church, and the Russian Red Cross. The group was to handle all matters connected with the erection of the commemorative objects in Katyn and Mednoye. Deputy Minister of Culture Vyacheslav I. Bragin was appointed plenipotentiary for the Russian side and chair of the coordinating committee (on 21 February 1998, he was replaced by Deputy Minister Natalya L. Dementieva and, later, by Culture Minister Mikhail Y. Shvidkoi).

On 19 August 1994, then-premier Waldemar Pawlak issued regulation number 23 concerning the establishment of the new Commission for the Commemoration of the Victims of the Katyn Crime, to be subordinated to the prime minister. It was composed of prosecutor Śnieżko as commission chair, CPSMS general secretary Przewoźnik as deputy chair and secretary, and one member each from the Main Commission for the Investigation of Crimes against the Polish Nation, the Institute of National Remembrance (INR), the General Staff of the Polish Armed Forces, the Ministry of Foreign Affairs, the Office of the Council of Ministers, and the Ministry of Culture and Art. The president of the board of the FKF and a representative of the Chancellery of the President were also invited to participate in the commission's work. Organizational and technical support was provided by CPSMS.

On 23 August 1994, representatives of the Polish commission and the Russian coordinating committee held talks in Moscow with the participation of Deputy Premier Y. F. Yarov and officials from the Russian Ministry of Foreign Affairs. The parties set a date for the beginning of surveying-topographical work (the Russian side did not agree to exhumations) to locate the Polish remains. The work was to begin on 5 September 1995. The Russians promised to provide broad assistance to the Polish specialists (accommodations, labor, heavy equipment). They also proposed—as an element of reconciliation—the construction of a joint cemetery to a design selected through a single Polish-Russian competition.

The work of the Polish specialists at Katyn and Mednoye continued during two summer field seasons in 1994 and 1995: in Katyn from 5 to 25 September 1994 and from 6 June to 8 September 1995, and in Mednoye from 6 to 22 September 1994 and from 7 June to 31 August 1995. The Katyn team was led by the archaeologist Marian Głosek, while the Mednoye team was headed by Prof. Bronisław Młodziejowski, an anthropologist. The 1994 work was of a surveying-topographical character, while the 1995 effort was of a surveying-exhumation nature.

The work at Katyn was almost prevented by an organized protest of a group of women from a nearby children's sanatorium housed in buildings along the Dnieper River. They had been misled by reports that the sanatorium would be closed down since the Polish investigation covered an area of ninety-five hectares, including the sanatorium (in reality, the area of the Polish archaeological work amounted to about two hectares, some distance from the sanatorium). Subsequent obstacles, such as the blocking of the Polish team's communications with the Polish embassy in Moscow and failure to provide transport, heavy equipment, and laborers, considerably reduced the effective time of the actual work. A visit to Katyn in 1994 by Russian prime minister Viktor S. Chernomyrdin had little effect. The situation was similar in 1995.

In 1994, the main goal of the Polish team was to determine if the remains of Polish officers were buried in Katyn, and if so, where. In 1995, the objective was to fully and accurately locate the so-called death pits and collective graves and delineate the area of the future cemetery. Both tasks were achieved, though the program of work could not be fully implemented due to the obstacles mentioned above.

Drilling and excavations conducted within the area of the memorial made it possible to locate six large collective graves and the separate graves of two generals, built by members of a Polish Red Cross technical commission in 1943. Also found and opened were all the death pits. The fence of the Soviet memorial traversed one of the graves; it was discovered that the remains in the upper layers of the graves had been breached (with the possible exception of one grave) after the 1943 exhumations.

The work conducted in the years 1994–95 proved the presence in the Katyn Forest—within the area of the memorial or its immediate vicinity—of the remains of Polish officers from Kozelsk, murdered in the spring of 1940. The Polish specialists also located forty-two smaller graves of Soviet citizens.

At Mednoye, the Polish team discovered twenty-three death pits. All were located within the investigation area fenced off by the KGB in 1991. No graves were found outside that area, and no graves of Soviet citizens were discovered.

In addition to the work of the two teams aimed at locating and marking the mass graves for the future cemeteries, other undertakings were also implemented with the ultimate purpose of establishing proper graves.

On 16 and 17 February 1995, the Polish commission and the Russian coordinating committee held talks in Warsaw. The Russians agreed to Polish proposals that efforts should be initiated to arrange the commemorative objects, delineate the areas of the future cemeteries, and lay their foundation stones in the spring of 1995. Agreement was also reached on the establishment of Polish military cemeteries at Katyn and Mednoye as part of a joint complex of commemorative objects honoring victims of the totalitarian system. The parties also adopted a relevant timetable.

The main documents pertaining to the construction of the Polish military cemeteries in Katyn and Mednoye were signed in Smolensk on 25 March 1995. Maps prepared by Polish geodesists, indicating the location of the graves, served as the basis for delineating the cemetery boundaries. The boundaries were to be detailed in line with terrain surveys initiated in 1994.

The parties also set the precise dates for the laying of the foundation stones (to be consecrated by Pope John Paul II) in the framework of the Katyn Year and ceremonies to mark the fifty-fifth anniversary of the crime. In the case of Katyn, it was 4 June 1995 (with the groundbreaking plaque signed by Pres. Lech Wałęsa, who was present at the ceremony), and in the case of Mednoye, on 11 June 1995. The ceremonies were attended by crowds of visitors from Poland, prominently including members of the Katyn Families, as well as government delegations from the two countries and clergy of different denominations.

Initially, the search for graves in Kharkov was conducted using the method of archaeological exploratory drilling over an area of almost 1.3 hectares, designated within the Ukrainian Security Service sanatorium park. During the 1995–96 seasons, the Polish team concentrated on archaeological-exhumation work, though within a substantially smaller area. Seventy-five graves on both sides of the so-called black road were discovered within a rectangle of fifty by one hundred meters. All of the large graves within the road loop, with one exception, contained the remains of Polish officers.

Altogether, fifteen collective Polish graves were located and examined in 1991 and in 1994–96. They contained the bodies of 4,302 persons, including a woman. Thus, the number of discovered bodies was higher than the number of prisoners who had been transferred from the camp at Starobelsk to the NKVD in Kharkov. The Kharkov graves probably also contain the remains of persons whose names are on the so-called Ukrainian Katyn list (see below).

The Polish specialists discovered signs of mechanical interference in the graves, from top to bottom, made at the beginning of the 1970s, with the use of soil augers of sixty and eighty centimeters in diameter. After attempts were made to cover up the traces, the area of the graves was again fenced off and a holiday home and KGB dachas built within its boundaries. In 1996, the Polish team also explored and exhumed sixty graves of Soviet citizens, containing the remains of 2,098 persons.

The names of 79 prisoners from Starobelsk were determined on the basis of objects and documents recovered during the 1991 exhumations. A further 347 names were determined during archaeological work in Kharkov in 1995–96 and during the conservation of the excavated personal effects. After the work was concluded in 1996, each of the Polish graves was marked with a wooden, Catholic-type cross and each Soviet one, with an Orthodox-type cross.

The original burial place within the 1.3-hectare area had the shape of a rectangle of 50 by 100 meters. The graves were dispersed along the fence, on both sides of the so-called black road.

The extensive specialist documentation compiled during the work was indispensable for the construction of the future cemetery. While the work was still under way, CPSMS representatives held several meetings with Ukrainian authorities to discuss issues connected with the project, including the construction of the cemetery. The Ukrainian side pressed for the construction of a joint cemetery of victims of totalitarianism, arguing that the Polish and Soviet graves were close to one another and interspersed. Furthermore, the Ukrainian authorities refused to allow the transfer of the remains of Soviet citizens buried among the Polish graves so that an exclusively Polish section could be created. The matter was resolved during a visit to Ukraine, including Kharkov, of a Polish government delegation. It was then decided to build a joint cemetery of victims of totalitarianism.

Katyn Cemeteries

After complicated and painstaking preparations, on 17 July 1995, the CPSMS announced an open competition for the design of the Polish military cemeteries in Katyn, Mednoye, and Kharkov. The competition was addressed to Polish sculptors and architects in Poland and abroad. The cemeteries were to be ecumenical in character and had to incorporate national, state, and religious symbols, with particular reference to the Cross of the September Campaign and the Virtuti Militari Cross.

Thirty-two competition entries were received from Poland and other countries, including France, Germany, and Norway. A twenty-two-member jury was appointed to select the best design. It was led by Prof. Maciej Gintowt from the Architecture Department of the Warsaw Technical University and included outstanding architects, sculptors, artists, and representatives of the Ministry of Culture, the Ministry of National Defense, the Catholic Primate of Poland, the FKF, the Police Family 1939 Association, the IHCIKC, and the Polish Katyn Foundation.

The winning entry was the collaboration of the sculptor Zdzisław Pidek from the Gdańsk Fine Arts Academy, the sculptor Andrzej Sołyga from the Warsaw Fine Arts Academy, and the architects Wiesław Synakiewicz and Andrzej Synakiewicz. The jury believed their design reflected great respect for the existing collective graves and death pits and the trees that were growing in the area. The jury was impressed by the idea of an underground bell. The central element of each cemetery would consist of a wall with the names of all the victims buried there, an underground bell, an altar, and a cross visible from afar, constituting a kind of open chapel for prayer and other ceremonies. Since it was impossible to build individual graves (most of the remains could not be identified), mass graves with crosses would be used instead. The design of the joint cemetery at Kharkov was particularly challenging.

An exceptionally important development was the signing on 19 October 1996 by Russian premier Chernomyrdin of resolution number 1247 of the government of the Russian Federation "on the establishment of memorial complexes at the burial sites of Soviet and Polish citizens—victims of totalitarian repressions at Katyn (Smolensk District) and Mednoye (Tver District)." The memorial complexes thus received the status of state institutions. The Polish military cemeteries were to be built within their boundaries, in accordance with the Russian-Polish protocol of 25 March 1995. The resolution also specified the tasks of the respective Russian institutions and services. The design of the Russian memorial complex was to be selected through a competition to be organized by the Russian Ministry of Culture. The Russian side also promised to convey to Poland by the end of September 1997 the complete official documentation concerning the allocation of land for the cemeteries and the final delineation of their boundaries.

Przwoźnik and the authors of the Polish design presented it at a meeting of the Russian coordinating committee in Moscow on 23 January 1998, attended by the Russian-appointed directors of the memorial complexes at Katyn and Mednoye, as well as representatives of Russian deputy premier Oleg N. Sisuyev, the Russian Ministry of Foreign Affairs, the Ministry of Internal Affairs, the Ministry of Finance, and the district authorities of Tver and Smolensk. Moreover, the CPSMS conveyed the project documentation to the Russian side and asked for its quick approval by the competent authorities and services and for the issuance of a formal permit for the construction of the cemeteries.

Those attending a meeting of the district Working Commission for the Implementation of Undertakings Connected with the Commemoration of Victims of Totalitarian Repressions in Mednoye, held in Tver on 5 February 1998, fully approved the architectural and conceptual design of the Polish military cemetery at Mednoye. Its mutual integration with the design of the entire memorial complex was stipulated as a condition of its construction.

The decision allocating land for the project at Mednoye was not issued until 1 June 1999 and the formal building permit, 2 July 1999. All this required numerous representations, talks, interventions, and arrangements.

On 23 April 1999, the CPSMS obtained the Russian decision allocating land for the construction of the Polish military cemetery at Katyn and, on 22 June 1999, the formal building permit.

On 27 June 1998, the presidents of Poland and Ukraine attended the ground-breaking ceremony and laying of the foundation stone for the cemetery at Kharkov. On 7–9 December 1998, CPSMS general secretary Przwoźnik hammered out with the Kharkov district authorities an agreement on the final boundaries of the cemetery and received from them a list of 2,746 names to be inscribed on the Ukrainian wall of the cemetery.

In 1994, the CPSMS signed an agreement with the IHCIKC for the preparation of inscriptions on the individual name plaques of the Polish officers and policemen resting in the three "Katyn cemeteries" and of cemetery books for Katyn, and later, for Kharkov and Mednoye. The Katyn cemetery book was published in 2000, Kharkov's in 2003, and the last, for Mednoye, in 2006.

Under decision number 271 of 24 March 1999, the Executive Committee of the Kharkov City Council allocated 4,248 square meters of land in section 6 of the forest park to the CPSMS and issued a design and building permit for the construction of the cemetery.

Construction at Kharkov started on 31 March 1999. The work on the construction of the Polish military cemetery at Katyn began on 18 May 1999 and ended on 17 July 2000. The work at Mednoye started on 2 July 1999. The formal acceptance of the cemeteries took place on 9 August 2000.

On behalf of the CPSMS, General Secretary Przewoźnik supervised all matters pertaining to the construction of the Katyn cemeteries. The presidents of the Federation of Katyn Families and the Police Family 1939 Association were present during the adoption of all key decisions and took part in inspections of the construction sites. All of the cemeteries were financed with Polish state funds, that is, the CPSMS budget and public funds collected by the Katyn Families and the Polish Katyn Foundation.

The Katyn cemetery has an area of 13,900 square meters. It is fenced with metal elements 470 meters in length. The graves, with monumental crosses lying on them, are enclosed with a wall to which individual epitaphic plaques have been attached. The altar complex consists of a wall with the names of those murdered in Katyn, a sacrificial table, a 9-meter central cross, and an underground bell. Opposite are obelisks with the Polish national emblem and the Virtuti Militari and September Campaign Crosses and vertical plates with the symbols of the four religions of the victims. The death pits are covered by cast-iron plates. Two individual graves, those of Gen. Bronisław Bohaterewicz and Gen. Mieczysław Smorawiński, are located beside the altar, along with a plaque that reads, "In tribute to the more than 4,400 officers of the Polish Armed Forces resting in the Katyn Forest—prisoners of war from Kozelsk camp, murdered in the spring of 1940 by the NKVD. Polish Nation."

Regretfully, it has proved impossible to this day to commemorate the Kozelsk camp or the Polish officers buried at the local cemetery, despite representations made since the early 1990s by the Polish embassy in Moscow and written consent given by Alexei, the patriarch of Moscow and All Russia. Any commemoration has been opposed by the monks from a monastery in Kozelsk, regained by the Russian Orthodox Church in 1987.

The cemetery in Kharkov has the shape of an irregular quadrangle with a total area of 2.31 hectares and the following dimensions: 143 meters (southern side), 134 meters (western side), 97 meters (northern side), and 64 meters (eastern side). Its main elements include seventy-five mass graves (fifteen contain Polish citizens, and sixty hold citizens of Soviet Ukraine); two cast-iron crosses, one Catholic and one Orthodox in design; the so-called black road (the graves and road are inlaid with basalt set stone); a Polish altar wall (similar to the one at Katyn) and a Ukrainian altar wall (a vertical cast-iron plate with the names of 2,746 murdered Soviet citizens of various nationalities—Ukrainians, Russians, Poles, Belarusians, Germans, Lithuanians, and others) with an Orthodox-type cross; and a main avenue connecting the two cemeteries, flanked with epitaphic plaques (mounted on the underpinning) and the Virtuti Militari and September Campaign Crosses on pedestals. Obelisks with the emblems of Poland and Ukraine stand at the entrance, with the symbols of the four religions of the victims farther to the left.

As a result of representations by the Polish Consulate General in Kharkov, a plaque commemorating the Polish officers imprisoned in Starobelsk was unveiled near the local monastery in 2005.

The Polish military cemetery in Mednoye occupies an area of about 17,000 square meters. It is surrounded by a wall 524 meters in length and, on the inside, a concrete-surfaced avenue flanked with epitaphic plaques. Twenty-five mass graves, each demarcated by cast-iron plates and marked with an 8-meter cross across the surface, are located behind the altar complex. Opposite the main entrance stand two obelisks. Bas-relief carvings of a Virtuti Militari Cross and a September Campaign Cross are displayed on pedestals. In addition to a plaque unveiled on 30 August 1991, another has been mounted with the following inscription: "In tribute to the more than 6,300 officers of the State Police and Silesian Voivodeship Police, the Border Guard and Prison Guard, soldiers and officers of the military gendarmerie, the Border Defense Corps and members of other military units, employees of state administration and administration of justice of the Second Republic, resting in Mednoye—prisoners of war from the camp of Ostashkov, murdered by the NKVD in the spring of 1940 in Kalinin (Tver). Polish Nation."

The cemeteries in Katyn and Mednoye have been transferred to the administrations of the Russian state memorial complexes, which are responsible for their ongoing maintenance.

Memorial plaques have also been mounted in Kalinin, on the former NKVD building, in whose cellars the Polish police officers were murdered. Today, it houses a medical institute. The Russian plaque commemorates those killed at the NKVD-MGB headquarters in the years 1930–50. The Polish plaque bears the following words: "In memory of the prisoners of the Ostashkov camp, murdered by the NKVD in Kalinin. A warning to the world. Katyn Family."

In August 1994, granite plaques, with Virtuti Militari Crosses and the following words etched in Polish and Russian into their surfaces, were unveiled at the monastery building in Ostashkov:

Officers of the State Police and Silesian Voivodeship Police, the Border Guard and Prison Guard, soldiers of the military gendarmerie, the Border Defense Corps and members of other units of the Polish Armed Forces were imprisoned at this monastery during the period from September 1939 to May 1940. 6,311 of them were sentenced to death. Kalinin (Tver) was the place of their murder. Next, in the summer of 1940, Polish soldiers from Lithuania and Latvia were brought to Ostashkov and in the years 1944–1945, soldiers of the Home Army. May all the Poles murdered, tormented, and imprisoned here rest in peace. Compatriots.

Forty-five prisoners died at the Ostashkov camp before the NKVD started transporting the other prisoners away to their deaths. They were then buried in a cemetery near the village of Svetlytsa. One of the Polish graves has been preserved at the Troyeruchitskoye Cemetery, where, in the early 1990s, retired teacher Boris F. Karpov put up a small cross with a metal plaque bearing the names of forty-one deceased Poles. After an inspection by CPSMS specialists, a design was prepared for the permanent commemoration of the grave with the names of all prisoners of the Ostashkov camp who had died before the other Polish prisoners were taken away to their deaths.

In the year 2000, on the sixtieth anniversary of the crime, the Polish military cemeteries were opened and consecrated: Kharkov on 17 June, Katyn on 28 July, and Mednoye on 2 September. Members of the Katyn Families were the main participants in the ceremonies. Tribute to those murdered was paid by Polish members of parliament and government delegations of Poland, Russia, and Ukraine. The Polish delegation was led in all three locations by Prime Minister Jerzy Buzek. The Kharkov ceremony was attended by Ukrainian prime minister Viktor Yushchenko, while Russian deputy premier Viktor B. Khristenko was present at Katyn and Russian internal affairs minister Vladimir B. Rushailo was at Mednoye.

Solicitations made by the CPSMS resulted in the Katyn cemeteries being granted the status of "cemeteries of state importance," maintained by the central authorities of the two countries in whose territory they are located—the Russian Federation and Ukraine. It is noteworthy that, on 16 April 2005, the president of Poland, acting on a motion submitted by the CPSMS and the Polish embassy in Moscow, conferred high state decorations on thirty-one Russians and Ukrainians for their services in revealing and documenting the truth about the Katyn crime and also for assistance in building the cemeteries.

The construction and subsequent opening and consecration in 2000 of the Polish military cemeteries at the final resting places of Polish officers and policemen from the three special NKVD camps in Kozelsk, Ostashkov, and Starobelsk, murdered by the decision of the Soviet Politburo of 5 March 1940, seemed to close the most important chapter of the Katyn case. Alas, though long awaited in Poland and unprecedented, it did not close the Katyn case.

Murdered in Ukraine and Belarus

The fate of Poles detained in NKVD prisons set up in areas annexed by the Soviet Union and incorporated into the Ukrainian SSR and the Belarusian SSR as western districts, and who were sentenced to death on the basis of the same Politburo decision of 5 March 1940, could not be determined before the construction of the Polish military cemeteries that became the final resting places of Polish officers from the special NKVD camps in Kozelsk and Starobelsk and policemen from the NKVD camp in Ostashkov.

At present, we have only the so-called Ukrainian list, containing 3,435 names of victims of the Katyn crime murdered within the territory of the

Ukrainian Soviet Socialist Republic. We still do not know the names on the so-called Belarusian list, that is, the names of Polish citizens detained in NKVD prisons in the western districts of Soviet Belarus and also murdered on the basis of the decision of 5 March 1940. Attempts to obtain any related documents have been unsuccessful to date despite repeated archive searches.

We also do not know the location of the mass graves of Poles murdered in Ukraine and Belarus. Documents discovered in Russian, Belarusian, and Ukrainian archives contain the names of places or localities that constituted the last stop on the martyr's journey of the Polish citizens. These places are Kuropati, near Minsk in Belarus; Bikovnya, near Kiev; Kherson; and probably also Kharkov, in Ukraine. Our knowledge is limited to the very names of the places, where searches need to be conducted (we know more only about Bikovnya). A more precise location of the graves themselves is not available. Surveying and exhumation works in Kuropati, for example, could probably yield answers to these and other questions.

The so-called Ukrainian wall, with the names of persons from the Ukrainian Katyn list, consecrated on 28 October 2005 and located at the field cathedral of the Polish Armed Forces in Warsaw at the Katyn chapel opened on 15 September 2002, has become a symbolic grave and memorial to those murdered in Ukraine. The chapel walls are covered with the names of the prisoners of Kozelsk, Ostashkov, and Starobelsk, and the altar features an icon with an image of the Holy Mother of Ostrobrama (twelve by eight centimeters) and a sign that reads, "Kozielsk. 28.02.1940 rok." The icon was made in Kozelsk by Lt. Henryk Gorzechowski (subsequently murdered in Katyn), on his son's birthday, using a pine board detached from a camp bunk. The chapel was established at the initiative of the field bishop of the Polish Armed Forces, Gen. Sławoj Leszek Głódź, in collaboration with the field ordinariate of the Polish Armed Forces, the CPSMS, and the Ministry of National Defense.

Attempts to determine the fate of Polish citizens detained by the NKVD in Poland's eastern territories occupied after 17 September 1939 encountered numerous difficulties after the disclosure of the key document of 5 March 1940 pertaining to the Katyn crime. The disclosure of Soviet documents made it possible to recreate the mechanism used to annihilate that group of Polish citizens, but the places where their bodies were concealed have remained a mystery to this day.

On 22 March 1940, Beria ordered the transfer of three thousand Poles, hitherto held in prisons in the western Ukrainian SSR to the NKVD district directorates in Kiev, Kharkov, and Kherson in Ukraine, and another three thousand prisoners detained in the western Belarusian SSR, to the NKVD in Minsk. The operation of murdering these prisoners started during the last phase in the liquidation of the POWs from the three special NKVD camps in Kozelsk, Ostashkov, and Starobelsk. The Poles arrested in Ukraine were killed on the basis of thirty-three so called "disposal lists." The first three lists were compiled on 20–22 April 1940 and the last ones, after 19 May 1940.

On 5 April 1994, the deputy head of the Ukrainian Security Service, Gen. Andryi Khomich, conveyed to Polish prosecutors copies of the so-called Ukrainian Katyn list, the basic document affirming the murder of 3,435 persons in Soviet Ukraine. In effect, it is a prison register of the personal files of 3,435 arrested Polish citizens. On 25 November 1940, with five bags of files attached, it was sent by the head of the First Special NKVD Department of the Ukrainian SSR, Senior State Security Lieutenant Tsvetukhin, to the head of the Special NKVD Department of the Soviet Union, State Security Maj. Leonid F. Bashtakov. That document and press articles in Ukraine and Russia indicated that the bodies of some of the victims from the so-called Ukrainian Katyn list (i.e., persons transferred to the NKVD in Kiev) had been buried at the hamlet of Bikovnya outside Kiev, situated within the territory of the Darnitsky forest park (today within the boundaries of the Ukrainian capital).

As early as March 1937, that area was set aside for the "special needs" of the NKVD and was used to store (conceal) the bodies of persons shot in NKVD torture cells, at the Lukyanov prison and the internal NKVD prison. The burial site at Bikovnya was set up during the second stage of the so-called Polish operation, implemented in the years 1937–38, which targeted Poles living in the Soviet Union. On 11 August 1937, the people's commissar for internal affairs, Nikolai I. Yezhov, issued NKVD operational order number 00485, which envisaged shooting "the first category" of arrested Poles, that is, "spying, subversive, pestilent, and insurgent cadres of the Polish intelligence service." As a result of that criminal operation, officially concluded in 1938, more than 111,000 Poles were arrested under false charges of crimes against the state and executed. Some of them were buried at Bikovnya.

In 1941, after Kiev was occupied by the Germans, local inhabitants started talking about the secrets of the burial site at Bikovnya, and some of the graves were dug up. After Soviet troops recaptured the city in 1943, the designated area at Bikovnya was no longer used by the NKVD for hiding victims' bodies. Trees were planted on the land. That, however, did not prevent the profanation of the burial site by grave robbers. Numerous written and telephone complaints by Kiev residents led to the establishment in 1971, 1987, and 1989 of government commissions concerned with "the mass burials in Sections 19 and 20 of the Dnepropetrovsk forest district, near the village of Bikovnya." The 1971 commission opened mass graves and "investigated" the human remains found at the burial site. Two hundred seven pits were discovered to contain the remains of NKVD victims. However, it was declared that those were bodies of prisoners of war and civilians—"victims of fascism," supposedly shot during the German occupation of Kiev in the years 1941–43. The excavated remains were placed in wooden crates and buried in a huge mass grave near the place of their discovery.

Various objects found on that occasion on the excavated bodies indicated that a large group of Poles and Polish citizens had been among the NKVD victims. This suspicion was affirmed through work conducted in Bikovnya by subsequent Soviet commissions in 1987 and 1989. The documentation collected during the 1990s, as well as the findings of Ukrainian prosecutors and information from families of Katyn victims whose names are on the so-called Ukrainian Katyn list, provided the basis for a request addressed to the Ukrainian authorities to allow surveying and exhumation work around Bikovnya. Polish specialists carried out such work in 2001 and in 2006–7, pursuant to an agreement concluded in 2001 between the CPSMS and the State Inter-Ministry Commission for the Commemoration of Victims of War and Political Repressions, attached to the Cabinet of Ministers of Ukraine.

The Polish team explored fifty-four Polish graves and extracted some four thousand objects of Polish origin, left behind after the graves had been dug up in the 1970s and 1980s. Some of these objects were inscribed with names that figured on the so-called Ukrainian Katyn list. The researchers discovered many important details supplementing previous knowledge on the subject and helping to expose the secret of that grim place. The work in Bikovnya needs to be continued. Contrary to hopes that the Ukrainian authorities would close the matter by the seventieth anniversary of the crime, the work had not been completed by the spring of 2012. The forest at Bikovnya contains the fourth burial site of the victims of the Katyn crime. The Katyn Families hope that here, too, another "Katyn cemetery" will be established and the victims of the crime given a dignified burial.

We know the least about the fates of the 3,870 Polish citizens transferred to the district NKVD in Minsk in March 1940. Despite efforts in recent years to obtain the "disposal lists" of those killed in Soviet Belarus, the list of those murdered—often referred to as the "Belarusian Katyn list"—remains unknown. Kuropati, on the eastern outskirts of Minsk, is mentioned as the place where the victims are buried. The area is forested, but even though it is known that tens of thousands of NKVD victims are buried there, it serves as a recreational area for inhabitants of the Belarusian capital.

The efforts of Polish authorities to obtain documentation concerning Poles murdered in NKVD prisons in Soviet Belarus in 1940, with special reference to the so-called Belarusian Katyn list, have been unsuccessful to date. A request for legal assistance and the provision of copies of documents, sent in 2002 by the Institute of National Remembrance to Belarusian justice authorities, has not received any response. Talks initiated by the CPSMS with the aim of gaining consent for exhumation work at Kuropati and commemoration of the victims of the crime committed there have similarly failed to produce positive results.

The Katyn Investigation

The Katyn crime investigation was supposed to answer many questions and resolve outstanding issues. Under public pressure, Polish general prosecutor Józef Żyto sent a request in October 1989 to Soviet general prosecutor Aleksandr Y. Sukharev to open an investigation into Katyn. In justifying the request, Żyto referred to the United Nations convention of 9 December 1948 on the Prevention and Punishment of the Crime of Genocide and the UN convention of 26 November 1968 on the Non-Applicability of Statutory Limitations to War Crimes and Crimes against Humanity, both of which had been ratified by Poland and the Soviet Union. However, the Soviet side insisted that it would be inadvisable "to settle vague issues relating to Polish-Soviet relations by instituting penal cases."

The manifestly negative attitude of the Soviet prosecutors (January 1990) changed after yet another request submitted by their Polish counterparts, coupled with diplomatic interventions. In December 1990, the Chief Prosecutor's Office of the Soviet army advised the Polish General Prosecutor's Office that Polish prosecutors would be allowed to conduct their investigations and that legal assistance would be provided along with support for the relevant proceedings. The Russian prosecutors who aided the investigation the most included Col. Stefan Rodziewicz, Colonel Tretetsky, and Anatoly Y. Yablokov. It is to their credit that the efforts designed to determine the circumstances of Katyn, despite numerous obstacles, produced such excellent results by significantly extending knowledge about the events under investigation, making possible the 1991 exhumations, and producing several dozen volumes of investigative files. On behalf of the Polish General Prosecutor's Office, the investigation was conducted by prosecutor Śnieżko.

The investigation had the goal of fully determining the circumstances of Katyn. This included identifying the names of all the Polish citizens who had become its victims, establishing previously unknown execution and burial sites, determining who was involved in adopting and implementing the decision of 5 March 1940 and the extent of their individual culpability, and also, if possible, bringing to justice any surviving perpetrators.

In August 1993, following criticism of the actions of Polish prosecutors, General Prosecutor and Justice Minister Jan Piątkowski instructed the Warsaw voivodeship prosecutor to establish a team of prosecutors to open and conduct an autonomous investigation into Katyn, under the special supervision of the general prosecutor. This "Polish investigation" concerning the Katyn case, launched by the justice minister, did not change anything in the ongoing cooperation between the Polish and Russian prosecutors. Yet, it provoked heated reactions and protests in Poland—and not only within the community of Katyn families—and resulted in Piątkowski's resignation and annulment of his decision to launch the independent investigation.

The Russian investigation, conducted in collaboration with Ukrainian and Belarusian military prosecutors, was yielding positive results until the mid-1990s—when it visibly slowed. The change in pace could be seen in the failure of Russian prosecutors to participate in the exhumation work in Katyn and Mednoye—something that might have been caused in part by the change in the political climate in Russia itself and also in Belarus. In Belarus, there was a complete atrophy of contacts and absence of any investigative results. Meanwhile, cooperation with military prosecutors in Ukraine produced ample documentation concerning the mass burials at Bikovnya and other likely burial sites. Simultaneously, contacts between Russian and Polish prosecutors were becoming looser. The departure of prosecutors Tretetsky and Yablokov—both much merited in bringing to light the circumstances of the Katyn case—affected the future progress of investigation number 159 into the Katyn case. The investigation was taken over by prosecutor Nikolai Anisimov, assisted by prosecutor Sergey Shalamayev—a move that did not stimulate action by the Chief Military Prosecutor's Office of the Russian Federation. The evident stagnation in Polish-Russian contacts provoked increasing criticism in Poland of the persons responsible for the Katyn investigation at the Polish prosecutor's office. Such criticism was voiced not only within the Katyn community but also in different political circles. The critics noted the ineffectiveness of the prosecutors and the absence of a satisfactory conclusion to an investigation conducted for several years and closely followed by Poles both at home and abroad.

In January 2001, Justice Minister and General Prosecutor Hanna Suchocka transferred all the Katyn-related documents and materials from the National Prosecutor's Office to prosecutors at the Main Commission for the Investigation of Crimes against the Polish Nation along with the task of preparing an overview of the state of the investigation and submitting proposals for further action. Henceforth, the Katyn investigation was handled by a new institution—the Institute of National Remembrance, which had incorporated the Main Commission for the Investigation of Crimes against the Polish Nation (MCICAPN).

In November 2001, the General Prosecutor's Office of the Russian Federation, responding to a request by Polish prosecutors to take a position on issues related to the Katyn investigation, advised that Polish authorities had received "a copy of the penal case along with all the protocols of investigative actions and other documents containing information about the participants in each action." It was further declared "that all actions required to make the final decision, possible within the territory of Russia, have been executed, though the final decision cannot be made due to the absence of materials from the preliminary investigation conducted by the General Prosecutor's Office of Ukraine." The Russian response indicated that the Russian prosecution would not be providing Polish prosecutors with further documents concerning the crime.

The several-year break in working contacts between the prosecutors of the two countries and, even more so, the lack of clear prospects for concluding the investigation conducted by the Russian prosecution for some dozen years, led the Katyn community to bring pressure on the Polish authorities. The slowdown provoked a public debate on issues that hitherto had been the domain of a narrow group of specialists and legal experts. The animated discussion, stimulated by the protracted investigation and the absence of clear results, focused on the following issues: the legal qualification of the Katyn murders, the moral assessment of the crime, compensation for the repressions against and death of thousands of Polish citizens, whose families had waited several decades for determination of their fate, and the matter of a fitting commemoration of all the victims.

On 21 September 2004, the Chief Military Prosecutor's Office of the Russian Federation issued a decision terminating investigation number 159. A portion of the evidentiary materials collected during the investigation and the very decision to terminate it were classified. Russian prosecutors denied requests by MCICAPN prosecutors to gain access to these materials and copy them.

On 30 November 2004, the Warsaw branch of the Commission for the Investigation of Crimes against the Polish Nation opened investigation number S 38/04/Zk "concerning the case of murders committed on at least 21,768 Polish citizens during the period from 5 March until an undetermined date in 1940, in the territory of the Union of Soviet Socialist Republics, by functionaries of that state, implementing a resolution of the Politburo of the All Union Communist Party (Bolsheviks), adopted in Moscow on 5 March 1940, which constitute a war crime and a crime against humanity."

The sovereign "Polish investigation" into the Katyn crime has the goal of fully determining its circumstances. Prosecutors have concentrated on hearing witnesses, most of whom are family members of Katyn crime victims, residing in Poland and other countries. A total of 2,522 witnesses have been examined. Another priority is searching for archive materials that might constitute evidence relevant to the investigation. MCICAPN prosecutors have searched for documentary evidence in German and American archives and in Polish émigré archives in London.

In September 2009, the Warsaw branch of the Commission for the Investigation of Crimes against the Polish Nation sent another request to Russian prosecutors for legal assistance in the ongoing investigation. The Polish prosecutors asked for access to and preparation of certified copies of the full files of investigation number 159 and the decision of 21 September 2004 to terminate the investigation. The Russian side has failed to comply with the request.

Despite multifaceted efforts by Polish prosecutors in the framework of investigation S 38/04/Zk, there is no doubt that, without access to materials collected by the Russian military prosecutors and without full access to Russian archives, a comprehensive determination of all the circumstances of the Katyn crime will be impossible. This state of veritable cold war over the matter, which has lasted for several years, needs to be ended. Only the cooperation of prosecutors from both countries, despite certain differences in their legal assessment of the Katyn crime, can lead to an elucidation of all of its circumstances, a precise compilation of the lists of victims and perpetrators, and the establishment of the locations of the victims' bodies.

The lack of cooperation over the past several years between Poland and Russia concerning the investigation and adjudication of the Katyn crime assumed a new dimension in 2005, after the chief military prosecutor of the Russian Federation, Aleksandr N. Savenkov, publicly announced on 11 March 2005 that the Katyn investigation had been terminated and most investigation files and the termination decision had been classified. Savenkov's statement and his public comments—particularly those about the legal qualification of the crime—had powerful impact and evoked indignation in both Poland and Russia. They also triggered action on the matter by the Russian Memorial Society, which had earlier given Poles invaluable assistance in exposing the truth about the Katyn crime. The Polish section of the Memorial Society, headed by Aleksandr E. Guryanov, addressed a number of questions to the Russian military prosecution concerning the legal qualification of the crime. On 4 April 2005, the Memorial Society issued a statement, "On the Investigation into the 'Katyn Crime' in Russia," in which it argued that it was unacceptable to terminate the investigation without a "processual" definition of the murder of thousands of Polish inmates and POWs without judicial sentence. The Memorial Society further demanded the rehabilitation of all the victims of the Katyn crime pursuant to Russian law on the rehabilitation of victims of political repression, and it called for public access to all materials of the Katyn investigation. Between 25 May and 2 October 2006, the Memorial Society addressed motions to the chief military prosecutor of the Russian Federation for the rehabilitation of eleven victims of Katyn, compiled on the basis of letters sent by the victims' families to the Memorial Society. Activists of the society are currently applying all possible legal measures in seeking before Russian courts the rehabilitation of this small group of Katyn crime victims.

In late 2009, the Chief Military Prosecutor's Office of the Russian Federation denied further applications submitted by families of the Katyn victims for declassification of the investigation files and posthumous rehabilitation of the Polish officers and policemen murdered by the NKVD. The Military Panel of the Supreme Court of the Russian Federation rejected all the relevant complaints lodged by Russian lawyers, arguing that there was no basis for treating the officers as victims of a crime because under the penal code of 1926, Katyn—as a common crime—was subject to the statute of limitations. It was further ascertained that foreign nationals could not be given access to the classified decision of the prosecution. Lawyers for the families of the crime victims have appealed the ruling of the Military Panel of the Supreme Court to the European Court of Human Rights in Strasbourg. A further thirteen relatives of the victims have also filed complaints with the Strasbourg court. Their number is likely to grow as families of the crime victims receive letters from the Russian prosecutors rejecting their applications.

The developments of the last few years have brought into focus a number of crucial issues, the settlement of which could close the Katyn chapter in Polish-Russian relations. These prominently include: the status of the investigation and legal qualification of the crime, rehabilitation of the crime victims, access to archives and disclosure of hitherto unknown documents, further searches for places where the NKVD hid the victims' remains, and a fitting commemoration of the victims.

Some of these issues have evoked animated debates in both countries, often inflaming bilateral relations. The attitude of the Russian authorities has caused irritation and bewilderment within the community of the crime victims' families, affiliated in the Federation of Katyn Families and the Police Family 1939 Association, which number several thousand persons. The Katyn Families have repeatedly demonstrated their moderation and appreciation of the fact that Russians and members of other nationalities in the Soviet Union had also been victims of Stalinist repressions. But the patience of people who lost their relatives seventy years ago as a result of a horrific crime has been put to a severe test by the Russian prosecutors. It is a test they are likely to pass successfully—considering what they have endured so far in the struggle for the truth about the fate of their loved ones.

The intensity of emotions that accompany the tense Polish-Russian relations concerning Katyn is well reflected by the debate on its legal qualification. A clear-cut position on the subject has been taken by the INR-MCICAPN in the justification of the decision to launch investigation number S 38/04/Zk. Minutely analyzing the facts and also the provisions of applicable Polish and international law, INR-MCICAPN prosecutors argued that Katyn is a war crime and a crime against humanity and as such is not subject to the statute of limitations. The prosecutors further hold that "the murders committed by NKVD officers on Polish prisoners of war and the Polish civilian population were motivated by an intent to destroy a part of the Polish national group.

For these reasons their actions meet the statutory definition of the crime of genocide, pursuant to Article 2 of the convention on the prevention and punishment of the crime of genocide."

An exceptionally interesting view on the subject has been expressed by A. E. Guryanov of the Memorial Society, in the bimonthly *Nowa Europa Wschodnia*. Commenting on the adoption by the Chief Military Prosecutor's Office of the legal qualification of Katyn as a common crime (abuse of power by a group of top NKVD officials), Guryanov noted, "Yet was it really genocide? It has certain traits of being that, but they can be challenged. . . . It would be much harder to challenge qualification of the Katyn crime as a war crime and a crime against humanity. Then, the prosecution would not be able to invoke the statute of limitations or to question that qualification, as it is doing in the case of Katyn treated as genocide."

The essence of the dispute concerns the legal qualification of the criminal act, arbitrarily applied by the Russian prosecutors to the Katyn crime. Its qualification as abuse of power allows the Russian military prosecution and courts to reject the successive applications of the families for reopening the investigation and rehabilitation of the murder victims.

It is hard to disagree with Guryanov that "the Katyn case is, first and foremost, our own [i.e., Russian] internal problem, and only after that an issue in Polish-Soviet relations. We need to confront the Katyn case not to improve relations with Poland but for our own sake. Naturally, this would facilitate relations with Poland, but the Katyn case is one of the Stalinist crimes and we need to confront the whole period of communism."

In the heated atmosphere generated by the visit to Poland on 1 September 2009 of Premier Vladimir V. Putin and the publication by the Russian Foreign Intelligence Service of the book *Sekreti polskoi politiki: Sbornik dokumentov 1935–1945* (edited by Lev F. Sotskov), the Polish Sejm adopted on 23 September 2009 a resolution "commemorating the Soviet Union's aggression against Poland on 17 September 1939," in which it addressed the problem.

Many persons involved in eastern issues and committed to building good bilateral relations, based on historical truth and mutual respect, have long sought ways out of the present situation, as well as the creation of a platform for open, substantive dialogue that would bring us closer to the truth about Katyn and free current Polish-Russian relations from the emotions caused by still-unresolved problems rooted in the past.

Poles are well aware that the nations of the Soviet Union, millions of ordinary citizens—Russians, Ukrainians, Belarusians, and dozens of other nationalities that found themselves under the rule of the Stalinist regime—were victims of many crimes similar to that committed in Katyn. To use the words of a Polish writer, a prisoner of the Gulag, "the inhuman land" contained tens and hundreds of execution sites such as those in Katyn, Kharkov, Bikovnya.

Our nations are linked by the common tragedies of millions of families, still experiencing a sense of grief and loss. Nothing can ever make up for it. And that alone is reason enough to pass political and moral judgment on the Katyn crime, in accordance with the law and elementary justice.

Poles still have a sense of pain after losing their loved ones. The attitude of the authorities of the new Russia is incomprehensible to many of them and only intensifies that pain. The sensitivities of Poles—and not only those touched by "Katyn syndrome"—are still being hurt by the lack of an official admission by the government of the Russian Federation that the Katyn crime was the result of a decision by the top state authorities of the Soviet Union and by the absence of an apology to the people of Poland for the crime and the sixty years of lies about it, instigated and disseminated by Soviet authorities. It is equally painful that documents of crucial importance to the case—and to the victims' families—are still being withheld. These includes the minutes of the "troika" meetings, confirmations of the fulfillment of its decisions (with respect to both POWs and civilian prisoners), the record files of the prisoners (particularly their personal files), the so-called Belarusian Katyn list, the dispatching lists of prisoners from Starobelsk, which should have been together with the similar lists of prisoners transported out of the camps in Kozelsk and Ostashkov, conveyed to the Polish side in April 1990. We still do not know the locations of the bodies of Poles whose names are on the Ukrainian and Belarusian Katyn lists. The military prosecutors terminated the Russian investigation and classified its decision and a large portion of the case files. Yet, it was the arbitrary legal qualification of the crime adopted by the Russian military prosecutors—divorced from morality and justice—that has caused the greatest pain to Poles. That decision has evoked impatience and irritation in Poland, as it is fully congruent with efforts to conceal and falsify the truth about the Katyn murders, and it has been undertaken since 1990 by historians and writers connected with the ruling circles of the Russian Federation.

The resumption of work by the Polish-Russian Group for Difficult Matters gives hope that the deadlock can be broken. It confirms that dialogue between Poland and Russia, though difficult, is possible and helps identify solutions to complex issues rooted in mutual historical experiences, which fetter present-day Polish-Russian relations. It would be a great achievement if all the circumstances of Katyn were brought to light, the classified documents made available, and issues that arose as a consequence of the crime finally settled. That is so because the crime still casts a shadow on relations between Poland and Russia. Respect for the victims of this horrific crime requires that all matters related to it find a quick and satisfactory solution.

NATALIA S. LEBEDEVA

THE PROCESS OF REVEALING THE TRUTH AND COMMEMORATING THE VICTIMS

DOZENS OF MONOGRAPHS and document collections study the Katyn issue. Hundreds of articles and thousands of informational reports are dedicated to it. And yet we still do not know the rationale behind the decision making of the Katyn crime. Who came up with the idea, Beria or Stalin? What drove them to that fatal decision? When did it come up? How was the operation that executed Polish officers, policemen, and prisoners prepared and run? What follows is another attempt to clarify these questions and demonstrate how the Soviet leaders (for half a century) tried to deny their responsibility for Katyn's execution and instead incriminate Nazi Germany.

On 7 September 1939, Stalin, in a conversation with Georgi Dimitrov, the secretary general of the Comintern Executive Committee, characterized Poland as a fascist country that oppressed Ukrainians and Belorussians, and he emphasized that "destruction of this state under the conditions of today would mean one less bourgeois fascist state! Would it be bad if resulting from Poland's defeat we extended the socialist system onto new territories and population?" This statement hides the deep reasons for the future decisions that led to the Katyn massacre. Stalin craved and strove for the liquidation of Poland as an independent state, and he planned the timely removal of those who could prevent him from succeeding in that, those who could fight for a revival of the country.

On 17 September, the day the Red Army invaded Poland, Vyacheslav Molotov, chair of the Narkomindel and the people's commissar for foreign affairs of the Soviet Union, in a radio speech, emphasized that the Polish state had gone bankrupt and had ceased to exist. The next day, a Soviet-German communiqué was signed that directly laid out the Soviet Union and Germany's mutual goal in the war against Poland. The goal implied "the restoring of order and peace in Poland, which had been violated by the dissipation of the Polish State, and helping the people of Poland to rebuild their statehood."

The Boundary and Friendship Treaty, signed by the Soviet Union and Germany on 28 September in Moscow, described the reorganization of occupied areas by Germany and the Soviet Union "as a reliable foundation for the further development of friendly relations between the people of those two countries." The secret articles contained a note of agreement of mutual assistance in the act of suppressing any Polish agitation.

From the first days of that "undeclared war," the Stalin administration closely looked into the issue of the Polish prisoners of war (POWs). Disregarding the rules of international law, prisoners were removed from the army's custody and entrusted to the home affairs authority. On 18 September, the Politburo of the Central Committee of the All-Union Communist Party (Bolsheviks) made the decision to give the guards of the Soviet Union's People's Commissariat of Internal Affairs (NKVD) the powers of martial law. On 19 September, Beria issued an order for the creation of the Prisoner of War Command. Maj. Pyotr Soprunenko became its commander, and Semyon Nekhoroshev was assigned as its commissar.

During the period between 17 September and 1 October 1939, the Red Army captured almost 250,000 soldiers and officers of the Polish army. Of those, 126,000 were sent to eight stationary prison camps, whereas the others were in transition camps or on their way there. But due to an inability to provide food, accommodation, or even fresh water to that many people, on 3 October the Stalin administration decided to dismiss the common soldiers and noncommissioned officers who lived in territories that had been annexed by the Soviet Union. In mid-October, the Politburo authorized an exchange with Germany of those same categories of military men who were from central Poland, that is, to exchange them for those from eastern regions. However, about 25,000 soldiers and junior officers were kept in the Rovno (Równe) camp and other camps of the People's Commissariat for the Iron and Steel Industry in order to build a strategic highway and to work at coal mines in Krivoy Rog and the Donbas. About 15,000 officers, policemen, prison warders, those serving in the Border Control Corps (KOP), and *osadniki* (Polish soldiers who had been given land in areas acquired in the interwar period) were detained in the Starobelsk, Kozelsk, and Ostashkov camps.

On 3 October, the Politburo gave the Military Councils of the Ukrainian and Belorussian fronts the right to "to approve the death penalty sentences by court-martials for counterrevolutionary crimes committed by civilians in Western Ukraine and Western Belorussia and military men of the former Polish army."

On 8 October, Beria forwarded a regulation to the special services of POW camps. The regulation specified the tasks for such services as being to create an informant network, to detect "counterrevolutionary formations" among POWs and those who had served in intelligence or punitive agencies, police, prisons, or KOP battalions, or who had been members of paramilitary formations, political parties, and so forth.

Soon, officials from the central office of the People's Commissariat for Internal Affairs were sent to Starobelsk, Kozelsk, and Ostashkov. On 31 October, one of the executives from the Fifth Division (Intelligence), Vasily Zarubin of the Main State Security Agency (GUGB), left for Kozelsk, while State Security captain Boris Trofimov, later replaced by State Security captain M. Efimov, went to Starobelsk, and State Security captain Antonov went to Ostashkov. They sent POWs to Moscow—Lubyanka and Butyrka—often without the approval of the Prisoner of War Command. Agents enrolled by those officials provided information about life in the camps, reporting on those who led active religious and spiritual lives, carried out educational work, or supported patriotic feelings for their comrades. All of the information was entered into evidence and kept by Special Services Departments in the camps, along with records kept by Registration Departments. Overall, materials from the agents and operational intelligence regarding Polish officers and policemen showed that the latter did not support the dividing of Poland and were ready to fight for the independence of their country.

On 3 December 1939, the Politburo affirmed the proposals by Lavrentiy Beria to arrest all registered regular officers of the former Polish army. The operation was put into action on 10 December, when 570 officers were arrested in one day. Earlier, 487 officers had been captured by investigators as "members of counterrevolutionary formations."

On 4 December, a new investigating team was sent to Ostashkov camp from Moscow. The team was headed by Stepan Belolipetsky, senior inspector of the Soviet Union's NKVD/GUGB investigation unit. The team was instructed to finalize the proceedings and indictments for all prisoners of the Ostashkov camp and to submit those findings to the Special Council (OSO) of the NKVD.

The Special Council had the right to try each case in the defendant's absence. The council could impose a sentence of placement in labor camps for as much as eight to ten years (for some causes). The council did not have the right to impose the death penalty until November 1941.

On 31 December 1939, Beria authorized the handing over of all cases for the Ostashkov camp, as well as the investigational activity of officers from Starobelsk and Kozelsk camps, to the Special Council by the end of January 1940. Soprunenko and a large staff from the central office of the NKVD were supposed to go to Ostashkov; Iosif Polukhin, deputy commander of the Prisoner of War Command, was to go to Kozelsk; and Commissar Nekhoroshev of the Prisoner of War Command was to head for Starobelsk. In the Kozelsk and Starobelsk camps, the investigation must have been completed by the end of January, and special attention would have been paid to prisoners' spirits and to detecting members of political parties, the General Staff, and so forth. It is worth noting that the Special Council was only mentioned in the order regarding the Ostashkov camp.

By the end of January, the majority of cases were in the Ostashkov camp, amounting to more than six thousand, and they were handed over to the Special Council. On 1 February 1940, Soprunenko and Belolipetsky reported to Beria via high-frequency transmission line: "Investigation [on] former Polish policemen kept [in] Ostashkov camp completed, 6 thousand 50 cases made up. Started [to] forward the cases [to] the Special Council. Forwarding will be completed by February eighth. Required investigative actions have been completed."

By the end of February 1940, the Special Council had examined six hundred police officers' cases and rendered sentences of three to eight years in a labor camp in Kamchatka. A meeting was held in Moscow to discuss the procedure for transporting the POWs from the Ostashkov camp to the Northern Far East camp. Grigory Korytov, head of the Special Services Department in the Ostashkov camp and one of those attending the meeting, reported to Vasily Pavlov, chief of the Special Services Department of the Authority of the People's Commissariat for Internal Affairs (UNKVD) in the Kalinin region, to this effect: "Out of 6,005 cases submitted, 600 have been examined so far, terms are 3–5–8 years (Kamchatka), for now, further examination has been stopped by the People's Commissariat. But by March we should have a lighter load and be ready to receive the Finns. There are instructions from the People's Commissariat to put several categories of prisoners of war in the local prisons."

Instructions from the Prisoner of War Command followed on 23 February. They authorized the procedure of the NKVD order dated 22 February concerning the transfer of "prison warders, agents provocateurs, osadniki, judicial officers, landowners, tradesmen, and major proprietors" from the camps to prisons.

Reducing the number of prisoners (a so-called unloading) of the Starobelsk and Kozelsk camps was initiated by Soprunenko. On 20 February, he addressed Beria, suggesting that about three hundred disabled, seriously ill retirees above sixty years of age and four hundred to five hundred reserve officers, residents of territories annexed to the Soviet Union (farmers, teachers, engineers, doctors) who did not have any discrediting records were to be released. At the same time, the commander of the Prisoner of War Command asked for permission from the People's Commissariat to finalize and submit for review to the Special Council cases "on KOP [Border Control Corps] officers, judicial and procuracy officers, landowners, active members of the 'POV' and '*Strelets*' parties, officers of 2nd Department of the former Polish General Staff, CCC officers (about 400 people)." The letter from Soprunenko has Beria's resolution: "Comrade Merkulov. Speak to me. L. Beria. 20.11."

After Beria spoke with his first deputy and head of GUGB Vsevolod Merkulov on 22 February, the latter signed the instructions, which declared, "Under the authority of the People's Commissar for Internal Affairs, Comrade Beria, I suggest that all former prison warders, agents provocateurs, osadniki, judicial officers, landowners, tradesmen, and major proprietors kept in Starobelsk, Kozelsk, and Ostashkov NKVD camps should be transferred to prisons and placed under the custody of the NKVD. All materials on those listed are to be handed over to investigational units of the UNKVD so they can carry out the investigations. Future procedures for such cases shall be additionally communicated. The number transferred will be reported."

What can be learned from this document? It mentioned only a relatively small number of the POWs kept in the Starobelsk and Kozelsk camps. The NKVD did not plan the repression against the majority of Polish officers, at least before 22 February. The Special Council was not mentioned in the instructions given on 22 February, although Soprunenko in his letter to Beria dated 20 February suggested that some of the cases concerning Polish officers were to be submitted to the Special Council. This indicates that the People's Commissariat had yet to make a final decision as to which authority would be in charge of examining the cases dealing with Polish officers transferred to prisons.

The letter from Korytov also contains an important remark that the "reduction" of the Ostashkov camp was caused by the necessity to accommodate imprisoned Finns. As early as 1 December 1939, the day after the Soviet Union's attack on Finland, Beria issued an order to the commanders of the reserve camps (Gryazovetsk, Yukhnovsk, Yuzhsk, Putivislk, Kozelschansk) to get ready to receive a large number of Finnish POWs.

On 21 February, Soprunenko signed a letter of information for the NKVD regarding the camps being ready to receive about twenty-five thousand POWs from Finland. A letter from Korytov confirms that, when Beria issued an order authorizing the urgent execution and handing over of all the Ostashkov camp cases to the Special Council on 31 December, he intended to free up the largest and best-equipped camp for the POWs from Finland.

While creating room for Finnish prisoners definitely was not the only goal, the mass execution was also aimed at clearing out one to three camps of the Poles. After the Soviet Union was expelled from the League of Nations (on 14 December 1939) following England and France's insistence, with the active support of the government of Władysław Sikorski, Stalin's anti-West and anti-Polish attitude intensified. Afterward, the Supreme Council made the decision to send a task force to Finland, and the Polish government insisted on including its forces in it. On 24 January 1940, during a Cabinet Council session, Sikorski declared that deployment of troops in Finland drew France and Great Britain into "actual war with Russia and the same would be rather desirable to us." August Zaleski, the Polish minister for foreign affairs, also indicated the necessity to be ready to defeat Russia at the moment the Allies declared war. Plenipotentiary Ivan Maisky informed Moscow that the sentiments of the British government had seriously shifted, to a desire for intervention in the Soviet-Finnish conflict, and that the government was ready to operate, "notwithstanding the risk of a severance in relations and even an armed confrontation."

The French-British plan of a military operation against the Soviet Union during the Soviet-Finnish War was closely connected with the idea of striking the Caspian oil fields that had been developed by the Soviet Union. Those plans had been detailed and laid out in the first months of 1940. On 19 January, within the framework of the Supreme Council session in Paris, France presented a detailed plan of attack against the Soviet Union in the region of the Caucasus and the Caspian Sea. The Supreme Council had been discussing it from February till March (the last time, on 22 March 1940). The plan provided for an intensive bombing attack against the Caspian oilfields.

The information coming to the Kremlin via diplomatic and intelligence channels solidified Stalin's hatred toward the Polish officers. He believed that, in case of a possible war launched by the Western countries against the Soviet Union, they could become a fifth column. Stalin never forgot the part that Czech POWs had played during the civil war in Soviet Russia from 1918 to 1920.

The Winter War with Finland affected the relations of Germany and the Soviet Union as well. The Hitler administration came to the conclusion that the combat worthiness of the Red Army was rather low; hence, it was possible to start preparations for an attack against the Soviet Union. The first of the German troop shifts to the western borders of the Soviet Union had been noted by Soviet intelligence services in the middle of February 1940. The weakness of the Red Army also promoted a revival of Polish underground resistance directed by the government of Sikorski.

All of these circumstances spurred the Stalin administration to take measures to strengthen security in the frontier areas, namely the western areas of the Ukrainian and Belorussian SSRs.

It is absolutely clear that, during the last ten days of February, Beria came to a certain conclusion about the prisoners of three special camps; such an idea needed to be discussed with Stalin. But having met with Stalin on 29 February, Beria would hardly dare to offer the idea of shooting all the Polish officers, policemen, and prisoners to the "Master." It is probable that he brought him this option, but most likely it was Stalin who formulated the decision.

On 26 February, under the order of the people's commissar for internal affairs, Soprunenko ordered the commanders of the Kozelsk and Starobelsk camps to quickly gather data on the POWs. There was also a proposal to send extended questionnaires to the Prisoner of War Command in order to obtain detailed information about the officers (duty status, command of foreign languages, visits abroad, and whether they had relatives in the Soviet Union). To do that, the camp's administration had to "mobilize all of the worthy camp personnel."

Verdicts on the Polish prisoners of war—the officers and policemen and the fate of the prisoners of the western areas of the Ukrainian and Belorussian SSRs and the families of all those subject to repression (both POWs and civilian prisoners)—were gathered. On 2 March 1940, the Politburo confirmed the proposal by Beria and Nikita Khrushchev, "On Security of the State Border in the Western Areas of the Ukrainian SSR and Belorussian SSR." Along with the deportation of inhabitants from an eight-hundred-meter-wide border zone, all the families of the following categories were to be deported to Kazakhstan for ten years: Polish officers, policemen, prison warders, gendarmes, intelligence officers, landowners, factory owners, and officials subject to repression and committed to camps (in total, twenty-two thousand to twenty-five thousand families). "The most malicious" of those were to be arrested and their cases brought to the Special Council.

The reaction of several thousand officers and policemen is easy to imagine if they had learned their families were being deported to the waterless steppes of Kazakhstan. However, if the relatives had learned about the massacre of their husbands, sons, and brothers, they would have become active participants in the underground struggle against the Stalin regime in the western areas of the Ukrainian and Belorussian SSRs. Therefore, the simultaneous execution of POWs (officers and policemen), prisoners, and their families was absolutely logical according to the mentality and methods of the Stalin administration.

On 2–3 March, at the order of Beria, a summary of the data about the presence of the Polish officers, policemen, priests, prison warders, frontier guards, and intelligence officers in the Prisoner of War Command camps was issued. The data given in the reports dated 3 March became the basis of Beria's note addressed to Stalin.

The categories of officers and other POWs identified in the reports dated 2 March and 3 March, and Beria's note to Stalin, are almost identical. In particular, those documents do not mention officer cadets, youth, refugees, and other persons Beria did not suggest shooting. The categories of POWs presented in the reports and the people's commissar's note are also almost identical.

Therefore, there is no doubt that the reports were prepared for Beria as a follow-up to his note to Stalin indicating that the very information dated 3 March was the basis for the people's commissar's note addressed to the "All-Union Communist Party (Bolsheviks) Central Committee Comrade Stalin" and printed on the NKVD's official letterhead. It is remarkable that Beria's note was registered under number 794/b, between the numbers 793/b and 795/b, both of which were dated 29 February. Evidently, this number was assigned to the first version of Beria's note. Apparently, its text was later modified to accommodate Stalin's remarks. The final version under the same number but dated March (the exact date was not typed) was the basis for the decision of the Politburo dated 5 March. This leads us to the conclusion that Beria's note was dated no earlier than 3 March but no later than 5 March 1940, while the decision-making process regarding the executions took place between 20 February and 5 March.

The decision-making process was likely influenced by Khrushchev's proposals that were received from Kiev at the end of February regarding reinforcement of the border protections, including the deportations of families of those who had been repressed, that is, prisoners, POW officers, and policemen. Having participated in the executions of the Polish officers and prisoners, the former first secretary of the Central Committee of the Ukrainian Communist Party (Bolsheviks) authorized in 1959 the destruction of all files on the officers and policemen, as well as the proceedings of the "troika" commission that had made the decisions to execute the POWs and other prisoners.

It is probable that, after receiving Khrushchev's proposal, Stalin instructed Beria to finalize both a draft decision on border security (its final version bears two signatures) and a note on the execution of Polish POWs (officers and policemen) and other prisoners. One fact that remains certain is the close connection between the 2 March decision, "On Security of the State Border in the Western Areas of Ukrainian SSR and Belorussian SSR," and the 5 March decision, "Issue of the USSR People's Commissariat for Internal Affairs"; both decisions were in the note signed by Beria. It was the first time that a close connection between Polish POWs (officers and policemen) and prisoners was seen.

In his note, Beria substantiated the need for executing POWs (officers, policemen, and staff of intelligence agencies) and regular prisoners in the western regions of Ukraine and Belarus by the fact that "they are all staunch enemies of the Soviet system, full of hatred toward the Soviet regime." The people's commissar stated, "Prisoners of war and policemen in camps try to continue counterrevolutionary activity, and carry on anti-Soviet agitation. Each of them cannot wait to be free, to have a chance to actively participate in the fight against the Soviet system. Agencies of the People's Commissariat for Internal Affairs in western regions of the Ukrainian SSR and Belorussian SSR have revealed a number of counterrevolutionary rebellious organizations. Officers of the former Polish army, former policemen, and gendarmes have all been leaders in these counterrevolutionary organizations." He stated that the camps for POWs contained 14,736 former officers, civil servants, landowners, gendarmes, prison warders, osadniki, and intelligence agents, 97 percent of them Polish, and that prisons in western regions of the Ukrainian SSR and Belorussian SSR housed 10,685 arrested Poles. He also emphasized that all these people "are old hopeless enemies of the Soviet system." Beria suggested that the cases of those people should be reviewed "in a special procedure and the supreme penalty, execution, should be administered."

It was suggested that the cases should be examined in the absence of the arrestees and without arraignment, with final resolution of the cases on the completion of the investigation and indictment. The fate of those kept in the prison camps was to be decided based on references compiled by the Prisoner of War Command and, of those arrested, based on cases submitted by the People's Commissariat for Internal Affairs in the Ukrainian SSR and Belorussian SSR. The examination of cases and the decisions were carried out by the "troika" commission, consisting of Beria, Merkulov, and Leonid Bashtakov, head of the First Special Division of the People's Commissariat for Internal Affairs. The document was signed by Beria. The first one to sign it was Stalin, noting "Pro." Then, having made final corrections, he crossed out Beria's name and replaced it with that of Bogdan Kobulov, head of the Economic Department of the People's Commissariat for Internal Affairs. The document then was signed by Kliment Voroshilov, Molotov, and Anastas Mikoyan. The secretary's notes in the margins read, "Kalinin pro, Kaganovich pro." Thus, the Katyn decision was made at a session of the Politburo, rather than by polling, the latter being the common method for the committee (as in, e.g., the 2 March decision on border security). Finalizing the decision based on the text of the initial document was a common practice extensively used at the time. The note by the people's commissar has a stamp, "Protocol No. para No." in the right hand corner; "13," the protocol number, and "114 O.P." (O.P. standing for "special folder") are handwritten in the stamp. The signatures of Beria, Stalin, Voroshilov, Molotov, and Mikoyan were acknowledged as authentic by the Military Prosecutor's Office in 1990–91, after it had received unambiguous reports from several independent specialists.

For more than a half century, Beria's note was kept in a sealed package along with the extract from the Records of the Politburo dated 5 March 1940, which was also drawn up per the requirements of that period. The latter was printed on a form specifically meant for extracts from the Communist Party's records of highest importance.

The notorious conspiracy theorist Yuriy Mukhin, who had never seen the phototypic representation of Beria's note, wrote that it was not written on an official form, did not have a number or date, and therefore was fake. His successors, Sergey Strygin and Vladislav Shved, who were familiar with the note, appealed for a more sophisticated explanation. Being unable to deny the authenticity of the signatures of those members of the Politburo who approved the execution on the first page of the note and Beria's signature on the last page, they attempted to convince readers that the second and third pages containing the execution decision were forged during either Khrushchev's or Yeltsin's time. However, the third page contains the words "OP [Special Folder]. Issue of the NKVD," hand-written by Aleksandr Poskrebyshev, who was in charge of the Special Sector of the Central Committee of the All-Union Communist Party (Bolsheviks). Similar writings by Poskrebyshev can be found in initial documents to the Special Folders of the Politburo. Therefore, the page on which the Politburo formulated the decision (para. 144, Record 13) dated 5 March, is authentic. Extracts from the Records of the Politburo dated 5 March 1940 (para. 144, Record 13), kept in sealed package number 1 and certified by the signature of Secretary Khryapkina, who signed many extracts from such records, also add to the authenticity.

The impossibility of forging that record of decision dated 5 March is also confirmed by filings of the original Records of the Politburo of the Central Committee of the All-Union Communist Party (Bolsheviks). There were three kinds: unclassified, confidential, and top secret. Each record of the Politburo, as a rule, included decisions from a period of two weeks to about one month prior. The numbering of items on the agenda in the unclassified "Records" was continuous, without any withdrawals. If a decision was confidential, the corresponding item had only a number and description, without the text of the decision on it. Unclassified Record No. 13, item 144, read, "144. Issue of the USSR People's Commissariat for Internal Affairs. Special Folder." In the special folders, Record No. 13 is referred to as: "144. Issue of the USSR People's Commissariat for Internal Affairs. Top Secret Special Folder." The folder of initial documents for the unclassified Records of the Politburo (F. 17, list 163) also has a page with item 144 from Record No. 13. In the right-hand margin there is an underlined notation that reads, "Note of comrade Beria." It means that the note by Beria was the initial document on which the decision (item 144) dated 5 March was based.

The sealed envelope with Beria's note to Stalin, two copies of the extract from the Record of the Politburo dated 5 March, and the sheets with the text of decisions dated 5 March, withdrawn from Record No. 13, with a note made by Aleksandr N. Shelepin, chair of the KGB at the Soviet of Ministers (Sovmin) of the USSR, dated 3 March 1959, was stored in the personal safe of the head of the General Department of the Central Committee of the Soviet Union Communist Party and then in a sealed room in the Sixth Sector of the Central Committee General Department. It had the notation, "Not to be disclosed for inquiries; no opening without the permission of the Head of the Central Committee General Department." It could be accessed only by the first persons in the party: Yuri Andropov, Konstantin Chernenko, and also

Valery Boldin, the head of Mikhail Gorbachev's administration (in 1987 and 1989). After that, the envelope was again sealed.

Plans for the "unloading" of POWs from the Kozelsk, Starobelsk, and Ostashkov camps and of prisoners from the western areas of Ukraine and Belorussia commenced directly after the fatal decision by the Politburo to execute 14,500 officers and policemen and 11,000 prisoners. From 7 to 15 March, meetings were held with the staff of the central office of the People's Commissariat for Internal Affairs and with the commanders of the Kalinin, Smolensk, and Kharkov Regional People's Commissariats for Internal Affairs, their assistants, commanders of internal prisons, and commanders and commissars of three special camps.

On 7 March, Beria ordered the people's commissars for internal affairs of the Ukrainian and Belorussian SSRs (Ivan Serov and Lavrentiy Tsanava) to be prepared for the deportation of twenty-five thousand families of those who were soon to be shot. It was planned for mid-April and was to be done in one day; the lists of people to be deported were made by 30 March. The addresses of family members were obtained from the officers and policemen; for that, special brigades from the Prisoner of War Command came to Kozelsk, Starobelsk, and Ostashkov. The lists were made not only for those who lived in areas annexed to the Soviet Union in September 1939 but also for those residing in central Poland, then occupied by the Wehrmacht.

On 16 March, reports on the POWs and prisoners detained in the three camps were drawn up. On the basis of those reports, the juridical "troika" (Merkulov, Kobulov, and Bashtakov) were to make the decisions about the executions. Reports on officers and policemen were prepared by the Prisoner of War Command and, on prisoners, by the People's Commissariats for Internal Affairs of the Ukrainian and Belorussian SSRs. The blank report was received by Soprunenko from Kobulov. Along with three columns to be filled out (first column: surname, given name, patronymic; second column: year and place of birth, family and social status, place of detention, and date of capture; third column: last position and rank in the Polish army or in police, intelligence, or punitive agencies), there was a fourth column for a conclusion. It was intended for the insertion of a brief description of the charges and the article of the Criminal Code of the Russian Soviet Federative Socialist Republic (for prisoners it referred to the Criminal Codes of the Ukrainian and Belorussian SSRs). The first three columns were filled in at the camps, the last column, by the Prisoner of War Command.

The Ostashkov camp was ordered to prepare reports with conclusions only on those for whom cases had not already been made by the Special Council, but the Kozelsk and Starobelsk camps were to prepare reports for all prisoners. That was done under high secrecy. It was strictly forbidden to order additional report forms from a print shop. When cases with completed reports were ready, they were forwarded to Moscow. By 23 March, the Starobelsk camp had already sent materials for 760 persons. On 30 March, Soprunenko demanded that he primarily be sent reports on general officers, then senior and mid-rank officers, and finally on doctors, teachers, farmers, and civilians for whom no discreditable data were available. If the cases sent to the Prisoner of War Command were short of data, particularly relatives' addresses, variations in surname spelling, or other details, they were sent back to the appropriate camp for clarification. Otherwise, the Prisoner of War Command filled in the last column (conclusion). After that, a case was forwarded to the First Special Department of the USSR People's Commissariat for Internal Affairs. There, it was studied under the direction of the deputy head of that department, State Security captain Arkady Gertsovsky. Some cases were "controlled." The decision on them was made by Merkulov personally. Other surnames were included on execution lists that were thereafter transferred for the approval of the "troika" commission, including Merkulov, Kobulov, and Bashtakov. After a list was endorsed by the trio, POWs or prisoners included on it were considered condemned to the supreme penalty (execution). The commission's decisions were drawn up in special "Records." After that, the lists authorizing the transfer of prisoners from a camp to the custody of the Regional Departments of the People's Commissariat for Internal Affairs were sent to the Kozelsk, Starobelsk, and Ostashkov camps. Those lists were signed by the commander of the Prisoner of War Command or by his deputy, Ivan Khokhlov, after Soprunenko left Moscow. Instructions about the executions were signed by Merkulov and directed to the commanders of the Kalinin, Smolensk, and Kharkov Regional Departments of the People's Commissariat for Internal Affairs.

The executions of those held in prisons in the western regions of Ukraine and Belorussia were carefully prepared, too. To centralize the execution of the Poles held in these prisons, and to minimize the number of persons involved in the operation, thus avoiding leaks, it was decided that the condemned should be concentrated in four prisons and the inmates who were already there would be transferred to Gulag, the agency that oversaw the forced labor camps. In accordance with Beria's order dated 22 March, Poles from prisons in Lvov, Równe, Wołyń, Tarnopol, Drohobycz, Stanisławów, Pińsk, Brześć Litewski, Wilejka, and Baranowicze were to be transported to Kiev, Minsk, Kharkov, and Kherson within ten days.

As files were compiled on the workers in the three special labor camps and on prison inmates, other measures were taken to prepare the execution operation. From 16 March, any correspondence between prisoners of war was banned. The administration tightened access control, increased the number of camp guards, and cut down on technical staff. The Main Department of Transport of the NKVD of the Soviet Union developed a highly detailed plan for transporting prisoners to the execution sites. For one and a half months, Solomon Milstein, head of the department, was sending reports to Beria and Merkulov on a daily basis, and sometimes twice a day, detailing each slight deviation from the transportation plan, the number of empty, loaded, and unloaded cars, and so forth.

Shortly before the start of the operation, State Security captain Efimov and Mironov, the officer of the Fifth Section of Main Directorate for State Security of NKVD, responsible for the secret service agents, arrived in Starobelsk. Zarubin again left for Kozelsk, and another officer, Dmitry Kholichev, went to Ostashkov. Throughout the entire operation, representatives of the Main Directorate of the Military Escort Guard were present in the camps.

During the operations in the camp at Równe and camps of the People's Commissariat of the Iron Industry (i.e., Krivoy Rog, Eleno-Karakubskom, and Zaporozhye), officers, policemen, and gendarmes were segregated from the others and immediately transported to Kozelsk, Starobelsk, and Ostashkov. Seriously ill Polish officers and policemen in hospitals were transferred to the same cities, with the ranks of other prisoners swelling, too. On 4 April, Beria ordered Ivan Serov and Lavrentiy Tsanava, commissars of internal affairs of Ukraine and Belorussia, to arrest every noncommissioned officer of the Polish army involved in "counterrevolutionary work" in the former Polish provinces and to keep a record and assign agents to look after all the others. The prisoners who had been Polish citizens in the recent past and now were being held prisoner in other regions of the country were taken to Kiev and Minsk.

The first execution lists were received in the labor camps from 3 to 5 April and in prisons, from 20 to 23 April. On 9 April, thirteen lists containing 1,297 prisoners' names were signed. Could the extrajudicial execution authority have substantively reviewed almost 1,300 cases in a single day? The answer "no" is obvious since it is physically impossible. And this was not a necessary step: the task of the "troika" was simply to approve the lists compiled in the First Special Department under Merkulov's supervision. As a rule, such a list would contain about 100 names and order the camp commander to immediately transfer the persons on the list to the authority of the corresponding UNKVD in Smolensk (or Kharkov, or Kalinin). On the lists were 97 percent of all the officers and policemen detained in the Kozelsk, Starobelsk, and Ostashkov labor camps. Among those sent to execution were professional officers in active service, reservists, retirees, and old-age short-timers; members of political parties and altogether apolitical people; and Poles, Jews, Belorussians, and Ukrainians.

For many years, the motivation behind keeping 3 percent of the prisoners alive remained unclear. While preparing the Katyn documents for publication, we came across a document disclosing the reasons for sparing the lives of the 395 persons. Following a petition filed by the Fifth (Intelligence) Section of the Main Directorate for State Security of the NKVD, 47 people were left alive, the same number requested by the German embassy; 19 prisoners at the request of the Lithuanian mission; 24 Germans by nationality; and 91 prisoners sent to Yukhnov on the personal order of Merkulov. Among the latter were prisoners valuable as sources of information and those who had openly declared their communist beliefs and provided various services to the camp administration. Of those remaining, 167 fell into the "other" category: privates, youths, noncommissioned officers, officer cadets, and refugees, as well as a few dozen informants.

The first three instructions for sending 343 people out of the Ostashkov camp were signed by Soprunenko on 1 April. On 3 April, they arrived in the camp, and, according to travel records, on 5 April at 9:30 a.m., the same 343 "deprived of liberty" arrived at Ostashkov in five cars. The same number of persons was accepted into custody by T. Kachin, assistant chief of the UNKVD in the Kalinin region. The same day, the head of the UNKVD, Dmitry Tokarev, sent Merkulov a coded telegram: "Executed per Detail No.1. Number 343. Tokarev." These documents can still be found in various collections and various archives, including the Central Archive of the FSB (Russia's Federal Security Service). Similar documents have been found intact, covering almost each day of the operation. All figures in the documents closely match. The last prisoners had been transported out of the camps by the end of May.

During questioning in the military prosecutor's office, Tokarev gave a detailed account of the execution process. The shooting was supervised by State Security major V. Blokhin, head of the Commandants Section of the NKVD and sent from Moscow. It was he who, together with the commandant of the Kalinin section of the NKVD, had developed a special technique for execution by shooting. One of the cells was sheathed with felted cloth to muffle the sound of gunshots. The prison was temporarily cleared of other prisoners. "From the cells, one after another, Poles were walked to the 'red corner,' that is, to Lenin's room, where the personal data were checked—name, surname, patronymic, date of birth. Handcuffed, they were walked into the prepared cell and shot with a pistol in the nape of the neck," Tokarev said. In Kalinin alone, thirty people took part in the executions, and fifty-three in the three camps. They shot the prisoners using German Walthers. "Through the second back door, the bodies were moved from the cell and then thrown into covered trucks waiting outside. Around five to six trucks transported the bodies to the burial site near the Mednoye village, which was near the summer cottages of the UNKVD and, in fact, near one of my two cottages. The site had been chosen by Blokhin. He had also brought two excavation operators from Moscow," Tokarev continued. It should be noted that German troops never occupied the location of those burial sites.

According to the security head of the NKVD, Mitrophan Syromyatnikov, the Kharkov executions, as was the case in Kalinin, were conducted at the NKVD's in-house prison located on Dzerzhinsky Street; prisoners of war were brought to the prison in black police cars of that time, so-called *voronoks*, from the railway station. By truck, the bodies were transported to the Sixth District of the local forest park, one and a half kilometers from the village of Pyatikhatki, and buried near the summer cottages of the NKVD. The superintendents of the execution were specially trained employees of the Commandants Section of the NKVD, with the active participation of the in-house prison warden, Timothei Kupriy, along with the head of the Kharkov UNKVD, State Security major P. Safonov, and his deputy, Pavel Tikhonov.

Officers from the Kozelsk camp were executed in both the Katyn Forest and, probably, the Smolensk prison as well. This is evidenced by Milstein's reports about the itinerary of the trains carrying prisoners, which repeatedly stated that cars were arriving at Smolensk *railway station,* specifically: "on April 6 this year, two cars, Nos. 602 and 673, arrived at Smolensk *railway station* at 12:15 p.m. in train No. 87 . . . four cars, Nos. 670, 351, 602, and 673, *are being unloaded* at Smolensk station." The report from 7 April noted once more, "Cars No. 670, 351, 602, and 673 *are being unloaded* at Smolensk station" (emphasis by author). This points to the fact that the cars were being unloaded at the station for a period of two days. Apparently, the officers were brought from train cars to the Smolensk prison as room was made available following the executions of another batch of Poles. Stanisław Swianiewicz, delivered to the Smolensk prison, discovered that it was completely cleared of other prisoners. In one of the eight graves of Polish officers at Katyn, bodies were positioned in neat rows, face down, in contrast to the other death pits, where the shot prisoners were found in random positions.

In the Katyn Forest, people were executed in groups, with deep graves right behind them, and all were wearing uniforms and medals; they were shot in the nape of the neck at close range—7.65-mm German bullets were used. Of the POWs, 20 percent had their hands bound with wire or a braided cord. In one of the graves, bodies were found with greatcoats wrapped around the heads and cords looped around the necks and connected with bound arms.

In accordance with a report compiled as a result of the operation by the Department for POWs, 14,587 people were executed by three regional UNK-VDs. At the same time, reports prepared for Stalin by the NKVD administration in 1941–43 mentioned a figure of 15,131 persons. Shelepin's note addressed to Khrushchev on 3 March 1959 indicated that those killed had totaled 21,857, including 8,348 officers of the Polish army, 6,311 policemen, and 7,305 prisoners. The differences between the figures contained in the May 1940 report by the Department for POWs and the NKVD figures of 1941–43 are likely because there were other POWs and policemen who had been transferred per

Merkulov's order of 22 February 1940 to the authority of the three regional UNKVDs, that is, to the prisons. Thus, they were not accounted for in the report compiled by the Department for POWs but were executed together anyway with the POW officers and policemen.

Among those sent to death were 11 generals, 1 counteradmiral, 77 colonels, 197 lieutenant colonels, 541 majors, 1,441 captains, 6,061 lieutenants, second lieutenants, cavalry officers, and flag-bearers, and 18 chaplains and other clergy representatives.

Immediately after the massacre of Polish officers and policemen, punitive measures were taken against other Polish prisoners of war. In late May, eight thousand privates and noncommissioned officers of the former Polish army from the camps of prisoners, who had worked at the factories of the People's Commissariat of Ferrous Metallurgy, were sent to Gulag's northern railway camp to construct the North-Pechorsk railway.

On 13 April, the families of Polish officers, policemen, and prisoners sentenced to death were deported. Some seventy thousand women, children, and elderly persons were banished to northern Kazakhstan, where they had no shelter, no jobs, and no means of living.

It should also be emphasized that, by executing Polish officers and policemen, Stalin's administration eliminated an experienced staff capable of contributing greatly to the fight against the Nazis by augmenting the combat capabilities of the Anders Army formed in 1941–42 and the forces under Zygmunt Berling's command. It is known, in particular, that many officers previously interned in Lithuania and Latvia and transferred in July–August 1940 to the Kozelsk camp had expressed their readiness to join the Red Army immediately after Nazi Germany's attack on the Soviet Union.

For more than half a century, the highest officials of the Soviet state and the Communist Party were making every effort to conceal the truth about the Katyn atrocities, thereby sharing responsibility to a certain extent.

In 1942, Polish members of German railway teams learned from local residents about the graves of their compatriots in the Katyn Forest. Near one of the graves they put up a wooden cross. In February 1943, the German leadership became aware of the fact, and they were quick to use the results of the exhumation to create discord among members of the anti-Hitler coalition by trying to shift attention from the crimes of Nazism to the actions of the Soviets. On 13 April, Berlin Radio informed the world about the Katyn Forest mass graves of twelve thousand Polish officers executed by the NKVD in the spring of 1940 (in fact, there were some forty-five hundred Polish prisoners of war).

In response, on 15 April, the Soviet Information Bureau accused the Nazis of the crime by alleging that the Poles had been taken prisoner by the Germans while working near Smolensk.

Neither Stalin's administration nor the democratic allies of the Soviet

Union in the anti-Hitler coalition wanted to deal with the issue, as it was undesirable. Winston Churchill wrote to his foreign minister, Anthony Eden, that "we should not pathologically remain hovering over three-year-old graves." The attempts made by Owen O'Malley, British ambassador to the Polish government, to prove the involvement of the UNKVD in the execution of Polish officers caused nothing but annoyance in the British cabinet. Franklin Roosevelt took a similar stance: the unity of the Allied coalition was a necessary prerequisite for the defeat of the Axis powers, and all the rest had to remain in the background.

Meanwhile, the German message came as a shock to the Poles. On 18 April, Gen. Władysław Anders ordered that a mass be said for the souls of the captives, prisoners, deported, and deceased in the territory of the Soviet Union and those who had lost their lives in the battle against the Wehrmacht. The Polish government turned to the International Committee of the Red Cross (ICRC) with a request to investigate the deaths of the officers in Katyn, and it was on the verge of recalling its ambassador from Moscow. However, Stalin's administration took advantage of Poland's appeal to the ICRC and accused the Poles living in London of supporting Hitler, which resulted in the suspension of diplomatic relations with Poland on 25 April 1943.

In the time leading up to the liberation of Smolensk, the head of the Agitprop of the Central Committee of the All-Union Communist Party (Bolsheviks), Georgy Aleksandrov, suggested setting up a special commission to "investigate" the Katyn case.

Stalin's administration liked the idea; however, it had to be reworked substantially. At first, it was decided, no one from the Extraordinary State Commission to Investigate Nazi Atrocities (ESC) would be allowed on the special commission. At the same time, at the end of September 1943, some of its members and forensic experts were sent to the Smolensk region with the task of investigating only the crimes of the Nazis against Soviet citizens. Among those sent was Nikolai Burdenko, the chief surgeon of the Red Army and one of the founders of neurosurgery in the Soviet Union, as well as an ESC member. On 27 September, Burdenko sent Molotov a letter:

> Dear Vyacheslav Mikhailovich,
>
> Yesterday I received your instruction from Professor Traynin regarding the conduct of the investigation in the Smolensk region and, in particular, investigating the Katyn tragedy. In regard to the latter, I kindly ask your permission (in view of the need to take out the corpses of Polish officers and accurately investigate the execution techniques and the nature of wounds) to invite, on your behalf, the Head of the Main Military Medical Administration of the Red Army, Lieutenant General Efim Ivanovich Smirnov[,] and his competent subordinates to take part in the operation. . . . I hope to complete the entire operation by 29 September. Sincerely yours, N. Burdenko.

After reading the note, Molotov issued a resolution addressed to his deputy, Andrey Vyshinsky: "I gave no instructions to Comrade Traynin about Katyn. It is necessary to think it over as to when and how this problem should be addressed. Comrade Traynin was too quick in giving orders to Comrade Burdenko. V.M. 27.IX." As a result, the chief surgeon of the Red Army and other members of the ESC left for Smolensk, but it was not until the second ten days of January 1944 that they were given access to the Katyn case. Stalin's administration decided to prepare thoroughly before granting the representatives of the ESC access. The "preliminary investigation" was headed by Merkulov, the people's commissar of state security, who, as mentioned above, in April–June 1940 was first deputy of the people's commissar of internal affairs and was in charge of the operation dealing with the execution of the Polish officers, policemen, and prisoners. The main task in this case was the destruction of evidence against the NKVD and the forgery of documents about the Nazis' responsibility for the Katyn crime. Merkulov's team prepared numerous false witnesses, forged the necessary "documents," and planted them in the graves. By 10 January, an elaborate report had been compiled and signed by Merkulov and Sergei Kruglov, first deputy of the people's commissar of internal affairs.

After the case was prepared by employees of the NKGB and the NKVD, on 13 January 1944 the Politburo made the decision to "set up a special commission to investigate the circumstances dealing with execution of imprisoned Polish officers by the German fascist invaders in the Katyn Forest (near Smolensk)." Burdenko was appointed chair of the commission, whose members included the following: the writer Aleksey Tolstoy; Metropolitan Kolomensky; Nikolai Galitsky, chair of the All-Slav Committee; Aleksandr Gundorov, lieutenant general of engineering troops; S. Kolesnikov, chair of the Executive Committee of the Red Cross and Red Crescent Society; Vladimir Potemkin, people's commissar of education of the RSFSR and academician; Yefim Smirnov, head of the Main Military Medical Workers and Peasants Red Army (WPRA); and P. Melnikov, chair of the Executive Committee of the Smolensk region. No representatives from Allied countries or Poles from the Union of Polish Patriots (UPP) living in the Soviet Union were included in the commission.

The reputation of the members of the Special Commission had to mask the falsifications mastered by the staff of the People's Commissariat for Internal Affairs led by Merkulov. Any doubt expressed by any member of the Extraordinary State Commission created such a strong reaction on the part of the state security people's commissar that Burdenko and other members were happy to finally sign the text prepared in the People's Commissariat for Internal Affairs and the People's Commissariat for State Security. The communiqué of the Special Commission published in January 1944 confirmed the lie that the mass killings of the Polish POWs in Katyn had been carried out by fascist aggressors.

The attempt to buttress this conclusion at the expense of the credibility exercised by the International Military Tribunal in Nuremberg failed. The sentence it handed down did not mention the Katyn executions.

At the height of the Cold War, in 1951, the US House of Representatives called a special commission on the Katyn case. Having heard numerous witnesses and investigated documents, including reports on the exhumations, diaries, and other records found in graves, the commission members came to the unequivocal conclusion that it had been the authorities of the People's Commissariat for Internal Affairs who had massacred the Polish officers and policemen, so as to eliminate all those who could prevent "complete communization of Poland." Moscow kept watching the process closely and called its own commission on the Katyn case within the Ministry of Foreign Affairs. The representative of the Soviet Union's Ministry of State Security, D. Grebelskiy, became a member of that commission.

The Katyn executions were quickly forgotten in the Soviet Union, and any references thereto were withdrawn from historical works and encyclopedias.

In pro-Soviet Poland, the word *Katyn* was treated as antistate. Repressions could follow if one dared to put a candle under a cross with such an inscription. The families of martyrs were compelled to hide any relics left by the victims. But the memory of those killed, despite all the exiles, prisons, camps, and prosecutions, was alive and bleeding, and it separated the Polish and Russian nations. And only truth could eliminate the yawning gap between them.

Poles in emigration clutched at every tiny bit of information on Katyn. Adam Moszyński had performed titanic work in drawing up a list of the executed Polish officers and policemen. In 1948, *The Katyn Crime in the Light of Documents* was published in London under the editorship of General Anders. That collection was reprinted thirteen times. In 1951, *Murderers from the Katyn Forest,* a book by Józef Mackiewicz, was published in London. Janusz Zawodny, a professor at the University of Pennsylvania in the United States, contributed greatly in terms of the scientific development of this topic. His work, *Death in the Woods,* was translated into many languages; it revived the interest of the world community in Katyn and gave strong impetus to new research papers. The most famous publications on Katyn were the four books by Louis FitzGibbon, an English historian, published from 1970 to 1979, which created a stir in the West. In England, a massive campaign was launched to raise funds to erect an obelisk in London in memory of the victims. The BBC aired a long program devoted to the Katyn tragedy. Airey Neave, the former Nuremberg process prosecutor, speaking in the House of Commons of the British Parliament, demanded that the investigation into this case be resumed.

In the Soviet Union, there were people who did not wish to put up with the government's lie about the fate of the Polish officers. In 1969, the Ukrainian poet and publicist A. Karavansky, who had spent twenty years in Soviet prisons, appealed to the Soviet Union Communist Party's Central Committee and Office of the Public Prosecutor demanding a new investigation into the Katyn case. In 1970, Karavansky was sentenced to an additional ten years' imprisonment, and he was not released until 1989. Aleksandr Solzhenitsyn wrote about the Katyn crime in the third volume of *The Gulag Archipelago*.

In April 1980, on the fortieth anniversary of the Katyn executions, a group of Soviet human rights defenders (L. Alekseeva, A. Amalrik, V. Bukovsky, B. Vail, T. Ventslov, A. Ginzburg, Natalya Gorbanevskaya, Z. and P. Grigorenko, B. Efimov, P. Litvinov, K. Lyubarsky, V. Maksimov, V. Nekrasov, and others) published a prophetic statement. They expressed confidence to the effect that soon the day would come when the people of the Soviet Union would pay what is due all participants (executioners and victims) in the tragedy according to their deeds—whether evil deeds or martyrdom. The signers assured the Polish people that responsibility borne by the Soviet Union for the crimes committed by its officials in Katyn was not forgotten and would never be forgotten.

In the early 1980s, the Katyn topic was discussed ever more persistently by human-rights defenders and supporters of Solidarność in Poland. In May 1981, a committee was set up to raise funds to erect a monument to the Katyn victims. The monument was erected in the Warsaw military cemetery in July. However, the state security authorities of socialist Poland destroyed it overnight. Martial law, declared in December 1981, suspended for a while any open expression of grief over the Polish citizens killed by Stalin's executioners; however, since the second half of the 1980s, the Katyn topic has received mass media attention, including TV coverage, and has made it onto screens with unprecedented force. Official Warsaw decided that it was impossible to tamp down the topic any longer and that it would be more reasonable to take the side of the truth seekers. The bilateral "White Spots" commission of historians of the Soviet Union and Poland was created in 1987. One of the most important tasks it was assigned was searching for the truth about Katyn.

However, for two years the commission members could not find common ground on the issue. In May 1988, the Polish historians presented an expert review of the conclusions drawn by the Burdenko Commission, proving inconsistencies. However, the Soviet researchers, led by Georgy Smirnov, director of the Marxism-Leninism Institute, were not authorized (by the Soviet Union's Central Committee of the Communist Party) to question the Hitlerites' responsibility for the Katyn executions.

A member of the Politburo, Alexandr Yakovlev, who supervised the work of the commission, wrote,

And then all the tedious palaver of the search process began. The Polish party of the commission pushed G. Smirnov; he in turn was phoning me asking to help him with searching the documents. Each time I turned to Mikhail Serge-yevich, he replied to my numerous requests with . . ."Continue the search!" I repeatedly asked Valery Boldin, head of the General Department of the Cen-tral Committee, who was the keeper of archives, where any documents on Katyn could be. He assured me that he did not have anything, with a slight ironic smile on his face. . . . This process went on and on and on. But one day it was suddenly over. I was approached by Sergey Stankevich[,] who told me that a historian named N. S. Lebedeva had unexpectedly found information about Katyn while going over documents of escort guard troops.

However, the Central Committee interfered with the matter. On 22 Feb-ruary 1990, the head of the Central Committee's International Department, Valentin Falin, sent Mikhail Gorbachev a letter containing the following passage:

A number of Soviet historians (Yu. N. Zorya, V. S. Parsadanova, N. S. Leb-edeva) . . . have discovered previously unknown materials on the Prisoner of War Command and Command of the Escort Guard Troops of the USSR People's Commissariat for Internal Affairs dated 1939–1940 concerning the so-called "Katyn case." . . . Based on new documented facts, the Soviet his-torians are preparing materials for publication. . . . Making public such ma-terials would turn the situation around, dramatically. Our argument to the effect that no materials were found in the state archives of the USSR that shed light on the true background of the Katyn tragedy will not hold water. . . . The materials discovered by the scientists, and in all truthfulness, they have un-doubtedly dug up only a small part of the many caches out there, combined with the data available to the Polish party will hardly allow us to stick with the old versions any longer and avoid drawing the line.

The situation was discussed during a session of the Politburo, and, as a result, the publication of the historians' articles was banned. Despite that, I asked Sergey Stankevich to give the article manuscript to Egor Yakovlev, the editor in chief of the *Moscow News* [*Moskovskie Novosti*]. The article was pub-lished in the newspaper on 25 March 1990 and was truly a bombshell. It took the highest authorities of the Soviet Union more than three weeks to issue the TASS statement admitting the responsibility of the People's Commissariat for Internal Affairs for the executions of the Polish officers and policemen. Polish leader Wojciech Jaruzelski received photocopies of several cases with orders on the transfer of prisoners from the Kozelsk and Ostashkov camps to the custody of the Smolensk and Kalinin Regional Departments of the Peo-ple's Commissariat for Internal Affairs, that is, for execution, and also the list of registration cases of POWs transferred from the Starobelsk camp. In 1994, the deputy chief of the Ukraine Security Service, Gen. A. Homich, transmitted to the assistant to Stefan Śnieżko, the general public prosecutor of Poland, a list naming 3,435 prisoners from western regions of the Ukrainian SSR featuring the number of orders, that is, the sentencing and execution list (the so-called Ukrainian list). The Belorussian list, with around 3,870 names, has not yet been found.

In September 1990, Mikhail Gorbachev suggested that the Military Office of the Public Prosecutor of the Soviet Union file criminal charges for the mass executions in Katyn, Kharkov, and Kalinin. Aleksandr Tretetsky, colonel of justice, was appointed head of the investigation team on that case.

The Soviet Union's Communist Party leaders continued to hide the most important materials: the top secret special folders of the Politburo. As indicated by Alexandr Yakovlev, in December 1991, as Mikhail Gorbachev turned the government over to Boris Yeltsin, he handed the latter an envelope with the Katyn documents and warned him to be very careful with it. After the Russian president had gone through the materials, he agreed that it was worth thinking over. Only in October 1992 were the materials—the decision by the Politburo dated 5 March 1940, Beria's notes to Stalin dated March 1940, and the notes of Shelepin to Khrushchev and others dated 3 March 1959—presented within the framework of the Soviet Union's Communist Party legal proceedings. At that time, authorized copies were handed over to the Polish president, Lech Wałęsa.

In 1990–91, the Polish Military Commission got an opportunity to make copies of a large number of the materials (more than one million pages) featuring information about the Polish POWs in the Soviet Union. In 1992, the archival services of the two countries signed an agreement on the preparation of a four-volume edition of documents about the Katyn crime under Stalin's regime. I was honored to become a compiling editor and a member of the main editorial board. Two volumes were published in Russian, four in Polish, and a one-volume edition was published in English.

On 13 July 1994, the head of the investigation team of the Military Prosecutor's Office, Anatoly Yablokov, who had replaced Tretetsky, passed a ruling on the termination of the criminal case due to the deaths of the guilty parties. The ruling stated that Stalin, Mikoyan, Mikhail Kalinin, Kaganovich, Beria, other leaders and personnel of the People's Commissariat for Internal Affairs, and the executioners were guilty of the crimes per clauses "a," "b," and "c" of Article 6 of the Charter of the Nuremberg International Military Tribunal, that is, crimes against peace, war crimes, and crimes against humanity. However, three days later, the Military Prosecutor's Office and General Prosecutor's Office canceled Yablokov's ruling, and another public prosecutor was assigned to continue the investigation. In 2005, the case was finally terminated and the decision was classified, as were the majority of the 182 other cases. At the same time, it is worth noting that the investigators of the Military Prosecutor's Office had never questioned the fact that the execution of the Polish officers, policemen, and prisoners was carried out by the People's Commissariat for Internal Affairs.

Russian mass media repeatedly informed the public of the Katyn executions. Memorial complexes were opened in Katyn, Kharkov, and Mednoye. The truth about the Katyn tragedy is vital not only for the families of the victims but for the peoples of Poland and Russia, too. Feeling the other's pain as one's own and being determined not to allow a repetition of a tragedy like that is the only way to build a bridge over the Katyn watershed. And it is also very important to keep this bridge from destruction by either party.

6

WORLD WAR II, 1941–1945

POLITICS AND ITS CONSEQUENCES

Wojciech Materski (Poland)

Professor, Institute of Political Studies, PAS, member of the Polish-Russian Group on Difficult Matters since 2008.

Valentina S. Parsadanova (Russia)

Professor and researcher at the Institute of Slavic Studies of the Russian Academy of Sciences.

WOJCIECH MATERSKI

. . . .

POLITICS AND ITS CONSEQUENCES

. . . .

SOVIET-GERMAN COOPERATION, BASED on the treaties concluded in August and September 1939—though it visibly cooled in time—precluded the prospects for Polish independence. That was obvious as long as Poland was torn apart by the two collaborating regimes of occupiers. Only conflict between them would create a chance for the Polish cause.

The situation radically changed in June 1941, when Germany invaded the Soviet Union. That shattered an alliance that had brought about the fall of the Republic of Poland. The signing of the Polish-Soviet normalization treaty (Sikorski-Maisky Treaty) on 30 July 1941 meant the restoration of diplomatic links between the two countries. Opportunities appeared for rescuing hundreds of thousands of Polish citizens deported deep into the Soviet Union and kept in harsh conditions, as well as for the development of Polish armed forces on Soviet territory.

The next two years were marked by conflicts and misunderstandings of varying intensity over the implementation of the July accord, particularly with respect to the amnesty decree and the organization in the Soviet Union of Polish armed forces. The position of the Polish side in that primarily diplomatic confrontation gradually weakened. Moscow's prestige and clout within the anti-German coalition was vastly enhanced by the breakthrough in the military situation and the assumption of a permanent combat initiative by the Red Army. The United States and Great Britain now considered the Soviet Union their number-one ally, playing a crucial role both in Europe and in the final showdown with Japan. Poland, meanwhile, was seen as an increasingly embarrassing burden in that decisive phase of the war and in the maneuvering over the future world order.

The Problem of Borders and Citizenship
after the Treaty of 30 July 1941

The Polish premier attached secondary significance to the issue of borders in the negotiations before the signing of the treaty of 30 July. He agreed to postpone the matter until after the war, restricting himself to the formula that "the 1939 Soviet-German treaties concerning territorial changes in Poland have lost their force." This, doubtless, was an extremely grave diplomatic mistake.

The first misunderstandings over the issue of borders and citizenship appeared in connection with the fulfillment of the amnesty decree. They concerned the interpretation of the term "Polish citizens." Beginning in late October 1941, local authorities in the Kazakh SSR, followed by their counterparts in other republics, started denying Polish citizenship to Belarusians, Ukrainians, and Jews from the territories in eastern Poland annexed by the Soviet Union. The Polish embassy repeatedly protested against localities in eastern Poland being treated as Soviet territory.

The embassy made the first formal protest over the matter to the People's Commissariat for Foreign Affairs (Russian acronym: Narkomindel) on 10 November 1941. The Russian response presaged a serious and protracted conflict. The Narkomindel advised that all citizens of the annexed territories of eastern Poland had acquired Soviet citizenship under the law of the Soviet Union, while "the question of borders between the USSR and Poland has not been resolved and will be considered in the future."

During his talks in Moscow in December 1941 with Premier Władysław Sikorski, Stalin attempted to introduce the topic of borders. He stated they should reflect the incorporation of Eastern Prussia into postwar Poland and should run along the Oder in the west. That show of generosity was obviously meant to weaken the Polish premier's resolve in upholding the inviolability of the border affirmed in Riga. Premier Sikorski—exhausted by the visit and in failing health—refrained from taking up the difficult subject of the borders. He restricted himself to the general declaration that Poland's eastern 1939 border could not be questioned.

Shortly after departing from the Soviet Union, Sikorski further argued that the time had not been right for discussing such a pivotal issue. He insisted that it would be better to wait for the spring of 1942, when the Germans were expected to launch their offensive. It is possible that Sikorski—with his cabinet sharply criticized for its eastern policy—wanted to avoid any liabilities inherent in internal political bickering.

The postponement of the border issue was to have grave consequences in the future, since it would prove difficult to address the question in a way consistent with the Polish *raison d'état*. Also, it had a highly adverse impact on Polish citizens in the Soviet Union. They were confronted with the official Soviet position that the inhabitants of Poland's eastern territories incorporated into the Soviet Union had acquired Soviet citizenship regardless of their wishes; that circumstance would result in thousands of personal tragedies.

In an atmosphere made tense by constant misunderstandings, on 16 January 1943 the Narkomindel informed the Polish embassy that, henceforth, all persons who had resided until 1 November 1939 in territories incorporated into the Soviet Union, regardless of their origin, would be treated as Soviet citizens. At that time, according to the NKVD, 215,000 former citizens of the Second Republic remained on Soviet territory; they included more than 92,000 Poles, more than 102,000 Jews, more than 14,000 Ukrainians, and 6,500 Belarusians. That great number of Polish citizens now faced the threat of having Soviet citizenship imposed on them and, thus, losing formal ties with their homeland and not being able to return to it in the future. Premier Sikorski's entire eastern policy was in tatters.

On 26 January, the Polish Ministry of Foreign Affairs—in a note handed to Aleksandr Bogomolov, Russia's ambassador to the Allied governments in exile in London—categorically rejected the new Soviet policy concerning the citizenship of people living in Poland's eastern territories. Premier Sikorski wrote a personal letter to Stalin on the subject, but it had no effect. The Americans and British also refused to intervene. Pres. Franklin Roosevelt was brutally frank: this was no time to take up the issue of citizenship and borders as long as the Soviets were winning battles.

The new Polish ambassador to Moscow, Tadeusz Romer, repeatedly tried to raise the issue with the Soviets. Romer took a conciliatory approach, but Commissar Vyacheslav Molotov consistently replied that there could be no negotiations with foreigners on matters that the Soviets considered their domestic business. Ukraine's deputy commissar for foreign affairs, Oleksandr Kornyichuk, charged the Polish government with imperialist strivings, such as plans to annex Ukrainian territory and move Poland's eastern border to the Dnieper and the Black Sea. The room for dialogue was gone.

Controversies over the Polish Army

The prime minister of the Polish government in exile, Gen. Władysław Sikorski, attached particular importance to the development of the numerical strength of the armed forces. The Polish army reconstituted in France in the years 1939–40 was a formidable force of some eighty thousand men, but, after the defeat of France, only a third had been evacuated to Britain. The treaty with the Soviet Union of 30 July 1941 contained provisions (Article 4) on the formation of a Polish army in the Soviet Union. That created the prospect of the Polish armed forces being expanded several times over, since the pool of potential conscripts was enormous.

Pursuant to Article 4 of the Sikorski-Maisky Treaty, a bilateral military accord was signed on 14 August, detailing the formation of the Polish force. A joint military commission optimistically predicted that it would take six weeks to mobilize, train, and prepare the first units of the Polish army for front-line deployment and that this would be achieved by 1 October 1941.

The formation of the force began on 22 August 1941, following the issuance of Order Number 1 by the commander of the Polish army in the Soviet Union, Gen. Władysław Anders. The operation ran into difficulties from the very outset. It turned out there was a dramatic shortage of officers among the men wanting to enroll. Also, several days later, the Soviets advised the Polish army command that, in view of the situation on the front, they could supply arms for only one division. The chances for rapid deployment of the army to the front line had practically disappeared.

In December 1941, Sikorski held talks with Stalin in Moscow. Referring to the harsh conditions in which the Polish army was being assembled, Sikorski suggested that it should be moved to Persia, where the climate was milder and where American and British assistance would permit the rapid creation of a powerful force. Stalin's reaction was sharp: he called the proposal British intrigue.

The constant problems with the provision of arms and equipment for the Polish divisions were key factors that Sikorski had to take into consideration. More important, it was not possible in the Soviet Union to expand the Polish army to the size he had envisioned, while the Americans and British guaranteed the possibility of that larger force in the Middle East. Yet, it was a political argument that proved decisive: the joint operations of the Polish and Soviet armies on the eastern front could have great impact.

It was agreed that the Soviet authorities would, after all, find the resources needed to maintain the Polish army at the level of 96,000 men and that the Polish side would determine the areas where it would be concentrated. Sikorski could hardly have hoped to obtain more. It was further determined that the target size of the Polish army in the Soviet Union would amount to eight divisions, or about 150,000 men under arms. Even though the details of its future combat deployment had not been settled, the Polish side made it clear that the army should be used in battle as an integral force, since its use was the only guarantee of optimal psychological impact on the people of Poland.

Sikorski also tried to raise the matter of the missing Polish officers, but he was told they probably had fled to Manchuria.

In early December 1941, it was of considerable importance to Stalin to ensure that the Polish army remained in the Soviet Union. As Sikorski and Stalin negotiated, the Red Army—suffering great losses—barely managed to stop the German offensive on the approaches to Moscow. The military situation would soon change, creating a new political context for the continued deployment in Soviet territory of a numerically strong and organizationally coherent army of a Western country. But, on 3 December, short-term considerations were decisive; Stalin was now willing to make the costly promise of equipping a hundred-thousand-strong Polish army in order to get the outcome he wanted.

After Premier Sikorski's visit, military issues initially gained some momentum. The State Defense Committee of the Soviet Union adopted a resolution on 25 December 1941 clearing the way for the expansion of the Polish army to six divisions and defining its new concentration points and equipment allocations. A loan of 300 million rubles was granted to finance the development of the force. The ranks of the army swelled rapidly and, by January, exceeded seventy thousand men. However, the promised arms and equipment were not being delivered. Despite that, the Soviet authorities demanded that the Fifth Infantry Division, which was the best-trained and best-equipped unit of the Polish army, be deployed to the front line. But even the Fifth Division was not sufficiently trained and armed. There was no doubt that, in early February, it did not meet the requirements of Article 7 of the military agreement, stipulating that "Polish units shall be moved to the front only after attaining full combat readiness." An astounded General Anders flatly rejected the Soviet demand.

Further developments seemed to indicate that, in bilateral relations or talks with the Americans and British, the Soviet Union needed to argue that the Polish army wanted to avoid going into combat shoulder to shoulder with the Red Army. In reality, sending the Poles into battle would have been quite a problem for Stalin: the true situation at the front line would have been exposed, along with the high losses suffered by the Soviets, their inept command structures, and the poor quality of training. Most important, Soviet citizens would then be exposed to contact with people who were extremely critical of the internal situation in the Soviet Union. The Soviet leadership had precise intelligence on the mood within the Polish army and was not willing to permit such an ideological confrontation.

The refusal to send the Fifth Division into battle provided the pretext needed to orchestrate a crisis. Without it, the Soviets would have found it difficult to block the further expansion of the Polish army and stop the outflow of unpaid Polish laborers from work camps, places of enforced settlement, work battalions, and collective farms already stripped of men.

The conflict concerning the Fifth Division was somewhat defused after an unexpected conversation between Stalin and General Anders on 18 March 1942. It was agreed that the Polish army's food rations were going to be given to forty-four thousand soldiers. Moreover, Stalin consented to the evacuation to Persia (Iran) of forty thousand Polish troops and, in a crucial move, withdrew the demand that Polish divisions be deployed to the front as soon as they were formed. On that issue Stalin was unequivocal: "We are not pressing the Poles to go to the front. The Poles can be deployed when the Red Army reaches the Polish border."

In terms of diplomatic custom, the meeting was remarkable. Deliberations between the commander of the Polish forces and the head, albeit informal, of the Soviet state—held in the absence of the Polish ambassador—were certainly thought provoking. Stalin was clearly playing up the divisions among the Poles.

The first evacuation of the Polish army to the Middle East began in late March 1942. More than thirty thousand troops and twelve thousand civilians left the territory of the Soviet Union.

The main goal of the Polish side, that is, Premier Sikorski and General Anders, apparently consisted of extracting from the Soviet Union the largest possible number of Polish troops and civilians. However, leaving one corps of the Polish army in the Soviet Union—as Sikorski was planning in late April 1942—would make it possible to keep the recruitment stations operating and send surplus troops to the Middle East. That would fulfill the promise of retaining a Polish military force in the Soviet Union and permit the continuation of the campaign to rescue Polish civilians stranded there.

Meanwhile, Polish-Soviet relations started rapidly deteriorating. The Soviets charged that the Polish embassy in the Soviet Union and its local missions were gathering intelligence and conducting anti-Soviet propaganda. Local Soviet authorities started confiscating previously issued certificates of Polish citizenship and forcing some of their holders to join the so-called construction battalions of the Red Army. In late April 1942, the Soviets blocked recruitment into the Polish army; they closed the registration points and resupply centers at railway junctions.

The issue of restoring recruitment gained top priority in Sikorski's dealings with the Soviet Union, and the latter dominated bilateral relations over the next few months of 1942.

On 2 July, the Narkomindel informed the British ambassador to Moscow, Archibald Clark Kerr, that the Soviet authorities had consented to the relocation of three Polish divisions to Persia (Iran). The British government then advised Sikorski that, if the Polish government agreed to this, Britain would quickly provide arms and other equipment for the troops.

A complete evacuation from the Soviet Union would have substantially weakened the international position of the Polish government in exile. The Polish army in the Soviet Union, a largely independent force, was an important asset. In an aide-mémoire conveyed to the Foreign Office on 4 July, Polish consent to the evacuation was linked to the fulfillment by the Soviet authorities of a number of conditions, including their formal agreement to the continuation of recruitment until the pool of potential recruits was exhausted.

The Soviet government did not react in any way to the Polish conditions. It merely issued a statement that it did not oppose the use of three Polish divisions, stationed at that time in the Soviet Union, in the Middle East. In other words, it presented the whole matter as if the Polish side were the supplicant.

On 31 July, the parties signed a protocol in Tashkent on the evacuation of the Polish army and the families of Polish soldiers to Persia (Iran). All units, without exception, were to leave the territory of the Soviet Union. The complete evacuation of the Polish army from the Soviet Union, to be conducted in two stages, marked a diplomatic defeat of the Polish government. Not only were the Soviets ridding their territory of a force they considered vexatious, but the Poles were leaving amid accusations of having shirked combat, reneged on the treaty of 30 July 1940, and cheated an ally.

The commander of the evacuation base at Krasnovodsk, Lt. Col. Zygmunt Berling, and two of his aides refused to be evacuated. Berling was to play a key role in the subsequent formation of a new, "correct" Polish army.

The departure of the force from the Soviet Union significantly weakened Poland's position within the anti-Nazi coalition. Various factors had contributed to the move, prominently including British diplomatic maneuvering and Soviet ideological motives. The Poles were divided on the matter, while Stalin—as early as the spring of 1942—was obviously seeking to end cooperation with them.

Origins of the So-Called Leftist Alternative

The establishment in the Soviet Union of the Union of Polish Patriots (UPP) was connected with Stalin's commitment to finding a leftist alternative to the Polish question. Formally, the union came into being in June 1943, but that merely marked the crowning of a process initiated in 1942. It was then that the conviction had started growing in the Soviet Union that the Red Army was likely to enter Central Europe first and be able to dictate its future.

Moscow used the Comintern and, after its dissolution in June 1943, the International Information Department of the Central Committee to lay the groundwork for communist rule in Poland, Czechoslovakia, and Yugoslavia and thus to create along its western border a band of states under Moscow's tight control. The policy was designed to protect the Soviet Union's territorial acquisitions, consolidate its world position attained by the end of World War II, and maintain its political power.

Soviet efforts to establish a community of subservient, politically active Poles were facilitated in late September when Lieutenant Colonel Berling, acting on behalf of a group of officers who had not left the Soviet Union during the second evacuation, conveyed to Stalin a seven-point program. It incorporated slogans about building "a free and sovereign parliamentary republic," completely independent of the Polish government in London, which "no longer represented the interests of the Polish people." The new, democratic Poland would not "advance claims to territories inhabited by Ukrainian, Belarusian, and Lithuanian majorities."

The elaboration of the program coincided with increased activity by the Polish communists in the Soviet Union. They were grouped around the editorial office of the journal *Nowe Widnokręgi* (New horizons), which sought to become a political counterweight to the Polish embassy. The newspaper published indiscriminate attacks against Sikorski's government along with political editorials advocating that Poland's prewar eastern border be given up in favor of "moving" the country westward. By the end of 1942, Soviet propaganda unabashedly promoted that political grouping as an alternative to the Polish government in London, relations with which were now considered an impediment. The Soviets were looking for a pretext to break off those relations—a situation that was obvious to the Polish side. Polish foreign minister Edward Raczyński recalled, "We had the impression that the time was coming when Stalin would sever relations with the legal Polish government. He only seemed to be waiting for an opportune moment."

The pretext to break diplomatic relations was provided by the reaction of the Polish government to the report by Radio Berlin that mass POW graves had been discovered in the Katyn Forest.

The Soviet authorities' severance of relations with the Polish government in exile dramatically marginalized the latter's diplomatic possibilities. Furthermore, the Comintern was disbanded in mid-May—a move the West received with enthusiasm, believing that the Soviet Union had abandoned the path of ideological confrontation and would be a trustworthy ally in the future. All this created an extremely adverse environment for the Polish government and minimized its chances of countering the concept of the leftist alternative.

In the dramatic days following the discovery of the Katyn crime and the severance of relations, the Soviet authorities consistently assured the Allies that they were not contemplating the establishment of a Polish communist government in Moscow. This assurance created the appearance that relations with the Polish government could still be restored; the Americans and British took that at face value and made diplomatic efforts toward that end.

The Union of Polish Patriots (Związek Patriotów Polskich, or ZPP), during an informal period of its activity prior to the congress in June 1943, espoused a broad political platform designed to appeal to both communists and people with center-left views. Its political program was reduced to a few catchy slogans: alliance with the Red Army in the struggle against the German occupiers, restoration of the Polish state within legitimate borders, and parliamentary democracy pursuing a progressive agenda of social and economic reforms.

In the spring of 1943, the ZPP—with the broad backing of the Soviet authorities—began laying the groundwork for its organizational structures. Using propaganda and currying goodwill by financing social programs (nursing homes, orphanages, and schools taken over from the Polish embassy), it gradually eroded the natural reserve or even hostility of the Polish exiles. With time, it won relatively large support in local Polish communities. That facilitated the launching of the next stage in the leftist-alternative campaign: the building of another Polish army in the Soviet Union—an army that this time would have a different ideological image.

The decision to again organize Polish armed forces in the Soviet Union was made in May 1943. The formation of the First Corps of the Polish Armed Forces in the USSR was launched in August 1943. Zygmunt Berling, advanced to the rank of general, became its commander, though most of the front-line officers were Soviets transferred from the Red Army. Polish communists, on the other hand, made up the majority of the political officers. In all respects, including political, organizational, and operational, the force was subordinated to the Soviets. At an early stage of its formation and training, in September 1943, the Polish Tadeusz Kościuszko Division was sent to the front and used near the village of Lenino in Belarus to attack strongly fortified German positions.

The operation had pivotal tactical significance: by feigning offensive action, the Poles were supposed to tie down German forces on the right wing of the western front, preventing German deployment in the direction of the main thrust of the Red Army, in the central part of the front. But the command of the First Division had not been advised of the true nature of the operation and doggedly attempted to break through the German positions—the possibility of which had not even been anticipated by the Soviet top brass. As a result, the Poles—practically deprived of Soviet backup and sent into combat without proper reconnaissance—suffered huge losses, exceeding three thousand men, or 25 percent of their battle complement. The division lost its combat capacity and was transferred to the front reserves.

The heavy losses of the Kościuszko Division at Lenino appear to have been intended. They allowed Stalin to argue at the Tehran conference that the ZPP and its military arm were playing an important role and, unlike the army of General Anders that had been evacuated from the Soviet Union, were not sparing blood for the sake of the Allied victory.

In March 1944, the First Corps was transformed into the Polish Army in the USSR, subordinated to the command of the First Belarusian Front. It was part of the second echelon of the front in Volhynia, and, without being assigned offensive tasks, it focused on training, with a special emphasis on ideological indoctrination. That force and the clandestine People's Army, which operated in Poland, merged in July 1944 to form the communist-controlled Polish Armed Forces.

The Kremlin planned to resurrect Poland as a satellite state that would be neither "very strong, nor very large." The first political outline of such a Polish state was made in a draft declaration by the Union of Polish Patriots in December 1943, which made friendship with the Soviet Union and Czechoslovakia the main goals of Polish foreign policy.

In order to create the appearance that the "Polish government" being set up in Moscow was not a puppet of the Soviets, work on its preparation was launched by subservient Poles, rather than by the Soviets themselves. This, however, was halted after news reached Moscow that some hitherto unknown structure, claiming to represent the leftist pro-Soviet option, had been established in Poland.

Indeed, the National Council of Poland (NCP) had been formed on the night of 31 December 1943, at the initiative of the communists. It was a quasi parliament of political forces willing to implement the Soviet plans for Poland. In a programmed declaration, the NCP denied the Polish government in exile the right to represent the nation and called on the Polish people to back the policy of a close alliance with the Soviet Union.

A lack of efficient communications and insufficient knowledge about the people forming the NCP were the reasons why the Soviet authorities were at first extremely distrustful, especially since the council had been founded immediately before the Red Army entered Polish territory.

In order to get its bearings in the situation, on 1 February 1944 the Central Committee of the Soviet Communist Party established a body called the Central Bureau of Polish Communists (CBPC), headed by Aleksander Zawadzki. It was a secret structure, the existence of which was unknown to either the Polish communists in the Soviet Union or the Central Committee of the Polish Workers' Party (or PWP, organized by communists in Poland under German occupation in January 1942). The CBPC was tasked with finding, vetting, and proposing to Soviet authorities trustworthy people who could be assigned to top- and mid-level posts in a new, pro-Soviet Poland. In late May 1944, the CBPC reconciled itself with the establishment of the National Council of Poland and pledged to recognize its future executive branch. That, however, did not end the misunderstandings between the CBPC and the communists in Poland, or the distrust toward PWP activists.

The Second Annexation of the Eastern Territories
of the Second Republic

On the night of 3 January 1944, the Red Army advanced into the eastern territories of the Second Republic. When the news reached the Polish government in exile, it issued a statement expressing hope that the Soviet authorities would "respect the rights and interests of the Republic of Poland and its citizens." The statement elicited a furious response on the part of the Soviets.

In a counterstatement published on 11 January, they flatly rejected any possibility of discussions on the basis of the Riga Treaty, dismissing it as "annexation," though at the same time raising the possibility of Polish territorial gains in the west at the expense of Germany.

On 15 and 16 January, the Polish government in exile addressed notes of protest to the governments of Britain and the United States, asking them to undertake immediate mediation in order to bring about direct Polish-Soviet talks. The cabinet in exile found itself in a desperate situation after the British tried to persuade Stanisław Mikołajczyk—who became the Polish premier after the death of General Sikorski in an air crash at Gibraltar on 4 July 1943—to accept the Soviet demands as the basis of any talks, and in particular, to agree to the Curzon Line as Poland's eastern border.

On 12 January, Sarny became the first large Polish town to be occupied by the Red Army. Soon afterward, the NKVD organized "a spontaneous rally of the population," who adopted a message of homage to Stalin. In it, they expressed joy at having become "free citizens of the Great Soviet Union" and confidence that they would soon lead "happy Soviet lives under the sun of Stalin's constitution." Similar rallies were routinely held in other towns, where similar resolutions were also adopted.

As the Red Army occupied successive areas in the former eastern territories of the Second Republic, the authorities set about establishing Soviet administrative structures in them, from the district level down to the respective villages. After the first Soviet occupation, the German occupation, and the deportations, few Poles lived in those areas anymore and those who did were not as well organized as those in central Poland. This was true in the southeastern territories of the Second Republic, where losses caused by the two occupations were further aggravated by mass murders perpetrated on the Polish population by Ukrainian nationalists.

When reinstituting the local civil administration, the Soviets were forced to bring in trusted cadres from the outside, particularly people who had already worked in Poland's eastern territories during the first occupation, of 1939–41. This approach was logical, yet it did not guarantee efficient governance since even their Soviet party colleagues considered these people "depraved bootlickers." It is estimated that, after the hostilities ceased, local administrative staff constituted not more than 10 percent of the total staff in these western borderlands of the Soviet Union.

The establishment of a network of Soviet civil administration advanced faster at the district and region levels, where the NKVD and the army provided direct cover. Progress was much slower in rural areas, particularly in the south (Volyhnia, eastern Galicia) where Ukrainian—and to a lesser extent, Polish—underground organizations were active. In some areas, the Soviets controlled the garrison town and little else. Mass repression of the population was the only effective remedy. Yet, that difficult situation in the reoccupied eastern territories of the Second Republic did not prevent the Soviets from pushing ahead with Stalin's plan of the "leftist alternative" for Poland. It was accelerated after the Polish government in exile launched an important political initiative.

On 26 April 1944, Polish president Władysław Raczkiewicz issued a decree on the provisional administration of the occupied territories, pursuant to which the government delegate in Poland (holding the rank of deputy premier) established on 4 May the so-called National Council of Ministers. Its primary task was to prepare for an armed uprising and to assume authority in areas vacated by the German occupation forces. That move seriously complicated the implementation of the Kremlin's plans in Poland. Stalin responded by reviving the idea of a Polish National Committee, abandoned after the creation of the NCP. Around 22 June, he assigned the task of working out the details to the Central Bureau of Polish Communists. Within a month, the work was done, and, after Stalin introduced the final touches, it took the form of the Polish Committee of National Liberation.

Stalin and the Warsaw Uprising

Units of the First Belarusian Front reached the eastern approaches of Warsaw in late July. Their appearance and the widespread conviction in the Polish capital that the Germans were pulling out prompted the commander in chief of the Home Army to order an armed uprising in the city. It was to constitute a key stage of Operation Tempest: attacks from the rear on withdrawing German forces, the assumption of control of main towns, and establishment of an administration in these towns by duly appointed representatives of the Polish state who would then be in a position to meet the incoming Red Army as the effective authority. Earlier attempts to implement Operation Tempest, despite initial combat collaboration with the Red Army, met with dramatic setbacks after the Soviets treacherously disarmed and arrested the Home Army fighters. Yet, there was no feasible alternative to Operation Tempest.

All the underground organizations active in Warsaw, including the communist People's Army, joined in the uprising, which thus gained an all-national character.

The decision to take up arms in Warsaw was sudden and based on assumptions that had not been fully verified. The uprising was launched without consulting the Red Army or the Allies in the West.

The very first hours of hostilities showed that the situation on the ground differed from what the intelligence reports had predicted. Far from being depleted, the German forces in the city had in fact been significantly strengthened. On the approaches to Warsaw, in the region of Radzymin-Wołomin, German divisions inflicted heavy losses on the Soviet Second Tank Army—a setback that stopped the offensive by the First Belarusian Front. The insurgents in Warsaw found themselves in a dramatic situation.

The Warsaw Uprising contravened Stalin's consistently pursued idea of resolving the Polish question by way of the so-called leftist alternative, particularly because the uprising had assumed such a broad, bipartisan character and received worldwide publicity. If the uprising succeeded and the National Council of Ministers was unveiled in Warsaw as the representative of state authority, it would be hard to legitimize the recently formed Polish Committee of National Liberation (PCNL).

It was symptomatic that, two days before the insurgents went into action, Radio Moscow broadcast a message from the ZPP to the inhabitants of Warsaw exhorting them to take up arms against the Germans. Furthermore, on 30 July, Radio Tadeusz Kościuszko repeatedly broadcast the following call: "People of Warsaw! To arms! . . . Attack the Germans! Help the Red Army."

In accordance with the original plan of the offensive, the Red Army was to take Warsaw on 6 August 1944. In the new situation, after the lost tank battle, Stalin ordered that the assault be stopped when the troops reached the approaches to the Polish capital. Meanwhile, active defense of the Magnuszew bridgehead created the appearance that the offensive was still under way, though that did not help the insurgents.

The Soviet side did not respond to attempts made during the first days of the uprising by the Central Command of the Home Army to establish communications with the staff of the First Belarusian Front. When Premier Mikołajczyk and the British Military Mission in Moscow brought the matter to Stalin's attention, there was no answer. The Soviets also ignored a cable sent by the uprising's commander, Gen. Tadeusz Bór-Komorowski, to the commander of the First Belarusian Front, Soviet marshal Konstanty Rokossowski, requesting that the two forces coordinate their combat operations. There was no reaction to the dispatch of several liaison officers to the right bank of the Wisła between 12 and 15 September in an attempt to establish contact.

Stalin ignored a request made by the British on 5 August for the Soviets to aid the uprising with airdrops of arms and ammunition. Worse still, he would not allow Allied aircraft carrying such supplies to the insurgents to land in Russian-held territory. Despite that, the British started making airdrops for the Warsaw insurgents in early August. However, the Soviet refusal to grant the Allied planes landing rights on the right bank of the Wisła restricted the scale of the operation and resulted in heavy losses. In making that decision, Stalin wanted to prevent effective assistance to the insurgents, thus diminishing the prospects of their victory.

That, too, was the purpose behind Stalin's order to senior Soviet commanders in Poland to intercept and disarm any Home Army units making their way toward Warsaw to help the uprising.

On 14 September, forces of the First Belarusian Front occupied the part of Warsaw on the right bank of the Wisła. Now it would be impossible, in propaganda terms, to keep ignoring the fighting city across the river, particularly in view of the solidarity that the soldiers of the First Polish Army felt with the insurgents. For these reasons, Stalin agreed to an assault landing of Polish army units on the other bank of the river.

A plan hurriedly prepared by General Berling envisaged that the assault would be conducted in three waves. However, due to the lack of support by the front command and a shortage of landing craft, just over four hundred troops were able to cross the Wisła during the first phase of the operation. Meanwhile, two Soviet armies (the Forty-Seventh and the Seventieth) and front reserves could have provided support.

The fighting between 17 and 23 September to hold the Warsaw bridgeheads proved bloody and ineffective, because the forces committed to the task were woefully inadequate. But the point was merely to demonstrate that the Warsaw insurgents had received aid; the success of the operation, however, would only have generated political complications.

The Polish troops, denied Soviet support, lost five thousand dead, wounded, and missing in action. On 23 September, Marshal Rokossowski ordered that the assault operation be abandoned and forces of the First Belarusian Front adopt defensive positions along the right bank of the Wisła. They would remain in those positions until January 1945.

In stopping the offensive of the First Belarusian Front at the gates of Warsaw, Stalin was obviously guided by political motives, more so than any military, operational, or even moral considerations. He allowed the Germans to suppress the uprising and thus prevented the creation of a center of Polish administrative authority that would have rivaled the PCNL installed in Lublin. He had used the Germans to get rid of a very serious problem.

The Polish Committee of National Liberation and Legalizing "Lublin Poland"

The formal pretext for launching an executive organ of the "leftist alternative" was provided to the National Council of Poland and the Union of Polish Patriots on 15 July 1945, when they officially petitioned Stalin about "the need to establish a provisional Polish government." Actually, the idea had been raised two months earlier by Stalin himself in a conversation with Oskar Lange, a professor of economics at the University of Chicago and a communist sympathizer. Stalin noted on that occasion that, since the Polish question was complicating relations between the Allies, "it would be best to establish in Poland some kind of a provisional government, such as a National Committee, which would then force England and America to recognize it."

On 19 July, the decision was made to establish a delegation of the National

Council of Poland for the Liberated Territories, tasked with organizing civil administration beyond the Curzon Line, as the Red Army pressed westward. However, two days later, on 21 July 1944, at Stalin's bidding, that was changed, and, instead of the delegation, a quasi government called the Polish Committee of National Liberation (PCNL) was formed. Its "manifesto," dated 22 July 1944, was cleared with Stalin in every detail.

The PCNL described itself as "a provisional executive organ of the National Council of Poland," established "at this historic moment" to "lead the liberation struggle of the people, win independence, and restore Polish statehood." Since the NCP aspired to the role of an underground parliament—as officially affirmed in its resolution of 15 August 1944—the declaration by the PCNL was tantamount to claiming the status of de facto government, thus undercutting the competencies of Mikołajczyk's government in exile.

By installing the PCNL on a strip of Polish territory and using it as a front, the Soviet "Big Brother" was able to avoid the embarrassing situation of having to introduce direct Soviet occupational administration.

At first, probably for tactical reasons, in its communications with the Western Allies Moscow sought to downplay the role of the PCNL, suggesting that, in the future, it might merely "constitute the core of a provisional Polish government made up of democratic forces." That clearly meant that the restoration of links with the Polish government in exile was out of the question, as was its reconstruction, and any compromise would have to view the PCNL as the basis of a future Polish government.

Later that month, a delegation of the NCP, now acting on behalf of the PCNL, visited Moscow and signed two key documents: on July 26, an agreement on relations between "the Soviet commander in chief and the Polish administration" after the entry of Soviet forces into territory both sides described as Polish and, on July 27, a bilateral agreement on the common border. The Soviet side had made an explicit link between its consent to the establishment of the PCNL's administration in areas occupied by the Red Army and confirmation by the committee, in the form of a secret document, of the postwar border between the two states.

The competencies of the PCNL, its mode of operation, and cooperation with the Soviet side were discussed with Stalin by PCNL head Bolesław Bierut and aides on a visit to Moscow from 4 to 7 August. Ostensibly, the PCNL delegation had come to Moscow to meet with representatives of the Polish government in exile to review the possibility of reaching some kind of political accommodation, forming a joint government, and settling the issue of the borders.

The NCP delegation was advised that Central Committee member Nikolai Bulganin would be accredited with the PCNL as the Soviet representative. That quasi-diplomatic Soviet representative—a general in active service—arrived in Lublin on 4 August. His true role was revealed by his attendance at

PCNL sessions and by regular contacts with the prime minister and leaders of the PWP. No important decision was made without his approval. Bulganin acted as advisor to and supervisor of the "Lublin" authorities until 20 November 1944. Formally, he was replaced by the former Soviet ambassador to the Allied governments in London, Prof. Victor Lebedev. In practice, the duties of Soviet representative to the PCNL (subsequently: Polish Provisional Government) were fulfilled by the head of the Soviet military mission attached to the PCNL, Gen. Sergey Shatilov, while Lebedev continued his posting in London. That arrangement functioned until the end of January 1945.

Bulganin, as a member of the War Council of the First Belarusian Front, had good insight into both military issues and overall Soviet policy concerning the Polish question. He had been sent to Lublin to supervise the installation of the government imposed by Moscow and to coordinate the relevant activities of the Soviet special services. He must have also followed the conflict between the CBPC and the Polish-based communist leaders (so-called natives).

Initially, the CBPC had the upper hand, since it enjoyed the trust, or rather less distrust, of Stalin. It had a part in drafting the PCNL manifesto and determining the committee's composition. The CBPC strived both to dominate the PWP by sharply criticizing its program and to limit the role of the NCP. After the Red Army entered Polish territory, some CBPC members joined the leadership of the PWP, constituting its most pro-Soviet faction; they wanted to cut short the transitional period and begin full sovietization of the country. In view of Stalin's well-known distrust of Polish communists, it is likely that maintaining tension between the two Polish groups was intentional, since it made it easier to keep things under control and efficiently steer the process of legalizing the leftist alternative.

The establishment of the PCNL constituted an early phase of that plan, though already it had yielded certain international benefits. These included de facto relations with several states from the United Nations group, prominently including France. Furthermore, the committee helped the international community—and especially the United States and Great Britain—become accustomed to the Soviet scenario of resolving the Polish question. At the same time, the PCNL played an important role in administering Polish territories after the Red Army entered them; its very presence helped eliminate any local representation of the Polish government in exile.

However, the continued existence of the committee hindered inter-Allied talks on the postwar order while contributing little to the international recognition of the "new" Poland. Accordingly, the decision was made to move to a more advanced form of government in Poland—a provisional cabinet similar to the solutions applied in France and Yugoslavia.

At Stalin's bidding, on 31 December 1944, the NCP replaced the PCNL (active since July 1944) with the Provisional Government of the Republic of

Poland, led by Edward Osóbka-Morawski as premier. In the run-up to the meeting of the Big Three in Yalta, that formula was meant to legitimize the Soviet Union's partial takeover of its zone of influence, already affirmed in Tehran. Stalin hoped that the new body would make it easier for Roosevelt and Churchill to withdraw their recognition of the Polish government in exile.

On 5 January 1945, the Presidium of the Supreme Soviet granted de jure recognition to the Polish Provisional Government. The Soviet cabinet (Council of People's Commissars) appointed Victor Lebedev as its diplomatic representative to the Provisional Government. Meanwhile, Zygmunt Modzelewski, a longtime activist with the Polish and French communist movements, became the Polish ambassador to Moscow. The Soviet delegation to the PCNL was transformed into the Soviet Military Mission in Poland. These changes had little significance when it came to practical governance in Poland. It still functioned within the prerogatives determined in Moscow. All current decisions were cleared with the Soviet representative in Lublin, then in Warsaw after 1 February 1945, when the administrative center moved to the Polish capital.

The international context was pivotal to all this. The maneuver was designed to demonstrate the consolidation of the Lublin administration and its durability beyond the provisional stage of a "committee." The objective was to change the negative attitude of the United Nations group of states, particularly the big powers, in favor of the government installed by Moscow in Poland and to further erode the international position of the Polish government in exile. Meanwhile, the leaders of the Big Three were to meet in Yalta soon, to decide on the postwar order in Europe.

The Yalta conference was held 4–11 February, when the Red Army was just sixty kilometers from Berlin. The political horse-trading over the future of Central and Eastern Europe was taking place without any involvement of the Polish government in exile, or even the Provisional Government. On Poland, the conference adopted the so-called Yalta formula, according to which the Polish Provisional Government could count on the recognition of the Big Three powers only if it was reconstructed "on a broader democratic basis, with the inclusion of democratic leaders from Poland itself and from Poles abroad." The process of reconstruction was to be coordinated by a Good Offices Commission (Commission of Three) composed of Soviet foreign minister Molotov and the ambassadors of the United States and Great Britain to Moscow, Averell Harriman and Archibald Clark Kerr.

The Yalta decisions on Poland were no doubt welcomed by the Provisional Government, though little attempt was made to exploit them in propaganda terms. That was not surprising, since it would have been tricky to present the success of the Lublin group concerning the controversial issue of government in Poland without addressing the topic of the country's new eastern border.

From 14 to 20 February 1945, a delegation of the NCP and the Provisional Government conducted tough talks in Moscow; they covered relations with the military administration set up by the Red Army in Polish territory and current economic problems. The delegation also raised the issue of the numerous, often dramatic incidents involving the NKVD and the Red Army in Polish territories occupied by the Soviet forces. In the course of the talks, prospects appeared for halting the mass-scale robberies, devastation of industrial plants and infrastructure (communications, transportation, transmission lines, mills, etc.), and the harassment of civilians by Soviet troops, including thefts, beatings, illegal detentions, and rapes.

Regardless of what the Polish government-parliamentary delegation actually achieved in Moscow, analysts agreed that the reception it was accorded showed that the Soviet Union was determined to treat the leftist alternative as a pillar of its policy rather than a short-term tactic. That augured badly for the future fulfillment of the procedures thrashed out in Yalta regarding the formation of a national unity government.

The first meeting of the Good Offices Commission, which was supposed to implement the Yalta formula on Poland, also indicated that the prospects for a rapid conclusion of its mission were dim. The Soviet Union was not about to relinquish the broad zone of influence in Central Europe it was granted in Tehran, nor would it allow a government in Poland it did not fully control. At the beginning of February, the crisis reached its culmination and paralyzed the commission's work.

The situation was soon further aggravated by the treacherous detention and abduction to Moscow of sixteen leaders of the underground Polish state. In June, a show trial was conducted in Moscow in which they were charged with subversion in the rear of the Red Army.

The involvement of the NKVD in terrorizing Polish society constituted a particularly grim chapter of mutual relations in 1944–45. The Lublin authorities, who did not have a security apparatus of their own, sought the longest possible deployment of the NKVD in Poland—even though the NKVD remained outside their control and conducted itself with total impunity, disregarding the Polish administration. The Sixty-Fourth Internal Forces Division of the NKVD remained stationed in Poland until March 1947 at the personal request of Bolesław Bierut, significantly contributing to the consolidation of the Provisional Government and, subsequently, of the Provisional Government of National Unity.

In April 1945, the Soviet authorities surprised the Allies with an important gesture toward the Lublin government, despite the fact that the Yalta formula had not yet been realized. This gesture took the form of an official international agreement: the Polish-Soviet Treaty, which pledged friendship, mutual assistance, and postwar cooperation. The accord specified mutual obligations connected with the ongoing hostilities and outlined the shape of bilateral relations after the war, subordinating them to the principle of close cooperation in implementing a common vision of security. It constituted an important regulation, and not only in the sphere of bilateral relations, though it determined the shape of the latter for many years to come.

The conclusion by the Soviet Union of this type of agreement with the Provisional Government was no doubt a demonstration addressed to the Allies. It undermined the sense of the Yalta formula, under which Poland could be a party to such an accord only after overcoming the duality of government and its "reorganization." In any event, that took place much later, in June 1945.

The continuing crisis in the work of the Good Offices Commission induced the US government to seek agreement with the Soviets by broadening the scope of a possible compromise. The new US president, Harry Truman, who took over after the unexpected death of Franklin D. Roosevelt, was as eager as his predecessor to involve the Red Army in the war against Japan. US military analysts predicted that the war in the Far East might drag on for months, or even years. Its quick conclusion and thus reduction of American losses would be possible only if the Red Army joined the battle. That was the main reason why, after the war in Europe ended, Truman decided to abandon the British and accepted far-reaching compromise with the Soviet Union. On 19 May, he asked Stalin to receive his personal envoy, Harry Hopkins, who was authorized to discuss all outstanding issues, including the deadlocked matter of a Polish national unity government.

On 26 May, Hopkins began informal negotiations in Moscow. They focused on ways of overcoming the impasse in mutual relations, including compromise over the most contentious issue—a Polish government of national unity. At the outset, Hopkins recognized the leading role of the Soviet Union in forming a Polish cabinet of national unity, in which Lublin officials were to have a majority. With that on the table, overall agreement was easily reached during the next session.

From 17 to 21 June, the Soviet capital hosted the Good Offices Commission, which held its final round of talks on implementing the Yalta formula for the establishment of a Polish national unity government. The participants, working under strong pressure from the Big Three powers, in effect put democratic window-dressing on the actual transfer of Poland to Soviet dominance. Of the twenty-one portfolios in the new cabinet, non-Lublin politicians received only six.

On 28 June 1945, a week after Moscow imposed an agreement on the Polish-Soviet negotiations, the National Council of Poland dissolved the Provisional Government. It was replaced by the Provisional Government of National Unity, which was soon recognized by the Big Three powers.

VALENTINA S. PARSADANOVA

POLITICS AND ITS CONSEQUENCES

THE GERMAN INVASION of the Soviet Union radically realigned the forces in the international arena. On 22 June 1941, Great Britain and the United States declared their support for the Soviet Union in its fight against Germany. This move influenced the position of the prime minister of Poland, Władysław Sikorski, who then followed suit on 23 June by making a statement of a possible renewal of relations with the Soviet Union. He preconditioned such a renewal on a formal recognition of the Polish-Soviet border as of 1 September 1939.

The Soviet party, represented by its ambassador in London, Ivan M. Maisky, showed its willingness to restore relations between the two countries and to sign an agreement of cooperation in the fight against Germany. However, he used a thesis of the consolidation of all Polish people within the "borders of ethnic Poland," or the determination of an interstate demarcation on an ethnic basis. In the course of bilateral negotiations mediated by British foreign secretary Anthony Eden, it was revealed that the parties were willing to compromise on current issues related to military cooperation in the war against Germany; however, they were not ready to solve the issue of a postwar Soviet-Polish border. In this sense, the agreement on renewal of relations and cooperation in the war, signed on 30 July, contained a compromise.

The essence of this compromise was that the resolution of the border issue would be postponed for better days. This was evidenced by the first clause of the agreement, in which the Soviet Union's government invalidated the Soviet-German treaties of 1939 in so far as they related to "territorial changes in Poland." As the future showed, each of the parties interpreted the text of this clause in its own way and to its own advantage. Stalin did not construe the clause as recognizing the border that existed on 1 September 1939. Indeed, there was no such recognition in this clause. Sikorski quite logically interpreted the phrase "the agreements . . . cease to be effective" as

290

the abandonment by Moscow of its territorial acquisitions made in autumn 1939, although there were no verbal "hooks" for such an interpretation in the clause. However, the wording contained in the agreement was, undoubtedly, satisfactory for both parties at that time. Moscow, understanding the dependence of the prewar Soviet-Polish border on the outcome of the war, evaded its earlier recognition without any risk for itself. In fact, it facilitated relations with the "Great Powers," who were the direct allies of Poland. In the event there was mutual desire on both sides, clause number 1 could not prevent bilateral cooperation, which was of particular importance for the Polish government, the representatives of which were admitted to the Soviet territory and received the ability to contact and provide assistance to their compatriots in that territory. According to Soviet statistical data, the number of Polish people deep in the Soviet region was about four hundred thousand.

The most significant provision of the agreement of 30 June 1941, which was subsequently developed and finalized by joint documents of the Military Convention of 16 August 1941 and a declaration of 4 December 1941, concerned the obligation of the parties to create a Polish army on the Soviet Union's territory. Both the Soviet and the Polish governments were interested in the existence of such an army, although for rather different reasons.

Sikorski considered the creation of a large Polish army in the Soviet Union as the acquisition by the government of both military and political strength, which would give weight to Poland in the international arena and make it more significant in its relations with the Allies in the developing anti-Hitler coalition. Undoubtedly, it was also taken into account that the presence of such an army in the country at the final stage of the war would guarantee the return of the government to Poland from London.

In the initial stage of positive changes in relations with its western neighbor, the Soviet party viewed the creation of this army as a fulfillment of its obligations to its new ally. There was a political aspect to this issue. But there was also a need, especially urgent in 1941 and the beginning of 1942, for additional troops to be available for battles at the Soviet-German front. The agreement specifically stated, "Polish Army troops will be sent to the front upon becoming fully combat ready. They will march out, generally, by large units of not less than a division in size and will be used in accordance with the operational plans of the Supreme High Command of the USSR." Agreements were reached on the number of troops (thirty thousand), ethnic composition, equipment/armament (by the Soviet and English parties), and combat readiness (by 1 October 1941), as well as a number of other issues.

It should be emphasized that discrepancies arose at once in the parties' interpretations of their obligations, which were not consistent in terms of either objective capabilities or intentions of the parties. Certain difficulties arose with officer staffing and weaponry in the Polish army. The shortage of officers according to the staffing tables was met with positions being filled with officers from England and the army's own cadre training. As of 25 October 1941, the army consisted of 41,500 servicemen. The situation with armaments was even worse.

Stalin agreed to satisfy the request of Gen. Władysław Anders to form additional divisions in excess of the number specified in the agreement, although with the reservation that the only obstacle might be the lack of armament in the Red Army. This was indeed the case. Over the most difficult months of the war, from June to December 1941, the Red Army lost more than three million combat soldiers, six million units with small-arms weapons, twenty thousand tanks and self-propelled artillery vehicles, and ten thousand airplanes. Industrial enterprises evacuated to the east had not yet been put into operation. There was a severe shortage of arms for the units engaged in combat operations, so Stalin informed the Polish ambassador on 8 September 1941 that it could not meet the obligations under the agreement in full: the Soviet Union could equip with arms just one Polish division. (Shortly thereafter, an opportunity was found to equip one more division.)

Difficulties equipping the Polish army were not the only reason for complications arising in the interaction between the parties. The most acute problem was determining who would be regarded as a Polish citizen and able to join the Polish army; citizenship would enable one to be drafted through the joint Soviet-Polish conscription offices or Soviet military enlistment offices. The Polish government considered as contrary to law the order of the Supreme Soviet of the USSR of 1939 to grant Soviet citizenship to all people of Western Ukraine and Western Belorussia, thus limiting the possible number of combat-ready men.

The problem was defused by an exception from the citizenship order made in December 1941 by the Soviet government, which made it possible to enlist in the Polish army all people of Polish origin, including those who had once lived in Western Ukraine and Western Belorussia. As a result, people of various political persuasions joined the army, including organizers and participants of the underground Union of Armed Struggle released from Soviet camps or exile, as well as representatives of different prewar right- and left-wing political parties. Opponents and adherents of Sikorski, teachers, representatives of Polish peasant parties, socialists, and communists—all were united under the Polish banner. Due to this commingling, the climate within the troops was quite complicated, but the soldiers were welded together by patriotism and striving for the liberation and restoration of Polish statehood.

The broadening of opportunities to draft Polish people into the Polish army after December 1941 may be regarded as a concession made by the Soviet party under the pressure of a number of circumstances. Most likely, it was induced by a message Sikorski sent from London at the end of October 1941 concerning the intention to send the embryonic Polish army to Iran instead of the Soviet-German front. Such a scenario was hardly in line with Stalin's reckonings at the moment, when the Soviet command counted on each soldier at the front, and it appeared that Stalin wanted to postpone, if not prevent, the withdrawal of Anders's army by placating Poland with an expansion of the draft for the Polish army. As evidenced by negotiations with Sikorski in Moscow at the end of December 1941, Stalin succeeded in this approach for a while.

Stalin received Poland's prime minister on 3 December. Their talk, somewhat harsh from time to time, was focused on the initiative of the Polish party in discussions about difficulties faced by Polish people in the Soviet Union and about the Polish army issue. Notwithstanding the extremely difficult economic situation in the country, Stalin agreed to improve the position of the Polish people by granting a loan of 100 million rubles to Poland. However, he responded quite harshly to Sikorski's statement concerning his plan to send the army to Iran: "We'll do without your help. You may take it all, and we'll manage on our own. We'll regain Poland and then give it to you." At the same time, Stalin made some other important remarks. After the war, he said, Poland's border would be along the Oder River and the Polish army would gain the right to be the first to enter liberated Warsaw. Stalin did not care what kind of government would take shape in Poland, only that it be friendly to the Soviet Union. (The Soviet leader pursued this policy up to the establishment of the Polish Committee of National Liberation.) He believed that the joint participation of Soviet and Polish troops in the fight against Hitler's forces at the Soviet-German front was much more important politically for improved relations between the two countries than it was militarily.

Sikorski, in spite of his promise to British prime minister Winston Churchill, agreed to leave the Polish army in the Soviet Union. He also received a loan of 300 million rubles from Stalin for the army and put aside the border and alliance issues, albeit promising to return to them later. Stalin touched upon the territorial problems and, in particular, spoke about the possible annexation of Lvov to Poland.

The Soviet government did consider an option of some territorial proposals at that time, as evidenced in the document delivered to British foreign secretary Eden during his visit to Moscow in December 1941. The Soviet government, interested in joint military operations of both Polish and Soviet divisions at the eastern front, considered it possible, according to Vyacheslav M. Molotov's words, to reach an "amicable and reciprocal solution" of the Soviet-Polish border issue through the simultaneous expansion of Poland's territory at the expense of Germany.

However, let's return to the negotiations with Sikorski in Moscow. When leaving the Soviet capital, he was convinced that "a long-term anti-German alliance with the USSR should be contracted to put a permanent end to the prewar policy of maneuvering between the two enemies and military adventures against the USSR such as the march on Kiev in 1920[;] it is necessary to lay out a roadmap to the future while smoothing the relations between us." The general believed that this move could neutralize the plans of Polish communists waiting for liberation from the east. At the same time, Sikorski did not believe that the Soviet Union should be let into Europe: "The Polish-Russian border should remain what it has been for centuries, namely, the border of Western Christian civilization."

When evaluating the issue of the withdrawal of the Polish army from the Soviet Union today, we probably recognize it as the largest mistake the Polish government made during the war. And it was a mistake that was soon realized. At the end of February 1943, just after the Battle of Stalingrad, the Polish ambassador in Moscow, Tadeusz Romer, proposed during his meeting with Stalin to return the army to the Soviet Union, but such a proposal was not accepted by the Soviet party.

It was then that the Soviet Union also reinstated the policy of citizenship (although, when Polish units were formed in 1943 under the patronage of the Union of Polish Patriots, citizenship status changed for the fourth time) and liquidated the network of representative offices of the Polish embassy. Soon, in April 1943, Moscow suspended relations with the Polish government. The reason for and history behind this breakup have been studied comprehensively by both Polish and Russian historians. The Nazis tried to use the growing tension between the Soviet and Polish governments to destroy the anti-Hitler coalition from the inside. On 13 April 1943, they published information that they had found the bodies of slain Polish officers near Smolensk and specified the date (1940) and those who had committed the offense (the NKVD). Moscow found itself in a vulnerable position. It found a way out by blaming Hitler's forces for the mass executions and proposed that the Polish party make a corresponding statement. Propaganda campaigns were soon launched in the press. A powerful anti-Soviet campaign in Polish newspapers circulating in London, as well as a furious campaign directed against the acts of the Polish government toward the Soviet Union in Moscow, generated an extremely tense situation between the two countries. All the efforts of Poland's main ally, Britain, to "hush" the Poles, thus keeping the Soviet Union from reducing its support and preventing an aggravation of relations between the coalition's leaders, were in vain. A request by the Polish party submitted on 17 April to the International Committee of the Red Cross to send a special investigative commission to Smolensk turned out to be a "trap," as it was made simultaneously with a similar request by Germany. The situation looked like Polish-German anti-Soviet cooperation, because Poland requested that Moscow "provide detailed and accurate information about prisoners of war and civilians" no sooner than on 20 April. This three-day "silence" by Sikorski's government was considered by the Soviet government as sufficient grounds for a decision to "suspend relations with this government."

Today, there are no discrepancies in the realm of political science as to the series of episodes related to the break in Soviet-Polish relations. First of all came the Katyn crime. However, we can note that the escalation of this situation by the parties up to the break in relations led to negative consequences for Poland's government.

On 4 May 1943, Stalin made a terse statement to Churchill that the existing Polish government had no chance to "return to Poland and remain in power." About the same time, he decided to give the opportunity to form Polish military units to other political forces on the territory of the Soviet Union. Sikorski, as both an experienced general and a far-sighted, clever, and pragmatic politician, and understanding the destructive consequences of the break in relations, believed that Poland inevitably would be included in the scope of operations of the Soviet troops. He expressed his hope that the break would be temporary. Certain actions and statements by the prime minister can be construed as signals of restored interaction as early as 1943. In particular, he agreed that negotiations would be held by his representatives in Poland and the Command of the Armia Krajowa with the leaders of the Polish Workers' Party (Polska Partia Robotnicza or PPR). The communists, for their part, intended to offer Sikorski the prime minister post in the government of Poland liberated by the Red Army. During his inspection tour of Polish troops in North Africa, and most likely in response to Stalin's words in May 1943 about his intention to build relations with Poland on a good neighborly basis and in the spirit of mutual respect, Sikorski said publicly that his next visit would be to Moscow, believing that the Soviet Union's attitude to Poland remained the same. According to the Polish journalist Ksawery Pruszyński, in Sikorski's speech on 2 July in Cairo, he recognized the need to accept the changes in Poland's eastern border and make a constructive turn in bilateral relations.

Leaving "out of the brackets" the reasons for Sikorski's death on 4 July 1943 (they are still being investigated), it should be recognized that there was no other equally influential and thoughtful politician in the Polish government able to smooth the controversies piled up in relations with the Soviet Union. After Sikorski's death, the existing controversies escalated into acute and open conflicts with the Soviet Union during the period, when the country's fate was hanging in the balance. The government in exile and its subordinate underground became more and more controlled by the right-wing, conservative, and apparently anti-Soviet forces.

The Western Allies unsuccessfully tried to force Stanisław Mikołajczyk, the new prime minister of Poland, to restore relations with and become a partner of the Soviet Union and to submit to its terms. Somebody had to fill the "emptiness" in relations between the two countries. For the Soviet government, this could be done and was done by the communists.

In Poland, the PPR became this active partner. In the context of new military and political conditions, the party was created through the organizational and political efforts and under the mandate of the Executive Committee of Comintern, and it declared its existence in January 1942. It arose from leftist and communist groups operating separately underground. Officially, PPR was not a member of the Comintern Executive Committee; the committee's resolution on the dissolution of the Communist Party of Poland (1938) was not yet canceled. The party declared itself to be an independent workers' party and a member of the world communist movement. Accordingly, it proclaimed that "full national liberation" would be possible only if it were accompanied by social liberation. The struggle for the new Poland should be implemented in stages: first, "lead the working people at the current stage of the historical national liberation struggle" and then launch a struggle for the new Poland.

In May 1943, the Executive Committee adopted a resolution on the dissolution of Comintern. All the communist parties approved the resolution. The organizational form of Comintern became irrelevant and prevented the further development of national parties and their national identities. The notorious "hand of Moscow" could not be allowed to impede the establishment of internal and international relations, including those between the Allies within the anti-Hitler coalition. The Comintern Executive Committee's rhetoric and its course toward world revolution were inconsistent with the new world growing out of the war.

The Polish Workers' Party pursued a policy of pooling all the antifascist forces into a single national front, trying to create it both "from below" and "from above." With reservations as to the Soviet-Polish border, the PPR affirmed its support for Sikorski's government and intention to reach agreement with its subordinate underground. However, this policy yielded no result for various reasons: the majority of Polish people supported the government's course, including opposition to the Soviet Union on the border issue. So, instead of pooling, the policy led to a sharp political division, including armed conflicts between the left-wing radical forces grouped around the PPR, on the one hand, and the government's underground, on the other. The image and objectives of the PPR were still identified with the Comintern Executive Committee and its world revolution tactics of mass repression and collectivization in the Soviet Union. As a result, the party took a new political direction, toward pooling the democratic forces into a national democratic front, and created its underground "parliament," Krajowa Rada Narodowa (KRN), and local government bodies at the turn of 1944. This was also the beginning of their guerrilla war. By the time the Red Army entered Poland, the PPR and KRN had considerable armed forces under the Armia Ludowa (People's Army).

The government's underground was prepared to take power in the country. It had a well-organized vertical structure of political and public administration—an "underground state"—as well as military structures, including the massive nationwide Armia Krajowa, which also had guerrilla forces. Command, though, had different instructions for it at times: in October 1943, it was recommended to "avoid conflicts with Soviet troops[;] . . . enter into cooperation . . . in case of restoration of the Polish-Soviet relations," and, in January 1944, it was pointed out that "the Soviet troops on Poland's territory should be deemed hostile." The break in relations between the Soviet Union and the Polish government severely limited the Soviet Union's ability to support the "underground state" with diplomatic instruments, while maintaining its own interpretation of the national and state interests of Poland.

A conflict between these two contenders for power, unequal in their weight in society and having a different understanding of the interests of Poland together with the Soviet Union (the PPR) or in opposition to it (the government and "underground government"), was becoming inevitable.

The success of the Soviet troops changed the international military, political, and strategic balance of forces in Europe in favor of the Soviet Union, outlining the prospect of Poland's liberation by Soviet troops. This activated the Polish, and more specifically the communist émigrés in the Soviet Union, who started their activities in 1943 by establishing a patriotic nongovernmental organization, the Union of Polish Patriots (Związek Patriotów Polskich, or ZPP). With the assistance of the Soviet government, the ZPP turned into a massive organization influential among the Polish population in the Soviet Union, and it had broad opportunities to stage military operations.

Pursuant to the Resolution of the State Defense Committee No. 3294 of 6 May 1943, the formation of the First Polish Tadeusz Kościuszko Rifle Division took place from 15 May to 5 June 1943 in camps at the village of Seltsy on the Oka River near Ryazan. The division was further reinforced with a 45-mm antitank gun battalion, an armored regiment, 120-mm mortar battalion, and an antitank rifle company.

In the middle of August 1943, Wanda Wasilewska, the ZPP president in the Soviet Union, and Zygmunt Berling, the division's commander, requested that Stalin send the division to the front on 1 September—the anniversary of the Nazi invasion of Poland. In connection with this effort, the operational readiness of the division was inspected. It was stated in the inspection report that the overall strength of the division corresponded to the established strength, but the shortage of commanding officers was considerable: 892 officers instead of 1,093, and 2,082 noncommissioned officers instead of 3,258, according to the established strength. The equipment and transport vehicles were considered to correspond to the accepted standards. However, it was noted that the combat training program was "mastered on a quite average level." The overall conclusion of the inspection officers was that the division was "ready to perform combat missions." On the night of 31 August–1 September 1943, the division loaded onto troop trains and departed to the reserve of the western front. It joined the Thirty-Third Army and was quartered in the Krasnoye district to the west of Smolensk, where it continued its combat training. By 9 October, according to the order of the commander of the Thirty-Third Army, Lt. Gen. Vasily N. Gordov, the division was repositioned to a district to the east of Lenino in the Mogilev region (Belorussia). It was followed by the First Armored Regiment.

The Thirty-Third Army was a part of the western front attack force (which also included the Tenth Guards Army and the Twenty-First Army), which had the mission to advance from the Lyady-Lenino-Driben military line toward Gorky and defeat the Nazi troops near Orsha. The army was positioned in the straightest, shortest, and most difficult Minsk-Warsaw-Berlin route.

The formations of the Thirty-Third Army had difficult terrain on which to operate, especially for tanks. A serious obstacle was the Mereya River. Although not wide, it had a muddy bottom and swampy floodplain. Its left bank was significantly higher than the right, thus making it easy for the enemy to maintain surveillance and arrange a counterattack against the approaching units of the Workers' and Peasants' Red Army.

The soldiers and officers of the Kościuszko Division entered their first battle 12–13 October 1943. The mission assigned to the division was, upon fording the Mereya River, to break through the enemy's defenses. On the night of 11–12 October, Polish combat engineers, with the assistance of Soviet gunners and engineers from adjoining units of the Red Army, built bridges for infantry, tanks, and artillery. At dawn on 12 October, in the thick fog, an exploratory attack on the enemy's defenses was performed. At 10:30 a.m., following an artillery barrage, the formations of the Thirty-Third Army went on the offensive. Having forded the Mereya River, the units of the First Polish Division crashed into the enemy's entrenchment. Stubborn, bloody battles lasted for two days. Jointly with Soviet soldiers, combatants of the division penetrated deep into the defenses of Hitler's forces to the west of Lenino and, although they suffered heavy losses, were able to hold their objectives.

On 14 October, the division was withdrawn from the front to the army's rear and quartered near Nikolenki, which was fifteen kilometers to the east of Lenino. General Berling concluded that "Polish units took well the experience of the Red Army combat operations and showed a high level of military skill just in their first battles with German invaders." Later, the division operated as part of the First Belorussian Front under the command of Konstanty K. Rokossowski.

While noting the heroism of Polish soldiers in the battle near Lenino, it is important to mention the heavy personnel losses suffered by the division. The high number of casualties was the result of their "greenness" and insufficient combat experience, the harsh nature of battles at the Soviet-German front, and the fierce resistance of the German Wehrmacht, which was striving to recapture the initiative from the Red Army after the crushing defeats near Stalingrad and on the Kursk salient. Undoubtedly, the fact that the Polish division was included in the Soviet forces was a circumstance that should have evoked a wide international and political response, in particular, in occupied Poland and Germany itself.

Hitler's headquarters realized the significance of the breakthrough toward Orsha and the participation of the Polish soldiers advancing along the shortest and most difficult path to liberate Poland. An order was received from Berlin to frustrate the offensive at any cost. Reinforcements, infantry, tanks, and artillery were moved up. Special efforts were exerted to break the will and desire of the Polish soldiers to fight at the eastern front with the Red Army. In Poland, a propaganda campaign taken up by the Polish reactionary forces was launched to falsify the events near Lenino and discredit the Soviet formations, particularly those under the command of General Berling. Unfortunately, the echo of that campaign has not diminished even today.

Soon, the Kościuszko Division grew into the Polish Corps. In summer 1944, when approaching the Western Bug River, it had become the Polish army, reinforced by Soviet officers and Polish commanders trained in Soviet military schools. Soon afterward, it was replenished with guerrilla units of Armia Ludowa formed by the Polish communists. This resulted in the formation of Wojsko Polskie, the armed forces of the People's Poland. At the end of 1944, it numbered 285,000 soldiers and officers, of whom 182,000 fought at the front. The Soviet Union spent 723.3 million rubles from the country's budget for the maintenance of Polish military units from their formation until 1 January 1945.

However, the attempts by ZPP to form a political mission in Moscow as an alternative to the government in London were not supported by Stalin, as it had been with the establishment of the Central Bureau of Polish Communists by émigré communists. Various researchers have diverse opinions as to what particular role Stalin assigned to such structures, and quite often they tend to explain his acts as a desire to create a certain reserved political "airspace" due to his distrust of the PPR and its leaders. This distrust did exist, but following the visit by a delegation of the KRN to Moscow for negotiations with Stalin in May–June 1944, it can be confidently stated that the emphasis was placed primarily on internal communist forces, although they were "diluted" by Moscow émigrés.

Stalin's "cautious" tactics with regard to the intentions of the Polish communists were explained primarily by serious disagreements with the Allies as to the Polish issue, the solution to which Moscow associated with the satisfaction of its national and state interests. It seems that it was most important for the Soviet leader to prevent possible "sharp edges" in relations with the Allies and to adhere to the idea of compromising political structures in the countries of the Soviet Union's future sphere of influence that were similar to the anti-Hitler coalition. With respect to Poland, there was no doubt that the influence of a Polish government on Poland's population was taken into account (this explains the meeting with communist sympathizer and economist Oskar Lange on 17 May 1944 and the numerous times Stalin consented to hold negotiations with Mikołajczyk in May, June, and October 1944).

The Soviet position on its main point (that is, ensuring the security of the Soviet Union after the end of the war) remained effectively the same during the whole of World War II. Secretary Eden clearly identified it as he was recalling negotiations held in Moscow in late 1941: "The Russians had already firmly established their goal[,] which changed only slightly in the following three years and was aimed at ensuring the utmost in security for Russia's borders in the future."

After having failed to prevent the rupture of Soviet-Polish relations, the Western Allies, as they had to give way to Stalin's demands at the expense of their staunch partner, Poland, sought to bring the Soviet leader into consensus on restoring ties with the Polish government in exile based in London. All that was clearly revealed—initially at the meeting held in autumn 1943 that included the Soviet foreign minister, the British foreign secretary, and the US secretary of state, and then at the Tehran conference of the Big Three between 28 November and 1 December 1943.

Shortly before the Tehran conference, Eden recommended that, in order to restore Soviet-Polish relations, the British cabinet should recognize the 1941 borders between the two states, compensate Poland for its territorial losses by establishing its borders along the Oder, and meet Stalin's demands to restrict the supply of arms to the "Polish underground resistance movement." This last demand was made because, as Molotov put it, the movement was "hardly likely to be useful[,] being not in good hands." In Tehran, Churchill illustrated this point with the well-known "three matches." Stalin agreed but emphasized that "the Ukrainian lands should go to the Ukraine, and the Belorussian, to Belorussia." In the end, Churchill's wording prevailed, saying that "the hearth of the Polish state and people must be situated between the so-called Curzon Line and the line of the Oder River." The question of transferring Germans from the territories to be passed to Poland prompted no disagreement. Talking about relations with the Polish government in exile, Stalin took a simultaneously cautious and firm stand. He said he was ready to begin talks on restoring relations but only if the composition of the government was changed and a guarantee was given that "the agents of the Polish Government will not kill partisans, and that the émigré Polish Government will, in earnest, call for struggle against the Germans, instead of engaging in machinations."

Here, Stalin referred to an order issued by the Armia Krajowa (AK) command to destroy "bandit groups"—which, among others, included Union of Polish Patriots partisans. Moscow had a copy of the document and showed it to the Allies.

Therefore, the Western Allies gave in to Stalin's demands. Strictly speaking, they did not attempt a serious show of support for Polish interests, as they saw the Red Army as a force capable of defeating the German army in Europe single-handedly. The Western Allies, especially Churchill, focused primarily on how to protect and not harm their own interests. On 1 September 1939, Great Britain betrayed its Polish ally for the second time. The Allies' memoranda, statements, and letters addressed to Stalin after the Soviet troops had crossed the 1921 border gave lip service to the Polish cause. However, the Western leaders understood there was no chance to change the situation in favor of the Polish government. Mikołajczyk was also well aware of this fact.

In the spring of 1944, Stalin's stance was more flexible. During a number of meetings between Soviet officials and the KRN delegation that arrived in Moscow in order to "establish relations with the allied powers' governments," the negotiators discussed the issues of KRN's international recognition and future governance, terms of the Soviet troops' entering the territory of Poland and their relationship with the new Polish authorities, as well as the question of to whom the Union of Polish Patriots (ZPP) and the KRN's First Polish Army would be subordinate. Stressing that the Polish government "in its current composition would never be recognized by the Soviet government," the Soviet leadership said it was ready to recognize the KRN but at the same time pointed out that "the Allies could face big difficulties" as they would have to deal with Mikołajczyk and the Armia Ludowa.

In other words, Stalin was contemplating various options for Poland's future power structure. The Soviet leader was probably just being tactical when he told Oskar Lange he was ready to deal with the Polish government and then asked Lange to take to Mikołajczyk Moscow's suggestions for forming a new Polish government or a committee "somewhere within Poland." The simultaneous directives to Soviet ambassador Victor Lebedev to hold talks in London with Stanisław Grabski, the leader of the "émigré parliament," and then with Mikołajczyk could also be seen as tactical steps. The Poles could have turned those steps to their benefit, but they did not. Mikołajczyk would not accept Moscow's key demand for establishing the border along the Curzon Line. As a result, Stalin concluded it was time he use Polish "internal" forces and create a government to which power could be passed and which could become a party to further negotiations with the Western Allies and Mikołajczyk.

The day of 23 June 1944 saw a number of important events. First, Ambassador Lebedev broke off negotiations with Mikołajczyk because of the Polish government's "incorrect" behavior in refusing to recognize the Soviet interpretation of the Katyn crime, which was obviously unacceptable to the Poles.

The second event was Operation Bagration, launched by one Baltic and three Belorussian fronts of the Red Army. Soon, the offensive developed along the whole Soviet-German front line. The objective of Operation Bagration was to clear the Soviet territories of the enemy's troops, restore the state borders of the Soviet Union, and proceed to liberate neighboring countries from fascism. The goal of the First Belorussian Front included in particular the liberation of Belorussia. This would include crossing the Bug River, reaching the Wisła River, seizing bridgeheads on its west bank to the north and south of Warsaw, and taking over one of its boroughs, Praga, located on the east bank.

On the night of 22–23 June 1944, the members of KRN and the UPP delegation visiting Berling's army were invited to the Kremlin. The question at issue was the creation of the Polish Committee of National Liberation (PCNL) and its program.

On 24 June 1944, Stalin sent a message to President Roosevelt in which he said it did not appear that Mikołajczyk had changed his point of view and that he had "made a step forward" in repairing Soviet-Polish relations and "a reconstruction of the Polish émigré Government." In Stalin's opinion, such a reconstruction "would ensure participation of Polish leaders in Britain, the US, and the USSR" in the reconstructed government; then Stalin went on to stress that it would also ensure the participation, "more particularly[,] of Polish democratic leaders inside Poland, plus recognition by the Polish Government of the Curzon Line as the new frontier between the USSR and Poland." Therefore, the Soviet leader pointedly saw the KRN as a contender for power in Poland.

It is tricky for Russian historians to reach an unambiguous conclusion on that point because of a lack of documents concerning the negotiations between Stalin and the KRN-ZPP delegation (apparently no minutes were recorded during the meetings, and historians do not have access to the Polish government's archives). However, we can consider the significant statement made by Churchill during his meeting with Stalin on 16 October 1944: "Mikołajczyk knows that he will not get Lviv [Lvov], and will have to accept the Curzon Line, but he said that if he is not able to prove to the Polish people that Poland was entitled to defend its case at the peace conference, the Polish people might not recognize Mikołajczyk himself." This statement explains why the Moscow negotiations in autumn 1944 were doomed to failure.

The negotiations between Stalin and the KRN and ZPP resulted in the creation of the Polish Committee of National Liberation (PCNL), with the Soviet leader having personally taken part in the elaboration of its composition and manifesto on the night of 21–22 July 1944. The definition of the new authority as the "legitimate but provisional government" perfectly suited Stalin's attitude, as he was hesitant to make a final decision on the issue of power in Poland that could unnecessarily strain relations with Western Allies while their troops were in action in Europe. In anticipation of the Allies' negative reaction to the PCNL, Stalin sent a letter to Roosevelt explaining that the new authority was more of a committee than a government and thus could constitute the core of a future democratic government. Therefore, Moscow made it clear that no recognition of PCNL was required, thus preventing any serious tension with the Allies. The next step in the process of creating alternative authorities was made on 31 December 1944, when the PCNL was transformed into the Polish Provisional Government. Its legitimacy was accepted by various nations and politicians, including Stalin, Czechoslovakia's Edvard Beneš, and Charles de Gaulle of France, which marked the beginning of the Provisional Government's international recognition.

In "response" to a new Polish international "subject" and Stalin's tenacity over the border issue, the Polish government in exile organized an uprising in Warsaw on 1 August 1944. The objective was to liberate the Polish capital ahead of the Red Army's advance and prevent Polish communists from coming to power in postwar Poland. The government and the Armia Krajowa command planned to take advantage of what they thought was a favorable situation at the front, namely the Red Army's swift advance toward the Wisła River. The Soviet Stavka (the High Command) ordered the First Belorussian Front to seize Praga, the final goal of the Soviet offensive, no later than 5–8 August 1944.

Decades on, experts have been arguing about why the Red Army did not take the city. Some researchers blame the Soviet leader for allegedly halting the Red Army's advance on Warsaw. If so, the Soviet High Command, and Stalin in particular, should be held morally responsible for the human losses. But such a conclusion seems to be an attempt to shift the blame, especially given the presence of such a controversial and notorious person as Stalin. Was it he who had planned and organized the uprising? Until now, historians have disagreed about whether the Soviet leader could have given his decisive support to the rebels, given the extremely difficult operational situation that developed in August and September 1944 at the front line on the outskirts of Warsaw, as documents suggest. Soviet advance armored units were defeated and troops had to retreat, suffering heavy losses in men (up to 50 percent) and materials. Support services lagged behind somewhere at about a six-hundred-kilometer distance, and front-line units were short of supplies. The Soviet troops managed to continue the offensive only in the middle of September as they captured Praga. An attempt to ford the Wisła River within the capital failed.

While planning the uprising, the Polish politicians did not concern themselves with the lives of Soviet soldiers as much as they did those of their fellow Poles. Indeed, if guided by the principle that ends justify means, Stalin was able to issue any order, as he enjoyed absolute power in his country. But what really guided the Soviet leadership in 1944–45 were geopolitical considerations. Supporting the uprising's objectives would have been contrary to those considerations and would have meant opposing the Soviet Union's own national and political interests.

If we consider scientifically the issue of politicians' responsibility for their decisions, then we have to say that the main responsibility for the deaths of two hundred thousand people in Warsaw rests on those Polish politicians who masterminded the uprising and urged Poles to fight without coordination with the Soviet command.

That the Western Allies loudly proclaimed they would support the uprising with airdrops of arms, ammunition, and food had a simple explanation. As for the United States, Roosevelt needed the votes of millions of citizens of Polish origin in the upcoming presidential election, and so American airplanes carried out one mostly symbolic airdrop over Warsaw. Great Britain was initially opposed to the uprising, but after it started, the British took the opportunity to gain more political capital among those supporting the Polish government in exile. However, it refused to send its troops, claiming the need to focus on other strategic goals. After losing several aircraft near Warsaw, Great Britain suggested the Soviet side should tackle the issue of aid. Stalin, who changed his opinion about the airdrops, believed that the best and most effective way to help the anti-Nazi Poles would be to crush the Germans at Warsaw and liberate it for the Poles. Secret documentary materials on the Warsaw uprising published by Polish and Russian archive researchers and experts back up this conclusion.

On 16 October 1944, Churchill wrote a letter to King George VI about the political views and perspectives (toward the Soviet Union) of Stanisław Mikołajczyk and members of the Polish delegation that had gone to Moscow for the Soviet-Polish negotiations in October 1944. Churchill described those views as "decent but incapable and silly." For objectivity's sake, it is worth mentioning that Churchill had described Bolesław Bierut and members of the PCNL as "toadies never yet seen." Under those circumstances, the attempts of the Polish politicians to use human lives in order to make Stalin "play by their rules" and put Poland in the path of the Kremlin's plans were doomed to fail. Stalin was focused on ensuring the security of the Soviet Union from a new German aggression that the Allies thought was possible and on making the Soviet Union a global power. As its leader, he would never have allowed any political force ready to confront or wage war against his country to take over in Poland.

On 20 March 1945, the commander of the First Belorussian Front, Marshal Georgy Zhukov, reported to Stalin that his troops had "liberated Warsaw and turned the enemy's flanks closed with an enveloping maneuver and had reached the Oder River." Thus, the Red Army had completed its mission to liberate the Polish people.

On 12 January 1945, a Soviet offensive toward Berlin was launched, and it would serve as the background for the Big Three meeting held in Yalta from 4 to 11 February 1945. Today, it is often believed that Stalin imposed on his Yalta counterparts his conditions for Europe's postwar resettlement and, in particular, the Polish issue. This interpretation appears to be one-sided. As had been the case in previous meetings, Allied states whose futures were to be decided by the big powers were not invited, but there are no documents suggesting it was because of Stalin's proposal or pressure.

The Polish issue was a key point at Yalta, with two aspects being discussed: borders and government. While agreeing on the borders relatively easily, the Allies encountered significant controversy about the government. The United States and Great Britain understood that having two governments, one based in Warsaw and another in London, would be a major obstacle to the still-desired cooperation with the Soviet Union.

The Soviet side believed that "the main point was not to hinder the Poles because they already had their country liberated," and the implicit message was that the issue had already been solved within the country. Roosevelt thought that "the most important matter was that of a *permanent* [emphasis by author] government for Poland." Both Roosevelt and Churchill sought to help the London-based government "save face" and regain lost influence. The Western Allies seemingly changed their tactics: instead of making the Soviet Union restore relations with the reconstructed émigré government, they suggested the replacement of the two existing governments with a united cabinet to be largely controlled by Mikołajczyk's group. By that, Churchill believed Poland's freedom and sovereign independence would be restored. The Soviet side, referring to the opinions of Bolesław Bierut (formally an independent activist), Edward Osóbka-Morawski (a socialist and chair of the interim government), and Michał Rola-Żymierski (a ZPP member and commander in chief of the Polish army, formally independent as required by the Polish constitution and political etiquette), agreed only to consider the participation of a limited number of other activists from inside and outside Poland. Stalin strongly demanded that Soviet security interests be taken into account.

After mutual concessions, the Allies agreed to reorganize the Warsaw government and leave the question of power to be solved later, in Poland. The Western powers believed the communists would soon lose control over the government. Stalin suggested creating a broader social base for the government, which he believed would bring more political stability to the country belonging to the sphere of Soviet interests.

A key success for Stalin was that Roosevelt and Churchill accepted NKVD (People's Commissariat for Internal Affairs) activities to secure the rear of the Red Army in Poland as complying with the laws of land warfare. Therefore, the Western Allies gave the Soviet side carte blanche to quell underground military groups, particularly those of the AK and NSZ (Narodowe Siły Zbrojne, or National Armed Forces). The major reasons for the NKVD's activity were the numerous attacks launched by underground groups against Soviet military checkpoints and supply facilities. Such attacks had killed many soldiers and officers, often brutally. Remarkably, this aspect of the Red Army's presence in Poland is generally ignored by researchers.

The death in April 1945 of Franklin Roosevelt, who had seen the opportunity and benefit in postwar cooperation with the Soviet Union, was followed by a more active anti-Soviet trend in Western policy, which became clear after Harry Truman took office in the United States and after the end of the war in Europe. The Soviet Union received some unfavorable "signals" from London seeking to regain its lost influence on the continent by supporting pro-Western political forces in the territories belonging to the sphere of Soviet interests. The London-based Polish government eagerly teamed up with British politicians, as it still remained a subject of international society. Besides, in the summer of 1945, a plan for war against the Soviet Union was being worked out. The plan included the involvement of the industrial and human resources of Germany and the Polish army under the command of Władysław Anders, as well as underground political and military groups still operating in Poland. Fortunately, the British and US commands were wise enough to have never put Operation Unthinkable into action.

Moscow was aware of this plan and viewed it as an attempt to revise the process of establishing spheres of interest in Europe started at Tehran and continued at Yalta. Accordingly, some military measures were taken, as Marshal Georgy Zhukov, the supreme military commander of the Red Army in Germany, was ordered by the Stavka to redeploy troops, reinforce defenses, and carefully examine the disposition of the western forces. Simultaneously, Moscow increased its support for the Polish army (numbering 315,000 troops), offering Warsaw a long-term loan (from 1 June 1945 till 1 January 1947) for arms, ammunition, and supplies. Therefore, it was not urgent for the Polish government to allocate its own funds for its military. On 21 April 1945, the Soviet Union and Poland signed the Treaty of Mutual Assistance and Postwar Collaboration, which drew an angry reaction from the Western Allies. Article 4 of the treaty guaranteed that Poland would receive immediate assistance from the Soviet Union if Germany were to resume its aggres-

sive policy, alone or united with some other state. In fact, it could be view
as a military alliance.

On 19–21 June 1945, the Military Collegium of the Soviet Suprem_
Court sentenced Leopold Okulicki, the former AK commander (he signed
the disbandment of the AK on 19 January 1945) and several leaders of the
London-based underground to various terms of imprisonment for "anti-
Soviet and anticommunist activities" and the disobedience of PCNL decrees.
They originally were arrested by the NKVD in Warsaw and on its outskirts
in March 1945 and immediately brought to Moscow for trial. In doing so, the
Soviet side excluded any discussion on the underground leaders' participa-
tion in a future coalition government to be created at Yalta.

Therefore, the Soviet Union used all political and diplomatic options available to maintain its control in Eastern Europe, and over Poland in particular.

The negative trends that appeared in the foreign policy of Great Britain
and the United States, on the one hand, and the Soviet Union, on the other, as
well as Mikołajczyk's refusal to accept the Yalta decisions, made it extremely
difficult for the special joint committee set up in Yalta to determine the composition of the Polish interim government of national unity. Nevertheless,
all the partners had interests to pursue and eventually reached a compromise. The United States and Great Britain sought Moscow's promise to enter
the fight against Japan, hence their concessions. The Soviet Union had the
1941 borders recognized by all would-be members of the new Polish government, making possible the end of the territorial dispute between Moscow and
Warsaw and serving to defuse political tensions in Poland. The new Polish
administration was keenly interested in withdrawing from the Western-
recognized, London-based government and its political and military units in
Poland, which was eventually achieved. On 28 June 1945, the composition of
the coalition government was formed and announced, which paved the way
for the new Poland to become an internationally recognized, legitimate state
and a member of the international community. The émigré government, with
its views on Poland's sovereignty and role in Europe, as well as its conception of confronting the Soviet Union, ceased to exist. Poland remained under
Soviet control, and Polish communists retained political leadership.

Stalin's firm stand and the tenacity of the Polish delegation headed by
Bolesław Bierut at Potsdam (17 June–2 August 1945) ensured the delimitation
of the Polish border along the western Neisse River. The Potsdam Agreement
said that the former eastern German territories, "including the area of the
former free city of Danzig, shall be under the administration of the Polish
State and for such purposes should not be considered as part of the Soviet
zone of occupation in Germany"; however, the final delimitation of that part
of Poland's frontier would await the peace settlement.

The Potsdam wording about the border did not give reason to believe the decision was final, but there was a chance to practically establish the border line, given another Potsdam decision requiring the forced transfer of German populations from the territories now belonging to other countries.

Establishing the German-Polish border without tripartite guarantees from the Allies was beneficial to Moscow and the Soviet Union, as Poland was not capable of protecting it as a secure frontier for both countries. For Poland, already under Soviet influence, that meant long-term dependency on Moscow. According to the Polish historian Włodzimierz Borodziej, the Soviet Union then "became the only guarantor of the Polish-German Oder-Neisse border line."

At the request of the British, it was noted that Warsaw should "hold free and unfettered elections as soon as possible" to become a free "game" in which all parties and political forces should have the right to take part, while "representatives of the Allied press shall enjoy full freedom to report to the world upon developments in Poland before and during the elections."

Those commitments to be fulfilled by Warsaw looked very "flexible" and, if not accompanied by the agreed measures of international control, could have been easily avoided by election authorities, which indeed was the case in January 1957.

Following the Potsdam conference, the Soviet Union and Poland signed, in Moscow, a border treaty and a reparation agreement compensating for losses caused by the German occupation. The new treaty with the Soviet Union was prompted by the international recognition of the new Poland and was meant to support the Agreement of 27 July 1944 concerning Poland's eastern border. Pursuant to the Potsdam Agreement, the treaty confirmed the border along the Curzon Line, thus passing Białystok back to Poland. But the Polish delegation failed to regain Lvov, which, if it had, could have drastically changed the opinion of many Poles toward the government. Stalin stood his ground: Wrocław should be Polish, Lvov should be Ukrainian, and the Curzon Line should be accepted as the border only with possible, insignificant local territorial concessions to Poland, and those indeed were given within thirteen to thirty kilometers of the border line.

There was another important decision regarding Poland's western border, which effectively closed on 10 June 1945, although the precise line was defined only later, at Potsdam.

Under the agreement of 26 March 1945, all German enterprises located in territories being handed over to Poland were understood to be "war trophies." Only those officially passed to the Polish government were regarded as Polish property. It is worth mentioning that the Soviet Union received only 6 percent of the confiscated value of such enterprises and 25 percent of the industrial equipment.

Initially, the rights to the trophies were regulated by the Stavka's order of 9 August 1944, under which property found within the "old" Polish territories was considered a trophy of war only if previously belonging to the Wehrmacht. Those violating the order and seizing property from people unlawfully were to be prosecuted and could face the death penalty by military courts, irrespective of rank or position. In practice, equal punishments were meted out whether the prize was a carload of property or a stolen chicken.

The Polish government and its supporters had a different view: all property located in the "new" territories should belong to Poland. Hence, there was significant backlash when people saw German machines and equipment being dismantled and moved to the Soviet Union. That caused resentment among the authorities, although Poles themselves practiced the so-called *shabrovnitstvo,* or trips for abandoned property, sometimes taking it away from German civilians by force.

That the Potsdam declaration pronounced that the territories being handed to Poland should not be considered part of the Soviet zone of occupation in Germany was expected to bring some tense disputes over the captured property. The Soviet delegation at Potsdam said the Soviet government "renounces all claims in respect of reparations to the property and shares of German industrial and transport enterprises located in Poland," including the "new" territories. At the time of the conference, the commander of the Northern Group of Soviet Forces was ordered by the State Defensive Committee (GKO) of the Soviet Union to pass to Polish administration all German enterprises until 15 August 1945, except for 102 facilities due to be dismantled through 7 August 1945. By signing the treaty of 16 August 1945, Moscow reaffirmed its renouncement of any claims to former German property located in Poland.

At the time, Polish authorities and repatriates settling down in the newly Polish lands were strongly opposed to dismantling German factories and moving them to the Soviet Union, and they considered it illegal. Even now we can see that those events are not always looked upon as a question of historical fact, and their echoes still negatively affect Polish public opinion of Russia to this day. Then, in 1945, both countries, devastated by war, were in desperate need of industrial machinery, raw materials, and food and obviously had legitimate rights to their share of trophies. Both then and now, after decades, the available data were and are not enough to find out who took what and whose share was more legitimate in the whirl of war and demographic chaos. Hardly anyone will deny that the Soviet Union's claims to the trophies were as justified as those of the Polish.

Bolesław Bierut, president of the Provisional National Council (KRN), referring to estimates by Soviet experts, said that Poland received property in the western lands worth $9 billion (in prewar prices, excluding war losses), including machinery and equipment worth $1.75 billion. The Soviet Union, according to Moscow, received German equipment and machinery worth $500 million.

The question of reparations was originally very complicated, in particular for Poland, as life did not wait for the Great Powers to come up with the right solutions. Back at Yalta, the Allies agreed that reparations should be exacted from Germany in three forms: removal within two years of national wealth from Germany with the purpose of destroying Germany's military power, the use of German labor, and annual deliveries of goods from current production for a period to be fixed. Following Potsdam, Moscow received the right for removals from the zone of Germany occupied by the Soviet Union and for 25 percent of usable and complete industrial equipment from the western zones, with 10 percent of it without payment or exchange of any kind in return.

Under the Agreement of 16 August 1945, the Soviet Union agreed to pass to Poland 15 percent of the removals from the Soviet occupation zone, as well as 30 percent of the equipment obtained from the western zones, with half of the 30 percent without payment or exchange in return, while the other half was to be exchanged for Polish products. Also, 15 percent of German ships were given to Poland. The Western powers soon began to disrupt deliveries to the Soviet Union from their zones, and, in May 1946, the United States stopped them completely.

That hampered Warsaw's efforts to find and regain property taken to Germany during the war. The Polish government estimated the industrial equipment taken by Germans and located in the western zones was worth some $2 billion. By 9 April 1949, after the United States had stopped restitution deliveries, the Poles had managed to regain less than $8 million of the lost property.

The problem of German assets was accompanied by another controversial issue, the so-called reparation coal supplied by Poland to the Soviet Union on terms still considered by Polish public opinion as evidence of the Soviet policy of exploitation and inequality toward Poland. Today, the coal story is well known to every Pole; nevertheless, it is worth a reminder. In 1945, Warsaw, for political and national reasons, turned down Moscow's offer to establish joint ventures in Lower Silesia for the development of coal mines, particularly near Wałbrzych (the Polish government was even ready to waive its right to German reparations from the Soviet zone to avoid any requirement to form joint ventures). It was finally agreed that Poland would sell its coal to the Soviet Union for a special price of $1.22 per metric ton, which, as Bolesław Bierut put it, was "the cost of mining the coal, no profit and no loss." Władysław Gomułka, a deputy prime minister and leader of the Polish Workers' Party, commended the Agreement of 16 August 1945, saying "the Polish delegation did a proper job for the benefit of Poland."

Given that the Poles had just begun to settle down in the newly Polish territories, the Soviet Union pledged to provide extra labor to Poland. For that purpose and at the request of Gomułka, the Soviet Union sent fifty thousand German war prisoners to work in Silesian coal mines and provided mine prop supplies. To ensure normal mining, the Soviet Union organized coal deliveries using their own transport, as Polish railways had been largely destroyed and were out of service due to direct military operations in 1944–45, as well as Allied bombing and years of German occupation. Those Soviet efforts have never been valued.

According to Hilary Minc, minister of industry, the daily distribution of coal production was as follows: 15,000 metric tons of daily production, totaling 106,000 tons, was transported by Soviet gauge tracks; 40,000, by European tracks; 20,000 tons were consumed internally; and 31,000 tons remained in piles. At the time, only the Soviet Union and Sweden bought Polish coal in quantity.

Nevertheless, the fact remains that Moscow paid less than the global market prices, which turned the original economic coal issue into a long-term national and political problem. It once seemed that Nikita Khrushchev and Władysław Gomułka had resolved it in 1956, but now it appears they did not.

There are two ways of dealing with such a complicated issues in our historic relations. The problem can be closed again, as it once was in autumn 1956, when the Soviet delegation, after considering the extremely difficult situation in the Polish economy (as Edward Ochab, first secretary of the Polish Communist Party put it, "You don't help, we go bankrupt"), suggested a political resolution to the "coal problem." The financial issues were considered mutually settled.

There are some data and numbers available, mentioned and discussed during the Soviet-Polish talks in November 1956. It is worth mentioning that, under the Agreement of 16 August 1945, Poland was to deliver coal annually to the Soviet Union for a special price, starting in 1946 and for as long as Germany was occupied: eight million metric tons to be supplied during the first year, thirteen million during each of the next four years, and then twelve million metric tons during each of the following years. The protocol to the agreement specifically mentioned that those supplies were "in compensation for the Soviet Union waiving its right to former German assets in Poland's territories." Both sides almost immediately began to change the terms of the agreement. First, they postponed the commencement of shipments. Then, in 1947, the amount was halved under a new agreement. Accordingly, Warsaw renounced half of its share of German reparations, namely, agreeing to 7.5 instead of 15 percent (the protocol of 5 March 1947). After the German Democratic Republic (GDR) was established, Moscow, with Warsaw's consent, halved the reparations imposed on the GDR and renounced them on 1 January 1954. On the same day, Warsaw renounced its share of reparations from the Soviet Union. Moscow ceased to buy Polish coal at preferential rates. Poland agreed to keep the quantity supplied to the Soviet Union the same but would sell it at the fair market price. On 25 November 1955, a protocol was signed terminating the Agreement of 16 August 1945.

The Poles' attitude toward this "Coal Agreement" was negative, especially in its early years, particularly because they saw it as an effort by the Soviet Union to restore the traditional supplies of Silesian coal to German territories.

Prior to the negotiations on economic issues scheduled for November 1956 in Moscow, the Polish government had prepared and submitted to its Soviet counterpart five documents concerning the Agreement of 16 August 1945, the quantity of coal supplied during the period between 1946 and 1953, a legal opinion on the Soviet-Polish agreement and recuperation of losses caused by the occupation, a statement on reparations during the period between 1946 and 1953, and the removals of equipment and assets from the western territories. The Poles insisted that the term "war trophies" did not apply to the property and facilities located in the former German territories, so they believed that Poland had incurred significant losses as a result of the removal of the former German machinery and its transfer to the Soviet Union.

The Soviet side came up with its own data and figures suggesting some Polish estimates were not correct. Moscow in particular said the amount of supplies delivered during the term of the agreement of 1945 totaled 49.5 million metric tons of coal worth $56.2 million, which, if converted accordingly, would be $577.3 million rather than the $691.6 million estimated by the Polish side. Besides, Poland had overvalued the actual coal supplies to the Soviet Union by five million tons and used $1.12 per ton as a single price, while the true price ranged from $1.12 to $1.17, subject to the type of coal and year of delivery.

All those issues were discussed by members of subcommittees and delegations, but Polish and Soviet experts failed to agree about the figures. Eventually, Soviet Minister of Foreign Trade Ivan Kabanov, an expert who prepared documents and materials for the Soviet side, lost his patience and arrived at the conclusion that the Polish government had no legal or moral grounds to claim compensation for the total value of the coal supplied to the Soviet Union under the Agreement of 16 August 1945.

Nevertheless, the Soviet side decided to close the discussion, and, after consideration of the balance between the Polish claims (2.1 billion rubles) and the amount of Soviet loans used by Poland (2.146 billion rubles), a political solution to the coal problem was devised. First Deputy Prime Minister Anastas Mikoyan announced the decision of the Soviet government: under the circumstances and given the difficult situation in the Polish economy, they agreed to meet the Polish side halfway and suggested that the Polish debt as of 1 December 1956 for loans granted by the Soviet Union be used as payment for the total cost of Polish coal supplied to the Soviet Union during the period between 1946 and 1953, and the debt should then be considered paid in full. In so doing, he concluded, the long-standing problem would finally be resolved.

Władysław Gomułka accepted the solution. He recognized that the Soviet proposals generally accorded with Polish interests; therefore, the Polish side welcomed them, especially because the coal question, which Poles considered the major political issue, was resolved to Poland's benefit. Nikita Khrushchev even went so far as to say that the Soviet Union could stop buying Polish coal so that Poland could sell it to Western countries for currency.

In May 1957, Polish prime minister Józef Cyrankiewicz submitted to Moscow a statement questioning Soviet estimates of the GDR reparations. Authors of the statement recalculated the amount of reparations received by the Soviet Union in 1950–54 and concluded that their value amounted to $4.292 billion rather than $3.081 billion, as the Soviet side had insisted. Therefore, the difference was $1.211 billion. The Soviet experts explained that the amount of $4.292 billion should be reduced by $746.4 million, as that was "the value of Soviet stock companies in Germany (including patent value) that the GDR returned in 1952–1953." The value of foreign German assets accepted as reparations in Austria, Finland, Romania, and Bulgaria ($463 million) was also to be deducted from the higher sum calculated by Poland. The result was thus $3.081 billion, in 1938 prices, to be taken into account as far as Poland's share was concerned, which in the period between 1948 and 1953 was $257.8 million, as the Soviet side had previously said.

On 31 May 1957, the Presidium of the CPSU's Central Committee passed a decree on preparing proposals for a settlement of reciprocal claims. Mikoyan was sent to Warsaw to ensure the resolution of all problems. On 15 June 1957, reporting to the Presidium on the results of his trip, he said that Warsaw had accepted the Soviet proposals regarding the mutual settlement on German reparations. This meant the question was closed. Searches of the "Presidium of the CPSU" authors in the Russian Presidential Archive and the Russian Archive of Contemporary History have not turned up any document revealing details of the aforementioned agreement.

The early postwar years in Poland saw a mass deportation of hundreds of thousands of major non-Polish ethnic groups. This effort was a national idea supported by all Polish political forces. Poles sought to revive a single-ethnic Polish state and thus wished to exclude any acute ethnic conflicts such as those that spread through Poland in the period between the two world wars and which led to enormous casualties, particularly during World War II. The methods to solve the ethnic issue proposed by the Big Three and put in place by Polish and Soviet authorities largely involved the use of force, which had become common during the war and early postwar years and was accepted by both the public and politicians.

Those methods affected some 3 million Germans expelled from Poland, mostly in 1945–46. The number of repatriated Poles was also significant (up to 1.5 million people). In total, some 3 million Poles came back home from both west and east. Some resistance was offered by Ukrainians who were to be deported to Soviet Ukraine (480,000), Belorussians (36,000 deported to Soviet Belorussia), as well as small groups of ethnic Czechs, Lithuanians, and Latvians to be deported to their ethnic homelands. Among other noteworthy events was the immigration of Polish and Soviet Jews to Palestine (140,000 people).

The reason for the use of force in all those decisions went back to the negative consequences of the peace settlement following World War I. The existence of relatively large ethnic minority groups having unequal rights in most European countries between the two wars led to acute ethnic conflicts. Those conflicts were later recognized as a key factor in the collapse of the Treaty of Versailles and in igniting a new war in 1939. Now politicians sought to avoid any similar recurrence.

The "migration of peoples," arranged by national governments, was organized according to the Potsdam decisions and regulated by international agreements defining specific conditions for the transfer of the people. But sometimes ethnic distaste turned to hatred, as was the case in the relations between Poles and Germans, as well as Poles and Ukrainians, and then cruel and inhuman reality differed from law and regulation, which left negative imprints in the memories of the neighboring nations.

Nevertheless, the creation of a single-ethnic state with new territories, later developed by Poles, should be recognized as a positive fact in the history of Poland in the twentieth century.

Let's remember Akcja Wisła (Operation Vistula). As a result of the resettlement, Poland emerged from the war as a different nation, with a different territory, population, and societal, political, and economic structures. It became smaller in terms of population and territory. At the same time, it received more resources and its industry grew. Its borders moved farther into Europe, and it gained a five-hundred-kilometer outlet to the Baltic Sea, instead of the narrow corridor it had had before the war. All those aspects changed the country's geographic position and turned it into a significant factor in European geopolitics, which prompted the bitter struggle for influence over it in the early postwar years.

7

THE POSTWAR DECADE, 1945–1955

VICTORY AND ENSLAVEMENT

Włodzimierz Borodziej (Poland)

Professor at the Institute of History, Warsaw University.

Albina F. Noskova (Russia)

Leading researcher, Institute of Slavic Studies of the Russian Academy of Sciences.

Yalta
February 4-11, 1945

Potsdam
July 18, 1945

WŁODZIMIERZ BORODZIEJ

VICTORY AND ENSLAVEMENT

"THE INFLUENCE OF the Soviet Union in all spheres of cultural life in Poland and Czechoslovakia increases daily, in line with the consolidation in these countries of the new system of people's democracy and appreciation of the leading role of communist parties in state government." That sentence, written by a mid-level staffer at the Soviet Ministry of Foreign Affairs in 1949, opens one of the most important compilations of source materials on the subject in question, translated into Polish. It originated in the middle of the postwar decade and accurately reflects the fundamental trend of that period: Moscow's growing domination over its satellites and an increasing willingness by the latter to transfer models developed in and by the Stalinist Soviet Union into their states. The first signs that the direction of development was changing did not appear until 1955, so practically this entire text on the postwar decade deals with a period when the curve of Soviet domination was rising.

Thanks to the relative (periodic) openness of the Russian archives and the full accessibility of the Polish ones, research during the period from 1990 to 2010 has made enormous advances. It is mainly thanks to Polish historians that we know so much today about the mechanisms by which the Soviet center steered and controlled the Polish periphery. Polish academics have received significant support from their Russian colleagues; without them, we would not have the key source publications, without which the present state of knowledge would be hard to imagine. Polish historians also made use of studies that did not focus on Polish issues but treated them as a component of the history of Stalinism and the Cold War. The role of historians from other countries was less significant. The most important international, US-sponsored project on the Cold War—the International Cold War History Project—has focused on wars and crises; hence, the "period of the rising curve" was not the primary focus of interest of the researchers involved. Its various aspects have been addressed occasionally by historians of psychology, propaganda, or science. Still, the current state of research primarily reflects the condition of historiography in Poland and Russia, or more precisely, Warsaw and Moscow.

The ascertainment of qualitative progress does not contradict the opinion that "a vast field of research still awaits the willing (and the courageous)." Andrzej Paczkowski made that observation in reference to substantial gaps in research on the transitional period (1945–47) and the years of Stalinism. That somber assessment largely applied to studies in economic history, in which the unfavorable situation persists to this day. Meanwhile, two monographs have appeared that significantly broaden our knowledge of the immediate postwar years and put in perspective the achievements of Polish and Russian historians concerning the whole decade. The intentions behind the present essay are similar: I wish to recapitulate the state of research regarding the subject in question. I will not attempt a fundamentally new approach but encourage reflection on the body of facts available and means of interpretation.

General Observations

During the decade after World War II, dependence on the Union of Soviet Socialist Republics was a constitutive and permanent trait of the Polish state established in 1944 and, from 1952, called the Polish People's Republic. Certain forms of dependence and the main themes of the relationship between Moscow and Warsaw underwent changes between the end of the Potsdam conference and the establishment of the Warsaw Pact, that is, the period I consider in this text. The years 1945–47 can be described as a transitional period during which the Polish Workers' Party (PWP), relying on diverse assistance from the Moscow center, eradicated the opposition and introduced a single-party dictatorship and hegemony of Marxism-Leninism-Stalinism behind a double façade (elements of parliamentary democracy, gradually evolving into a "people's democracy"). In the area of external relations, the rejection of the Marshall Plan symbolized Poland's severance from the West, which extended far beyond the economic sphere. The year 1948 marked the culmination of these processes and a turning point in the history of the Stalinist state: while the less-visible foundations had been laid in the preceding period, after that year the time came to raise the walls of the first floor—something that had to be obvious from any distance. The seven years since the end of the 1940s, roughly coinciding with the Six-Year Plan, were (with the exception of the ten-month existence of the Polish Committee of National Liberation and the Provisional Government of the Republic of Poland) a period of the greatest subordination and—unlike in 1944–45—the closest emulation by Poland of the Soviet model. The Polish authorities concentrated at that time on the eradication of institutions, social groups, and social phenomena incongruent with the Stalinist prototype. This deracination particularly applied to the Catholic Church and the peasantry, seen as a holdover from the times of the free market economy, though the "relics" that had to be eliminated also included the petit bourgeoisie, regional traditions, remnants of the market, thinking that did not conform with the currently binding version of Marxism, autonomy of social organizations, historical remembrance, foreign ties, and others. It was a period of the most widespread, most acute daily terror.

In the economic sphere, the 1950s were dominated by preparations for war and ever-closer links between Polish and Soviet industries. Vestiges of Poland's national distinctiveness were reduced to the role of props along the only true path to socialism. The creeping disintegration of Polish Stalinism was characteristic of the last year of the period in question. That process began with factional infighting among the leadership of the Polish United Workers' Party (Polska Zjednoczona Partia Robotnicza, PZPR), mirroring the fragmentation of the Moscow center brought on by the struggle to succeed Stalin.

Dependence in the years 1945–55 extended to ideology (including the model of the state), the law (including the constitution), domestic and foreign policy, defense and security, the economy and—from the end of the transitional period—culture. Below, I present the elements of that construction in chronological order. The decisions made by the Allied powers during the Potsdam conference (17 July–2 August 1945) constituted the point of departure.

Dependence on the Soviet Union in the Transitional Period

Foreign Policy and Economic Relations Due to Potsdam

After the Polish Committee of National Liberation (PCNL) relinquished Poland's eastern territories, subsequent to Yalta and the establishment of the provisional Polish Government of National Unity (PGNU), the matter of Poland's western frontier remained open. As early as December 1944, the eminent diplomat and historian George F. Kennan warned that "the farther the western frontier of Poland is advanced into Germany, the greater will be the dependence of the Poles, economically and militarily, on the Soviet Union. . . . The line of the Oder as the westernmost limit of Germany must inevitably bring this dependence to a point where no Polish regime in the territory east of that line can be anything more, in effect, than a local authority, and where the Polish territory must become by the unalterable logic of events the military, economic, and political responsibility of the Soviet Union." Half a year before the end of the war, Kennan had no way of knowing that Great Britain and the United States would strengthen that dependence at Potsdam by consenting to the most western version of the Polish border while simultaneously refusing to sanction it conclusively. The intentionally ambiguous wording of point 8.b of the final communiqué (coupled with US and British support for the definite incorporation of the northern part of East Prussia into the Soviet Union) left the matter of the Polish-German border, to some extent, in suspension. The first controversies over the nature of the Potsdam decisions appeared as early as 1946. Meanwhile, Moscow unequivocally endorsed their permanence, thus becoming—at least until 1970—the sole guarantor of Poland's western border.

The decisions made at Potsdam were of fundamental importance because the Allies endowed the new Polish state with Germany's eastern provinces, which henceforth constituted one-third of Polish territory. In effect, Poland was shifted geographically westward by two hundred to three hundred kilometers and found itself—for the first time in its history—politically in the East. The weight of the territorial compensation was such that, in the coming decades, the defense of the border along the Oder and Neisse constituted one of the few political issues on which Polish political émigrés and the Warsaw government agreed.

Moscow had a different reading of the new border's significance. It calculated the value of the so-called recovered territories at $9.6 billion, that is, three times the value of the Soviet-annexed eastern Polish provinces ($3 billion to $3.5 billion). The Soviets added to that tally a further $500 million—as debatable as the other amounts—in lieu of lost reparations from formerly German territory. As compensation for themselves, they proposed to Warsaw the establishment of mixed Polish-Soviet coal companies. Even though, at that point, nothing was known about the performance of such enterprises (which in the future German Democratic Republic [GDR], eastern Austria, Romania, and Hungary would soon come to symbolize exploitation of the local economies), the Poles rejected the offer. However, two weeks after Potsdam, they did agree to conclude an agreement with the Soviet Union on remuneration for losses incurred as a result of the German occupation. Under the accord, the Soviet Union relinquished "all claims to post-German property . . . in the entire Polish territory, including the part of Germany that is being transferred to Poland." That provision remained largely unfulfilled, as did Article 2, pursuant to which Poland was to get a 15 percent share of the German reparations to the Soviet Union. Under the deal, Poland was to supply the Soviet Union with eight million to thirteen million tons of coal a year, the price of which was set in a secret protocol at less than 10 percent of the market price. Since coal was Poland's top export commodity (in 1949, output reached seventy-four million tons, of which a total of twenty-six million tons was exported), Polish losses due to the use of the "special contractual prices" were enormous and totaled between $500 million and $800 million. That, however, was still substantially less than what would have followed from the agreement on compensation for wartime losses signed on 16 August 1945, since Warsaw managed to negotiate the deliveries down to 50 percent (1947) and then to 25 percent (1950) of the originally stipulated amounts. That chapter was closed when the Soviet Union and, as a result, Poland relinquished the reparations from the GDR (agreements of 22 and 23 August 1953). Attempts to reach a settlement regarding the consequences of the Agreement of 16 August 1945 ended in 1957 with no resolution.

To recapitulate: the consequences of the decisions made at Potsdam concerning Poland's western border were felt throughout the entire existence of the Polska Partia Robotnicza (PPR), though with diminished intensity after the years 1970–75. The incorporation into Poland of the former German provinces in a way resurrected the post-Versailles constellation, constituting a structural antagonism between Poland and Germany (West Germany, from 1949). Thus Poland—much weaker than in the 1920s—was forced to curry favor with the only power that had forced through its new western border and subsequently supported it. Furthermore, unlike during the interwar period, Poland's new border tied it to another issue that was to become the most profound problem in European politics—namely, the German question. The PPR, as a beneficiary of Potsdam, became a part of that question and remained so until the end of its existence. That situation—further deformed by Stalinism, based in the sphere of foreign relations on the principles of boundless distrust and strict subordination—led to the atrophy of Polish foreign policy after 1947. It did not exist until 1955 and will not be further discussed in this essay.

The ostentatious prevention of Poland from participating in the Marshall Plan had multifaceted, mainly political consequences, though also long-term economic ones: after the UN Relief and Rehabilitation Administration program ended, Poland not only was deprived of further economic assistance but also a gradual shift took place in the main directions of its foreign economic policy. The period immediately following the war was marked by a clear tendency to rebuild ties with the West: in 1945, the Soviet Union accounted for 90 percent of total turnover in foreign trade; in 1946, that figure fell to 58 percent, then to 27 percent in 1947, when the Marshall Plan was launched. Contrary to common wisdom, the change of orientation did not occur abruptly; over the next two years, Polish trade with Western countries continued to be substantially higher than with socialist countries. This trend did not reverse until 1950.

It would be impossible to put together even an approximate balance sheet of mutual losses and profits. There is no ambiguity about the dismantling and requisitioning of property conducted in the former German territories by the Red Army and other Soviet organs in the spring and summer of 1945 (continued, to a lesser extent, in subsequent months); both Władysław Gomułka and Bolesław Bierut protested against that. The situation was similar with regard

 he's on Ellis Island

to the post-German ports along the Baltic coast, which the Soviet Union was loath to hand over to Poland and did so with considerable delays: the last port, at Szczecin, was only taken over by Poland in September 1947 and was leased to the Soviet armed forces. In addition to that, the Red Army exploited industrial plants, farms, river craft, and maritime vessels in the former German provinces. It is obvious who lost, and who profited. Yet, even here it is not clear how to calculate the losses resulting from the looting, retention, and exploitation of property, which constituted a substantial element of the balance sheet of losses and profits. Mariusz Lesław Krogulski, who studied the consequences of the Red Army presence in Poland in the years 1945–55, compiled hundreds of pieces of data concerning the dismantling of major objects, unpaid electricity bills, the use of rolling stock and tracks, illegal exportation of diverse goods, poaching, and common crime. But even he did not attempt a summing up. There is no doubt, however, that the presence of the Red Army had particularly adverse consequences for Pomerania, particularly its western part.

Internal Policy and the Soviet Role in the Ascent to Power of the PWP

The literature on the subject has focused on classical political themes: the mechanism of the creation of the Polish Government of National Unity; the Polish-Soviet treaty of friendship, mutual assistance, and cooperation of 21 April 1945; and the Trial of the Sixteen. However, it would be *useful* to keep in mind the less publicized, even forgotten, background of the political developments at that time. I refer to the sweeping "operation to cleanse the rear of the active fronts of hostile elements," during which the NKVD arrested and deported by the end of March 1945 more than 170,000 persons, including almost 35,000 Poles. Two weeks later, that number had risen to 210,000, though the percentage of Poles among the repressed persons clearly decreased, having gone up by "only" 3,000 (to 38,000). After the wave of terror in the territories of "Lublin Poland," the "cleansing operation" in the first quarter of the year dashed any hopes that Poland would be treated as a sovereign ally and that the measures applied to its citizens, considered suspect for any reason, would differ from the methods used against the citizens of the Soviet Union. The scale of the undertaking and the position of the perpetrator toward the victim were different in each case: the repressions affected millions of Soviet citizens and were meted out by the security apparatus of their own state. In Poland, the repressions—even if less prevalent—made that apparatus a representative of an occupier rather than a liberator.

The arrest of sixteen leaders of the Polish underground state and their trial in Moscow (the Trial of the Sixteen) constituted the most publicized example of that policy line. The case, due to the positions held by the persons involved and their number, had symbolic significance. The point was to mete out spectacular and exemplary punishment to representatives of the old elite. However, the trial constituted just one instance of a campaign of terror that was much broader in numerical terms and thus unpredictable and ungoverned by any regulations (tens of thousands of repressed, deported, and arrested persons were denied the right of defense). The psycho-social damage was unimaginable. In his now-forgotten novel, _Zdobycie Władzy_ (The seizure of power), Czesław Miłosz presented a literary image of an all-powerful steamroller driving across Poland and crushing everything that still survived in a landscape devastated by six years of wartime occupation. In historiography, Krystyna Kersten was the first to render the ambivalence of Polish recollections of the spring of 1945, expressed by the confluence of liberation and new subjugation, or of victory and defeat. Her path was followed by authors of subsequent syntheses of Polish history, today used as academic textbooks. That ambivalence will probably long continue as the main point of contention in Polish anniversary disputes over the place of 1945 in the history of the state and society. In any case, current studies into the disorientation of Polish society at the end of the war indicate that, unsurprisingly, it coped with the new situation with great difficulty.

The next stage and dimension of the establishment of communist rule involved the participation of the Soviet Union in eliminating armed opposition in Poland.

The ample literature on the subject lacks precise (or more accurately, synthetic) data concerning the participation of the Red Army and Soviet internal security troops in the installation of the PWP. It would have been hard to imagine that process in the spring and summer of 1945 (and the autumn of 1944) without Soviet involvement: neither the Polish Armed Forces, nor the Internal Security Corps, nor the People's Militia displayed much ability (or willingness) to conduct effective anti-insurgency operations. There is much evidence of their avoidance of combat, desertions, and passiveness when threatened with disarmament. Even in the late summer of 1945, three or four months after the war ended, members of the underground were capable of capturing prisons in the provincial capital of Kielce (the night of 4 August) and in the city of Radom (9 September).

Regrettably, no one has yet calculated the "man-days" spent by Soviet soldiers and internal security troops on anti-insurgent operations, as Norman Davies did in relation to the fronts and campaigns of World War II. Obviously, the results of any such calculations will not be precise, though in Davies's case the results provided a rather clear idea of the contribution of the respective countries and the impact of the respective fronts or campaigns on the final outcome of the war. As for the NKVD and other security formations, only fragmentary data are available. Certain conclusions can be made on the basis of comparisons with other countries occupied by the Red Army.

Of the thirty-five NKVD regiments dispatched in June 1945 to the Soviet occupation zones in Austria and Germany, and to Poland, Czechoslovakia, Romania, Bulgaria, and Hungary, fifteen (or more than 40 percent of the total) were deployed in Poland.

Many reports mention or even describe extensively the participation of Soviet troops in the physical, armed suppression of the anticommunist underground. For at least a year after the publication of the PCNL manifesto, that participation was pivotal (during the so-called Augustów sweep in July 1945, units of the Polish Ministry of Public Security (MPS) and of the Polish army played an obviously auxiliary role, though later the role of the Soviet forces gradually diminished). However, also in July 1945, the Polish border guard took over frontier posts that the Soviets had held along the border with Czechoslovakia, while Soviet-trained officers of the MPS assumed protection of the top officials of the new system. By May 1946, there remained in Poland the Sixty-Fourth Division of the Soviet Ministry of Internal Affairs (forty-two hundred men) and four other units (a total of nine thousand troops). Moscow realized that the use of Soviet internal security troops in Poland, especially in armed operations, was costly in propaganda terms since it undermined the theory that the "people's democracy" had local roots. In spring 1946, the Soviet Ministry of Internal Affairs (MIA) even had the idea that "units of the MIA deployed in Poland should wear the uniforms of Red Army infantry." However, over the next few months, some of the internal security units were withdrawn from Poland. Plans to also withdraw the Sixty-Fourth Division met with resistance from Bierut, who argued that "the MIA troops are essential and [requested] that they remain at least until 1 March 1947," which indicated that the infamous unit still played a key role within the security apparatus. Moscow had little confidence in the competence of the Polish authorities (including the security forces), as indicated by the fact that the chief task of the NKVD units in 1946 consisted of guarding elements of Moscow's system of communications, with top officials in the Soviet occupation zone in Germany and with the Northern Group of Forces.

The use of force played a fundamental role in installing the PWP in power. However, the Soviets also possessed an array of nonrepressive instruments to ensure their indirect control of the western neighbor. These tools included population exchanges along the new eastern border and fulfillment of the so-called evacuation agreements of September 1944 and the Polish-Soviet accord of 6 July 1945 on the right to change citizenship. These matters have been studied in detail by Wrocław historians, so I will restrict myself to some basic facts: about 1.5 million Polish and Jewish people were repatriated to Poland, several hundred thousand (up to a million) remained in the Soviet Union, and more than half a million Polish citizens (of whom more than 90 percent were Ukrainians) were deported to the Soviet Union. It would be hard to find a single common denominator in the mass trans-frontier migrations of the Poles, Ukrainians, Jews, Belarusians, Czechs, and Lithuanians, which combined elements of direct coercion and free choice. In many cases, "situational duress" played a role: people preferred to give up their "local homelands" in order to live in a new state; in others (e.g., the Lithuanian and Belarusian SSRs), hundreds of thousands wanted to leave but were stopped by the authorities. Those developments reflected Poland's subordination to the Soviet Union and constituted a component of the history of Poland's relations with its neighbors; they exemplified ruthless, totalitarian disregard for human rights and the legacy of the war and occupation, when persecutions and the use of force to resolve old ethnic conflicts reached unimaginable proportions. However, those population exchanges today do not constitute a "difficult matter" from the point of view of Polish-Soviet relations: the brutal division of population along ethnic lines has been accepted as a historical fact and has not produced bilateral (or international) obligations or claims.

The Soviets used the nonrepressive instruments to influence Polish internal policy throughout the transitional period. In the autumn of 1945 and the spring of 1946, Stalin even advocated that the Polish communists display moderation in dealing with the legal opposition. Still, it was the mission of Col. Aron M. Palkin, sent from Moscow, which is believed to have forged the referendum results. Successive decisions to grant Poland economic aid (e.g., loans in 1945, 1946, and 1947, grain supplies, and the cancellation in spring 1946 of war debts) helped stabilize Gomułka's and Bierut's regimes. However, the decision to move ahead with rural collectivization surely had the reverse effect, since it had not been triggered by international tensions (which largely explained the grandiosity of the Six-Year Plan) or other current circumstances. The reason was ideology, that is, the unassailable laws of Marxism-Leninism-Stalinism. Alas, their interpretation changed frequently, so adjusting one's conduct to the current line was a profound challenge posed by Stalinism for its politically active adherents.

To recapitulate: it is impossible to write about Polish affairs in the immediate postwar period without taking into account the often decisive and direct influence of the Soviet Union. However, no serious historian would classify that ascertainment as a "difficult matter" or a contentious issue. It remains a joint task of Polish and Russian historians to campaign for further access to Moscow archive materials, without which the picture of the issues addressed in this essay will remain incomplete.

Stalinism on the Periphery (1949–1955) and the Soviet Model

Socialist Multilateral Organizations and Economic Ties

Even after the foundations of Stalinism had been laid, bilateral communications were primarily conducted through party channels, that is, by means of telephone conversations between top officials in the PWP/PZPR and the All-Union Communist Party (Bolsheviks)/Communist Party of the Soviet Union. The bureaucracies behind the decision makers continued to have relatively little influence, and that is why leading Polish politicians took up many questions directly with Stalin, negotiating on issues that apparently could not be resolved at lower levels. In the preceding period, some of these matters were of key significance: Stalin became personally involved in such pivotal conflicts as those pertaining to relations between the PPR and the Polska Partia Socjalistyczna, or PPS (1946), or the nationalist deviation and Gomułka's position (1948). During the period of "classical" Stalinism, its author occupied himself with amending the draft of the Polish constitution (1951) and setting the exchange rate of the Polish currency to match that of the ruble (1952). According to research conducted by Krzysztof Persak, economic issues dominated in top-level relations during the early 1950s: Bierut repeatedly asked Stalin for help with the development of the Polish arms and coal industries and for Soviet engineering specialists to be sent (in his last letter to Stalin, dated 2 March 1953, Bierut also requested Soviet agricultural advisors). Bierut not only contacted Stalin to discuss such major projects as the Palace of Culture and Science or the Warsaw subway but also in connection with drought, food shortages, and minor changes in the Polish-Soviet border (including Bug River crossings).

For this postwar period (up to 1953), virtually no information is available about visits to Warsaw by Soviet decision makers (not to mention visit by Stalin himself). The only exception was a visit in July 1951 by Deputy Premier Vyacheslav Molotov and Marshal Georgy Zhukov on the occasion of the seventh anniversary of the PCNL manifesto. The frequency of visits is one indicator of the extent of subordination. That rule changed to some degree in 1954 during the post-Stalin succession struggle (Nikita Khrushchev attended the Second Congress of the PZPR, and Nikolai Bulganin, formally a mere deputy premier but in reality a member of the "collective leadership," also visited).

The two embassies—classical instruments of contact in the mid-twentieth century—played a somewhat atypical role. The Polish mission to Moscow in 1945 could not enlighten the hosts about the tenets of Polish foreign policy—because such a policy simply did not exist. It limited itself to gauging the Kremlin's intentions and obtaining its opinions. No wonder that, with the passage of time, the Moscow embassy came to be seen as an increasingly unattractive posting: among the Polish ambassadors who held that post after the departure of Zygmunt Modzelewski in August 1945, only Marian Naszkowski (ambassador to Moscow in 1947–50) gained promotion after returning to Warsaw. The names of the three other ambassadors (Henryk Raabe, 1945–47; Kazimierz Jasiński, 1950–52; and Wacław Lewikowski, 1952–57) are known only to specialists; neither they nor their associates went on to play significant roles.

Meanwhile, the situation at the Soviet embassy in Warsaw was nothing short of amazing. Victor Lebedev was a significant player, though not "an all-powerful figure"; he was recalled to Moscow because he was too heavy handed in his attempts to interfere in the internal affairs of the PZPR leadership. The reasons why the other Soviet ambassadors did not last long in their posts are not that obvious: Arkady Sobolev (1951–53) was followed by Georgy Popov (1953–54), Nikolai Mikhailov (just thirteen months), and Panteleimon Ponomarenko (1955–57). Thus, in the relatively short period of seven years of classical Stalinism, Moscow "used up" five ambassadors in the capital of its western vassal. What happened?

One clue is contained in the guidelines (which I know only from a summary) adopted by the Politburo in October 1951 for advisors of the Ministry of State Security attached to state security institutions of the socialist countries, including Poland. Apparently, the objective was to put a stop to the imperious attitudes of the Soviet advisors and thus reduce the number of conflicts with the local authorities, by respecting their will with regard to specific matters. It is hard to imagine that Soviet diplomats, and particularly ambassadors, were immune to overbearing conduct (Lebedev's recall is a good example). In any case, the game of musical chairs at the Warsaw embassy does not testify to a prudent and far-sighted policy of an empire.

We reach the same conclusion when examining the institutional framework of Poland's dependence. The Soviet Union did not feel compelled to put in place a legal basis for the stationing of its garrisons in Poland, and it was only in the post-Stalinist phase that it initiated the establishment of the Warsaw Pact, supplemented—in Poland's case—with an agreement on the status of Soviet troops provisionally stationed in Poland. Naturally, the situation in the early 1950s could be seen simply as affirmation of the obvious truth that the Soviet Union could deploy whatever it wanted in the subordinated countries. However, that was hardly rational, since the relevant legal basis was easy to create, and, considering the nature of the mutual relationship, the PPR would not have been capable of effectively exacting the provisions of any accord in a conflict situation.

The situation was similar with regard to the Council for Mutual Economic Assistance (CMEA or Comecon). It was set up in 1949 as counterweight to the Atlantic organizations launched in connection with the Marshall Plan, and it remained practically dormant in the early 1950s. Comecon's revival in the spring of 1954 probably stemmed from the awareness of Moscow decision makers that the bilateral steering mechanisms used at that time were no longer sufficient in view of the relatively high level of mutual economic dependency achieved over the preceding years. In the case of Poland, the share of trade with the Soviet Union doubled between the year Comecon was established and the year it was resurrected, accounting for one-third to two-fifths of all Polish foreign trade.

In revisiting the subject, it is essential to point out that the balance sheet of profits and losses for either side is still unclear. This view even applies to the most spectacular investment projects: the production in Poland under Soviet license of the Pobyeda automobile (called "Warszawa" in Poland) and the T-34 tank, or the erection of the Palace of Culture and Science in the Polish capital and the Nowa Huta steel plant outside Kraków. How much more would it have cost to buy Soviet oil or Polish processed goods at free-market prices? How should you calculate the true cost of transit across Poland between the Soviet Union and the Soviet occupation zone/GDR? How should you convert transfer rubles into hard currency and how should you compare the value (or rather the feasibility of the conversion rate) of the currency złoty and the circulation złoty? We do know that, in 1951, Stalin personally ordered that the new złoty-to-ruble exchange rate be lowered by two-thirds, which no doubt significantly affected mutual settlements. It is unclear if the move was motivated by an economic need or prestige (originally, the exchange rate had been set at one złoty to one ruble). The original, even rate of exchange clearly favored Poland, and the attendant prestige factor had its weight. It is noteworthy that both central banks had endorsed that even exchange rate, contrary to the opinions of economists who thought it did not reflect economic realities. In any event, Moscow arbitrarily imposed a different exchange rate, which in a normal economy would have had disastrous consequences. It remains a mystery why that did not happen in the case of trade between Poland and the Soviet Union.

Imitation, Dependence, and the National Question

It would be hard to enumerate the diverse expressions of dependence that often amounted to a more or less mechanical replication of Stalinist patterns. Starting with the office hours of Polish decision makers, adjusted to Stalin's daily routine, practically everything was imitated: the tenets of ideology and forms of its propagation, the cult of personality (as it later came to be called), the realm of aesthetics (including the prevalence of the color red), philosophy (or rather its lack), the norms and practices that characterized daily life, from kindergarten and workplace to university, the spy mania and fetishism for secrecy in the armed forces, doctrine, arms and organization, and everywhere the image of the enemy and the notion of the "camp of socialist countries" as the cornerstone of peace and security. In the 1945–46 academic year, the Russian language became an obligatory subject in public schools. Other replications of the Soviet model included not only the striving for actual autarchy but also the rules of planned economy, the nomenklatura, and, to a certain extent, the "permanent purge" as a key element of keeping members of the nomenklatura on their toes.

All this (much more could be enumerated) had its shadings and accentuations, though certain digressions from the norm were possible. For example, because two famous architectural designs, in Poland and East Berlin, had been modeled on the same Moscow original, the MDM in downtown Warsaw resembled the Stalinallee in East Berlin but was not identical, just as it was not identical to its Soviet point of reference. The decoding of public space (monuments, street names, etc.) proceeded in the same way, though with room for certain local peculiarities. The slogan "socialist in content, national in form," explains some of these distinctions. Certain symbols of national tradition were considered suitable for domestication, particularly if they could be interpreted as synonyms of progress and, better still, as forerunners of the idea of a "people's Poland." That was why the presentation of the images of Tadeusz Kościuszko and Adam Mickiewicz was exclusively positive and why the Sejm building on Wiejska Street was reconstructed, while the meaningless institution within its walls did not change its name to a "People's Assembly" or something of that sort. The prewar national anthem, national colors, and the state emblem (the white eagle, alas, without its crown) were all retained, though not the state holidays of 11 November and 3 May.

While, during the transitional period, the PWP had tried to invoke as many icons and forms of prewar statehood as possible—on condition that they did not collide with the new ideology—it did not feel compelled to do that when Stalinism proper was in place. Stefan Korboński penned a description of the swearing-in ceremony of Bierut as president on 5 February 1947 and concluded with an insightful observation: "The point was to ensure that the only outward difference was that instead of [Ignacy] Mościcki it was Bierut who had arrived in the black Cadillac." Soon enough, however, some of the Moscow overseers of Polish affairs decided that that façade was superfluous, irritating, and—worse yet—an expression of a genuine, traditional nationalism by their Polish comrades. In view of such accusations, the PWP made its well-known policy turn in 1947–48, recognizing that national trappings were a hazardous substance, difficult to handle and potentially harmful.

When, in November 1949, Soviet marshal Konstanty Rokossowski was appointed commander in chief of the Polish armed forces and marshal of Poland, dependence (i.e., the opposite of the prewar principle of sovereignty) gained a symbol that would have been unthinkable two years earlier. Thus, in the autumn of 1949, that dependence, even in the most sensitive sphere of national dignity, was only barely camouflaged (by highlighting the supposedly Polish roots of the new marshal). In effect, it came to be displayed openly and persisted, without much modification, for the next six years.

That situation had its consequences for the leaders of the PZPR: Jakub

Berman, who was the second- or third-ranking state official, continued to meet with the counselor or first secretary of the Soviet embassy—something that was unprecedented in the history of international relations. This also meant that even the most preposterous accusations against the PZPR leadership were not simply filed or thrown away but ended up on the desks of top decision makers in Moscow. The editors of one of the most important compilations of source materials point in this context to "the feeling of superiority and know-it-all attitudes of the Soviet authors of these reports and evaluations," also rightly noting that "distrust toward the Poles, who—after all— were still comrades, was a highly distinct trait of the documents produced within the Soviet apparatus." Let me add that the distrust was mutual and contradicted the official image of good-neighborliness in every possible way. Still, it remained the unwritten rule of bilateral relations for decades, if not until the end of the PPR. Meanwhile, ordinary citizens, who were not privy to that state of affairs, scorned the overt dependence and made jokes about it, though, at the same time, they felt humiliation, injustice, and even hatred.

Soviet specialists played a more discreet role in perpetuating Poland's dependency. They were occupied in diverse fields. Most prominent in the armed forces, they were also notable in the major investment projects of the Six-Year Plan and even provided advice on jamming Polish-language radio broadcasts from the West (utilizing their own "technical means"). They were employed in all the key industries and in agriculture and the railways. While their overall number was relatively small among the constantly ballooning civil service, Soviet advisors, commanders, and senior Ministry of Defense officials in 1949 constituted a highly visible group in the armed forces, exceeding 7,000 men. Even though the percentage of Soviets diminished in the rapidly expanding officer corps (the corps grew from 19,000 in 1950 to 47,000 four years later), their importance did not; throughout the period in question, they held most of the top posts. Simultaneously, the number of prewar officers decreased to a symbolic few—240 by 1956. At that time, the growing armed forces and arms industry—the top beneficiaries of the Cold War and the Soviet strategy in Europe—consumed an unknown proportion of the state budget, probably corresponding to the proportion before the war (i.e., 35 to 50 percent). Here, too, no credible research has been conducted to determine the cost of militarization relative to the state's overall expenditures.

Soviet citizens were much less evident at the Ministry of State Security, where there were about fifty of them. However, the ministry was a copy of the Soviet model: it was big and unhindered by law. Formally, it was in charge of prisons and, informally, of the judiciary. It intruded into every sphere of life, striking fear in all, including members of the PZPR. Andrzej Paczkowski made an apt distinction regarding the postwar decade: until 1948, we were dealing with mass terror, intended to intimidate the society at large rather than to suppress the already weak and dissipating underground. Later, the terror still served the original goals, but—true to the Soviet model from the 1930s—it became universal: "not even the highest post held, not even the greatest services rendered, not even the most servile sycophancy gave you protection." If we add Paweł Machewicz's reflection that the network of informants had reached exceptional proportions by that time, and Dariusz Stola's observation that the borders had been sealed almost hermetically, then we get an idea of the role the so-called security organs played in the Polish edition of Stalinism. That topic is likely to continue fascinating historians in the future, though it does not appear to constitute a "difficult matter"; for that to happen, we would need two different viewpoints, and that is not the case here.

The Crisis of Stalinism in Poland in Reaction to the Soviet Crisis of Power

The beginnings of de-Stalinization in the center and the mechanisms of their transfer to the Polish periphery in 1953–55 do not yield interesting material relating to our chief point of interest, that is, the structure of Poland's dependence/subordination. The role of the respective factions in Warsaw and in Moscow, the nature of their ties, the progress of the infighting—all these issues hardly function as "difficult matters" in Polish-Russian relations. Furthermore, without access to the Moscow archives, little more can be said on the subject. We do know that the losers included the security apparatus and, to a certain extent, the armed forces, though not necessarily the military-industrial complex (it is unclear if, in the Polish conditions, it constituted an identifiable, self-aware lobby).

Events that occurred 10–14 May 1955 seem more relevant to our topic: when Khrushchev came to the Polish capital to sign the Warsaw Pact, he was accompanied by Molotov, still the Soviet foreign minister. One of the greatest achievements in Molotov's career was the conclusion of the Ribbentrop-Molotov Pact, including the infamous secret protocol. Sixteen years later, it was one of the many fundamental historical facts zealously denied throughout the bloc. In May 1955, the Soviet Union was consolidating and bringing order to its "external empire" in Europe, which it had partly acquired in 1939 and 1940 under the 1939 treaties and partly conquered militarily in 1944–45. Molotov's presence was supposed to lend credibility to stabilization, the creation of a legal network, and a reduction of tensions (the Soviet Union had proposed a conference on peace and security in Europe), that is, *sui generis détente* in Europe. It was irony at its finest and, at the same time, convincing proof that de-Stalinization, with its inevitable impact on relations between the Moscow center and the European periphery, remained, at least until the Twentieth Congress of the CPSU, a process that was uncertain, unclear, and equivocal.

Conclusions

There has been no development after 1989 of the discussion—quite vigorous in the previous two decades, particularly among Western historians—on the mechanisms (e.g., reactive) or the inevitability of the Stalinization of the Soviet Union's foreground in Europe. In this situation, an interpretation of the transitional period, formulated a quarter of a century earlier by Dietrich Geyer, has retained its validity:

> From Moscow's point of view, the methods of indirect rule constituted the only political alternative to annexation and sovietization, the only one elaborated by communists in the interwar period. They built on elements of the earlier practice of the popular front. They were sufficiently pliable and flexible to cope with the national and regional distinctions within Eastern Europe. Little indicates that in order to ensure its rule and loyalty outside the Soviet state, Moscow had at its disposal methods and instruments different than those applied in establishing the Stalinist system in the USSR itself. As concerned the practice of government, Stalinism . . . in Eastern Europe could not be different than in its homeland.

Regarding the practice of government in mature Stalinism, that is, after 1948, that interpretation needs to be supplemented with two equally classical components. Even before World War II ended, Kennan predicted that relations between the center and the peripheries would become one of the profoundest challenges for Moscow as the quasi government of the external empire, when confronted with the ambitions and interests of the local elites. A quarter of a century later, Johan Galtung argued that the essence of the cliental international relations consisted of a community of interests of the elite/rulers of the peripheries and the elite/rulers of the center. In the specific case of the Soviet Union and its satellites, Galtung underscored the high level of coercion, the relatively limited benefits obtained by the elite/rulers of the peripheral state, and the unpredictability of the patronage in its original edition, authored by Stalin. Galtung further pointed out that the cliental relations between the center and the peripheries were characterized by a permanent conflict between the "periphery of the periphery" (i.e., the society of the peripheral state) and the "elite of the periphery" (i.e., the authorities thereof). That observation, like Kennan's prediction, leads us to the year 1956, which is the subject of the next chapter.

ALBINA F. NOSKOVA

· ·

VICTORY AND ENSLAVEMENT

· ·

A Democratic Regime for a Society in Transition

Modern scholars are still debating many of the critical issues relating to what happened in Poland after the war ended. Did the Red Army bring liberation or Soviet occupation? Did Poland win or lose the war? Was the regime the result of violence and treachery on Stalin's part? Were the Polish communists mere puppets?

The answers to the questions about liberation and victory are obvious enough: the Red Army, alongside the Polish army, brought liberation, not occupation, and this was a victory because it saved the country from being destroyed by the Nazis. Confirmation for such a view can be found by reviewing those half-forgotten German policies of "Lebensraum" and the "Eastern Master Plan." Speaking on 11 January 1960, Cardinal Stefan Wyszyński recalled such policies in a conversation with Władysław Gomułka: "During the war, the Nazis thought, 'We'll win the war and the rest will be taken care of by the crematoriums, because we do not want the Poles, we need only their land[;] they would do the same if we lost the war.'" The only way to win the war was by uniting with the Soviet Union at the cost of millions of soldiers' lives.

For those Poles who had lived through the nightmare of Nazi occupation, the experience determined their attitude toward the Red Army in 1944–45. They welcomed the Soviet troops with open arms, greeting them as liberators and in no way perceiving them to be invaders. This was a commonly held view of the Red Army's arrival, although some people were of a different opinion. The latter were defined by Soviet intelligence officers as anti-Soviet and hostile.

Although academics acknowledge the fact of the Red Army's liberation of Poland, they also conclude that there were violations of Poland's right to make its own decisions, independent of the Soviet Union. Indeed, many felt that, with liberation, came a threat to national freedom, and the government in exile, trusted by the Poles to bring about a Polish revival, began to foster a bitter feeling of defeat. Fears began to mount concerning the Soviet presence. People remembered the events of 17 September 1939. They knew about the Katyn massacres. There was the painful memory of the defeat of the Warsaw Uprising, a defeat that many blamed on Stalin. There was also growing indignation regarding the actions of the NKVD, which suppressed the armed underground forces that were trying to resist Soviet occupation and the establishment of communist rule. All this had a negative effect on the atmosphere in Poland and created a climate of anxiety that led to mistrust between the Provisional Government and a large part of the population. However, as suggested by the well-known Polish scholar Krystyna Kersten, for most people this mistrust and prejudice toward the Polish Workers' Party (Polska Partia Robotnicza, or PPR) did not develop into a perception of the new government as a non-indigenous regime, and that was important.

It would appear that Stalin's actions can be largely explained by geopolitical reasons as well as the desire to guarantee security in postwar Europe. Along with his coalition partners, the Soviet leader was convinced that Germany would make a rapid recovery, something he repeatedly mentioned. He believed that the next *Drang nach Osten* campaign would need a much shorter time frame, and, following that logic, Europe and the country that defeated Nazism needed a strong, geopolitically allied Poland. Stalin declared Russia ready to provide Europe with this version of Poland, adding that anyone in Poland who did not want to work in tandem with the Soviet Union (such as the government in exile) under the proposed conditions would be defeated and that those who attempted to interfere with these efforts (such as the underground forces) would be suppressed.

One must pose another pertinent question: at that time, given the conflict between Polish and Soviet opinions on matters of national and state interests, was there ever any real possibility of Poland shaping its own destiny and creating ideological imperatives and a social system that differed from those of the Soviet Union? The Hungarian writer Sándor Márai lived through this era and provided the answer to that question in the spring of 1945: "At Stalingrad, that great nation, at the cost of unprecedented casualties, changed the flow of events. . . . Her young soldier(s) brought salvation and liberation from the Nazi terror to all those who had been persecuted by fascism. But he could not bring freedom, because he himself did not have it."

We may agree and recognize that the fate of Poland depended not only on the Poles but also on various leaders of the coalition who monopolized the right to determine the future of "minor" countries. Poland's allies were guided by their own interests.

The Soviet Union resolved its security issues by expanding its territory and creating a "security belt" of allied countries along its borders. In accordance with the spirit of the times, Stalin's plans for Eastern Europe were colored with geopolitical concerns. Meanwhile, for a limited period at least, his partners in the wartime "Big Three" were ready to accept anything, provided Germany was defeated. One need only recall the 1943 meetings in Moscow and Tehran or the "dirty" document, which Winston Churchill gave to Stalin in Moscow in October 1944. Discussion of the "Polish question" gave Stalin grounds to believe that the West would accept his terms for settling the question of Soviet-Polish relations, not because Russia was strong, as Churchill acknowledged, but because it was right. For the Western Allies to have adopted a different stance, British and American troops would have needed to have played a much more active role in the ground war on the continent prior to the summer of 1944.

However, that course of action would not have suited the Allies' intention to use political and economic tools as their predominant contribution to the defeat of Germany in Europe. There was the lend-lease program of assistance to Moscow, put in place, as Roosevelt wrote to Churchill in October 1942, to "provide, provide, and provide" in order to "consistently keep Russia at war with Hitler," since "the Russian front today is our biggest support." This is why they breached agreements concerning the opening of the second front in 1942, 1943, and 1944. It also explains the lack of support for the Polish government in its opposition to the Soviet Union and leads one to question whether the Polish government's uncompromising stance toward the Soviet Union was in any way constructive. Is it not fair to say that Polish premier Stanisław Mikołajczyk's rejection of the Soviet terms in the autumn of 1944 was beneficial to Moscow? Averell Harriman, the US ambassador to Moscow, believed that the Polish government's anti-Soviet stance was "irreconcilable, and strongly spiced with Russophobia" and that it made it impossible for Stalin "to deal with the London government." To this end, it was decided to hold the Yalta conference, where the Allies had no option other than to give away parts of Europe. In the summer of 1944, the Allies accepted a transfer of power to the communists (Polish Committee for National Liberation, or PCNL), although it went against what the Polish government in exile and people actually wanted and jeopardized efforts to disarm the Armia Krajowa (AK) and the rebels of the National Armed Forces. In the spring of 1945, the Allies actually agreed to the dominant position of the PPR in the Polish government, at least until an election.

The Allies did not respond to the NKVD's and the defense ministry's actions during "Smersh"—an attempt to prevent the security of the Red Army's rear from being undermined. US president Franklin D. Roosevelt recognized the right and determination of the Soviet leader: "your rear flank should be secure as you move your army on to Berlin." However, in essence, the purpose of Smersh was to forcibly resolve the question of power in Poland and to suppress the fighting of units of the Ukrainian Insurgent Army (UPA), the military arm of the Organization of Ukrainian Nationalists (OUN).

At the Yalta conference, the Allies did not identify the mechanisms for mutual control in "their" zones, so agreement was at the discretion of those parties involved. Moscow was endeavoring to keep Poland in the Soviet zone and thereby prevent the resurgence of a hostile Poland. In achieving its goal, the Soviet Union demonstrated its ability to secure control of large border areas important to its postwar defense strategy.

So, it would be simplistic to lay responsibility for the lack of freedom in Poland on Stalin. The rules of the "big politics" game were applied; hence, the deliberately "abandoned" opportunities of the Western powers. As a result, Poland, awaiting liberation from the West, got it from the East. The Polish government was defeated in all major policy areas, particularly in the national (independence from the Soviet Union) and geopolitical (barrier against Bolshevism) spheres.

One must also consider the reasons for which Stalin implemented this direct transfer of powerful positions to the communists in Poland but not in other countries, such as Yugoslavia and Albania. Why was the Soviet presence there so profound? The answer lies in the fact that no conclusion was offered to the question of Poland's geopolitical position in Europe or to that of the Soviet Union's role. The two parties who failed to provide the needed conclusion were the government in exile (those "doomed representatives of the doomed regime," as George F. Kennan put it) and the influential political forces that sought a return to prewar living circumstances and a defense of the disputed eastern border (which was viewed in Poland as a symbol of independence). Of the "two enemies" (the term used to describe Poland's concept of security in the prewar years), only one was left. That enemy was winning the war and was preparing to begin negotiations. There were two alternatives: (1) compromise at the cost of territorial and political concessions, which would have meant a betrayal of Poland in the government's eyes and would have run the risk of losing contact with society, or (2) refuse to compromise and prepare the nation to resist "the occupation." They chose the latter option, but, at a time when Poland and the Western Allies were in no hurry to defend the sovereignty of the country, a third option—the loss of political power by the Polish government in exile—emerged and was becoming more and more attractive.

The Polish communists decided to accept a compromise based on the new situation and the interests of the country. Guided by a program of creating new Polish borders through changes in the population's interests, they formed a coalition with the Left Socialists and the members of the "people's" parties (*ludowcy*), establishing the Krajowa Rada Narodowa (KRN) as a center of power. It was the left-wing alternative to the government in exile and a modest social force made up of the "underground state." The communists claimed a share of power, knowing that their chances grew in inverse proportion to the legitimate government's chances to return to Poland. They were ready to come to power, and they garnered success under favorable conditions.

The communists' willingness to accept power was explained by their ideological similarity to the Soviet regime and by their own understanding of the country's interests, including the political and territorial aspects. PPR easily won second place, a position assigned to the Polish government by the Western powers. Demonstration of the government's intransigence would only weaken its reputation; the country was rapidly becoming the subject, rather than object, of coalition politics, and future territorial losses were imminent. The Polish left wing believed it was possible to avoid any such problems by acting together with the Soviet Union, gaining wider access to the Baltic Sea and securing guarantees for the newly established borders. Acceptance of these terms involved a transition into the zone of Soviet interests, as well as an agreement that limited national sovereignty.

Therefore, in giving his approval of the Polish Committee for National Liberation lineup, Stalin, who still believed that it was possible to establish contact with the Polish government, represented a blend of ideas from the Polish left wing, who were ready to share the burden of responsibility for a successful outcome of the war, and from the Soviet desire to avoid installing a military government in the liberated countries, leaving strong geopolitical and ideological partners to assume power.

Yet, it was not as simple as just transferring and assuming power. Power had to be secured in order to fulfill the Soviet Union's strategic goal of keeping Poland in its orbit of influence and under control. It is clear that one also needed to resolve the issue of the nature of power itself. It was impossible to achieve this goal without resolving at least two short-term domestic tasks. First, it was necessary to neutralize those forces that might try to resist Poland's transition to Soviet control. This problem could be resolved by the PPR and the Soviet Union together. Second, the PCNL needed to obtain the confidence of those who were ready to cooperate for the sake of national goals. Here, the PCNL (more precisely, the PPR) had a chance of success.

During the Nazi occupation, the social structure changed and there was a further impoverishment of the working class, accompanied by growing left-wing sentiment among the workers. Farmers, whose representatives were *ludowcy* in various political groups, suffered less, but the looting of farms by the Nazis led to bankruptcies and new forms of land redistribution. Many intellectuals who had possessed unorthodox political views had been exterminated or had lost their jobs and professional status. The position of urban landlords and property owners and landowners changed, because they lost their influence and property during the war. After the war, the social status of the survivors was never restored.

The war led to an increase in the number of low-income and impoverished people in all social groups. Those social strata that were unwilling to return to the Second Republic (the antagonisms of capitalism may have retreated into the background, but their memory remained) or to live under a Soviet model of socialism were offered a way out. The socioeconomic changes advocated by the socialists before the war and the *ludowcy,* which were now implemented by the communist-led government, suited the needs of the poor and were appropriate to the "time and place." In connection with the repatriation of the Poles to their homeland, as well as those who had been driven to Germany, and Poland's development of the eastern and northern German territories, the targeted nature of the reforms became more prominent. They either fully or partially met the interests of a majority of the population. It should be noted that the reforms were not accompanied by significant social and political conflicts.

For a significant portion of the population, physical survival was more important than national losses, personal tragedies, or plans for the future. During social and territorial changes, voluntary and forced migration, and transformations in the ethnic composition and size of the population, citizens developed a special way of thinking that made them ready to cooperate with the government and to take advantage of changes in their lives. In such an environment, various movements began to emerge, many of which expressed radical sentiments and social impatience; revolutionary slogans were about justice and freedom, with a particularly acute reaction to injustice and lack of freedom. Various political parties were upholding these sentiments, and the communists, socialists, and *ludowcy* were among them. The new government provided the opportunity for landless peasants to acquire land and for their children to study and live in town, while workers were able to gain qualifications, earn a salary, and move on to higher positions. Intellectuals were able to return to their original professions. The government also provided land and contributed funds to the Roman Catholic Church for the restoration of churches and religious life.

Filling national and local government posts were representatives of those social groups who had no experience in running the country. The latter also entered into posts in the army, police, industry, schools, and hospitals and settled and developed new territories. Impelled by the basic need to improve their everyday lives and to raise their social status, Poles had to work well with government. For its part, the government started to make use of these sections of society. In 1945–46, the coalition, which was later transformed into an electoral bloc led by the Polish Workers' Party, was supported by 25 percent of the population. That was a significant share if one considers that the figures reflect the stated political positions, which, in a country dependent on the Soviet Union, defined the PPR as a party following the will of Moscow. We may assume that, in such circumstances, latent support could have been greater. It seems that those who insist that Polish society was in conflict with the authorities were in fact incorrect.

It should also be noted that attitudes toward the authorities ranged from resistance to rejection (in 1947, Gomułka believed that "enemies of the people" and "reactionary elements" constituted about 20 percent of the population), suspicion and indifference, to a conscious political choice in favor of the government. Workers' parties were joined by those who saw the reforms as the creation of a fair system and by those who were motivated by career opportunities. It is hard to say which group was more numerous, but considering the rapid growth of the PPR, the PPS (Polska Partia Socjalistyczna, or Polish Socialist Party), and the SL (Stronnictwo Ludowe, or Polish People's Party), the proposed social benefits were readily accepted by the working classes, farmers, intellectuals, and left-wing intellectuals and by young people in particular. Apparently, this increasing acceptance gave life to the concept of a "democratic stage."

Support for the socioeconomic transformations did not mean that the government was gaining trust. Many Poles based their political positions on their desire for a peaceful life and a natural protest against violations of their right to organize their own domestic life, something which was understood as the return of the legitimate government to the country and restoration of the 1921 eastern border.

While the communists were in power and Poland lived under Soviet control, any alternative mode had no real prospects. In the specific environment of the mid-1940s, it would only have been possible to form a left-wing or center-left coalition government with lots of scope for the Communist Party to gain decisive positions. Such a political system was called a democratic regime.

According to the communists, the political system in such a democracy could include a working party and, according to Gomułka, "liberal parties" or farmers' parties, as well as the "bourgeois-liberal" parties that would form a legal opposition. However, right-wing groups consisting of former political elites were to be excluded. Such a system represented the various sociopolitical interests of a large section of Polish society. Its primary goal was to avoid civil war by using the Soviet Union's help—a high price to pay. They also wanted to restrict independence through the use of force, including Soviet forces, and to preserve the Polish state geopolitically and geographically (in the postwar mold), as well as to resolve national problems.

By the middle of 1945, the real model of power was significantly different from the democracy "ideal" declared by Gomułka. The multiparty system that included the PPR, PPS, and SL was based on interparty agreements, often made under pressure from their powerful ally. Such agreements were often breached by hegemony, and even outright dictatorship, on the part of the PPR, which supported the entire political structure and controlled all the power levers of the executive branch of government. In the middle of 1945, when the Provisional Government of National Unity was founded, the coalition was expanded. Positions in the Krajowa Rada Narodowa, the government, and local government were taken by representatives of the SL "Roch" (right wing of the Polish People's Party). The Polish People's Party (Polskie Stronnictwo Ludowe, or PSL, sometimes translated as Polish Peasants' Party) was joined by the socialists, who had come out of hiding. The representative nature of the political system became stronger, but its representation was largely determined by the strong potential of the PPR.

Polish communists, Comintern "old-timers," activists of the emigration and occupation period, and the radically minded youth, who poured into the party after liberation, controlled state institutions and political processes in the country. Their ideological views, which included intolerance toward "aliens" and a manifestation of an "ends justify the means" approach, were apparent in the legislation on government and state apparatus, in decrees on protection of the state, and in the most severe penalties for disobedience.

Violence is an inherent trait of authoritarianism. Elements of this method of government were present in Poland. The power-play agencies, including the army, police, internal troops, and state security agencies, occupied a special place in the emerging government. They turned into party-ruled political agencies, created according to Soviet patterns before them. The commanders who arrived along with the first "draft" were trained in the Soviet Union and, for the most part, were members of the former Polish Communist Party. They were ideologically and politically close to the advisors and instructors of the Soviet NKVD-KGB, which, as of February 1945, participated in the formation of the vertically structured Ministry of Public Security (Ministerstwo Bezpieczeństwa Publicznego, or MBP). At the same time, ideological imperatives were introduced into the system of state security in the interest of serving one political force. These structures were continuously expanding.

The model of power had been put in place and was partially supported by Polish society and based on the hegemony of the PPR and the interaction and predominance of the workers' parties. The authorities used repression as a means of exerting pressure on the population. Violence was turned into a tool for destroying the disintegrating "underground state" and intimidating the politically neutral. Thus, the PPR was creating an inner "safety cushion" within a new state, making it impossible to return to the prewar order of things or to pursue a different foreign policy course. These manifestations of authoritarian government were perceived by many to prove the existence of a PPR dictatorship based on borrowed Soviet techniques.

After the war, many nations saw a rise in such violence, not just Poland. The war gave life to the belief that violence was justified and acceptable in peacetime as well. The communists and their opponents were equally convinced that the use of force in the political struggle was permissible. A new Poland had already come to pass—a Poland within new borders, with a government led by the communists and protected by the Soviet Union.

In the towns and villages within operating army zones, the military commandants' offices in the liberated Polish territories were performing a number of tasks, according to Marshal Konstanty K. Rokossowski's order of 28 July 1944. The offices were to ensure discipline in the army, stop the unlawful actions of service members, communicate with local authorities, confiscate weapons from the population, carry out restoration operations, make inventories of abandoned property, maintain law and order, and suppress small, armed resistance groups.

Although the demobilization of Soviet soldiers and officers was under way (the number of those in uniform had shrunk from 11 million to between 3 million and 5 million), the Red Army stayed in Poland, situated beyond the Oder. Its presence in the region guaranteed the Soviet Union's claim concerning its sphere of interests and the need to ensure a balance of power and security in Europe so as to fend off the German threat. Poland was located in the rear flank of the Soviet forces, within the eastern zone of occupation in Germany, and it was a major component of any European balance. Moscow's task was to secure its own geopolitical interests and Poland's new geopolitical and territorial status.

Thus, the Soviet Union carried out the role of ensuring security by creating optimal conditions for the existence of a new state and the establishment of a pro-Soviet, legitimately founded government, hence the contribution to the suppression of the armed underground forces in the rear of the multimillion-member regular army, made in 1944–45. The Sixty-Fourth Division of NKVD domestic troops, as well as Smersh operational groups, were carrying out massive operations to disarm the population in a number of Polish provinces, taking underground activists to the Soviet Union, thereby simultaneously resolving operational and geopolitical tasks.

The underground movement was weakened, but in Polish national memory it is still seen as a strong force consisting of Armia Krajowa fighters in opposition to the Soviets. The suppression of the AK was the price paid by Moscow and the Polish communists to limit Polish sovereignty and maintain the social transformations and Soviet presence while protecting the national borders.

In western and northwestern Poland there was the Soviet Northern Group of Forces (NGF), which in 1945 numbered three hundred thousand. These troops served not only in the important task of ensuring a liaison with the Soviet troops in Germany but also as a guarantee of the Soviet-Polish Treaty, signed in Moscow in April 1945 and encompassing the stability and security of the Polish borders and of the German lands handed over to Poland for management.

The Soviet presence was also backed up by the service of thousands of Soviet officers in the Polish army. They reported to the Polish command, occupied commanders' positions, and performed the task of creating a capable and politically reliable army along the borders of the Soviet sphere of influence. In 1948, however, the officer corps was replaced in favor of prewar Polish officers. The state system, designed primarily to defend the external frontiers of the country, had service members of a different nationality and who had not taken the Polish military oath. Therefore, this regulated army could not be used against the Soviet Union. The opportunity for turning it into a destructive internal political factor did not exist.

The national government gained a share of the sovereign right to manage the means of protection against external threat in return for guarantees for statehood within the western borders, as yet not legally recognized by the international community. The country could not protect the western borders on its own. A long-term dependency on Moscow was emerging.

The Soviet military presence ingrained a feeling of sustained irritation in Polish society. Cases of looting and violence by Soviet soldiers caused protests and indignation. The dehumanization of the army, typical during any war and especially for an army that had spent four years in the trenches battling for a devastated country that had seen hundreds of thousands of families killed, had led the soldiers to believe that everything was permitted. Once they had returned to a peaceful life, it was difficult for them to refrain from criminal acts. The Soviet leadership sought to put an end to this tendency. The order of the Supreme Commander of 19 January 1945 ordered military tribunals to impose capital punishment. That order was put to paper, and several thousand soldiers were shot accordingly. Rokossowski was a general who would punish his subordinates in the most severe way. It is known that Stalin, aware of the inherent "winner takes all" instinct of the people, made two public pleas for forgiveness for the Soviet army.

It is impossible to delete any evidence of wrongdoing from history, but it would be a mistake to focus exclusively on the discussion of the Soviet presence and thereby diminish the human dimension of war, as can be seen in the lives sacrificed by the Red Army's soldiers in order to liberate their own country, and other nations, from the Nazis.

Due to the efforts of Gomułka, the scope of the Soviet presence was gradually subsiding. Under his agreement with Stalin, in 1945–47, the vast majority of Soviet officers (seventeen thousand) returned to the Soviet Union. In autumn 1946, the NGF MVD (Soviet Ministry of Internal Affairs) rear troops were withdrawn, and the NKVD division left on 1 March 1947, at the request of then-president Bolesław Bierut. The MGB (Soviet Ministry for State Security) advisors (trainers) who worked in Polish state security were recalled from inferior posts, but they stayed in the provinces (until 1950) and in the central apparatus of the Ministry of Public Security. The main burden of struggle against the Polish underground and the Ukrainian underground (OUN-UPA) was carried out by the Polish security services and the army. The strength of the Northern Group of Forces was gradually reduced (from one hundred thousand troops in 1946 to sixty-four thousand in 1956). Less land was used by these forces, and, in 1949, about 70 percent of occupied properties were transferred to the Polish authorities.

The Soviet military presence and the complexity of Soviet-Polish relations, such as the work of trophy teams in 1944–45, the unauthorized dismantling of equipment at former German factories, and the coal problem, all posed an obstacle for the PPR, limiting its appeal with the public. The consequences were clear to Moscow. Considering this alongside his international obligations, Stalin, knowing that he would never allow the communists to be ousted from power, agreed at Yalta to the extension of the coalition and the return of Mikołajczyk to the country as the deputy head of the Provisional Government of National Unity (June 1945). Having honored the condition of public recognition of the Polish state, including the boundary along the Curzon Line, and of the opposition democratic parties that emerged from underground (the PPS-WRN, which was the Polska Partia Socjalistyczna–Wolność, Równość, Niepodległość [Polish Socialist Party–Freedom, Equality, Independence] and SL "Roch"), Stalin had ensured recognition of the new Poland by all the Great Powers, doing away with the subjectivity of the government in exile in terms of international law and turning the latent opposition to the left-wing forces into an open opposition force. But the emergence of a legal political opposition did not change the situation with the workers' parties or the nature of the political regime.

Stalin knew that it was "impossible to have a Poland without opposition[;] . . . if there were no Mikołajczyk, we would have to invent him." Stalin allowed Mikołajczyk and his associates to come to power as a political magnet, which, together with other opposition leaders released as a result of a government amnesty, would take people out of hiding, after which the scale of the opposition could be seen clearly. This did take place, and, by early 1946, Mikołajczyk's party, PSL, was more than just the leader of a farmers' movement; it started to express anti-Soviet and anticommunist sentiments felt by various social groups. Directly or indirectly, PSL supported the underground activists, still significant in numbers, but quite scattered about. The fact that the PSL leadership distanced itself from these people did not convince the population, government, or the Soviet Union. This put the party under attack from the security forces. Yet, public support gave the PSL the hope that, after winning the elections to the Sejm (Poland's lower house of parliament), it would remove PPR from power.

The PSL offered a version of a political system that could work as an alternative to the democratic regime, a system in which the principles of Western democracy would be adjusted in line with the PSL's desire to be the "first among equals" and continue the country's development in accordance with an agrarian doctrine. They proposed a "third way" of "neither Capitalism nor Bolshevism" in which the farmer would be the leader of the nation. The political essence of the PSL program was not to be found in its model for internal development but in its attitude toward foreign policy.

Generally speaking, Poland was to hold a rightful place in the system of West European alliances, with a balanced East-West orientation of policy and good relations with its eastern neighbor, something that corresponded to the covenant of the patriarch of the *ludowcy* movement, Wincenty Witos (which could be summarized as "you have to be friends with the Soviets, without hugging with them"), and was in line with the policy of interaction between the Great Powers. But this ambiguity in terms of Poland's external interests from 1945 to 1946 was incomprehensible to those who supported PSL as an opponent to the communists and the Soviet Union and to those who demanded independence from the Soviet Union and the removal of PPR from power. Such sentiments positioned PSL as an anti-Soviet force, disavowing the frequent assurances of its leaders about loyalty, departure from the underground forces, and condemnation of anti-Soviet feelings. The Polish communists saw these assurances as a mere tactical cover, as did Moscow.

It is clear that the leaders of PSL could not openly demand the reorientation of the country toward the West. There was cautious talk about the experience of the Finnish liberal elite (led by Juho Paasikivi). The elite, fearing an invasion of Soviet troops, made concessions to Moscow and retained power by exchanging a foreign policy drift toward the Soviet Union for domestic political freedom, which diffused the anti-Soviet sentiment among the people. Apparently, Moscow was satisfied with some territorial gains, such as the ice-free port at Petsamo/Pechenga, the presence of Soviet troops on the Finnish border, the Soviet naval base in Porkkala Udd, and the foreign policy of Finnish neutrality. It did help that Finland did not have a common border with Germany and was located on the periphery of the European continent.

Poland had no chances to pursue the Finnish way. Its geographical location as an invasion corridor and then a transit road to Germany was paramount for Moscow's geopolitical plans. The anti-Soviet orientation of the Mikołajczyk-led government in exile, as well as the presence of the anticommunist underground forces, left no hopes for PSL to copy the Finnish version and led to a strengthening of Soviet control through direct military presence in the country.

In terms of public sentiment, despite the administrative steps of the authorities and mass-scale arrests of party activists, the PSL's pre-election position was strong enough for it to count on a majority in the new parliament. Yet, Mikołajczyk's firm belief in his own success and uncompromising demands (75 percent, then 40 percent of the mandates) brought about some countermeasures on the part of the communists. Through political pressure and Moscow's support, they prevented the transformation of the socialists into a "third force." The tactics of the electoral bloc allowed for the organization of a political scene on the eve of the election, and no results of the vote in January 1947 could reverse the "failure" at the elections and the beginning of PSL's disintegration, not even the repressive and administrative pressure of the authorities. The Western Allies limited their response to the falsification of election results to official protests.

From 1945 to 46, the population manifested considerable support for PSL, and this support was further strengthened in the workers' parties during debates on the prospects of the democratic regime that had discredited itself through repression and dependency on the Soviet Union. This was claimed to be a third way, deviating from the Polish policy of the past, with its agrarian focus, and also from the Soviet way. The emphasis was placed on defining popular democracy as a transitional stage to socialism.

At meetings with the leaders of PPR and PPS, held at the Kremlin in 1945–46, Stalin described popular democracy as a special, evolutionary "national road" to socialism "without the dictatorship of the proletariat and through the use of such institutions of bourgeois democracy as the parliament and other institutions."

Often, researchers attribute these and similar characteristics to a sort of mimicry of a political leader, who was actually stubbornly following ideological doctrine. They wrongfully deny Stalin something that his contemporaries called the pragmatic policy of a dangerous partner who possessed an "abyss of wit" and the "diabolical art of tactics" (George Kennan). Without denying his ideological goals, deferred until "better times," we must admit that the tactics of party blocs across the entire Soviet zone matched the wartime, and, as Stalin expected, postwar realities of interaction between the Great Powers. Stalin's words about a non-Soviet path to socialism were addressed not only to his comrades in Eastern Europe but also to communists in the West. Perhaps, in response to Churchill's "Iron Curtain" speech, Stalin was giving a signal to the partners in the coalition, something like, "Your man Mikołajczyk may still be the deputy prime minister, but you can forget about the plan to split Poland away from the USSR and alter its western border." These deviations toward international issues while also discussing internal problems showed that the idea of a national road to socialism was correlated with the interest and expectation of the Soviet Union to cooperate with the West.

"Hints" were provided in the form of joint reflections and were perceived by the PPR and PPS as an opportunity for independent decisions on solutions to domestic problems. Like other leaders of the Soviet zone of control, Gomułka championed the concept of the national "Polish path to socialism" and was convinced of its viability. The year 1947 showed that his position was a combination of the historic mission of communists, Stalinist innovation, and his own understanding of the movement toward socialism through a popular democratic system. The socialists (Julian Hochfeld, Oskar Lange, and others) were in favor of the Polish way, which "reduced the price of revolution for the Polish people." They brought the problem of democracy to the forefront, fearing rejection of the popular democratic model by the PPR and referring to the latter's dictate and the presence of pro-Soviet elements in its leadership.

Thus, both parties saw the Polish path to socialism as a chance for an independent policy with continued movement toward "non-Soviet socialism," involving a reduced dependence on the Soviet Union. But the concept of the PPR was more realistic, if it is seen in light of the international situation in 1947 and with consideration of the historical fact that the Western Allies and the Soviet Union were moving from cooperation to a state of relations that would soon be called the Cold War.

Historians almost unanimously agree that both parties accomplished this transition. The two parties traversed a parallel course, neglecting points of mutual interest. Each party was actively looking for both a way to ensure its own safety and a political object to call an external threat. For Moscow, the United States, as it built up its military and economic strength and global presence in the world, became one such object. For the United States, the number-one enemy could only be the Soviet Union. The Soviet system was centered on one man, Stalin. The "man of steel" had defeated Germany and taken part in the war against Japan; he had an operational military industry as well as natural and human resources; he had also shown enough strength to keep Eastern Europe. In all, he was a dangerous person. The West was also taking into account the considerable social impact of the international communist movement.

Stalin's intention to maintain the Soviet position of the wartime "power center" in western and southern Europe, Iran, and Turkey and his statements about the inevitability of conflict of interest and war in the capitalist world (February 1946) were qualified as a Soviet challenge by British and American politicians. The latter attributed to Stalin an insatiable desire for unlimited expansion and saw a potential threat that Soviet influence would spread around the world. As a result, the Soviet Union was recognized as the only power with which the United States might come into conflict should dialogue fail. There emerged the "long telegram" from George Kennan in February 1946, the Iron Curtain speech by Winston Churchill in March 1946, and US secretary of state James Byrnes's speech in September 1946.

Moscow's interest in furthering cooperation with the United States was based on the need to restore the European part of the country and overcome the drought of 1946–47 (when one million people starved to death). In such circumstances, Stalin was unlikely to pursue a conflict with the West. Another question is whether he could get away with it without the Allies realizing; there were strong communist parties in France and Italy, and he needed to uphold the law in Eastern Europe. The policy of German unity would be possible only later. Stalin's conversations with various politicians in 1946 showed that he was hopeful that Western powers would not break their relations with the Soviet Union. ("They keep intimidating us, but if you do not let yourself be intimidated, they'll make some noise and then calm down.")

Changes occurred in 1947: the Truman Doctrine was put in place in March–June, communists were ousted from the governments of France and Italy in the spring, and the Marshall Plan was implemented in the summer. In September, Cominform was founded. The Truman Doctrine did not cause great concern in Moscow, unlike the Marshall Plan. According to Bernard Baruch, the US diplomat, the plan was to turn the United States into a "gendarme of Europe" in order to save "Western civilization" and, most importantly, "our money."

It is known that the West, inviting the Soviet Union to participate in the Marshall Plan, expected a rejection, and that was exactly what happened. In Moscow, the plan was seen as an invitation to participate in a US plan to use money to reconstruct Europe along geopolitical terms that were detrimental to the Soviet Union and therefore unacceptable. The Soviet leadership, resisting economic temptations, refrained from participating and then made steps to prevent "their" countries from joining the plan.

Allies in the emerging "socialist camp" were pressured. What could Moscow offer? First of all, loans. Poland soon received loans worth $450 million, then another worth $100 million for industrial projects. What political arguments could be provided? A full answer cannot be found in Soviet documents. Nevertheless, Moscow's position is largely explained by the plan's intentions to interfere in the domestic, economic, and (consequently) political affairs of the member states, as well as by the US focus on staking out Germany as the core of organization and the heart of Europe's restoration.

The German factor, which had only recently united the efforts of all partners in the coalition, lost its binding function and gradually turned into a major problem of the Cold War. The prospect of creating a Western bloc and a separate West German state did not square with Stalin's idea of transforming a united and neutral Germany into a buffer zone between Western powers and the Soviet Union's East European zone of influence.

The mass consciousness of the Slavic people made no distinction between Nazism and Germany. The Nazi image of Germany was alive in the minds of the Poles and, because of the ominous, revanchist tones, was perceived as an inherent threat. Hatred toward the Germans was a sustained phenomenon. It fully manifested itself during the deportation of the Germans, which was accompanied by looting, robbery, rape, and murder.

Poland, with its anti-German sentiment, could play the role of a frontier zone between East and West. The Polish government was comfortable with that role: the German factor consolidated the nation and strengthened domestic stability. As for joining the Marshall Plan, the question of the status of the western border could arise, and the legitimacy of deportation of the Germans and development of new territories could be called into question. Any attempt to address the issue of the western border was fraught with the risk of mass exodus of the Poles from the new lands and a national political collapse.

Rejection of the Marshall Plan and the creation of the Cominform meant a rigid foreign policy and an ideological link between the region and the Soviet Union. The result was a change in the strategy of the Kremlin. In Eastern Europe (as in the West), the time had come to eliminate the variability of political development. The communist leadership's hopes of forging a special route to socialism, as opposed to the Soviet path, were rapidly falling away. By the end of 1947, there were external and domestic prerequisites for such a process.

After the "defeat" of PSL in the Sejm elections, the PPR's position strengthened: in order to correct the results of the vote and destroy the popular PSL, a significant effort was required at all levels of government and the state apparatus. The Soviet presence naturally contributed to that. The socialists were not allowed to free-float politically. Secret services and the army crushed the Polish underground. The task of creating a mono-state, through the deportation of Germans and Ukrainians and the repatriation of Poles, was implemented with the approval of society. The economic recovery process was gaining momentum. The PPR held discussions that attacked the economic attitude of capitalism and encouraged the expansion of government control over the popular democracy. At the same time, advocates of "Stalin-style socialism" became more active.

Nevertheless, in the early postwar years, Poland's politically structured society was involved in a process of transformation. Polish society was polyphonic in its philosophical orientations. The economy had various sectors and various forms of ownership that determined the social structure of the population. Numerous publications associated with Polish political movements and parties were quick to report everything that happened in the country. There was no monopoly on the truth, not only from the viewpoint

ALBINA F. NOSKOVA

of Marxism-Leninism but also in the social-democratic interpretation of socialism. Political censorship permitted public criticism of the government but suppressed calls to overthrow it and break away from the Soviet Union. The Catholic Church had firmly established positions and posed an unquestionable threat to the regime. Catholic press and Catholic organizations enjoyed near total freedom. In other words, there was a multifaceted ideological and political depth in Polish society. Legal opposition forces were tolerated by the authorities, but obviously illegal forces were unacceptable. There was a multiparty political system within government, parliament, and local governments.

Thus, there was a transitional social model in Poland that was significantly different from the Soviet model, although the power levers and the Soviet protective function could ensure a rapid (by historical standards) transition to another stage in the country's development. The "sovietization" of the country, if that term is understood as the establishment of a different social system, occurred at the next stage.

Manifestations of authoritarian elements within the "package" of methods applied by the communists were associated with the assertion of a geopolitically justifiable Polish state and with the emergence of Poland within its new borders, as guaranteed by the Soviet presence. The Soviet involvement in the crackdown in Poland could not be directly associated with plans to introduce a Soviet-style regime. The general geopolitical line of the Soviet Union left several issues to be resolved: the need to ensure the safety of the rear flank of the active army in 1944–45 (any objective historian would need to recognize this fact), to keep Poland within the Soviet sphere of interests of the Soviet Union, and to have a trusted neighbor and ally in Warsaw. All these issues were resolved satisfactorily.

The Polish Version of Stalinism

The year 1948 began the period of Western European consolidation against the "Communist East," as seen in the creation of a Western alliance and the steps taken to unite the western zones of Germany. The North Atlantic Treaty Organization (NATO) would soon be founded. Moscow's attempts to resist the idea of pushing the Soviet Union behind the Iron Curtain and limiting Soviet influence in Eastern Europe ended in failure, perhaps because they were accompanied by a desire to hide behind that "curtain," away from the temptations of the Western world. In contrast, they found success through their efforts to link Eastern European countries in the region with a Kremlin-controlled network of bilateral military-political treaties and commercial agreements. At the end of a long epoch, a bipolar world was beginning to emerge and it gave way to a special period of transition in Europe.

Instead of attempts to improve relations with the West, the region began a social transformation on the basis of extensive forced industrialization in the Soviet style. Were these countries, including the Soviet Union, prepared to accept and, more importantly, to realize the possibility of improvement along different lines, as had happened in Germany? Today, it would seem like this important issue needed to be properly discussed, but, at the end of the 1940s, the communists knew only one way of ensuring Soviet-style forced economic growth, and that was through the development of heavy industry and military potential. Instead of launching market mechanisms, which the Soviet leadership could not and would not allow ideologically, it was necessary to carry out all forms of management from one center. Therefore, the main questions were the future of private property, the possible establishment of an absolute monopoly of power, the unification of politics, and the ideological content of the communist parties. Any discussion about development that was inconsistent with the Moscow version was regarded as a dangerous manifestation of independence. Dependence on the Soviet Union was turning from possibility into reality. A favorable background for the new strategy was created by the Soviet-Yugoslav conflict, geopolitical in origin, but turned by Moscow into an ideological struggle against the apostasy of Belgrade.

With the communist parties transformed into monolithic organizations, the radical left-wing impatience on the part of the postwar "recruits" was growing, and the communists continued to spread illusions of achieving rapid progress for any country that had withstood the military trials. A considerable left-wing radical potential was replenished from the grass roots with activists recruited by communists who had passed through the Comintern school in Moscow. Many would identify the new order with its Stalinist version and with the implementation of a just society, in which they fervently believed. Therefore, Moscow's expectations for the project's success were not groundless, although in the Kremlin were still aware that political movements in the region included a considerable number of those who did not accept these ideas. An analysis of the position of the Communist Party of Yugoslavia shows that Moscow used clan fighting in the leadership of the communist parties to allow advocates of the Soviet path to have a chance to defeat nationalists, who wanted their own way of development.

Poland was no different from the other countries that continuously edged closer to Stalinism. In 1948, the communists (Gomułka and others) were encouraged by Moscow to exert unprecedented pressure on the socialists. Several of their leaders took part in the process of unification with the Communist Party, abandoning the ideological, political, and institutional identity of the party, an identity centered on national independence and democratic socialism. They conducted a massive purge of the party ranks, the results of which were equal to the crackdown on PSL. The national path to socialism lay beyond this threshold, and it can be seen as the beginning of the introduction of Stalinism into Poland, something that was completed by the unification congress of the PPR and PSL in December 1948. There was a new united party (Polish United Workers' Party [Polska Zjednoczona Partia Robotnicza, or PZPR]) headed by the former Comintern apparatchik, Bolesław Bierut. The key positions were taken by the "die-hard" activists, that is, the orthodox communist-Bolsheviks, as well as the members of PSL, headed by Józef Cyrankiewicz, who set to work on implementing Stalinist policies in Poland.

Together with the PPR-PSL unification, they started to copy the in-house principles, ideology, and politics of the All-Union Communist Party (Bolsheviks), or AUCP (b). There were no PZPR congresses for five years after 1948, and, instead of four annual plenums of the Central Committee at the usual times, four plenums were held in from 1951 to 1953. The direct participation of party members and their involvement in politics soon became simply consenting to the directives. Socialist ideology was the main doctrine in Stalin's mind. He used dogma to ensure that the guidelines of the party were carried out scrupulously, while acting as a political hypnotist and using the "stick" to suppress dissent. These were all signs of the bolshevization of the PZPR. This game was easy for the junior partner of Moscow who still maintained political leadership and contacts along many channels.

The formation of a united party spelled the end to any alternatives in the Polish labor movement, and social democracy as an ideological trend in Polish Marxism disappeared. In 1949, there was a mass-scale unification of farmers in Poland, who had been supporters of the communists since 1920. For the right to exist, the United People's Party (Zjednoczone Stronnictwo Ludowe, or ZSL) paid the price of seeing the agrarian doctrine rejected and Stalinist policy approved, which meant collectivization. A no less traditional but numerically small representation of the democratic intelligentsia and small urban strata, the Alliance of Democrats (Stronnictwo Demokratyczne, or SD) found a place on the periphery of the political system. Stronnictwo Pracy, a labor party, "decided" to disband. The project of forced liquidation of those political parties and movements that contrasted with the Soviet model was complete.

Why was a multiparty system retained in Poland? Why did Moscow allow that situation? Perhaps, these were the "traces" of the concept of the Polish road to socialism, the idea of the national front, instead of the "bloc of communists and nonparty members" formula, as was the case in the Soviet Union. Probably, the psychological factor, as well as the traditional politicization of Polish society, was also taken into account. Perhaps it was a harmless imitation of the real past political process, an imitation that can be recognized as the most important feature of totalitarianism, specifically, in its left-wing variant.

Multiparty functionality under socialism was not determined by a set of parties but by the completeness of those powers established by the Communist Party. The communist rule, understood as the right to manage the development of the country and to govern the state and national treasures, was now a monopoly. If a monopoly is understood as the absolute power that, according to the Polish-American historian Jan Tomasz Gross, means "deprivation of access for other forces, elimination of freedom of actions for the existing or potential centers of collective life (or power), organizations, independent from those authorized by the state," then PZPR rule was not absolute. It was limited by the existence of the Catholic Church, a powerful enemy that remained a potent religious and political institution. Thus, the specific authority of the PZPR, compared with the Soviet model, was not only that the party's policy was consistent with Moscow and was implemented directly and through the multiparty system but also in the fact that another societal entity existed and tried to express the interests of the nation. Although it had been ousted to the periphery, the Church remained influential.

A special trait of the political regime in Poland was the absence of a charismatic party leader, normally typical of a classical totalitarian regime. Bierut lacked the qualities of the "leader." His creditability in the eyes of the party members was based on propaganda and a biased approach. A big obstacle was the figure of his predecessor, Gomułka, whose removal added to his reputation the aura of a social fighter for the right to be independent from Moscow.

The upper echelons of power in Poland were represented by a small group (a triumvirate, according to the definition of A. Werblan) of Communist Party members: Bierut, Jakub Berman, and Hilary Minc. The origins of this specificity lay in the traditions of the Polish Communist Party, then the PPR and the PPP (Polska Partia Pracy, or Polish Labor Party). There were groupings at various levels in the PZPR. Moscow was satisfied with the person-specific "erosion" of power. It was quite fine to have a group of rulers in Warsaw. Together, they created the convenient image of a collective party leadership. In Moscow, Bierut was distinguished from the others, as they realized that Berman and Minc, next to the Pole Bierut, were not dangerous.

Above the Polish leadership was another tier, and no one was supposed to be higher. Only the top person in the party had direct access to Stalin. Meetings of the leadership with the Soviet leader eventually became less and less frequent. Regular interaction was going on between the leadership of the Central Committee of the AUCP (b) and the Central Committee of the PZPR. The problem of relations with the Soviet apparatus and the problem of the need for a relevant national unit with a specified level of independence are difficult to analyze from a scholarly standpoint due to the abundance and, at the same time, shortage of specific materials. It is similarly problematic to find information concerning the level of interdependence between the parties. Such study requires multidisciplinary professional approaches and is still limited in the national historiography to general statements relating to dependence on the center in Moscow, which undoubtedly was the case. It would seem that there could be no equality between the party apparatuses. At the same time, documents suggest that, although the Moscow center was dictating to its partners, the latter also carried some influence. Each party was defending its own interests, had a specific "weight," and was playing its own games.

The new course was intended to replace the ruling elites and was carried out under the direct influence of the Soviet side. As in the Soviet Union, leaders emerged from society's "lower layers" and thereby gave legitimacy to the PZPR. That typical feature of a Soviet-style regime was entirely present in Polish Stalinism. In the late 1940s to early 1950s, there was a "peak" in the variety of personnel placement techniques, which not accidentally coincided with an increase in public support for the PZPR. New managers were sourced from the party, which was structured as a rigid vertical system. In the early 1950s, there were almost 1.2 million people in the party (workers, 44.5 percent; farmers, 13.4 percent; intellectuals and civil servants, more than 36 percent). There were more than three thousand party committees and around two hundred thousand party activists.

Personnel "quality" was based on whether their educational and cultural level differed from their social status or the public's expectations. Party members were mostly unskilled workers who were unemployed and desperate or poor farmers—often young men and less-educated people (in 1945, education restrictions were lifted for workers and farmers) who were professionally untrained but welcomed for reasons of class theory.

The class approach to the nomination of leaders (70 to 80 percent were recruited from among workers) established an authoritarian and totalitarian type of party with a state leader, who brought the party's decisions to life. In the first half of the 1950s, workers started to be replaced by intellectuals in the party committee. This shift indicated the establishment of a "new" intelligentsia. These people filled the executive branches and formed the Polish corps of public officials in the central and local governments, contributing to the establishment of a special clan—the party and state *nomenklatura* (bureaucracy), which was a sociopolitical phenomenon created by Stalinism.

The system of Soviet job placement was that the appointment to key positions was carried out based on political loyalty, which was equal to party affiliation. That model of power was special in that it gave birth to the "party state" in which government positions, jobs, and functions would be merged and overlapping. The effect of intertwining party and state power was combined with the unquestionable superiority of the party's authority.

In Poland, the nomenklatura was introduced gradually (as of 1944, command staff from powerful agencies were in charge of the party's Central

Committee). By this stage of Stalinism, no appointment could be made without the mandatory sanction of party authorities. In 1949, lists of positions that required approval of the PZPR Central Committee were received from Moscow. In 1950, the same principle covered the provincial and district committees, and then the system was extended to the municipal and district levels.

The actual priority of the party over any public authority allowed the professional party bureaucracy to take on the critical functions of public administration and to adjust laws in accordance with what was deemed expedient. That was certainly the point of both the administrative reforms of 1950 and the constitution of 1952. The local and executive authorities had a very formal and symbolic role, being separate from the party. Party directives regulated court proceedings, as was obvious during political repressions and trials. The system of job placements for public officials, centralized decision-making methods, and bureaucratic means of executing decisions was an imitation of the Soviet system, and it showed the increasing role of the party. The Polish historian Antoni Dudek was right when he said that the introduction of the nomenklatura principle into staff policy was evidence that the political regime had stability.

Poland had the objective preconditions for the transition to an industrial-agrarian stage, including a vast territory with rich natural resources, a lengthy seacoast, "old" and "new" industrial centers, lands for development, and lots of labor. But there were factors that impeded economic breakthrough: the lagging stage of capitalism, wartime destruction that affected social psychology, human losses (especially among the intellectuals), mass-scale migration of the population, overpopulation in the backward rural areas with land-hungry villages, the low educational level of the main source of labor in rural areas, and a lack of financial capital. All of this prompted the authorities to pursue an extensive development effort using a modernization project imposed by the bureaucracy. However, there were limited resources available to the political center, another factor that limited economic growth.

The party's political and state dependence on Moscow was aggravated by the dependence of the Polish economy on Soviet credits and raw materials (in 1950, 100 percent of the imports of manganese, 80 percent of cotton, 70 percent of fat products, and 65 percent of iron ore came from the Soviet Union). Poland also relied on the Soviet Union for energy and supplies of production equipment and documentation for the reconstruction of two hundred power plants and the construction of thirty new ones. Technical and technological assistance was supported by training in Soviet schools. The equipment supplied and installed by Soviet experts, as well as the professionalism of those experts, was not always on par with world standards. That was manifested, in particular, when the economic plan for 1950–55 was drafted.

The crucial revision of the plan followed a meeting that took place 9–11

ALBINA F. NOSKOVA

January 1951 in Moscow. The attendees included the Soviet leaders and top officials of the satellite states. Poland was represented by Edward Ochab and Marshal Rokossowski. The documents of the meeting are not yet available, but, according to some participants, Stalin formulated the following goals: to mobilize all resources and, in two to three years, launch coordinated military production to reequip the armies, multiply their strength, prepare the territory in military-operational terms, and thus raise the defense potential of the bloc. According to Georgi K. Zhukov, speaking in November 1956, it was decided that each country was to identify the capability scope of its defense industry. Poland was to carry a large share of the task because the country was considered to be a "corridor" for thwarting aggression from the West. Yet, the capital investment in the defense industry, which Poland did not have earlier (1951, 3.7 percent; 1952, 7.4 percent; 1953, 7.2 percent; 1954, 3.9 percent; and 1955, 3.2 percent of total investments), was not fundamentally different from the level of investment in other countries of the bloc. The size of the army in 1954 came close to the wartime figure, totaling 331,000. This was in line with the government's desire to accelerate the modernization of the economy and increase industrial development through militarization, thus cutting production of goods and reducing the standard of living. The consequences of that policy have been mixed.

Industrialization changed the Polish economy in many ways. Gross industrial output at the end of 1953 exceeded the 1939 result by a factor of 3.6. The high growth rate was accompanied by rapid urbanization, and the social and professional structure was improving; there was a need for universal literacy and a comprehensive general and vocational education system for "new" workers and farmers (in 1939, illiteracy in the country amounted to 8.2 percent overall, with much higher levels in rural areas). The share of scientific and technical intelligentsia also needed to increase.

The long-awaited exponential growth did take place, resulting in a situation in which Poland no longer lagged behind other Western countries, at least in certain areas. Over a short time, Poland turned into a strong industrial and agricultural country; industrial complexes were built and new industries were emerging. Millions of jobs were created in new towns, with a system of social protection and guarantees earlier unknown to the "weaker" social strata. As a result, important changes took place, which, just like in the Soviet Union, created the objective conditions for electoral support of the party and the socialist model created by the efforts of the authorities. This support could be seen most clearly on the part of the workers (especially those who emerged in the postwar period), employees, young workers and farmers, and the "new" intelligentsia.

However, in these years, the weaknesses inherent in the centralized operation of a socialist economy became obvious. Implementing the Soviet model without Western technology and capital, faced with the failure of the system of collectivization in the rural areas, which the Soviet Union used to finance industrialization, the leadership of the PZPR could get the required capital only by withdrawing funds from the consumer sector (increasing discontent and reducing labor enthusiasm and productivity) and using Soviet credits (growth dependency). Of course, the resources of Moscow were not limitless, but the Soviet Union's vital allies had to be supported. As an example, there was a meeting with the party and a government delegation of Poland in Moscow on 16 January 1948, during which nearly all the requests of the Polish side (to build a steel plant, supply cotton and corn, and provide credit) were met. Stalin, who attended that meeting, remarked, "You are interested in our weaponry, our models of weapons. We will not hide them from you. You need jet aircraft. We'll provide. We'll help your industry as best as we can." By the mid-1950s, the volume of Soviet loans (with a very attractive interest rate, from 0 to 2–3 percent per annum) to Poland was enough to cover the supplies of equipment, including military hardware, food, consumer goods, and raw materials, and amounted to 5.2 billion rubles. The Soviet Union provided loans and technical assistance to Poland to build sixty-nine production facilities, including six mines, three coal mines, eight metallurgical plants, seventeen engineering plants, and twelve hydropower plants.

There was a focus on the directive/distribution mode of centralized management, the potential of which, with limited capital investment, seemed to be superior to the free-market growth opportunities. However, this mode was faulty in the main aspect. An economy based on forced administration and politically driven allocation of capital in favor of production of capital goods and defense industries suppressed consumption and created limits to the system's existence. According to Paul Gregory, an American expert in the history of economics, the system was in a state of suspended animation. Without creating the conditions for consumption growth and lacking any incentives for improving labor productivity, which was 2.5 times lower than even in the Soviet Union, Poland had acquired Soviet spending mechanisms that blocked the process of sustained economic growth.

Negative processes were developing in the country. Targets for the production of consumer goods were not met, in contrast to quotas for military products. Prices were rising. Promises to improve living standards were not fulfilled. Imbalances in various sectors and insufficient investment combined with low gross domestic product yield became major factors in the PZPR crisis that had developed by the mid-1950s. The rhetoric of the party did not match the results, and the demands of the people were greater than the potential and vision of those who were at the top. There was "equality in poverty" (Mikołajczyk), with a parallel, layered system of social privileges for select categories, which violated the principle of equal access to social guarantees.

The working class started to reject the living conditions resulting from PZPR policies. Documents show that Moscow and the leaders of the PZPR had no illusions as they began to assess the situation. It was known that a major element of the growing public discontent derived from the nation's dependency on the Soviet Union, the violation of civil liberties, and the unequal distribution of limited assets. However, there was a belief that the discontent could be quieted, just like it was in the Soviet Union, through repression. Repressions to quash discontent and search for those who were "guilty" form an important element and serve an important purpose at this stage in the monopoly of the sole party. Repressions have always been an integral feature of left-wing totalitarian regimes.

Historians often view the repressions in Poland as a single process covering the period between 1944 and 1956. In my opinion, their history can be divided, albeit conditionally, into two stages. The second stage came in 1948–49. To date, academics have roughly drawn up a sequence of events. They try to understand the tragic phenomena and to widen scholarly access to the available material. There is no disagreement among scholars that the installation of a system of terror ensured the implementation of "easy" control mechanisms in a society where there was no freedom, thus forcing it to accept the ideology of the communist elite. Given the variety of the targets, the repressions were aimed at preserving the regime, creating the required quality of readiness to respond to signals from "above," and providing an atmosphere of mobilization, sacrifice, and fear, perfectly in tune with the climate of the Cold War.

Party-backed repressions were a specialty of the PZPR. They were part of a large-scale campaign in the region, carried out by the AUCP (b). The preparations for this campaign started in the spring of 1948. The communist parties were told to remove members who had allegedly taken an antiparty or anti-Soviet stance or who had underestimated the historical role of the Soviet Union and were "infected" with the ideas of Trotskyism, nationalism, and Yugoslavia's Josip Tito. In fact, the idea was to get rid of any remaining diversity in the understanding of socialism at the "top" and among the "lower classes," thus turning the Communist Party into a monolithic power base pursuing ideological unification and identification of national and state interests for each country in the Eastern bloc.

Gomułka was ousted from the party just before the PZPR was founded. He was a strong supporter of communism. He was also an author and a staunch advocate of the "Polish road to socialism," as well as a politician capable of taking independent actions. He understood the reasons for the justifiable and inevitable limitations of Poland's sovereignty, but he was unhappy to see his country's dependency on Moscow and thus sought to reduce it, while still acknowledging the national and state importance for Poland to maintain its alliance with the Soviet Union.

Among historians, there is a prevalent view that Gomułka came into sharp conflict with Stalin and that his resignation was orchestrated by Moscow, while Warsaw only executed the instructions. The documents found in the Russian archives may adjust such judgments. Gomułka's withdrawal was in line with Moscow's plan to restructure the elite of the communist parties. Bierut would not have dared to take action if Moscow had not supported the pro-Moscow group in the People's Republic of Poland. Additionally, Gomułka had a personal and political conflict with this group on the issue of the "Polish road to socialism" and whether it should be a strategy or just a tactic. Bierut's struggle for supreme power in Poland concealed from Stalin what had been going on since the war. Archivists have studied Bierut's report about Gomułka, which was received by Georgi Dimitrov at the Department of International Information, Central Committee of the AUCP (b), in the summer of 1944. The document was never seen by others, and the same happened to W. Kowalski's report of 1945, sent to Soviet foreign minister Vyacheslav Molotov. These compromising allegations were coming from Warsaw, either directly or through the embassy, and they formed the basis of the notice issued by the Central Committee of the AUCP (b) of 5 April 1948. The opponents of Gomułka used that notice to their advantage. It was used as the basis for the decisions of the Central Committee of the PPR, which ousted Gomułka from the party's top position.

Gomułka's position on the Yugoslav question irritated Moscow, but Stalin's position was quiet and determined. It was significantly different from his reactions to other, similar cases, such as that of Traicho Kostov in Bulgaria or László Rajk in Hungary, who were both put on trial and executed. The leader of the PPR was replaced in a surprisingly mild way, considering these precedents. Bierut was constantly in touch with Stalin about Gomułka's case, and he made a trip to Moscow immediately after Rajk's execution in Hungary. There was undoubtedly a leading hand in Bierut's transition to power, but it was as if someone (it could not have been Bierut) "opened a rescue parachute" above "Comrade Wiesław" (Gomułka). The retired head of the PPR, charged with being a right-wing sympathizer and nationalist, was received by Stalin in December 1948, and the latter listened to the former Polish leader, responded to the letter, then kept him in the Central Committee of the party, and, after Gomułka's arrest, did not allow his execution. It is also interesting that, even in the days after Gomułka's resignation in 1948 and after his arrest in 1951, none of his friends or family faced execution. In October 1956, Khrushchev insisted that this "issue" be resolved in Warsaw so that everyone knew that the initiative to arrest Gomułka "came from Warsaw, not Stalin": "We did everything to save you." Gomułka never refuted that statement.

The plot of the story calls for further document-based justifications, but it seems that it was not accidental that, after the appropriate preparations in 1949–53, arrests were carried out in Poland, and several close associates of Gomułka (M. Spychalski, Z. Kliszko, G. Korczyński, Władysław Komar, M. Rola-Żymierski, and others) were taken, although there was no major "party case," as usually happened in other countries. There was no openly anti-Semitic trial, although the Polish "impulse" was there at the plenum of the PZPR Central Committee in May 1950. We may assume that Moscow, aware of the sentiments in the Polish party and the country, discouraged those "initiatives" of Warsaw that could jeopardize the "appeasement," which had taken so much effort and blood to achieve.

With the establishment of a monopoly on power having taken place during a divisive period in world history, the motivation for repressions in Poland became much stronger. From the very start, a presumption of guilt accompanied the repressive policies because the PZPR leadership did not have any substantial arguments with which to destroy the multiplicity of ideological views and orientations toward Western democracy. The forced activation of the population (with agitation and propaganda about a brighter future) was loud but heeded by very few people. Western broadcasts that were technically impossible to jam were also quite successful in opposing those calls.

Toward the end of 1949 and early in 1950, the policy of tethering Poland to the Soviet Union and its international interests was becoming increasingly predominant at the same time that Poland's sovereignty was increasingly being restricted. Many Poles found it hard to accept that policy, especially those who had recently formed the electoral base of the PSL, as well as the members of the parties allied to the PZPR and intellectuals with backgrounds in humanities, science, and engineering. Industrial workers and many PZPR rank-and-file members could not understand why Poland was becoming so dependent on the Soviet Union. Discontent was brewing in the lower ranks of the party machinery, as material benefits available to them were becoming increasingly scarce. The repressions were now targeted at members of social strata across the board, both those who were capable of resisting and those who were considered a potential or real hindrance to the transformation of society.

The leaders of the PZPR were getting ready to organize a terror campaign on a party-wide (see plenary meetings of the Central Committee of the PZPR in 1949 on party cadres and vigilance) and a statewide (see laws on antistate activities) scale, imitating the repressive machinery used in the Soviet Union. The kingpin of state security, Ministerstwo Bezpieczeństwa Publicznego

(MBP), and its branches were becoming increasingly active as the number of personnel swelled. It had a force of 300,000 in 1953, and, of this number 125,000 were members of the Volunteer Workers' Militia. Governments have generally never done without security forces, but Stalinism perverted basic kinds of security, and it meant that political repression was the order of the day. The Polish state security service was controlled by a select committee of the Politburo of the PZPR, headed by Bierut. He controlled the agency, whose central apparatus employed advisors from the security agencies of the Soviet Union. Soviet officers who commanded military counterintelligence and army justice reported to him (and to Moscow), though formally they were subordinate to the Polish defense minister. This arrangement was a source of tension between Rokossowski and Bierut.

Repressions within the party and outside it were initiated on behalf of the party itself, and appropriate instructions and orders were issued in the same manner. By 1954, the state security files had a list of 6 million people under suspicion. According to Polish historians, in 1951, 110,000 people were in penitentiaries, 14,000 of them serving sentences for antistate activities. The figures for 1953 were 162,000 imprisoned, with 9,000 of that number incarcerated for political crimes. The network of informants numbered more than 70,000 mobile agents. The density of the network enabled the security services to penetrate various layers of society while the state obtained additional and varied support from dependent persons.

The repressions during the Stalinist phase became even more severe as the protests of urban workers were neutralized and the active resistance of farmers was crushed by force (for instance, the Gryfino events in the fall of 1951). Administrative and criminal punishment was meted out to tens of thousands of politically inactive people, but those repressions had a special kind of impact. The sheer scale of the "dekulakization" (repressions) of Russian farmers had created a tense atmosphere that the nomenklatura needed in order to run the country; similarly, the repressions in Poland were used as a means of controlling the population.

The idea of purging society dictated the need to wipe out real or imaginary dissent, and those considered to belong to a fifth column were repressed as a preventive measure. By that time, there was no organized military political underground in Poland, and even minor protest groups, usually consisting mostly of young people posing no real threat, were repressed. The fact that such groups even existed served as the pretext for show trials of members of parties from the "underground state," such as the "Freedom, Equality, Independence" faction of the Polish Socialist Party (in the arrest and trial of K. Pużak and others), the National Party or Stronnictwo Narodowe (the trials of A. Doboszyński and others), the Socialist Party (the case of J. Kwasiborski and others), and PSL or Polish People's Party (the trials of M.

Gulewicz, Wincenty Bryja, and others). The officers of the AK who had been amnestied and who had abandoned underground activities (for instance, K. Pluta-Czachowski, J. Mazurkiewicz, J. Gorazdowski, and E. Fieldorf) were re-arrested. The courts served tough sentences, and death sentences were carried out (e.g., Fieldorf). In that manner, the PZPR was hoping to crush the self-expression of those who were, in one way or another, related to the former regime and to isolate the old elite regardless of the attitude some of its members had toward the new regime.

There is no doubt that the Soviet embassy and its officers in Wojsko Polskie (the Polish army) reported to Moscow about the "special measures," but there are no documents conclusively revealing the part played by them in the Ministry of Public Security of Poland. Clearly, however, the Soviet Union was directly involved in the political repressions in Wojsko Polskie that Moscow considered to be of key importance. The personnel policy, counterintelligence activities, and military courts were controlled by Soviet officers who were on the staff of the Polish army and were on the membership lists of the PZPR.

At the same time, a confrontation between military blocs was taking place as NATO and US military bases were being established around the world and as the war in Korea was beginning. The high-level conference mentioned earlier was held in Moscow with the aim of discussing the re-armament of the bloc's armed forces and preparing the territories of member countries to repel outside aggression. This discussion raised the issue of the political and military reliability of the Eastern bloc's armies and, above all, that of Wojsko Polskie, deployed at the front line of defense. In 1948, the majority of the officers of the Polish army had joined before the war. More than 50 percent of them had served in army staffs. That was a source of grave concern on the part of Moscow and the PZPR leadership. At the end of 1948, and then at the beginning of 1949, Polish army headquarters sent its analysis of the situation in the army to Moscow, and the embassy later sent Molotov a plan for restructuring the Polish army, worked out no doubt in collaboration with Warsaw. The idea was to reorganize, in cooperation with "Polish friends," the politically unreliable top brass of Wojsko Polskie. Bierut was to be involved in any discussion of purging the General Staff and Ministry of Defense departments of "enemies wearing officers' uniforms." Measures were taken to limit the powers of Defense Minister Michał Rola-Żymierski and to place loyal subjects in command positions. Then, the rear flanks of the Soviet army in Germany would be peopled by "an ally that would not let us down at a moment of need." It was recommended that the Politburo of the Central Committee of the PZPR create a national defense commission headed by Bierut and made up of Minc, A. Zawadzki, Franciszek Jóźwiak, and S. Matuszewski. Later developments would indicate that these proposals were accepted by Moscow. On orders from Davidov, the advisor of the MGB of the Soviet Union, the Polish state security services placed Rola-Żymierski under systematic surveillance.

Preventative purges of the prewar army generals and officers went ahead in 1949–50, as did purges of officers of the Armia Krajowa and Peasants' Battalions who served in Wojsko Polskie, General Staff officers, officers of district commands and services, and the General Staff Academy. Well-known generals and officers of the old army who had joined Wojsko Polskie, guided by the interests of the state, were repressed. Some of them were in positions of responsibility.

Stanisław Tatar, F. Herman, Marian Utnik, S. Nowicki, J. Kirchmayer, J. Kuropieska, and S. Mossor were accused of engaging in espionage, making connections with émigré circles, and setting up clandestine organizations in the army. Accordingly, the "trial of the generals" was organized. The trial went on for almost three years, administered at first by state security and then by army counterintelligence. A total of ninety-three people were in the dock, and thirty-seven death sentences were handed down, with twenty of those proceeding to execution. Displayed to society at large was an "army conspiracy" to justify the dismissal of the prewar cadre of officers.

The "trial of the generals" was coordinated with Moscow. At the end of October 1949, Stalin received information about the pending arrests, and it must be assumed that he gave his permission for this trial to proceed because, at the beginning of November, the main figures of the trial were arrested. Moscow received information about the interrogations, and a draft of indictment was delivered. Stalin's response to these documents is unknown, as is the involvement of Soviet officers in interrogations. The instructions of the Soviet MGB banned them from being involved in interrogations. However, based on the experience of other countries, it is clear that Stalin's opinion would have been sought in such cases and that, on occasion, Soviet advisors were present at interrogations.

The arrests of the prewar military figures were motivated by mistrust and the idea that, if you repress the dissenters, you will thereby destroy the will to dissent. The arrests of PZPR members among the Polish generals had a different motive. They targeted those who had come to power with Gomułka and those who were (or at least were considered to be) his allies. By contrast, they were also accused of cooperating with the old intelligence services, as shown by Soviet ambassador Victor Lebedev's reports to Moscow. The Polish state security service, MGB advisors, and Soviet officers in counterintelligence were keeping a close eye on Defense Minister Rola-Żymierski and vice-ministers M. Spychalski (who replaced Soviet officers with Polish officers in 1945–47) and Korczyński. Also under surveillance were the head of the second directorate of the General Staff, W. Komar and others. During 1949, the advisor Davidov and Ambassador Lebedev were looking for a candidate to replace Rola-Żymierski, but as the ambassador claimed, there were "unhealthy relations" between "our Polish generals" (S. Popławski, A. Zawadzki, and W. Korczyc). That was probably the reason why Rokossowski was suggested for the post.

The repressions against the communist generals were a continuation of the clan struggles within the party. Party leaders believed that those arrested could provide evidence for the Gomułka case and demonstrate to party members that the Gomułka era was over. A younger cadre of officers—coming from humbler "workers and peasants" origins—could fill the vacuum, ready to carry out the party's orders without questioning them. The PZPR was making sure that the key agency would not offer any surprises.

Moscow was acting with the same goals in mind. The reason for the new "call-up" of Soviet officers into Wojsko Polskie was the growing bloc confrontation. The roster of duties of Soviet officers who worked in the armies of allied nations, as dictated by the instruction issued by the Politburo of the Central Committee of the AUCP (b) in November 1949, mainly focused on canvassing support for the national command on military issues, and that support was to be administered by replacing the national command in order to concentrate on political objectives. The officers were supposed to monitor the status of the army and the sentiments of its commanding officers on a day-to-day basis, as well as to influence the positioning of key figures, ensuring that they were faithful to the government and the Soviet Union. The chief military advisor was to inform the defense minister about the army's state of readiness and morale and about discipline and sentiments within the officers' corps. Between 1949 and 1952, 160 Soviet officers were sent to serve in the Polish army; that number was lower than in 1948 (when there were 1,652 and 21 generals among them), but they took up command positions. At that time, several thousand Soviet officers were serving in the armies of China and North Korea, hence the decrease in the size of the Polish army. By mid-1949, of the 192 command positions, 84 were filled by Soviet officers in the General Staff, services, districts, academies, and aviation divisions. By the summer of 1953, there were 37 generals and 630 officers who had not pledged allegiance to Poland. Being members of the AUCP (b), they were not on PZPR membership lists because the rules of accounting for party members introduced by the Comintern were in the process of being revised.

The new call-up coincided with Rokossowski's tenure as Poland's defense minister. The post was taken by a marshal of the Soviet Union, an outstanding Soviet army commander who had liberated Poland from the Nazis and was of Polish background. The Polish Sejm endorsed the appointment of a foreign national to a key state post in violation of the laws of the land and in clear breach of Poland's sovereignty. The appointment was justified by the need to uphold the security of the Soviet Union and Poland, as well as that of the military bloc as a whole. Strategic operations were going ahead on Polish territory. Rokossowski inaugurated several military-technical educational institutions of the kind that Poland had not had in the past.

Relations between Rokossowski and the leadership of PZPR experienced conflict from time to time. The minister was not happy with his post. He was aware of the problems it created and insisted that the pay of Polish officers be raised and that Soviet officers should have the internationally accepted status of military advisors. That option was considered in Moscow, but it was only after Stalin died that on, 14 August 1953, the Presidium of the Central Committee of the CPSU decided to withdraw all Soviet generals and officers and gradually replace them with Polish officers and Soviet advisors. This process was under way from 1953 to 1955. At the request of Bierut and Rokossowski, Moscow decided to dispatch to Poland a total of 269 chief and senior advisors (the former attached to the minister) to the General Staff and central directorates of the National Defense Ministry, districts, army formations, and air force, navy, and anti-aircraft defense units, colleges, and military schools. The Soviet Ministry of Internal Affairs (MVD) sent 44 officers (16 to counterintelligence, 8 to the districts, 5 to interior troops, and 15 to the frontier guards). The tours of duty of 156 officers and generals were extended. Similar to the situation with state security, this number was a reduction but not a withdrawal of the Soviet military presence in Wojsko Polskie. By the mid-1950s the withdrawal of Soviet officers had accelerated. In 1956, there were 28 Soviet generals and 52 senior officers serving in the Polish army; by 1 November 1956, there were 32 generals and 39 officers. Plans were also made to withdraw 17 generals and 21 officers.

The proposal by Ochab, made to First Deputy Prime Minister Anastas Mikoyan on 11 September 1956, concerning the withdrawal of state security advisors, was in line with Moscow's general policy geared toward dismantling the institution of state security in the satellite states. Moscow was coming to realize that the Soviet military presence did more harm than good. In the fall of 1954, the issue was brought before the Central Committee of the CPSU. The state security agencies and MVD were planning to withdraw twenty-one of the eighty-nine officers and, in 1956, to cut twenty-one of the forty-one military advisor positions. This decisive move was made in October 1956. All Ministry for State Security advisors and most army officers returned to the Soviet Union together with Rokossowski. Wojsko Polskie—the symbol, attribute, and guarantor of state sovereignty—was now coming under the control of the Polish government, in keeping with the constitution.

The constitution approved by the Sejm in 1952 imparted the force of law to the party's plan to build socialism in Poland and legalized the transfer of the Soviet regime to Polish soil. The fundamental democratic norms (equality of citizens and rights and freedoms) were proclaimed but not implemented; they coexisted in the document with class emphases on the workers' republic, the people's state, the people's government, the leading role of the revolutionary working class and peasantry, and the right to labor free from exploitation.

Just as in the Soviet constitution, the Polish one established no guarantees for separation of the functions of bodies of power or for the realization of civil rights. The proclaimed electoral procedures for representative power (the Sejm, Rada Narodowa) in fact boiled down to the distribution of posts and positions by the party, while legislation was replaced by rule by decree. The Stalinist definition of the government—not as the executive branch of the Sejm but as the "supreme executive and directive body of state power"—was in force, directly violating the principle of the separation of powers and nullifying the rights of the Sejm. The right to work, general education, and health care was in real life distorted by a system of class and nomenklatura privileges, while the independence of the judiciary existed only on paper, as the courts performed repressive and punitive functions as a matter of top priority. The constitution fixed the status quo and also defined a course toward the "realization of the socialist course" and the "liquidation of the exploitative class." Rural dwellers were in confrontation with the farmers' cooperatives, and the relevant article of the constitution on "assisting the farming reform" seemed symptomatic. The fundamental law was therefore called upon to assist the building of Soviet-style socialism, just as was the case with the Soviet Union.

Some national deviations from that model—such as prewar state symbols, army ranks and uniforms, and the existence of noncommunist parties and organizations that posed a threat to the state—were designed to emphasize the continuity of Polish statehood and "decorate" the constitution, thus concealing the Soviet master plan behind them. These deviations from the model paid homage to national values and traditions that were not considered to be dangerous. The specifics of the Polish variant of Stalinism were taken into account in Moscow. The Soviet Union supported the preservation of national symbols dating back to the struggle for independence and the Second Republic. It comes as no surprise that Stalin, who at one time had held the post of nationalities commissar, was emphasizing the national features and outlines of sovereignty in the Polish constitution as edited its text. His edits essentially changed nothing.

The article of the constitution stating that the church is separate from the state and proclaiming freedom to practice religious rites was a clear sign that the Soviet model of relations between state and church was being enforced in Catholic Poland. The strategy of the communists was to turn the Roman Catholic Church, the main confessional institution of the country, into a factor of social discourse independent from the Vatican but dependent on the state. The goals set were implemented one after the other.

From 1944 to 1948, the state assisted the clergy in performing confessional functions as destroyed churches were restored and new ones built, the episcopate received funding, and the Church retained the right to own land, although members of clergy who opposed the state were still repressed. Secular attributes, such as the priority of the secular registrar's office over church records and the optional course of religious instruction in schools was promulgated by the anticlerical socialist and "people's" movements. They also initiated the breaking of relations, namely the concordat with the Vatican, in the fall of 1945, which enabled the government to make decisions without consulting the Holy See.

In 1949, the government adopted a course that involved forcing the Catholic Church to recognize the regime and the leading role of the PZPR. The Soviet interest in the confessional policy of the PZPR heightened. The conformity between the two forces was closely monitored, and Moscow's influence over confessional policy grew considerably. In his correspondence and meetings with Bierut, Stalin offered the latter his advice. The PZPR began to enforce a tough policy aimed at ousting the Roman Catholic Church from politics, repressing the opposition inspired by the Church, controlling the personnel policy of the episcopate, and restricting requests from members of the clergy. The secret service treated the Church as a collective suspect, and deportations, arrests, and trials of the Church hierarchy went ahead, along with attempts to split the lower ranks of the clergy and isolate them from the bishops.

The episcopate was seeking ways of assuring the survival of the Roman Catholic Church as an institution. It accepted compromises and made political concessions, hoping to reduce the losses from repressions. It even gave up unimpeded communication with the Vatican in order to be able to communicate freely with the believers. In the spring of 1950, in a bid to stop the repressions, it signed an accord that played into the hands of the state, and, in the summer of 1951, it signed the Stockholm political appeal to avoid a conflict with the antiwar sentiments of the Poles. Cardinal Wyszyński, guided by the interests of the state (the western frontier) and by the unity of the clergy, bypassed the Vatican and recognized the government's decision on elections to church administration in the western lands and agreed that new vicars should pledge allegiance to the "Polish Republic and its popular democratic power," which was clearly secular in form and political in content (1951).

The changes in the rights of the Catholic Church in the 1952 constitution, the usurping of the prerogative of confessional appointments of the Vatican and episcopate, the introduction of a mandatory pledge of allegiance to the state for the clergy (the State Council decree on appointment of clergy to positions in the Church, dated 9 February 1953), on the one hand, and the episcopate's *non possumus* response to the government on 8 May 1953, on the other, caused tension between the Church and the state to mount. Convinced that its days were numbered, the episcopate made it clear that the time when it maneuvered and attempted to prevent conflicts with the state for the sake of the Church and believers was over. The communists responded by stopping the party's concessionary policy toward the Church. Accordingly, Wyszyński was arrested, Bishop M. Klepacz was elected head of the Roman Catholic Church in agreement with the will of the state (why he accepted the post is a different matter), and the bishops pledged allegiance to the People's Republic of Poland on 17 December 1953.

In that manner, using a variety of tactics, the PZPR achieved the goals it had set in 1948. The Church recognized the political regime and party rule and retreated from confrontation with the state, which had imposed its right to decide confessional appointments and had violated the economic independence of the Church, thereby establishing control over it. By the mid-1950s, the Church's presence in state and public structures was noticeably weaker. It concentrated its activities in churches, since religious instruction in schools was restricted. The Polish episcopate, the Russian Orthodox Church, and other churches in the region were forced to accept the model of relations with the state imposed on them in order to be able to preserve the church as an institution and fulfill its duties to believers.

Having prevailed over the Church on political, socioeconomic, and state levels, the party still managed to remove only the external attributes of the Church's real worldview and moral influence on the nation. Although the people had become somewhat less religiously active, the Church managed to retain its sway over confessional communication with believers and proved to be stronger than a state dependent on Moscow. The Church influenced the patriotic sentiments of parishioners and preserved the deep-rooted fundamentals of the faith of an absolute majority of Poles, as well as their attachment to Catholic values and trust in the clergy.

Toward the end of the 1950s, the Polish government, aided by the Soviet Union, had created the fundamental structures for a Soviet model of society. The PZPR had a monopoly of power, and the core nomenklatura of the party and the state had emerged. A Soviet-style system of government was formed, based on top-down rule by decree, and it assured that the party clan, headed by a select few leaders, could dictate its terms. The country's economic mobilization was ruled by decree in the same manner.

The policy of accelerated extensive industrialization on the eve of the scientific-technological revolution opened up the prospect of modernization but at the same time restricted the chances for it. The disproportions grew with the country's dependency on Moscow. The policy of waiting for a breakthrough strengthened the hand of the bureaucracy in the pursuit of its collective interests. The disparity between the living standards of the bureaucracy and ordinary people became ever clearer. Living standards stagnated, showing the flaws of the artificially induced "labor enthusiasm." The image of a system of social justice (proposed by the PZPR as a national idea) lost value when confronted with the realities of the day.

Mass political repressions characteristic of the Stalinist model were used to make the whole structure stable. The subsystem of fear created a short-term prospect for relative civil accord. The Soviet role in the repressions of the 1940s and 1950s basically boiled down to ideological and political guidance of the national cadres.

There were geopolitical reasons for the transition from authoritarian tendencies to Stalinist totalitarianism in the late 1940s. At the same time, the type of rule in Poland displayed certain historical features that distinguish it from a replica of the Stalinist Soviet system. During the popular democratic phase, the political sphere became structured along party lines, and there emerged ideas and concepts characteristic of the struggle to form a civil society during an industrial transition. Later developments indicated that the introduction of the Stalinist model did not turn the PZPR into an ideological monolith similar to the AUCP (b), nor did there emerge a consistent image of the national leader. Propaganda was no substitute for the multitude of ideas and national convictions in society at large.

The merging of the geopolitical interests of the Soviet Union and Poland after the war followed from the need to ensure the political security of the two countries in the international arena. As the weaker state in that alliance, Poland soon found out that this merging of interests was transformed into long-term political, ideological, and economic dependence on the senior partner. This was something the Poles were painfully aware of, and it is the reason why the PPR-PPS, and later PZPR, was constrained in attempts to reach out to the masses and turn them into a readily controllable, Soviet-style society. The desire to become independent of the Soviet Union was a long-term factor, both overt and latent in society at large as the Poles put more trust in Western democracy. Those public forces capable of understanding the destructive potential of the Soviet model remained intact. After the death of Stalin, the short-lived Polish Stalinist regime gradually became a Polish form of authoritarianism that survived for thirty years, apparently to the satisfaction of at least some Poles. Occasional spells of de-Stalinization could not, however, remove the discontent of other parts of the population, a sentiment they readily demonstrated throughout 1956 and through the elections to the Sejm in 1957.

8

THE THAW

THE TWENTIETH CONGRESS OF THE SOVIET COMMUNIST PARTY, THE POLISH OCTOBER, AND THE STRUGGLE FOR AUTONOMY

Andrzej Paczkowski (Poland)

Professor, Modern History Center of the Institute of Political Studies, PAS, member of the council of the National Institute of Remembrance.

Nikolai I. Bukharin (Russia)

Leading researcher at the Institute of Economy of the Russian Academy of Sciences.

ANDRZEJ PACZKOWSKI

THE TWENTIETH CONGRESS OF THE SOVIET COMMUNIST PARTY, THE POLISH OCTOBER, AND THE STRUGGLE FOR AUTONOMY

IT IS GENERALLY believed that 1956 marked one of the most important junctures in the latter half of the twentieth century due to the changes that took place at that time within the communist camp and in East-West relations. It needs to be pointed out, however, that two crucial developments that year—Nikita Khrushchev's address, "On the Cult of the Individual and Its Consequences," delivered at a closed session of the Twentieth Congress of the Communist Party of the Soviet Union (February), and the Soviet army's suppression of the national revolution in Hungary (November)—carried quite different, even contradictory, messages. The former supposedly testified to the "opening up" of communism and its inherent capacity for self-criticism and self-improvement. The latter demonstrated that the Soviet Union was capable of deceit and violence if its leaders thought the national interest and ideological dogma were under threat, and that, despite de-Stalinization, the Soviet Union had not ceased being imperial and aggressive. The Hungarian lesson (and indeed the Czechoslovak lesson twelve years later) left a deep imprint and became a key factor enhancing the stability of communism in all of Central and Eastern Europe until 1989. That dual image of the Soviet Union was also evident in its relations with Poland. In 1956, it expressed itself in the deep inertia of the Soviet system, the Soviet leaders' predilection for ordering the satellite states around, and the imperative of maintaining internal discipline and unity.

The pace of de-Stalinization in Poland substantially accelerated in the spring and summer of 1956 as a result of several factors, including growing public disaffection. The latter reached its peak in late June, when economically motivated strikes in several factories in Poznań evolved into street demonstrations and riots (public buildings were attacked, including the local headquarters of the Security Office) and were violently suppressed by the army. The workers were singing "The Internationale" as they marched out of their plants but switched to the national anthem and religious-patriotic songs after tens of thousands had gathered in the city center.

Perhaps the revolt would not have taken place or assumed such dramatic scale if it had not been for the rift within the party leadership following the unexpected death of the "Polish Stalin"—Bolesław Bierut—who died on the night of 12 March in Moscow, where he had gone to attend the Twentieth Congress of the CPSU. On 14 March, the Presidium of the Central Committee of the CPSU decided that Khrushchev would personally take part in Bierut's funeral in Warsaw and discussed his likely successors: Edward Ochab and Aleksander Zawadzki. In his memoirs, Khrushchev cited concern over rumors circulating in Poland that Bierut had been murdered in Moscow as the reason he chose to make the trip. However, beyond ceremonial considerations, it is certain that succession issues were more important to him. Khrushchev took part in the funeral and stayed on in the Polish capital to attend the session of the Central Committee of the Polish United Workers' Party (PZPR) that was to elect the party's new first secretary. His participation in the meeting on 20 March took an unexpected turn: Khrushchev did not restrict himself to the role of observer but joined in the debate about the addition of Roman Zambrowski—a Politburo member and close Bierut aide—to the CC Secretariat. Khrushchev took the floor after one of the speakers asked how the appointment "would be received by the people," which raised tempers in the auditorium because Zambrowski was of Jewish origin and some of those present thought the statement smacked of anti-Semitism. Khrushchev insisted that he "had not the slightest intention of interfering in your personnel policy" and delivered a protracted exposition on the technical division of competencies in the top Soviet party and state leadership, offering it as a model. However, the mere fact that he took part in the session and became involved in an internal conflict within the PZPR evoked adverse reactions. A press communiqué on the meeting did not even mention Khrushchev's presence, though a rumor that he had attended and spoken out against Zambrowski's candidacy quickly made the rounds, reinforcing the conviction that Moscow was calling the shots. Hardly anyone believed that Khrushchev had come to Warsaw to admire the recently opened, pompous Palace of Culture and Science (named after Stalin).

It is possible that Khrushchev cleared the surprising decision of the PZPR leadership to translate, print, and distribute to party cells the text of his "secret speech" at the Twentieth Congress of the CPSU. It attracted such intense interest that party meetings at which the speech was presented "were of a truly mass character, with thousands of people—not only party members—attending across the country." The brochures with the speech "were passed from hand to hand," read out loud at neighborhood meetings and community centers, and even hawked in marketplaces. Poland's subjugation to the

Soviet Union was one of the main themes of these discussions: the exploitation by Moscow of the Polish economy, the presence of Soviet officers in the Polish army, Katyn and the deportations of Poles in 1939–41. Polish historian Paweł Machcewicz believes that "it was characteristic that the ferment was marked by negative attitudes, expressed by the rejection of the existent reality rather than by the formulation of alternative political concepts."

The reach and heated nature of the debate were such that Ochab tried to stop it, but it was too late. Moreover, the authorities made further decisions that only increased the pressure. These included an amnesty in April that led to the release of thousands of political prisoners and the dismissal of the general prosecutor, the chief military prosecutor, and the justice minister, coupled with the arrest of several senior security officials. The public largely received these moves as an indirect admission of guilt and a sign of weakness. Magazines published articles demanding the rehabilitation of the Home Army, a convention of economists sharply criticized the way the economy was being managed, and dissenting voices were raised within artistic associations and academic communities.

Yet, all that did not seem to cause concern in the Kremlin and at the CPSU headquarters in Moscow's Old Square. In any case, analyses of the available documents conducted to date do not indicate that developments in Poland caused anxiety among the Soviet leadership, which was kept up to date on events by the Soviet Union's diplomatic and consular missions. Practically all the dispatches from Poland, including an extensive memo by Communist Party Central Committee staffer Jan Dzerzhinsky, who spent two weeks in Poland in April and May, painted a grim picture of the situation. Yet, no action seems to have been taken; in any case, no evidence has been discovered to date that the Polish comrades were warned and told to mend their ways. It was only the Poznań revolt that set alarm bells ringing: the Presidium of the CPSU decided to publish a report in the government-run *Izvestiya* headlined, "Hostile Provocation of Imperialist Agents in Poznań," and, more importantly, it adopted and published on 2 July a Central Committee resolution "on overcoming the cult of the individual and its consequences." The document toned down the message of the Twentieth Congress, highlighting the bipolar alignment of forces in the world, and again described the Poznań riots as being the result of imperialist scheming.

At the same time, the Soviet leadership, recognizing Poland's economic and social difficulties, decided to "extend to Poland comprehensive economic assistance, both in the form of goods [and] supplies and a gold loan." That commitment led to a series of talks and the initialing on 18 September of an agreement under which the Soviet Union granted Poland a credit in gold (which Poland was to sell in the West) and pledged deliveries of goods. Earlier yet it was agreed that Prime Minster Józef Cyrankiewicz would visit Moscow in October. Poland's image in the communist camp was also adversely affected by friction with the leaders of Czechoslovakia and the German Democratic Republic (GDR) over Poland's failure to supply coal to the two countries, which came to a head during a Comecon session in June. Meanwhile, the Soviets were also displeased by the disclosure on that occasion that the Soviet Union had been buying Polish coal for many years (1945–54) at a fraction of world prices. The Poles also raised the matter of payments for Soviet transit to the GDR, which had reached an enormous volume since half a million Red Army troops were stationed west of the Oder.

Ultimately, Cyrankiewicz did not go to Moscow. Instead, Soviet premier Nikolai Bulganin and Defense Minister Georgy Zhukov arrived in Poland. Ostensibly, they came to attend the state holiday celebration of 22 July, but that was obviously only a pretext since such high-ranking delegations had never previously visited Warsaw on similar occasions. It is likely that the visitors wanted to hold confidential talks with Polish leaders, or to indicate that Poland remained a crucial link in the socialist community, or both. At the event, Bulganin held official talks with Cyrankiewicz while Zhukov and Marshal Konstanty Rokossowski reviewed a military parade, and then the delegation toured Poland for eight days, visiting Silesia, Łódź, and Nowa Huta.

During an official meeting, Bulganin delivered an address laced with criticism of the situation in Poland. He particularly targeted the Polish press, a part of which—he claimed—was unfriendly toward the Soviet Union. He even spoke of "poisoned seeds" being sown by enemies working for certain newspapers. The speech was published in both *Trybuna Ludu* and *Pravda*. Bulganin also held talks with Ochab and possibly even with the entire Politburo, but he did not show up at the Seventh Plenum of the Central Committee of the PZPR, which took place at the same time (it lasted from 18 to 28 July, with a two-day break for the state holiday). I was not able to determine whether Bulganin had been planning to attend the CC meeting and changed his mind or, more likely, if his participation had not been anticipated. In any case, that spared him the embarrassment of having to witness a debate that at times resembled a free-for-all and that might have even shocked him since he was hardly used to such spontaneous party gatherings. During the meeting, a head-on collision took place between the "liberals" (also known as the Pulawians) and the "hardliners" (Natolinists), who were accused of anti-Semitism. The future of Władysław Gomułka was another contentious topic. The PZPR leadership had been holding confidential talks with Gomułka for several months, but these had only led to his partial political rehabilitation and the restoration of his party membership, even though the hardliners were demanding that Gomułka—Bierut's former prisoner—be immediately readmitted into the CC. The heat of the debate was reflected by the fact that ninety-five speakers took the floor and numerous statements were submitted as well.

ANDRZEJ PACZKOWSKI

Bulganin missed all this, but there is no doubt that the Soviet leadership received detailed information on the dispute and thus had a thorough understanding of the conflict tearing apart the Polish communist leadership. The intensity of the conflict was also apparent to many Poles: even though official press releases were laconic and much of the debate was confidential, people got information—and numerous rumors—through the grapevine and in broadcasts by Radio Free Europe (RFE), which used copy supplied by Western journalists based in Warsaw. At that time, RFE had a particularly large audience in Poland, especially after autumn 1954, when it started broadcasting sensational reports based on information supplied by a security apparatus defector (Lt. Col. Józef Światło). The news that Gomułka had been readmitted into the party sparked rumors and even speculation of his imminent return to power, and this belief gradually became a postulate in various communities. Meanwhile, signs of dissatisfaction intensified within such organizations as the Union of Polish Youth and the trade unions, which had hitherto served as docile "transmission belts" for the party. Acrimonious exchanges took place at various party gatherings over such subjects as anti-Semitism, "young" Marx, and the issue of freedom in Marxist theory.

Still, the focus remained on the responsibility for the "errors and distortions" of the Stalinist period. Demands were voiced for a return to "Leninist norms," seen as the cure for all ills, which would also allow for improvement of relations with the Soviet party. The hardliners—taking their cue from Bulganin—attacked the press, blaming it for the current turmoil, while the liberals sought to defend it. Indeed, a number of newspapers (mainly weeklies) had published articles that were sharply critical and nonconformist, for example, praising the Yugoslav model of worker self-management. Meanwhile, the censors—deprived of coherent guidelines from the CC—allowed the press more freedom than it had enjoyed since 1947. Some of the Home Army veterans released from prison considered the possibility of resuming public activity, which alarmed security officials. Unexpectedly, the "party pluralism dummies," that is, the United People's Party (Polish: Zjednoczone Stronnictwo Ludowe, ZSL) and the Democratic Party (particularly the former), came alive, as did PZPR activists with Polish Socialist Party roots but sidelined since 1948 (they included Edward Osóbka-Morawski, who had served as prime minister from 1944 to 1947). The annual pilgrimage to Jasna Góra on 26 August attracted at least half a million worshipers; an empty chair placed on a rostrum reminded those present that the primate of Poland was still in prison. In September, peasants started deserting collective farms in mass numbers. The PZPR leadership attempted to defuse public unrest: administration of prisons was transferred from the Ministry of the Interior to the Justice Ministry, letters sent abroad could now be dropped in any mailbox and not only at designated post offices, while the Sejm started debating its own role—which was a most timely move, since parliamentary elections were due in November. Certain initiatives of a confidential or even secret nature were also conducted. The Politburo decided to ask the Kremlin to recall Soviet advisors assigned to the Polish security apparatus and to give Poland full jurisdiction over the port of Świnoujście, then under total control of the Soviet Baltic Fleet. The problem of Soviet officers holding most of the top positions in the Polish armed forces was also put on the agenda. These issues were raised in Moscow personally by Ochab, who stopped over in the Soviet capital on his way to Beijing (11 September) and on his way back (18 September).

Ochab later recalled that, during his visit to China, "the Soviet ambassador did not leave us for a moment. . . . Whenever he could, he pushed his way toward me," which at times disrupted Ochab's talks with the Chinese hosts. The Soviets did not have much confidence in the Polish leadership and felt it was losing control of the situation. Yuri V. Bernov, a counselor at the Soviet embassy in Warsaw, recalled that Ochab had disclosed in Moscow that the Polish Politburo intended to offer Gomułka a seat on the Central Committee and the post of deputy premier. In any case, Gomułka was receiving quite a few visitors at that time, among them party officials of diverse rank (including members of the Politburo) and his former comrades (e.g., Gen. Grzegorz Korczyński, who was one of the few people who did not turn their backs on him in prison). The visitors also included Soviet diplomats, though Ambassador Panteleimon Ponomarenko was not one of them.

It was not an easy time for the Kremlin leadership: it was shaken by internal friction and strife, there was local social and ethnic unrest in the Soviet Union, and the future generation of *shestidyesyatniki* (literally, the Sixties people) was increasingly vocal among the young intelligentsia (while it never directly challenged the leadership, it did make its life more difficult). The external situation was not calm, either. When Soviet-supported Egyptian president Gamal Abdel Nasser nationalized the Suez Canal, tensions rapidly increased in the Middle East. In late July, the threat of upheaval loomed in Hungary, where Matyas Rakosi unexpectedly quit as general secretary of the Communist Party. As in Poland, Hungarian intellectuals were clamoring for liberalization. The name of Imre Nagy, the former premier recently expelled from the party, increasingly appeared in political discussions. On 6 October, several hundred thousand people attended the reburial of László Rajk, executed in 1949 as one of the first victims of the "Great Purge" in Central Europe; the ceremony turned into an antigovernment demonstration.

The political crisis in Poland was deepening. For the time being, it did not prompt external repercussions, though naturally it attracted growing interest. Soviet diplomats in Poland kept sending critical memos to headquarters, though, according to the Polish historian Andrzej Skrzypek, the Soviet ambassador "advised the CPSU leadership to let things run their course and refrain, for the time being, from giving advice." Indeed, there is no indication in any available publications or known documents that developments in Poland provoked increased interest among the Soviet leadership or party apparatchiks, not to mention any practical actions on their part. I have been unable to ascertain if the Soviet embassy restricted itself to information gathering or if it conveyed specific signals to its Polish contacts. However, it appears certain that—in line with the sentiments expressed by the leadership in Moscow—it was sympathetic toward the hardliners, who were clearly more pro-Soviet, than to the liberals.

By early October, nothing indicated that the Kremlin was alarmed by the Polish situation, even though, in September, Khrushchev had received at least two memos dedicated to "the unhealthy tendencies in Poland" and the mounting "anti-Soviet campaign of slander." However, on 4 October, the Presidium of the Central Committee of the CPSU limited its discussion to Polish grievances concerning coal prices and decided to acquiesce to the request for the withdrawal of the KGB advisors. It was also agreed that no action should be taken in response to cables from the Warsaw embassy, again sharply critical both of the Polish press (particularly the weekly *Po Prostu*) and a delegation of Soviet journalists, who had spoken warmly of their Polish colleagues. It was probably assumed that the maneuvering of the Polish leadership was tactical and meant to defuse tensions by partly appeasing public expectations. Moreover, the Kremlin appeared unimpressed by reports on meetings of the Polish Politburo (8 and 10 October), which, due "to the lack of unity within the P[olitical] B[ureau]," "increasingly anti-Soviet attitudes," and the still unresolved problems of "coal and Soviet officers," had decided to convene a plenary session of the Central Committee. Apparently, Moscow was still unaware that the crisis in Poland was entering its final stage.

I have not discovered any information on reactions in Moscow to Gomuł-ka's appearance at another meeting of the Politburo (12 October), at which he delivered an extensive address, thus assuming—for all practical purposes—the role of the party's first secretary. On the same occasion, the Politburo decided to make Gomułka and two of his closest associates, Zenon Kliszko and Gen. Marian Spychalski, members of the Central Committee. At its next meeting (15 October, again with Gomułka present), the Politburo rejected Ochab's draft address that was to be delivered at the upcoming plenary session of the CC. However, the turning point came on 17 October, when it was agreed that the entire Politburo would resign and that the plenary meeting of the CC would elect a new Politburo, with Gomułka as first secretary. The proposed lineup of the future Politburo and CC Secretariat did not include several leading, Moscow-backed hardliners, among them Franciszek Mazur, Franciszek Jóźwiak, Władysław Dworakowski, and Zenon Nowak. However, what incensed Khrushchev and his aides the most was the absence on the list of candidates of Marshal Rokossowski's name. Adding insult to injury, the proposals were sent out to all the members of the CC, which meant they would be publicized, since no one believed that leaks could be avoided.

Rokossowski complained in an emotional, even hysterical telephone call to Moscow. According to Khrushchev, he supposedly suggested that the Pulawians had won Gomułka over and intended to make a power grab, which carried the threat of Poland leaving the Warsaw Pact. Khrushchev immediately called Ochab and proposed that the CC session be postponed so that a special delegation of the Soviet Central Committee could first come to Warsaw. Ochab replied that he had nothing against the Soviet visit taking place, if it took place after the meeting of the Polish CC. Khrushchev later admitted that he lost his temper and ordered Marshal Zhukov to put Soviet troops in Poland and the Baltic Fleet on alert. The next day it was decided to immediately dispatch to Poland a top-level delegation, including Khrushchev, Molotov, Kaganovich, and Mikoyan. First, however, Khrushchev went to Brest for a meeting with the commanders of the three Soviet military districts bordering Poland (the Baltic, Belarusian, and Transcarpathian).

Meanwhile, the commander in chief of the Warsaw Pact, Marshal Ivan Konev, ordered two Soviet divisions stationed in Poland to march on Warsaw and dispatched several vessels of the Baltic Fleet into the Bay of Gdańsk. On the same day, following an order by the chief of the General Staff of the Polish army, Soviet general Jerzy Bordziłowski, small Polish units arrived in Warsaw or took up positions in its vicinity. Much indicates that the movement of the Soviet forces did not constitute the beginning of an armed intervention but was designed to put pressure on the Polish leadership. However, the deployment of the Soviet units in central Poland (in the vicinity of Włocławek and Łódź), gave them an operational advantage in the event action needed to be taken. It has not been established to date if the Soviet command had ready a plan of aggression at that point, though it seems unlikely.

On the morning of 19 October, a few hours before the scheduled opening of the Central Committee session, two planes landed at the Warsaw airport, one from Moscow and the other from Brest, with Khrushchev on board. Thus began a day that was to endow Gomułka with hero status comparable to that of Józef Piłsudski. It would also be remembered for Khrushchev's outburst at the airport—"You won't get away with this!"—which came to symbolize the attitude of Big Brother toward his Polish vassals. The content of the Polish-Soviet talks—which were the subject of numerous rumors and a few myths—was recently detailed thanks to the publication of notes made at the time by Jan Dzerzhinsky, son of the infamous head of the Soviet apparatus of repression, Felix Dzerzhinsky. Khrushchev wasted no time in laying his cards on the table with regard to the planned reshuffle in the Polish leadership: "We won't allow it, and if you do it anyway, we'll be forced to make a brutal intervention." The Soviets complained of anti-Soviet sentiments in Poland, supposedly expressed even in party papers, and underlined the importance of the Soviet Union in preserving Poland's "independence and inviolability of borders," since "the revanchists in West Germany are becoming increasingly impudent."

The tone and temperature of the talks was aptly reflected by the following exchange:

Gomułka: If we see eye to eye . . .

Khrushchev: What if we don't?

Gomułka: Are you allowing that possibility?

Khrushchev: Yes, I am, if you follow the present course. The situation is very serious. You have to draw some conclusions.

Gomułka: You have to draw conclusions, too, and stop interfering in our affairs.

Almost all those present took the floor and tough language was used in many of the exchanges, but ultimately it was a clash between Gomułka and Khrushchev—two politicians with vivid, authoritarian, and impulsive personalities. Naturally, it would be hard to gauge the impact of their character traits on the outcome of the talks on 19 October and the future of Polish-Soviet relations. In any case, the Pole emerged victorious: Khrushchev ordered all troop movements halted (though troops were not ordered back to their barracks), and the parties agreed on an obtuse communiqué ("the talks were held in an atmosphere of partylike and comradely sincerity"). Without achieving much of anything, the Soviet delegation departed on the night of 19 October.

Alas, that did not end the Polish-Soviet "cold war," so Skrzypek seems to have been exaggerating when he claimed that "on the night of 19 October, Khrushchev and Gomułka created a fact of irrevocable consequence in the history of the communist system, comparable to the importance of the reconciliation of Gregory VII and Henry IV at Canossa to the history of the struggle between the empire and the papacy." In any event, the showdown lasted several more days. Shortly after the Soviet delegation returned to Moscow, the Presidium of the CC of the CPSU held a meeting (with the participation of Ivan Serov, chief of KGB). It was agreed that any further action would hinge on Rokossowski's fate: "If Rokossowski stays on [as Politburo member and cabinet minister], we'll have to hold back a little longer." The Presidium also decided to invite the leaders of Czechoslovakia, Hungary, Romania, the GDR, and Bulgaria to Moscow and to send a CC envoy to Beijing to brief the Chinese. This meant that allies would be consulted before a key decision was adopted and that they might even be given a role in its implementation. Hungary was another topic on the agenda; it was decided to send Mikoyan there, though reports from Budapest were not yet alarming. The Soviet leadership seemed to be wavering in its response to the situation in Poland. The deliberations continued for another day. The minutes of the meeting indicate that two alternate approaches were under consideration: either "to influence and monitor developments" or "to take the path of intervention." Also, the invitation list of the "fraternal parties" was slightly altered: Romania was dropped in favor of China.

Later that day (21 October) the tone at the evening session was different. Khrushchev indicated that, "taking the circumstances into account[,] we should forgo armed intervention and show patience," while Molotov declared that "changes have taken place in CPSU policy." Those statements appeared out of step with events in Warsaw that same day: during elections to the Politburo, Rokossowski got only twenty-three votes out of seventy-five cast in a secret ballot, which amounted to a humiliating defeat. It was an obvious snub, to both Rokossowski and the Kremlin. The outcome of the vote demonstrated that the majority of the CC members were willing to risk confrontation with Moscow or simply wanted to show loyalty to Gomułka. But Khrushchev telephoned the new first secretary to congratulate him and apparently did not divert from the norms of diplomatic protocol. Meanwhile, the Presidium agreed that the Poles should themselves propose a solution concerning the Soviet officers in the Polish army: "We are even prepared to withdraw them," it was noted in the minutes. The Soviets kept their cool: they decided not to publish Gomułka's speech and then drafted a letter to CPSU party cells, explaining the situation in Poland. The meeting with the "fraternal" leaders went ahead, though the Chinese were received separately. The European visitors naturally were not enthusiastic over what had happened in Warsaw but also did not contest Moscow's decisions on the subject. Liu Shao Tsi followed suit, though Beijing had already advised Khrushchev—through the Soviet ambassador—that it was against interference in Polish affairs.

It is hard to conclusively verify the theory that it was China that "saved Poland," since we do not know what kind of clout Beijing had with Moscow at the time. In any event, the growing instability in Hungary probably had greater claim on the attention of Moscow's decision makers. Certainly, after 23 October, when firearms were used against demonstrators in Budapest, events in Hungary became dominant and within a few days completely overshadowed the situation in Poland. In view of the developments in Hungary, it is not surprising that Moscow swallowed without protest Rokossowski's dismissal from the posts of deputy premier and defense minister ("due to the erosion of his authority"). On the same day, Gomułka was triumphant at a huge rally in Warsaw, where several hundred thousand people sang "May He Live a Hundred Years" to the new leader.

At that point, the crisis in Polish-Soviet relations was effectively over, as affirmed by the fact that, at a secret meeting on 1 November, Khrushchev briefed Gomułka on Soviet plans for an armed intervention in Hungary. Although unrest continued in Poland for some time yet, partly with anti-Soviet motivation (e.g., a Soviet consulate was set on fire in Szczecin), mutual relations were quickly refocused on economic issues. In mid-November, an official Polish delegation led by Gomułka secured an agreement in Moscow on railway and financial settlements, coal prices, reparations, arms production and strategic investments in Poland, and other matters. December saw the signing of agreements on the status of Soviet forces stationed in Poland and on repatriation, which led to the return to Poland of almost 225,000 people. In the final account, the Soviets—though they never ceased complaining— accepted the "Polish specificity."

But a lack of confidence persisted, and Khrushchev—in his impulsive way—was given to criticizing Polish politicians and expressing opinions without mincing words. At a meeting with Gomułka on the Black Sea in late summer of 1957, he told the Pole, "We have good relations with all countries, but with Poland they only get worse. . . . You keep spitting on us and yet you expect our aid. . . . You got rid of all the supporters of the Soviet Union and replaced them with enemies, all kinds of Jews and others." I am not familiar with the minutes of Khrushchev's meetings with other communist leaders, so I am not in a position to judge if that was his normal conduct and he berated everyone, or if that kind of treatment was reserved only for the Poles. However, he seemed completely sincere in his outbursts, so his willingness to be so explicit—obviously without the intent to break relations—may have been a sign of a certain trust. Gomułka, himself an explosive person, probably found it extremely hard to stomach Khrushchev's tirades, but he had no choice since he really did keep asking the Soviets for economic aid. Nothing is known of any scheming by Khrushchev to remove Gomułka from power, especially since Gomułka was gradually "turning the screws" and eliminating "the Jews and others" from the PZPR leadership.

However, when, in late 1970, following factory strikes and a bloody suppression of demonstrations, Poland descended into a deep political crisis, the Soviet leadership—this time with Leonid Brezhnev at the helm—did not hesitate to administer the coup de grace to Gomułka: on the evening of 18 December, the Soviet ambassador handed Prime Minister Cyrankiewicz a letter from the Presidium of the Central Committee of the CPSU demanding that the crisis be resolved by political means. That amounted to a vote of no confidence in Gomułka, who, a few days prior, had ordered the use of firearms against the protesters. In a sense, history had come full circle: Gomułka, who had assumed power against Moscow's wishes, was now being removed with its participation.

NIKOLAI I. BUKHARIN

· ·

THE TWENTIETH CONGRESS OF THE SOVIET COMMUNIST PARTY, THE POLISH OCTOBER, AND THE STRUGGLE FOR AUTONOMY

· ·

THE HISTORIC TWENTIETH Congress of the Communist Party of the Soviet Union (CPSU) was held in Moscow from 14 to 25 February 1956. On the last day of the closed session, Nikita Khrushchev, first secretary of the Central Committee of the CPSU, gave a secret speech titled, "On the Cult of Personality and Its Consequences," in which he condemned the cult of personality of Stalin. The speech expressed a landmark view of the country's recent history, which had been defined by the "cult of personality" and various kinds of Stalinist repression. It rejected the Stalinist theory of intensifying the class struggle in the course of socialist development. It also raised the issue of rehabilitation of party members, statesmen, and military figures who had fallen victim to Stalinist repressions.

The Twentieth Congress of the CPSU was a milestone in the history of the Soviet Union that divided the Soviet epoch into two halves. The launch of de-Stalinization began the era now referred to as the "thaw." Khrushchev's de-Stalinization, with its fluctuations and half-hearted character, was the first stage of this thaw (the next stage came in the latter half of the 1980s).

The Twentieth Congress and Khrushchev's reforms fundamentally changed life in the Soviet Union. There was a certain liberalization of the Soviet regime. Changes affected all areas of life: the party and the state, the economy and social relations, science and culture.

The darkest sides of the repressive totalitarian system were the first to be eliminated. Critical measures were taken to remove the distressing consequences of the lawless Stalinist repressions and restore law and order, as well as the constitutional rights of citizens.

Hundreds of thousands of innocent people were released from prisons and labor camps. Bylaws of the party and collective leadership were restored. The state machine's activity was put into working order. The rights of the Soviet republics were extended. Tough totalitarianism evolved into a milder authoritarianism, since Khrushchev and his associates were not concerned about consistent democratization but rather the preservation of the foundations of the old system.

However, the process of demystification had begun. Some monstrous facts of the state's terror toward its citizens were disclosed. During the "Great Terror" of 1937–38, 1.34 million people were sent to prison, of which 682,700 were shot. According to the Interior Ministry of the Soviet Union, on 1 April 1954, Gulag (the Soviet labor camp authority) had 1.36 million prisoners. Of those, 448,000 had been sentenced for counterrevolutionary crimes. Altogether, Khrushchev's revelations, the terrifying details of murders, tortures, moral neglect, and lack of humanitarian behavior had a dramatic impact upon the Soviet psyche. This was the greatest of national tragedies.

An integral part of the de-Stalinization process was the rehabilitation of those citizens who had been repressed under Stalin. Within the period from 1956 to 1961, nearly seven hundred thousand people were rehabilitated; the victims of repression had their good names restored. Those who were alive came back from the labor camps. After the Twentieth Congress of the CPSU, the Chechens, Ingush, Karachai, Balkars, Kurds, Koreans, Buryats, and other ethnicities that had been illegally deported during the Great Patriotic War were repatriated to their homelands.

It was in February 1956 that the "thaw" in the inner life of the Soviet people began. The fear disappeared. The Soviet people could breathe freely. They believed the brutality of Stalin's time would never come back. The censorship threshold was dramatically lowered. The notion of public opinion was restored, even though it was virtually ignored by the authorities.

The ideas of freedom spread among students and clerisy. Creative life became rich and eventful. The people of dominant influence for the youth and the clerisy were the "children of the Twentieth Congress"—poets and writers such as Yevgeny Yevtushenko, Andrei Voznesensky, Vasily Aksenov, B. Okudzhava, Bella Akhmadulina, Vladimir Voynovich, and Aleksandr Solzhenitsyn, stage directors such as Georgy Tovstonogov, A. Efros, Y. Lubimov, and O. Yefremov, and film directors such as Grigory Chukhrai and Andrey Tarkovsky. The official periodicals of the democratic writers were *Novy Mir,* edited by A. Tvardovsky, and *Yunost,* edited by V. Kataev and B. Polevoy. All the same, party "guidance" of literature and art remained. By 1957, the party and the KGB had begun to interfere with the democratic mood.

Stalin's death and the Twentieth Congress of the CPSU, along with the uprisings in Poland and Hungary, resulted in a reevaluation of Soviet policy toward the satellite states. Consequently, from the middle of the 1950s, the Soviet Union and the Eastern European bloc countries entered a new phase of political and economic relations. The development of relations was greatly influenced by Khrushchev's personality, with all its positive, and negative, traits. It was Khrushchev who led to the significant upturn in relations between the Soviet Union and the socialist countries in 1956–57, a change that set them free from Stalinist oppression and let them initiate political renovation. In his summary report at the Twentieth Congress of the CPSU, Khrushchev stated, "The development of the socialist countries is distinguished by their absolute independence, both politically and economically." It is believed that the countries themselves understood that thesis as a sign of withdrawal from Stalinist policy.

The events of 1956 in Poland and Hungary urged the Soviet government to revise the Soviet Union's policy toward the socialist countries. Early in the morning of 20 October 1956, the Presidium of the Central Committee of the CPSU began four days of discussions on the situation in the Eastern bloc countries, and in Hungary and Poland in particular. The Soviet government came to the conclusion that relations with the socialist countries had to be based on equality and that no interference in their internal affairs was permissible. The results of the Presidium's sitting and the appraisal of the situation in Poland and Hungary were communicated to the leaders of the European socialist countries (Walter Ulbricht, Otto Grotewohl, Willi Stoph, T. Zhivkov, Anton Yugov, E. Staykov, A. Novotny, Viliam Široký, and Antonín Zápotocký), who had been invited to meet in Moscow on 24 October.

After the Presidium adjourned, a document was prepared detailing the new principles of relations with the socialist countries, namely the Soviet government's declaration of foundations of development and further consolidation of friendship and cooperation between the Soviet Union and the other socialist countries. It recognized that the previous period "had experienced quite a lot of difficulties, unresolved problems and outright mistakes, including in the area of relations with the socialist countries. Those mistakes and violations diminished the principle of equality in regards to the aforementioned relations." This document highlighted the importance of general democratic standards and principles such as absolute equality, respect for territorial integrity, independent statehood and sovereignty, and non-interference in each other's internal affairs.

The declaration laid the foundation for bilateral negotiations between the parties and governmental delegations of the Soviet Union and the European socialist countries that took place at the end of 1956 and the beginning of 1957. In the course of the negotiations, Khrushchev "spoke about lots of questions concerning the concept of sovereignty of the countries with popular democracy, the essence of equality, and the Warsaw Pact." The negotiations resulted in the Soviet Union canceling debts of several billion rubles owed to them by the socialist countries and giving them credit of several more billion rubles as well. It was satisfaction for the "sins" of Stalin's era and a consolidation of the socialist countries' shattered unity.

During the Soviet-Polish negotiations in November 1958, Khrushchev gave the following definition of Soviet policy toward the European socialist countries: "As for internal affairs[,] we will never impose, only give straightforward advice. You make your own decisions. As for foreign affairs[,] we will express our opinion and consult with you. It is neither guidance nor control, it is political accountability." Khrushchev declared an end to Stalin's policy of dictatorship and to Moscow's control over the socialist countries from Moscow.

Khrushchev's secret speech was a great surprise for the Communist Party and Labor Party leaders of the European socialist countries and also for the parties themselves. The chief negotiators who attended the congress received a slightly revised version of the report. In Poland and Yugoslavia, the report was immediately made public. As opposed to the other socialist countries, the Poles made multitudinous copies of the speech and it was widely distributed. Meanwhile, the party leaders of Czechoslovakia, the German Democratic Republic (GDR), Romania, Bulgaria, Albania, and Hungary tried to conceal its contents. The Chinese government denied its existence. However, it was impossible to stop the end of Stalin's cult of personality. It gave rise to the liberalization process in the socialist countries, particularly in Poland and Hungary, and also evoked hope for a democratic renewal of socialism and liberation from Moscow's excessive dictatorship.

The Polish incidents and the "Polish October" in 1956 were the first things that prompted a meeting of the massive movement of "the ruled" with the acute crisis of "the rulers." However, the incidents had nothing to do with an antisocialist movement. The aim of their participants was to return to a democratic path to socialism and form a Polish model on that order. The Polish historian A. Frischke believes that the incidents of 1956 presented "the first major attempt to gain freedom and sovereignty." At the same time, the Soviet "thaw" was not supported by a massive movement. It was initiated from above as an outcome of the de-Stalinization process, whose boundaries were defined by the government. That is why the Soviet "thaw" was a less profound process than the "Polish October."

News of Khrushchev's report came at the same time as Polish premier Bolesław Bierut's death on 12 March 1956. On 20 March, a plenary session was held in order to elect a new first secretary of the Central Committee of the PZPR, the Polish version of the Communist Party. The Soviet party and state delegation was in Warsaw from 15 to 21 March. Khrushchev took part in the plenum's work. In his improvised speech, he did not mention the new leader's election but confined himself to some remarks on the staff of the Central Committee Office and the functions of that party body. Khrushchev's presence at the plenary session was resented by some Central Committee members, who took it as interference in the affairs of the PZPR.

The plenum had unanimously elected Edward Ochab the new party leader. In his memoirs, Khrushchev noted, "We weren't worried about Ochab's nomination[;] he was our friend and had the right notion of that friendship." During his visit to Poland, the Soviet leader brought up the matter of Gomułka, namely his return to the party and state leadership. The Polish leaders objected to that.

The Polish historian and publicist Wiesław Władyka wrote that "the introduction to Khrushchev's secret report became one of the crucial factors and motives for the big 'moral revolution' of spring 1956 in Poland." In March and April, a wide discussion began, fueled by criticism at thousands of party meetings and clerisy and work meetings. The government had to accept criticism, make concessions, and withdraw from Stalin's ruling methods. The party leadership had split into two parts: those who tended to preserve the administrative-command methods of the ruling members (Natolinists) against the supporters of moderate democratization of the party and society, as well as political independence from Moscow (Pulawians). All that resulted in a growth of political tensions within the country. The public discussion was also focused on the possibility of Gomułka's return to power after he had been removed from the party leadership in 1948 and then arrested in 1951. After his release in 1954, Gomułka stayed away from politics.

Further aggravation of the crisis was caused by the massive disturbances in Poznań in June 1956. They were provoked by dissatisfaction among the workers of the city's largest enterprise, the Cegielski plant. The workers believed that there was an unjust compensation scheme, that the living conditions were too hard, and that the management had no regard for the requirements of the workers, junior engineers, and technicians. Although the governmental authorities were aware of the employees' feelings, no satisfactory action was taken to ease the situation. The workers' patience was totally exhausted.

At six o'clock in the morning on 28 June, several thousand people gathered to hold a meeting. They left the plant's premises and headed for the city center, singing patriotic and religious songs on the way. At several other enterprises, a work stoppage was followed by the formation of large groups of mostly workers who then headed to the offices of the local party and state authorities. It was a peaceful manifestation of protest. Its major slogan was "Give us bread and freedom!" The secret service also recorded a large number of anti-Soviet slogans. About 100,000 people gathered on the square in front of the castle where the provincial committee of PZPR and the municipal people's council met. Among those gathered, many had antigovernment sentiments, and some were actually criminals. Several hundred young radicals and anarchists attacked the city prison, releasing the prisoners and seizing firearms and ammunition. After that, the armed youth and the released criminals attempted to capture the facilities of the provincial department of public security. Despite the order not to use weapons, the troops guarding the department opened fire. Regular troops were brought into the city and suppressed the attackers' nests. In the course of the armed conflicts, 74 people were killed, including 66 civilians, 3 officers of the security department, 1 policeman, and 4 soldiers of the Polish army. There were 575 people injured, with varying degrees of severity. Late on 30 June, the troops were withdrawn from the city.

The Poznań incidents were immediately qualified by the Polish government as "a provocation of imperialistic agents, the reactionary underground, and hostile agents." The Soviet government shared that view. Later on, PZPR renounced that qualification, attributing the disturbances to certain economic reasons, acknowledging the spontaneous character of the incidents and the fact that the thesis that there was external provocation of the incidents was false. According to the Russian historian A. M. Orekhov, the Poznań disturbances were a spontaneous and ruthless riot of hopeless and enraged people.

The Poznań incident sped up the worsening political crisis in the party and in the country. The Seventh Plenum of the Central Committee of the PZPR, which took place from 18 to 28 July, aggravated the political polarization in the Central Committee and the disjointedness of the party leaders. The new first secretary of the PZPR Central Committee, Ochab, was regarded as an interim party leader. When the party split into two groups, he took up a centrist position, trying to bridge the gap. At first, he opposed Gomułka's return to power, but then he gave up and played an important part in transferring power to Gomułka. Some party leaders thought that Gomułka was the only politician who was able to take control of the situation in the country. Negotiations for the terms of Gomułka's return to the party leadership began. He agreed only on the condition that he become first secretary.

On 1 August 1956, Gomułka was reinstated in the PZPR, and, on 12 October, he began to work with the Politburo. In the eyes of the people, Gomułka symbolized the Poles' aspiration for de-Stalinization and greater autonomy in their relations with the Soviet Union. Gomułka's approval among the people was steadily growing, and his supporters prepared the Eighth Plenum of the PZPR Central Committee in order to formalize their leadership in the party, and, contrary to the established procedure that dated back to the time of Stalin and Comintern, he purposely failed to coordinate the nominations to the party's governing bodies with those of the Soviet government. For the Kremlin, there seemed to be even more defiance in the predetermined elimination of Marshal Konstanty Rokossowski from the Politburo of the PZPR Central Committee. The Soviet embassy informed Moscow of the regular gatherings of certain leaders of the PZPR and other parties in Gomułka's flat in Warsaw's Saska Kępa district. The behind-the-scenes preparation for the Eighth Plenum was in progress, and posts in the party and the state apparatus were filled. The Soviet-Polish bipartisan conflict developed at an ever-increasing rate. The Soviet government's interference in the situation was more and more inevitable.

The Soviet executive branch of power was particularly anxious about the growing anti-Soviet feeling both in the party and among the people. This anxiety was perfectly justified. The Soviet Union still interfered in a number of important spheres of Polish life. Most notably, their regular interference in staffing policy (when determining the composition of the Politburo, the Office of the Central Committee of the PZPR, and the government) was regarded by Polish society as a considerable restraint on the country's sovereignty. The presence of Soviet troops in the country—two armored divisions and two aircraft divisions—had no legal grounds. The Polish government had not even been informed of their numbers.

Poles were resentful of the appointment of Soviet marshal Rokossowski to the post of defense minister of the People's Republic of Poland (PRL) in 1949. Rokossowski, having acquired Polish citizenship, still retained his Soviet citizenship. They were also annoyed about the appointment of a number of Soviet officers of Polish origin to leading positions in the Polish army (in 1956, there were 49 Soviet citizens among the officers) and the presence of Soviet advisors in the army (about 150 in 1954 and 26 in 1956) and security bodies (89 in 1954). Apart from that, 700 Soviet officers had acquired Polish citizenship. The national security bodies, therefore, had a conflict of interest. The military intelligence service of the PRL was controlled by the officers of a special NKVD department.

At party meetings and youth gatherings, be it in media, at colleges and universities, at enterprises and institutions, or even within family circles, everyone was discussing the bitter truths of recent history. There was an abundance of distressing facts: the Molotov-Ribbentrop Pact, the Red Army's invasion of the eastern Polish provinces on 17 September 1939, the deportation of Poles to northern parts the Soviet Union and Kazakhstan, the Katyn massacres, the suppression of the Warsaw Uprising, and the tragedy of the Armia Krajowa. The Poles insisted that Lvov and Vilnius should be given back to Poland. It was the only moment in the history of the PRL when the territories lost in the course of World War II were demanded back with a certain clamor.

According to the memoirs of Khrushchev (and backed up by the memoirs of both Khrushchev's son Sergey and the first advisor of the Soviet embassy in Warsaw, Yuri Bernov), the cables sent by P. Ponomarenko, the Soviet ambassador in Warsaw, were of a more and more alarming character. At first, he frightened Moscow with reports of the intensification of anti-Soviet and revisionist feelings in the Polish government and party as a whole, and then with reports of the threat of a counterrevolutionary coup d'état, which, according to the embassy, was being arranged by some anti-Soviet and antisocialist forces that wanted to dismiss the government elected after Bierut's death and bring Gomułka back to power.

Gomułka himself was characterized as a right-wing revisionist who was both a nationalist and anti-Soviet. The embassy thought that Gomułka "blamed and resented the USSR for the fact of his dismissal on Stalin's command and then also for his arrest on a charge of right-wing nationalistic deviation." It was also known that he disagreed with Stalin's stand on Yugoslavia. All that suggested the idea that Gomułka and his supporters would start making their own domestic and foreign policy, thus adopting Yugoslav practices. The embassy also predicted that "Poland might withdraw from the Warsaw treaty and venture to risk the socialist achievements."

On 15 October, a meeting of the Politburo of the Central Committee of the PZPR was held in Warsaw and devoted to a convocation of the Eighth Plenum of the Central Committee. A storm ensued in Moscow as a result of the following highly unusual postscript: "Gomułka took part in the Politburo's session." It could only mean a takeover of power. The fact that the nomination had not been coordinated with Moscow disturbed Khrushchev very much. It contravened the adopted Stalinist/Comintern practice of coordinating nominations. The information received from the embassy concerning an article that had been published in the weekly magazine *Nowa Kultura* poured oil onto the flames and cast doubt on the credibility of the slogan "Workers of the world, unite!" in this new context. The article made Khrushchev furious.

He had come to the conclusion that the situation in Poland was very serious and that immediate action had to be taken. Late on 17 October 1956, Khrushchev telephoned Ochab and declared his intention to visit Warsaw in order to conduct negotiations, because Poland was of strategic importance to the Soviet Union. The point he wanted to make was that the presence of the Soviet Northern Group of Forces (NGF) in the PRL ensured that communications that went through Polish territory and provided connection to the Soviet troops in Germany were functioning. All this was in accordance with the Potsdam Agreement of 1945. Ochab replied that he had to take counsel. He soon called back and said, "We would like you not to come before we finish the session of the Central Committee." Recalling this incident, Khrushchev wrote, "We were insulted by that. Insulted by the way the Soviet Union was abused and the fact that the Poles repudiated the casualties our people had suffered fighting for Poland's freedom. We had the impression that[,] according to the publications and the statements at the meetings, Poland wanted to break off relations with us."

Early on 18 October, during a session of the Presidium of the Central Committee of the CPSU, opinions were exchanged and a delegation was sent to begin negotiations with the Polish government. The group included Khrushchev, Foreign Minister Vyacheslav Molotov, Deputy Prime Minister Anastas Mikoyan, and Lazar Kaganovich, deputy chair of the Council of Ministers. By 18 October, by command of Marshal Georgy Zhukov, defense minister of the Soviet Union, the NGF in Poland, the Baltic Fleet, and parts of the Baltic military district were brought into a state of high alert for combat.

Despite objections on the Polish side, early on 19 October 1956, the delegation from the Presidium arrived in Warsaw. Galvanized by the Soviet embassy's communications, Khrushchev shook his fist at the Polish government as soon as he went down the boarding ramp. By that gesture, the Soviet leader tried to show that he was going to take rough and decisive action. First, Khrushchev greeted Rokossowski and the generals. Ivan Konev, commander in chief of the Joint Armed Forces of the Warsaw Pact, reassured Khrushchev that Soviet troops were moving toward Warsaw. Then, Khrushchev addressed the Polish government authorities, who had come to meet the Soviet delegation: "Comrade Ochab's treacherous activity has been revealed. You won't get away with this." In response to that, Gomułka suggested going to Belvedere, the residence of the president of the State Council of the PRL, and having a peaceful talk. The Soviet leaders demanded that the plenary session of the PZPR Central Committee be adjourned, but the Polish leaders refused to do so.

Before the negotiations started, the Soviet delegation took counsel with Rokossowski and Konev, and the former confirmed that antisocialist and anti-Soviet forces were building up in Poland. In order to stop their activity, it would be necessary to rely on the armed forces. Rokossowski placed himself at the disposal of the Soviet government. According to Sergey Khrushchev, in response to the question of how the Polish army would behave, Rokossowski honestly stated, "Not all of the Polish troops will obey my orders now, but . . . there are some parts that will execute my orders. I am a Soviet citizen and I believe that certain measures have to be taken against the anti-Soviet forces which are striving for power. It is vitally important to preserve the communications with Germany through Poland." When he went on to specify which parts would obey his orders and which would not, Khrushchev was convinced that "the situation would not turn out well."

At the Eighth Plenum of the PZPR, the Central Committee convened as scheduled (19–21 October 1956), and Gomułka and his supporters were co-opted as members of the Central Committee. The plenum and negotiations were held in a dramatic situation, reflecting tensions within both the party and society. Soviet troops were already on the march. Some of the members of the Central Committee were so apprehensive of arrests that they stayed away from home overnight.

Minutes (rather than shorthand reports) of the meetings held between the leaders of the CPSU and the PZPR and published by Russian historian Orekhov, show that the negotiations were very arduous. The first secretary of the CPSU Central Committee maintained an offended attitude. He later recalled, "The conversation was rude, with no diplomacy." In response to Gomułka's assurances that the Polish leadership did not want to break off friendship with the Soviet Union, Khrushchev declared, "You will not get away with this; we are prepared for active interference."

As a result, the negotiations turned into acute polemics and accusations from both the Soviet and the Polish leaders. Members of the Soviet delegation demanded an explanation of those actions, which they saw as being aimed against the Soviet Union. They insisted that Rokossowski, who was seen as a guarantor of control over the Polish army, retain his position as the national defense minister and also remain a member of the Politburo of the PZPR. They also demanded the election of pro-Soviet politicians to the Polish Politburo. The Polish leaders tried to explain to their Soviet counterparts the complexity and specificity of the political and economic situation in Poland and the inequality inherent in Soviet-Polish relations. They asserted their right to make domestic policy independent of Moscow.

By the evening of 18 October, Defense Minister Zhukov had ordered a tank division from the cantonment of the NGF to proceed toward Warsaw. Almost simultaneously, at the order of Rokossowski and with the consent of Ochab, units of the Polish army quartered in the territory of the Warsaw military district advanced in the same direction. They were instructed to ensure increased security of the capital's strategic facilities and to block the city's thoroughfares in the event of unforeseen mass rallies. Soviet warships, headed by the cruiser *Zhdanov*, entered the waters off Gdańsk. All over Poland there were rumors of Soviet military units concentrating along the border of the GDR and Poland and also along the Soviet-Polish border.

NGF units left their bases in Pomerania and Silesia on 18 October and reached the Włocławek-Łęczyca-Łask line, keeping away from major settlements. On 19 October, the tanks stopped in the vicinity of Łęczyca waiting for further orders and then moved on, completing their push toward Warsaw and covering the areas of Łęczyca-Łowicz and Włocławek-Gostynin. A distance of fifty to eighty kilometers lay between them and the Polish capital. The tanks remained there until 24 October.

At around 2:00 p.m., Roman Zambrowski, a member of the Polish Politburo, read out a recently received message saying that Soviet and Polish troops were nearing Warsaw and that workers at a car factory in Żerań had decided to hit the streets to block them. At around 4:00 p.m., Gomułka announced receipt of a new message on the advancement of Soviet and Polish tank units. "We request the Soviet comrades to instruct Comrade Konev to suspend the troops' advancement," he said excitedly. As Khrushchev wrote in his memoirs, Gomułka was speaking passionately and uttered some words that won over the Soviet leader: "You think that only you need friendship with the Polish people? As a Pole and a communist, I swear that Poland needs friendship with the Russians more than the Russians need friendship with the Poles. Do you think we do not understand that without you we would not be able to survive as an independent state? Everything will be all right between us, only please do not let the Soviet troops enter Warsaw, because then it will be extremely difficult to keep the situation under control." Khrushchev and other members of the Presidium of the CPSU Central Committee started to explain that it was a matter of regular maneuvers that always took place at that time of year, and they agreed to instruct Konev accordingly.

After 4:30 p.m., the Soviet delegation left for the Soviet embassy in order to confer; Rokossowski was also invited. Having thought it over, Khrushchev suggested to his colleagues that they should support Gomułka. The Soviet leader said, "Comrades, I trust Gomułka, I trust him as a Communist. He is in a difficult situation. He will not do it at once. However, gradually, if we express our confidence in him, withdraw the troops, [and] give him time, then Gomułka will cope with those forces, who are on the wrong side now. . . . I believe it is necessary to support Gomułka." There were no objections from the other members of the delegation.

Khrushchev proposed to stop the advance of the Soviet tank troops but not to bring them back to the barracks. They were to be deployed along those same lines they had passed during their march. However, they were not to be stretched along the line but ordered into groups. Konev immediately ordered the troops to stop their advance toward Warsaw. If the Russian troops had entered the Polish capital, it could have caused irreversible damage. Khrushchev recalled, "Rokossowski received the same instruction from us through Konev. I am using the word 'instruction,' because at that time Rokossowski obeyed us more than he did his own government. The government was at a transitional stage and had little influence over him." The troops remained in their positions until 24 October when, at 10:00 a.m., Khrushchev called Gomułka to inform him that he had ordered the troops to return to the cantonment, and, in turn, Gomułka announced this news to thousands of Poles at a gathering in Warsaw.

This same remarkable day, 19 October, also saw a renewed and heated dispute during the Soviet-Polish negotiations that resumed after 7:00 p.m. There was a distinct lack of trust on both sides. Most likely, the Polish authorities had seen the relocation of the Soviet troops as a continuation of the march toward Warsaw. Due to this notion, Gomułka stated that the advance of the Soviet and Polish tanks continued. He addressed Khrushchev: "I am asking what do the words uttered this morning mean: 'We are prepared for decisive interference?'" Khrushchev went on accusing the Polish leaders of departing from the policy of friendship with the Soviet Union. Rokossowski submitted a request to the Polish Politburo and the Soviet Presidium. The request was for them to consider his resignation.

The situation was defused by Gomułka, who proposed sending out a joint communiqué, stressing that "socialism is the foundation of the friendship between Poland and the Soviet Union and it is also the common objective, a cause served by both parties." He also suggested, in the second part of the communiqué, that it should be noted that "both parties confirm that each of them must deal with their own internal affairs independently, taking into account the common interests of socialism." Khrushchev addressed him in a conciliatory manner: "Comrade Gomułka, we see you as a major public figure. I had shared this view with many of those present here even before you were nominated."

The Soviet-Polish conflict was settled by a revision of Soviet policy toward Poland. The PZPR leaders got their way at the negotiations, managing to combine loyalty to an alliance with the Soviet Union with the right to an independent domestic policy. Moscow yielded; it renounced its former direct guidance of Poland through its embassy, Soviet advisors, and agents of influence. At the Eighth Plenum of the PZPR Central Committee, Gomułka stated that relations between the parties and the states of the socialist camp "must be based on mutual trust (and) mutually constructive criticism . . . within the framework of such relations each country must enjoy full independence and autonomy, while the right of each nation to sovereign governance in an independent country must be respected fully and by both parties."

Discussions between the Soviet and Polish leaders were completed at 1:00 a.m. on 20 October, and at 6:45 a.m. the Presidium delegation took off for Moscow by plane. According to the recollections of Mikoyan's son, Sergo, Khrushchev and Mikoyan flew on the same plane and spoke of a successful settlement of the conflict. However, immediately upon arrival in Moscow, Khrushchev changed his mind, most likely prompted by Molotov and Kaganovich. When Mikoyan came to Khrushchev, he was told of a majority decision of the members of the Presidium to bring Soviet troops into Warsaw and to hand power over to obedient members of the PZPR Central Committee (though Khrushchev failed to name any truly obedient individuals). Draft minutes of the meeting of the Presidium held on 20 October stated, "There is only one way out to put an end to what is going on in Poland. If Rokossowski stays on, then we can wait." However, on 21 October, at another Presidium meeting, Khrushchev, proceeding from the developments in Poland and Hungary, changed his point of view again: "Taking into account the situation, we should renounce military interference. [We should] have tolerance." This approach was shared by all members of the Presidium. On 21 October,

Gomułka was elected first secretary of the PZPR Central Committee. On the evening of the same day, Khrushchev telephoned Gomułka to congratulate him on his election.

Complications continued to disturb the situation. On 24 October, a group of Poles broke into the Soviet consulate building in Szczecin and set it on fire. On the same day, a four-hundred-thousand-strong rally was held in Warsaw and addressed by Gomułka. Participants in the rally voiced their support of the new leadership of the PZPR. Following the completion of the rally, a crowd of several thousand people with white-and-red flags shouting anti-Soviet slogans headed toward the Soviet embassy and soon encircled the building. The Warsaw authorities reacted promptly. The embassy was surrounded by armored personnel carriers and motorcycles. The crowd trying to burst into the building was dispersed.

Two days after the plenary meeting, in a telephone conversation with Gomułka, Khrushchev confirmed that he "saw no obstacles to stop party and state relations between the USSR and Poland from being based on those principles laid by the 8th Plenary meeting of the PZPR Central Committee."

At the negotiations between the party and government of the Soviet Union and the PRL, held in Moscow from 15 to 18 November 1956, delegates adopted a joint declaration on the issue of Soviet-Polish relations. It stated that interstate relations between the Soviet Union and the PRL would be based on the principles of full equality of rights, inviolability of territorial borders, independence and sovereignty of the contracted parties, and non-interference in each other's affairs. Gomułka called the declaration "an expression of a fundamental turning point in relations between Poland and the USSR," as well as between the PZPR and the CPSU. Khrushchev recalled, "We withdrew everything that could evoke an idea of unequal relations, that could give the slightest reason to think that we treated Poland as a dependent state, abusing our power and imposing our conditions."

The CPSU leadership accepted the fact that Gomułka had become first secretary of the PZPR Central Committee in spite of Moscow's will. Thus, the Kremlin was forced to reconcile itself to the "Polish path to socialism," a path that provided for a renunciation of wide-scale collectivization, preservation of small-scale private property in urban areas, a specific multiparty system headed by the PZPR, greater freedom for cultural and scientific creativity, and a greater openness to the outside world. The compromise between the Soviet leaders and the reformist wing of the PZPR allowed for the preservation of peace and stability in Poland.

This conclusion to the crisis was viewed by the other countries of the socialist camp as a victory by the Poles, while the soft attitude of Khrushchev, who had failed to use the armed forces, was later rebuked by the conservative elements of the Presidium of the CPSU Central Committee.

The developments in Hungary that started on 23 October pushed the Polish issue to the sidelines. Unlike in Poland, the situation in Hungary got out of control and called for special attention on the part of the Soviet leadership. The Kremlin realized that saving socialism by way of armed interference in two countries simultaneously was an impossible task. As likely as not, it was the Hungarian events at that time that saved the "Polish October" from violent suppression.

Poland freed itself from the odious signs of dependency on Moscow. At the Eighth Plenum, held on 20 October, Rokossowski was not elected to the Politburo. Out of the seventy-five members of the Central Committee, his nomination was supported by only twenty-three members. The Polish side demanded that Soviet advisors be removed from the Polish army and state security bodies. In a letter dated 22 October 1956, addressed to the PZPR Central Committee and signed by Khrushchev, the Soviet side gave consent to the abolition of the institute of Soviet advisors of the PRL's Public Safety Committee and the withdrawal of Soviet officers and generals from the Polish army.

On 13 November 1956, Rokossowski asked the Polish government to release him from all his positions. His request was satisfied. Gomułka went to great lengths to talk the marshal out of leaving Poland and offered him a considerable pension and a government mansion. Rokossowski said in reply, "I was sent to work in Poland at the request of the Polish government by the CPSU Central Committee, and I am reverting to its control." Shortly before his departure, a government certificate of merit was delivered to him, and in it the Polish authorities expressed appreciation for his contributions to strengthening the Polish army. Rokossowski and Soviet military advisors left Poland, and Khrushchev had to admit that, though Rokossowski was "a Pole by birth, he is not a Polish Pole, but a Soviet Pole."

In Warsaw, on 17 December 1956, a treaty between the Soviet government and the PRL government on the legal status of Soviet troops temporarily stationed in Poland was signed. The treaty clearly formalized two important provisions: the stationing of Soviet troops was temporary and would not in any way affect Poland's sovereignty or lead to interference in the country's internal affairs. The troops mentioned in the treaty were the contingent in the western and northwestern parts of the PRL and the units linking Moscow with the Soviet task force in Germany. The treaty fixed the total strength of the Soviet troops in Poland at between sixty-two thousand and sixty-six thousand, with thirty-nine cantonments. Any movement of the Soviet troops outside their cantonments required the consent of the PRL government, even for exercises and maneuvers. The Soviet troops stationed on Polish territory, the personnel of the military units, and the family members of Soviet servicemen were obliged to respect and comply with all requirements of Polish law. The Soviet troops enjoyed the same privileges and benefits as the Polish army.

In 1957, Khrushchev proposed to withdraw Soviet troops from Poland. His reasoning went as follows: "Why should we give rise to reproaches about keeping the Soviet army in the territory of Poland and thus allegedly compelling the Polish people to be under the constraints of Soviet policy?" However, Gomułka vehemently opposed this idea. It turned out that it was economically advantageous for Poland to have the Soviet troops pay for their stay in hard currency. Despite these objections, the Soviet contingent stationed on the territory of Poland was halved at the end of the 1950s.

On 5 March 1957, the "Demarcation Treaty for the Existing Soviet-Polish State Border in Its Section Adjacent to the Baltic Sea" was signed in Moscow. This Baltic seacoast section was described in detail in the treaty. Thus, all issues associated with the postwar identification of the border between the Soviet Union and the PRL were finally settled.

After the war, in the period from 1945 to 1947, not all the Poles remaining in the territory of the Soviet Union were able to return to their homeland. Therefore, as early as 1955, the Polish authorities raised the issue of the need to organize a new repatriation wave. In May 1955, the Soviet Foreign Ministry relayed to Vladimir Lebedev, Khrushchev's assistant, a memorandum from the Polish Foreign Ministry stating that, "in connection with military and postwar conditions[,] a considerable number of persons matching the criteria of the 1945 Treaty could not use the possibilities offered by the Treaty due to reasons beyond their control." This situation separated families. The Polish side was especially insistent on addressing the needs of children who had been separated from their parents.

First, the Presidium of the Supreme Soviet of the Soviet Union issued, on 13 July 1955 and then on 14 January 1956, resolutions to expand the following decree of the Supreme Soviet:

> On Withdrawal from Soviet Citizenship of Persons of the Polish and Jewish Nationalities, Former Polish Citizens, and Members of Their Families Resettling from the USSR to Poland and on Acquisition of Soviet Citizenship of Persons of the Russian, Ukrainian, Belorussian, Rusyn, and Lithuanian Nationalities and Members of Their Families Resettling from Poland to the USSR to include persons of the Polish and Jewish nationalities willing to evacuate from the USSR to Poland, as well as Soviet citizens of the Polish and Jewish nationalities who did not avail themselves of the right to evacuation to Poland under the Soviet-Polish agreement dated July 6, 1945.

Then, on 25 March 1957, the Soviet Union and PRL governments signed the "Agreement on the Time Schedule and Procedure of Further Repatriation of Persons of Polish Nationality from the USSR." The right to repatriation was granted to the following: (1) persons of Polish nationality who had been Polish citizens before 17 September 1939; and (2) children or persons of Polish nationality who had been Polish citizens before 17 September 1939 or those born afterward who did not have close relatives in the Soviet Union but did in the Republic of Poland and were petitioning Polish authorities for repatriation.

The agreement stipulated that anyone who had the right to repatriation and wanted to use this right but was serving in the Soviet army would be discharged and repatriated, while anyone who had the right to repatriation but was detained in a penal institution would be released before their term expired and would be repatriated or handed over to Polish authorities.

In addition, anyone of Polish nationality who was repatriated under that agreement would be deemed to have abandoned Soviet citizenship from the date of their departure from the Soviet Union and to have acquired Polish citizenship upon arrival in the PRL, while family members of repatriates, since they were not of Polish nationality, could retain or forgo Soviet citizenship in accordance with their desire as expressed in immigration documents. All provisions of the agreement relating to persons of Polish nationality also applied to persons of Jewish ethnicity who had been Polish citizens before 17 September 1939.

As a result, forty thousand people left the Soviet Union in 1956 and ninety-four thousand in 1957. By the beginning of 1958, there were still some three hundred thousand persons who were entitled to immigration but remained in the Soviet Union. At the request of the Polish authorities, the flow of immigrants was reduced to eight thousand persons per month. The Polish authorities indicated to their Soviet counterparts that they were unable to accept repatriates in municipal areas due to lack of jobs and decent living conditions.

The only thing Moscow was worried about was the use of Poland as a transit point for immigration to Israel, especially immigration of anti-Soviet-minded elements. Therefore, the parties soon agreed not to request and allow immigration for these former Polish citizens. Despite all these measures, at least fourteen thousand Jews of those repatriated from the Soviet Union to Poland in the 1957–59 period later immigrated to Israel via the PRL.

The number of applications for departure to Poland started to decline. By 1 May 1958, the Soviet Union's Ministry of Internal Affairs had only 22,000 applications under consideration. However, 86,000 persons left in 1958 and 32,000 in 1959. The second repatriation wave was completed in 1959. All in all, from 1955 to 1959, 245,500 people returned to the PRL. Through the fault of the Polish side, some Poles remained in the Soviet Union, primarily in Kazakhstan.

All of the formerly problematic issues concerning Soviet-Polish economic relations had by this time been resolved. Khrushchev wrote in his memoirs,

"Together with our Polish comrades we have reviewed everything meticulously and repaired injustices wherever we found them. The world prices were an indicator for us, a litmus test. We used this litmus test to check our economic relations and to set them right. If we had to pay anything additionally, we agreed and paid."

First of all, this matter of world prices concerned deliveries of Polish coal. According to Soviet statistics, from 1946 to 1953, Poland supplied the Soviet Union with 49.5 million metric tons of coal at special prices—$1.14 per ton—for a total of $56.2 million. The cost of that coal expressed in world prices would have been $577.2 million. The Soviet side alleged that the reason for special coal prices related to compensation for German assets in the territory of postwar Poland that had been ceded by the Soviet Union under a Soviet-Polish agreement dated 16 August 1945 and under protocols related to it and dated 25 November 1953. Having grasped the idea of the coal problem, Khrushchev arrived at the following explanation of its origin: "We gave the Poles the coal-abundant area of Silesia, an area we had taken from Germany and which they would not have were it not for us. Stalin believed that the coal delivered from there was, to a certain extent, payment for the blood our soldiers shed in the liberation of Poland." At the same time, the Soviet leader was compelled to acknowledge that such justifications were somewhat emotional and subjective, depriving them of legal value. At the time, with the Donetsk Basin's coal industry not yet rehabilitated, the Polish coking and coal power plants played an important role in ensuring the functioning of the Soviet economy in the Soviet Union's European sector.

There were also problems with settlements for Soviet commercial transits between Germany and the Soviet Union for the period from 1 January 1946 to 1 July 1954 with regard to Poland's defense industry (mainly military supplies from the Soviet Union) and construction of strategic facilities in Poland's territory (military airfields, railways, etc.).

A final settlement of the issue of Poland's reparations and associated issues about the mutual settlements of both sides also needed to be found. At Soviet-Polish talks in Moscow in November 1956, PRL prime minister Józef Cyrankiewicz stated that, immediately following the war, more material value had been moved out of Poland's western provinces than from the Soviet occupation zone in Germany. Eugeniusz Szyr, a member of the PZPR Central Committee, claimed that Poland had received considerably fewer reparations considering the losses caused by the artificially lowered coal prices. Soviet leaders contested these claims made by the Polish side.

According to Soviet estimates, the German assets ceded by the Soviet Union to Poland were valued at about $8.9 billion at prewar prices. As for the repatriation supplies the Soviet Union moved to Poland, the amount provided fully met Soviet obligations and amounted to $257.9 million at 1938 prices, or $595.4 million at the prices for the corresponding years, calculated using the United Nations' price indexes.

The claims associated with the special price of coal were settled by the Soviet side's forgiving of Poland's debt under Soviet loans (civil and military loans, worth $261.2 million and $276.8 million, respectively, and totaling $538 million, were written off). In November 1956, Cyrankiewicz reported to the Sejm on the Polish-Soviet negotiations held in Moscow on 15–18 November 1956 and underscored that, as of 1 November 1956, the Soviet side had written off Poland's debts and that this act "constitutes a full conclusion to the issue of the costs associated with coal supplied" at artificially low prices.

However, Poland's economic claims were not fully settled until the middle of 1957. On 31 May 1957, a meeting of the Soviet Presidium discussed the results of the Soviet-Polish talks on mutual economic relations that had been held in Moscow on 24–25 May. A resolution adopted at the meeting recommended "making steps to effectively settle any claims between the USSR and Poland" and to send Mikoyan to Warsaw "to inform the PZPR Central Committee of the decisions made by the CPSU Central Committee in connection with the talks."

In June 1957, an unofficial visit to Warsaw by the first deputy chair of the Soviet Council of Ministers highlighted the discussions taking place between Soviet and Polish leaders concerning previous difficulties in Soviet-Polish economic relations. Claims were finally settled. In a report given to a meeting of the Soviet Presidium on 15 June 1957, Mikoyan detailed the results of his visit and said that the Polish side had accepted the Soviet proposals to give up any mutual claims under Germany's reparations. On 4 July 1957, the "Final Protocol on Supplies Relating to Germany's Reparations in Favor of the USSR and Poland," as well as a number of other state documents regulating economic relations between the two countries, were signed in Warsaw.

The "Polish October" of 1956 had a significant impact on the democratic-minded Soviet intelligentsia, and it also sparked political interest in the more open and Western-oriented elements in the Polish mass media. Its impact was also felt in the fields of science and culture in Poland. The second half of the 1950s saw a repetition of the situation in the seventeenth century, when the cultural and political influence of the West penetrated Russia through Poland. The Soviet Union saw the emergence of the generation of the 1960s, who largely supported Poland.

In conclusion, it should once again be underscored that, fortunately, the Polish crisis, unlike the Hungarian one, was resolved using political means. The Poles managed the crisis themselves without military interference from the Soviet Union but at the cost of the revision of Soviet policy toward Poland. In 1956, Polish leaders used their own resources to settle a difficult situation in the country, and this independence had a great significance and impact on the Kremlin's policy with regard to subsequent political conflicts in Poland, especially in 1980 and 1981. Through the events of October 1956 and thanks to changes in Soviet-Polish relations, the Polish leadership won the right to an independent domestic policy. Poland's sovereignty had been strengthened.

9

THE DISSIDENT MOVEMENT

THE WAY TO FREEDOM IN CULTURE

Jerzy Pomianowski (Poland)

Professor, editor-in-chief of the monthly *Novaya Polsha*, member of the Polish-Russian Group on Difficult Matters since 2008.

Andrei V. Vorobyov (Russia)

Envoy extraordinary and plenipotentiary.

Aleksandr V. Shubin (Russia)

Director of the Center for the History of Russia, Ukraine, and Belarus, Institute of World History of the Russian Academy of Sciences.

JERZY POMIANOWSKI

THE WAY TO FREEDOM IN CULTURE

EVERYTHING THAT OCCURRED during the postwar half century in Polish-Russian cultural relations is distinguished by the absence of certain features in areas that might appear to be more profound or have greater impact on the daily lives of the two societies, such as the economy, governance, legislation, and security.

Culture has grown in significance everywhere, if only because the twentieth century saw a dramatic growth in the volume of information potentially accessible to everyone. The rapid development of media—radio, television, the Internet—meant that news, commentary, and related artistic works could bring awareness to everyone. Attempts by foreign occupiers or native authoritarian regimes to halt the process ultimately proved futile, despite their efforts, expenditures, and repression.

In Poland, this process had a distinct tradition. The period when Poland was partitioned by foreign powers had deprived Poles of influence over the legal, administrative, and, as a result, material conditions of their existence. This gave greater significance to cultural activity and, hence, to the authority and influence of its representatives, including the unmatched adulation of national poets, the struggle to keep national themes in official education programs, and the determination to provide private and clandestine schooling and skills to publish and distribute illegal media. The failure of several successive armed uprisings only enhanced the importance of culture as a battlefield for preserving national identity and, importantly, for ensuring social development congruent with the vectors of Western civilization. The six-year period of German occupation convincingly demonstrated the significance of that tradition. The Polish network of clandestine schools (including universities), the number of underground newspapers, numerous lectures, "home" theaters and self-published books, and the wealth of young talent that appeared in the process was unmatched elsewhere in a terrorized Europe.

Salvation and Liberation

The post-Yalta period did not allow us to forget that tradition. This author is not a proponent of the following assertion, which is rather widespread in Poland: "The end of the war meant the replacement of one occupation with another." I believe that both we and the Russians should be more inclined to say that "the Poles were saved, but not liberated."

The Polish People's Republic was a state politically, militarily, and economically dependent on the imperial center—the leadership of the Communist Party of the Soviet Union and its executive body, that is, the government. Yet, we must not lose sight of the significant differences in the weight of that dependency during the pre- and postwar periods and within various areas of Polish life. For example, the extent of Polish dependence on Russia's strategic fuel supplies has remained the number-one problem for the present-day Polish economy, long sovereign in other areas. However, what happened with culture, even in the so-called previous period was—in contrast to the economy or government—more overt and thus better known to the public, even abroad. Moreover, at least in Poland, it was not subject to such close supervision or, in the event of divergence from the prescribed line, such harsh retaliation as was the case in other areas. That might have been because a measure of relaxation by the People's Republic of Poland (Polska Rzeczpospolita Ludowa, or PRL) in matters of culture, and art was intended to be a showcase of the country's autonomy.

Thus, the period of the PRL must not be considered a black hole in Poland's history. The eradication of illiteracy was not the only lasting example of corrected prewar negligence, and the collaboration of Polish and Soviet nuclear scientists at Dubna was not the only instance of fruitful cultural cooperation in that first postwar decade, when repression was so prevalent.

Paradoxes of Indoctrination

It was culture and education that became more important to the communist authorities—in theory, if not in practice—than the system of repression. By this, I mean "indoctrination." Originally, it was intended to exhort people to build—collectively and willingly—a world without exploitation, violence, racial prejudice, religious superstition, class privileges, or, above all, fear of the authorities. Alas, by the time Poland became involved in the operation, any chance of conducting this transformative education through persuasion had been exhausted. Soviet practice had effectively compromised the founding tenets of communism, and all attempts to put the system in place around the world produced the same results. The most visible feature was the need to use coercion and force in every sphere, from the economy to science to art.

Admittedly, force in these areas was used sporadically in the People's Republic of Poland, though coercion was widespread. The tools of coercion and force included censorship and the imposition of prescribed methods, styles, and doctrines in research and art. Whoever did not espouse the Lysenko doctrine in biology or socialist realism in art was banned from public activity, which left such scientists and artists to work without acclaim and in fear. In the Soviet Union, such restrictions were applied consistently and for the duration of the union. In Poland, communist cultural dogma produced results that were transitory and, at times, paradoxical:

> Socialist realism (proclaimed in 1949) in literature, music, and painting did not survive the thaw of 1956 (and came to be defined as "the poetization of sham statistics").

> Lavish festivals and visits by superbly trained (and usually uniformed) Russian choirs and ballet companies were seen as a show of force. Attendance was ensured by schools and army troops.

> Polish drama theaters were officially mandated to include in their repertoires a specific percentage of Soviet plays. Thanks to the resourcefulness of their directors, the works of Sukhovo-Kobylin, for example, had broader distribution in Poland than those of Sofronov.

> Obligatory teaching of Russian language and literature in schools (widely seen as a form of the russification of Poland) contributed to an almost total ignorance of the enormous Orthodox cultural tradition and Russian philosophy.

> Censorship continued to be diligent, but it was precisely its intrusiveness that led, with time, to the remarkable development in Poland of underground publications. The existence in Poland of legal enclaves of free thought and speech, where the access of censors was hindered, was equally important. These processes, which will be further discussed, were enhanced by the existence in Poland of the Catholic Church and the social stratum known as the "intelligentsia."

The Church as Refuge for the Regime's Heretics

Both Warsaw and Moscow realized the power and influence of the Church and its natural ties with the West in the only country of the socialist camp where the Roman faith was followed by an absolute majority of the population. Also, Poland was the transit country between the Soviet Union and East Germany, where more than twenty heavily armed divisions stood guarding the Soviet zone of influence.

Accordingly, social calm was essential to the Kremlin. As a result, attempts were made to divide the Church (e.g., the PAX Association, the transfer of "patriotic priests"). However, its outstanding dignitaries, including Cardinal Adam Stefan Sapieha and Primate Stefan Wyszyński, proved more skilled than their political antagonists in exploiting the ongoing changes to expand the Church's influence and widen the cultural boundaries laid down by the regime. The "thaw" (after the Twentieth Congress of the CPSU) restored Primate Wyszynski's freedom and returned *Tygodnik Powszechny*—a quality journal—to its founders (later, it would publish the writings of outstanding lay intellectuals, after the censors had closed down other "excessively liberal" periodicals). Publishing houses such as the Catholic Znak and the Dominican W Drodze issued (even during martial law) the writings of banned authors and the works of Second Russia writers and philosophers—either emigrants or persons banned in their own country—such as Vasily Rozanov, Nikolai Berdyaiev, and Dmitry Filosofov. Catholic "intelligentsia clubs" were established under the Church's aegis and played host to highly valued artistic events and scientific conferences. In those crucial decades preceding Karol Wojtyła's pontificate, the Church in Poland was cultivating the cultural elite and links with the intelligentsia.

The Role of the Intelligentsia

The intelligentsia in both Poland and Russia plays a special role that is more prominent than in other countries. Even if social classes, estates, guilds, and religious communities in Poland and in Russia managed to raise their voices, they did it exclusively in defense of their own sectional interests and aspirations. In Poland, this was caused by many centuries of foreign occupation and, in Russia, by the nearly timeless inability of subjects to influence the decision making of autocratic political power. The state of the country and the prospects of society were determined by these autocratic rulers who, alas, had no monopoly on wisdom—something that became increasingly obvious with the development of education and mass media.

In these circumstances it was inevitable that, sooner or later, a certain number of people would appear in both societies who, on the one hand, did not have particular interests and privileges and thus did not seek to defend them and who, on the other hand, were aware of the needs of the society at large and wished to advance them. Some people describe this as concern for the national interest, though in essence we are talking about interference in matters that hitherto had been exclusively reserved for the authorities. That circumstance and not the intelligentsia's sins—true or imaginary—was the root cause of the numerous campaigns against it, campaigns that usually signaled a rise in autocratic tendencies among the authorities.

In the West, the term "intelligentsia" is often placed inside quotation marks, signifying its foreign origin. Rightly so. The citizens of Western countries obviously cultivate their interests and those of their group, but they know that these rights are guaranteed by institutions established in the past (the Magna Carta or the American constitution) to protect them from abuse by the government. That, too, is the reason why citizens are often capable of relinquishing particular claims in defense of their state and thus feel no need to have a separate group of intellectuals preoccupied with the good of society as a whole.

The societies of Poland and Russia were long deprived of the right to "interfere"—to determine the fates of their countries. That may be the reason why group, party, and corporate claims often prove to be more important in our countries than the general interest. That is also the reason why Solidarity seemed a fortunate exception to that pattern. Indeed, its success was unprecedented in the history of our glorious defeats. Solidarity was not a movement in defense of material claims. Its crowning achievement—the compromise reached in the Round Table talks—became a watershed because of a phenomenon long awaited by generations of utopists: an alliance of working-class leaders and the elite of the Polish intelligentsia.

That phenomenon materialized after a long half century of setbacks and disappointments, in the presence of foreign troops and native administrators of the country, amid stinging poverty and a sense of isolation. Still, it was the Polish stone that set off the whole rockslide that went on to obliterate the walls and bars of communism.

The role of people of culture in that endeavor and the mobilization of critical minds determined the success of the project as much as the fortunate confluence of material circumstances. The Soviet leadership was loath to intervene in the country of uprisings, of which Gen. Aleksandr Lebed had written, "It was Russia's nightmare in the nineteenth century." In turn, the Polish United Workers' Party leadership overestimated its ability to maintain the status quo. Yet, it was also crucial that far-sighted strategists became involved so that the strike package of worker and union demands could be armed with a political warhead.

On 4 June 1989, parliamentary elections were held, resulting in the unavoidable defeat of the regime.

Resistance of the People of Culture

The path to that semifinal was not as straight as it might seem. It was marked by major military encounters, including armed clashes until the 1950s between sizable insurgent units (led by Warszyc, Łupaszka, and Szary) and security forces, by bloody suppression of worker revolts in large cities (Poznań in 1956, the Pomeranian tri-cities area in 1970, Radom in 1976), and by massive strikes—particularly in Łódź and along the Baltic coast—that almost evolved into a general strike. Here, however, we are concerned by other acts of resistance against the regime, undertaken by the unarmed authors, publishers, printers, and distributors of illegal brochures, newspapers, and periodicals, by the lecturers of "flying universities," by the actors who recited and sang in churches and private homes. A special place among them is occupied by the organizers, writers, commentators, news readers, and technicians of radio stations and editorial offices outside Poland. Despite the diligent jamming of their broadcasts, they had large and enthusiastic audiences in Poland. The Polish section of Radio Free Europe was especially noteworthy (particularly when it was led by Jan Nowak, i.e., Zdzisław Jeziorański). Its listeners constituted a veritable army of silent resistance.

These efforts were characterized, first of all, by the remarkably high number of publications and their relatively large print runs; second, by the spontaneous engagement of top Polish artists and specialists; and, third, by their effectiveness, that is, their substantial impact on public opinion. The handful of intellectuals who were involved in this work on a full-time basis remember the 1970s and 1980s as the most eventful time of their lives.

These people produced more than twenty-seven hundred different current-events and political newspapers, weeklies, and other journals, distributed clandestinely (particularly during martial law). In Wrocław, the weekly *Z dnia na dzień* had 524 issues over a ten-year period. The weekly *Hutnik* was published outside Kraków for eight years, until 1980. The Białystok *Solidarność* had 180 issues in the years 1980–90, while the Gdańsk *Solidarność* appeared 229 times within the same period. The literary-social journal *Krytyka* was published for thirteen years in a row, starting in 1977. *Obserwator Wielkopolski* appeared from 1981 until 1990. *Karta,* a book-format periodical, collected and published key government and underground documents and is still doing this today. The most important among these publications, *Mazowsze* (a Solidarity press organ), brought out 290 issues over eight years, beginning in February 1982. It was headed by Helena Łuczywo, and the authors included Adam Michnik, who contributed to the newspaper between his stays in prison.

The catalog of the National Library contains the titles of fifty-five hundred books published illegally in Poland in the years 1976–90.

Young Polish expatriates were not idle, either. *Aneks,* launched by Aleksander Smolar and continued by his brother Eugeniusz Smolar and Nina Smolar, achieved a prominent position. In Paris, Barbara Toruńczyk published the first editions of *Zeszyty Literackie,* which are still thriving. The Catholic *Spotkania* was published in both Lublin and Paris. Also in Paris, the monthly *Kontakt* had twenty issues; it was ingeniously smuggled to Poland. Its publisher, Mirosław Chojecki, established an efficient film studio. It produced a unique documentary about Józef Czapski and, importantly, a film about Jerzy Giedroyc and his *Kultura*.

The Role of the Paris *Kultura*

This wealth of publishing and conceptual initiatives was largely inspired by Jerzy Giedroyc and the Paris monthly *Kultura,* which he founded after the war. It was his example and cool-headed persuasion that convinced Polish intellectuals of the power of well-chosen words and arguments, even if expressed in isolation but with the certainty of being right. That attitude was exemplified by the consistent campaign in the 637 issues of the journal to gradually convince thinking Poles that Vilnius and Lvov, both jewels of Polish culture, were due the Lithuanians and Ukrainians so they could regain their former capitals. With those capitals ceded, Poles would have by their side allies instead of oppressed and hostile minorities.

The circulation of *Kultura* did not exceed seven thousand, but the journal had disproportionately high influence, since it was addressed to the intelligentsia—a stratum that enjoyed authority despite the attacks and cajoling of the government. *Kultura* published the works of the most outstanding expatriate and domestic writers, which removed the compulsion for the latter to choose between silence and hypocrisy. It was *Kultura* that published the diaries of Witold Gombrowicz and Gustaw Herling-Grudziński and the essays of Jerzy Stempowski. It was *Kultura* that allowed the likes of Konstanty Jeleński, Stefan Abner, Antoni Pospeszalski, and Leopold Unger to bring Polish journalism out of its backwater.

Kultura oversaw the elaboration of a future democratic vision of the country. It was based not on delusions but on precise calculations that may have appeared dubious at the time since they assumed thwarting the pressure of the geopolitical vise gripping Poland and thus depriving the country of lasting independence. Giedroyc lived to see that vision fulfilled. The relevant guidelines had been formulated earlier by Juliusz Mieroszewski, a spokesman for Giedroyc. This catalog of principles of Poland's eastern policy should form the core of Polish strategic doctrine if foreign policy were to be granted its due priority, preceding internal intrigues.

The first component of this concept consisted of the postulate of seeking the best possible relations with Russia, as long as that did not happen at the expense of the independence and vital interests of Ukraine, Lithuania, and Belarus. After all, the centuries-long, bloody conflicts between Russia and Poland were rooted in the striving of both to achieve domination over these countries.

A second equally important element was the conviction that only the citizens of Russia could change the country, its politics, and its relations with its neighbors. Assuming mutual regard, no intervention, pressure, or sermons were permissible, which ruled out any deliberations on hegemony and zones of influence.

Both these initial postulates are still valid. Their fulfillment depends not on agreements and declarations but on the consolidation of mutual respect in the sphere of Polish-Russian relations. This, in turn, necessitates an essential change of content and instruments in the areas of culture, information, and education. And here, we approach the crux of the matter: the state of affairs does not have to be ominous if we see Russia as something more than just a *pays légal*.

Literature and Relations between Societies

While relations between Russia and Poland have been tense on occasion and are still cool, contacts between Poles and Russians have been subject to completely different and quite paradoxical norms. This especially true of the intelligentsia of the two countries. Let us spare ourselves journeys into history and peruse a few examples from these regions.

When the PRL was still analogous to a klutzy teenager and censors played its zealous chaperone, brilliant writers who could not publish their own books without experiencing debasing hypocrisy earned their living as translators. As it turned out, Russian literature was something more than just the darling of subservient state publishing houses. It was discovered anew by demanding readers. One of the reasons was that in the previous (nineteenth) century, it just wouldn't do for a patriot to know the language of the foreign occupiers. As a result, Dostoyevsky had to be retranslated in Poland from its translations into French. In the 1920s, it was mostly the works of contemporary writers that were translated, and rather selectively at that. And then, in the 1950s, thanks to good translations, Grushenka and Prince Mishkin became the heroes of conversations and dreams (even though both characters abhorred Poles, as did Fyodor Mikhailovich himself). Even literary right-wingers translated masterpieces hitherto unknown or poorly translated. Paweł Hertz did a beautiful translation of Muratov, while Maria Dąbrowska herself tackled Chekhov. At a time when Soviet advisors—the likes of Dmitry Wozniesienski and Antoni Skulbaszewski—reigned supreme in the Polish secret service, Russian literary classics saved Poles from sinking into russophobia.

When the thaw began after Stalin's death, rehabilitated Soviet writers turned out to be a greater revelation for Polish readers and publishers than James Joyce or Françoise Sagan. People in love were not the only ones who raved over Akhmatova, while the magnificent Ewa Demarczyk received ovations in Krakow's Piwnica pod Baranami (Cellar under the rams) venue and at the Olimpia in Paris for her sung rendition of Osip Mandelstam's poem about a Gypsy girl. Sayings from the Odessa short stories of Isaac Babel made their way into the language of the Warsaw streets. Evgeny Schvartz's *Dragon* premiered in Warsaw long before it was staged in Moscow. The story with Ilya Ehrenburg's *The Stormy Life of Lasik Roitschvantz* was the same: it became a literary hit in Poland in the late 1950s, while in Russia it remained practically unknown until the disintegration of the Soviet Union.

Giedroyc and his Literary Institute did more than anyone else to help Poles discover that other Russia. Mikhail Heller was editor of the regular "Russian Notes" feature in *Kultura*. In addition to *Kultura* and *Zeszyty Literackie,* Giedroyc published 541 books banned in Poland by censors. Polish translations of Russian works were prominent among them. They included

Boris Pasternak's *Doctor Zhivago,* Aleksandr Solzhenitsyn's *The Gulag Archipelago, The First Circle,* and *Cancer Ward,* writings by Andrei Sakharov, and historic works by Mikhail Heller. Some Russian authors, such as Andrei Sinyavsky and Yuri Daniel, sent their manuscripts to Giedroyc for translation before submitting them to émigré Russian publishers.

The Russian *samizdat* (the practice of copying and passing along censored materials) no doubt served as inspiration for Polish clandestine publishing. The extent of the latter was impressive during martial law. The NOWA publishing house alone issued and illicitly distributed more than five hundred Polish translations of Russian books. They included works by Akhmatova, Brodsky, Bunin, Pilnyak, Zamyatin, Mandelstam, Shalamov, Voinovich, Yerofeyev, and Solzhenitsyn.

Skeptics might say, "But all this is just food for the elite"—that narrow stratum of the intelligentsia dismissed even by such democratic scholars as Józef Chałasiński as "a foreign body, an illegitimate offspring of the gentry." Let us then point out that this intellectual Polish elite in its absolute majority hailed from villages, small towns, and working-class suburbs; credit for its social advancement is due to the period of the People's Republic of Poland. As for the attitude of the average Pole to Russians, from the moment they started visiting Poland, not in uniforms but in civilian clothes, we didn't hear them complaining about the xenophobia of the local population.

The Mutual Influence of People of Culture in Poland and Russia

It probably would take a Russian scholar to describe the Russian response to Polish cultural initiatives and the related obstacles that can be conquered only through joint efforts. Yet, certain characteristic and uncommon phenomena are already evident.

Official Soviet undertakings in the sphere of culture and art did not have their intended propaganda and ideological effects. This was determined by the contrast between the message of the propaganda and the reality Poles knew from personal experience. The obvious fundamental function of films, plays, most contemporary books, and artistic performances was the promotion of the Soviet system and its attributes. This was totally out of step with the Polish gift to recognize—after the experience of the German occupation—the sinister marks of looming violence. Even those who believed that Bolshevik ruthlessness was the only effective antidote against a possible regression of the fascist scourge soon learned that the cure was not necessarily better than the ailment. Such was the fate of Tadeusz Borowski, a prisoner of Auschwitz and one of the greatest talents of postwar Polish literature, who committed suicide after many years of defending the PRL regime.

The thaw opened the door to artistic exchanges, though true change only took place thanks to the diffusion into the Soviet Union of Polish versions of

Western books, music, and news about the cinema and theater that had been cleared for distribution in Poland, while their Russian translations—or even reports about them—were still banned in the Soviet Union.

The monthly *Polsha* (Poland) proved to be a valuable vehicle. Although subject to censorship, it was edited intelligently and offered a richly diverse fare, including foreign news. Its top circulation reached a dizzying 350,000 copies. Alas, mass demand for the journal ended with the implosion of the Soviet regime: Russian windows and ears were now wide open to news from the West, so this Polish vent became redundant. But Poles still have reason to share their experience, reflections, and works of their artists with the Russians. That was the reason why Jerzy Giedroyc persuaded me to launch and edit *Novaya Polsha* (New Poland). After ten years of publication, its editors have two reasons for satisfaction: it is dependent only on its readers and is the sole platform for dialogue between the Polish and Russian intelligentsia (a third of the authors are Russian). It would be highly desirable if a similar magazine appeared in Poland to provide reliable information to the Polish intelligentsia about the problems of the new Russia.

To return to the thaw and the celebrated cohort of the *shestidyesyatniki* (literally, Sixties people): that was the time when a veritable explosion of Polish-mania took place in the Soviet Union. Iosif Brodsky commented, "We needed a window to see Europe, and the Polish language opened that window for us." It so happened that the magnificent poet read Joyce's *Ulysses* (in Maciej Słomczyński's translation), Faulkner, and even Proust in Polish. Thanks to his command of self-taught Polish before leaving Russia, he translated poems by Wat, Herbert, Kubiak, Staff, Harasymowicz, Rymkiewicz, Gałczyński, and even Norwid. It was only in the United States that he started translating Czesław Miłosz, found the Pole to be a brilliant poet, got to know him personally, and, doubtless, was highly instrumental in Miłosz being awarded the Nobel Prize.

While there were many more such examples, works with "Polish themes" written in the final period of the Soviet Union seem mostly superficial.

The events of 1980–81, followed by martial law and the watershed years of 1989–91 in both countries, opened the way for Russian works connected with Poland that were written without a hint of coercion. Understandably, it all started with journalism. A campaign by the Paris weekly *Russkaya Misl*, edited by the magnanimous yet uncompromising Irina Ilovayska-Alberti, had the greatest impact. It published the remarkable story of Solidarity, penned by the eminent poet Natalia Gobanyevskaya; her articles, later collected in a separate volume, had the character of an ideological wake-up call rather than a chronicle. The Moscow monthly *Innostrannaya Literatura* also made a great contribution, thanks to such experts on Polish culture as Ksenya Starosyelskaya, Andrei Yermonsky, and Asar Eppel.

Alexander Galich wrote *Ballad about the Eternal Flame* in the same spirit and at the same time, though as an émigré, as poems written by Boris Slutsky, Iosif Brodsky, and Vladimir Britanishsky, replete with Polish motives, which were published in a free Russia. It was then that Russian writers could for the first time address topics such as Katyn or the secret protocols of the Ribbentrop-Molotov Pact. However, accounts authored by such outstanding Polish reporters as Ryszard Kapuściński, Wojciech Jagielski, Krystyna Kurczab-Redlich, Wacław Radziwonowicz, and Marcin Wojciechowski demonstrate that the interest of Poles in present-day Russia is growing, regardless of any changes in the political climate.

Past Tense—Future Tense

The dialogue on these crucial issues is not over. It is hindered by a tradition of communist propaganda and mental habits rooted in the forty-year period of Soviet domination over the entire bloc. Admittedly, this situation has aroused in Poles a desire to separate themselves from Russia and its influences. We have also witnessed the swelling of an antagonism that could dominate the mood in a once-conquered country. But that is not the only Polish tradition: in 1830, Polish insurgents inscribed the words "For your freedom and ours" on their banners—something unprecedented in the struggles of subjugated nations against their conquerors. Their contemporary descendants—and we underscore this without any undue pride—likewise did not turn their resentment, disappointment, and hostility against Russians but, as a rule, against the imposed system and manifestations of the Bolshevik order. It needs to be emphasized *sine ira et studio* that even in numerous underground press and literary publications previously mentioned one would be hard put to discover deliberations generally hostile or insulting to Russians, that is, imbued with russophobia.

The bandying about of that term has regrettably become the trademark of xenophobic and chauvinistic groups among the ascendant right- and left-wing extremists and thus a problem for the government of the Russian Federation (see the Levada Center report of October 2008, discussed in the *Novoye Vremya* issue of 16 March 2009). Those displaying these tendencies are easily identified by their attitude toward the subject of our deliberations. Until recently, their attacks against Poland as the standard-issue enemy of Russia coincided with periods of economic or political controversy between Russia on the one hand, and the European Union and North Atlantic Treaty Organization, on the other.

Even verified facts (such as Lavrentiy Beria's proposition and Stalin's decision of 5 March 1940, which led to Katyn, or the conviction of sixteen leaders of the underground Polish state for treason against the Soviet Union) have been negated by representatives of the red or black reactionaries. A good example is Stanislav Kunyayev's *The Gentry and We*—a bizarre caricature of the history of Polish-Russian relations. I'll pay a king's ransom to the person who can find anything in the Polish press or prose written in a similar tone about Russia. It is not enough to engage in reasoned polemics—as we tried to do on the pages of *Novaya Polsha,* with the involvement of credible experts. A good example of what I mean is an article by Prof. Andrzej Nowak about the fates of Russian prisoners of war in Polish captivity in 1920, headlined "Ten Questions to Russian Historians"; to date it has not elicited any response.

The avoidance of similar issues has prevented frank dialogue between Russians and Poles. Yet, such dialogue is necessary and should not be hindered, seeing as how the historic bones of contention have disappeared and the intellectual opinion makers of the two countries have cultivated mutual amity and common traditions. Thus, we have created a pool of tested experts and talents, capable of productive endeavors in the realm of culture. Even in periods of political tension, this terrain has never been a wasteland. Thus, whatever happens within its bounds deserves stronger, consistent political support on both sides. That is what we have attempted to demonstrate.

Concluding Remarks

The above developments and political circumstances, their evolution and consequences, lead to conclusions that might be reduced to the following straightforward observations:

> The official attempts during the existence of the bloc to use the realm, assets, and cadres of culture in order to stiffen political discipline and boost the propaganda of the mandated ideology had, as a rule, effects opposite to what was intended. The reason for that was not the Poles' supposedly innate russophobia or their yearning for the prewar order but the obvious contradiction between theory and reality. The falsehood was particularly striking in descriptions of recent military history and the Polish resistance movement, served up by the media and taught in schools. In Russia, that situation has not changed to date.

> Despite this situation, Poles' interest in Russian culture and its assets has not dissipated, largely thanks to the animated and growing development of informal links with independent creators and activists of independent culture, barely tolerated in the Soviet Union. Pasternak, Okudjava, Visotsky, Galich, Maximov, Sakharov, and Solzhenitsyn kept citizens of the People's Republic of Poland from disrespecting Russia.

> A special role in this cultural ferment was played by Polish opinion-making expatriate institutions. Giedroyc's *Kultura* and Radio Free Europe never stooped to attacks against Russians, accentuating the difference between the Soviet order and state violence on the one hand and the Russian people and its intellectual leaders on the other. Works of Russian writers and historians

published by the Paris Literary Institute made Poles aware of another Russia, one that instilled respect rather than fear.

The stance of the Roman Catholic Church in Poland—particularly during the pontificate of John Paul II and thanks to his profound thesis about the "two lungs" of Christianity—contributed to an important breakthrough in research and publications concerning Russia's spiritual life and the part of its tradition that Soviet propaganda sought to stifle.

The intelligentsia of both countries has been the mainstay of a spontaneous cultural exchange, as evidenced by the popularity in the Soviet Union of the Polish language, the considerable readership of *Polsha,* and the renown enjoyed by Polish writers and artists (Brylska, Demarczyk, Olbrychski, Wajda, Zanussi). Similar phenomena occurred in Poland. Even after the transformations and disintegration of the bloc, the press runs of translations of Yerofeyev, Pyelevin, Babel, Tsvyetayeva, Solzhenitsyn, and nineteenth-century classics have remained as high as before. Polish theaters certainly are not adverse to productions of Russian drama. *Novaya Polsha*—with its online edition—has become a vehicle for unrestrained Polish-Russian dialogue.

The circumstances previously set out clearly indicate where we should focus our endeavors. Without expecting a mass response and rapid results, we need to consolidate and deepen the ties between the Polish and Russian intelligentsia as the stratum of opinion makers traditionally committed to an exchange of ideas and experience.

Conflicts of interest are unavoidable in international political life. It would be futile to hope that Polish-Russian relations will be immune to them. However, it is the task of politicians to find civilized channels for the amicable resolution of conflicts, rather than try to sweep them under the rug. Culture and science assume a special significance in this, for theirs is a realm not only of artistic performance and research but also of conflicting political concepts, often contradictory by their very nature. These contradictions not only concern theoretical issues but also current economic interests and political plans. In order for them not to degenerate into conflict, it is essential that they first be debated by experts, before being addressed by politicians. Today, this rule applies only to members of the European Union; indeed, the EU was established to implement such principles. It would be expedient at this point to find a similar institutional solution in order to remove from the field of Poland's relations with Russia various fossils and to keep it from becoming overgrown with weeds.

Examples of "weeds" include such incomprehensible situations as the retention in Russia of treasures of Polish culture removed from our country at the end of World War II. The library of the Brothers Zaluski, patrons of the Polish Enlightenment in the eighteenth century, is just one instance. Polish scholars are denied access to the library, even though it is stored in Saint Petersburg, the capital of the Russian Enlightenment.

It is of upmost importance to cultivate links with those in Russia who wish to exchange ideas, not just exhibits or goods. Cooperation between nongovernmental organizations, artistic associations, academic schools, scientific institutes, and societies is no longer subject to government control and does not require an official seal of approval. We should exploit this unprecedented opportunity without delay. Regardless of fluctuations in intergovernmental links, we should use this path to enhance the understanding of Polish views and objectives by Russians at large.

ANDREI V. VOROBYOV AND ALEKSANDR V. SHUBIN

· ·

THE WAY TO FREEDOM IN CULTURE

· ·

WHILE ARGUING ABOUT the intellectual influence Poland and Poles have exerted on Russia and Russians (as well as vice versa, since the process can only be seen as an interaction between the two great peoples and their brilliant cultures), it makes sense, we think, to consider a broader historical background, rather than just the early postwar years. That interaction and historical relationship have rarely been mentioned in recent years, at least in the mass media. Certainly, our countries have always had essential differences in civilization, their development paths being opposite. But it is on the boundaries of nations and ethnic groups that unique cultural phenomena and processes often appear, as proven by plenty of evidence in Russian-Polish history, including names, events, and archaeological and cultural finds. Regretfully, in remembering and realizing all that, we are much worse than the two previous—let's call them "socialist"—generations and much worse than those who lived in the two decades between World War I and World War II or earlier.

Why is it so? That's a different question, but it seems like this mutual ignorance and misunderstanding still affects today's political and journalistic analysis of bilateral relations, making it poor and superficial. The "old guard" clashes of opinions sounded much more expressive and thorough, both philosophically and literarily. Czesław Miłosz, never sentimental about the eastern neighbor, wrote picturesque memoirs about Russia. "The Russian language," he writes in *Rodzinnej Europie*, "was an appeal to Poles as it unleashed the Slavic part of their souls. The language contained everything worth learning from Russia. Learning the language, Poles learned how not be too serious about themselves." Today this notion is gone, unfortunately. Sometimes one can feel that those Poles who lived through the disasters of the twentieth century or suffered in a Gulag prison had a better attitude toward Russia and better understood it than some recent members of former communist youth organizations or graduates of prestigious European universities. Wojciech Jaruzelski in the early 1980s, on the way from an officers' cemetery in Powązki after the funeral of a fellow soldier with whom he had served in the Polish First Tadeusz Kościuszko Division, uttered a noteworthy phrase: "We just paid our last respects to Wacek, and I remember me wrapping my father like a dog, in a *Pravda* newspaper[,] after he died in Siberia in 1942." Nevertheless, General Jaruzelski never hated Russia.

Russia has always held appeal for Poles, as well as for Europeans, with their mixed feelings about the eastern neighbor. As one modern philosopher aptly put it, Russia has been and will be "the subconscious of the West." The Russian attitude toward Europe, of which Poland has always been an integral part, even when in the Russian Empire, was expressed long ago, and the man who did it was not a Westerner: "Oh, gentlemen, do you know how dear Europe is to us . . . ? Europe is a terrible and a sacred thing." This statement belongs to Fyodor Dostoyevsky, one of the "pillars" of slavophilism.

Many Russians had periods of passion for Poland. For some, it was like the first step toward European ideas and values, while others came to a deeper understanding of Russia's original values. One of the authors of this book, while in his twenties, learned Polish and once was surprised by a Polish translation of the work of Bulat Okudzhava, a Russian poet and songwriter, as he could see a clear difference between the original, "When victory's over, we foolishly mount a statue. And fame of the statue is over the victory's fame," and the Polish translation, "Pedestals remain, but figures are gone" (Górują cokoły, na których nie stoi już nikt).

On reflection, it is this difference that, to a great extent, has determined our eternal and deep curiosity about each other, our mutual affinity and interaction in intellectual dissidence in the two nations.

Not surprisingly, the terms "dissident" and "dissidence movement" originally came to Russia from Poland. Drowning in information presented by today's mass media, we lost the origin of the term long ago, but Russia still remembers that, in the past, it referred to those Orthodox Christians who opposed forced conversion to Catholicism. This "aggravated" etymology is likely to have affected the way the term "dissident" was perceived in Russia in the 1960s after it appeared again but in reference to members of intellectual movements opposed to the official socialist doctrine, as they were treated with prejudice. Most people in the Soviet Union did not care about dissidents, despite the efforts of Radio Liberty, and numerous underground publications paled in comparison with multimillion-copy print runs of the official press.

For a better understanding of the dynamics of the dissident movement, one should realize that the Russian version, unlike that in Poland, originated and developed all along as a natural part of Soviet socialism. It could not have been otherwise, as Russian dissidents were under the influence of the victories of World War II, which has always been seen in Russia as the Great Patriotic War. Even now, the tragedy of 1941 and the victory of May 1945 still affect the mentality of Russian society and its political elite, and it undoubtedly had a greater influence on the war generation and its descendants. Not surprisingly, during the first postwar decade, those who would doubt the official ideology would be clearly considered traitors to their country. The phenomenon of Soviet dissidence goes back to First Secretary Nikita Khrushchev and his "secret speech" at the Twentieth Communist Party Congress, which became the first major blow to the seemingly monolithic Soviet ideology. People understood that, from then on, socialism could be subject to criticism, although criticism was to be limited to Stalin's time and aimed at improving the Soviet system and its position in the global competition. Yet, it was the beginning. Civil unrest in Poland and Hungary shortly after the Twentieth Congress shocked many Soviet people even more.

This dramatic turn may be illustrated by interviews conducted with a large group of Soviet dissidents and political prisoners, recorded by Tatyana Kisinova for a project titled "Dialogue: Soviet-Polish Dissident and Cultural Relations and Interaction in 1950–1980," organized by the Memorial Humanitarian Society of Russia and the Eastern Archive of Poland in 1992–94.

In particular, Boris Pustintsev, a former Soviet dissident, recalled that

> all the developments taking place in Poland at that time were extremely interesting for us. It looked like the Bolshevik regime was about to transform. Poland has always been a bulwark of opposition to Russian regimes, whether before or after the Bolsheviks. After 1956, many Russians saw Poland as, if not an island of freedom, at least that of semi-freedom. It had nothing to do with political freedoms, as differences between the two regimes were negligible, if any. But there was something in the air, this free spirit intrinsic to Poles which engaged and attracted us.

Yet, Pustintsev admitted he appeared to be a "white crow" among his associates, oriented toward "a more progressive model of socialism," according to him. Marat Cheshkov, a postgraduate at the Moscow University economic school in the mid-1950s, found that, "while we were well versed in Marxist theory and liked to argue about its dogmas, Poles preferred to distance themselves from all that theoretical speculation, as if they didn't take it seriously." Those facts can be viewed as indirect evidence that most Russian dissidents were holding firmly to socialist beliefs. Even later, in the 1960s, Soviet revisionists still remained sure about their supremacy over Polish counterparts, as far as Marxist theory and methodology were concerned. But Poles still had an advantage; neither in 1956, nor later, did they openly stand up to Marxism. Instead, they downplayed its significance, preferring other theories and ideas adopted, of course, from the West. It should be recognized that, after

1956, Poland saw quick progress in the social sciences. Achievements by Polish social scientists were closely examined, if not followed, by their Russian counterparts.

The repercussions of the Hungarian uprising, with its disastrous magnitude, somehow became more significant for the time being, but Poland still remained closer to Russians, and it seems it will stay like that, since we have a common historical experience. This is exactly where the problem is: up to now, many have viewed relations between Russia and Poland through the lens of that past experience. Today, Russian researchers are lucky to have various historical judgments and points of view to consider. But, back in 1956, the new generation was well aware of the attitude of Aleksandr Herzen, Nikolay Chernyshevsky, social democrats, and even Mensheviks toward Poland, while they could be totally ignorant of what Fyodor Dostoyevsky or Mikhail Katkov thought about it. The likes of Lev Krasnopevtsev and Nikolay Obushenkov (both arrested in 1957 as members of an "anti-Soviet group consisting of professors and students of the Moscow State University related to Polish reactionaries") had considered it natural, since their school years, to enthusiastically support Polish liberation movements and cooperation with Polish opposition groups, and they gratefully remembered the role of Poles in fighting the Russian tsarist regime. That attitude toward Poland had been traditional for the Russian democratic intelligentsia, of whom many Soviet dissidents perceived themselves the successors. Time after time, blatant contradictions between democratic beliefs and national interests brought historic disasters to Russia. In particular, those contradictions were reflected in the fact that, in 2009, Lenin was still, as he was in 1956, portrayed as a democrat opposed to "totalitarian" Stalin—strangely enough, given that the tally of Russians killed during the Bolshevik Revolution and the subsequent civil war is hardly less than the number of people who fell victim to the purges in the 1930s. The very same contradictions contributed to some people connecting Lenin to democratic traditions established by Herzen (thankfully, that misconception was gone with the dissident discussions of the 1950s and 1960s). During the Soviet period, and because of those contradictions, the Soviet people confronted Soviet socialism. (Recall that Mikhail Gorbachev said in 1987, "We are all Soviet people.") People were destroying Soviet socialism while chanting, "We want more socialism!" Today, those nuances, even if remembered by some, do not puzzle anyone. That is regrettable, because many issues—technologies of perestroika in the 1980s, the transformation of political and party elites, and their incorporation into new social, political, economic, and financial structures throughout the Soviet bloc—did not receive scientific scrutiny.

Plainly, Soviet dissidents can no more be credited with the collapse of communist ideology and the Soviet communist state system than members of the Decembrist revolt in 1825 could be credited with the fall of the Romanov dynasty in 1917. But as was the case with the Decembrists, who, as Lenin put it, "awakened Herzen[,] who launched revolutionary agitation," Soviet dissidents played a major role in changing the political orientation of the Soviet elite and, to some extent, the Soviet people, in no small part due to the so-called *samizdat* (forbidden literature self-published by dissidents in the Soviet Union or smuggled from abroad) and its unique literary style. Vasile Ernu, a winner of many literary awards and an immigrant to Romania, raised an interesting point in his book *Born in the USSR*, saying that a Soviet dissident was "a product of collaboration between Soviet and anti-Soviet ideology," while dissidence was "art, a kind of common language, accepted *by both sides*." Many criminal files of Russian dissidents are not available for archival research, simply because some of those people or their relatives are still alive. This situation is sure to change over time, and then cryptograms of yet *another* side of Russia's history of the twentieth century will become more understandable.

Admittedly, in Poland they speak another political language, and Poles thus did not have to create an alternative mode of political thought, because there had always been the alternative—Polish émigrés in Europe. The only thing to do was to bring that alternative to the banks of the Wisła River. That goal was achieved as a Polish-émigré journal called *Kultura* came into being in 1946. Natalya Gorbanevskaya, a Russian poet and civil rights activist, described *Kultura* as "the best émigré journal in the world." The journal brought together prominent Polish intellectuals, and it was no wonder that the Paris-based *Kultura* was considered in Poland to be the most important repository of Polish thinking in the second half of the twentieth century. Its pages featured the work of many high-profile authors, including Czesław Miłosz, Witold Gombrowicz, Jerzy Stempowski, Marek Hłasko, Andrzej Bobkowski, and Konstanty Jeleński. Publishers from the beginning paid attention to Russia and kept in touch with Russian authors, whether residents of the country or emigrants. *Kultura* was edited and produced by Jerzy Giedroyc, the spirit and brain of the journal and a brilliant Polish intellectual who was born (ironically) in Minsk and had been a student (ironically) in one of Moscow's grammar schools. So, as nothing ever happens by accident, it was no wonder that relations with the eastern neighbors, their history, and their future had always been in the focus of *Kultura,* and Jerzy Giedroyc, apparently, was the first who called on his fellow Poles to forgive the injuries of 1939.

Paris-based *Kultura* managed to raise at least two generations of Polish intellectuals, and it became a veritable university for alternative thinking in Russia. Gorbanevskaya recalled a remarkable fact: Vladimir Maximov, a Russian émigré writer, decided to publish a journal that would differ from numerous Russian journals that already existed in Europe and would bring together all Russian emigrants. He asked Aleksandr Solzhenitsyn for advice. Solzhenitsyn answered without hesitation: "Talk to the people in *Kultura.* They will teach you." That was how the major Russian émigré dissident journal *Kontinent* started in the 1970s. Tatyana Maximova, the widow of its publisher, recalled that it was Solzhenitsyn himself who suggested the new periodical be named *Kontinent,* perhaps as a symbol of the face-off against the "Communist Archipelago." The journal was meant to bring together authors from all of Eastern Europe. Once again, Poles were the first to take part in the new project, as Vladimir Maximov had followed Solzhenitsyn's advice and told Giedroyc, Józef Czapski, and Gustaw Herling-Grudziński of *Kultura* about his idea. All three of them immediately joined *Kontinent*'s editorial board and worked there as long as it was published, though rumors circulated that they could not help envying *Kontinent*'s financial wherewithal, as it was sponsored by Springer, a global publishing company.

Kultura's ideological influence on Vladimir Maximov's *Kontinent* was obvious, though not that visible compared, for example, with the role it played in the development of Polish foreign policy after 1989, particularly since the mythological concept of the so-called Kresy (historical eastern territories), once followed by the London-based government in exile and some influential Polish intellectuals, today is seen as no more than nostalgia. The independence of Ukraine, Belarus, and Lithuania is no longer questioned by the Polish political establishment, even by extreme rightists, because they no longer consider it incompatible with Polish interests, and our Polish neighbors can take advantage of the geopolitical situation that appeared in Eastern Europe after 1991, as they still have other ambitious concepts from the 1920s to put into practice.

Maximov's *Kontinent* accepted the independence of Ukraine and other Soviet republics and even tried to promote it, but Soviet political elites would not change their view on the issue, which was quite natural in the 1970s, even with the influence of émigré journals that made Russian, Ukrainian, and Belarus political elites in the 1980s adopt a "graceful divorce" decision. Even Solzhenitsyn, with his own concept of rebuilding Russia and opposition to the partition of the Soviet Union, had no impact on those elites.

When, in the 1980s, the Solidarity movement emerged to challenge the communist nations' governments, as well as the old-style opposition, the importance of émigré and dissident publications completely faded.

Lyudmila Alexeyeva, a famous Russian dissident, recalled that, in the late 1970s, "the core of Moscow human rights activists included founders of this movement, who saw their activity as a purely moral opposition and didn't intend to pursue any political goals or a public following. Nor did they aim at turning it into a broader movement through involving other social groups, as the Polish opposition did, and when it just happened on its own they didn't appreciate it and, in fact, backed away from newcomers." Here lies the key difference between dissidents and the later generation of civil activists who set up opposition organizations in the 1980s.

It was the Solidarity movement that inspired young dissidents in the Soviet Union to look for ways to use the Polish experience of 1980–81. Unlike traditional human rights activists, these young people were ideologically slanted and somehow reminiscent of the underground groups of the late 1950s who had tried to follow the Polish and Hungarian experiences of 1956. For example, one of these organizations operating in the 1980s was called "Marxist Social Group 68–80."

In December 1980, chief editors of the samizdat journals announced the creation of the Free Cultural Trade Union. Although the idea eventually failed, it indicated a clear desire to get more social groups involved.

It is worth mentioning, however, that even before Solidarity emerged there had been attempts to create independent trade unions in the Soviet Union. For instance, in January 1978, Vladimir Klebanov, an engineer who had already "served a term" in a mental institution for his attempt to set up a committee to control labor conditions, tried to register a purely legal and loyal free trade union to protect workers' rights. He was immediately arrested, and the trade union, already consisting of two hundred relatively law-abiding citizens, broke down. Then, on 28 December 1978, a group of dissidents, including Lyudmila Agapova, Lev Volkhonsky, Valeriya Novodvorskaya, Vladimir Skvirsky, and others, announced the creation of the Free Interprofessional Association of Workers (SMOT).

Although not very successful, SMOT became the first dissident attempt of the so-called going to the people type (a reference to a Russian revolutionary movement of the nineteenth century), as well as a clear message to Soviet authorities that dissidents would not stay in the niche prepared for them by the communist system. "The mission of SMOT was to provide legal, moral, financial, and other assistance to its members. That included plans to create 'cooperative' units such as mutual aid funds, saving funds meant to buy or rent villas for joint use, [and] nursery schools if needed in some areas. There was even an idea of barter deals for goods [that were] in short supply. Suppose one could buy tea and condensed milk in Moscow and swap it for canned pork bought by someone else in Eastern Siberia, where it was occasionally available," Alexeyeva wrote.

However, some SMOT leaders adopted the radical views of the Solidarity movement, which led to failure of moderate ideas. In particular, Valery Senderov, who took part in publishing the *Information Bulletin,* SMOT's only successful project, proclaimed himself a member of the émigré National Alliance of Russian Solidarists. For him and the likes of Novodvorskaya, another prominent radical member, their association was no more than a tool that allowed them to turn to more aggressive activity. This is how Novodvorskaya explained the logic of the radical SMOT members:

> Kościuszko and Dąbrowski awakened the Committee for the Defense of Society (KOS) and Workers' Defense Committee (KOR). KOS-KOR in their turn awakened the Solidarity movement. In the Soviet Union, the 20th Congress of the Communist Party awakened Bulat Okudzhava and Yuri Lyubimov, who then awakened dissidents, but dissidents failed to awaken anyone, because the society was fast asleep. There was no awakening. The idea of independent trade unions in the USSR that inspired Vladimir Skvirsky ("granddad" as we called him), was just a platonic idea. Our Free Interprofessional Association of Workers (SMOT) was just a desperate Stakhanovite attempt of the forlorn intelligentsia to spawn a labor movement, in addition to its own dissident activity.

The Polish experience had an impact on the so-called young socialists movement. In the late 1970s, new samizdat "left-oriented" journals emerged, including *Left Turn,* published by Boris Kagarlitsky, and *Varianty* published by a group of fellow university graduates, including Andrey Fadin, Pavel Kudyukin, Mikhail Rivkin, Vladimir Chernetsky, Yuri Khavkin, and I. Kondrashyov. The journals covered a broad ideological spectrum, from right social democracy to European communism, though the left socialist orientation was predominant. Pavel Kudyukin described his views of that time as

> left social democracy with elements of revolutionary social democracy. Andrey Fadin and I didn't look at the West as something different. For us it was a part of the Third world. In this regard, our revolutionary activities targeted the West as well as the USSR, as we thought the West had its dead ends, which couldn't be fixed just by evolutionary development. Nevertheless, talking about revolution we didn't mean violence. In that we were definitely close to western "new leftists." We recognized that a crisis in the USSR could spark an explosion of violence and destruction. We wanted the Soviet empire to be replaced by a commonwealth with a plural economy consisting of public, municipal, and private sectors to be flexibly regulated by indicative planning. We wanted economic democracy, free trade unions, western-style political democracy, and democratic development at [the] grassroots level to get more people involved in public decision making.

Boris Kagarlitsky of *Left Turn* was a bit more leftist. Those journalists or "young socialists," as they would later be called, concurred there was a need for reforms at the top under pressure from below to make the socialist system more efficient and democratic.

In 1985–89, the designers of perestroika made similar ideas their official policy, but back in 1982, the plans of the "young socialists" caused concerns for the KGB. The young socialists criticized the regime, questioning whether it was indeed socialism. They hopefully followed the developments in Poland in 1980–81 and discussed the chances of the Polish experience being replicated in the Soviet Union. They intended to create a federation of socialist-oriented democratic forces as a core organization of the future revolution (earlier, the Revolutionary Communist Union had also planned to hold a conference of leftist groups). Traditional Soviet dissidents had abandoned any attempts to create a national political organization long before. No wonder the KGB focused on cracking down on the leftists. Only in 1987 was it made possible to legally set up the Federation of Socialist Clubs; back in 1982, the "young socialists" had been arrested. In a report to Yuri Andropov (who then was about to become secretary general, officially leaving the position of KGB chief), his successor Vitaly Fyodorchuk wrote that the detainees "took measures aimed at organizing in the country an underground movement, the so-called 'Federation of socialist-oriented democratic forces,' to actively fight the Soviet government, as they claimed in one of their 'theoretical' documents that 'Soviet Communism is a crime against human and humanity, and the USSR is a moral torture chamber for millions of people.' . . . The investigation found that Fadin on a regular basis passed to Maidannik, Sheinis, Vorozheikina, Rzhevsky, Daniliv, Ivanova, and Skorokhodov various anti-Soviet literature for studying."

"Young socialists" were thus connected to the scientist intelligentsia, who, in turn, had contacts with "liberals" in power. The KGB viewed their joint efforts as "subversive activities" aimed at creating an organization akin to KOS-KOR in Poland.

During the "normalization" period of 1982–84, Polish and Soviet opposition activists developed their ideas in a similar direction. Gleb Pavlovsky, a cofounder of *Poisky* (The quest), a samizdat journal, recalled:

[Mikhail] Gefter, [Vyacheslav] Igrunov, and I were seeking ways to a broader reality. At the same time, dissidents [Václav] Havel and [Adam] Michnik in Czechoslovakia and Poland, respectively, launched a discussion on a compromise that would lead their activities out of the isolated environment. For me, the Soviet Union was a result of compromise between real policy and social idealism that I wouldn't sacrifice. I believed the Soviet society was a society of equal individuals. If so, it made sense to go in for other political stuff, or else what is the use in going on if the social equality and empire of knowledge and education ceases to exist? After all, the Russian classic literature with its ideal of equity is a source of Russian Marxism. This is where our identity is.

But new radical groups interpreted the Polish experience as proof that a revolution was possible in order to overthrow the regime. Unlike the opposition groups of the 1950s through 1970s, radicals of the mid-1980s were lucky to see some of their plans turn into reality. For example, organizers of the famous Obshchina (Russian for "community") club during perestroika had planned to establish a structure akin to the Polish KOS-KOR—Solidarity

First. They were going to set up a lecture society ("Lektsyonnoe obshchestvo," LO) for the promotion of their ideas among workers and employees. If that was successful, the next step was to create labor social unions ("Trudovoy obshchestvennyi soyuz," TOS) to become instruments for oppositional activities such as that of Solidarity, including rallies, strikes, and so forth. The whole system was dubbed "Lotus" for the time being. "Lotuses" were expected to be set up in different Soviet cities to make up a national organization. Looking back at the revolutionary experiences of Russia, Nicaragua, and Poland, young leftists thought their first "attack" would create a system of connection and communication between various civil movements, and hence they would gain more freedom than before the revolution. That would allow them to redeploy their still semi-underground groups and then deal a fatal blow to the regime sometime at the turn of the next century.

The most striking thing is that the tactics of 1986 partially bore fruit. The second half of 1986 saw the creation of a discussion club that started to promote ideas. Some opposition activists used "Knowledge," the public educational organization, as a shelter for their opposition activities, as they managed to give hundreds of ideological lectures in the 1986–89 period. The year 1988 saw the formation of the Union of Opposition Socialist Political Clubs. Propaganda activities reached factories and offices in 1987. In 1989, activists established close ties with labor movements. In 1988–89, opposition activities in which the so-called social socialists played a key role turned into a mass grass-roots movement.

With the beginning of Gorbachev's perestroika, opposition activists, relying on the "Polish scenario," were purposefully looking for and quickly found one another. The site where their first contact took place was the Social Initiative Club (SIC), created in 1986 by G. Pelman, who managed to engage in its work B. Kagarlitsky. Kagarlitsky recollected his cooperation with Pelman as follows:

> At this time, we did not realize how different our vision was. We both wanted to have a place for communication, able to attract people of a certain type and to create a wider social milieu, open on the borderline between legal and illegal. This would appeal to both "status intelligentsia" like academician Zaslavskaya and "lumpen intelligentsia" ousted from the official system, like myself. As a result, I would like to form something like Polish KOS-KOR to reach the general public, not pure intelligentsia. Status intelligentsia can bring people together legally, while we can undertake organizational work. In a parallel way, similar work was being done by a club of friends of the *Echo* magazine, initiated in this case by the "status ones." Out of it in 1987 grew *perestroika*. I wanted it to be a chain of social initiative clubs that would have no clear ideological coloring. People were supposed to get to know each other in this open space. This indeed happened.

In 1987, the SIC engaged in its work the organizers of Obshchina. A participant with negotiations between the SIC and Obshchina, A. Isayev, recollected,

> There we started to present our Komsomol project [a program of opposition agitation under the guise of discussion at Komsomol, the All-Union Leninist Young Communist League] again and we received a lot of attention. It was clear from some remarks that the audience was radically anticommunist. When we mentioned methods of forbidding the discussion, we heard, "Oh, that's clear, the triumph of 'social democracy,' as usual." Least of all could we guess, for example, that M. Malyutin was a member of the CPSU. And after certain comments by Kagarlitsky we decided that this was a blatant hotbed, and an organization like Polish KOS-KOR. We have detected it quickly.

KOS-KOR for Russia became a kind of slogan of informal self-organization and its prospects. But opposition structures were formed under the conditions of acute competition aggravated by prior dissents that had taken place before perestroika and had been tearing the oppositionists apart. As a result, KOS-KORs were coming to the surface of social life one after another. On 21 May, Obshchina, via the SIC, established contact with the Baltic Club of Socially Active People (CSAP), the Extramural Social Political Club, and the Moscow club Perestroika. They all were striving to establish contacts with workers, and each of them had several activists from industrial enterprises.

However, the developments of 1988 showed that the democratic movement in the Soviet Union was not developing according to the Polish scenario. Attempts to create alternative trade unions were being made, but without much success. More promising was the organization of mass demonstrations. Nevertheless, leftist members of unofficial organizations did not forget about the importance of the labor movement. Thus, *Nezavisimy Vestnik*, the first opposition publication with a print run in the thousands, on 5 December 1988 published the article "Polish Cause," written by anarcho-syndicalists, on the summer strikes in Poland in 1980. On 18 December 1988, Obshchina members distributed a leaflet headed "For our and your freedom!" devoted to the anniversary of the suppression of Solidarity in 1981.

With the commencement of mass labor actions in the Soviet Union in the summer of 1989, the participants of KOS-KORs in 1987 rapidly established contacts with the leaders of the mass labor movement. Obshchina members, who created at that period the Confederation of Anarcho-Syndicalists (KAS), established a labor movement information center, which they defiantly called KAS-KOR (by analogy with KOS-KOR). In spite of the outrageous image of anarchism, labor leaders accepted the informational support of the Left. A representative of KAS became a member of the Council of Labor Confederation, established by miners and other industry movements.

This was the climax of the "Polish model" in the Soviet opposition. In the future, the KOS-KOR supporters and labor movements started to drift apart. The miners' leaders reoriented their sector toward a populist democratic movement headed by Boris Yeltsin, which was criticized intensively by the young Left. KAS-KOR began to cooperate not only with new trade unions but also with those All-Union Central Council of the Trade Unions members that had started to reform their structures and were released from direct supervision by the Communist Party. Subsequently, the KAS-KOR publishers joined the editorial staff of the newspaper of the Moscow Trade Union Federation, *Solidarity* (in the 1990s, the press organ of the Federation of Independent Trade Unions of Russia).

Simultaneously, with the implementation of the "Polish model," attention was focused on the situation in Eastern Europe, which determined in many aspects the success of the common struggle against the communist regime. Oppositionists in the Soviet Union and throughout Eastern Europe believed in networking events on both sides of the Soviet border and were helping each other as much as possible. The possibilities of "people's diplomacy" were used in official diplomacy as well.

As Pavlovsky recollected,

> KOS-KOR creator Adam Michnik came here, met with Chernyaev through Gefter, and presented his proposals on the compromise. They were accepted here, in the Central Committee, and this course was being pursued, until it was discovered after the election that there was absolutely nobody behind the communists in Poland. If the Soviet administration had realized that the situation in Eastern Europe was critical and it would be necessary to leave this territory anyway, it could have used the "people's diplomacy" channel to promote compromise counterproposals, which could be fixed in international treaties prior to the inevitable collapse of the Warsaw Pact bloc. But neither Gorbachev nor his more conservative colleagues realized these prospects. As a result, "people's diplomacy" was first and foremost used by the USSR opposition.

The 1989 revolutions were greeted by the Soviet opposition very enthusiastically, and meetings were held to show solidarity with Czechoslovak students (as well as Chinese students). The idea of the "roundtable" was adopted, brought forward for the Soviet Union by a KAS representative at a giant opposition meeting in Luzhniki in May 1989.

The magnitude of the events in the Soviet Union caught up with and overtook the scale of the opposition movement in Eastern Europe. The battle "for our and your freedom" was won the way fighters against the communist regime understood it. And our peoples were to struggle on their own for social rights and freedoms in the globalization era.

10

THE SOVIETS AND THE POLISH CRISIS

THE ROAD TO MARTIAL LAW, 1980–1981

Andrzej Paczkowski (Poland)

Professor, Modern History Center of the Institute of Political Studies, PAS, member of the council of the National Institute of Remembrance.

Inessa S. Yazhborovskaya (Russia)

Professor, Institute of Sociology, RAN.

ANDRZEJ PACZKOWSKI

THE ROAD TO MARTIAL LAW, 1980-1981

POLISH-SOVIET RELATIONS DURING the period between the wave of strikes in July 1980 and the introduction of martial law in December 1981 were exceptional in many respects. Never before had direct contacts between the state and party leaders of the two countries been so frequent—with the possible exception of the 1944–46 period, when Stalin simply dictated many key decisions to the Polish communists, while many others were made only after consultations with him. Furthermore, the top Soviet authority—the Presidium of the Central Committee of the Communist Party of the Soviet Union (CPSU)—had never before occupied itself so intensely and systematically with Poland: Polish issues constituted separate points on the agenda of at least twenty to twenty-five Presidium meetings. This frequency was connected with the fact that the economic crisis in Poland, which had lasted since 1976, triggered a social crisis that found expression in widespread strikes. Symptoms of no less than a systemic crisis appeared after August 1980 and the emergence of Solidarity as a multimillion-person social movement, independent of the authorities. The rise of Solidarity had a number of causes: in addition to the prevalent dissatisfaction with living standards and the arrogance of the government, other contributing factors included the activity of the democratic opposition (rightly considered antisocialist) and the influence of the Catholic Church, which in 1978 had gained powerful authority in the person of the "Polish pope," John Paul II. The pope's 1979 visit to Poland—described as "a pilgrimage to the Homeland"—demonstrated conclusively who really held sway in the country.

The strikes in mid-July 1980, including a several-day work stoppage at the Lublin railway junction, which handled much of the transit traffic for Soviet army troops stationed in the German Democratic Republic (GDR), evoked concern in both Warsaw and Moscow. Soon after Edward Gierek, then on holiday in Crimea, met with Leonid Brezhnev, who was critical of the Polish comrades, accusing them of having incurred excessive debt to Western countries, abandoning the active struggle against political opponents, and "obscuring the class sense of socialist patriotism with slogans like 'All Poles are brothers.'" Still, up to mid-August there was no reason for alarm or extraordinary measures. The situation changed on 14 August when, for the first time ever, a sit-in strike began at the Lenin Shipyard in Gdańsk that was not spontaneous but organized by opposition groups. From that day on, the Politburo of the Central Committee of the Polish Workers' Party met daily, a special panel (the so-called Kania Commission) was established to monitor the situation and draft response measures, a crisis team (known as Summer-80) was set up at the Ministry of Internal Affairs, and the General Staff of the Polish Armed Forces had officers on special standby. At last, Moscow also responded: on 21 August, Gierek received a personal letter from Brezhnev, and a few days later the Soviets established a commission on Poland, headed by Mikhail Suslov. It included Foreign Minister Andrei Gromyko, KGB chief Yuri Andropov, and Defense Minister Dmitry Ustinov. Their presence demonstrated the importance of the commission and the fact that Moscow was not ruling out the "force option."

On 27 August, Brezhnev sent another letter to Gierek, demanding firm measures to bring the situation under control. The Suslov Commission was obviously alarmed by the developments in Poland: on 28 August, it prepared a draft decree on the mobilization of three armored divisions and one motorized division, which were to attain combat readiness by evening the following day. As if that were not enough, the plan envisioned the mobilization of a further five to seven divisions, "if the main forces of the Polish Army take the side of the counterrevolution." Although in light of subsequent events those proposals appear bizarre, they certainly reflected the attitudes and fears of the Soviet leadership. It is little wonder: at that time, the strikes had engulfed practically the entire country (some 750,000 workers were involved). On 29 August, the Polish leadership decided not to suppress the strikes by force and to sign agreements with the major strike committees.

That opened a new chapter in the history of communist Poland, which, for all practical purposes, ended only in 1989. Because of Poland's size and location, everything that happened in the country was of vital significance to the entire Soviet bloc in Central and Eastern Europe and thus had an impact on the Soviet Union's security. Although the Soviet Union had great military potential and massive economic leverage, that did not mean that its leaders would be willing to use that power or even be capable of doing so. Without going into the details of the Soviet Union's complicated relations with the West (primarily the United States)—which, to some extent, restricted the Kremlin's room to maneuver—it should be noted that the Soviet army was bogged down in Afghanistan in an increasingly costly and unwinnable war.

Thus, opening a "second front" through military intervention in Poland's internal affairs carried considerable risk. Furthermore, since the Polish communist leaders had decided on a formula that Gierek described as "the lesser evil," that is, the gradual restoration of control and stability, Moscow could ill afford to openly undercut them or, less still, do the job for them. The only thing to do was to support the Polish communists in their efforts to restore the *status quo ante*. Their first move consisted of replacing the first secretary of the Polish Communist Party, who thus joined the list of top-level scapegoats first identified on 24 August. Gierek on 5 September was replaced by Stanisław Kania, hitherto responsible for the security apparatus—a move that must have received Moscow's discreet and informal consent, though this has not been conclusively verified.

Although the strategic goal, that is, the elimination or total subordination of Solidarity, remained unchanged, it is possible to distinguish two fundamental phases in Soviet policy at the time, preceded by a preliminary period when it was not yet obvious what size the independent union would ultimately reach and when hopes could still be entertained for bringing it to heel before it gained too much momentum. One thing remained constant: the Kremlin wanted any action to be as tough and quick as possible. Still, the first recommendations for the Polish comrades drafted by the Suslov Commission on 3 September were rather general and moderate: they advocated "flexibility" and suggested that "balanced administrative measures" should be applied only "when necessary." The commission focused on propaganda and such enigmatic initiatives as "boosting the fighting spirit of the party cells," the "organizational strengthening of the local PZPR committees," and "exposing the political image and intentions of opposition leaders." The only innovative recommendation concerned the "involvement of the [military] command cadre in party and economic work." It was assumed, however, that the new (or, rather, renewed) Polish leadership—where the top roles, alongside Kania, were played by Gen. Wojciech Jaruzelski, Kazimierz Barcikowski, Interior Minister Mirosław Milewski, and several hardliners (including Stefan Olszowski, Stanisław Kociołek, Andrzej Żabiński, and Tadeusz Grabski)—would take resolute action to stop the development of Solidarity. However, despite repeated prompting, conveyed directly during Kania's visit to Moscow (30 October), the Polish leadership could not bring itself to take radical measures. Those of its members who pushed for confrontation were in the minority. Kania—supported by, among others, Jaruzelski—was not making the expected decisions. As a result, on 10 November, a Warsaw court registered Solidarity, which thus became a completely legal organization. Solidarity numbered seven million members at that time, while the old trade unions were falling apart.

At that point, Moscow was not yet certain what further steps to take. On the same day that Solidarity was registered, the Soviets decided to grant Poland economic aid: this aid package included cash credits worth $150 million, credits for the purchase of grain, food, and raw materials, and the postponement of debt repayment. The Kremlin realized that improved consumer supplies could significantly influence the public mood in Poland. At the same time, however, moves were taken to limit the impact of the situation in Poland on Soviet citizens: the distribution of Polish press in the Soviet Union and tourist exchanges were both sharply reduced. Czechoslovakia took similar measures, while the GDR suspended a bilateral agreement that had permitted travel between the two countries without passports and visas.

Without access to Soviet military and KGB documents, it is hard to determine when the policy line that meant the initiation of this "first phase" started taking effect. Perhaps it was set off by the registration of Solidarity, a development received with misgivings in Moscow—but even more so in East Berlin and Prague, both of which felt threatened by the "Polish disease." In any case, the first impact of the events in Poland was evident in the Soviet Union by October. A major cause for even greater concern over the situation in Poland was the appearance within the Polish United Workers' Party (PZPR) of a reformist trend. It was a grass-roots movement without support among top officials (as had happened in Czechoslovakia in 1968) but was seen, nevertheless, as potentially dangerous in view of the increasingly urgent need to convene an extraordinary congress of the PZPR. It was feared that the movement, known as "horizontal structures," would be able to influence the selection of congressional candidates. It was also feared that, at a time when party discipline was weak and the authority of the top leadership was being challenged, the movement might determine the composition of the party leadership and push the PZPR onto the "social-democratic" path.

The policy line adopted by Moscow in November was based on the assumption that Warsaw Pact war games would be conducted in Poland (with the participation of Soviet, Czechoslovak, East German, and Polish troops), providing cover for the suppression of Solidarity, which—as the Soviets imagined—would involve the detention of several thousand union and opposition activists. The foreign (though "fraternal") forces would intimidate Polish society, encourage Kania's team, and help it pacify any resistance. That line of action was advocated by East German leader Erich Honecker in a letter to Brezhnev.

In late November, tensions in Poland increased dramatically after an incident that led to the arrest of two staffers at the Warsaw branch of Solidarity. Although the incident was papered over, the tense atmosphere remained—and that may have been the true goal of the authorities. In any event, on 1 December, representatives of the top army brass from Poland, Czechoslovakia, and the GDR were urgently summoned to Moscow and received by the

Soviet chief of staff, Marshal Nikolai Ogarkov, who handed them maps of the planned Soyuz-80 war games. The exercises were to begin on 8 December with the participation of eighteen divisions (eleven Soviet, four Polish, two Czechoslovak, and one East German). The troops were to be deployed near major towns and industrial centers. Simultaneously, the Polish leaders and the leaders of all the other Warsaw Pact countries were invited to Moscow on 5 December for a conference on Poland. All this resembled the events of 1968, when "conferences" were being convened while Warsaw Pact countries held war games in Czechoslovakia. During the Moscow gathering, Kania made an extensive address, followed by speeches of the other first secretaries, who emphatically declared that the situation in Poland was hazardous, that counterrevolution was in the air, and that robust measures were needed to suppress it. Yet, the matter of the war games was not on the agenda: Brezhnev had decided to postpone them and give the PZPR time to cope with the situation. It is not clear to me if the plan for the war games unveiled on 1 December was simply a bluff designed to force the Poles into action or if Brezhnev was treating it seriously. According to some American historians, the position taken by Pres. Jimmy Carter and his letter to Brezhnev of 3 December crucially influenced the decision to call off the games; in the letter, Carter warned that "foreign military intervention in Poland would have [very] negative consequences for East-West relations." Moscow certainly took note of the letter, though it is not clear that it had a decisive impact.

Moscow neither definitively abandoned the plan nor stopped worrying about Kania's indecisiveness and the insufficient clout of the hardliners. The state of affairs in Poland was extremely alarming, and Moscow's determination was further stimulated by the conviction that Poland was engulfed by a wave of anti-Sovietism that the authorities were incapable of stopping. Indeed, anti-Soviet sentiments were strong in Poland and prone to be manifested in periods of political unrest—as in 1956. Yet, such attitudes were not provoked by specific situations; they had always existed and only manifested themselves when the circumstances were conducive. Thus, it could be argued that anti-Sovietism—the successor, in a way, to old anti-Russian sentiments—was deeply rooted in Polish society. Yet, it was verbal anti-Sovietism, not backed by any acts of aggression. Moreover, much indicates that at least some of the signs daubed on monuments connected with Soviet traditions (these were mainly monuments commemorating World War II but also included those of Lenin and Felix Dzerzhinsky, who was a Pole) may have been security service provocations, designed to give Solidarity's opponents reason to clamp down on the movement. The moderate leaders of Solidarity, led by Lech Wałęsa, were usually critical of such expressions of anti-Sovietism, though their influence was limited in this sphere. They could hardly fire the editor of a local union newspaper for running a caricature of

Brezhnev (pictured as a growling bear) or for publishing articles about the Ribbentrop-Molotov Pact and Katyn. I am not sure that Soviet leaders viewed such excesses with the same seriousness that the Soviet press suggested they did, but they censured Kania over their appearance nevertheless. The coverage of such events was addressed to Soviet citizens for the purpose of turning them against Solidarity and Poles in general; these efforts—as in the case of most East Germans, Czechs, or Hungarians—were largely successful.

Although preparations for martial law were moving ahead rapidly at the General Staff and the Ministry of Internal Affairs, the plans were being constantly updated and no deadline had been set for their implementation. The impulse again came from Moscow. On 22 January 1981, a member of the Suslov Commission, Leonid Zamyatin, reported to a meeting of the Soviet leadership on his recent visit to Poland. His assessment was relatively calm: he noted that "the party cells are gradually invigorating their activity" and suggested that "constant pressure should be exerted on the [Polish] party," the leadership of which was free of obvious divisions. However, in the final part of the meeting, Marshal Ustinov—referring to the opinions of Marshal Viktor Kulikov, who was at that time in Poland—said that "there has been no meaningful breakthrough in Poland" and announced that Warsaw Pact armies would hold war games in Poland in March. He further underscored that "we need to upgrade the status of the games, in other words, to let [the Poles] know that our forces are on standby." That is to say, the December initiative was being revived—this time under the code name Soyuz-81.

The appointment on 11 February of General Jaruzelski as prime minister was probably a step in the Polish leadership's preparations for the possible introduction of martial law under cover of the war games and, at the same time, the implementation of one of the September directives issued by Moscow. Never before had a career officer been made premier in a communist country. Usually, things worked the other way around: it was civilians who were appointed to senior military rank. A few days later, several dozen officials from the Ministry of Defense, Ministry of Internal Affairs, and the Central Committee took part in a "staff exercise" devoted to the imposition of martial law. The elevation of the defense minister to the premiership was welcomed in Moscow, though its doubts and concerns were not completely dissipated.

On 4 March, during official Polish-Soviet talks, Marshal Ustinov "lost his temper," and—according to an eyewitness—reportedly screamed at the Poles, "You've got two weeks to get things in order in Poland." Soyuz-81 began on 17 March, and two days later an incident took place in Bydgoszcz: some Solidarity activists were forcefully removed from a local council meeting, and three of them were severely beaten in the process and had to be hospitalized. That assault was seen as an attack on Solidarity itself. The union leadership demanded that the guilty be punished, and, when the authorities tried to justify the police action, they proclaimed a warning strike and threatened a general strike. Although no Polish or Russian documents confirm that the incident was in fact a provocation, it is highly probable that it was intended to provoke street protests, which then would have been used to validate martial law. In any case, the timing of the incident, the fact that Jaruzelski and Kania signed on 27 March the fundamental martial law documents ("Guidelines for the introduction in the territory of the PRL of martial law for reasons of state security," "Framework plan of action for the armed forces"), and the arrival in Warsaw of both Marshal Kulikov, with a large staff, and KGB deputy chief Vladimir Kryuchkov appear to indicate that Moscow felt the time was opportune for a showdown with Solidarity.

In effect, the Soviets had picked the time for martial law when they had set the date for the war games. The Polish mass media, including television, provided daily coverage of the games, creating an atmosphere of threat. According to the CIA agent Ryszard Kukliński—at the time an officer with the General Staff and personally involved in the preparations for martial law—Kulikov and Kryuchkov advocated suspension of the constitution and assumption of power by the military. In a telephone conversation with Kania, Brezhnev demanded resolute action; "things are at a critical stage," he insisted. But the Polish leadership again backed down: Kania and Jaruzelski thought the preparations were not yet complete and, more importantly, feared that Solidarity could mobilize itself rapidly, particularly since the PZPR branches in major industrial plants—where Wałęsa's union enjoyed the greatest backing—had come out in favor of Solidarity.

Cardinal Stefan Wyszyński sought to cool the militant attitudes on both sides. As a result, a provisional accord was reached on 31 March: Solidarity called off the general strike, while the authorities consented to register the Solidarity of Private Farmers and to investigate the Bydgoszcz incident. That forced Moscow to review its tactics. In a nervous, at times dramatic conversation held in a railway coach at Brest, Andropov and Ustinov—acting with Moscow's authorization—accepted Kania and Jaruzelski's position: martial law was to be introduced by Polish forces, without the participation of Warsaw Pact troops, though the latter would be ready to provide support if the operation appeared headed for failure. Thus began the second stage of the Soviet policy on Poland.

Alas, that did not mean that the pressure on the Polish leadership had eased in any way. On the contrary, after that conversation, the Soviets started preparing for the ouster and replacement of Poland's ruling duo, with particular energy displayed in these endeavors by the Soviet ambassador to Poland, Boris Aristov, and the Warsaw KGB station chief, Vitalii Pavlov. Honecker was also exceptionally active, with both the East German Communist Party

(SED) and Ministry of State Security (Stasi) providing the strongest backing for the Polish hardliners (known in Moscow as the "healthy forces"). On 16 May, a top-secret meeting was held in Moscow at which Honecker (the meeting's initiator) and Czechoslovak leader Gustav Husak attempted to persuade Brezhnev that Kania had to go. According to former KGB officer KGB Vasili Mitrokhin, nine Polish generals had approached Moscow with a plan that envisioned a coup d'état, the installation of a military junta, removal of the Politburo from power, introduction of martial law, and a request for Warsaw Pact military assistance. This may sound like political fiction and seem like the concoction of unreliable KGB informers, but it certainly illustrates the tensions that existed within Poland's broadly conceived communist establishment. Without going into detail, it is enough to note that the "healthy forces" suffered a stinging setback: the motion of its leader Grabski for dismissal of the Politburo made at a plenary meeting of the Central Committee got the support of only twenty-four members, with five abstaining and eighty-nine voting against. The outcome was probably the result of misguided tactics by Moscow, such as simultaneously attacking Kania and Jaruzelski, and of divisions within the ranks of the hardliners. In any case, Kania's line was upheld and Brezhnev acquiesced; at a Soviet Politburo meeting on 18 June, he remarked, "We'll just have to wait and see."

The failure of the "Central Committee putsch" and the decision not to introduce martial law in March exposed Moscow's limited ability to influence events in Poland, even including the Communist Party. Indeed, without sufficient backing inside the country, the Soviet Union could rely only on the use of military force—something it wanted to avoid at any cost. The defeat of the "healthy forces" demonstrated that Moscow did not have that kind of backing and was forced to look for other people who would be prepared to introduce martial law without vacillating (as was the case with Kania and Jaruzelski). Kania's reputation in Moscow was deteriorating steadily, and his passiveness was treated as bordering on treason, so finding a suitable replacement was the order of the day. Moscow was not partial to the ideas of Honecker and Husak, who were still betting on the same people that had proved so inept in June. Contacts were still maintained with them, but it was obvious that they could be trusted only to provide auxiliary services and were incapable of putting forward a leader with the desired authority and talent.

Meanwhile, the passage of time was relentless: the list of Kania's transgressions only grew longer, and Solidarity managed to conduct its national convention and elect national leadership (with Wałęsa as chair), which gave it additional legitimacy. Worse still, the union—feeling that its power had made it invincible—wandered beyond the realm of "self-limiting revolution," despite such Soviet gestures as the holding of the largest-ever military exercises on the Baltic Sea and in Lithuania, Belarus, and Ukraine. Delegates to the Gdańsk congress of Solidarity could watch the huge aircraft carrier *Kiev* at anchor in the Bay of Gdańsk without having to use binoculars. An important signal to Moscow, amounting to *casus belli,* was the adoption by the Gdańsk congress of an "Appeal to the Working People of East Europe," who were exhorted to emulate Solidarity and were promised support. In response, Poland's government-controlled media launched a fierce propaganda campaign, while Moscow and the "fraternal parties" followed suit and sent a sharply worded letter to the Central Committee of the PZPR. Still, no resolution was in sight.

On 21 October, the CPSU's Konstantin Rusakov reported to Honecker, "We note that clear differences have recently appeared between Kania and Jaruzelski in their approach to fundamental issues." That was because Jaruzelski "was largely prepared to take a tough stance against the counterrevolution," so "we started working with Jaruzelski" and for that purpose the assistance of "good Polish comrades" was enlisted and they held talks with him. Jaruzelski was reminded of his "party obligations" and the high stakes involved; the Soviets also promised that he could "count on the support of the fraternal parties." Along with the invocation of ideological and political *imponderabilia* and playing on the general-premier's personal ambitions, economic blackmail was also applied. This was easy because Poland depended on Soviet energy supplies, and its industries were geared to the needs of the Soviet market. In any event, Jaruzelski agreed to play along. On 18 October, the Central Committee accepted Kania's resignation (104 in favor, 79 against) and a few hours later elected General Jaruzelski as first secretary (this time with a unanimity more congruent with party custom: 180 in favor, 4 against).

From that moment on, Jaruzelski held three key posts: he was first secretary of the party, prime minister (which meant he chaired the National Defense Committee), and defense minister. This was crucial because it ensured full consistency of power—something that could not be guaranteed by even a perfect collaboration of two or three different people. Moscow, which had never shed its suspiciousness, a constant dating back to the struggle for the succession to Lenin, was not completely confident of Jaruzelski's determination—as indicated by the minutes of Soviet Central Committee meetings held in November and December 1981. Yet, Brezhnev realized that, if martial law were to be imposed and administered, there was no alternative to Jaruzelski—even if he had to be prompted and supervised. On 7 December, Marshal Kulikov made another visit to Warsaw, followed the next day by Nikolai Baibakov, head of Gosplan, who assured Jaruzelski of Soviet economic aid and additional supplies of meat. Although the Kremlin still did not know when martial law would be imposed and what some of its provisions would be, it decided to bet on the general and his aides. There simply was no new concept for dealing with the situation in Poland, which, however, did not mean that one—including military intervention—could not appear at any time.

In any event, there was no need for it: shortly before midnight on 12 December, special army units, the security service, and police started imposing martial law, which was officially announced in General Jaruzelski's radio speech on 13 December at 6:00 a.m. The Kremlin welcomed the operation with relief, since it made it more difficult to charge the Soviet Union with direct interference. In a telephone conversation, Brezhnev congratulated Jaruzelski. Moreover, Moscow sent the same cable to all the fraternal parties—including the Cuban, Vietnamese, and Laotian parties but not the Romanian—asking them "to extend political and moral support to the Polish comrades and to provide additional economic assistance." Three days later, Marshal Kulikov flew back to Moscow. His supervision was no longer needed in Poland.

Moscow protested vehemently when Pres. Ronald Reagan blamed it for martial law in Poland, but he certainly had a point. Although it was likely that, even without outside coercion, the Polish communists would have imposed martial law or used some other radical means to deal with the Solidarity "counterrevolution," there was no denying that the Soviet Union had incessantly exerted extreme pressure, tried to influence top-level appointments, repeatedly resorted to economic blackmail, and threatened to send in tanks and special forces until it got the result it wanted. However, it was no accident the Polish communists had pursued the same goals.

ANDRZEJ PACZKOWSKI

INESSA S. YAZHBOROVSKAYA

THE ROAD TO MARTIAL LAW, 1980-1981

THE EVENTS OF 1980–81 were a manifestation of another socioeconomic and political conflict in the history of the People's Republic of Poland (PRL). The turmoil arose from the failure of the Polish United Workers' Party (PZPR), led by Edward Gierek, first secretary of the PZPR Central Committee (CC) to modernize the country's economy using major loans from the West and to acquire new technology. The turmoil escalated into a crisis of "real socialism." The so-called downward period of the "long waves" of the Kondratieff cycle in the global market of the 1970s, when the world economy was in a recession, contributed to the deepening of the crisis that destroyed the system of incentives for economic growth, hindered scientific and technological progress, increased the failure of Poland's command economy in coping with the challenges of the day, and doomed the country to collapse. The crisis froze political progress and impaired communication with the public authorities, which gave rise to increasingly acute clashes and conflicts, accompanied by mass worker demonstrations. In the early 1980s, the sociopolitical conflict was supported by Solidarity, a multimillion-strong protest movement that identified itself as an "independent labor union."

In July 1980, several brief strikes in Lublin to protest rising prices of meat and meat products remained outside the concern of Soviet leadership, which had not yet perceived them as a symptom of the festering mass protest movement. The wake-up call came suddenly on 15 August 1980, when Gierek, who had been vacationing in Crimea, returned to Warsaw. On the previous day there had been a strike at the Gdańsk shipyard, which employed sixteen thousand people. The growing mass strikes on the Baltic coast and the appearance of pockets of self-organized workers and cells of independent labor unions quickly escalated the political conflict. Information received in Moscow showed spreading "antisocialist" sentiments. There were growing economic hardships and decreasing standards of living caused by the alienation

of the party's leadership and the entire party from the people, bureaucratiza-
tion of the leadership and their unrestrained greed, and the party's rejection
of democratization and free-market reforms.

After 20 August, CPSU secretary general Leonid Brezhnev sent a letter
to Gierek expressing the Soviet leadership's concern regarding the events
unfolding in Poland. In accordance with Brezhnev's notion, which Western
politicians called the Brezhnev Doctrine or the "doctrine of limited sovereignty" and which was based on the experience of Czechoslovakia's "Prague
Spring," the Kremlin was guided by the following idea: "When the internal
and external forces hostile to socialism are trying to turn the developments
in some socialist country toward the restoration of a capitalist system, there
is a threat to socialism in this country, a threat to the socialist community as
a whole; and therefore, it has become a problem for the people of this country
and a common concern for all socialist countries as well." The adoption of
this doctrine, proclaimed in November 1968 at the Fifth PZPR Congress, was
an important factor in maintaining unity in the socialist community. Under
this doctrine, the Soviet Union embraced the right to intervene, using military force if necessary, in the internal affairs of the Warsaw Pact (WP) allies
in order to reverse these events.

The Soviet foreign policy doctrine was based on the assumption that it
was the duty of the Soviet Union to engage in actions of varying intensity "on
the basis of proletarian internationalism," including the suppression of "antisocialist" and "anti-Soviet" actions through the WP's military apparatus.
At the same time, that doctrine also embraced peaceful coexistence, noninterference in the internal affairs of other countries, and peaceful settlement
of international disputes. Consequently, the incongruity between these principles deepened the "root of conflict between the class and state approach."

The events in Poland were perceived by the Soviet leadership as a threat
to the existence of socialism, the "socialist commonwealth," the strength of
the Warsaw Pact, and stability in Europe. The largest country in Central and
Eastern Europe, with the second-largest army in the WP, Poland held a leading geopolitical position in the "socialist commonwealth" and had special
political and strategic-military importance. Vital communications channels
passed through Poland, connecting Moscow with the Group of Soviet Forces
in Germany; it was the bridge between the Soviet Union and the German
Democratic Republic (GDR). Soviet nuclear weapons were deployed in Poland. It provided control over Czechoslovakia and Hungary. The Baltic coast
linked the joint actions of the allied fleets of the Soviet Union, GDR, and
Poland.

When the question of developing the Soviet position on the Polish situation arose, it was based on an application of the Brezhnev Doctrine to these
events. In a telephone conversation, Brezhnev assumed the traditional mili-

tary option and warned Gierek, "You've got rebels, they have to be taken by the snout, we will help you." As early as 25 August 1980, following Brezhnev's statement on the evolving situation in Poland, the Soviet Politburo passed a resolution, "On the Situation in the Polish People's Republic." According to the Soviet geopolitical doctrine, the overriding sentiment was "we must not lose Poland." A special committee, the so-called Suslov Commission, was secretly formed by the Central Committee and headed by a member of the Politburo, Central Committee secretary Mikhail Suslov (after his death in 1982, it was headed by Mikhail Gorbachev). The commission included the most important party and government officials: A. A. Gromyko, Yuri Andropov, Defense Minister D. F. Ustinov, K. Chernenko, Mikhail Zimyanin, Ivan Arkhipov, L. M. Zamyatin, and O. B. Rakhmanin. The objective of the commission was to monitor the situation and to propose necessary actions by the Soviet Union as the guarantor of the integrity of the socialist community, especially in regard to the preservation of Poland in the WP. The commission worked continuously, led by Rakhmanin, first secretary to the deputy head of the CPSU Central Committee on Relations with Communist and Workers' Parties of the socialist countries. The commission's recommendations formed the basis for the decisions made by CPSU management. Beginning at that time, the situation in Poland occupied a significant place on the meeting agendas of the Politburo and the Central Committee Secretariat, initially once a month but then more frequently (four times in January 1981 and five times in April of that year). Brezhnev would often start his day with the question, "How are things in Poland?" As the tension increased, Andropov (based on the experience of the 1956 suppression of events in Hungary) would frequently request reports from the KGB's representative in Poland, Gen. V. Pavlov, who would call him several times a day.

A large-scale deployment of Soviet troops to suppress the "counterrevolution" was not ruled out. On 28 August, the chair and members of the committee—Suslov, Gromyko, Andropov, Ustinov, and Chernenko—in a note addressed to Brezhnev, asked him to raise a full alert for three armored and one motorized division "in the event of military assistance" to the PRL, to call up one hundred thousand men from the reserves, and to mobilize fifteen thousand vehicles. Further aggravating the situation, the plan included mobilizing divisions in several military districts to wartime levels. In the event of reactions by the "counterrevolutionary forces" and the "main forces of the Polish Army," the army group was to be expanded by five to seven divisions. Brezhnev, who during the events of 1968 in Czechoslovakia was in no hurry to sign a similar order to deploy troops, said at the time, "Let's wait a little bit more." Nikolai Ogarkov, chief of the General Staff of the Soviet army, was also against yet another military operation that would further burden the economy.

On 31 August 1980, one of the CPSU Central Committee's main newspapers, *Pravda* (Truth), published an article headlined "The Enemies of Socialist Poland," signed by A. Petrov (the signature under all articles that were approved by the Politburo). The article said that the emergence of Solidarity had been declared by "subversive forces" that were represented by the Committee for Protection of Workers' Rights and Western special services. Any compromise with such forces, according to the Soviet leadership, was out of the question.

The minutes of the 3 September meeting of the Politburo and the attached transcripts of talks with representatives of the Polish leadership contain the negative reaction of the Soviet party and state leadership to the events of "an antisocialist orientation" in Poland, the emergence of Solidarity, and the dynamics of the situation in the PZPR. Initially, the Polish leadership was invited to start working inside Solidarity, with the hope that this phase of the conflict could be slowly neutralized. However, it only escalated. Soviet troops were moved close to the Polish border in an attempt to weaken it.

Gierek's behavior exhibited confusion and a desire to keep waiting. The Soviet leadership bet on new first secretary Stanisław Kania, who in the 1970s supervised the Special Services, internal affairs, and the army. At a plenary meeting of the PZPR Central Committee on 5 September, he replaced Gierek. At meetings in Moscow, members of the PZPR leadership, Mieczysław Jagielski (10 September) and Andrzej Werblan (17 September), received instructions from Brezhnev and Suslov regarding the resources and methods needed to overcome the crisis and were encouraged to prepare a counteroffensive ("if necessary, use administrative tools"), to implement "steps and take the necessary measures to strengthen the socialist rule of law," and to vigorously influence public sentiment using ideological methods in order to prevent any bias about "real socialism," the excitement of public opinion in other countries of the "community," and the undermining of its political system. The policy of the PZPR was viewed as "counterconcessions." Moscow was especially concerned about the Gdańsk, Szczecin, and Jastrzębie-Zdrój agreements between representatives of the party and Solidarity, which were viewed as legalization of "antisocialist opposition," and the proclamation of Solidarity in 17 September 1980 as a nationwide structure that jeopardized "leadership in society and leadership in the state" (which is exactly how the Polish cliché sounds). Subsequently, even greater dissatisfaction was caused by the political demands to establish a self-governing commonwealth, to prosecute party and government leaders responsible for the difficult economic situation in the country, and to establish democratic rights and freedoms.

Several times, the Soviet leadership discussed the possibility of directly using the military and political might of the Soviet Union. The strength of the troops remaining in Poland after World War II was expanded in 1970 at the request of Gierek. But the weight of the arguments against further engagement of Soviet forces to change the situation in Poland was also increasing. The Soviet Union's difficult economic situation, the high cost of the war in Afghanistan, the threat of bloodshed in Poland, and the introduction of Western economic sanctions increased discussions within the international communist movement. And there were serious objections to Soviet military intervention. Moscow began to shape public opinion in favor of resolving the conflict and restoring the party and state's "leading and guiding role" in Poland. It also began to use Polish resources—discrediting opposition leaders, introducing independent labor unions, and using the presence of Soviet troops and their concentration on the Soviet-Polish border, as well as rumors of their deployment into Poland, to put pressure on the Polish leadership, Solidarity, and Polish society. At that time, the idea emerged of using martial law in the country to defeat Solidarity. The Kremlin saw its key task as persuading the leaders of the PRL to use security forces "to restore law and order in the country" as soon as possible.

The PZPR leadership relied on purely political methods to resolve the crisis situation, hoping to lower the level of unrest by requesting economic assistance from the Soviet leadership. Poland received help from the Soviet Union and other socialist countries. But that was the only thing Kania did, which angered Brezhnev. Moscow was waiting until the situation was ripe for a military solution and pushed the Polish government to take action.

The two countries began to search for ways to resolve the crisis on a constitutional basis. In line with the interests of the Suslov Commission, the constitution of the PRL was found to contain an article regarding a "threat to the security of Poland" and an article that could provide a legal basis for martial law. From then on, the Kremlin's policy for the Polish conflict to be resolved forcefully with Polish resources became a key strategy. At a Politburo meeting on 29 October 1980, on the eve of the visit to Moscow by Kania and Józef Pińkowski, chair of the Council of Ministers of the PRL, Brezhnev worded his assessment and recommendations regarding the situation very harshly: "In Poland we are witnessing rampant counterrevolution, and statements in the Polish press and by Polish comrades downplay that fact, no mention of the enemies of the people. . . . Why?" Citing the experience of Yugoslavia, where striking workers were suppressed and some were jailed, the Soviet leaders felt the need to encourage the use of similar measures in Poland. The CPSU general secretary posed a fundamental question: "Maybe we really need to impose martial law?" Gromyko took up his idea, proposing to use the "measure to save the revolutionary achievements" and to "support" and "reinforce" the Polish leadership. Marshal Ustinov, thinking as a military man, clearly and resolutely justified the desired Soviet position in a more traditional way: "If we do not introduce martial law," the situation will become very difficult, especially because the Polish army has people who are still undecided. The Soviet Northern Group of Forces (NGF) "is fully prepared and is in full combat readiness." Gromyko was more careful, proposing to introduce martial law, "not right way" and "not right after the return of Kania and Pińkowski from Moscow . . . but within some time after that."

Politburo meetings yielded all sorts of suggestions for tactical solutions: Polish forces were the preferred way for "armed intervention by the Soviet Union or jointly with the Warsaw Pact countries, in case of emergency." If no change in the situation in the country was possible without the involvement of Soviet troops, direct Soviet military intervention into the events in Poland was increasingly viewed as a potential, yet unwanted and forced option. It would be appropriate to give importance to the evidence of the 1990–91 chair of the Commission of the Supreme Soviet of Russia on the transfer of the CPSU and the KGB archives to scholars and the public. Volkogonov argued that, according to these documents, the Soviets continued to prepare for an armed invasion of Poland.

The entire course of the Politburo meeting on 29 October meant that the Polish leadership was to ensure that Soviet leaders were dissatisfied with the agreement made with the moderate element of Solidarity. They were irritated by the indecisive Polish leaders, described by CPSU secretary Konstantin Rusakov as follows: Kania does not accept "international aid," and the "too passive" defense minister, Wojciech Jaruzelski, said that Polish military units would not act against Polish workers. "The Polish comrades say," said Rusakov, "that they do not have a situation similar to that in Hungary and Czechoslovakia." In other words, in their view, the situation in Poland was not so acute as to necessitate martial law and the use of force applied by either the Poles or others. It was decided to propose "comprehensive assistance" to the "Polish friends" in order to "normalize" the situation to guarantee the PRL's membership in the WP.

Kania and Pińkowski arrived in Moscow the next day and were invited to talk to Brezhnev. He addressed them as follows: we must immediately "roll back the counterrevolution," utilizing the state apparatus, the army, the police, and security agencies, relying on the "healthy forces in the party and the people," and struggling using peaceful and nonpeaceful means; the Soviet side will provide the necessary support. Meetings in Moscow and visits by representatives of the Politburo and the Central Committee Secretariat to Warsaw, and subsequent analysis and assessment of the position of the Polish leadership, were followed by this phrase uttered by the Soviet secretary general: "the Polish comrades cannot understand the simple truth that they are dealing with an uncontrolled counterrevolution." Andropov was particularly infuriated that Polish leaders, instead of employing strictly military, administrative, and judicial measures, had been trying to launch a so-called political settlement. On 31 October, Brezhnev displayed an expanded approach and recommended and "encouraged more decisive action," calling for them to "cheer up and strengthen their confidence in their potential and their capabilities." He also mentioned reasonable economic help, "which would allow the Poles to survive in this difficult time." To mitigate the crisis, the Polish leaders continued to ask for economic aid. That assistance was promised by Brezhnev during a meeting with the Polish leaders. According to the decision of the Central Committee "on the provision of economic and financial assistance to Poland in 1981," dated 11 November 1980, that assistance was provided in the first quarter of 1981.

Having acquired some Cold War experience of resolving (including through the use of force) the crises in Poland and Hungary in 1956 and the Prague Spring in 1968, the Soviet Union and other socialist countries applied it toward settling the situation in Poland. A unified approach to the Polish crisis was adopted based on the Warsaw Pact. In November 1980, the Central Committee discussed the possibility of involving, according to the Czechoslovakian example, "healthy forces" in the PZPR and Poland to overcome the social and political conflict. On several occasions, Moscow invited the leaders of socialist countries who were particularly concerned about the prospects of Poland dropping out of the security system of the socialist countries. For that reason they were very much involved in exerting pressure on the Polish leadership. On 5 December, at a meeting in Moscow, they responded to the call of Soviet leadership to stay loyal to the mutual alliance and not to "abandon" Poland. This move suggests two possible interpretations of the Warsaw Pact effort: as a scheme to work out a joint plan between socialist countries to perform a military operation and bring troops into Poland (this interpretation is in line with the US government's position at a 7 December meeting at the White House) or as a maneuver to intimidate Kania and his government and push them to begin extreme measures.

Czechoslovakia's Gustáv Husák, recollecting the experience of 1968, and Hungary's János Kádár, recalling the experience of 1956, advised taking forceful action. The GDR's Erich Honecker recommended changing the Polish leadership and bringing in troops. Brezhnev emphasized that those intentions would do no harm. In talks with Polish leaders, Soviet leaders deliberately maintained the possibility of Soviet military intervention in order to push them into taking forceful action. On the same day, 5 December, in a personal conversation with Kania, Brezhnev did not rule out a Soviet military intervention: "If we see that you are overcome, we'll act." In other words, if the "healthy forces" suffered a defeat, the Soviet troops would step in, compelled to do so. Kania warned that Polish society would react strongly to military intervention—the whole nation might rise up. In his memoirs, he interprets Brezhnev as follows: "Well, we won't enter. If it gets difficult, we'll enter. But not without your consent." Polish leaders tried to reassure their colleagues in the socialist community that they could handle the situation in their country and that there was no need for military intervention. On the same day, in a meeting of party and state leaders of the commonwealth of socialist countries, Jaruzelski made a statement proposing to resolve the crisis in Poland using Polish resources by gradually reducing tension in the country.

Soviet leaders were becoming increasingly aware that the situation in Poland was much more complex and contradictory: on the one hand, the protest movement of workers was unusually widespread, and there was no confidence "in the necessary loyalty" of other Polish forces and their ability to avoid negative international consequences. At the same time, Polish leaders told their Soviet colleagues, "Poland has always been and will be a socialist state, a strong link in the general family of socialist countries." The Soviet leadership soon realized that this was a misunderstanding of the seriousness of the situation, but they had to accept the assurances of the PRL leadership that they would cope with the crisis themselves, without support from an external power. Summing up the 5 December meeting, the CPSU Politburo agreed on 12 December to resolve the situation using Polish forces. That was a crucial test for Soviet policy regarding Polish events. The Soviet leadership had decided that the PZPR leadership had to deal with the turmoil in the country. The Kremlin wanted Polish leaders to introduce martial law in Poland as soon as possible, to gain control of the political situation. Therefore, it was decided to very actively influence the internal balance of forces and support the party's "healthy forces."

In early 1981, the Polish government still maintained a dialogue with Solidarity, trying to resolve the conflict by political means and to reach a compromise with Solidarity leaders. That was a subject of concern and irritation for the Soviet leadership. On 22 January 1981, there was a meeting of the Politburo regarding a visit to Poland (13–20 January) by a Soviet delegation led by the head of the Office of the CPSU CC, L. M. Zamyatin, wherein Gromyko stated, "Our Polish friends, despite our recommendations, do not want to use extraordinary measures—that idea is essentially out of the question for them." Brezhnev, constantly monitoring the situation in Poland, would call Kania every two weeks to remind him of the need to take decisive action against "counterrevolution." On 30 January, he insisted on the need for such action and added that "mortal danger" hung over socialism in Poland.

It was difficult to find a sound rationale for effective action by the "healthy forces." As of the second half of November, the Polish military was preparing to introduce martial law. First, they put together a package of documents dealing with the legalities of the issue. According to V. L. Musatov, a very competent officer of the Soviet Ministry of Foreign Affairs and the Office of the CPSU Central Committee, a state of emergency plan had been finalized at the end of the year by the Polish military and the intelligence officers who were being supported by Soviet specialists from the ministry and the KGB.

To enhance control over the situation in Poland, as well as prepare for the possibility of using Soviet troops and troops from other countries of the Warsaw Pact, Soviet authorities created a plan for joint military exercises. This plan, called Soyuz-80 and submitted to the Polish military on 1 December, called for bringing fifteen Soviet, one East German, and two Czechoslovakian divisions into Poland under the command of the allied armies and fleets. During these exercises, the objective was to be ready on 8 December to cross the Polish border and surround major cities and industrial centers. Meanwhile, the start of the exercises was repeatedly delayed by the Poles, and there was further foot dragging. After two and a half months, the allied forces' headquarters was gradually eliminated, and the flags of the Warsaw Pact countries were removed from the flagpole in Legnica in May.

In Washington, according to the memoirs of former US defense secretary Robert Gates, then a senior CIA officer and later director of the agency, there was an opinion that the Polish authorities would cope with the situation in the country. At the end of January, after regularly receiving information from Col. Ryszard Kukliński, a CIA agent in the Polish military leadership, and acknowledging a significant escalation of tensions, the CIA predicted an increase in Soviet pressure on Polish authorities. By the beginning of February 1981, there was another opinion: if the internal confrontation continued, there would be a shift toward Soviet invasion. When Prime Minister Jaruzelski replaced Pińkowski on 10 February, CIA director William Casey reported to Pres. Ronald Reagan that the situation had become extremely aggravated and that the military option in the conflict through an invasion by Warsaw Pact troops was imminent. Most likely, neither the US government nor the Polish government predicted the Kremlin's actual tactics. In February 1981, Jaruzelski told Mieczysław Rakowski, "Our historic mission is to prevent the Soviet invasion."

The Soviet authorities were preparing measures to impose martial law in Poland and "normalize" the situation. Soviet agencies studied measures aimed at weakening and then defeating the "counterrevolution" in Poland and discussed the model of socialism to be adopted there. To this end, the Soviets established a working group comprising members of the CPSU Central Committee, the KGB, the Foreign Ministry, and the General Staff at the level of deputy heads of departments. In early February, the group presented recommendations on how to defeat Solidarity, gain control of and influence in the economy, streamline cooperation with "healthy forces" in the Polish United Workers' Party through martial law, and establish an appropriate regime. In February, due to the deteriorating situation in the country, Polish law enforcement agencies conducted "staff war games" to prepare for a possible general strike on the eve of the declaration of martial law throughout the country.

In mid-February, the Politburo commission on the Polish question approved the "Program of Consolidation of Socialism in Poland" and the appropriate policy steps, including the elimination of "traces of capitalism," collectivization of the rural areas, adoption of a "plan-based" economy, and reorientation of foreign economic relations with a focus on the Soviet Union, along with measures to restrict the Catholic Church, destroy political opposition, and form a "socialist intelligentsia." Among the most important measures were a purging of the party ranks to remove all revisionists, opportunists, and those who supported a compromise with Solidarity and the enactment of "profound reforms" of the PZPR.

On 23 February, addressing the Twenty-Sixth CPSU Congress, Brezhnev said that "socialist Poland, fraternal Poland, will not be abandoned!" On 4 March, during a meeting of top Soviet and Polish leaders, the conversation took a hard turn when the leadership of the Communist Party accused its Polish counterparts of conducting a "rotten" policy of compromise with the "class enemy" and of being lenient toward Western interference in internal affairs. The Polish delegation was requested to restore law and order in Poland within weeks: "Our patience is running out! We have someone to rely on in Poland!" yelled Ustinov. Published in *Pravda,* an official statement following the meeting reiterated the ideological tenets: "the integral socialist community and its protection is a matter not only of each state, but of the entire socialist coalition."

On 12 March 1981, summarizing the results of meetings with the leaders of socialist countries during the party congress, members of the Politburo had to admit that they were even more fearful of the implications of the events in Poland and of a repeat of the situation in their own country with the same undesirable, large-scale consequences.

The Politburo continued to play up the possibility of an invasion into Poland. Ustinov, as the defense minister, proposed to reinforce Polish fears with a demonstration of Soviet military power, and maneuvers in Poland were to be "somewhat stepped up, in other words, to make it clear that we have our forces on standby." Along with the command and exercises of the allied armies and fleets, reports were leaked to the media about preparations for the invasion of Poland by Warsaw Pact troops, emphasizing the fact that the country was in the Soviet Union's sphere of influence.

The "Bydgoszcz events" of 17–24 March (in which three workers were beaten at a local Solidarity office) triggered preparations for a general strike on 31 March and gave the Soviet leadership a new impetus to exert massive pressure for the immediate application of force. The question of immediately imposing martial law came up. Rumors were spread that several Soviet divisions were ready to move into Poland.

On 27 March, the WP chief, Marshal Viktor G. Kulikov, arrived in Warsaw. Polish leaders, aware of the way the crises of 1953, 1956, 1968, 1970, and 1976 had been resolved, were expecting similar developments. However, the incident was resolved peacefully. At the same time, the abolition of the general strike through an agreement between the state commission headed by M. Rakowski and the Polish Conciliation Commission of Solidarity was perceived in Moscow as a sharply negative development. In the last days of March, faced with a general strike scheduled for 31 March, Brezhnev repeatedly demanded, under the pretext that the strike was illegal, that Polish authorities begin a direct confrontation, without concern for shedding blood. However, Solidarity canceled the strike. Martial law was never imposed. The Soviet efforts to create additional support for martial law during their maneuvers failed. But the first phase of preparations for imposing martial law was carried out.

The situation in the Polish army was ambiguous. Information was spread about possible armed resistance if allied armies invaded. The Soviet military attaché, Col. S. J. Rytov, withdrew from Warsaw, but he insisted on his assessment of the situation: "Poland is not Czechoslovakia, and here it can get to bloodshed." The CC CPSU apparatus continued to analyze the crisis in Poland. It was seeking a way out and discussed the possible scenarios. One of these meetings was described by the Soviet scientist and publicist Robert (Rudolf) Boretsky, who was working in Poland at that time: "Once it was agreed that the situation in Poland was deteriorating . . . I ventured to mention, in an environment where the sparks of aggressiveness were already strong, to say something like we already know about the experience of Czechoslovakia in 1968. That experience may be viewed as successful. The troops were moved in and peace was achieved. But that's not the way for Poland. It's gone too far there. The magnitude of Solidarity's popularity was already too great. And the Poles aren't the Czechs."

Boretsky continued, "I noticed right away that the audience went silent. And there were no other questions."

The Communist Party leaders of the socialist community were kept informed of the situation in Poland. In the period from January to July, a detailed analysis of the situation was sent out six times to Honecker, Husák, Kádár, Bulgaria's Todor Zhivkov, and Cuba's Fidel Castro, who were also drafted to put pressure on the Polish leadership.

Meanwhile, tension was growing. It became increasingly clear that the moment had come when the price of suppression—of individuals, grass-roots efforts, and mass social movements, in a rather large country this time—was too high and the results of outside interference could be more than problematic. In the extreme, it could threaten the international situation, result in severe economic sanctions, and even lead to an outbreak of armed conflict between the two blocs. The United States received information about the assignment of three task forces of the Soviet General Staff to Poland and the expansion of the network controlling the invasion of troops. On 28 March, a team of high-level representatives of the KGB, the Soviet Ministry of Defense, and the State Planning Commission arrived in Warsaw to counsel the Polish leadership on the introduction of martial law. They criticized the Polish plans and demanded a transfer of sovereign power to the military, with appointment of Soviet military advisors at all levels. The Polish authorities did not accept that demand and, after they had agreed to a number of concessions, insisted they had exclusive responsibility for the outcome of the situation.

According to Gates, Washington was waiting for martial law to be introduced in Poland—possibly accompanied by a deployment of Soviet troops. Former British prime minister Margaret Thatcher wrote in her memoirs that the Western allies were ready to respond to the Soviet invasion. NATO had been discussing possible sanctions.

Although martial law was not imposed after the incident in Bydgoszcz, the Soviet leadership continued on their course. On 2 April 1981, the Politburo again discussed the situation in Poland. Brezhnev opened the discussion of the "Polish problem" with these words: "We all have great anxiety about the future course of events in Poland. Worst of all, my friends listen to and agree with our recommendations, but do practically nothing. The counterrevolution is coming on all fronts." The Soviet leadership feared that the opportunity to impose martial law might be lost and Solidarity might take over the country. It sought new arguments to persuade the Polish government to introduce martial law. The Polish leadership's line on political resolution of the conflict with Solidarity was criticized. The general secretary proposed scheduling another meeting with seven member countries of the WP to review the "Polish question" at the highest level. There was also a decision to schedule a meeting with Andropov, Ustinov, Kania, and Jaruzelski, in Brest, to discuss the economic issues associated with the imposition of martial law.

The general secretary said that, on 30 March, during a telephone conversation with Kania, he recommended taking "resolute measures" at the plenum of the PZPR, "not just to criticize, but to take the baton in their hands." He continued with the comment that "you keep talking about the path of peace, not realizing or not wanting to see that the 'peaceful way' you stick to may cause bloodshed." Condemning the "surrender to the opposition," he still proposed a plan to the Polish leadership for mutually accepted measures through the Sejm, although he expressed doubt as to "whether the measures will be taken in full" and whether "there will be enough determination and effort to implement these measures in practice."

For his part, Ustinov offered to "take all necessary measures to ensure that Polish comrades act on their own" and indicated he would exert economic pressure on Poland, which was paralyzed by strikes and dependent on Soviet supplies of food (the Soviet Union's consent for Poland to join the International Monetary Fund was never received). Ustinov viewed introducing martial law in terms of the situation in the Polish army, pointing to the deterioration of its combat readiness resulting from Solidarity's appeal to young service members. He doubted that Kania and Jaruzelski would "go for confrontation," believing that, given Solidarity's highly mobilized state, "it will not be possible to avoid the inevitable bloodshed."

Foreign Minister Gromyko had a somewhat reserved view, being concerned about a possible deterioration of relations with the West and likely sanctions. He mentioned the repeated warnings of the West that the Soviet Union was not supposed to interfere in Polish affairs using armed forces. However, Gromyko thought it necessary under "any circumstances" to tell "the Polish comrades" that there was "a need for more severe . . . emergency measures to restore order," because a further retreat was "totally unacceptable." At the same time, he cautiously urged them to figure out what the real situation in Poland was, "along with the situation in the armed forces." "The army is the main force," he said, "and can we rely on it—if the Polish leaders will at least partially accept the introduction of emergency measures, if they are convinced that the army, the Interior Ministry, and the security agencies will be on their side[?]."

Andropov was ready, fearing a peaceful takeover by Solidarity during the extraordinary congress planned in June. In a personal meeting with him, the Polish leadership was advised to adopt "tough measures . . . without fearing that it may bring about bloodshed." Instead of strict measures, he said, "they propose their so-called political settlement. We talk to them about taking military action, and administrative and judicial steps, but they always limit everything to political measures."

Brezhnev continued this idea, believing that the Polish leaders apparently did not understand what martial law meant: "I'll have to tell them what martial law means, and explain that properly." Andropov went further: "That's right, it should be explained that imposing martial law means establishing a curfew, restricting street traffic, and strengthening protection for state and party institutions, enterprises, etc." The recommendation was incorporated into a draft document for the introduction of martial law, intended to assist the Polish leaders.

A meeting with the Polish leadership was held in a railcar near the border on 3 April in Brest between 9:00 p.m. and 3:00 a.m. so Polish comrades taken to the meeting in a Soviet Tu-134 airplane, as Andropov explained, "could have their attendance avoid detection and then leave unnoticed." On 9 April,

Andropov and Ustinov presented a report on the meeting to the Politburo. The Polish leaders were "in a [state of] stress, and nervous." Kania admitted that the counterrevolution was becoming stronger, the antisocialist forces were pressing, and Solidarity's authority was not subsiding. On the contrary, its position was getting stronger. Therefore, "with regard to sending troops, they just said it was quite impossible, just impossible to introduce martial law"; "they do not understand, and they will be powerless to do anything."

By the way, expert estimates show that, at that time, the strength of forces poised to invade in the event of Warsaw's failure to cooperate was clearly insufficient. At least thirty divisions were necessary, and, if fighting armed resistance were necessary, at least forty-five divisions would have been needed. Such strength was not available. The situation in Poland did not look to be improving, and improvement was necessary if martial law were to be more or less imposed; the crisis turned into a chronic process.

Kania and Jaruzelski once again assured their counterparts that they would restore law and order on their own. Andropov and Ustinov, according to the meeting report, criticized the Polish leaders for indecisiveness and explained to them that using force was a very common political practice, including in the socialist countries. They cited the example of Yugoslavia and other countries where, "if a minor rebellion breaks out, or if there's some sort of confusion, a state of emergency or martial law is immediately introduced." They insisted that the Polish government was wasting time, since martial law could have been introduced as early as September 1980. They further insisted that it was wrong to separate military action and administrative policies: "We must combine everything reasonably." The Polish representatives were invited to sign a draft document on the introduction of martial law. They refused to do so without a Sejm decision. In that situation, Andropov proposed to treat the document as a guideline for the future application of the measure, with a tentative date of 11 April, but he insisted on signing it, "so that we know that you agree with this document, and you know what should be done during martial law." The Poles took the paper without reading it but did not sign it (later, it was discovered that they had no intention of using an immediate military solution in the worsening situation). They developed a new proposal for a political settlement of the conflict in the country. In the discussion of political issues, emphasis was placed on strengthening the party and state. The plan to establish a National Salvation Front to find appropriate policy decisions was endorsed by Soviet authorities, provided that "this front should not replace the party and government." They hinted at the possibility of using the threat of the return of Silesia and Gdańsk to Germany (which could be played up to encourage feelings of unity among the people) in order to exert pressure on public opinion, and they emphasized the importance of the Soviet economic aid that could be lost.

Following the meeting, the Politburo discussed the struggle against Solidarity in the Sejm and the split in the party leadership. The Kremlin was quite worried about the mood in the Polish United Workers' Party; the hardcore party representatives offered to organize an underground Politburo (as it turned out, on the advice of Zhivkov). The idea was rejected, as it could have led to surrendering positions and a defeat. Suslov offered to stop such initiatives and prepare information for the fraternal parties. In mid-April, the Politburo discussed the next steps, "without the discharge of nervousness," but also the need to trust the Suslov Commission to prepare and make a "broader, strategic analysis, so to speak, that would make it possible to break away from current events and assess a longer-term prospect for the development of the situation in and around Poland."

A most important event in the history of the PZPR and the country was the Ninth Party Congress, which was held in June 1981. Preparations for the congress and its progress were the Kremlin's focus. The Soviet leadership thought that the main objective was to strengthen the positions of the party's conservatives (the "healthy forces") and to weaken party reformers, the "revisionists." Therefore, on 23 April, the Politburo of the CC CPSU was reviewing not only the general situation in Poland but also first and foremost the situation in the PZPR. The attached note said that the political crisis "has acquired a protracted, chronic nature." And, if Solidarity was not going to take power at that moment, "it is primarily because of the fear of a Soviet invasion, and because it hopes to achieve its goals without bloodshed, through their creeping counterrevolution . . . seizure of power in 'a lawful manner.'"

The analysis of the balance of power within the PZPR was objective and evenhanded. The fact that forces closest to the Soviet Union (the "diehards") were all set for a "head-on" action was emphasized. On the one hand, the diehards ignored the balance of forces in the country and, on the other hand, did not see "the possibility of improving the situation without a Soviet invasion. That position objectively leads to a greater isolation of the party and the country." That meant that it was difficult to rely on the Poles, because a lot of effort was needed for an election to the congress and the governing bodies (if it were ever possible). The reformist wing of the PZPR was defined as the carrier of an alien ideology, as being close to the leaders of Solidarity and to the concept of restructuring the socioeconomic sphere "in approximately the same way as in Yugoslavia," and as being in the spirit of Eurocommunism, social-democratic pluralism, and the partnership of various political forces.

In preparation for the congress, the Politburo plan was consistently implemented to assist PZPR leadership in strengthening the party's organization and ideology. There were visits and consultations with leading Soviet figures (Suslov, Gromyko, and Viktor Grishin) and party delegations at various levels, as well as with journalists, editors of party publications, labor unionists, and others, in order to explain "the basic laws of Marxism-Leninism."

Before the congress, on 5 June, the CPSU Central Committee directly addressed the PZPR activists. The appeal stated that Soviet comrades were seriously concerned that the revolutionary achievements of the Polish nation were "in great danger" and that there was a "threat to the very existence of an independent Polish state." The committee then asked, "And who could then ensure the independence, sovereignty, and borders of Poland as a state? No one." That statement was accompanied by the standard ideological message: the offensive by antisocialist forces in the PRL "threatens the interests of our entire community, its unity, integrity, and the security of its borders."

During that period, public discontent was at its peak. According to polls conducted in June, the PZPR had 6 percent public support and the government, 24 percent, while Solidarity came in at 62 percent. The Ninth Plenum of the PZPR, held 9–10 June at the request of the CPSU Central Committee, showed the balance of power in the Central Committee and in the entire party; the "diehards" received less than a quarter of the votes. In this situation, the Kremlin found it expedient to continue supporting Kania and Jaruzelski. The resolution of the plenum was focused on the "convergence of views in the evaluation of the current situation in Poland" with those of the CPSU and on continuing the process of socialist renewal by uniting all the forces of the People's Unity Front "in implementing a policy of social reconciliation and reforms." At the same time, the question of suppressing the "rebellion" in Poland by force remained on the agenda in numerous intense contacts with the Polish leadership. Marshal Kulikov, the commander of the Warsaw Pact, arrived in Warsaw and kept insisting on decisive action by mid-June, as he negotiated with Kania, Jaruzelski, and the Polish army chief of staff, Gen. Florian Siwicki.

A report on the Polish question by the Suslov Commission recommended exploiting fears of "internal reactionary forces" and "international imperialism" as much as possible to deter the counterrevolution, stemming from the fact that the Soviet Union might bring in troops. Speaking at a Politburo meeting two days after a 16 June telephone conversation with Kania, who was also scared by the prospect, Brezhnev expressed his hope that "maybe they will eventually begin to think and act forcefully." Soviet army commanders were very active, and, in July, six hundred more tanks were brought into Poland without the consent of the Poles, thus tripling the number there.

The Ninth Congress of the Polish United Workers' Party brought no significant changes, including any alignment of forces within the governing bodies of the party. Yet, by August, there was increased convergence between the leadership of the party, Solidarity, and the Catholic Church.

In August, Marshal Kulikov asked the commanders of the Polish army for consent to add Soviet military advisors to its ranks, from the General Staff to the division level. That idea was rejected. Anticipating an imminent military confrontation, and under an agreement between the KGB and its Polish equivalent, the MBP, a statement on martial law of the State Council was secretly printed in Moscow (without specifying the date or the name of the council chair) and forwarded to Poland. In September to early October, near the Polish border in Belarus, in the Baltic military district, and along the Baltic Sea, Soviet troops held their "West 81" exercises, timed to coincide with the First Solidarity Congress.

Representatives of the two General Staffs continued to develop emergency plans. According to Colonel Kukliński, who was working as an American agent, General Siwicki shared with his entourage his information about the "institutionalization of the coming martial law" and about the likely Soviet assistance if the domestic operation failed. Media immediately set out to provide information about potential "international aid." However, in mid-September, Poland's political leadership once again rejected the plan proposed by the military to introduce martial law.

A new round of intense Soviet pressure on Polish leaders to declare martial law has been associated with the decisions made by the First Solidarity Congress.

An analysis of the congress's ideological and political positions was carried out by the Suslov Commission during the development of its executive report for the plenum of the CPSU Central Committee. That report offered one conclusion: the First Solidarity Congress had approved a plan for how to assume power, change the social system, eliminate existing forms of ownership, carry out centralized planning, and control the party membership, as well as establish workers' self-management. The objectives of holding free elections for parliament and local governments, ensuring that all political and social forces had free access to media, and eliminating political censorship were interpreted as the elimination of the PZPR and the transformation of the nation into a multiparty, bourgeois parliamentarian republic. The congress's appeal to the peoples of Eastern Europe "to exchange experiences in fighting for the establishment of free labor unions" was described as an assault on the principles of the "socialist community" and the Warsaw Pact. This proposed political assault could provide grounds for an immediate imposition of martial law. On 17 September, the Soviet ambassador to Warsaw, Boris I. Aristov, and Jaruzelski submitted a statement to Kania from the Soviet leadership protesting the "provocative activities of antisocialist forces" that were harmful to Soviet-Polish relations and ran counter to Poland's obligations as an allied state. Moscow strongly protested bringing back the celebration of the anniversary of the revival of an independent Polish state on 11 November and the opening of the official Powązki Cemetery in Warsaw, with its sign that read "Victims of Katyn" and "1940."

No significant steps were taken by Kania. The Soviet leadership decided that he was psychologically and politically demoralized and unable to cope with the challenge of martial law in the country. At the Fourth Plenum of the PZPR Central Committee on 18 October 1981, Jaruzelski—who was prime minister, defense minister, and chair of the National Defense General—was appointed first secretary of the party's Central Committee. He was a very well respected leader in the party and had significant weight in the army. On 19 October, in congratulating him on his new position, Brezhnev strongly reminded him of the need for immediate action against the "counterrevolution" with the help of the "healthy forces." Preparations for imposing martial law, it seemed, were entering their final stage, with increasingly intense pressure on the Polish government and society. At the army post in the Polish town of Żagań, Soviet and Polish troops held tactical maneuvers accompanied by a demonstration of new Soviet weapons, with the military leadership of Poland, the GDR, and Czechoslovakia in attendance. The question of moving in allied forces was not discussed. At a 21 October meeting of the main team of commanders in the Ministry of Defense, Soviet Chief of Staff Marshal Ogarkov never raised the issue of the situation in Poland directly, focusing instead on protecting and promoting the interests of the Northern Group of Forces situated in Poland, and employing safer routes for troops and inventory when moving strategic reserves in the event of a war. Marshal Kulikov, chief of the Warsaw Pact forces, said he was concerned about the future of Poland as an ally and about the preparations for an invasion by troops located along the perimeter of the Polish border (Jaruzelski strongly objected to moving in German troops from the GDR). At the same time, the WP chief of staff warned of the unpredictable consequences of such actions and was supported by Marshal S. L. Sokolov and Gen. A. A. Epishev. In autumn of 1981, the operational plan focused exclusively on the mission of the Polish armed forces. Other WP forces were to provide assistance only relative to the risk of aggravating the situation throughout the "socialist community" and were thus viewed as a reserve force. These troops remained on combat alert at the borders of Poland until April 1982.

There were other options for action in the event Polish forces failed to impose martial law, a fact confirmed by several Soviet military leaders. One of them, Gen. Viktor P. Dubinin, who developed and carried out similar actions in the 1990s, said in an interview with Boretsky, "In 1981, military action was planned if Polish leadership failed to take decisive steps toward restoring the stability of the system, and law and order in the country. I'm not saying that we were talking about full-scale military operations, yet the presence of our troops was supposed to stabilize the country." The commander of an armored division that was involved in moving tanks into an area south of Warsaw recalled, "I was aware of the mission's objectives, and knew where to go and all of the settlements that we were to enter." In 1992, he told the press that preparations had been completed by the end of November 1981 and that, if the plans for martial law did not "work," the invasion was planned for 14 December. Similar evidence came in the book *I'll Tell You the Truth*, by Gen. Vladislav A. Achalov, who at the time was a young paratrooper unit commander trained in the "West 81" operational-strategic exercises to engage a hypothetical enemy after troops had been moved into Poland. His task was to enter Warsaw and Łódź, seize key strategic points there (the PZPR Central Committee, the Sejm, Gostsentrobank, the Ministry of Interior, the Ministry of Defense, etc.), and arrest General Jaruzelski and other government and army leaders. To prepare for the operation, Achalov dressed as a civilian and toured all of those key facilities with a Russian group in August 1981. Other military officers provided further evidence of the readiness to deploy troops from other military districts in November–December 1981: Gen. Vladimir Dudnik, Gen. Dmitry Sukhorukov, Col. Viktor Alksnis, Col. I. Kachugurny, Col. V. Konovalov, and others.

At the Politburo meeting on 21 October, in a discussion of "the Polish agenda item" following a visit to Warsaw, CPSU secretary Rusakov voiced the following position: all of the Poles' requests must be answered by saying that the Soviet Union would not move troops into Poland. Ustinov, who had arrived from a military meeting, justified this statement by saying that "our troops should not be moved into Poland. The Poles are not ready to receive our troops."

Suslov insisted that no troops should be moved into Poland under any circumstances, "even if the Polish leaders ask us to take this step." He added that "we need to cooperate with all political forces there, even with the social democrats." He told the Polish leadership that Soviet troops would guarantee Poland's security in the event of an external threat, but under no circumstances were they to be used for domestic purposes. Such actions, concluded Brezhnev, did not give a clear idea of what was going to happen in Poland. For the Soviet leadership, a qualitatively new situation had emerged, spinning developments out of control.

While continuing to put pressure on Jaruzelski, Brezhnev spoke to him through the ambassador, "urging" him to consider that it was not a question of whether a confrontation would take place but who would start it, what means would be used, and who would retain the initiative. On 29 October, while discussing the situation in Poland following Rusakov's trip to the GDR, Czechoslovakia, Hungary, and Bulgaria, Andropov insisted that, if Polish leaders were talking about military assistance from fraternal countries, one line must be maintained: troops will never be moved into Poland.

General Jaruzelski, continuing to investigate the dynamics of the senti-ments and intentions of the Soviet leadership and still in no hurry to intro-duce martial law, continued probing and searching for a political agreement with Solidarity, seeking negotiations that would extinguish the conflict. The final, unsuccessful attempt to negotiate with the opposition was the meet-ing of 4 November in Warsaw between Jaruzelski and Cardinal Józef Glemp, successor to Cardinal Stefan Wyszyński as primate of the Polish Catholic Church, and Solidarity leader Lech Wałęsa, who was considering the idea of a Front of National Accord. However, the increasingly tense situation was pushing both sides toward confrontation. At an expanded meeting of the Presidium of the National Commission of Solidarity, that idea was rejected.

Of particular concern to the Soviet leadership was the decision, prompted by Poland's economic situation, to join the International Monetary Fund, which resulted in economic aid being provided, though not right away.

Jaruzelski's hesitation to impose martial law was causing a growing dis-trust on the part of the Soviet leadership. On 11 November, Suslov spoke at the plenum of the CPSU Central Committee and gave a secret presenta-tion about the situation in Poland, thus preparing Soviet party activists for the approaching decisive action. In addition to "Plan A" (martial law), the CPSU Central Committee was prepared for "Plan B," according to which the "healthy forces" in the PRL were to take power, with the assistance of Soviet troops in Poland, if anarchy developed in the country. Information was also presented about the readiness of the security forces led by Gen. M. Moczar to ensure that Jaruzelski would retire and be replaced by a stronger supporter of the effort to suppress the opposition. On 19 November, there was a nationwide conference of the "healthy forces" in the army and security agencies, which demonstrated a willingness to launch a decisive attack against the counter-revolution. The PZPR, which was practically split into groups, discussed not only reform but also a plan to form a new party as well. That party's found-ing congress was planned for 15 December. Replenished with new military contingents, the Northern Group of Forces was to ensure the suppression of Solidarity's rear guard, if escalation of the conflict dictated such a course.

Confusion and uncertainty about the situation and outlook caused quite a few obstacles to clearly defining and refining the options available to the Soviets. Several versions of the minutes dated "21 November" from the Polit-buro were substantially different. The published version had clearly been ed-ited. The archived "working record" lacks the crucial fifth page. (That page is actually missing from the archive of the Presidential Collection of Polit-buro Minutes.) In one version, the text describes a discussion of a military assistance issue with Jaruzelski; in another, he insists that Poland would cope with the situation on its own.

It is impossible not to point out the following statement by Suslov: "Jaru-zelski is playing tricks with us." And the general himself, in an interview with Boretsky, commented on this as follows:

> It was really so. . . . We had to play two games, which was hard and took lots of wisdom. Incidentally, the game was played on both sides. They were probing us on the subject of martial law. We, in turn, tried to find out how much of a threat their "fraternal assistance" was to us. It was especially difficult with Suslov, who played with a variety of options—"And if you start, and then we move in?" [he asked]. "We'll handle this ourselves," I answered. "And if the situation becomes complicated?" [Suslov asked]. I recalled the words Brezh-nev said to my predecessor, First Secretary of the PZPR S. Kania[:] "If the situation is complicated, then we'll go." That was back in 1980. But, hardly anything had changed a year later. Therefore, I insisted that we would man-age ourselves.

At the 21 November meeting mentioned above, the Politburo decided to organize a reception in the Soviet Union for the government delegation led by PZPR leader Jaruzelski. And on 22 November, an oral message from Brezhnev requested that he immediately begin a military confrontation with Solidarity.

From 2 to 4 December, there was a meeting in Moscow of the Warsaw Pact's Committee of Ministers of Defense. The central item was the Polish question. Kulikov, who "was convinced that the troops would have to be moved in" and who "made no secret of his position" (which was that collapse was inevitable if the community, led by the Soviet Union, no longer had the power to maintain "law and order in our surroundings"), spoke with Jaruzel-ski on 3 December about allied forces entering at midnight (00:00 hours) on 8 December. Because of the complexity of the situation, Siwicki, who repre-sented Poland, raised the issue of moral and political support in the form of a statement condemning the actions of the counterrevolution in Poland and NATO interference in the country's internal affairs. When that proposal was not approved due to a "lack of authority" by the defense ministers of Hungary and Romania, Jaruzelski expressed great surprise that the allies "do not want to assume at least some of the responsibility, even when they constantly say that the Polish problem is a problem for the Warsaw Pact, and not only a Polish problem." He added that "the allies are driving us into an impossible position," [so] "leave us alone." In this context, the question arose about pos-sible military aid from the Soviet Union, when martial law "failed" and the situation became "critical."

On 7 December, Marshal Kulikov and Nikolai Baibakov, the chair of Gos-plan, once again went to Poland at the request of Brezhnev. Baibakov was instructed to promise economic aid to Poland if martial law was imposed. Ku-likov proceeded from the "clear line of CPSU Central Committee general policy" and tried to force General Jaruzelski to immediately impose martial law. Urging Jaruzelski to introduce martial law, Brezhnev warned that, "if appropriate measures were not taken immediately, it would be too late; it will turn into our common concern," he said, as quoted by Vladimir I. Voronkov. Thus, the plan to move the WP troops in was once again announced. Talks in Warsaw did not lead to any concrete result. Even the attempts to find out the timing of the martial law declaration did not give results. The Polish leaders continued to raise the issue of providing political support. On 9 December, General Siwicki appealed to Moscow on behalf of Jaruzelski with an urgent request for the state to make an official announcement or at least for TASS to issue a statement about the situation in Poland. These statements were never made.

On 10 December, according to draft minutes of the Politburo, the last recorded before the introduction of martial law, it was proposed to quickly resolve the matter of moving the troops stationed on the border into Poland, along with the WP troops already stationed there.

Musatov draws attention to many factors, such as the nonlinearity and complexity of the situation and scenarios that could subsequently develop: the military had ideas on how to secure the GDR's key communications and what steps might be needed to counter NATO activities. The KGB resident in Poland, General Pavlov, wrote about plans to "build a channel" to maintain communications with the Soviet armed forces in western Poland and Germany.

Still very confusing were the questions of the Polish leadership's intent and commitment to martial law, as well as of the position of Marshal Kulikov, who was in Warsaw at the time on a mission to encourage the process. The working group of the "Polish committee" discussed the alternative of using the Poles (and a corresponding plan existed for that) to establish a political-military dictatorship by the general—or without him—a so-called collective junta; the people appointed would be directly responsible for the internment of General Jaruzelski and other Polish leaders who were Soviet military service members.

Information about these issues in the two versions of "working drafts" is contradictory and dubious (the originally brief archive was expanded later, with volumes being added; it was prepared for publication and submitted by Boris Yeltsin to Wałęsa in August 1993). On the one hand, there was a constant emphasis on the fact that restoring order in Poland was the objective of the PZPR, its Central Committee, and the Politburo. On the other hand, the version sent to the Poles emphasizes the alleged Polish requests to bring in Soviet troops, apparently as an excuse to later justify implementing this option.

In the drafts, Jaruzelski talks about probing the situation and denies that there were such appeals. Rusakov claims, however, that, according to him, the general had hoped for help from other countries until the allied forces entered, relying on Kulikov's assurances. As for the general's probing the conduct of those bearing "international aid" after Polish forces failed to implement their plan, he said, "It seems . . . like he's trying to cheat us." In an interview with Boretsky, Jaruzelski drew attention to the fact that only one "false . . . working record," which "really talks about something wrong," indicated that he expressed his intention, if necessary, to request "fraternal assistance" and "contact with allies" in order for troops to be moved into Poland. He also indicated their expectation that such assistance "will be provided to and from the USSR," referring to Kulikov's promises.

At a Politburo meeting on 10 December, Rusakov was quick to clarify that Kulikov had simply repeated the words of Brezhnev that "we would not abandon Poland in trouble." Andropov, who contacted Minister Mirosław Milewski, stated otherwise: "They do not yet have a firm decision to impose martial law and no firm date has been set. Moreover, they will start operation 'X' when it is 'imposed' by Solidarity." Andropov stressed that Kulikov's statement above "would be wrong"; the operation "must entirely be the decision of our Polish comrades; as they choose, so be it. We will not insist on this and will not be discouraged." He explained the meaning of the Soviet position:

> We cannot risk it. We do not intend to move troops into Poland. This is the correct position, and we must adhere to it to the end. I do not know how things will turn against Poland, but even if Poland is under the rule of Solidarity, it will be one thing. But if the Soviet Union collapses under the capitalist countries—and they already have a relevant agreement regarding various economic and political sanctions—it will be very difficult for us. We must care about our country and strengthening the Soviet Union. This is our main focus.

In another version, that statement reads as follows: "Jaruzelski again raises the question of our military intervention. We have already told him that we cannot interfere in Polish affairs; we will not do this, but this does not add hope for his army. And so, he would like to have our assurance that we will intervene as a guarantee. . . . He must rely on his resources. It's one thing if Solidarity wins in Poland, but quite another thing if we move in and the entire western world comes down on us with sanctions and everything."

The Soviet leaders decided to inform Jaruzelski that he could count only on himself. Defense Minister Ustinov confirmed that the general was counting on them alone and that Kulikov "knows perfectly well that the Poles themselves asked not to move the troops in."

Later, there were questionable attempts to attribute a request for armed assistance to Jaruzelski, making references to unofficial notes that were made on unnumbered pages on inserts in "workbooks" taken "from the archive of" Kulikov's adjutant general, V. Anoshkin.

Ustinov made a statement at a meeting of the Politburo on 10 December regarding Jaruzelski's consistent position with regard to rejecting the "international aid" that they had been unequivocally denied. The general clearly defined his position on engaging WP armed forces while responding to Boretsky's question: "Can you briefly say, in yes or no terms, whether you asked for direct 'fraternal assistance'[?] And in general, is there a single answer to that question?" Ustinov stated,

> There is a definite answer—no. Many times I have said and written this about it. The fundamental always boiled down to saying that Polish affairs were to be resolved by our own efforts. . . . The army enjoyed unprecedented support—according to opinion polls, 93 percent of Poles trusted the army! So, why would we call up "big brother" to rescue us? . . . And I didn't want to commit suicide. Since calling in another would not help martial law, but would instead trigger a national revolt and would, in fact, start a war. And such a war would involve not only civilians; it would also lead to a split in the army. And the first bullet would have been mine.

Kulikov and Baibakov were sent to Warsaw after Ambassador Aristov made comments that differed from those of Polish security officials: the decision to impose martial law was made at a meeting of the PZPR Politburo on 5 December, or it was not; it was planned to be introduced on the night of 13 December, or no specific date had been slated; there were still doubts about the need to introduce it; it was going to be announced in a radio and television broadcast "around 20:00" by State Council chair Henryk Jabłoński; and General Jaruzelski believed it was only possible to pass a law after it had been discussed in the Sejm, which was to meet on 15 December (but there was no such item on the Sejm's agenda).

According to G. H. Shakhnazarov, deputy head of the Department of the Central Committee for Cooperation with the Communist and Workers' Socialist Countries, a little later Suslov emphasized the need to keep the Poles and the world convinced that martial law imposed by Soviet troops "had not been ruled out" and that the threat of force was to be used to demonstrate that in every way ("whether Jaruzelski believed in that or not, he emphasized, did not really matter; as the country's leader, he was obliged to not rule out such a possibility"). But at the Politburo meeting on 10 December, Suslov set the record straight: "If the troops are introduced, it would spell disaster. I think we all have here a broad consensus that moving the troops in is out of the question." Other members of his committee—Gromyko, Grishin, and Ustinov—spoke against the invasion and strictly in the spirit "of noninterference." A relevant decision was made, encouraging the long-awaited settlement of the Polish issue using Polish forces.

The situation becomes clear from Mikhail Gorbachev's official letter of 31 August 1995 to the Sejm commission on constitutional responsibility, which had reviewed the issue of imposing martial law. In particular, Gorbachev's letter stated the following: "The Soviet leadership has been desperately trying to find a way out of the two equally unacceptable options: to agree with the chaos that has engulfed Poland, which may entail the disintegration of the socialist community; or to respond to events in Poland using force. . . . Nevertheless, our troops and the armored convoys along the Polish border, as well as the relatively strong Northern Group of Forces in Poland[,] could be activated under certain extreme circumstances." As for the role of Jaruzelski in the process of democratization, in the opinion of Gorbachev, he was by no means inclined to instigate a large-scale repression of Solidarity, which had gained unprecedented support and had been produced by a combination of various factors calling for systemic change. General Jaruzelski deserves credit because he rejected using force and WP troops to resolve the conflict. One cannot ignore the fact that the relocation of Polish units and their concentration ruled out amassing allied units in Poland that would be ready to provide "fraternal assistance." At the same time, Jaruzelski managed to maintain social progress in the context of the discourse at the time of the inevitable, peaceful, and optimal preservation of the "socialist community."

On the same day, 10 December, Jaruzelski asked the Soviet government to send a member of the Politburo of the CPSU Central Committee to Warsaw. In his memoirs, General Gribkov recalled a telephone conversation between Rusakov and Ambassador Aristov that included a request to inform the Poles that, in the near future, none of the Communist Party leadership would be visiting Poland, and with regard to government statements, "action will be taken"; the troops would not be moved into Poland; the Poles would have to solve the problems on their own; and the Gosplan chair was working on additional economic assistance. Jaruzelski saw that as an attempt to walk back the Polish problem. Siwicki's emotional comment was, "If you do not provide the required assistance to Poland, it will be the end of the Warsaw Pact." At the same time, the Soviet units tapped for the invasion of Poland stayed combat-ready until the spring or summer of 1982.

On 12 December, Moscow discussed sending a delegation headed by Suslov to Warsaw. On the scheduled date of the visit, Ustinov called Kulikov, who was in Poland, and said that the visit by Suslov, Chernenko, and Rusakov was still under consideration. The visit never took place. The Soviet leadership "did not want to show their cards" in a tense moment, hoping to maintain complete freedom of action.

On 13 December, 1981, at 00:00, Poland began to introduce martial law. The announcement was made six hours later.

On the same day, the PZPR Politburo notified all other WP parties about the introduction of martial law in Poland, emphasizing that, prior to these events, in response to a message from Jaruzelski about his intentions, "he was told that the Soviet leadership had received the decision of the Polish comrades with understanding" and that it approved of General Jaruzelski's address to the nation. Acknowledgment of the party's leading role and evidence of the PRL's allegiance to its obligations under the Warsaw Pact were also welcomed.

Meanwhile, the Brezhnev Doctrine was losing strength. The following aspects of the operation were apparent: the introduction of martial law because of a political decision made by General Jaruzelski and his team saved the country both from the "healthy forces" that would have come to power and from the inevitable bloodshed. They also saved the country from the deaths of hundreds or, more likely, thousands of people. A competent analysis of the international situation, which was so essential for future progress, was combined with political plans and maneuvers that hindered controversial options that were explosive and fraught with armed conflict and civil war. This made it possible to initially remove the excessive tension and eventually put everything into the mainstream of peaceful negotiations. The knot of contradictions was cut with violence applied, but the peaceful introduction of martial law was acceptable to the Soviet Union and the United States. The Soviet leadership did believe that the new political regime was not strict enough, and during a visit of a Polish delegation to Moscow on 1 March 1982, the Soviet leadership sought to redirect the Polish authorities toward restoring the party and political structures by using the "healthy forces." Jaruzelski did not accept that dangerous course, which might have incited a new period of confrontation. A relatively calm, "cool" regime of martial law made it possible to keep the economy from backsliding, to look for ways out of the crisis, and to carry out democratic reforms in the political sphere and the market economy. That gradually led to a reduction of social tensions, and, as a result, in 1989, a political compromise was reached between the government and the moderate part of the opposition, which opened up ways to bring about a systemic transformation.

11

REGAINED FREEDOM AND SOVEREIGNTY

TRANSFORMATION PROCESSES IN POLAND AND RUSSIA

Włodzimierz Marciniak (Poland)

Professor at the Jesuit University Ignatianum in Kraków, member of the Polish-Russian Group on Difficult Matters since 2008.

Vladimir G. Baranovsky (Russia)

Full member of the Russian Academy of Sciences, deputy director of the Institute of World Economy and International Relations, professor at the Moscow State Institute of International Relations (MGIMO University).

Boris A. Shmelyov (Russia)

Professor and director of the Center for Political Studies at the Institute of Economy of the Russian Academy of Sciences.

WŁODZIMIERZ MARCINIAK

TRANSFORMATION PROCESSES IN POLAND AND RUSSIA

THE POST-1989 POLITICAL experiences of Poland and Russia are comparable to some extent, since both countries dealt with changes in the political regime during conditions of deep economic and social crisis. Furthermore, in both instances, we witnessed the dismantling of a system of Communist Party rule. Poland, however, developed a political system based on checks and balances, the political involvement of its citizens, interparty competition, and alternating governments. Russia, however, has not been consistent in separating the branches of government, and political competition is played out not between parties but within a hierarchical power structure. There has been no change of government since 1991, and society has been effectively depoliticized. If, in the case of Poland, one might speak of a transition from authoritarianism to democracy, in the case of Russia we have seen a transition from authoritarian mobilization to oligarchic competition. The new regime might be considered a kind of elitist government in which the sham character of the democratic institutions prevents genuine control over the people in power.

The tumultuous developments of 1989 in Eastern Europe set in motion deep political, economic, and social changes, the scope of which roughly overlapped with the geopolitical structure of the Soviet Empire. However, the political process followed a different course in the heart of the empire, that is, Russia, than on its periphery in Central and Eastern Europe. Systems in which the parties in power changed evolved only to the west of the Soviet Union's pre-1939 border. The eleven states that were part of the Soviet Union before World War II now have presidential systems. The parties in them are very weak, and the opposition has seldom managed to win the presidency through elections. Within that group of countries, only Ukraine conducted political reforms, establishing a more balanced political system.

The Soviet Empire and Its Ideological Mutations

The Soviet Union was not an ordinary territorial state with national interests, a political system, and bureaucratic mechanisms for decision making. First and foremost, it was an ideocracy and an exterritorial state-party. The teleology of that structure and the types of strategic and tactical decisions made were rooted in its archetype. In fact, decisions were not so much made as they were interpreted by the hierarchy of competent organs in a process of ceremonial rites (*arcana imperii*). The Communist Party in its various versions had always been a homogenous and centralized organization, international with regard to its goals and functions and constituting merely a part—though the victorious part—of a greater global entity. The Union of Soviet Socialist Republics never consisted of just its fifteen member republics. Rather, it resembled a geopolitical system comprising several concentric circles. At its center was the Russian Soviet Federative Socialist Republic (RSFSR), where the Communist Party ruled directly, without having to establish branches in the republics. The second and third circles consisted of the union's republics and socialist countries, with increasingly complicated systems of government. The system also had its exterritorial peripheries, in the form of legal and illicit organizations that "had not yet" assumed power. As Alexei Salmin points out, the ideological "mutation" of policy constituted an exceptionally rare phenomenon in the communist world system and involved a fundamental renewal of the ruling elite, including the replacement of the leadership of the ruling party and the physical—or merely political—liquidation of a part of the previous elite. During the period of Soviet rule, only two such "mutations" occurred: in the mid-1920s, when the ideology of building socialism in one state was adopted, and in the late 1950s, when the concept of the peaceful coexistence of different socioeconomic systems was formulated.

In each instance, the ideological "mutations" were accompanied by certain alterations in the practice of government. In the 1930s, it was decided that a formal distinction between the legislative branch (Supreme Soviet) and the executive branch (Council of People's Commissars; from 1946, the Council of Ministers) would be introduced. The first elections to the Supreme Soviet were preceded by a self-criticism campaign and a purge, generally referred to as perestroika, the goal of which was to awaken the criticism of the masses. That is why Mikhail Gorbachev's reforms might be interpreted as the third—this time, unsuccessful—attempt at the ideological "mutation" of Soviet communism through a renewal of the way of thinking and of the elite, or part of it. The basic difference between Stalin's perestroika and Gorbachev's consisted of the fact that the former involved terror, while the latter relied on massive criticism of party dignitaries, which rapidly transformed into criticism of the system.

Each time, the institutional changes were coupled with the idea of establishing an office of president, elected by universal suffrage. This happened during the discussion preceding the adoption of the 1936 constitution and in 1962, in the final stage of reforms intended to decentralize the administration. The idea was revived after the failure of economic acceleration, when Gorbachev initiated political reforms designed to institute a new organ of government—the presidency. That goal was facilitated by the relatively competitive election of people's deputies in 1989 and the establishment of a supreme state authority—the Congress of People's Deputies.

Gorbachev's Reforms

Political reforms in the Soviet Union were launched in the late 1980s, somewhat earlier than in other countries in the communist bloc. The reasons for initiating the reforms were similar to those in Poland, the German Democratic Republic (GDR), and Hungary: the failure of attempts to boost the effectiveness of central planning, coupled with a dramatic drop in oil prices in 1985 and the rising cost of foreign debt service. In the years 1987–88, the economic crisis evolved into three structural crises: a crisis of loyalty among the empire's provinces, a crisis of loyalty among the population, and a crisis of loyalty among the apparatus of repression.

The crisis of loyalty among the empire's provinces reflected the geopolitical structure of the Soviet Empire, with the Communist Party at its center and the successive circles formed by the Russian republic, the other republics in the union, and the socialist countries. The years 1987–88 marked the beginning of systemic changes in Central and Eastern Europe. At about the same time, conflicts started between the republics and the Soviet Union over declarations of state sovereignty within the framework of the Soviet Union that envisaged the primacy of republic law over union law and the primacy of republic budgets over the union budget. The crisis of loyalty among the provinces proceeded in waves. By the time it reached the territorial center of the empire, declarations of independence had been made by Lithuania, Latvia, Armenia, and Georgia. Meanwhile, the Warsaw Pact was nearing collapse.

The crisis of loyalty among the population was primarily caused by shortages of consumer goods, the budget deficit, inflation, and the freezing of savings deposits. In 1987, individual business activity was legalized and state enterprises were given increased independence. However, the deteriorating economic situation triggered increasingly massive protest actions, including political strikes in the spring of 1991.

The crisis of loyalty among the apparatus of repression stemmed from the "military revolution" and drastic cuts in allocations for the arms industry. In 1988, when the pullout of Soviet troops from Afghanistan was under way, discussion began on the conversion of the arms industry. The crisis of loyalty among the apparatus of repression was of pivotal importance to the

Communist Party because of the systemic memory of the illegitimacy of its rule and the role that force had played in retaining it. In this context, it is noteworthy that, in the late 1980s and early 1990s, the communists showed restraint in using force. That crucial innovation—not only in the history of communism but also, indeed, in the annals of revolution—made itself evident for the first time in the course of the so-called "Velvet Revolution" of 1989 and was repeated in the Soviet Union in August 1991 and during the "color" revolutions in Georgia and Ukraine. The phenomenon of restraint by the apparatus of repression indicated that the disintegration of the Soviet Union had progressed beyond the framework of political transition, since it now concerned the issue of sovereignty, that is, something much more fundamentally significant than the political regime.

Gorbachev attempted to avert the crisis of sovereignty by initiating political reforms in the summer of 1988. At that time, the constitution was amended, making the Congress of People's Deputies the supreme organ of state power. The congress was tasked with appointing two other organs of state power: the Supreme Soviet and the chair of the Supreme Soviet and, from March 1990, the president of the Soviet Union. The elections of people's deputies took place in March 1990, when the Round Table talks were still under way in Poland. Two-thirds of the deputies were elected in their respective constituencies, while the remaining third were appointed by social organizations (the Communist Party, the Komsomol, trade unions, and others). Each seat was contested on average by two candidates, though in some constituencies there was just a single candidate.

The elections of people's deputies had dual consequences. First of all, a mechanism of political competition was set in motion and consolidated a year later, in the spring of 1990, during the republics' parliamentary elections. Secondly, the elections instituted the Congress of People's Deputies, which had the prerogative of legalizing the new organ of power, that is, the president of the Soviet Union. Gorbachev decided to establish the presidency in March 1990, thus undermining the Communist Party's monopoly on power. A month later, the Congress of People's Deputies elected Gorbachev the first president of the Soviet Union, simultaneously amending Articles 6 and 7 of the constitution, which had guaranteed the political monopoly of the Communist Party. The confluence of these developments is symbolic because they tellingly illustrate the intention of replacing the dictatorship of the Communist Party with a "strong" presidency.

It soon became evident that the new president felt constrained by the constitution. After a short spell of democratization, he reverted to the practice of concentrating power. He asked for special powers to run the economy by decree. Since none of the competing concepts of economic reform had gained majority support, in October 1990 the Congress of People's Deputies granted the president special powers in the area of economic reform, including the prerogative of issuing decrees equivalent to laws. Thus, actual power started shifting from the Communist Party to the president. Furthermore, talks with the leaders of the respective republics concerning a new union treaty were conducted without the knowledge of the deputies. On the day Gorbachev wrapped up secret negotiations on a new treaty, the president's chief of staff called for the introduction of a state of emergency.

Gorbachev's actions encouraged other politicians to follow suit. Almost immediately after Gorbachev became president, the leader of the communists in Kazakhstan, Nursultan Nazarbayev, proposed that the union's republics should also have presidents. That declaration changed the logic of the ongoing transformations, since political competition began shifting from the realm of interparty rivalry to the sphere determined by the institutional structure of the Soviet federation. The political landscape underwent a fundamental change: the political parties began disappearing and their functions were taken over by the republics' legislative assemblies, elected in the spring of 1990.

Russia's Sovereignty

March 1990 saw elections to the Congress of People's Deputies of the RSFSR, that is, elections to the supreme organ of state power, empowered (in line with the logic of "Soviet democracy") to establish other organs of government. The first Congress of People's Deputies of the RSFSR elected a Supreme Soviet and its chair, though it was the adoption of a declaration about the state sovereignty of the RSFSR that became the focal point of political competition. Initially, the idea of state sovereignty for the RSFSR within the Soviet Union was put forward by Aleksandr Vlasov, a communist and the prime minister of the RSFSR. He called for a separation of the competencies of the Soviet Union and the RSFSR. In response, Boris Yeltsin—Vlasov's rival for the post of Supreme Soviet chair—floated the idea of Russia's economic sovereignty. He insisted that RSFSR independence made sense only if republic ownership of assets was instituted.

The declaration on state sovereignty for the Russian Soviet Federative Socialist Republic, adopted on 12 June 1990, triggered the so-called "war of the laws," which lasted for several months. Its first salvo was the law on the separation of the management of institutions on the territory of the RSFSR, which separated the Council of Ministers of the RSFSR from the government of the Soviet Union, and the last—the law of January 1991—on the assets of the RSFSR, which provided for the transfer of all union assets to republic jurisdiction.

The adoption in 1990 of declarations of state sovereignty by Belarus, Moldova, Russia, and Ukraine amounted to a pivotal turning point in the development of the political situation in the Soviet Union. The question of sovereignty of the Soviet republics—rather than their democratization—was at the core of this process. The opposing factions did not reach compromise, so the escalation of tensions became a key factor in the political process. The system of Soviet democracy, based on the Congress–Supreme Soviet formula, collapsed twice, with tragic consequences in August 1991 (Soviet Union) and September 1993 (Russian Federation).

In Russia itself, the confrontation between the union and republic leaderships evolved in early 1991 into an open rift within the Russian Congress of People's Deputies. Taking that into account, Yeltsin, whose power totally depended on the people's deputies, attempted to make popular support a permanent component of political legitimization. It was in those circumstances that there appeared the idea of establishing the office of president in the RSFSR/Russia, elected by universal suffrage. It was a novel idea in Russia with regard to the method of creating a supreme authority and the source of its legitimacy. Alas, that great victory of Russian democracy turned out to be its last utterance, since, as early as August 1991, the victorious political camp proclaimed a moratorium on elections and the president of Russia started "requisitioning" the prerogatives of his rival, the president of the Soviet Union, in the form of a creeping coup.

Yeltsin's election as president and the victory of the democrats in 1991 not only revolutionized the method of creating and legitimizing state authority but also initiated the process of concentrating power in one hand. The process of reproducing the cultural archetype of authority was also enhanced by institutional factors. The Russian presidency emerged in the course of political struggle as the means to overcome the crisis in the Soviet system and was deprived of the sturdy skeleton of the Communist Party. The presidency occupied the spot in the political system vacated by that party, thus entering into an automatic conflict with the Soviets and the Congress of People's Deputies, endowed by the constitution with unlimited powers. In the absence of a public rivalry between the parties, political rivalry metamorphosed into a struggle between the organs of power. However, the institutional conflict was not over the division of power between the executive and legislative branches but over who would be dominant in the hierarchical power structure. The conflict led to the crisis of 1992–93 and armed clashes in Moscow on 3–4 October 1993.

Immediately after the August 1991 events, the Supreme Soviet of the RSFSR passed a law changing the system of territorial authorities in the state. The executive committees of the Soviets (*ispolkoms*) were replaced by the new office of the heads of administration. Under the act, the heads of administration were to be elected by universal suffrage, but the Supreme Soviet introduced a moratorium on elections during the transitional period (in practice, until 1996), authorizing the president to appoint administration heads by decree.

The office of the President's Administration was established in August 1991 to supervise the work of local authorities. At first, it was not considered a player on the political scene, but the rapid acquisition by Yeltsin of the prerogatives previously held by the president of the Soviet Union (defense, foreign policy, security services) made it the second most powerful power center after the president himself. In effect, all the political institutions in Russia depend on the president and the President's Administration. The informal character of the functioning of the administration as a covert organ of power in Russia closely resembles the operation of the apparatus of the Central Committee. The President's Administration, along with the Security Council and the president's representatives in the regions (and from 2000, in federal districts), constitute an autonomous, extensive network of executive power, the role of which is rooted in the president's central position in the political system of the Russian Federation.

In November 1991, the Congress of People's Deputies empowered the president for one year to decide by decree all matters pertaining to economic reforms and the formation of the executive branch. Furthermore, the congress appointed Yeltsin prime minister. Over the next few months, the organs of executive power of the Soviet Union were transferred to the jurisdiction of the RSFSR/Russia, including the armed forces, the foreign service, the security agencies, and the functional ministries (e.g., finance, economy, railways). Most of the economic ministries of the union were transformed into state companies (e.g., Gazprom). It was characteristic of the time that this process had no legal basis in the RSFSR constitution or the law on the presidency of the RSFSR. The relevant transformations were conducted on the basis of special legislation, resolutions by the Congress of People's Deputies, and presidential decrees.

Political power in Russia was shaped amid the transfer of political rivalry from the realm of interparty competition to the sphere of two institutional conflicts: one between the union and republican authorities, and the other between the president of Russia, on one hand, and the people's deputies and the Supreme Soviet, on the other. The absence of fundamental consensus concerning the transformations distinguished the political processes in Russia from those in other postcommunist countries. In Russia, an ascendant minority imposed its will on the majority in August 1991 and then failed to legalize—in the form of a referendum or parliamentary elections—the consequences of the disintegration of the Soviet Union. In March 1991, 71.3 percent of the voters in Russia came out in favor of preserving the Soviet Union. In Ukraine, the results of the March referendum were invalidated by a referendum on independence, held on 1 December 1991. In Russia, the Supreme

Soviet merely renounced the union treaty of 1922 without even adopting an independence declaration.

Once it decided not to seek democratic legitimization of the new order, the new leadership was forced to look for support among the old party nomenklatura, the provincial bureaucracy, the new class of entrepreneurs, and the security forces. The victorious minority, which had assumed power following the failure of the communist coup and the success of its own "creeping coup," could only strengthen its rule by consolidating the "no-alternative" character of the president's power and his circle, which gradually contracted to include only members of the "family." Dmitri Furman has commented that, "in that system, there is no room for 'unchanging rules of the game,' thanks to which different forces can win power. On the contrary, it ensures that power is held by one person (or his successors) thanks to the 'rules of the game' that change in accordance with current circumstances." Democracy is a system in which parties win and lose elections. In Russia, however, the victory of the democrats resulted in the institution of a system in which those in power have never lost an election and changes at the top amount to a game of musical chairs.

Political Stabilization in Russia

Pres. Boris Yeltsin's decree of 21 September 1993, which put an end to the Soviet constitution and dissolved the related representative bodies, was titled "On the Gradual Constitutional Reform of the Russian Federation," thus heralding reforms of the political and legal system of postrevolutionary Russia. The adoption of a new constitution in December 1993 ended a two-year crisis of diarchy that had triggered armed clashes in Moscow on 3–4 October 1993. The preamble of the constitution speaks of "reviving the sovereign statehood of Russia" and "preserving the historically established state unity." Thus, the authors assumed there had once existed a sovereign Russian state and that its territorial continuity had been maintained. Rejecting the Soviet past, the new authorities did not claim legal continuity either with the Russian Empire or with the short-lived republic. The idea of electing a constitutional assembly was also abandoned. The new constitution was adopted in a national referendum on 12 December 1993, held simultaneously with elections to the Federal Assembly. The presidential poll was held in 1996 and was largely stage-managed. Finally, Yeltsin returned to the monarchic practice of appointing the ruler's successor.

The system of direct, two-round presidential elections in Russia was instituted in 1991, even before the disintegration of the Soviet Union. No representative of the opposition has ever won the presidency. In 1991, Boris Yeltsin—the then-chair of the Supreme Soviet of the RSFSR—became president. In 2000, the presidency was assumed by Acting Premier Vladimir

Putin, and in 2008, the election was won by the official "successor," Deputy Premier Dmitry Medvedev. Twice, in 1996 and 2004, the incumbents were reelected. On four occasions, the favorite won in the first round, and, in 1996, Yeltsin needed two rounds.

The method of electing the State Duma was laid down in a presidential decree of 1 October 1993 and remained in force, with certain amendments, until 2005. Half of the deputies were elected by simple majority in single-seat electoral districts, while the other half—in the federal electoral district—were elected proportionately according to the number of votes cast for the respective federal election lists. The Hare method is used to determine the proportional division of seats in the Duma. The use of that method and the 5 percent election threshold ensured a good representation of party leaders in the Duma, granting them considerable autonomy and facilitating the conclusion of compromises with the government. The autonomy of the political leaders, the limited prerogatives of the Duma, and the weakness of civil society all contributed to the fact that Russia has not seen the emergence of bona fide political parties. The role of spokespersons for the interests of the voters was assumed by deputies from the single-seat districts, which hardly enhanced the consolidation of the party system.

The application of a mixed election system in Russia meant that the rest of the 1990s passed in relative calm, at least as compared to 1990–93. The antireformist opposition always won the vote in the federal district but never managed to form a government. As a rule, the opposition struck compromises with the president on substantial issues, limiting criticism to his more propagandistic moves. Under the mixed election system, only one attempt was made to impeach the president; earlier, in the years 1990–93, the Congress of People's Deputies systematically threatened to take such action.

After the adoption of the new constitution, the president's policy addresses to the Federal Assembly became an important means of influencing political strategy. They were prepared by the president's aides and advisors, who used government-supplied data to elaborate concepts of strategic forecasting and policy planning. The first presidential addresses in the 1990s were devoted to the consolidation of the state and the enhancement of the executive branch. They served as the basis for a decree, issued in July 1995, on the concept of legal reform of the Russian Federation. The concept, drawn up in 1997–99 by a group of experts from the President's Administration, focused on the following crucial areas: the reorganization of the state in line with the concept of a division of the branches of government, a guarantee of constitutional coherence of the executive branch at all levels, the elaboration of a concept of civil service, adjustments of the management system to conditions of a market economy, and transparency in decision making.

Concepts for administrative reform were rooted in the conviction of many experts that the political system that evolved in Russia after the volatile period of 1991–93 was ineffective. The dominant view was that the ineffectiveness was caused by the excessive concentration of power in the hands of the president. During the 1990s, the primary political problem consisted of the mode in which the federation functioned, rather than in the establishment of a more balanced system of government. An attempt to alter the situation was only made amid a deep crisis caused by the financial collapse of 17 August 1998. The mass protest actions on 7 October that year were marked by demands for Yeltsin's resignation. The president responded with an announcement of plans for a power-sharing arrangement and even for an amendment to the constitution. In a compromise move, the cabinet headed by Yevgeny Primakov became the first—and last—cabinet in Russian history formed at the initiative of the parliamentary majority.

The significance of that development can be compared to Yeltsin's election as president in 1991 in a universal poll, particularly since the formation of a parliamentary majority government was coupled with a pledge of constitutional changes. Yet, the installation of the Primakov cabinet in September 1998—and, indeed, Yeltsin's election in 1991—carried with it the germ of regression, stemming from the historic and political circumstances of the development of the Russian Federation's political system. The president's move was a tactic to share responsibility for the crisis with the Duma; he was not seeking a fundamental revamping of the constitution. In any event, the Primakov cabinet lost its parliamentary majority in December 1998, which illustrated the weakness of public politics in Russia and, especially, of party politics.

Yeltsin's policy line at the time constituted a reaction to the financial crash of 1998. If Yeltsin thought federalism was the cure for the crisis of 1991, in 1998 his team decided that fomenting a "catastrophic" mood in the country was the best way of addressing the crisis of that year. The concept of the "power vertical" (*vertikal vlasti*)—that is, a peculiar melding of the cabinet and the President's Administration—was formulated in 1998. In essence, it again invoked the archetype of "concentrating" full power in one hand and rejecting administrative reforms that would have consolidated the institutionalization of the executive branch in Russia. The appointment of Vladimir Putin as prime minister in August 1999 and his subsequent elevation to the presidency indicated a return to the informal concentration of power in the hands of the president and the President's Administration.

Putin did not become president to implement the political reforms promised during the crisis; he became president to stabilize Yeltsin's political system by limiting political pluralism. In May 2000, federal districts were established along with the office of plenipotentiary representative of the president in the various districts. Changes were made to the procedures for appointing members of the Council of the Federation and the heads of the republics, provinces (*oblasts*), and territories (*krais*), leaving the local administration unchanged. The president was empowered by law to appoint the heads of the republics and provinces. This considerably extended the competencies of his office, as enumerated in chapter 9 of the 1993 constitution. In 2004, the government was reorganized, and three types of government administration units were established: ministries, services, and agencies. Their total number was raised from fifty-nine (in the cabinet of Mikhail Kasyanov) to seventy-five (in the cabinet of Mikhail Fradkov).

The years 2001–5 also saw the introduction of numerous changes that restricted political competition: the election threshold was raised from 5 to 7 percent, and single-seat constituencies were scrapped, while the mixed election system was replaced with an exclusively proportional one. This change increased control of the federal authorities over the composition of party lists, the process of voting, and the functioning of parliament.

The most important change introduced during Putin's presidency consisted of the reconstruction of the covert power infrastructure, composed of a huge number of officers of the security agencies deployed in all government institutions, social organizations, think tanks, media, and diverse private companies. This state of affairs was not brought on by any real successes of the security agencies; on the contrary, their performance throughout the 1990s was marked by a string of spectacular setbacks.

In the process of these transformations, how one defines the problems confronting society is a crucial matter. During the first half of the 1990s, there occurred a temporary collapse of political power and a partial loss by the state of its monopoly on the legal use of force. Although the collapse of the state was not total, the experience of living with a sense of endangerment may have shaped a new perception of the foundation of social order. A political theory that emerged in the 1990s highlighted the need for protecting the public order due to its natural frailty and the fear of chaos. The very description of the crisis during the 1990s as "chaos" implied the need for granting the broadest possible powers to the security agencies, which exist "somewhere on the borderline of two worlds, with one foot in the reality of primeval struggle, and the other in the reality of everyday life."

Freedom Regained

If, in the case of the Soviet Union and Russia, we were dealing with a failed attempt at a political transition from authoritarianism to democracy involving the nonlegitimization of the disintegration of the empire and the resultant failure to develop a mechanism for the alternation of power, then, in the case of Poland, the process of emancipation from the empire encountered problems rooted in the relative weakness of the political parties and the acrimonious character of dualism in the executive branch. An animated debate has been under way in Poland for several years concerning the beginning of the systemic changes, including any links between Gorbachev's reforms and transformations in Poland. In particular, it has repeatedly been claimed that the changes in Poland were imposed on Gen. Wojciech Jaruzelski by the leaders of the Soviet Union. Chronologically, the constitutional reforms and elections of people's deputies in Russia preceded the Round Table Agreement in Poland, the replacement of the constitution of the People's Republic of Poland (Polska Rzeczpospolita Ludowa, PRL), and elections to the Sejm and Senate. But, in conceptual terms, only the initial phase of the changes in Poland can be considered a part of the empire's ideological mutation. The June 1989 elections in Poland substantially accelerated the pace of developments, though the demise of communism in Europe was definitely sealed by the eradication of the Soviet Piedmont in the heart of the continent and the reunification of Germany. The June elections in Poland set in motion the process of the gradual introduction and consolidation of a mechanism of political competition, which collapsed in Russia in dramatic circumstances in September 1993.

The existence of a well-organized, mass-scale opposition—affiliating workers of state enterprises belonging to the Solidarity trade union—was a unique feature of the Polish transition compared to changes taking place in other states of the empire. The worsening economic crisis and lack of prospects for its solution within the Soviet Empire motivated the communists to seek the PRL's greater integration into the world economy while retaining political power in the country. Initial attempts to draw selected opposition groups into controlled political dialogue ended in failure. The communists—acting under limited though constant public pressure—then launched a strategy to co-opt the reform movement. In the summer of 1988, talks began between Czesław Kiszczak, the internal affairs minister, and Solidarity chair Lech Wałęsa, leading to the Round Table negotiations. That, in turn, resulted in general elections to the Sejm and Senate on 4 June 1989; the poll resembled the "curial" elections conducted in many European countries during the final phase of absolutism.

The two-chamber parliament then elected the leader of the Communist Party, Gen. Wojciech Jaruzelski, to be the country's president, while the Sejm made General Kiszczak the prime minister (he failed to form a cabinet due to resistance from Solidarity). The opposition entered into a coalition with the communists' previous satellite parties, the United People's Party (Polish: Zjednoczone Stronnictwo Ludowe, ZSL) and the Democratic Party. On 24 August 1989, the Sejm appointed Tadeusz Mazowiecki prime minister, and he formed a coalition government. The first universal presidential election, won by Wałęsa, the legendary Solidarity leader, was held on 25 November (first round) and 9 December 1990 (second round). The first fully democratic parliamentary poll took place on 27 October 1991.

The elections of 1989 had a dual effect: on one hand, they stimulated the substantial expansion of public participation in political life, and, on the other, they activated the mechanisms of political competition and alternation of power. Regardless of which party won the elections in subsequent years, political competition always existed in the form of party rivalry. The progress of democratization in Poland was influenced by the specific conditions that had existed at the point of departure. Political parties were established as a result of the crisis of participation and a crisis of legitimization with the previous system. Their establishment had been preceded by a fundamental change in public attitudes toward political authority and increased activity by the counterelite connected with the Solidarity opposition. Parties were built both by elements of the old nomenklatura and by the Solidarity counterelite. They were usually established from the top down, with the successive parliamentary elections and the work of the legislature providing the stimulus for their formation. The institutional weakness of political parties in Poland was determined by their elitist and parliamentary roots, the absence of party traditions and lack of links with uncrystallized social interests, and the power of independent trade unions and pressure groups for certain industries. The peculiar conditions at the point of departure were the reason why strong, mass-membership parties did not emerge in Poland. Today, Polish political parties are closer to the model of a cartel or catch-all party.

Despite these weaknesses, Polish political parties undeniably do channel the dispersed political will and meet their basic definitional requirement by successfully seeking to win and hold decision-making powers. They have also ensured the legitimization of the new order. The burdens attendant in the transfer from pretensions of unity to open competition, from a monoparty to a multiparty system, have stimulated social disorientation and, from the very beginning, hindered the task of legitimizing the new system. Furthermore, the new governments were hobbled by the influence of the old bureaucracy, and their members became entangled in settling complicated relations with the old nomenklatura, which generated a high dose of uncertainty. Still, the Polish political system has proven its viability. Repeatedly, elections have resulted in transfers of political power between parties in the framework of the political system. In two instances, coalitions of post-Solidarity parties yielded power to the party of the old nomenklatura, which was a particularly trying test of democratization. Similar transfers of presidential power have also occurred.

Despite these virtues, Polish political parties have proven exceptionally impermanent and incapable of entering the institutionalization phase. The break-up of large anticommunist coalitions in the early 1990s resulted in the fragmentation of the party landscape, frequent fusions, and further splits. Not a single anticommunist grouping present in the 1991 Sejm managed to last more than ten years, and their leaders have dispersed among various other parties and today frequently attack each other. In the 2001 election, Sejm seats were won by deputies representing parties that had earlier existed merely as electoral committees (Civic Platform and Law and Justice).

Polish political parties are extremely unstable. Only two groupings have contested all parliamentary elections since 1991 under the same name: the Polish People's Party and the Democratic Left Alliance. All the other parties underwent frequent organizational metamorphoses. Many of the parties that achieved good results in the 1991 and 1993 elections have ended their political existence (e.g., Freedom Union). New political groupings appeared practically before every election, and many proved ephemeral. The fact that they gained considerable support even though their platforms were largely unknown illustrates the frailty of the ties between parties and voters. A good example of fluctuating support is the coalition of Solidarity Electoral Action and Freedom Union; in a 1997 poll, the coalition had garnered a spectacular 47.2 percent of the vote, which just four years later plummeted to 8.7 percent.

Despite such negative tendencies, the Polish party system is stabilizing—as evidenced by its concentration, that is, the growth in support for the two parties that achieved the best results in each election. The winner of the 1991 election, Freedom Union, received just 12 percent of the vote, while the winner in 2001, Democratic Left Alliance, scored more than 40 percent. The percentage of votes collected by the two top-scoring parties continued to grow until 1997, when it equaled 60 percent. In the next election, it dipped to 54 percent and then rose again in the subsequent election. In the 2005 and 2007 elections, the top two spots were claimed by the same parties, Law and Justice and Civic Platform, which appears to affirm the increasing stabilization of the party landscape.

Political Stabilization in Poland

The post-1989 transformations not only activated the mechanisms of political competition and alternation of power in Poland but also changed the mode of the creation and operation of the executive branch. The cabinet is appointed by the parliament and is politically accountable to it, so the quality of the executive branch depends on the electoral system. As a rule, the less proportional the electoral system, the stronger the position of large parties, including the ruling party. The absence of an election threshold, even at a low level, increases parliamentary fragmentation. The division of seats by the Sainte-Laguë method instead of the d'Hondt method has a similar effect. A good illustration of this was provided by the 1991 elections, when representatives of twenty-nine groupings made it into the Sejm. Three prime ministers held office between December 1991 and May 1993. In 1997, on the other hand, when the d'Hondt method was applied, only three groupings won Sejm seats, while Premier Jerzy Buzek stayed in office—though not without problems—for four years.

During the period of the People's Republic of Poland, the government did not govern; instead, it administered. It merely carried out the decisions of the Polish United Workers' Party (PZPR), which functioned in accordance with the logic of *misterium imperium*. That is why the government did not need an analytical base in order to prepare political strategies or procedures for settling conflicts between cabinet members from different parties. Finally, it did not have to persuade citizens to accept its decisions since it would not be subjected to electoral verification. Successive democratic governments after 1989 attempted to develop modern instruments of governance, but a fundamental change in the executive branch did not take place until 1997. From then, the prime minister would be the unquestioned head of government and not merely chair of the Council of Ministers. The problem is that, in postcommunist states, the core of government is an isolated island in a sea of administration, one that tends to passively implement decisions from above instead of becoming involved in the fulfillment of cohesive political strategies. The core of government has no influence on decisions made by other subjects, while its legal instruments for exacting coordination are ineffective.

There are several reasons for this in Poland. First, the absence of a single executive center means there is a chronic conflict between the president and the prime minister. Second, the existence of a large number of ministries and other central institutions means that administration is institutionally fragmented. Third, the chaotic character of government coalitions is particularly burdensome since the parliament has much greater influence on policymaking than in most countries of Western Europe. All governments in Poland after 1989 have been formed by party coalitions that enjoyed minimal majorities, which in conditions of deep ideological divisions excluded the creation of syncretic coalitions and destabilized all the ruling coalitions. Intracoalition conflicts caused most cabinets in Poland to effectively stay in power for only about sixteen months. After that time period, they rapidly lost public support and drifted aimlessly instead of governing. This happened to the cabinets of Waldemar Pawlak (even though it had an almost two-thirds majority in the Sejm), Jerzy Buzek, and Leszek Miller.

Jarosław Kaczyński was the first prime minister who intentionally wanted to beat "the law of the sixteen months" and tried to boost the steerability of the coalition cabinet he headed. He wanted to avoid the fate of the cabinets led by Buzek, Miller, and Marek Belka, which had struggled against a backdrop of political scandals, party splits, and media leaks. The strategy of avoiding entanglement in an agenda imposed from the outside was pursued through the triggering of political crises that the government felt it could control and through the formulation of catchy slogans directed against the opposition, coalition partners, and selected professional communities. All this was designed to distract the media and the opposition from the decisions the government was actually making. Kaczyński's strategy eroded the mutual confidence of the coalition partners, decreased public support, and, ultimately, undercut the cabinet's steerability. The resulting credibility crisis was the reason for the election defeat of Law and Justice in 2007.

The monopoly of the Communist Party, enshrined in the constitutional principle of homogenous state power, was replaced in Poland after 1989 by the principle of checks and balances among different authorities, though this has been interpreted exclusively in negative terms—as a constraint placed on each authority, with minimal cooperation between them. The rule of mutual blocks not only applies to the executive and legislative branches but also to relations within the legislature, between the Sejm and the Senate, and in the executive branch, between the prime minister and the president.

The dualism of the legislative and executive branches is rooted in the systemic solutions adopted in 1989. The office of president and the Senate were formally introduced through an amendment of the constitution adopted by the last Sejm of the PRL on 7 April 1989. Its provisions were the result of a compromise reached during the Round Table talks between the Solidarity opposition and the Polish United Workers' Party. The Senate would be elected by universal suffrage, but without the curial quotas for different political forces applied in the elections to the Sejm. The president, however, was to be elected for a six-year term by the National Assembly. That formula indicated that the new institutions were meant to protect specific interests. The Senate was intended to ensure the opposition's participation in the legislative branch—to a greater degree than provided by the Sejm electoral rules. In turn, the presidency, which was to be held by General Jaruzelski, would protect the interests of the nomenklatura.

Political practice has consolidated this formal dualism. The adoption in autumn 1989 of the rule "your president, our prime minister" was meant to resolve a specific political problem. In hindsight, that concept, as Maciej Drzonek points out, "became a catalyst of divisions and the creation of a tense dualism based on opposition rather than cooperation." Since then, relations between the prime minister and the president have been marked by almost constant political antagonism.

The first years of the systemic transformations were decisive in determining the rules for the functioning of this executive dualism. The law amending the constitution in 1989, in addition to addressing ceremonial competencies, endowed the president with three significant prerogatives: the possibility to veto legislation, the right to designate the prime minister, and the power to dissolve parliament in strictly specified instances. In September 1990, the Sejm shortened Jaruzelski's term of office and amended the constitution, introducing direct presidential elections. Tadeusz Mazowiecki's defeat in the presidential contest later that year undermined the position of the prime minister in favor of the new president, Lech Wałęsa.

The law of 17 October 1992, on the mutual relations between the legislative and executive branches and popularly known as the "little constitution," was the key document defining the new alignment of political forces in Poland. Overall, it strengthened the position of the president; in addition to having the right to designate the prime minister, the president was given the power to appoint a cabinet for a period of six months. Furthermore, the prime minister was obligated to seek the president's opinion concerning the appointment of ministers of defense, internal affairs, and foreign affairs. The president executed "general leadership" in the spheres of external relations and in the internal and external security of the country. The "little constitution" envisaged the use of the "unconstructive" vote of no confidence, which in crisis situations would further strengthen the president's position.

The new constitution adopted on 4 April 1997 had been conceived with the intent of diminishing Wałęsa's political role. It deprived the president of the right to appoint a presidential cabinet and to assess candidates for the posts of defense, interior, and foreign ministers. The prime minister was not obligated to inform the president on the work of the cabinet. The "general leadership" of the president on foreign and security matters was replaced with the president's duty to collaborate with the premier and relevant ministers. The new constitution also restored the constructive vote of no confidence, which strengthened the premier. Still, the president retained many of his previous competencies, which meant that the dualism of the executive branch was preserved.

Executive dualism is quite frequent in the practice of democratic states and has a tradition in the Polish political system, since it functioned during the period of the Second Republic. The problem is that it often took the form of political rivalry, which—paradoxically—was most acrimonious when the prime minister and president had the same ideological orientation. For this reason, boosting its effectiveness will probably require the relative strengthening of one of the two centers of executive power.

The problem of major reforms for streamlining the operation of the political system appeared in Poland and Russia in the late 1990s. Numerous changes were made in Poland at that time with the objective of streamlining the dualism of the executive function and boosting its capacity to formulate political strategies. In practice, the changes had the effect of enhancing steerability within political parties, parliamentary coalitions, and the government. Yet, this enhancement was achieved not through the establishment of a core of government, capable of elaborating and implementing coherent political strategies, but through the strengthening of the position of the leader of the ruling party and head of government.

Besides the absence of a government core, an additional problem that undercut the effectiveness of political reforms in Poland was the model for adjustment to European Union requirements adopted in the accession process. It imposed on the underdeveloped postcommunist peripheries the necessity to introduce institutional and procedural changes congruent with stages of development they had not yet achieved. Jadwiga Staniszkis contends that "the example of Poland shows how structural coercion destroys steerability and at times even eradicates the autonomous, systemic character of peripheral states and economies. They become transformed into a loosely connected arrangement of networks that spill beyond the nominal borders of the nation state, implementing goals more characteristic of other regions or stages of development."

In Russia, the concept of systemic reform that emerged in the late 1990s was rejected in favor of strengthening presidential power. However, the system in place hardly resembles a classical presidential republic whose distinguishing feature is separation of the executive and legislative branches, which guarantees the independent and strong position of the latter. The constitution of the Russian Federation in many places resembles the constitution of the French Republic, though the dualism of power characteristic of semi-presidentialism has been replaced by monocentrism, further strengthened by informal links within the syndicate of the security agencies. The establishment of a monocentric system of government not only excluded the political system from the processes of modernization but also created conditions for the revival of archaic ideas about the nature of power (e.g., demonization of external threats, cult of the national leader).

Thus, as a result of the social and political reforms made in the late 1990s, Poland has found itself in a situation in which the nominal borders of the nation-state are being blurred by the processes of globalization, and the country is grappling with the problem of the imposition of institutional solutions and procedures characteristic of highly developed postindustrial capitalism. In Russia, however, the political system—after a period of deep convulsions in the late 1990s—has quickly returned to a typical monocentric construction, with the attendant dilemma of its legitimacy.

VLADIMIR G. BARANOVSKY AND BORIS A. SHMELYOV

TRANSFORMATION PROCESSES IN POLAND AND RUSSIA

IN THE MID-1980S, the Soviet Union entered the era of perestroika, or reform. It began as an attempt to provide momentum to national and international policy changes, as well as to develop social relationships with Soviet satellite nations in Eastern Europe. The logic driving perestroika became counterintuitive to reform. The consequences quickly escalated on an ever-increasing scale. This chapter traces the emergence of the political and social reform efforts and discusses the disastrous results of the reform policies. In particular, the chapter addresses the Soviet policy toward and social relationship with Poland.

Events emerging from the Soviet Union's international relationships were paramount throughout perestroika. The "Polish component" was only one element of the problems that emanated from dramatic changes that occurred within and around the Soviet Union.

The General Dynamics of the Soviet Bloc

By the mid-1980s, relationships between the Soviet Union and other socialist nations in Eastern Europe faced multiple issues. The issues derived from growing social and economic unrest. The existing economic and political systems required radical reforms to overcome impending crises.

The existing socialist community models required drastic changes. In particular, the underpinnings of the "Comecon operation" needed review. The Comecon model, derived from an integration of scientific and technical development, became a hindrance to progress rather than a positive, driving force. The Institute of Global Socialists Economic System at the Soviet Union's Academy of Sciences grew aware of the model's inadequacies and apprised the Soviet government of the problem. The institute emphasized that the mechanistic managerial approaches utilized by Comecon did not accommodate input from smaller economic influences within the Soviet network.

Government agencies at higher levels excluded satellite nations' input from the decision-making process. Economic suggestions from internal nations were ignored. Instead, higher-level agencies within the Soviet system merely imposed policy measures. The Soviets failed to consider either the sociological and sociocultural interests of the bloc nations or their manufacturing abilities. Consequently, the approach resulted in long-term inefficiency.

Commodity instruments were also inadequate. The instruments failed to promote mutual cooperation, adequate supplies of products, or economic import/export gains. Nations experienced either economic gains or losses. The economic system was unbalanced, and the lack of balance was unjustifiable.

Higher government levels dominated decision making. Even minor economic issues were micromanaged. This persistent pattern created political discontent among national leaders.

Socialist economic research scientists proposed comprehensively restructuring the existing economic models. Their proposed model would be more open, would be implemented multilaterally as well as bilaterally, and would coordinate managerial planning and credit, monetary, and financial instruments. The new model would be implemented among collective international institutions, including joint undertakings among satellite nations and Comecon projects. In addition, the model would be implemented within the legal system and be used to regulate international communication procedures, determining, for example, how scientific and technical documents would be released.

The premise of the new model was grounded in assumptions that effective, cooperative, functioning systems could indeed be established among socialist nations. Although the assumption can no longer be verified, it is noteworthy that the scientists emphasized within their proposal that economic and social reform within the bloc's nations was crucial. Furthermore, scientists asserted that "the success of restructuring is primarily dependent on creation of adequate prerequisites in [the] internal processes of fraternal countries."

The restructuring of the entire economic system across the socialist countries could not be expected to take place without encountering some resistance. Entering into new degrees of cooperation required profound reform in each nation. Because of conditions in the mid-1980s, Soviet leaders reasoned that restructuring satellite nations could be accomplished only within the framework of the Soviet system. Leaders reasoned that the Soviet Union had to take a proactive role in initiating reform. They believed that it was essential that the Soviet Union assume the role of the primary builder of a "socialistic commonwealth."

Mikhail Gorbachev provided two essential political and ideological prerequisites for reforming relationships between the Soviet Union and its allies. He would have to initiate policies to modify the existing socialism, then create policies to stimulate "new political thinking." In either circumstance, the existing relationship would undergo a complete transformation. Conceivably, throughout each stage of the transformation process, debates and controversies could unfold.

Gorbachev's formula involved two essential components: maintaining continuity and addressing the need for change. His premise was based on a belief that change emerged by establishing equitable relationships, respecting national sovereignty, and recognizing national independence, while simultaneously acknowledging mutual interdependence and cooperation in every part of the political and social arenas. Gorbachev implied that, once a nation concurred with his principles, it would then necessarily assume complete responsibility for situations that occurred within the country. Gorbachev's proposition was the most important attribute within the emerging policy changes. From his perspective, the changes signified a new transition, as well as a rejection of the "Brezhnev Doctrine." That doctrine was an accepted idea that had never been officially proclaimed. Nevertheless, the doctrine had defined the Soviet Union's approach to allied nations. In May 1985, at the Soviet Ministry of Foreign Affairs, Gorbachev presented his ideas in an open forum. During his speech, Gorbachev stated quite openly,

> Our relationship with our fraternal socialist countries has entered into a new historical era. It will be an area where societies have full rights. We can no longer lead them by leashes. Our association should be refreshed. We need to give maximum attention to our friends as well as to their needs. In the past, disparities existed between our nations. We declared friendship without recognizing the true spirit of friendship. We need to respect the sovereignty and dignity of our allies. Respect should be extended to even the smallest nations. We should purge our illusion that we should lecture anyone.

However, despite the proposed changes between the Soviet Union and satellite nations, Gorbachev did not abandon the socialistic premise. He believed that socialism merely needed restructuring, that the socialist regime's potential had yet to be exhausted, and that socialism could solve the most complicated tasks. Increasingly active cooperation could multiply socialism's effectiveness and become a catalyst for ongoing development. Unfortunately, the underpinnings for conflict had long been established. Inevitably, crises would emerge. Conflict stemmed from two incompatible dilemmas: the need for "socialist renewal" and the fact that factions rejecting socialism existed throughout the bloc.

Despite the reform efforts, Gorbachev was still not going to allow ally nations the freedom to create political movements independent of Soviet regulation—he would not allow satellite nations to drift away from the safety of "Big Brother." In April 1986, at the Eleventh Congress of the Socialist Unity Party of Germany, Gorbachev said, "In our future, we do not foresee a Soviet Union existing apart from close cooperation with the GDR and our other fraternal nations." He added, "This is based on existing principles within our international policies. It is also evident that it would be impossible to find solutions or complete the tasks at hand apart from our guiding principles."

Essentially, the Soviet Union would maintain the leading position, while satellite nations would undertake internal economic and political reforms. The new direction would free Moscow from bearing all of the economic burden and internal political headaches of the "brotherhood nations." The idea was to promote internal reform while requiring satellite nations to take responsibility for reform. Moscow would then be free to concentrate on broader issues across the Soviet community. In theory, Gorbachev envisioned that new progressive-minded leaders from "fraternal countries" would support Soviet reform endeavors. Progressive leaders would then create a strong political and ideological foundation for new relationships within the socialist community. A new era of mutual cooperation would begin.

Gorbachev wanted to abandon the established traditions of past years. Under those traditions, the Soviets had essentially informed the satellites' leaders of foreign economic decisions. The nations would then formally approve the Soviet decisions and declare their allegiance to the Political Consulting Committee (PCC) of the Warsaw Treaty Organization (Warsaw Pact). Under the emerging policies, the Soviet government would allow a nation's leaders to discuss Soviet policy proposals. The Soviets expected their allies to accept Soviet diplomats and recognize that the reform measures were more practical than prior, propagandistic approaches. Reform would lead the union in a peaceful direction, provided that the leaders of satellite nations took the reforms seriously.

In October 1985, the Communist Party met during a PCC gathering in Sofia. Government officials wanted to "compare notes" before the upcoming Soviet-US summit in Geneva. Gorbachev wrote, "It was probably the first time in years that the Soviet government did not force its allies to just face the facts before getting their formal approval. Instead, the Soviets decided that it was necessary to discuss initiatives. . . . Everyone there truly appreciated the decision."

Gorbachev detailed his vision of drastic changes to the practice of socialism in the treatise "On Certain Aspects of Cooperation with Socialist Countries." The Politburo of the CPSU prepared the document and concluded that the Soviet Union needed an "actual turning point in the entire system of cooperation with allies."

The main focus of the document was foreign economic reform. The motivation of the reform was to address serious economic problems, as well as practical cooperation between the Soviet Union and its embedded socialist nations. From the beginning, potential problems existed that could complicate political relationships and weaken mutual trust. The potential for failure

VLADIMIR G. BARANOVSKY AND BORIS A. SHMELYOV

grew increasingly obvious. Failure could emerge in any arena, including economic, scientific, and technical cooperation. Attempts to satisfy the developing needs of socialist countries could also fall short. The existing structure had remained virtually unchanged for years. Some fifty-six resource-intensive industries provided the industrial, transportation, and industrial needs of two-thirds of the cooperating European socialist nations. Most resources were in heavy industry.

The Institute of the Economy of the World Socialist System published "On the Effectiveness of Economic and Technical Assistance of the USSR to Socialist Countries." The document asserted that the scientific and technical assistance the Soviet Union provided to its allies failed to meet the allies' needs. Since the early 1980s, ally nations had been experiencing significant economic restructuring. Satellite nations also had reduced energy development, despite enhanced resource endeavors and technological advancements. However, the Soviets did not support new trends in technology. The institute concluded that increasing the efficiency of economic and technical cooperation between the Soviet Union and socialist countries was an important component for restructuring economic life in the union. The union and its nations needed an urgent solution for mobilizing all of its reserves.

At the "socialist summit" meeting in Moscow in November 1986, the Soviets addressed cooperation issues regarding current economic problems. Attending members questioned the foundational socialist principles of previous decades. However, the existing principles defined Communist Party policies. Participating members pointed to inadequacies in the current economic models used by nations within the "socialist commonwealth." Participants spoke of the "evils of economic policies that failed to provide optimum efficient balance in social justice, social programs, and workforce incentives."

The Moscow meeting was among the last attempts to find a mutual economic and social solution to escalating difficulties within the Comecon nations. The concern was that the difficulties would turn into unpredictable crises. Gorbachev later reflected, "No one at that time understood the full extent of the crisis." It was becoming clear that giving socialist satellite nations a voice within the Soviet Union would not be possible without profound changes in economic systems and mechanisms.

Vadim Medvedev, a member of the Politburo, believed that the Soviet Union's "need to restructure the political system, primarily the Party itself, was delaying reform." What the nations really needed was "profound democratization of society, openness, and freedom of speech. . . . The economic reform could only exist as a component of comprehensive restriction of society." Gorbachev's government, as well as most European socialist leaders, had a significantly different approach.

The leaders were not fundamentally opposed to reforms in society. National leaders alleged that they had solved many of the political problems that had prevented the reform of socialism within their countries. The leaders of communist parties in the Czechoslovakia, Bulgaria, Romania, and the GDR were especially strong in these assertions. Consequently, differences in opinions strengthened negativity toward Soviet perestroika policies. Nevertheless, Gorbachev stood firm in his belief that perestroika should underpin reform in each socialist nation as well as the entire socialist commonwealth.

The assumption the Soviet government held was that satellite leaders would display traditional loyalty to "Big Brother." Reforms would become self-supportive and continue through political "inertia." In exchange, the Soviets would support the regimes of allied nations. The Soviets presumed that they would gain respectful support. Instead, the Soviet government received contentedness. Over time, opposition to perestroika grew. Leaders wanted personal democracy and openness.

The Plenum of the CPSU of the Central Committee met in January 1987. After the meeting adjourned, GDR leader Erich Honecker dedicated himself to democratization and developing policies that would advance human resource issues. Honecker declared that the perestroika route was not suitable for the GDR and then prohibited the publication of the plenum materials within the GDR.

Romania's Nicolae Ceaușescu also rejected the plenum's decisions. The Romanian public never knew what was discussed in the meeting. Ceaușescu openly told the Soviet ambassador that he could not agree to the statements made at the plenum and that "the Communist Party was getting on a dangerous path." Czechoslovakia's Gustáv Husák and Bulgaria's Todor Zhivkov both expressed reservations about Moscow's new reform policies.

However, according to Gorbachev, Poland's Wojciech Jaruzelski "strongly supported changes in the Soviet Union." So did Hungarian leader János Kádár. It is noteworthy that only the Polish and Hungarian leaders found Gorbachev's policies favorable. It is not likely a coincidence. Socialist reform in both Poland and Hungary was in an advanced state. Although reforms in both nations developed differently and were subsequently advanced by different events, neither set of reforms could have been a substitute for changing the entire Soviet socialist system. The resonance of the processes initiated in the Soviet Union was more obvious in Poland and Hungary than in hard-line communist nations such as the GDR and Czechoslovakia.

Twenty-five years later, Jaruzelski admitted that the underlying influences for Poland's compliance were based on a military event of a few years earlier. If a military emergency had not been declared in 1981, the forces of the Warsaw Pact would have entered the country. Such an event would have "inevitably strengthened the position of hardliners in the USSR government. Gorbachev would not have been able to come to power to start his reforms."

Jaruzelski's statements can be neither confirmed nor refuted. There is a notable absence of clear analysis about the Soviet Union's relations with its allies in Eastern Europe at the time of perestroika. Apparently, the possible consequences of the policies established in both Eastern Europe and the Soviet Union were not anticipated or analyzed to any degree. Policies often appeared to be based on idealistic, wishful thinking rather than on an empirical analysis of existing conditions. For instance, it was assumed that changes in the Soviet Union would result in a favorable "wave of imitation" throughout ally nations. The assumption was supported and even pushed by the Soviet leadership, even when leaders of "brotherhood parties" expressed reservations rather than the expected enthusiasm. The Soviets soon contemplated replacing insubordinate political leaders with a new generation of politicians. Ideally, the Soviets sought out less conservative politicians who were more open to new reform ideas.

Did regimes within most Eastern European countries waver? Did they have the resources to survive despite growing difficulties? If the Soviets had not initiated reform, how long could leaders have stayed in power? Soviet Minister of Foreign Affairs Eduard Shevardnadze wrote, "We clearly saw that in almost all Eastern European countries political leaders were quickly losing control of the situation and could not find a means to adequately respond to [the] demands of those who supported democratic changes." Furthermore, he added, "Stubbornly unwilling to implement reforms, conservatives were forced to use measures and methods, which regardless of their will and intention brought organized opposition closer together. The refusal to reform contributed to the development of a nationwide democratic movement." Conservative forces within socialist countries sought and found support among perestroika opponents in Moscow. To oppose perestroika, the traditional party hardliners and government elite were willing to undertake true consolidation on the scale of the entire "socialist commonwealth."

Moscow thus faced challenges from leaders within "fraternal countries," as well as from within the Soviet Communist Party. The growing opposition gained more and more support. None of the policies seemed completely satisfactory. If Moscow supported the authorities of any particular country, it would become ostracized for dominating public opinion. That would jeopardize its relations with future governments. If Moscow took a strong, straightforward approach and replaced the existing authorities, then Moscow would be interfering in the internal affairs of "fraternal countries." The policy of "no interference" or "dissemination of ideas" could be an advantage in political propaganda. It also could fit well with the logic of "new thinking." However, it could also result in a complete loss of control.

The current popular opinion is that the Soviet government was incapable of preventing this collision. More precisely, the popular view is that a resolution resulted from a series of events that grew beyond the control of perestroika's initiators. One should not overlook the impact that resulted from the rejection of the Brezhnev Doctrine. The rejection was fundamentally important. Even if one doubts that, in the late 1980s the Soviet Union was capable of implementing perestroika in practice. After the fact, it seems obvious that Moscow was probably not capable of repeating the 1968 scenario. In the spring of that year, an uprising in Prague had been suppressed directly by military force. Conservatives in the Kremlin government could have had a different position. The odds that "fraternal parties" in Eastern Europe could maintain power without political support, economic aid, and military assistance from the Soviet Union were becoming more and more improbable. They needed comprehensive support. Attempts to save the communist regimes or prevent their reformation would still have obvious consequences.

Moscow's behavior was indecisive and inconsistent. Some could interpret the behavior as cautious and responsible. Beginning in 1987, interest in removing some of the top leaders of "fraternal countries" gained support. The Soviet leader, however, refused to help the Romanian opposition overthrow Ceaușescu based on the fundamental policy of non-interference in the internal affairs of other countries.

A dramatic scenario that could have resulted in a crisis between the Soviet Union and Eastern Europe countries did not unfold. There is reason to believe that it was the Gorbachev government that managed to avert the crisis. A paradox was that, although Moscow refused to guarantee support to existing regimes, Moscow was not concerned with the future of Eastern Europe until the very end. A statement by Gorbachev in 1988 reveals the Soviets' confidence. Gorbachev said that "the socialist world is undergoing a process of transformation and reform which should give a new beginning to the new public order and take it to new levels in all dimensions economic, political, ideological." According to the Soviet leader, "The processes of reforms and drastic changes in socialist countries confirm the viability of socialism and its readiness to answer the call of time."

In reality, the viability of the "new public order" was moving as quickly away from Soviet hands as fast as a pebble skips across water. The Soviets could no longer justify the reforms. Their aspirations that the reform would become an incentive for socialist nations to transition in a new direction had faltered. The Soviets attempted different reform approaches. Nevertheless, economic and social conflicts within the nation were escalating. Satellite leaders would not carry out the reforms or apply Soviet economic policies. Therefore, long-term goals could not be reached, there would not be an immediate solution to existing economic problems, and there would not be cooperation among the nations.

The previous economic model was now exhausted. Under it, satellite nations had received raw materials and energy in exchange for manufactured products.

VLADIMIR G. BARANOVSKY AND BORIS A. SHMELYOV

The Comprehensive Program for Socialist Economic Integration adopted in 1986 was not as effective as its authors expected. The Soviet Union was going through a social and economic crisis, and that crisis was growing. The Soviet Union could no longer be the driving force of socialist economic integration.

The Soviet Union also no longer had the financial means to supply raw materials or energy at discounted prices. Moscow officials began to view the allies as a "burden" and wanted to "distance" the center from the satellite states and their problems. The Soviet leaders decided to no longer be responsible for the socialist nations' issues. Instead, the Soviets would focus on reforms for the union as a whole. Furthermore, the Soviet government decided to move from a trading-oriented economic relationship to a currency-oriented relationship. The Soviets then issued hard currency for Comecon nations. The decision resulted in a severe blow to reform endeavors.

Consequently, Comecon was disbanded. The collapse resulted from the growing distinctions among socialist nations, their unwillingness to adopt a new, more restrictive model, and their inability to manage various aspects of trade, industry, or scientific and technological advancements.

In the late 1980s, both the Soviet Union and the nations that made up the region began experiencing turbulent economic conditions. Hungary, Poland, and Yugoslavia were the first to officially declare that an economic crisis existed. A year later, Bulgaria, Romania, Czechoslovakia, and the GDR acknowledged the crisis as well. Evidence of a systemwide economic crisis across the Soviet community soon became more evident. It became obvious that the theory of "real socialism" was not being put into practice in the ostensibly socialist nations. It was also apparent that socialism, in either theory or practice, did not correspond with the emerging economic and social trends of nations outside the Soviet system. "Real socialism" had reached a historical peak. Socialism could no longer provide socioeconomic direction or flexible and effective responses to the challenges of the time.

In the fall of 1989, Moscow recognized that epiphany. The CPSU Central Committee discussed the situation in Eastern Europe, and Secretary Valentin Falin warned that "the specific social developments within Poland and Hungary revealed that the postwar order we established is now in crisis. The entire socialist system and socialist community are in crisis. We need to be ready for an impending explosion. However, it is not clear where the explosion will occur first."

The Soviet Union could no longer stabilize the socialist community. Furthermore, the Soviets planned to significantly reduce economic assistance and opportunities. Then, in 1989, a series of events in Eastern Europe unfolded and became a test of Moscow's new policies of social and political recognition. The events also tested Moscow's affirmation of national freedom in the Soviet bloc. Moscow passed the test.

Gorbachev later summarized his Eastern European policies. He said that "the regime that existed in Eastern and Central Europe was condemned by history just as it condemned our country. The Soviet Union has exhausted itself and oppressed the nations. Saving such a system or trying to preserve it would mean further weakening the positions of our own nation and compromising it in the eyes of our own nation and the entire world."

The refusal to preserve Soviet hegemony in Eastern Europe was not a result of conscious and well thought out policies. It was a result of historical consequences. Moscow could not or did not want to "compete." It is meaningless today to wonder if the Soviets could have acted in a different way. The dismantling of socialism in the region happened peacefully and without dramatic perturbations.

International Political Conditions

To understand the scale of changes in the late 1980s and 1990s, one should remember that the control established by the Soviet Union over Eastern Europe was a result of its victory over Germany in World War II. The Soviet Union legitimized its claim on the region through the Soviet liberation of Eastern Europe from the Nazis. This experience was also a foundation for the considerable support that Eastern Europe gave to the Soviet Union for such a lengthy time. However, Eastern Europe suffered hardship at the hands of the Soviets. The Soviets squelched the social, political, and cultural development of its European satellites, while those Eastern European nations also neutralized negative attitudes toward the Soviets' ambitious imperialism.

The Soviet presence in Eastern Europe was also based on military and political imperatives. Moscow saw Eastern Europe as a security belt. The Soviets considered it necessary to dominate the region in order to secure its position in case of a confrontation with the West. It was a strategic, defensive position. The Soviets' presence in Eastern Europe provided additional structure and strength. Furthermore, Soviet domination over Eastern Europe put military and political pressure on Western Europe.

The Cold War was primarily the result of a clash of interests between the Soviet Union and the West, and the Soviet presence in Eastern Europe played a significant role in the conflict. The Soviet Union's efforts to maintain its Eastern European presence influenced interactions between the Soviet Union and the West during the postwar era.

The signing of the Helsinki Final Act signified the West's recognition of Soviet territorial control of Eastern Europe, which the Soviet Union considered its compensation for defeating Nazi Germany. Moscow interpreted the Helsinki Act as consent to dominate the Eastern Europe satellites. Western nations did not share the same view. On the contrary, the West viewed the occupation as a way to gradually "soften" the Soviet camp and weaken the

Soviet Union's control over the eastern nations. The Soviets would have to provide economic, political, and humanitarian assistance to those countries. The West felt that, in time, the Soviet Union would be forced to redirect its economic and social policies.

Moscow used its assistance to argue for stricter policies with Eastern Europe and as a basis for justifying its actions to the West. This line can be historically traced to the early days of perestroika. Gorbachev's "new political thinking" required changing how the Soviets dealt with the West. A significant problem that Gorbachev faced was how the Soviets would tell the West that the Soviet Union was taking measures to free Eastern Europe from Soviet domination. The task proved difficult. The Soviets could no longer use universal human principles as a talking point. It was now a matter of the Soviets protecting their geopolitical interests and security. Yegor Ligachev, Gorbachev's number-two man in the party leadership, clearly expressed his positions. Ligachev believed that the Soviets should strengthen the socialist community and develop interconnections and cooperation with all socialist countries. Ligachev made this a primary goal of Soviet foreign policy.

Were the geopolitical transformations of the region west of the Soviet Union inevitable? This is yet another question that does not have conclusive answers. One would have to consider all the contributing factors. Some scholars believe that the changes, as well as the scale and pace of the changes in Eastern Europe, occurred because of perestroika. Some scholars also believe that neither Gorbachev nor the West predicted the way events would ultimately unfold.

In the mid-1980s, Soviet dominance in the region was almost taken for granted. Obviously, no one openly discussed the matter in "decent" society much less in any official or semiofficial setting. Such a discussion was considered taboo and "politically incorrect." At best, Western European capitals as well as Washington yearned for more liberal policies within the socialist regimes and reductions in the police forces and repressive factions. None in the West expected complete independence, a termination of the Warsaw Pact and Comecon, or the elimination of Soviet control over the "socialist community." The Western world would be astonished that "normal" conditions could give rise to destabilization and unforeseen consequences.

However, by the end of the decade, conditions were obviously no longer "normal." Others hold different opinions, asserting that traditional Western vigilance brought an end to the Soviet stranglehold on the region. A surge in this attitude occurred within the Soviet Union in the years immediately preceding perestroika. One can read it as early as 1984 in reports by the Institute of the Economy of the World Socialist System of the Academy of Sciences of the USSR that address this discussion.

One of the institute documents states, "Current conceptual and strategic policy guidelines in the USA and among [its] allies demonstrate Western intentions to increase confrontation with the socialist community and escalate the arms race. They intend to pressure radical change in Eastern Europe throughout [the] 1980s in order to tip the balance of power in their favor. Reagan's current political rush to American imperialistic extremism reflects a 'crusade' against communism. Reagan's long-term goal is the elimination of both socialism and communism by the end of the 20th century."

The West focused on a strategy that would make it the final winner of the global tug of war: weakening the Soviet Union by depriving it of international political influence. The West appeared to advance this agenda at any opportunity and made it the single most important foreign policy priority, pushing other foreign or economic policy opportunities into the background. That agenda led the Soviets to pursue a drastic path, while the West worked to eliminate resources of potential use to the Soviets.

One Russian scholar has noted that the West realized that Soviet control over its satellites was a significant resource. Moscow used its control of the region to influence foreign policy decisions. The West needed to eliminate that source of power and did not want to wait around for the results of the Soviet Union's social restructuring experiments. The Russian who was deputy director of the CPSU CC International Department at that time was part of the highest echelon of power that existed at the "Old Square." When Gorbachev publicly declared his "new thinking," the United States and its closest allies made conscious efforts to weaken the Soviet Union's role and influence in Central and Eastern Europe. The United States applied a wide range of tools during the Cold War to oppose the Soviet Union. It used baiting tactics, political pressure, financial leverage, and propaganda to influence government leaders. The United States' goals were always the same: use any opportunity that came out of Gorbachev's policies to create favorable outcomes for the West. Step by step, the United States spun Gorbachev's agendas into Western advantages. The deputy director cites the views of Pres. George H. W. Bush and US national security advisor Brent Scowcroft. Bush wrote that the first priority of the US administration was Eastern Europe. The president wrote that he took advantage of any "reform measures that would give the United States opportunity to benefit from the Soviet's 'new thinking' policies and then weaken Moscow's grip." The deputy also notes that Bush considered the goal of "separating" the Soviet Union from its allies a higher priority than controlling nuclear and conventional armaments. Regulating nuclear arms would ensure the safety of the United States.

Beginning in the early twenty-first century, some Russians developed a restoration mentality. That mindset represented nostalgia and was gaining momentum in Russia, especially in light of the cunning agenda of the West. Contemplating the idea seems completely pointless. The restoration premise is based on the idea that the Soviet Union had a legitimate right to control and influence the "socialist community." The mindset, though, steadily continues to disappear. The Soviet Union experienced an ideological crisis and loss of capacity to implement reform strategies in Eastern Europe. Moscow was forced to constantly improvise and adjust to rapidly changing conditions and the "natural" course of events.

In particular, two factors made endeavors to retain Eastern Europe within the Soviet Union impractical.

First, even if an East-West confrontation existed, by the end of the 1980s the Soviet Union did not have the resources to maintain a confrontational stance. The Soviet Union was steadily going down a path of economic degradation. The Soviets faced challenges simply to maintain military and strategic uniformity. Significant internal political problems were emerging. In such conditions, the Soviet Union did not have the resources to deal with Eastern Europe, even if it had wanted to maintain control.

Second, Gorbachev's "new political thinking" underpinned his foreign policy. He focused on ending the arms race and developing a constructive relationship with the United States and Western Europe. He also sought cooperative efforts to strengthen international security, terminate policies of isolation, and develop scientific, technical, and cultural cooperation. Gorbachev advanced a de-idealization of Soviet foreign policies, but, instead, he focused on human and social values. Gorbachev abandoned enforcement policies in favor of political methods. Global interdependence would replace peaceful coexistence. The Soviet leader promoted the construction of a "common European house" throughout Europe. Gorbachev hoped that his foreign policy would help the union manage essential tasks, give a powerful impulse to internal development within the country, and overcome increasing economic decay. Furthermore, he hoped to reduce the economic burden of the complex military industry. Supplying the military "put pressure on every economic sector. It crippled the economy and decreased the standard of life, which was already astonishingly low."

It was logical to include the Soviet Union as well as the Eastern European nations in the world economy. It was also logical to integrate the Soviet Union into Europe. Soviet control over its allies was no longer politically acceptable. More importantly, developing a relationship with the United States was a higher priority than developing a relationship with Eastern Europe. The Soviet course of action addressed problems related to matters of war, peace, and global security. Moscow considered these issues to be vital.

The Soviets thus moved into political realism. The price of success would be concessions, flexibility, and a rethinking of interests in other areas. According to the former deputy director, the time would come "when Eastern European countries, mere satellites of the Soviet Union, would become a bargaining chip in negotiations with the West." Bargaining would boost Moscow's policies, support perestroika, and promote continued financial and economic assistance. The move into that new reality arrived in 1989. Allegedly, Henry Kissinger attempted to motivate Moscow into reducing communistic elements in Eastern Europe. In exchange, Washington promised not to act against Soviet interests. Potentially, Soviet-American cooperation could emerge.

In 1989, rapid political and social changes in Eastern Europe began to snowball. The fact that the Soviet Union did not interfere indicated that the Cold War was over. It was indisputable. The changes began in association with Soviet policy shifts, progressed rapidly, and ended without any international political turmoil.

One reason was the fact that major international foreign policy makers were focused on other issues. Eastern Europe benefited from being a "side issue." Early in the development stage, the Eastern bloc nations were not "divided." There were not any hard choices to make or ultimatums to face. However, no one had considered a cautious, well-balanced, and well thought out adjustment of the international and political status of Eastern Europe. It had not been long ago that Moscow was the main player in this region, so Moscow felt forced out of the political arena in Eastern Europe. The situation created political discomfort. Nations were ready to take counteroffensive positions or at least build a solid defense.

The Bilateral Context

The Soviet leaders paid special attention to Poland in the Soviet Union's Eastern European policies. A number of emerging circumstances also demanded the Soviets' attention.

Compared to other Eastern nations, Poland's crisis of "real socialism" was the most extreme. Hardliners and traditionalists considered Poland to be a "weak link." It was the most vulnerable to outside pressure and the most at risk of the "destructive actions" of the internal opposition.

The Soviet government had a long-standing bias against the Polish model of socialism. The view was still strong during the first half of the 1980s. The Soviets felt that the Polish model failed to meet the fundamental principles of socialism. They also believed that the reason Poland was experiencing crisis was that the Polish United Workers' Party did not consistently implement the ideas of Marx or Lenin. The Soviets, by contrast, had "correctly" and "fully" implemented Marxist-Leninist principles in the Soviet Union.

The Soviets continually admonished the Polish government. Moscow gave the Poles specific advice on strengthening socialism within the country and hoped that Poland would develop stronger political positions. Konstantin Chernenko, general secretary of the CPSU Central Committee, told Gen.

Wojciech Jaruzelski "to root out antisocialist elements, limit church political interference, liquidate multiformity in [the] national economy, and direct villages to the socialist track." The practical implementation of such advice would only accelerate the country's path to chaos and national catastrophe. In reality, the advice was mostly ignored. This strengthened Poland's reputation as a "willful brother" in the minds of Kremlin leaders.

Moscow believed that keeping power in the hands of the Polish United Workers' Party was a fundamental condition for preserving socialism at the national level. If Solidarity came to power in Poland, it would symbolize the failure of socialism. Poland would leave the Warsaw Pact and orient itself to the West. That reorientation would have major economic consequences.

After the "Polish experience," Moscow became concerned about how other socialist nations would react. Poland proposed a new political force and a self-governing trade union that was openly supported by workers but not regulated by authorities. The workers openly and successfully opposed the ruling party. A new labor movement that opposed the authoritarian system had emerged in a socialist country. This circumstance itself was disconcerting to the ruling Soviet elite. More democratically minded leaders realized that reforms were necessary. Traditional hardliners went on the defensive. In August 1980, Soviets created the Suslov Commission to monitor Poland.

Despite the emerging contradictory influences, the Soviets managed to create an official policy. The Soviet government flatly refused any communication with Solidarity's leaders, whose supporters seemed to openly strive for the dismantling of the socialist system and removal of communists from power. Therefore, dialogue with them was out of the question. Moscow saw any opposition to socialism or communism as dissent. Nevertheless, Moscow still wanted to avoid bringing its troops into Poland. Publicly suppressing the opposition would bring negative political consequences and irreparable damage to the Soviet image.

Moscow believed that, if the crisis could be solved with proactive measures, then the Polish government should be the one to implement and oversee them. Moscow started to rely on the political leaders in Poland who favored stricter policies. The Soviets even pushed them in that direction. General Jaruzelski was one such political figure and became the leader of the Polish United Workers' Party with Moscow's support. On the eve of 13 December 1981, the Polish government declared a state of emergency, or martial law. The Soviet government supported the decision.

Soviet troops were ordered not to interfere with the events in Poland. However, that decision did not prevent a new wave of mutual alienation. The Poles believed that the Soviet Union was responsible for declaring martial law and wanted to prevent any reforms in the country. Moscow feared that these measures would not be sufficient and that the new government in Warsaw would not have enough determination to put an end to the antisocialist tendencies. Furthermore, Moscow feared that the destructive elements in Poland would continue to grow, become even stronger, and start to influence other "brotherly countries." Moscow thus "sanctioned Poland for its rebellious actions. The Soviets either froze or drastically reduced humanitarian and non-humanitarian aid." Soviet media did not mention the "socialism renewal" policies implemented by the Polish United Workers' Party under Jaruzelski. Gorbachev's "fear of Polish contamination" eclipsed even the fact that Polish society had isolated itself from its eastern neighbors. Poland identified with the West and defended Western confrontation with the Soviet Union. Furthermore, Poland used the situation to "stir up anti-Soviet and anti-Russian sentiment."

Major problems emerged within bilateral Soviet-Polish economic trade negotiations. It became increasingly clear that the Soviet export and commodity structure was ineffective. From 1980 to 1984, machines and technical product exports dropped from 25 to 12 percent. Exports of fuel, raw materials, and other supplies increased from 60 to 75 percent. Soviet interests were not being met. The situation also hindered Polish economic improvements.

Under perestroika, the Soviet Union had a chance to positively influence emerging bilateral relations. Gorbachev and Jaruzelski took advantage of the opportunities. The personal relationship and mutual understanding between the two was better than the relationships Gorbachev had with political leaders of other socialist countries.

In April 1987, Poland and Moscow developed and signed the Declaration of Soviet-Polish Ideological, Scientific, and Cultural Cooperation. The declaration was initiated by Poland, and it revived communication among social scientists, writers, journalists, scientists, the creative community, and youth in the two countries. The document asserted that history should not be a subject of ideological speculation and a pretext for stirring up nationalistic conflicts. Signing of the declaration also revived the work of Soviet and Polish historians. Historians set a goal to eliminate "gaps" in the social histories of the nations. Some important topics included the Soviet-Polish war of 1920, Stalin's massacre of the Polish Communist Party, the tragedy of the Warsaw Uprising of 1944, and the Katyn massacre. Katyn was an issue that was particularly sensitive for Poles. Gorbachev insisted that archived documents on Katyn be transferred to Poland.

These actions, as well as others, positively contributed to restoring trust between the leaders of the two countries and their parties. Public sentiment toward the Soviet Union had been improving in Poland for some time, and perestroika in the Soviet Union gave Poland momentum to create liberal policies. Poland used the momentum to make drastic changes.

However, hardliners opposed these changes. The improving sentiment in Poland toward the Soviet Union did not eliminate negative attitudes toward socialism. Traditionalists remained cautious. The Soviets expected that a new economic era would emerge. However, although Poland signed the Comprehensive Program for Scientific and Technical Cooperation in 1986, Soviet-Polish trade and economic development never took off.

Moscow had another concern over the Polish situation. Poland was the largest socialist nation in Eastern Europe. If it left the socialist commonwealth, then there would be devastating consequences for the state of affairs there. It would also have a significant impact on the Soviet Union's security. On 30 June 1986, Gorbachev addressed the Tenth Congress of the Polish United Workers' Party. He emphasized that close cooperation between the Soviet Union and Poland was essential for both nations' security. Both states represented two of the largest European socialist political entities. Gorbachev stressed that, before stability or peace could exist in either nation, both the Soviet Union and Poland had to mutually strengthen and assist the development of each other. Gorbachev called it the "Polish factor" and believed that it could positively or negatively impact the Soviet Union's future.

Perestroika's goals seemed to focus on new approaches to socialism. The Soviets reconsidered former dogmatic notions of socialism. In this sense, the Polish experience could be very useful and instructive. In reality, the scale of its application was more than modest. In theory, the Soviet Union was supposed to lead, and the "brothers of the socialist community" were supposed to follow. The Soviets would not accept overt leadership of a subordinate satellite. Poland's skepticism toward Moscow's plan was disconcerting to the Soviets because Poland's reform actions could influence others to veer in the "wrong" direction as they implemented their own reforms under perestroika. In other words, another potentially "difficult problem" emerged here, namely, the nature of the transformations the public and political system required.

Poland's problems developed more rapidly than Moscow could develop positive political relationships. In the late 1980s, the Polish crisis escalated. The crises merged with deteriorating economic conditions. The Polish United Workers' Party (PZPR) was boxed in and had little room to maneuver politically. In order to continue reform, the party needed to include oppositionists in the political system. Taking such an action implied that the PZPR would have to relinquish its monopoly. That event was a milestone in Poland's history. The resulting Round Table talks included members of the reform wing of the PZPR and moderate Solidarity members. At the final meetings, the political assembly officially signed a new representative government into existence. The new government would be supported by democratic elections.

Moscow gradually established unofficial contacts with select Solidarity representatives. It did so out of respect for Poland and the need to keep a stable Poland within the Soviet sphere of influence. The Soviets thus became open to noncommunist forces possibly coming to power. However, the Soviets would enter into the final agreement only if Poland remained within the Warsaw Pact. In June 1989, parliamentary elections began. It was a significant success for Poland and a huge upset for opposition party members. The Soviets' plans for a gradual transformation to democracy had not come to fruition.

Poland became the "trigger." Free elections in Poland resulted in a season of so-called "color revolutions" throughout the region. During that time, a new era began in Soviet-Polish relationships. However, it ended quickly, replaced by new relationships between a new Russia and a new Poland. In the midst of change, both Moscow and Warsaw had plenty of experience dealing with "difficult problems."

The relationship between the two countries had to be fundamentally changed. Their relationship could also no longer be used to cultivate a model of relations between the Soviets and socialist nations within a "socialist commonwealth." A wide range of issues emerged. The nations had to revise legal documents, regulate political and psychological instincts, and overcome stereotypes. The situation resulted in disputes and conflicts.

Warsaw and Moscow had different opinions about the direction that the two countries should take. Liberal-minded Soviet leaders intended to develop a "true partnership" with the former satellite and make Poland a "true ally." Poland wanted to minimize contact.

In 1990 and 1991, Poland emerged as a driving force in an effort to disband the Warsaw Pact and Comecon. In the meantime, Moscow drafted a new agreement to demonstrate friendship between the two nations. Moscow particularly encouraged Poland not to enter political agreements with other nations that would jeopardize the Soviet-Polish relationship. In particular, the Soviets did not want Poland to join NATO.

The reform momentum in the Soviet Union gradually began to fade. The results were unexpected. Poland dismantled socialism. Tadeusz Mazowiecki became the first postcommunist leader in Poland. Jaruzelski said that Mazowiecki wanted to introduce capitalistic laws but did not want massive unemployment. Mazowiecki also wanted to preserve the government's role in continued reform and to overcome potential stagnation. Mazowiecki searched for a "third" way to deal with the situation. Gorbachev dubbed Poland a "laboratory for reform."

However, experience and experiments were no longer in demand in the Soviet Union. The economy of the country was still managed by Soviet executives who did not know any other management approaches. The emerging elite were incapable of putting the reform interests ahead of their own needs. In Poland, Leszek Balcerowicz, the new deputy prime minister and finance minister, started reforms, which prompted the Soviet embassy to begin sending frantic telegrams back to Moscow. That is when the political and economic trajectories of the two countries really started to diverge. This divergence did not become a new "difficult problem" in the relationship between the two countries. Instead, two decades later, it had produced radically different results in the two countries. Authoritarian-oligarchic capitalism triumphed in Russia. A liberal capitalistic market model emerged in Poland. The Polish model still holds significant social-reformist components in Poland.

Poland terminated its alliance with the Soviet Union, and the Warsaw Pact dissolved. The question of Soviet troop withdrawal remained. The problem quickly became politically acute and needed a faster resolution. New approaches also were needed to deal with the common cultural heritage of the two countries, as well as displaced values. Furthermore, both nations needed access to archives.

Finally, because difficult problems had yet to be fully resolved, new disruptions could bring about new interpretations of current and past problems. Subsequently, this was exactly what happened.

Three stages in the relations between the Soviet Union and Eastern European socialist countries in the era of perestroika can now be distinguished.

In the first stage, Moscow's policies underwent no change. The policies were very similar to ones that existed in earlier Soviet governments. The dynamic personality of the new Soviet leader surely brought the unique elements to the forefront with regard to Soviet allies.

In the second stage, the emerging relationships were under the powerful idealistic influence and practices of perestroika, which eventually resulted in radical social, political, and geopolitical changes throughout the region. Furthermore, perestroika strengthened the position of the reformist wing of the PZPR. Soviet perestroika was a decisive factor in the transformations of the region. The Soviet government applied these principles to its relationships with its allies. The application of the principles began with a goal to renew socialism and ended with democratization throughout the Soviet Union. The Soviet Union recognized its satellite nations' right to self-determination and freedom to choose their own path. The Soviets did so in both word and deed. Gorbachev openly renounced the concepts of "limited sovereignty, collective responsibility for socialism," and other ideologies that justified intervening in the internal affairs of allies.

Gorbachev believed that he could reform the Soviet Union as well as the Soviet satellite states. He believed that a revived socialism would strengthen Poland and other Eastern European nations. Ultimately, the alliance between the Soviet Union and the European socialist nations would grow. The Soviets believed that reform-minded leaders such as Jaruzelski would give the socialist regime a fresh start. However, resources within the socialist nations were smaller than the Soviets anticipated. The reform movement exhausted its potential and was doomed.

In the third stage, the PZPR's power was revoked through parliamentary elections. Power was seized by the "nonsystemic opposition." Cooperation with and interest between Moscow and the new Polish government sharply declined. The new political forces in Poland were oriented toward the West, which Poland hoped could help solve numerous political problems and lead the country out of crisis. Poland ignored the Soviet Union. The Soviet system itself was in a state of decline.

Problems emerged within both Poland and the Soviet Union. Change indelibly emerged from the conflicts in both regions.

12

ASSISTANCE OR EXPLOITATION?

ECONOMIC RELATIONS BETWEEN POLAND AND THE SOVIET UNION

Janusz Kaliński (Poland)

Professor at the Warsaw School of Economics.

Leonid B. Vardomsky (Russia)

Professor, director of the Center for Post-Soviet Studies at the Institute of Economy of the Russian Academy of Sciences.

JANUSZ KALIŃSKI

ECONOMIC RELATIONS BETWEEN POLAND AND THE SOVIET UNION

AFTER WORLD WAR II, economic relations between Poland and the Soviet Union passed through several stages that differed in character, the closeness of the links, and their economic effects. They were under the powerful influence of political relations, which were also subject to evolution. In this chapter, I distinguish six such stages: the first two (1944–49 and 1950–55) corresponded to the Stalinist period, and the others cover, respectively, the latter half of the 1950s, as well as the 1960s, 1970s, and the 1980s together with the early 1990s. Although the distinctions between some of these phases might appear excessively formal, I believe they did have specific traits.

The period up to 1949 was ambivalent as, indeed, were relations in Poland in general. Elements of Soviet assistance for the war-ravaged country coincided with large-scale exploitation of the Polish economy, while attempts to establish economic contacts with Western countries were coupled with a growing dependence on the Soviet Union. The latter trend found its full expression during the implementation of the Six-Year Plan and was stimulated by the Cold War. During the first half of the 1950s, bilateral economic links were harnessed to the establishment of Poland's industrial and military potential and the exploitation of the country's resources and infrastructure for the needs of the communist empire. A system of prices and payment settlements—divorced from the world market and clearly advantageous to the Soviet Union—was imposed upon Poland.

The years 1956–59 saw an attempt to critically address the Stalinist period, also in the economic sphere, and to launch partnerlike relations, while simultaneously developing contacts with the West. The return to close ties between the Polish and Soviet economies in the 1960s took the form of "socialist integration" under the auspices of the Council for Mutual Economic Assistance (Comecon), resurrected after years of lethargy. The push for "integration" isolated the Polish-Soviet economic relationship from the mechanisms of the world economy and led to the appearance of autarchic tendencies. A new stage in bilateral relations emerged in the 1970s, when both Poland and the Soviet Union were expanding their links with Western countries. That did not weaken mutual contacts but rather augmented them with new forms of cooperation. The difficulties encountered by both economies during the 1980s had a similar effect. Both the 1970s and 1980s brought a growing lack of transparency in economic relations, particularly as concerned payment settlements. That provoked much speculation and controversy over the benefits of such cooperation. The fall of communist rule in Poland and the gradual disintegration of the Soviet Union created new conditions for trade, characterized by the transition—challenging for both parties—to hard currency settlements and world prices.

First Contacts and Problems, 1944–1949

In the period immediately after Stalin ordered the establishment of the communist-controlled Polish Committee of National Liberation in July 1944, economic relations between the two countries did not have a treaty basis. Poland supplied the Red Army with food and fodder, with the volume of these deliveries substantially higher than that directed to the Polish army or the Polish civilian population. The Red Army was also supplied with industrial goods, including textiles. For its part, the Soviet side extended food and sanitary assistance to the population of certain cities and organized the reconstruction of infrastructure and industry. At the same time, there occurred massive requisitioning of property on Polish territory and its incorporation into the military potential of the Soviet Union. The restoration of Poland's sovereignty, particularly in the area of transportation infrastructure, took several years.

The first trade accord between postwar Poland and the Soviet Union was called the "Agreement of 20 October 1944 on Deliveries of Goods and Terms of Settlement between the Polish Committee of National Liberation and the Government of the Union of Soviet Socialist Republics." Further regulations followed from the "Treaty on Friendship, Mutual Assistance, and Postwar Cooperation between the USSR and the Republic of Poland" of 21 April 1945. It served as the basis for the conclusion on 7 July of the "Trade Agreement between the Republic of Poland and the Union of Soviet Socialist Republics." The documents included a most-favored nation clause and envisioned the clearing method of trade payments, based on the US dollar and world prices.

In the years 1944–46, Polish-Soviet trade agreements were based on a barter system, which eliminated cash payments. However, Poland needed to obtain Soviet credits and loans. In April 1945, the Soviet Union granted the Polish Provisional Government a loan of $6.5 million for economic reconstruction. It was to be repaid over ten years, beginning in 1950, in hard currency or goods. In May 1946, during a visit to Moscow by a Polish government delegation, the parties annulled mutual liabilities connected with the supply of arms to the Polish army and expenditures incurred by Poland for the maintenance of Soviet forces and Soviet transit across Polish territory. The Soviet Union agreed to credit arms deliveries to Poland and to provide financial aid for economic development. Additional credits of 15 million rubles and $500,000 were granted to Poland in September. The annual interest rate was set at 2 percent, with repayment scheduled to begin in April 1947.

In March 1947, Poland received a loan in gold worth $28.8 million, at 2.5 percent interest. Sale of the gold in the American market permitted purchases of machinery, food, and other goods. The military part of the agreement constituted its key component. It provided for a ten-year credit of $100 million, to be repaid in Polish złoty and goods and services for the Northern Group of Forces of the Soviet army. Agreements on deliveries of Soviet grain, half of which were to be repaid with industrial goods, were also of considerable importance to Poland.

Alas, trade with the use of Soviet financial and commodity credits did not complete the picture of the overall Polish-Soviet economic relations. Negative phenomena, such as numerous robberies, instances of arson, and the devastation of municipal infrastructure, committed by Soviet troops as the front moved westward, should also be mentioned. Particularly in areas within the borders of the Third Reich, the army and military administrators requisitioned fixed assets, including both plant and consumer goods. Rolling stock, communications gear, industrial equipment, and farm livestock were all taken to the Soviet Union. That kind of activity caused especially high losses in the western and northern territories, which were incorporated into Poland after the war. It is calculated that the total losses in that part of Poland may have reached $2 billion.

Under the agreement of 16 August 1945, the Soviet government officially ceded to Poland all claims to formerly German property and other assets within Polish territory. The accord further determined that Poland would receive 15 percent of the reparations obtained by the Soviet Union from its occupation zone in Germany and 30 percent of the reparations from the Western occupation zones, with half of the latter to be repaid with deliveries of Polish products. The Polish government, in recognition of the Soviet efforts to obtain in talks with the Western powers a more advantageous western border for Poland, including the incorporation of Lower Silesia, committed itself to deliveries of coal and coking coal to the Soviet Union. Special prices were imposed on Poland: it was to receive $1.22 for one metric ton of coal and $1.44 for one metric ton of coking coal, which amounted to one-tenth of world market prices. The deliveries made at these prices amounted to about fifty-four million metric tons, generating a loss of more than $630 million. This constituted a kind of tribute imposed by the Soviet Union, and it restricted the possibility of developing contacts with Western countries, which at that time were experiencing coal shortages.

The reparations received by Poland through the Soviet Union reached a value of $228 million and included machinery and industrial equipment as well as complete industrial objects, though these goods in many cases were highly decapitalized. Merchant vessels, rolling stock, and deliveries of goods from then-current German production constituted a further, important part of the reparations. They also included publications on Marxist ideology and the history of the Soviet Union, printed in Polish. The reparations ended in 1953, when the Soviet Union relinquished the compensation it had been receiving from the German Democratic Republic. At the same time, the Soviet Union also raised the drastically unfair prices it was paying for Polish coal.

Immediately after the war, a confluence of factors made the Soviet Union Poland's number-one trading partner. In 1945, it provided 91 percent of all Polish imports and received 93 percent of Polish exports. Such high participation in Polish trade was an exceptional and transitional phenomenon. As Poland established economic relations with other countries, the role of the eastern neighbor diminished in favor of Western countries. Bilateral trade was at its lowest level in 1949, when imports from the Soviet Union accounted for 18.8 percent of all foreign purchases, while exports to the Soviet Union constituted 19.4 percent of all sales. The corresponding data for Western countries came in at 57.4 percent for imports and 54.6 percent for exports.

Poland imported the following commodities and products from the Soviet Union: iron and manganese ores, cotton, grain, flax and tobacco, asbestos, aluminum, copper, synthetic rubber and tires, and tractors and trucks. Soviet deliveries accounted for 60 percent of Polish iron ore imports and 70 percent of cotton imports. Exports to the Soviet Union included coal, zinc, ash, cement, rail freight cars, sheet glass, sugar, and silk fabrics, as well as metallurgical goods and cotton, linen, and wool fabrics produced from Soviet-supplied raw materials. Despite systematic growth in Polish exports, the volume of imports continued to be substantially higher, which led to a persistent trade deficit, covered with credits. As a result, Poland's debt to the Soviet Union reached $58 million in 1949.

Toward Dependence, 1950–1955

After Moscow coerced Warsaw into rejecting the Marshall Plan, Poland embarked on a path of strengthening economic links with the Soviet Union, at the expense of links with the West. January 1948 saw the signing of a package of accords that constituted a kind of compensation for not partaking of the American aid. The trade agreements were underpinned by Soviet credits worth $450 million, at 3 percent interest, to be repaid over five years with goods deliveries. The "post-Marshall" package also included a second loan in gold worth $20 million, granted in September 1949 on terms specified in the 1947 agreement. By offering financial and technical assistance, the Soviet Union was again becoming Poland's main supplier of raw materials, complete industrial plants, machines, equipment, and arms. The Soviet Union continued seeking to restrict Poland's contacts with the West, as illustrated by forcing Poland to abandon plans to build a Fiat-licensed car factory; instead, Poland launched automobile production based on an outdated Soviet design. At the same time, Poland undertook production of maritime vessels for the Soviet market.

The close links between the Polish and Soviet economies were further consolidated by the abandonment of the US dollar in mutual settlements and the introduction of the clearing ruble in that role. The use of current world prices was also dropped in favor of 1949 prices. The exchange rate of the Polish złoty to the ruble was determined in the course of monetary reform in Poland in October 1950. The rate was set at one złoty to one ruble, with four złotys and four rubles to one dollar. Even though the Soviet Union oversaw the monetary reform in Poland, the exchange rate that was actually adopted turned out to be unfavorable to the Soviet side due to differences in domestic prices in the two countries and the falling purchasing power of the złoty. Stalin intervened and the Polish authorities agreed to introduce a "special" exchange rate of three złotys to one ruble. The system of prices and settlements adopted in the early 1950s was advantageous to the Soviet Union and constituted a kind of tribute to the communist empire.

As the Cold War progressed and the Korean conflict heated up, the Soviet Union attached growing importance to the development of arms production in Poland. The relevant tasks were included in the Six-Year Plan for the years 1950–55, forcing changes in the agreement of January 1948 on deliveries of industrial equipment. Expansion of the arms industry was substantially accelerated, and plants were built for the manufacture of combat jets, tanks, and radars. Railway lines, roads, bridges, and airfields were modernized or built in line with the requirements of the Soviet General Staff. Military investment projects were facilitated by the signing in June 1950 of further accords on the mutual delivery of goods in the years 1953–58, on Soviet deliveries of industrial equipment on credit, and on credits for the supply of arms.

The "Agreement between the Government of the Republic of Poland and the Government of the Union of Soviet Socialist Republics on Credit Deliveries to Poland of Arms and Military Equipment in the Years 1951–1955" was of particular importance in this context. It also provided for the supply of components needed in the industrial assembly of arms. Moreover, the Soviet side agreed to transfer to Poland, free of charge, licenses for the production of arms, ordnance, and military equipment. One-third of the deliveries were to be repaid with exports of Polish goods and two-thirds by a credit worth 1.2 billion rubles, at 2 percent interest. It was determined that the credit and interest would be repaid with deliveries of Polish products.

The Soviet Union's share in Polish foreign trade started rising again in 1950, though it was still substantially lower than immediately after the war and amounted to 37.3 percent in exports and 37.9 percent in imports. Simultaneously, the share from Western countries was reduced to, respectively, 28.9 and 29.7 percent. The proportion of machines, equipment, and transportation gear in imports from the Soviet Union was rising rapidly. That group of imports also included arms, the value of which amounted to $56 million in 1952, accounting for one-fifth of all Polish imports from the Soviet Union. The deliveries of plans for investment projects were coupled with the transfer of technologies (occasionally outdated) and with an influx of Soviet specialists into Poland.

Change was also evident in Polish exports to the Soviet Union. Poland started exporting maritime vessels and increased deliveries of consumer durables, including china, textiles, clothing, and furniture. Butter, bacon, and fresh and canned meat were also supplied to the Soviet Union in certain years. Arms exports were initiated and reached the value of $7.5 million in 1952. Uranium ores from Lower Silesian mines constituted another, little-known item on the list of Polish exports to the Soviet Union.

An Attempt to Square Accounts, 1956–1959

The new Polish leadership, headed by Władysław Gomułka, brought to power by the events of October 1956, opened talks with the Kremlin, focusing on the contentious aspects of Polish-Soviet economic relations, such as the underpriced coal exports, war reparations, transit payments, and Polish debt to the Soviet Union. No agreement was reached on the different Polish and Soviet estimates of the war reparations. As for the unfair coal prices and the Polish debt, the parties decided on a zero option: it was agreed that the losses Poland incurred due to the coal exports had offset Poland's credit debt to the Soviet Union. Furthermore, the Soviet Union granted Poland credits worth $286 million and transferred $60 million in payment for transportation and communication services to the Soviet army in the years 1946–54.

The years 1956–59 in Polish-Soviet trade were marked by high fluctuations of turnover and a persistent deficit on the Polish side. From 1955 onward, the Soviet Union's share in Polish foreign trade steadily diminished. It reached its lowest level in 1958, when the Soviet Union accounted for 27 percent of Polish imports and 25 percent of Polish exports. Western countries clearly gained in prominence as trading partners.

Revival of Comecon, 1960–1970

In the late 1950s, the leadership of the Polish United Workers' Party (PZPR) decided to again accelerate the country's industrialization, with particular focus on the fuels and raw materials sectors. Similar efforts, prompted by Nikita Khrushchev's call to overtake the West, appeared in the Soviet Union. Comecon livened its attempts to coordinate five-year and longer-term development plans of the member states, with special focus on cooperation and the specialization of production. The areas of specialization assigned to Poland included rolling stock production, machine tools, and the steel, chemical, and textile industries. A 1961 document called "Basic Principles of International Socialist Division of Labor" envisioned the development in Poland of a commodity sector and steel and chemical industries.

The launching of the International Bank for Economic Cooperation, affiliated with Comecon, in 1964 and the introduction of the transfer ruble were important developments in the sphere of payment settlements. The transfer ruble (with parity of 0.987412 grams of gold)—equivalent to the circulation ruble after the 1961 monetary reform in the Soviet Union—replaced the clearing ruble as the currency used for settling accounts. Simultaneously, bilateral clearing was replaced with multilateral clearing. The changes in the system of settlements were coupled with the introduction of more flexible prices within Comecon. As a result, Comecon used the average world prices from the years 1957–58 until the end of 1964, and, starting in 1965, it used the average prices from the years 1960–64. That amounted to a certain progress compared to the rigid price system from the early 1950s and meant more favorable terms of trade for Poland. However, substantial differences between world prices and those applied in trade within the Soviet bloc still remained, which obscured economic effectiveness.

Polish-Soviet consultations and economic accords concluded at the turn of the 1950s helped accelerate investment programs in Poland. The year 1960 saw the signing of agreements on Soviet assistance in the construction of industrial plants, on mutual deliveries of goods for 1961–65, on deliveries of natural gas in exchange for Polish pipe, and on payment settlements. Relations with the arms industry—strained in the latter half of the 1950s—improved, which led to the launching in Poland of the production of Soviet-licensed missiles, helicopters, and tanks.

The year 1960 also marked the beginning of a rapid expansion in Polish-Soviet trade. Polish imports had doubled by 1967 and tripled by 1970, as compared to the 1960 level. Exports also surged and, in 1970, were more than three times higher than in 1960. However, Poland had a deficit in its trade with the Soviet Union throughout the decade, with the exception of

1964, 1965, and 1968. The deficit was offset by exports of services, chiefly in the construction sector. In trade negotiations, the Soviets increasingly demanded that higher deliveries of commodities and energy to Poland be coupled with Polish credits for related investment projects in the Soviet Union. During the 1960s, Polish credits were used to boost the production of potassium salts imported from the Soviet Union, while gas and oil deliveries were linked to Polish exports of pipe for these industries.

In the years 1960–70, the Soviet Union consolidated its position in Polish foreign trade. In imports, its share increased from 31 to 38 percent and, in exports, from 29 to 35 percent. As in the past, this increase came at the expense of trade with Western countries.

Developing Contacts with the West, 1971–1979

The 1970s brought warming of relations between the East and West, reflected by the invigoration of economic links. The Polish leadership, headed by Edward Gierek, displayed a particularly strong pro-Western orientation. That, however, did not undermine economic ties with the Soviet Union. On the contrary, accords concluded in 1971 provided for increased trade in machines and equipment needed for the modernization of output, as well as in the fuels and raw material sectors. The beneficial impact of increased contacts with the West on trade between Poland and the Soviet Union was illustrated by the cooperation of Polish brake-system manufacturers with Westinghouse, which led to exports of Polish-manufactured brakes to the Soviet Kamaz truck factory. Also, the production of Fiat-licensed cars in both Poland and the Soviet Union enhanced cooperation between the automotive industries of the two countries.

In the years 1971–75, Polish imports from the Soviet Union shot up by 80 percent and exports doubled. The rapid expansion of exports meant that Poland had a trade surplus from 1972 onward. However, despite the growing turnover, a trade deficit again reappeared from 1976 forward (with the exception of 1979). It was generated by difficulties the Polish economy encountered in connection with the country's increasing debt to the West and the related necessity of channeling additional exports to Western countries. Overall, between 1971 and 1979, Polish imports from the Soviet Union trebled, while exports to the East increased by three and a half times. This was stimulated by the high growth rates in both countries, maintained until the late 1970s.

In the 1970s, Poland was the largest supplier of raw materials and fuels to the Soviet Union among the Comecon countries. Coal exports dominated and accounted for 25 percent of all Polish coal sold abroad. The Soviet Union was buying 90 percent of the rolling stock produced in Poland and 55 percent of the ships launched from Polish yards. Other exports to the Soviet Union included aircraft and helicopters, construction and agricultural machines, machine tools, and trucks. Complete industrial plants and technological lines also figured prominently in Polish exports. During the 1970s, the Soviet Union bought twenty-eight Polish sulfuric acid plants, sixteen sugar refineries, several refrigeration plants, and lines for the production of fiber- and mineral board. In 1975, the Soviet Union was the recipient of 85 percent of all Polish paint and varnish exports (which accounted for 22 percent of Soviet imports in that sector). Poland also became the leading Comecon supplier of consumer durables to the Soviet Union (15 percent of Soviet imports in this area).

Imports from the Soviet Union included steel industry products, machine tools, transport aircraft, trucks, automobiles, diesel locomotives, agricultural tractors, and mining and construction machines. The Soviet Union also supplied equipment for steel mills, coking plants, cement factories, and pre-cast-building-unit plants. Poland was the largest buyer of Soviet consumer goods, including refrigerators, radio and TV sets, bicycles, watches, and cameras.

Poland's participation in the development of the Soviet extraction industry constituted another form of cooperation. Poland was a party to thirteen agreements and injected a total of 1.1 billion rubles into related projects. That resulted in increased deliveries of Soviet oil, natural gas, asbestos, and ferroalloys. Polish companies also participated in the construction of wood-pulp plants, asbestos factories, and gas and oil pipelines. Poland's participation in the building of the Khmelnitsky nuclear power plant and related transmission grid secured guarantees of higher electricity supplies from the Soviet Union. Western credits granted to Poland were used to finance some of these investment projects. This investment involved, in particular, purchases of specialist equipment from the West or production of it in Poland under Western licenses. The credits Poland extended to the Soviet Union carried lower interest rates than the Western credits Poland received.

Poland and the Soviet Union were both interested in upgrading their transport systems, including the military component. With that in mind, the two countries expanded and modernized railway transfer stations on their border and built, with Soviet participation, a broad-gauge track into Polish Silesia. The Steel-Sulfur Line, as it was known, facilitated the transportation of iron ore, potassium salts, grain, and machines to Poland. The trains carried Polish coal and sulfur in the other direction.

Soviet aircraft constituted the backbone of the fleet of the Polish national airline, LOT. Deliveries of Soviet aircraft had begun in the 1940s; initially, these were propeller-driven airliners, with jets added in the late 1960s. In the early 1970s, LOT took delivery of six long-range IL-62s, which permitted the launch of transatlantic routes.

The dynamic development of Polish-Soviet trade in the 1970s was undercut by deteriorating terms of trade. The delayed consequences of the first world energy crisis had then begun to take their toll. Initially, the crisis did not affect the prices of commodities imported from the Soviet Union since Comecon used world prices from the years 1965–69. As a result, the 1973 prices of Soviet fuels, commodities, and production materials were 11 percent below world prices and, in 1974, 41 percent below world prices. The situation changed in 1975, when it was decided to introduce annual price adjustments in transactions between the Comecon member states. Contract prices were determined on the basis of the average world prices for the preceding five-year period (staggered price base). This resulted in radical price increases, especially for imported oil and gas, which worsened Poland's terms of trade. In 1975, the exchange rate of $1.00 to 0.62 ruble was adopted, which meant considerable losses for Polish companies that exported goods with Western components to the Soviet Union.

Agony in the Communist System, 1980–1991

The social and political developments in Poland in the early 1980s had a significant impact on Polish-Soviet trade. Turnover expanded in 1980, though Poland had a high trade deficit. In 1981, Polish exports stalled while imports from the Soviet Union increased, which resulted in a doubling of the Polish trade deficit.

In autumn 1980, the Polish authorities—faced with a dramatic economic crisis and mounting public unrest—asked the Soviet Union for financial aid. It is estimated that, in the early 1980s, Poland received Soviet credits worth 4.9 billion transfer rubles and $1.8 billion. After the imposition of martial law, Western sanctions against Poland led to further growth in trade with the Soviet Union. In 1982, the Soviet Union sold Poland an additional half million metric tons of grain, along with maize, rice, and other products worth 130 million rubles. Western sanctions also forced Polish producers to buy components made in the Soviet Union for automobiles, telephone switchboards, and varnishes, which were subsequently exported back to the Soviet Union.

In the years 1982–86, imports rose by 40 percent while exports surged by almost 90 percent. Polish exports continued to expand year to year while imports from the Soviet Union began shrinking in 1987. Due to internal economic problems, the Soviet Union was failing to fulfill its contracts for the supply of oil, gas, and electricity. Unexpectedly, this problem helped the Polish balance of payments: starting in 1988, Poland had a surplus in trade with the Soviet Union, since the imports of Soviet raw materials and fuels were lower than the exports of Polish processed goods.

Both the recession that appeared after the launch of systemic reforms in Poland and the progressing disintegration of the Soviet Union contributed to the reduction of imports from the Soviet Union by 44 percent in 1990. Remarkably, Polish exports increased by 22 percent, largely as a result of Soviet companies—in collaboration with Polish partners—using reserves of transfer rubles to buy food and to reexport consumer electronics from Poland. These were often shady transactions, though they boosted Poland's trade surplus.

Payments were still being made in transfer rubles in 1990, though a gradual transition was taking place to hard currency settlements and the application of market rules. In the last year of the Soviet Union, trade turnover shrank to $2.2 billion, with a deficit of $600 million on the Polish side. The collapse of Polish exports was connected with restrictions on hard-currency imports in the Soviet Union (payments freeze). Many Polish companies, unable to extract payment for their deliveries, went under.

The Soviet Union's share of Polish foreign trade gradually decreased starting in 1984: exports had gone from 29 to 24 percent by 1988 and to 11 percent by 1991, and imports dropped from 35 to 23 to 14 percent over the same periods. Western countries were the chief beneficiaries. In 1990, after decades of Soviet domination, Germany became Poland's largest trading partner.

The 1980s were marked by a persistent trade deficit on the Polish side and an abundance of Soviet credits. As a result, by the end of 1990, the Polish debt—as calculated by the Soviet side—totaled 4.5 billion transfer rubles. Poland questioned this figure, insisting that the Polish input into raw material investment projects in the Soviet Union should have been properly taken into account. According to Polish assessments, the true value of Polish investment contributions was triple the Soviet estimate made for the purpose of settling mutual accounts. That translated to 3 billion transfer rubles, which, combined with the relevant interest, practically offset the Polish debt. In turn, the Soviets claimed that the services of Polish companies had been priced 15 to 20 percent above those of other foreign enterprises. A special intergovernmental commission was established to address these discrepancies.

An Assessment

Bilateral economic relations after World War II have always provoked controversy in both Poland and the Soviet Union (Russia). It was commonly believed in the Soviet Union that exports of oil, gas, industrial commodities, and grain to Poland in the framework of Comecon, combined with credits, amounted to a subsidization of the Polish economy. Some Western analysts have also attempted to calculate the losses that the Soviet Union supposedly incurred in its trade with Comecon member states.

Contrary opinions were expressed in Poland, in underground (uncensored) publications. Trade and other forms of economic relations with the Soviet Union were treated as an ongoing exploitation of the Polish economy, designed to advance the Soviet Union's imperial goals. There was a widespread conviction that trade with the Soviet Union was unprofitable, since it forced Poland to engage in energy- and material-intensive production. The peculiar needs of the Soviet economy caused products manufactured for the Soviet market to be uncompetitive in Western countries. Furthermore, the model of economic relations used only reinforced autarchic tendencies in both countries and strengthened Poland's dependence on the Soviet Union.

Generally speaking, economic relations between Poland and the Soviet Union were congruent with the system the Kremlin had put in place in the entire Eastern bloc. It was a system subordinated to the ideological tenets and imperial goals of the Soviet Union. Immediately after World War II, reparations, "contributions," and "spoils of war" were used to facilitate the reconstruction of the Eastern power. In the late 1950s, that approach was replaced by trade and cooperation on terms determined by Moscow. The artificial conditions of cooperation were totally opaque and divorced from world markets, which prevented a reasonable assessment of their effectiveness. Mutual deliveries of arms, licenses, and equipment for the military sector remained shrouded in secrecy. That stimulated an atmosphere of mutual suspicion and distrust. Political factors also continued to play a key role, as evidenced by attempts to defuse recurring socioeconomic crises. The Soviet Union extended economic aid to its vassals when political stability was under threat. Moreover, it did not obstruct their economic relations with the West if it thought that its own interests could be served.

In light of the above analysis, it is impossible to provide an unequivocal answer to the question in the title of this section of the present publication: was it assistance or exploitation? The main reason is that there is no way of assessing the benefits of bilateral economic cooperation in the conditions imposed by a centrally steered economy, isolated from world markets. The flawed Polish-Soviet economic links were a result of overall postwar relations between the two countries, in which the imperial interests of the Eastern power were decisive. As a result, the political and economic system and model of cooperation imposed on Poland caused the bankruptcy of the Polish economy in the late 1980s.

JANUSZ KALIŃSKI

LEONID B. VARDOMSKY

· ·

ECONOMIC RELATIONS BETWEEN POLAND AND THE SOVIET UNION

· ·

THE ECONOMIC COLLABORATION between Poland and the Soviet Union dating back to the period of "building socialism" has generated fewer conflicting assessments and less political speculation than the Katyn executions or the Red Army prisoners of war (in Polish camps), let alone the secret Molotov-Ribbentrop Pact. By and large, this period gave rise to no major issues that would overshadow relations between the two countries today. Economic cooperation was based on bilateral accords whose general provisions were in the public domain, though their content was not fully transparent. There are numerous academic publications from both Poland and Russia that deal with economic cooperation dating back to the socialist and market-reform years.

The papers written during the socialist and market-transition periods are very different. The former are characterized by informative research describing the substance of cooperation, debating certain issues of the day, and detailing the new avenues and vehicles of that cooperation. The papers written during the market-transition period, of which there are few, are characteristically analytical, investigating the reasons for the failure of the socialist economic integration project and evaluating its pros and cons and the benefits and losses for both countries. It is perhaps worth mentioning here the three-volume study, *Central and Eastern Europe in the Second Half of the 20th Century,* published by Nauka in 2000 and 2002 and compiled by the Institute of International Economic and Political Studies of the Russian Academy of Sciences.

Viewed from a modern-day standpoint, the results of the economic cooperation between Poland and the Soviet Union in 1945–91 defy an unambiguous assessment. On the one hand, the Soviet Union helped Poland restore its economy in the early postwar years and during the subsequent industrialization, which brought Poland's economy closer to those of the most economically advanced members of Comecon: the German Democratic Republic (GDR) and Czechoslovakia. Poland was fairly actively involved in developing natural resources in the Soviet Union, modernizing certain branches of its industries, and supplying consumer goods to the Soviet market. The Druzhba oil pipeline, Yamal-Europe gas pipeline, and Ust-Ilim pulp mill still operate today. On the other hand, cooperation failed to bridge the gap between the economies of the Soviet Union, Poland, and other Comecon members and the leading world economies. On the contrary, that gap continued to grow. By placing large orders with Poland in the absence of competition, the Soviet Union could not stimulate modernization in manufacturing in Poland, which contrasted with the Western nations that leaped forward through innovation in the 1970s and 1980s. The Soviet Union also could not supply new technologies to its Comecon partners, since it was running short of them itself. Some Polish studies point out that, in the postwar years, the Soviet Union kept Poland in an economic stranglehold, exploited its human and natural resources, and sought to stifle its development.

Be that as it may, partly in response to the needs of Poland and other Comecon members, the Soviet Union was forced to emphasize developing its raw materials (a trend that has persisted to this day), defined Russia's specialization in the world marketplace, and caused all the problems and imbalances we see today.

In my view, Soviet policies toward Poland and other Comecon members were defined by the logic of a bipolar world order, geopolitical rivalry, and confrontation between the military alliances. The Soviet Union was prepared to sustain huge material costs and to increasingly lag behind in order to try and keep up with the competition from the West. This situation could not last forever. By the late 1980s, the economic and political crisis in the Soviet Union released its partners in Comecon and the Warsaw Pact from the Soviets' political grasp, and the "need to pay for their political loyalty was no longer there."

The defeat of the Soviet Union in the Cold War meant that the assets invested in the "people's democratic" countries were for all intents and purposes thrown down the drain, since the political and economic clout of the Soviet Union and its successor, Russia, over these countries was so weakened as to be negligible.

At the same time, there is reason to believe that the geopolitical price paid by the Soviet Union and the potential advantages lost by Poland in dropping it as an ally were not so high if one is to assume that the parity between the military alliances prevented a world war whose costs would have been incomparably greater. In other words, at a certain stage, cooperation between the Soviet Union and Poland and other countries of the "socialist camp" helped maintain geostrategic stability in the world and promoted economic growth and an increase in human resources, which played an important role during the market transition.

Economic cooperation between these countries throughout the period under review was marred by clashes of conflicting interests. Poland was not prepared to kowtow to the Kremlin all the time. Neither Władysław Gomułka nor Edward Gierek can be thought of as dumb Kremlin puppets. Poland's former president, Wojciech Jaruzelski, said that Poland "experienced Soviet pressure at times bordering on *diktat,* but it did not experience exploitation; even during the worst of times, the Poles lived better than the Russians." Poland's leaders were well aware of the geopolitical significance of their country to the Soviet Union and acted above all in the national interests as they understood them at the time. Poland learned to take advantage of its geopolitical situation and had continued successfully to do so until Comecon and the Warsaw Pact collapsed. Polish specialists overseeing bilateral cooperation better understood the interaction between planned and market economies, as well as national and world economies; they were less conservative and likely to stick to dogmatic ideologies. Moreover, Poland was among those members of Comecon that could influence the policy of the Soviet Union and persuade it to introduce some economic innovations, belated though they were. During perestroika, Polish experts and entrepreneurs were very instrumental in developing Russia's "market."

At the heart of the economic contradictions that arose between the two countries was the ideology of centralized planning and the fact that the "real ratio between the market values of prices and spending was ignored in favor of the calculated value." Bilateral trade was an extension of the centralized economy that served to balance national production and consumption. That was done as part of a coordination of economic plans, key parts of which were the bilateral trade agreements drafted for five-year periods and annual protocols listing the commodities to be supplied and contracts on the supply of specific goods.

Foreign trade acted as a balance because the administrative command economic model was dogged by deficiency. The countries concerned imported the goods in short supply instead of expanding exports. Under these circumstances, trade exchanges were divided into "hard" goods, which were in shorter supply and for which there was demand on the world market, and "soft" goods, which were in short supply and for which there was no demand on the world market. The countries concerned attempted to balance bilateral trade over both categories. However, they did not always manage this balancing act, and this imbalance became a basis for reciprocal complaints.

Before Comecon was formed in 1949, trade between countries of the "socialist camp" was based on current world prices. In 1950–51, the war in Korea caused the prices of raw materials on world markets to rise by 50 to

100 percent. It was not clear how to respond to that change, since centralized planning required price stability in bilateral trade. A consensus was reached that the 1949–50 prices would be retained in bilateral trade. These prices were maintained until 1957. Following the closure of the Suez Canal in 1956, world coal prices rose dramatically. However, they fell just as dramatically in 1957. This shift induced Comecon members to change the pricing of the goods and commodities they supplied to each other.

In 1958, a policy to set the trade prices was agreed upon, and it was in force until the mid-1970s. Contract prices for one five-year term were agreed to bilaterally based on the average world prices of any particular good for the previous five-year term. That policy worked if world prices were relatively stable. If the prices for various categories of goods started to fluctuate, particularly to varying degrees for different goods, then the arrangement faltered, which significantly changed the terms of trade within Comecon, causing some Comecon members to sustain major economic losses.

In response to dramatic world price fluctuations in 1975, Comecon upgraded its pricing policy and introduced so-called annual incremented prices. The contract prices were revised annually by averaging the world prices over the previous five-year term. This practice served to somewhat cushion the price fluctuations on the world market, but it could not resolve the problem altogether. That contract price-setting policy therefore inevitably led to a non-equivalent exchange of merchandise.

The predominant view at that time was that the issues arising from the non-equivalent exchanges of merchandise could be resolved through cooperation and mutual assistance, the main instrument of which was the coordination of national economic plans. Controversies over trade issues stemmed not so much from the contract price-setting as from currency conversion.

A system of payments was introduced to specially service bilateral trade schemes that relied on the transfer ruble, whose gold value per unit and rate of exchange to the US dollar were equal to the ruble. The idea was that the transfer ruble would be an international socialist currency supporting multilateral payments within Comecon through the International Bank for Economic Cooperation (IBEC). In reality, though, the transfer ruble could only support bilateral trade. Since one and the same kind of goods had to have several price tags attached to it with respect to the different countries of the Commonwealth of Independent States, the transfer ruble had variable purchasing power depending on what pair of Comecon countries traded with each other.

It made no sense to accumulate transfer rubles; they came into play only when a transaction was recorded and existed only as records in the accounts of Comecon members at the IBEC under the contracts they signed.

The increasing fluctuations of world prices in the 1970s and 1980s led to a situation in which exchanges of merchandise could not be balanced fairly; one side was always on the losing end. A sort of balance was achieved by either lowering or upping the contract price below or above the agreed upon contract price level. The trade balance in transfer rubles represented phantom assets that could not be spent because they were attached to nonexistent merchandise on hand. The main supplier of fuel and raw materials, the Soviet Union, amassed 15 billion illiquid transfer rubles between 1975 and 1985. The European Comecon members formed assets worth 10 billion transfer rubles as a result of trading with the Soviet Union in 1986–90 as the prices of fuel and raw materials dropped.

The illiquidity of transfer rubles was, of course, caused by the state monopoly over foreign trade. There had been no real rates of exchange between national currencies and transfer ruble hard currencies until the late 1980s, which actually meant that the national economies were isolated from one another and the world economy. The national economies received distorted signals from the world and Comecon markets, and therefore the efficiency or lack thereof in bilateral trade and economic activity as a whole could not be assessed properly, thus blocking industrial specialization and modernization. Exchange coefficients were introduced only at the final phase of Comecon's existence. What feeble monetary regulation tools there were for regulating cooperation cemented the outdated industrial infrastructure and precluded its modernization and production of quality export goods. As enterprise self-financing was introduced in the national economies, the crippled payment mechanism could not catch up with the new realities, thus decimating the profits of individual enterprises and depriving them of the smallest incentives to build up trade relations.

Three phases can be identified in the evolution of trade relations between Poland and the Soviet Union.

The initial phase lasted until the early 1960s. During it, *the purpose of cooperation was determined by the need to go ahead with postwar industrial reconstruction, the transition to socialist industrialization, and, last but not least, the confrontation between the military alliances.* Cooperation proceeded while the economies of the countries concerned were ravaged by the recent world war and the beginning of the Cold War, when the West imposed an actual embargo on trade with these countries that lasted from 1948 to 1954. The Export Control Act, adopted by the United States in 1949, legally framed the Truman Doctrine aimed at simultaneously restricting the economic development of socialist countries and encouraging the economic development of Western European economies.

During this period, economic cooperation emerged in the socialist group of nations, with the Soviet Union enjoying a clearly dominant role and the Polish state system and economic management assuming the Soviet model.

Aware of Poland's role in its confrontation with the West, the Soviet Union extended to Poland extensive economic aid in the form of interest-free or low-interest commodities or monetary credits. According to the Polish scholar Marian Wilk, the Soviet Union credited a supply to Poland of nine hundred thousand metric tons of grain between 1946 and 1949. The Soviet Union extended total credits worth 4.1 billion złotys ($1 billion) between 1947 and 1957. Soviet credits accounted for 10 percent of investment in Polish industries between 1950 and 1963. Those credits provided supplies of raw materials for the textile, leather, smelting, and chemical industries. The Soviet Union extended technical aid in the form of technical documentation and equipment to help create two hundred industrial enterprises in Poland; it also helped Poland restore its transport infrastructure, communications, and health care and offered free training for Poland's work force in the growing economy.

It should be stressed that this Soviet economic assistance was a form of payment in return for Poland's refusal to join the Marshall Plan, which was aimed at, among other things, checking the growth of Soviet influence in West European countries. As a result, Poland was for several years laboring under severe restrictions in its trade with the United States and other Western countries. The interest rates on Western credit to Poland were three to four times higher than the interest rates on Soviet credits (2 to 3 percent).

The first major economic controversy between the Soviet Union and Poland arose in 1945 over property reparations for the western territories joined to Poland under the Yalta and Potsdam accords. The Soviet side suggested that Polish-Soviet societies be formed to develop the coal mines of Lower Silesia; however, Poland declined. Addressing a Polish-Soviet government meeting in August 1945, Vyacheslav M. Molotov spoke of a considerable imbalance in Poland's favor and quoted property valuations conducted on the former Polish territories ceded to the Soviet Union ($3.6 billion) and former German territories ceded to Poland ($9.5 billion, inclusive of machinery and equipment worth $1.75 billion). By August 1945, the Soviet Union had brought home property as reparations worth $500 million from Poland's western territories.

Differences over the valuation of the property as reparations were inevitable since they were merely approximate, while the parties concerned were naturally keen to quote values that would benefit them. There were no independent auditing procedures at the time.

After Poland declined to set up joint societies, Molotov proposed that the property losses could be offset if Poland supplied coal to Russia (eight million metric tons in 1946, thirteen million metric tons in the four subsequent years, and twelve million metric tons until the end of the occupation of Germany) at a special price of $1.20 per metric ton. That price was a mere 10 percent of the global price for coal at the time. Poland agreed, and an agreement to that effect was signed on 16 August 1945. Under that agreement, the Soviet Union was also obliged to hand over to Poland fifty thousand German prisoners of war to be sent to the coal mines, to give up claims to any German property on Polish territory, and to recognize Poland's rights to one-seventh of the reparations received by it.

In 1947, the coal deliveries were halved to 6.5 million metric tons and, in 1950, were reduced by a further 25 percent. The special coal price was in place for ten years, and Poland's losses from not selling coal on the European market at normal prices amounted to between $500 million and $800 million. In 1956, the Soviet government recognized Poland's claims worth $500 million, or 2 billion złotys, in connection with the increase in world coal prices and reduced by that sum Poland's debt, which developed after it took credits over the previous period.

Transit tariffs were another source of antagonism. Poland pointed out that the Soviet Union underpaid it for freight and passenger transit to the GDR. In 1957, these claims were settled as a result of negotiations. The Soviet Union assumed the obligation to hand over 182 million rubles' worth of commodities to Poland as compensation.

As it insisted on prices and tariffs that gave it an advantage, the Soviet Union was trying to alleviate the burden of the Cold War it had to bear, just as Poland as a country had borne the burden of being ravaged by war. However, in the final analysis, the importance of Poland as an ally forced the Soviet Union to make concessions.

Another problem in Soviet-Polish relations arose from the transition in payments from the US dollar to the "clearing ruble." If the two sides were to stick to the gold parity of the ruble to the złoty in 1950, one złoty was to be exchanged for one ruble. That exchange rate was unacceptable to the Soviet Union since domestic prices in the two countries differed considerably and inflation in Poland was running high. Finally, the two countries agreed to introduce a special rate of three dollars to one złoty to account for the different national pricing policies and the model of commodity exchange of that period. That was an artificial exchange rate that gave rise to complaints from both sides about non-equivalent exchanges of merchandise.

On the whole, cooperation between Poland and the Soviet Union during that phase complemented the industrialization of both economies. Development proceeded based on domestic sources as part of the concept of "autonomous development."

In the early 1950s, the Soviet Union accounted for a third of Poland's foreign trade turnover, whereas Poland accounted for an 8 to 10 percent share of Soviet foreign trade overall.

The exports were made up of national production surpluses that very often were appropriated at the expense of domestic consumption, further intensifying internal imbalances. Polish imports from the Soviet Union were designed to meet the need for industrial equipment and raw materials, whereas Soviet imports from Poland came in the form of consumer goods. Over that phase, Poland experienced difficulties in its balance of payments that arose from a shortage of export resources. These problems peaked in 1955–57.

The next phase, which lasted until the late 1970s, was characterized by a desire to replace autonomous development with the so-called international socialist division of labor and economic integration and an emphasis on co-operation with third countries. During that phase, Polish-Soviet cooperation was closely integrated into Comecon activities. It received a major impetus by the adoption of the new Comecon charter at the end of 1959 and, in 1962, of the "main principles of the socialist division of labor." Starting from 1962, attempts were made to draw up plans for specializing production in the countries concerned. Specialization was viewed as a means of making full use of the available industrial potential and of developing it further. In reality, however, specialization ran into serious difficulties since the Comecon countries were keen to develop manufacturing industries above all and were reluctant to make investments in capital-intensive raw materials industries. This reluctance was partly explained by the disparity of prices on the world market; the prices of manufactured goods were growing steadily, while the prices of fuel and raw materials were unstable. That was to the disadvantage of fuel and raw materials exporters. It should be noted that manufactured products were categorized as "soft" commodities and sold above all on the "goods-hungry" Soviet market at prices that were often higher than those of similar Western products of far better quality.

In the early 1960s, the cofinancing of fuel and raw materials projects in exchange for the supplies of fuel and raw materials to investor countries became a growing practice in the cooperation between Poland and the Soviet Union. In 1963, Poland granted the Soviet Union 70 million rubles' worth of credit for the expansion of the production of potassium salt in Soligorsk. Poland also invested in the production of phosphorites in Kingisepp, the construction of the Ust-Ilim pulp mill, an asbestos plant in Kiembay, a gas pipeline between Orenburg and the western border, the Polotsk-Biržai-Mažeikiai oil pipeline, and other projects. The credits were granted in the form of investments and consumer goods, as well as construction services. In exchange for participation in the expansion of production capacities, Poland was getting an additional annual supply of forty thousand metric tons of pulp, fifty thousand metric tons of asbestos, and one million metric tons of oil. These projects, based on the principle of investment for fuel and raw materials, created considerable problems in mutual payments and settlements.

The price ratios of these exchanges changed substantially as these projects were implemented. Increases and decreases in the global prices of fuel and raw materials upset the initial equivalence of the exchanges and gave rise to differences between the partners. It was also rather hard to assess the investment contribution from the partners. Resolving the problems that arose was complicated by a delicate balance of manufacturing and consumption of certain types of goods in the domestic markets.

Joint raw materials investments in the Soviet Union promoted its fuel and raw materials specialization not only within Comecon but on the world market as well, whereas in relation to the Soviet Union, Poland specialized in shipbuilding, manufacturing construction and road-building machinery, producing equipment for sugar refineries, and so forth. It also produced military hardware based on Soviet licenses.

Starting in the mid-1960s, technological specialization geared to the production and supply of particular kinds of units and assemblies was adopted in the cooperation. Poland and the Soviet Union signed an agreement on cooperation in the automobile industry in 1968. Under it, the Polish foreign trade company Polmot and the Soviet Avtoexport agency signed a contract for production parts and assemblies for the Fiat 125p and Zhiguli (Lada) cars.

At the same time, international economic organizations were set up with shared ownership and production in the interests of the participating countries. Poland and the Soviet Union were actively involved in the activities of these organizations, among them Intermetall, Organization for Cooperation in the Ball-Bearing Industry, and Interchem, to name a few.

The introduction of new forms of cooperation made it even more difficult to balance the exchanges of commodities for the five-year planning term, since the issue of recalculating the transfer ruble into national currencies was not resolved. The situation remained under control for as long as the need to balance cooperation prevailed over the need to raise the efficiency of production and trade. That began to change in the late 1960s. Poland was running short of export resources, and imports had to be restricted. Its external debt was growing, and the balance of payments was shaky. Attempts to resolve these problems by cutting domestic consumption led to a political crisis in the late 1970s. When Poland refused to raise food prices in February 1971, the Soviet Union had to "transfer $100 billion to Polish accounts at a Swiss bank."

Early in the 1970s, a series of world events took place that had a profound impact on further developments. Among them were the recession in the capitalist economies, the hard currency crisis at the beginning of the decade, the 1973–74 oil crisis, the easing of military-political tensions in Europe, and the success of the European Economic Community as a trade and economic alliance, as well as the effect that that success had on public opinion.

In 1971, Comecon adopted a package program for socialist economic integration to coordinate the economic development plans of the participating nations. The program was viewed as a viable alternative to the European Economic Community and a means of further integrating the economies of Comecon members. The program listed a coordinated plan for international integrative activities, long-term target cooperative programs, and international economic agencies. It provided mechanisms for accelerating the processes of intra-industrial specialization, which was viewed as the prime mover of "socialist economic integration."

Polish-Soviet cooperation centered on major projects requiring large investments, such as the construction of Poland's first nuclear power plant in Żarnowiec (it never got off the ground, though), a modern smelting plant in Katowice, an aviation plant in Mielec, and others. Poland became a main supplier to the Soviet Union of complete plant equipment. Between 1971 and 1975, it supplied equipment for twenty-two wooden slab plants, twenty-five silicate brick factories, and thirteen sulfuric acid plants.

Being aware of their restricted technological potential, the Soviet Union, the other Comecon members, and Poland attempted to take advantage of détente in the early 1970s to rapidly modernize their economies, especially the consumer goods industry, by importing Western technologies and borrowing abroad. The idea was that modernization would pave the way to intensive development.

Over that time, the Soviet Union also started to attract foreign investment but in a more cautious way; it returned equipment and material credits by supplying appropriate products such as natural gas, oil, coal, pulp chips, ammonia, and so forth. That cooperation was dubbed "gas for pipes."

Between 1970 and 1975, Poland's negative balance in trade with industrialized Western countries grew from 239 million złotys to 749 million złotys in hard currency. According to the Polish economist Leszek Balcerowicz, the country's foreign debt grew from $1 billion to $8.5 billion.

The new wave of industrialization based on Western technologies coincided with the worsening of the economic situation in the West following the oil crisis of 1973–74. The creditor nations began to import and consume less, Poland's debt grew, and another crisis developed in the country. Poland started having problems in balancing imports from the Soviet Union. By the end of the decade, the economy had overheated, causing a serious recession and a political crisis.

The price dynamics on the world and Comecon markets were different, and that differential had a profound impact. The crises in the West caused prices to go down, whereas, on the Comecon market, they were going up because they were based on projections made five years previously. The sharp oil price increases in 1973 affected the acting contract prices. Clearly, that situation, detrimental to national interests, gave rise to much criticism of Polish-

Soviet trade. These issues were never publicly discussed in Russia, but in Poland they were discussed in the press in the 1980s (for instance, in the publications of Marian Rajski). It cannot be ruled out that Polish authorities were interested in such publications since they created an appropriate psychological atmosphere for negotiating price and commodity supply corrections in Poland's favor.

In the second half of the 1970s, greater socialist integration efforts and the expansion of economic ties with the outside world led to more problems over the equivalence of exchanges. In particular, specialization in the supply of parts and assemblies led to problems in setting a fair price, since contract prices could not always be determined based on foreign equivalents. Another problem was related to reimbursement of the costs of imported parts and assemblies set for jointly supplied and prepared machine building production. The re-export of Soviet oil by Poland was causing problems in bilateral relations, too.

The final phase saw *a decline in cooperation within the framework of the socialist paradigm as transitions were made to market-driven economies and Comecon countries became integrated into the world economy.* During this phase, the rate of growth in bilateral trade declined. Between 1970 and 1980, bilateral trade grew by a factor of 3.4, from 2.35 billion rubles to more than 8 billion rubles, according to Soviet statistics, whereas between 1980 and 1990 it registered growth of only 50 percent, from 8 billion rubles to 12.066 billion rubles. The declining rate of foreign trade growth reflected the serious structural problems in cooperation. The share of fuel and raw materials in Russian exports to Poland reached two-thirds, 40 percent of which was hydrocarbons. Machinery and technological products accounted for 60 percent of Polish exports. There was some growth that proceeded on an interindustrial basis. The commodity composition of imports and exports was different, and it was therefore hard to balance them since the prices were fluctuating. Bilateral trade could not play a balancing role as the imbalances on the national domestic markets continued to grow. The Soviet war in Afghanistan and the world economic recession created a negative background in 1980–83. The drop in world fuel prices in 1986–90 proved fateful for the Soviet economy.

Both the Soviet Union and Poland were accumulating foreign debt over that period. Poland's debt in 1980 reached $25 billion and grew to $41 billion toward the end of 1989. Of the credits that Poland received in the 1970s, only 20 percent were spent on investment products. The greater part, 65 percent, was spent on purchasing materials and parts; 15 percent of all imports consisted of consumer goods.

The economic imbalances in Poland in 1980–81 caused a political crisis. The economic reform that was started and aid that began to come from the Soviet Union in the shape of $2 billion and several billion rubles enabled Poland to halt the economic decline.

Comecon attempted to revive cooperation and thus initiated a series of major investment projects. In 1985–86, Poland was supplying the Soviet Union with goods and services as part of the development of the Yamburg gas deposit, where large-scale production began in 1987, and it constructed a gas pipeline from Yamburg to the western Soviet border. Another major project that involved Poland was the construction of the Khmelnitsky nuclear power plant, whose first generating unit was launched in 1987. In 1984, a 750-kilowatt power transmission line was built from the Khmelnitsky plant to Rzeszów.

In 1986, Comecon adopted a package for scientific-technological development until 2000 and decided to form a united market. Poland was one of the most active members of Comecon. It contributed to agreements on industrial cooperation among international economic organizations and was in favor of developing direct trade and economic relations between economic organizations and regions. But it was too late. Both countries were gripped by a growing debt and economic crisis. Between 1985 and 1987, the total positive balance of the Soviet Union in trade with Poland amounted to 1.892 billion rubles; between 1988 and 1990, there was a negative balance in trade, which reached a total of 6.274 billion rubles. The negative balance in trade between the Soviet Union and Poland in 1990 accounted for 38 percent of the total negative foreign trade balance. In 1990, according to official Soviet statistics, Soviet exports to Poland were worth 4.121 billion rubles while imports from Poland were worth 7.946 billion rubles. Soviet exports to Poland declined from 6.814 billion to 4.121 billion rubles between 1986 and 1990, whereas Polish exports to the Soviet Union grew from 6.127 billion to 7.945 billion rubles. The growth of Polish exports in 1989–90 was the result of Polish companies re-exporting consumer goods from East and Southeast Asia to the Soviet market.

The re-export of Asian goods came as a result of the liberalization of Poland's foreign trade. Poland started market-driven reforms much earlier than did the Soviet Union and pursued them far more vigorously. Back in 1982–83, centralized planning had been replaced with government orders. Industrial ministries were dissolved, a banking reform took place, and opportunities for private business interests were expanded. The reforms became systemic in 1989. The Balcerowicz plan introduced hard currency and foreign trade liberalization, and the złoty was devalued. In January 1990, the złoty became convertible and foreign trade liberalization was completed. Systemic market reforms in Russia began in 1992 against a totally different geopolitical background.

In response to the changes that had occurred, the Soviet Union proposed to Comecon partners in 1989 that average world prices denominated in hard currency be introduced in mutual settlements. That transition was started in 1990, and an appropriate agreement was signed by the Soviet Union and Poland on 13 November 1990. Events started to develop rapidly after that. Early in 1991, Comecon's monetary unit, the transfer ruble, was abandoned. On 28 July 1991, Comecon itself was dissolved at its forty-sixth and final session.

Settlements were now made in hard currency, and the volume of trade between the Soviet Union and Poland shrank dramatically. According to the official Soviet State Statistics Committee, Soviet exports to Poland reached 4.037 billion rubles, while imports from Poland were only 3.473 billion rubles. Running short of gold and hard currency reserves, the Soviet Union was forced to restrict centralized importation and forgo its obligations under the contracts signed. Private Russian business had narrow opportunities in foreign trade since the importers had no hard currency to spend. The problem was alleviated in part by barter deals as part of direct trade links. The declining turnovers were pushed down further by the economic recession. The dramatic decrease of imports from Poland had a direct impact on Polish companies that operated in the Soviet market, especially those in the defense industry, and the decrease in imports caused production to decline in Poland.

Debts were also a central problem in economic relations between Poland and the Soviet Union at the final phase of their socialist cooperation. At the end of 1989, Poland's debt to Soviet and Comecon banks whose charter capital was owned by the Soviet Union was estimated at $2.1 billion and 4.5 billion transfer rubles, respectively.

Balcerowicz recalls that, during talks on settling the debts, Poland was insisting that its debts be recalculated into transfer rubles and was pointing out that it had sustained losses in the past. These losses were largely due to the fact that the investment made by Poland in the Soviet raw materials sector in the 1970s and 1980s was not compensated for equivalently. According to Polish estimates, the Soviet Union owed 3 billion transfer rubles' worth of uncompensated investments. The Soviet side pointed out that, according to its estimates, Polish companies exaggerated their costs by 15 to 20 percent compared to proposals from third countries.

Poland also used as an argument its expected losses from the transition to hard currency in mutual payments as of 1 January 1991. The Russian side would not agree to convert the Polish debt to transfer rubles and pointed to substantial losses in current exchanges as a result of the different dynamics of prices for the goods supplied. The prices of fuel and raw materials supplied to Poland were much lower than world prices, in terms of the prices for the goods the Soviet Union exported from Poland. Neither side would budge.

The problem was eventually resolved when the transfer ruble was devalued against the dollar in October 1990, from 56 kopecks for one dollar to one ruble 80 kopecks for one dollar. This change was assisted by a major Polish positive balance in its trade with the Soviet Union estimated at 7.5 billion transfer rubles in 1991. This figure somewhat straightened out the debt balance between the countries. According to Marek Wróblewski, Poland owed Russia 4.7 billion in transfer rubles and $2.3 billion, while Russia owed Poland 7.9 billion transfer rubles, 300 million clearing dollars, and 30 million rubles. The mutual debt claims were finally settled according to a zero base plus $20 million in Poland's favor in November 1996.

In conclusion, we can make several generalizations and deductions.

First, Poland's administrative command economy displayed considerably greater readiness to take economic risks, experiment, and modernize compared to that of the Soviet Union. Poland's socialist leaders apparently assumed that the Soviet Union would be prepared to share those risks. If the economic policy they pursued had achieved the desired results, their positions within the country would have been strengthened, the influence of the internal opposition would have been curtailed, and ultimately Poland's dependence on the Soviet Union would have decreased. The risks were certainly worth taking. Poland started the reforms before the Soviet Union did and enjoyed a certain advantage. It was better at counting its money and did not engage in ideology-driven charities. In the final analysis, Poland emerged from "socialism" in pretty good shape and became a full-fledged member of the European family.

Second, the Soviet Union failed to become the leader of Comecon because of the conservatism of the Soviet leaders and the enormous inertia of its political and economic system. The Soviet Union lagged behind both Poland and Hungary in its readiness to accept new ideas and introduce social, political, and economic innovation. Significantly, the system of contract prices and transfer rubles invented in the Soviet Union ultimately brought Comecon down and contributed to the collapse of the Soviet Union itself. As it emerged from Comecon, the Soviet Union owed its erstwhile partners a huge debt, and the total advantage gained by East European countries from trading with the Soviet Union between 1970 and 1984 amounted to $196 billion, according to the American scholars Michael Marrese and Jan Vaňous. That advantage arose because the East European countries got a better deal from trading with the Soviet Union on a bilateral basis than vice versa. Poland's particular advantage accounted for a large measure of that total.

Third, it makes no sense at all, in my view, to try and calculate a balance of economic gains and losses for the period of socialist cooperation since states were the actual subjects of international economic relations. The lists and quantities of goods traded, prices, and exchange rates were not based solely on economic considerations, as they were intertwined with political, defense, and ideological issues. Up until the mid-1980s, the efficiency of economic solutions was often sacrificed for political and defense concerns. That was business as usual for the Soviet Union, faced with the confrontation between East and West.

I believe that the Soviet Union could not afford to exploit Poland and other East European countries by gaining an additional advantage over them derived from trade. Poland's internal political stability was crucial for the Soviet Union during the Cold War, and, also, the Soviet Union was totally committed to dogmatic ideology and "proletarian internationalism." Its aid to its economically weak satellite countries was an extension of its policy of helping develop its "ethnic outlying regions." The acting mechanism of socialist economic integration redistributed the gross income in favor of the Soviet Union's partners in Comecon. As a result, the Soviet Union was increasingly lagging behind the more advanced Comecon members and could not perform as an effective technological or, later on, political leader. In the final analysis, the Soviet Union paid the ultimate price for its conservatism and its failure to become economically efficient and accept reforms—it ceased to exist.

Fourth, Comecon did not contribute significantly to the technological development of the world economy. The expansion of trade and economic relations with the Western nations beginning in the 1970s revealed the inefficiency of Comecon as an organization for regional economic integration. The system of bilateral trade was not transparent; it was politicized and dogged by the question, "Who is feeding whom?" The European Economic Community aimed to raise the competitiveness of national economies, and the disparities that arose in trade relations were resolved through specially formed European funds. At the initial stage, the Western economic blockade consolidated the European socialist countries somewhat, but, during the period of détente, the expansion of trade between the two economic organizations contributed to the decline and fall of Comecon.

Comecon's experience indicates that an isolated regional group guided by a set of rules and principles totally different from those of a dynamically developing world economy is doomed to failure.

Fifth, the efficiency of economic cooperation between the Soviet Union and Poland is reflected to a certain extent by the composition of their trade turnover, which has retained really competitive goods. Throughout the post-socialist years, Russian exports to Poland exceeded Polish exports to Russia. Machinery accounts for a far smaller percentage of today's composition of the trade turnover between the two countries. Soviet "hard" goods remained hard as the geopolitical situation changed. Hydrocarbons came to dominate Russian exports, while consumer goods prevail in Polish exports. During the years of socialist cooperation, they accounted for the "hard" part of Polish exports as well.

13

RUSSIA VERSUS SOVEREIGN POLAND

POLITICAL RELATIONS BETWEEN POLAND AND RUSSIA SINCE 1990

Katarzyna Pełczyńska-Nałęcz (Poland)

Doctorate in sociology, ambassador of the Republic Poland to the Russian Federation, former undersecretary of state at the Ministry of Foreign Affairs, former deputy director, Center for Eastern Studies, member of the Polish-Russian Group on Difficult Matters, 2008–12.

Artem V. Malgin (Russia)

Vice-rector of the Moscow State Institute of International Relations (MGIMO University).

KATARZYNA PEŁCZYŃSKA-NAŁĘCZ

. . . .

POLITICAL RELATIONS BETWEEN POLAND AND RUSSIA SINCE 1990

. . . .

MORE THAN TWENTY years prior to 2010, Poland was the largest satellite within the global Soviet Empire centered on Russia. Today, the Republic of Poland is Russia's largest European Union (EU) neighbor, while Russia is Poland's largest non-EU neighbor. The line that used to separate the People's Republic of Poland and the Soviet Union inside the Eastern bloc has become a section of the European Union's external border. Depending on one's vantage point, it is a border between the Western world and an area seen as the EU's neighborhood, of which potential future members (looking from Brussels and Warsaw) are a part, or as a border with Russia and its zone of privileged interests (as seen from Moscow). The history of the border symbolically illustrates Polish-Russian relations over a twenty-year period—relations that have not been related to these two nations alone but which have been implicated in broader issues of significance to all of Europe.

This chapter reviews the first two decades of relations between independent Poland and the Russian Federation (RF). They are primarily presented through the lens of difficult matters, since our mutual relations have indeed focused on contentious issues. The time that has elapsed makes it possible to address questions that have been posed since the early 1990s (though they have often elicited superficial or stereotypical answers): What is the essence of the problem in Polish-Russian relations? Are these problems rooted in historical phobias and prejudices, or do they reflect actual contradictions of interest? And finally, do the difficult relations amount to treading water or do they constitute a process that imbues bilateral relations with a new quality?

It would be in order at this juncture to make two points that tend to be ignored in discussions on Polish-Russian problems but that need to be remembered in order to fully appreciate the momentum and meaning of interactions between Moscow and Warsaw.

First, present-day problems must not obscure the fact that, in historical terms, the period from 1990 to 2010 may well be considered a golden age in Polish-Russian relations. For the first time in centuries, a sovereign Poland has managed to build mutual relations with Russia without resorting to force. Moreover, the two countries have created a bilateral legal base, the provisions of which concerning "the inviolability of borders, territorial integrity, non-interference in internal affairs, and the right of nations to decide about their future" have been implemented, albeit not without problems. This new circumstance is, naturally, the result of many factors, not just of Polish or Russian decisions. Still, what we perceive today as being difficult and deeply unsatisfactory already constitutes a watershed and testifies to the enormous progress that has taken place in Moscow's policy toward Warsaw, and vice versa.

Second, Polish-Russian links must not be reduced exclusively to the intergovernmental sphere. The unquestionably difficult relations between the two governments have had little impact on the much better cooperation among business communities, social organizations, academics, and artists. Though initially after the disintegration of the Soviet Empire the scope of such cooperation diminished, that change was brought on mainly by the new social and economic circumstances and not by any tensions between Warsaw and Moscow.

Four Problems

In October 1990 in Moscow, the foreign ministers of Poland and the Russian Soviet Federative Socialist Republic (RSFSR) signed a declaration of friendship and good-neighborly cooperation. The document, adopted even before the disintegration of the Soviet Union, is considered the symbolic beginning of the new, post-Soviet Polish-Russian relations. Since then, there have been moments of correct relations, but, for the most part, the atmosphere of bilateral contact was cool and tense: on several occasions top-level visits were canceled or cut short, for nine years (1993 to 2002) the president of Russia avoided visiting Poland, Moscow introduced economic sanctions against Poland, there were numerous diplomatic and political clashes, and media in both countries engaged in campaigns critical of the other.

In hindsight, it is apparent that the recurring tensions have always been caused by the same set of issues: (1) the dismantling of the Soviet domination of Poland and Polish policies toward the EU and North Atlantic Treaty Organization (NATO), (2) the policies of the two countries toward the states of Eastern Europe, (3) their relations in the energy sphere, and (4) the interpretation of their common history and related undertakings. Looking back over those twenty-odd years, it can be ascertained that these four long-term processes constituted the pivotal and most challenging areas of mutual relations.

The Dispute over Poland's Sovereignty

Most Polish decision makers agreed that, after 1989, the strategic goal of the country's foreign policy consisted of eradicating all vestiges of Soviet and, subsequently, Russian domination and in preventing the appearance of new forms of dependence. This was considered an essential condition for ensuring the independent existence of the Polish state, so the motive was not to undermine the Russian Federation. In his policy address to parliament, the first noncommunist prime minister, Tadeusz Mazowiecki, was emphatic: "We have opened a new chapter in Polish-Russian relations. They are no longer determined by ideology and the Communist Party. . . . These are normal relations between states and their governments guided by the welfare of their nations and their *raison d'*état. Our point of departure in mutual relations is the independence of the Polish state."

It rapidly became apparent that the freedom to choose one's allies would be a pivotal manifestation of that independence, since, in Poland's geopolitical situation, neutrality would have meant continued dependence. Accordingly, nothing less than membership in the Euro-Atlantic structures was considered tantamount to the full military, political, and economic sovereignty needed for the country's modernization and systemic transformation.

Moscow, however, saw the Polish drive for independence and the country's resulting approximation to the West as something that eroded Moscow's influence in Europe and enhanced the position of the Western "camp." That divergence has been the main source of Russian-Polish friction that has continually resurfaced for twenty years, with varying intensity.

As early as 1989, Premier Mazowiecki received assurance that Soviet troops would leave Poland by 1991. That pledge was soon forgotten as hardliners got the upper hand in the Kremlin. For many months there was no progress in negotiations on the subject. The turning point came after the August putsch. October 1991 saw the initialing of an accord on the withdrawal of troops, under which the last Soviet soldier was to leave Polish territory by the end of 1993, though property issues remained unsolved. The Russians proposed the establishment of mixed-capital companies, the assets of which would include property left behind by the Northern Group of Forces of the Soviet army. Former army officers working for such enterprises were to have the right of residence in Poland. At first, the Polish side agreed to incorporate provisions on the mixed-capital companies in the accord on the withdrawal of forces. That, however, drew very sharp criticism from most of the Polish political establishment as something that undermined Polish sovereignty and preserved bridgeheads for a Russian politico-military presence in Poland. As a consequence, during Polish president Lech Wałęsa's visit to Moscow on 22 May 1992, shortly before the signing of the agreement, the Polish side demanded that the provisions on the joint companies be deleted.

During his May visit to Moscow, President Wałęsa also signed a new treaty on Polish-Russian bilateral relations, negotiations on which had started in 1991. At that time, the main sticking point was Moscow's insistence that either party should not be able to join a military alliance or pact without the consent of the other. In any event, that demand was subsequently dropped and the first article of the treaty read, "The Parties shall shape their relations in a spirit of friendship, good-neighborly partnership[,] and equality."

Membership in NATO and Military Cooperation with the United States

The implementation of these provisions turned out to be problematic. Even as the two presidents put their signatures to the treaty, a debate was in full swing regarding the accession to NATO by Poland and other countries of Central Europe. Moscow's opposition to the process was voiced from the very moment of the establishment of the Russian Federation and assumed particular intensity in 1993, as the approximation of Poland, the Czech Republic, and Hungary to the alliance became increasingly obvious. Mindful of such attitudes among Russian politicians, Poles enthusiastically welcomed the Polish-Russian declaration adopted during the visit to Poland in August 1993 by Russian president Boris Yeltsin. It read in part, "A future decision by sovereign Poland [to join NATO] shall not contradict the interests of other states, including Russia." Alas, the declaration did not change Russian policy. Before the year was out, President Yeltsin had sent a confidential letter to Western leaders in which he highlighted dangers supposedly connected with the integration of Central European countries into NATO. He argued that the expansion of NATO carried the threat of Russia's isolation and of worsening its relations with the West. Meanwhile, it was more important for European security that NATO have good relations with Russia; relations with the countries of Central Europe were thus of secondary importance.

The Russian stance was reflected in strategic documents. The new foreign policy, unveiled in January 1993 by the Russian Ministry of Foreign Affairs, and the new military doctrine of November 1993 both contained references to "Russia's historic interests" in the region and the need to preserve its "friendly neutrality."

The attempts to halt NATO's expansion not only were related to the question of influence in Central Europe but also constituted an element of a broader Russian strategy concerning a new architecture of security on the continent that would give Russia the right of codecision on political and military matters while limiting the American presence in Europe.

Russian foreign minister Andrei Kozyrev presented that position in Kraków in February 1994. He advocated restricting the role of NATO and the transformation of the Commission on Security and Cooperation in Europe (CSCE) into the main institution coordinating security issues in Europe. Furthermore, Kozyrev offered the Czech Republic, Slovakia, Hungary, and Poland the possibility of overlapping Russian and Western security guarantees.

Those proposals were received in Poland as indicating Russia's refusal to accept the former's political emancipation. Warsaw tried to persuade Moscow that it should not take the expansion of NATO as a threat but, on the contrary, as an opportunity to establish closer relations with the alliance. At its Madrid summit in July 1997, NATO decided to admit three new members, including Poland. Henceforth, the matter of NATO's expansion no longer drew such strong Russian criticism.

After ten years of Poland's NATO membership, it became clear that the arguments of both parties have not been fully validated. Although NATO's expansion changed the geopolitical situation in Europe, it did not have a defining impact on the alliance's policy toward Russia or on Russia's internal situation and foreign strategy. While the new members tend to be distrustful of Russia, NATO's expansion has neither exacerbated relations with Russia nor led to their long-term improvement (as Poland had argued). The crises in relations over the first ten years of Poland's NATO membership primarily arose from differences in the parties' strategic goals (in the Balkans, in Georgia). As the Kremlin had anticipated, the alliance's new member states—prominently including Poland and, later, the Baltic States—became the most fervent advocates of the alliance's integration with Ukraine and Georgia, something the Kremlin flatly rejected.

In recent years, the plans to deploy elements of the US missile defense (MD) system in Poland became a prominent point of contention. Throughout the Polish-US talks on the subject (2006–8), Russia kept expressing its firm opposition, arguing that in fact the system would be aimed against it. In retaliation, Moscow threatened to point its missiles at the MD installations in Central Europe and to deploy a new generation of short-range missiles in Kaliningrad. The Russian criticism was not so much directed at the United States as at Poland and the Czech Republic (where the system's radar station was to be located).

For its part, Poland insisted that the project was defensive and designed to intercept a possible attack by Iran. Poland also referred to its sovereign right to conclude bilateral accords with the United States. Warsaw further pointed out that Russia's opposition exposed its peculiar treatment of Central Europe, including Poland, since it had not objected to the deployment of MD elements in Denmark or Great Britain.

In reality, the quarrel over missile defense was not related to the installations or their character but marked a continuation of the strategic dispute over the degree of US military presence in Poland and Central Europe as a whole. Russia was opposed to the permanent stationing of any US forces in the region. The Polish government, however, believed that such a presence was an additional guarantee of security. It was assumed that the presence of American military infrastructure in Poland would make the United States more likely to become engaged in Poland since that would mean the defense of the United States' own forces in Polish territory.

Integration with the EU

The process of Poland's integration with the EU was less problematic, though it did cause a certain controversy. At first, the Russian side believed that the EU's enlargement did not threaten its interests—in contrast to the expansion of NATO. That appeared to echo the Soviet perception of zones of influence chiefly in terms of military presence. However, as Poland moved closer to the union, Moscow realized that the process could have negative consequences and started expressing its concern. The way the Russian demands were formulated and the sharpness of the rhetoric revealed that, apart from addressing the matter of the negative effects of EU enlargement, Russia wanted to make a political statement. It had the goal of showing that, despite the enlargement of the EU, the Russian Federation had not been marginalized; on the contrary, the European community had to respect the interests of Moscow as a key player on the continent.

The problem of Kaliningrad proved to be one of the most contentious issues. Enlargement meant that the Russian exclave would be completely surrounded by EU member states. Even before the accession of Poland and the Baltic States, the Russian side started highlighting the adverse effects of that for the ties between Kaliningrad and Russia proper (such as hindered movement of persons). That resulted in serious friction between Poland and Lithuania on the one hand and Russia on the other. Lithuania firmly resisted any arrangements that could complicate its future accession to the open-border Schengen zone, while Poland rejected Russia's proposal for an exterritorial corridor across its territory. Warsaw pointed out that, because of existing infrastructure, the transit route to and from Kaliningrad would not run across Poland anyway. The European Commission became a de facto mediator in the dispute. As a result, the parties reached a compromise, which took effect in June 2003: transit would take place exclusively across Lithuania, on the basis of cost-free and readily available special permits (facilitated transit documents).

The economic consequences of EU enlargement for the former Republic of Yugoslavia (FRY) constituted another issue raised by Moscow. Economic relations between the EU and Russia were regulated by a partnership and cooperation agreement (PCA); new EU members automatically became signatories upon their accession. Yet, the process was far from smooth. A few months before the 2004 enlargement, Russia demanded the signing of a statement that would deal with issues it considered sensitive in mutual cooperation. In April 2004, the parties signed a protocol to the PCA and a statement. The union acquiesced to most of Russia's economic postulates, though it rejected the possibility of liberalizing or waiving the application of union norms (e.g., sanitary regulations) to goods imported from Russia.

Paradoxically, Poland's membership in the EU proved to have greater impact than its accession to NATO on Russia's overall relations with Poland and with the West as a whole. Obviously, the presence of Poland in the union did not bring about any breakthrough in the community's policy on Russia, though it influenced the EU's strategy in some areas. These areas include policies on energy, the "Eastern Neighborhood," and the economy.

As for economic cooperation with Russia, Poland was provoked into action by the so-called "meat crisis." In November 2005, Russia slapped an embargo on Polish agricultural produce and meat, justifying the move by pointing to supposed forgeries of export certificates for these products. The losses Poland incurred as a result were not staggering ($300 million a year), but the Polish side felt the embargo was largely motivated by political considerations and that it was aimed at undermining the union's single-trade policy and dividing member states into preferred and unapproved partners. In that situation, the main Polish objective was to obtain the support of the European Commission, formally charged with trade policy, and the backing of other member states as an expression of European solidarity. On 13 November 2006, Poland blocked the European Commission's mandate for opening talks on a new agreement on the legal framework of relations between the EU and Russia. That forced member states to focus on the problem and take specific measures addressed to Moscow.

Initially, the EU took a two-track approach: it tried to persuade Poland to withdraw its veto and Russia to lift its embargo. The union only displayed greater solidarity after Russia stiffened its stance; at an EU-Russia summit in Samara, in May 2007, German chancellor Angela Merkel declared that the affair had all-European implications rather than being merely a bilateral dispute.

In any event, the meat embargo was lifted (depending on the product category, between December 2007 and November 2008) only after parliamentary elections in Poland and the formation of a new cabinet by parties that favored warmer relations with the Russian Federation (RF). At the same time, Poland withdrew its veto against the EU-Russia talks on a new agreement.

Contradictory Visions of the Neighborhood

Unlike the process of Poland's political and military emancipation and the attendant approximation to NATO and the EU, the question of Eastern Europe has never been formally identified as an important area of relations between Poland and Russia. In reality, both sides were aware of the divergence of their interests in this sphere. Tensions rooted in that latent conflict affected bilateral relations, producing conflicts of a secondary character. The dispute stemmed from different visions of the preferred order in Eastern Europe, with both Poland and Russia attaching pivotal importance to the region's future.

Warsaw focused its interest on Ukraine and Belarus and, later, also on Georgia and Lithuania. The latter, however, stopped being perceived as part of the "neighborhood" when it joined Euro-Atlantic structures. Poland wanted these countries to be sovereign (i.e., free of Russian, Polish, or any other country's domination) and to follow the path of systemic transformations chosen by Poland—which involved building democracy and a free market and seeking integration with Euro-Atlantic structures.

That vision constituted the implementation of a fundamental Polish political concept, authored many years before the fall of communism by two outstanding émigré writers, Jerzy Giedroyc and Juliusz Mieroszewski. They argued that the situation in Ukraine, Lithuania, and Belarus (referred to as ULB in their writings) had a fundamental bearing on Russia's policy toward Poland. Russia's control of ULB opened the way to the subjugation of Poland, while sovereignty of the three countries enhanced Poland's independence.

From Russia's point of view, it was of secondary importance what political or economic systems evolved in these countries as long as they retained strong political, economic, and military ties with the RF, though Moscow was not thinking in terms of a partnership but rather of its own domination. Accordingly, Russia was firmly opposed to the integration of these countries with NATO and, to a lesser degree, with the EU. Moscow treated the emancipation of countries in the Commonwealth of Independent States (CIS) as a threat to its own security, leading to its marginalization in Europe.

That perception of post-Soviet states, including East European ones, is enshrined in Russia's "Strategy toward the Member States of the CIS," approved by presidential decree on 14 September 1995. Point number one of the document, devoted to the goals and tasks of Russian policy toward the CIS, makes no mention of democracy or the free market. It does underscore that Russia is seeking the political and economic integration of the CIS. The process should be implemented with due consideration of Russia's interests and with the objective of "strengthening Russia as the main force shaping the new order of international relations in post-Soviet space."

Disagreements concerning Eastern Europe have surfaced with varying intensity over the first two decades since the end of the Soviet Union. However, the asymmetry of Poland's and Russia's potential and policy instruments has been evident from the very start of this period. The Russian Federation was the key player, as were the countries of the region themselves. Poland, however, played a secondary role, apart from a few specific situations. Warsaw thus realized very quickly that it would be unable to support the democratization of Eastern European countries and their approximation to Euro-Atlantic structures without involving Western states in the process. An opportunity for such involvement presented itself when Poland joined NATO and the European Union. The strategy of seeking allies, rooted in Poland's awareness of its own limitations, was misinterpreted by some Russian journalists and politicians as having been inspired, or even "ordered," by Western powers.

Tensions related to Poland's policy on Eastern Europe had already become apparent in 1990. At that time, Poland adopted a two-track strategy, aimed at developing a dialogue with the Soviet republics while maintaining the best possible relations with the Kremlin. The practical implementation of this strategy created dilemmas for the Polish authorities as to which relations should be prioritized. The decisions that were made often amounted to a rotten compromise. Fearing complications in its relations with Moscow, Poland procrastinated on the diplomatic recognition of Lithuania (it was only the twenty-sixth country to grant such status). In the case of Ukraine, the Polish authorities acted differently: Poland was the first country that recognized Ukraine's independence, even before the meeting at Białowieża where the decision was made to terminate the Soviet Union.

In the early years after the disintegration of the Soviet Union, Polish-Russian tensions over the question of Eastern Europe were not conspicuous. Russia sought to preserve its domination in the region. Assertions of "Russia's special responsibility in the near abroad" appeared in the concept of the Russian Federation's foreign policy and 1993 military doctrine. Poland was troubled by such signals. Yet, the international climate was not conducive to the fulfillment of Polish policy objectives. Most Western states did not perceive the countries of Eastern Europe as important European actors. "Russia and only Russia" was the prevalent attitude, which effectively gave President Yeltsin the position of chief guarantor of stability in the post-Soviet space.

Friction between Poland and Russia increased at the beginning of the new century, when Poland—a rookie member of NATO—became an enthusiastic advocate of Lithuania's accession to the alliance (Lithuania was admitted in 2004), which ran very much counter to Moscow's ideas.

The crunch came in 2004. Poland had just become a member of the European Union after a drawn-out integration process. Russia, politically boosted after a presidential poll that resulted in a spectacular victory for Vladimir Putin, intensified its campaign to shore up its influence in the CIS countries. That was the setting for an acute social-political crisis in Ukraine: the opposition (and its candidate, Viktor Yushchenko) accused Ukraine's president at the time and the candidate he was backing, Viktor Yanukovych, of election fraud. Furthermore, there were many indications that Yanukovych was also supported by Moscow (he was promoted by Russian media and politicians). Hundreds of thousands took to the streets to protest the abuses and irregularities committed by the authorities during the voting.

It was crucial for Poland that the Ukrainian election conformed to international standards. The conviction was that any other scenario, particularly the use of force to resolve the crisis, would undermine Ukraine's sovereignty and pave the way for Russian domination. At the same time, Kiev's cooperation with the EU, NATO, and the Western states would be impeded, if not made outright impossible. That belief was the primary motive for the engagement of Polish politicians, including most prominently Pres. Aleksander Kwaśniewski, in efforts to settle the internal crisis in Ukraine. The Polish side was instrumental in bringing about the three sessions of the Ukrainian Round Table, which produced a compromise and agreement to repeat the second round of voting. It is noteworthy that Poland was careful to act primarily as a representative of the European Union, highlighting (successfully) the community character of the mediation mission (it included Javier Solana, the EU's high representative for common foreign and security policy [CFSP]) rather than its own role.

Russia perceived the Polish efforts as being directed against Moscow, with the purpose of establishing a Polish zone of influence. Russian media charged that Poland's involvement amounted to de facto support for the pro-Polish Viktor Yushchenko.

The conflict did not find direct expression at the diplomatic level. When the Polish foreign minister visited Moscow on 17 December, that is, before the second round of voting in Ukraine, both he and his Russian counterpart agreed that the Ukrainian people should choose their president independently, without outside interference. However, it was President Kwaśniewski of Poland who defined the true essence of the dispute: in a statement surprisingly candid for a head of state, he opined that "any great power [implying the United States] would prefer a Russia without Ukraine than a Russia with Ukraine." That provoked an equally blunt response by President Putin, who read Kwaśniewski's declaration as an intention to restrict Russia's contacts with its neighbors or even to bring about its isolation.

The cooling of relations caused by the controversies over the Orange Revolution was echoed the following year by several seemingly insignificant developments unconnected with the Ukrainian crisis. These "secondary" conflicts found their culmination in Warsaw on 31 July 2005 when a group of toughs beat up and robbed three teenaged children of Russian diplomats. Despite expressions of regret by the Polish Ministry of Foreign Affairs, the Russian side insisted on treating the incident as an intentional anti-Russian move rather than a chance encounter. Russian media launched an anti-Polish campaign. Within several days (5–10 August), two Polish embassy workers and a Polish journalist were roughed up in Moscow.

In subsequent years, Poland—now a member of the EU—tried to influence community policy on Eastern Europe. These efforts became more effective as Poland's representatives learned to navigate the shoals of union diplomacy. All the Polish initiatives, including assistance for the Belarusian opposition in 2006 during and after the presidential election, the unfulfilled idea of the so-called "Eastern Dimension," already put forward by Poland in 1998, and the successfully promoted initiative of the Eastern Partnership, were seen by Russia as directed against its interests and intended to minimize its influence in Eastern Europe.

The question of the region's relations with NATO continues to provoke much greater controversy than does union policy on Eastern Europe. Warsaw officially supported the accession of the Baltic States into NATO and later—though not as unequivocally—the admission of Ukraine and Georgia. Meanwhile, Moscow considered Georgia's and Ukraine's accessions as an absolutely unacceptable "crossing of the red line." Warsaw, in turn, was critical of that position, interpreting it as a lack of acknowledgment of the two countries' full sovereignty.

Energy Geopolitics

Due to their geographic location and the layout of their infrastructures, Poland and Russia have considerable potential for mutually advantageous cooperation in the energy sector. In a way, they appear predestined for such cooperation. Yet, this area of relations has seen enormous controversy since the early 1990s.

The level of tension and the importance assigned to the respective points of contention have shifted considerably in recent years, in line with the evolution of the Russian strategy on the one hand and the changing priorities of successive Polish cabinets on the other. However, conflict over certain issues has remained more or less constant. Most of all, the Polish side feared that its energy sector would become excessively dependent on Russia, which might lead to monopolistic practices and disadvantageous solutions and might also be used as an instrument of pressure outside the economic sphere. Meanwhile, Russia was interested in preserving its monopoly on supplies and obtaining maximum control over energy infrastructure, especially the transit pipeline.

It is noteworthy that Polish-Russian relations in the energy sphere and the attendant disputes were not of an exclusively bilateral nature. Over a five-year period they largely extended to the broader European scene, becoming a component of both the Russian agenda for the EU and the Polish strategy as a member of the community.

On the bilateral level, the terms on which gas was supplied to Poland and the related problem of building a new transit pipeline across Polish territory aroused the most acute controversies.

In the early 1990s, it was a Polish priority to negotiate new terms for gas supplies from Russia. During the few last years of the existence of the Soviet Union, gas deliveries were governed by the so-called "Yambursk agreement" (1987–96), which provided that gas would be supplied in exchange for Polish construction services in the Soviet Union. Soon, that component of the deal was linked to the construction of a new pipeline designed to link the Yamal gas fields with customers in Belarus, Poland, and Germany. After protracted negotiations, an accord was concluded on 25 August 1993 (during Yeltsin's visit to Poland) for the construction of a system of gas pipelines for the transit of Russian gas across Polish territory and for supplying Poland. The plans provided for the construction of two branches of the pipeline with a combined capacity of 62 billion cubic meters. In September 1993, the Polish Ministry of Industry and Trade approved the status of EuRoPol Gaz—the company tasked with the construction and management of the Polish part of the Yamal pipeline. Contrary to the provisions of the agreement, under which shares in the project were to be split between Gazprom and Poland's PGNiG SA, 4 percent of the shares were allocated to Gas-Trading, a company with mixed Polish-Russian state-private capital. In September 1996, PGNiG and Gazprom concluded a twenty-five-year contract for the supply of 250 billion cubic meters of gas, worth, according to the Russians, $21 billion. The agreement on the construction of the pipeline was only partly fulfilled: only one branch was built. It was completed in 1999 and attained its target capacity of 32.3 billion cubic meters in 2005.

The Yamal agreement aroused much controversy inside Poland and weighed on the relations between Warsaw and Moscow. That situation was mainly caused by the ownership structure of EuRoPol Gaz, which, in effect, allowed Gazprom to assume control: Gazprom was collaborating with the private shareholder of Gas-Trading—an arrangement that gave it effective control of Gas-Trading and, by, extension, all of EuRoPol Gaz. In Poland, this circumstance was seen as contrary to the national interest. It was believed that the Yamal pipeline, like the whole transmission infrastructure, should be under Polish control. Paradoxically, the matter of the Yamal pipeline ownership structure was raised again at the initiative of the Russian side during Premier Putin's visit to Poland in 2009. Putin suggested that Gas-Trading should be removed from EuRoPol Gaz—probably because Gazprom had decided it no longer needed to collaborate with the controversial company. The removal of the private part-owner slightly increased the share-holding of the Russian monopolist in EuRoPol Gaz.

Another point of contention concerned the broader problem of diversifying the sources for gas supplies in Poland. Domestic discussion on the issue had already flared up in 1993 on the question of whether the Yamal accord ensured the country's energy security by providing long-term supplies and balancing Poland's dependence on Russian supplies with Russia's dependence on transit across Poland, or whether it sealed Gazprom's monopoly, precluding any diversification initiatives for many years to come. The dilemma constituted one of the main challenges of Poland's energy policy. Yet, the strategies of successive Polish cabinets were incoherent and marked by abrupt turns. In 2001, when the post-Solidarity coalition of AWS-UW (Solidarity Electoral Action, or Akcja Wyborcza Solidarność, and Freedom Union, or Unia Wolności) was in power, Poland signed a provisional agreement for the purchase of five billion cubic meters of gas from Norway, beginning in 2012. The next government, dominated by former communists, abandoned the deal. The matter of diversification again became a priority when the right-wing Law and Justice Party took power, but it again lost prominence under the center-right coalition of PO-PSL (Civic Platform, or Platforma Obywatelska, and the Polish People's Party, or Polskie Stronnictwo Ludowe) that formed the next cabinet. The latter strived to prolong the Yamal accord up to 2037 and increase annual supplies by 20 to 30 percent. Meanwhile, the Russian side was consistent in its position: it wanted to preserve its monopoly and curtail other sources of supply for the Polish market.

Poland has been engaged in the debate on EU energy policy from the moment it joined the union. That process coincided with a clear invigoration of Russia's efforts to advance its own interests in the union. In particular, Moscow boosted its campaign to gain access to the retail gas market in the member states and started promoting the idea of building new pipelines that would partly cross the territories of EU member states. As a consequence, many of Poland's postulates relating to the union's energy policy constituted in effect a response to Moscow's overtures and in most cases ran counter to the interests of Gazprom.

At the EU, Warsaw focused on the following goals:

To protect the liberalizing union energy market from investments by the Russian gas monopoly, which, due to its combined production and transport potential, could gain an advantage over other market players and pose a threat both to the functioning of the developing market and to the energy security of individual countries.

To seek European Union support for infrastructure projects conducive to the diversification of gas and oil supplies to Central and Eastern Europe, that is, projects that would offer EU market access to energy resource suppliers other than Russia. The main project promoted by Poland in this context has been the Odessa-Brody-Gdańsk oil pipeline, intended to carry Caspian oil (mainly from Azerbaijan) to Ukraine and Poland and possibly to other countries in Central Europe (Germany, Slovakia, Lithuania).

To prevent any projects that would deepen the EU's dependence on supplies from the RF and on Russian investments in the energy sector.

To perpetuate Russia's reliance on the transit countries, including EU non-members, such as Ukraine and Belarus.

The latter two points are the main reasons why Warsaw has opposed the Russian-sponsored Nord Stream pipeline on the bottom of the Baltic Sea between Russia and Germany. From Moscow's point of view, the Nord Stream project will make it possible to avoid the troublesome transit across not only Ukraine or Belarus but also Poland, permitting direct supply to a key customer, Germany. Warsaw, on the other hand, believes Nord Stream will undercut the position of the transit countries vis-à-vis Russia and diminish the maneuverability of the whole community, including Poland, in seeking alternatives to Gazprom.

History as a Political Instrument

The dispute about history has undoubtedly been one aspect of mutual relations that clearly extends beyond the sphere of bilateral relations. On the one hand, this dispute has been part of each country's efforts to enhance its international position, and, on the other, it has been deeply entangled in their internal affairs. However, the significance of this dispute (in both the international and domestic spheres) has been completely different in Poland and Russia.

For Russia, historical disagreements with Poland have been just a small fragment of a wider process, involving—among other things—the use of history, whereby the Russian Federation has been defining its new, post-Soviet identity. That identity, especially between 2000 and 2010, has increasingly come to be built around Russia's great-power aspirations, with reference to the achievements of the Soviet Union. That is why the Russian leadership has rejected those elements of the past that undermine the image of the Soviet Union as a constructive global power.

For Poland, the historical disputes with Russia have been important in their own right as yet another area of emancipation from the dominance of the former empire—hence the particularly emotional attitude toward the question of clarifying and publicizing facts concerning Soviet acts of violence against the Polish state and nation previously ignored or distorted.

The beginning of the historical problems can be traced back to the controversies that arose during negotiations on the 1992 Polish-Russian treaty. Warsaw wanted the document to include references to Stalinist crimes and reparations for Polish citizens. The Russian authorities flatly rejected this stance. In subsequent years, the Polish side regularly though unsuccessfully argued that the matter needed to be settled through an accord between the two states. Gradually, Warsaw's commitment to the subject flagged, though formally it still figures on the list of unresolved bilateral issues. The Russian authorities have consistently claimed that these matters are covered by Russia's domestic legislation, under which Polish nationals, too, may claim compensation. However, obtaining compensation by that route would be impracticable in the majority of cases (the victims have not obtained court rulings pertaining to their cases and without them are not eligible for compensation).

Another bilateral legal dispute of much greater significance for the Polish side concerns the final clarification of the Katyn case. In the early 1990s, the Russian authorities made a number of gestures that seemed to indicate their intent to settle the matter. In 1990, Soviet president Mikhail Gorbachev conveyed to Pres. Wojciech Jaruzelski a number of NKVD documents from the years 1939–40 concerning Polish prisoners of war. In 1992, Yeltsin transferred additional files to the Polish side, affirming the responsibility of the Soviet leadership for the Katyn crime. A year later, Yeltsin—as the first leader of the new Russia—laid a wreath at the foot of the Katyn cross in Warsaw's Powązki Cemetery. However, contrary to what is widely believed in Poland, no official apology was made on that occasion. According to eyewitnesses, the Russian president whispered when laying the wreath, "Prostite, yesli smozhete" (Forgive, if you can).

Exhumation work was under way around that time. Military cemeteries were established in Kharkov, Katyn, and Mednoye and opened in 2000. Serious disagreements emerged later, in 2004, when the Military Prosecutor's Office of the Russian Federation closed the Katyn investigation initiated in 1990. Contrary to Poland's expectations, the crime was not recognized as genocide, and 116 out of the 183 volumes of files were classified. Moscow also refused to rehabilitate the victims of the Katyn murder, claiming that action could not be taken since they had never been convicted. Poland has repeatedly raised these issues, especially the question of the declassification of the files, but they remain unresolved.

These disagreements closely relate to a much wider debate, one that touches on national prestige and symbolism, concerning the origins, beginnings, and consequences of World War II. The debate has been fueled primarily by commemoration activities during anniversaries connected with the war.

The first major differences in connection with the anniversaries of World War II surfaced in 1994 and 1995. Wałęsa did not go to Moscow for the fiftieth anniversary of the victory over fascism (Poland was represented by Premier Józef Oleksy), while Yeltsin did not attend the ceremony for the fifty-fifth anniversary of the crime in Katyn. Among other things, the parties disagreed on the meaning of the end of the war. To Wałęsa, it marked the beginning of a new occupation of Eastern Europe—a view that offended Russia. The Russians, however, claimed that Warsaw sought to diminish the historical role of both the Soviet soldiers and the Polish soldiers who had fought shoulder to shoulder with them.

The anniversary quarrel heated up in 2004–5, particularly in the media, in connection with the sixtieth anniversary of the Warsaw Uprising, the sixty-fifth anniversary of the Katyn crime, and commemoration of the outbreak of World War II, all marked in Poland, and the sixtieth anniversary of the victory over fascism, celebrated in Russia. After much hesitation, President Kwaśniewski decided to take part in the Moscow ceremonies. However, the conduct of the Russian side in connection with his visit was received in Poland as an intended slight: President Putin made no mention of the contribution of the Polish forces to the Allied victory. Since Poland had no opportunity to present its position in Moscow, Foreign Minister Adam D. Rotfeld communicated it to the international community in his address at a special session of the UN General Assembly, convened to commemorate the anniversary of the victory.

Poland and Russia subscribe to different interpretations of the role of the Soviet Union in starting the war. The Polish side has emphasized the Soviet Union's co-responsibility and its cooperation with Nazi Germany (in the Ribbentrop-Molotov Pact), while Russia has been outraged by the equating of Soviet and Nazi totalitarianism. The two sides also differ about the Yalta conference: the Poles see it as a symbol of the division of Europe into spheres of influence, while the Russians believe that view distorts the outcome of the conference, which "reasserted the desire to make Poland strong, free, independent[,] and democratic" (the Russian Ministry of Foreign Affairs released a special statement on the subject).

The seventieth anniversary of the outbreak of World War II, marked in Poland, also provoked heightened emotions on both sides. Russian premier Vladimir Putin attended the ceremonies. In a statement on that occasion, and in an article published earlier by the daily *Gazeta Wyborcza,* Putin addressed a number of historical issues and condemned the Ribbentrop-Molotov Pact, albeit noting that it had been preceded by the signing by France and Great Britain in Munich of a "treaty with Hitler that ruined any hope of a joint front of struggle against Hitler." He also expressed understanding for Polish sensitivities over Katyn. However, the balanced message delivered by Putin in Poland coincided with a number of tough official and media statements in Russia, worded in the spirit of Soviet historiography. Documentaries broadcast by state television contained some of the most stridently anti-Polish material. The films portrayed Poland as a country that cooperated with Hitler during the 1930s for the purpose of, among other things, engaging in aggression against the Soviet Union.

Neither Russia's official position nor the message conveyed by Russian media in the run-up to the seventieth anniversary of World War II focused exclusively on Poland. They were part of a broader concept of the origin of World War II, which the Russian authorities had been promoting for several years. It was argued that, apart from Germany, other countries—including France, Great Britain, and Poland—bore responsibility for the outbreak of the war because they had struck compromises or collaborated with Hitler, thus contributing to the strengthening of Germany on the one hand and the marginalization of the antifascist Soviet Union on the other. Thus, the Soviet Union was forced to start talks with Hitler as a preventative measure.

Two Decades of Difficulty as Neighbors

The experience of the 1990–2010 period leads to some interesting conclusions that challenge the various stereotypes about Polish-Russian relations.

First of all, the oft-repeated view that Polish-Russian conflicts mainly stem from a genetic russophobia on the Polish side or irrational prejudice on the Russian side is unfounded. The underlying causes of the Polish-Russian problems are real and concern strategic issues. At the deepest level, there is a dispute about the borders of the Western world and about the Russian Federation's sphere of influence. The dispute is being played out at many levels. It pertains to historically defined identities, economic assets, and the political sphere. Obviously, it does not relate to Poland and Russia alone. Moreover, Poland is certainly not the most important actor in this regard, although, due to the historic context and its geographic location, it is one of the countries closest to the "line of scrimmage," which determines Poland's particular involvement.

Second, it is untrue that all of the fundamental problems between Poland and Russia remain unsolved. On the contrary, the most important contentious issue of the 1990–2010 period—the question of Poland's emancipation and its integration with the Euro-Atlantic community—can in fact be considered settled. This situation demonstrates that Polish-Russian frictions should not be considered totally unproductive but rather part of a difficult process that generates a new quality in relations between the two countries.

Third, the manner in which the dispute over Poland's sovereignty was resolved demonstrates that dealing with strategic problems does not require—as is often believed—an approximation of the parties' foreign policy priorities. When the question of Poland's Euro-Atlantic integration was being decided, Russia stepped up its "great-power" rhetoric. However, after Poland's accession to NATO and the EU, when the situation had become unequivocal, the parties adjusted their positions to the new realities within a couple of years. It could be argued that the tension subsided when the "zone of uncertainty" shrank. Moscow came to accept Warsaw's political emancipation, and Poland gradually softened its stance toward its eastern neighbor, thus meeting the expectations of its more conciliatory Western partners.

Fourth, the same pattern applies to the other still-unresolved dispute concerning Poland's and Russia's contradictory visions of the future of Eastern Europe. In the past, the problem gained intensity whenever uncertainty arose as to which direction Eastern European countries would take, for example, during the Orange Revolution or when NATO was deciding whether to award membership action plans to Georgia and Ukraine. This observation has interesting implications for the future of the dispute. Assuming that neither Poland (and, more broadly, the European Union) on the one hand and Russia on the other are likely to redefine their interests, it can be predicted that uncertainty (the two-track strategies pursued by the countries concerned, the ambiguous strategies of the EU and NATO) will only add fuel to the dispute. Meanwhile, a resolute stance might heat up the conflict when things come to a head, but in the long term it might produce a settlement.

Fifth, the dynamics of Polish-Russian relations from 1990 to 2010 have shown that relations between Warsaw and Moscow are not doomed, as often believed, to a state of permanent crisis. The political climate has improved on several occasions since 1990. However, the periods of better relations usually were not occasioned by real change but rather by redefined tactics, when the parties displayed greater moderation in the perception and presentation of outstanding problems. Thus, a less confrontational treatment of disagreements (by both Poland and Russia) is likely to enhance the atmosphere. However, it is also true that the periods of relaxation have always been followed by new crises. Such fluctuations can also be expected in the years to come, for it would be an illusion that serious disputes can truly be solved just by changing form, especially since the disagreements about the future of Eastern Europe, the interpretation of history, and energy security certainly qualify as serious disputes.

Sixth, unexpectedly, along with Poland's membership in NATO (the subject of the fiercest battles), its accession to the European Union has also had a crucial impact on Polish-Russian relations. This impact refers not only to the widely noted civilization changes that have increased the distance between Poland and Russia in terms of legal, political, social, and economic systems but also to the less frequently noted interconnection between Poland's policy within the union and relations between Warsaw and Moscow. Upon becoming an EU member, Poland gained additional vistas for building relations with the Russian Federation, with the backing and mediation of Brussels. Paradoxically, Poland's integration with the EU has also expanded the range of instruments available to Russia, which the Polish side had not anticipated. The quality of relations with Russia has become a factor that could either enhance or undermine the credibility of Warsaw and its representatives within the EU. The years from 2005 to 2010 have indicated that this interdependence may generate two kinds of effects. On one hand, it may stimulate the two states' determination to maintain good relations by restraining their confrontational rhetoric (in order to avoid being labeled as irrationally russophobic, in the case of Warsaw, or to prevent Poland from taking "anti-Russian" actions within the EU, in the case of Moscow). On the other hand, it may trigger an escalation of the conflict if it becomes used instrumentally, by Russia to discredit Poland in the European Union in order to create divisions within the community, or by Poland to unite the EU in opposition to the Russian Federation.

ARTEM V. MALGIN

....

POLITICAL RELATIONS BETWEEN POLAND AND RUSSIA SINCE 1990

....

AN INVESTIGATION OF Russian-Polish relations during the existence of postsocialist Russia and Poland within the framework of a relatively short text requires a certain level of schematics. The author could take the liberty of outlining a straight-line methodological approach to analyzing these relations by expanding upon those items that fit within the general logic of this book.

Despite the name of the book, the author supposes that the recent period of Russian-Polish relations stays fairly well within the conventional scenario of cooperation between two independent countries and has no "black spots." The difficulties arising in modern Russian-Polish relations hardly fall into the category of the tragic or dramatic. They form a constituent part of the dynamic international processes of the two decades from 1990 to 2010 and are only partially a legacy of the past.

The Formation of Post-Soviet Identity and Foreign Policy

The formation of post-Soviet identity and new foreign policy priorities, as well as the formation of new national and international identities, started almost simultaneously in both Russia and Poland.

In fact, the two-and-a-half-year period that passed between the June 1989 electoral victory of the noncommunist coalition led by Solidarity in Poland and the December 1991 dissolution of the Soviet Union is insignificant from a historical point of view.

In Poland, however, for almost ten years, the active formation of a new political class, new types of social relations, and civic institutions in the form of free trade unions and prototypes of modern political parties preceded the regime change.

The preparatory period for post-Soviet Russia's existence was much shorter and in fact started with the unexpected progression of independence in conjunction with tremendous territorial and demographic losses in Russia's traditional areas of political, economic, and cultural existence.

In other words, compared to Poland, Russia was faced with a much more difficult task: to create not just a new regime but an absolutely new national identity within newfound borders.

It is obvious that such encumbrances intensely influenced both the path and the dynamic for Russia in foreign affairs, particularly in European policy.

Along with changes in geopolitical frontiers during the 1990s, both Russia and Poland surprisingly got new common neighbors (Ukraine, Belarus, and Lithuania). Moreover, in the case of Poland, the new neighbors (almost at the moment they emerged) became a constituent part of the diversification of its foreign policy and provided additional room for international maneuvering, which consequently improved Polish performance in European affairs. For Moscow, on the other hand, the emerging neighbors caused an additional set of responsibilities and encumbrances across the broader range of issues related to legal succession from the former Soviet Union into the new independent republics.

The post-Soviet era governing efforts consumed great amounts of staff time, as well as both diplomatic and other resources in Russia, during the first half of the 1990s. To a large extent this situation persists to the present day.

During the era's turning point, the Western orientation was undoubtedly chosen in both Russia and Poland to be the major direction for social, economic, and foreign political development.

Following the global parameters of the Western experience, each party in its own way reformed all aspects of its own existence.

During the period between 1991 and 1993, many people in Moscow thought that such a universal movement toward a single developmental paradigm would help to overcome all interstate and international conflicts. History now shows that such was not the case. National interests were still present, and they started to play a significant role as foreign policy developed for the new states.

For the first time in modern history, Russia attempted to formulate its strategic international priorities within the Foreign Policy Concept of 1993. It clarifies that a European orientation and European institutions form an integral part of the system of foreign political values and objectives. Moscow (primarily the professional diplomatic community) took a range of principal steps, while struggling with a variety of tactical problems and objectives. These steps determined the vector of European policy we are still following.

Russia actively participated in converting the Conference on Security and Cooperation in Europe into the full-scale Organization for Security and Cooperation in Europe: in 1993, Russia submitted an application to join the Council of Europe; expressed the intent to join the General Agreement on

Tariffs and Trade (now the World Trade Organization, or WTO); and established basic relations with NATO by both joining the North Atlantic Cooperation Council (recently the Euro-Atlantic Partnership Council) in 1992 and signing the framework document "Partnership for Peace" in 1994.

Russia worked intensively with the European Bank for Reconstruction and Development, which was cofounded by the Soviet Union shortly before it dissolved. The country was covered by the activities of the European Investment Bank. Moscow established a dialogue with the Organization for Economic Cooperation and Development, closely cooperated with the International Energy Agency, and joined the Energy Charter.

The signing of the Cooperation and Partnership Agreement with European Communities in June 1994 is now regarded as the main "European event" for Russia.

The Cooperation and Partnership Agreement was not just a recognition of the new day-to-day realities of an integrated Europe. It defined a framework for economic relations with all member states of the European Union, which by 2004 included Poland. Although in its broader strokes, the Cooperation and Partnership Agreement allowed, as early as 1994, for the possibility of creating a common economic space and a free-trade zone between Russia and the European Union, it also provided a forum for ongoing dialogue on political issues on the European and international agenda.

During the mid-1990s, through membership in various European institutions, Russia began to adopt a system-wide modernization of its legal, economic, and political frameworks and to address strictly technical issues related to European standards and regulations.

Those who are unconscionably self-critical (in Russia) and critical with respect to Russia in Poland should keep in mind this fifteen-year experience of European modernization in Russia.

Polish activities toward Europe were much more purposeful. The entire period from the early 1990s until entry into the EU on 1 May 2004 was characterized by the Polish intent to "return to Europe."

Although for the Russian reader it may seem counterintuitive, "returning to Europe" was not only a foreign policy objective, and a minor one at that, but also an important part of the formation of a new national identity.

The Polish return to Europe gradually changed the internal organization of the country's public policies. Moreover, the process itself was relatively simple. Poland made efforts to gain membership in existing European and Euro-Atlantic institutions as soon as possible. In 1991, Poland became a member of the Council of Europe. In 1994, Poland joined the Partnership for Peace, a NATO program, and afterward started to consider the prospects for full-scale membership in the North Atlantic Alliance (NATO). In March 1999, Poland became a member of NATO. On 1 July 1995, Poland joined the

World Trade Organization, which was recognition of the full-scale inclusion of Poland into global economic relations. Moreover, this membership cleared the way for it to join institutions such as the Organization for Economic Cooperation and Development and the European Union. Poland participated in or acted as an observer of the entire variety of subregional European institutions, from the Council of Baltic Sea States to the Organization for Black Sea Economic Cooperation.

Poland enthusiastically supported Václav Havel's idea on the form of integration and cooperation within Central Europe, which was implemented by the Visegrad Group and in the Central European Free Trade Agreement. The Polish regions were included within the cooperative network of the European regions. This arrangement gave Poland the opportunity to activate its economic life within the border areas, to expand social contacts, and to eliminate the population pressure on the labor market.

The variety of emerging prospects was puzzling, but Warsaw discovered the main path for developing an effective European political and economic self-identification.

On 1 January 1994, Warsaw started to carry out the European Agreement that provided for Polish inclusion in the European communities. The intent to join the European Union was demonstrated by the National Integration Strategy of 1996.

The four-year period of negotiations for entry into the EU, which had started in 1998, ended with success on 13 December 2002. The Athenian Agreement on EU entry was signed on 16 April 2003. In contrast with other historic precedents, this reduction or liquidation of Polish sovereignty (by virtue of joining the European Union) was preceded by a referendum. A significant 58.85 percent of the population took part in the referendum, and 77.45 percent of Poles supported Poland's entry into the European Union.

On 1 May 2004, Poland became a full-fledged member of the European Union.

Therefore, in fifteen years Poland had completed its political, economic, and social transition, received a new international identity, and fulfilled all the tasks the country had faced at the beginning of the reforms. Generally speaking, it is only from this point in time that we can recognize the history of the new Poland as a conventional European country characterized by a relatively stable pattern of internal and international development. We will later try to consider possible exceptions to this principle, how serious they might be, and what exceptions actually occurred in reality.

By 2004, Russia also had had a significant number of achievements regarding its interests in Europe (related to bilateral relations). Russia and the European Union *exchanged* development strategies for relations with each other. Traditionally, Russian diplomacy has had little taste for excessive detail in its plans regarding a certain direction. However, an exception was made for the European Union. The development strategy for relations with the European Union from 2000 to 2010, which was approved by presidential edict, unmistakably identified the European Union as a priority Russian partner in Europe, not only in terms of economic relations but also for establishing a system of security.

Moreover, the strategy emphasized that, for the foreseeable future, Russia was seeking neither membership in the European Union nor association with it. This stance was taken because of the geopolitical advantage of the country's non-allied existence. The completion of negotiations between Brussels and Moscow for Russia's entry into the WTO can undoubtedly be referred to as an achievement. The position of the European Union as the main Russian partner was a critical point in the country's advance toward full-scale participation in the global economy.

Russia and the European Union developed *road maps* for creating four common spaces, with common economic space surely being the most important. The common economic space, if it is eventually implemented, could signify a formal association between Russia and the European Union. From the author's point of view, Russia's strategy for not establishing a formal association revealed the ambivalence of Russia's political class in its attitude toward the range of European problems.

By the way, it is worth mentioning that both Russian and European officials are apprehensive about formalizing a relationship by way of an "association." This is the particular psychological border beyond which relations do not expand.

It is counterintuitive, but the expansion of the European Union, moving this integration closer to Russia, restored Moscow's close relations with even those countries that had distanced themselves from Russia for other reasons. It is a well-known fact that Poland's entry into the European Union gave an absolutely different feel to relations between Moscow and Warsaw.

Nobody can deny the fact that European interests influenced internal Russian affairs, but during this period the next stage of efforts toward creating a Russian state identity was mostly related to internal political events. Those efforts were mainly based on creating a vertical power structure, concentrating the regions around the federal center, pacifying the Islamic underground in the North Caucasus, and doubling gross domestic product, with considerable effort related to consolidating the national energy sector. The Russian administration managed to eliminate the most noticeable gaps in social policy in a relatively short period of time, which slowed down the growing demographic disaster.

Without excluding the strategic European influence, Russia's foreign policy at the turn of the century was oriented to the concept of a multipolar world, which gained popularity within society and among the political class. Moscow reasonably regarded itself as one of the key poles.

This concept was implemented within a whole range of more or less successful constructions: the Russia-India-China "triangle"; the Shanghai Cooperation Organization; full-scale membership in the Group of Eight, which culminated in the Saint Petersburg summit of the Group of Eight (G8); and implementation of a political dialogue in the form of BRIC (Brazil, Russia, India, China).

It is obvious that these constructions are much wider than just the European element of Russian foreign policy. When we add the traditionally complex international security agenda regarding relations with the United States and the multifaceted relations with the closest post-Soviet neighbors, it becomes clear why Poland was able to concentrate on European influence and achieve primary successes there, while Russia was not afforded that luxury.

In other words, Russian society and the political class, in contrast with Poland, were faced with a range of tasks that could have answered the question of a new Russian identity, including its international elements, only through their difficult and prolonged solutions.

In contrast to Poland, Russia did not have a single leading factor that could have been the engine of development in re-creating the country's essence and image.

The Problem of Historical and Foreign Political Self-Consciousness

In terms of their historical and foreign political self-consciousness and self-perception, both modern Poland and Russia are alike. This similarity arises from the stability of ideologies drawn from history and implemented in modern, internal, and especially foreign policy with an art worthy of a better cause. Not least of all, this applies to bilateral relations.

The list of ideologies common to Russia and Poland includes an overestimated view of their place and role in international affairs; the view that their closest neighbors are countries that need the guardianship of Moscow or Warsaw; and an excessive recourse to such concepts as morality, ethics, spirituality, suffering, martyrdom, and heroism with regard to themselves. There is a list of deeper historical myths and concepts, similar for both countries, which are partly based on reality and undoubtedly form this reality. Among them, we can mention the Sarmatism concept, which explained to Russians and Poles both the necessity of reclaiming "lost" territories and the existence of certain elements of social and day-to-day patterns that were uncommon in other parts of Europe. Other prevalent concepts are that of a bridge between the East and the West and, without a doubt, a historic pride for having saved Europe from the Tatar invasion. All of these ideologies are common and equally important, if not popular, within Polish and Russian historical self-consciousness.

In other words, both Russia and Poland have an irrational, phantomlike self-sentiment for being specific, unique countries or states in the way these concepts were understood between the seventeenth and nineteenth centuries. Moreover, in Russia, the words for "state" or "empire" are often used in semiofficial discourse as a self-designation.

In Polish foreign policy, phrases meaning "great power statehood" and "imperial complex" are mainly implied and the democratic traditions of the noble-aristocratic Rzeczpospolita are considered to be a limiting factor. The historical term "Rzeczpospolita" is much broader in its essence than the term for "republic" in other European languages. Incidentally, Russian historians and journalists have always understood the term "Rzeczpospolita" and transliterated it as the name of the Polish state. Moreover, "Rzeczpospolita" during certain historical periods was used as a synonym for "Poland."

In the Russian historical perception and Polish self-perception, the term "Rzeczpospolita" is smoothly conjoined with the self-perceived concept of "the clearest," a country "from sea to sea," a state that historically included the territories of Rus, which were listed in the title of the Russian autocrats.

Russia and Poland are afraid to recognize their similarities. Indeed, if they are so similar, then what is their uniqueness in this part of the world? In general, Russia and Poland, being young states in their present forms, are characterized by a penchant for nationalizing history, seeking to explain present-day events through direct reference to convenient historical evidence or a convenient historical interpretation. It is possible to argue with the author or to regard his assertions to be a primitive, flattened interpretation of the national consciousness, a grotesque form, which has nothing in common with the official position. But, unfortunately, this particular grotesqueness, uncritically introduced by historical stereotypes, dominated Russian-Polish relations from the mid-1990s to 2010. It occurred alternately, due to the fault of one party and then another. During this period, the similarities between Russia and Poland did not bring the countries closer but stuck them together just as equally charged particles collide with each other.

Again, it is counterintuitive, but the disappearance of the Soviet (i.e., late Soviet) historical paradigm, which explained the same Polish events in terms of class and the struggle for liberation of a suppressed nation, reduced the level of pro-Polish support from historical Russian indoctrination and reverted to historical paradigms of a strictly "statist" nature. Russian public opinion automatically returned to the outdated perception of Poland, which was formed in tsarist Russia during the nineteenth century.

This perception, clearly unacceptable from the point of view of the Polish political class and society in general, was supplemented by sentiments and tags related to the People's Republic of Poland, which operationally were of little use from the point of view of modern Poland. Also, clumsy propaganda campaigns from 2005 to 2007, attempting to create an antagonistic image of Poland, were extremely negative elements.

It is equally necessary to mention that, from the author's point of view, the denial by the modern political class of the People's Republic of Poland ("unnumbered" Rzeczpospolita) cannot be advantageous for the historical and foreign political self-consciousness of modern Poland. Such a denial deletes an entire historical layer and makes Warsaw the successor of foreign political concepts from the 1920s and 1930s, which are far from blameless. The author may receive an objection that the social ideas of the postwar Polish emigrant community may be fairly well included in the modern consciousness. However, any unbiased observer can see that, unfortunately, the main line of thinking of the Polish political class is much more monochromatic than the heritage of Jerzy Giedroyc or of the collective mind of the Parisian *Kultura*. Moreover, due to the fact that the serious return of émigré thought occurred during the difficult postreform period during the early 1990s, we can state that it hardly gathered any new supporters beyond intellectuals from middle-aged and older generations. All of this was superimposed on the growth in popularity of "historical foreign policy" in Poland, which burgeoned during the first two years of the term of (deceased) Pres. Lech Kaczyński. With regard to Russia, the "historical foreign policy" mobilized all negative stereotypes that had formed over decades, if not centuries. The "historical foreign policy" is far from being just a Polish phenomenon, but only in Poland did it become a constituent part of the official political doctrine of the dominant party, at least for some period of time, and was developed as a historically based foreign policy.

Dr. Dariusz Gawin and many famous Polish historians and journalists have noted that "the present day wave of a universal historic revisionism is a unique event which leads to the substantive re-evaluation of the values and reference points not only in liberal sciences, but also in politics. This critical wave is targeted not only against widespread notions and stereotypes but also against the truths which play a fundamental role in the feasibility of the set forms of the collective memory, a phenomenon important for any political order."

In general, the "historical foreign policy" settled on the blessed ground of Central and Eastern Europe and the Baltic States. The political life in this part of the world, including Russia, came to be literally invaded by the shadows of the past. According to a quote by Jacek Żakowski, "the skeletons' march" began in Europe. During this time, both public and nonpublic historical interpretations became targets for rude rebuffs from the foreign affairs institutions. The interpretations themselves were naïvely regarded as a powerful foreign policy weapon.

Any milestone date gave a pretext for historical and political provocations. Some acquired a long-lasting and completely sophisticated "network" nature, such as, for instance, the continuous disparagement of the part Russia played in the victory over fascism or the anti-Katyn project, contradicting obvious historical facts.

The "historical foreign policy" trend is currently dying off. It appears the cause originated in both Poland and Russia, in which both found strength and due inventiveness to create a specific protocol for handling politically sensitive historical issues. This refers to the Group for Difficult Matters, which will be described later.

To assess the historical consciousness of contemporary Russian and Polish societies, one principal aspect needs to be considered related to the environment in which they form.

Poland started reforms after ten years of economic crisis, which affected everyday life for its citizens. The liberal reform originated by Leszek Balcerowicz turned out to be much less shocking on a day-to-day basis for the average Pole than the reforms carried out by his Russian counterpart, Yegor Gaidar. The everyday economic crisis struck the vast majority of Russian families in the first years of modern Russian history, rather than during the Soviet period. The "practical socialism" of the Khrushchev and Brezhnev eras undeniably won the comparison with the first half of the 1990s in terms of public order, social security, and the absence of internal military conflicts, as well as organized crime.

It often happened, either because of ignorance or due to purposeful myth making, that the comparative advantages of the late period of socialism were unjustifiably overshadowed by the horrors of the Stalinist period. To tell the truth, both Nikita Khrushchev's "thaw" period and Mikhail Gorbachev's perestroika inoculated a significant part of the population against such extrapolation, when the range and tragedy of Stalin's crimes were demonstrated in the fate of the country. In other words, objective and subjective weaknesses and failures of the Russian reforms made the Soviet period comparatively attractive. For the vast majority of Russians, the disconnect from the Soviet past was and still is a completely artificial process. It should be well understood by anyone who would criticize the well-known statement by Vladimir Putin, who referred to the breakdown of the Soviet Union as the major geopolitical disaster of the twentieth century. Though being overly emotional, the statement was accepted by the majority of Russians as perfectly natural.

Simultaneously establishing a state and international political identity, both Russia and Poland had experienced the influence of almost every prominent ideology and political regime during the twentieth century and could not avoid active and often aggressive myth making. Moreover, such myth making was based on a traditionally uncritical attitude toward their own history (in both countries) and on genuinely tragic chapters in their mutual history, including Katyn.

The attempts to break the deadlock of mutual historical prejudices, undertaken during the epochal turning point, were left incomplete for a number of reasons and did not stick in people's minds. That incompleteness resulted from the very peculiarities of the highly dynamic and unstable life in those days, as was previously mentioned. That did not help the recognition of even the most adequate steps in the public consciousness. For instance, no one but historians seems to remember that a historic meeting between Putin and Donald Tusk took place in Katyn on 7 April 2010, almost exactly twenty years after Gorbachev handed Wojciech Jaruzelski, on 13 April 1990, the lists of the names of Polish soldiers who had been sentenced to execution. Who remembers that, in 1992, Boris Yeltsin handed over all principal documents incriminating Stalin and his associates in that villainous action? Only historians do.

It looks as if the external context constituted the principal difference in the Russian-Polish historic dialogue from Polish-German or French-German relations, which started in the comparatively quiet background of the 1960s and 1970s. From 2008 to 2010, both Poland and Russia made systematic efforts to overcome complicated historical and psychological problems. A huge role was played by the Group for Difficult Matters. The author, who was a counselor to the copresident and executive secretary of the Russian delegation, was privileged to witness its activities from within, knowing more than outsiders. The political decision in 2007 to change the group's status, which practically meant reorganizing it, happened because of the history of Russian-Polish relations and was the first contribution to creating a mutual understanding on sensitive matters related directly, as one would think, to national pride or national tragedy.

When the group was founded, nobody had a clear vision of the character and procedure of its work or the exact range of problems to consider. There were, and still are, no written powers or obligations. The group was organizing its work based on political intuition and mutual apprehension. It is important to note that, from the very beginning, unlike many other groups and commissions, the group established constructive but not obsequious relations with the foreign departments of both countries on the most complicated issues. Hence, the group was better equipped to feel out the international fabric, while still preserving the pragmatic logic of its activities.

The group did not set political goals but solved them in practice, simultaneous with its main aim to make the truth—currently known only to professional historians—available to the general public and particularly to the ruling elites of both countries. However, there were virtually no serious disagreements between the Polish and the Russian participants regarding the interpretation of events, the point being to make those interpretations public in our countries.

The work concentrated on two principal objectives. First, we aimed to prepare joint publications on the mutual history of our two countries from 1917 until the present day. Paradoxically, when we tried to identify the most critical issues of debate, we realized that the book in fact was becoming a sequence of essays on relations between our countries. The chapters on all issues of dispute or mutual interest were evenly arranged in chronological order. On each issue the authors prepared two essays, one in Russian and one in Polish—the authors included both group participants as well as outside experts.

The reader may judge the result. The publication was preceded by a book, published with the support of the group, also based on two points of view and dedicated to the genesis of World War II. The book received substantial reader support in both Russia and Poland.

The other side of the group's activities was of a less continuous and more nonpublic nature. It dealt with promoting the initiatives born inside the group to the level of foreign policy departments and to the level of political decision making. A great role in the process was played by the copresidents of the group: Anatoly V. Torkunov, an academic and the rector of the Moscow State Institute of Foreign Affairs, and Prof. Adam Daniel Rotfeld, the former Polish minister of foreign affairs. Their academic backgrounds and high public status enabled those people to break through the wall of mutual prejudices built up by agitators and to calm the political intrigues scarring the pages of our tragic common history.

The major goal, however, was purely positive: to explain, to tell, to convince people who, not maliciously, but because of their remove from political and historic problems, did not understand the poignancy of a given issue or could not appropriately express their thoughts on sensitive historical questions. Many people did not seem to understand that understatement in history could have a negative impact on society in the present and future.

It seems difficult to overestimate the importance of multiple references to the group's activities made by the prime ministers of both countries at their meetings in Sopot and Smolensk. When Putin used the phrase "as our historians told me," it said a lot. But even more important was the fact that Russian and Polish high authorities (particularly the Russian ones) were able to absorb the new information and to be flexible in addressing the problems, which were seemingly remote from their current concerns.

Can we say that, after 7 April 2010, we have closed the problem of Katyn and effectively expunged all historical issues from the political agenda of our relations? We can, with respect to Putin's sincere and emotional gestures and words, obviously resulting from serious inner effort, at the memorial in Katyn. We can, if we consider the fact that the head of the government of modern Russia confirmed all of the statements of his predecessors, but in much stronger and clearer terms. We can, if we remember that, at the memorial ceremony, both prime ministers confirmed an absolutely identical approach to understanding the question of who was the victim and who was the criminal. We can, if we introspectively peer into the anti-Stalinist message of Putin's declaration, which was much wider than just the Polish question. We can, if we remember that the Polish Catholic bishop took part in the ceremonial laying of the cornerstone of a new Russian Orthodox church in Katyn. And we can, because the ceremonial brigade of the Polish army took part in the annual Victory parade on Red Square in Moscow on 9 May 2010, thus reminding everyone that our countries were allies in the war with a common enemy.

A new tragedy near Smolensk literally shocked Russia when, on 10 April 2010, Polish president Lech Kaczyński and several dozen prominent state and public figures were killed in a plane crash. Public feelings toward Poland and the Poles attained an attitude of compassion, sympathy, comradeship, and solidarity in grief. Hardly any other event could have attracted more warmth from Russians toward Poland. It might seem cynical, but the response to the catastrophe on 10 April could have been very different if it were not for the words of truth declared by both presidents, united in joint memory and grief, on 7 April in Katyn.

It was very important that the Russian authorities, Pres. Dmitry Medvedev and Prime Minister Putin, not just personally responded to the tragedy but gave clear political signals for future convergence with Warsaw. It obviously referred to a whole range of questions, including the ones related to historical problems. It was clearly declared during the negotiations between Medvedev and Bronisław Komorowski, acting president of Poland, on 18 April 2010 in Kraków and on 9 May 2010 in Moscow.

The positive strategic answers given by the author to the question of whether historical issues have been eliminated from the political agenda must, unfortunately, be supplemented with a number of negative tactical answers. Negative, because there are currently a number of claims under consideration in the European court on human rights, initiated by claimants dissatisfied with Russian court decisions regarding the "Katyn cases." Negative, because the historical refrain is customarily exploited in internal Polish and Russian political struggles, particularly before parliamentary elections in our countries. Negative, because, regardless of the facts, Russian radicals are still repeating the version of the Katyn events outlined by the Stalin-era Soviet diplomat-prosecutor Andrzej Wyszyński. Fortunately, those are questions of a tactical nature, and time, common sense, and political will are bound to eliminate them soon enough. I hope that the joint centers of dialogue and agreement, being organized according to decisions by the prime ministers of Russia and Poland, would duly rely on the above three elements in their activities. The consultations and exchange of letters in July 2010 between the two Ministries of Culture, which were put in charge of providing activities for the centers, gave us hope that the institutions would soon be able to start functioning.

The Changing Context of Bilateral Relations

Russia and Poland have experienced such a wide variety of scripts in their historical relations that it is hardly possible to identify any historical or legal form they have not covered. These forms have included voluntary and compulsory cooperation, attempts to create and to impose rulers and governments on each other, relations with governments in exile, forced or nearly voluntary inclusion of historic parts of one country within the territory of the other, as well as periods of equal relations between the two European players, such as the one that started after 1991.

The major factor in modern relations between Russia and Poland is, and will be for the foreseeable future, the difference in potential determined by Russian preeminence in territorial, natural, military, and demographic resources.

On the other hand, Poland, being a member of the close-knit association of the European Union, which exceeds Russian potential in every parameter but the military, can summon joint EU capacity in case of crisis. At the same time, the two countries' difference in potential causes an asymmetry of mutual attention and mutual interest in Russian-Polish relations. Russia accounts for a third or even up to half of Poland's foreign policy efforts and concerns. Poland would hardly ever rise to that level of significance in Russian foreign policy concerns, even for a very short period. The classical bilateral relations that prevailed between our countries over the centuries ended in 1991, in conjunction with the loss of a major portion of common border. The Kaliningrad section of border will never compensate for the loss. Modern bilateral relations will increasingly center on the common (judging by the range of issues) international, particularly European, agenda. The small Kaliningrad and coastal border sections shared may serve an as indicator and catalyst of relations in the "big agenda" framework.

Russian-Polish relations during the 1990s revolved around issues of the legal transition from the Soviet Union–People's Republic of Poland tandem. A number of practical questions had to be solved, including those related to the shared border, legal issues, and property rights, including foreign property owned by the state. One of the major elements was the question of the withdrawal of the Soviet Northern Group of Forces from Polish territory. The withdrawal was completed in 1993. Both parties were in search of systematic solutions for transporting Russian gas and oil through Polish territory and trading in those commodities. Perhaps, from today's perspective, many agreements achieved at that time now seem unprofitable to both parties, but that is why there is a bilateral commission; it works to develop mechanisms for continual correction and consideration of new realities. The problem was that these mechanisms functioned with long pauses.

During the 1990s, Poland learned how to make use of "geopolitical rent." This reserve created during the Soviet period started to work in the 1990s. The first stage of the Yamal-Europe pipeline construction was completed in that decade, and Polish pipelines were included in Russian oil transit. As a result, 30 percent of Russian oil and 16 percent of Russian gas exports passed through Polish territory. During that time, the Polish transport companies became some of the region's largest road transport operators, conveying goods and food products from Western Europe to Russia.

It should be mentioned that the old infrastructure was used during the first decade of the market economy, with lucky exemptions for newly built and renovated border crossings. It is already forgotten that there was a visa-free regime between Russia and Poland until 1 October 2003. Everyone who has had the experience of applying for a Schengen or American visa can appreciate the greater degree of openness and freedom between our countries.

One notable post-Soviet phenomenon of the 1990s was the mass diversification of individual, often half-legal, cross-border commerce (the so-called "shuttle trade"). It enabled Poles and Russians who, as a result of market reforms, found themselves outside the organized economy to have the means to survive. In border regions, shuttle trade and related services quickly became serious business. Apart from the often negative image of a small middleman, it became possible for broad groups of the population in Russia and Poland to get acquainted with life in the neighboring country. Until the tightening of the border by the regime in January 1998, Poland drew almost four million tourists and merchants annually. Shuttle trade revenues reached several billion dollars per year. From 1992–2003, the "gray" imports from Poland exceeded the official trade figures.

In evaluating bilateral relations during the 1990s, it is important to remember that the whole region of Central and Eastern Europe, including Poland, was not at the top of the list of international priorities.

Surprisingly, the new democratic elite ushered in a new political-ideological aspect to relations with Europe. The international priorities of Yeltsin and his circle could be considered liberal and US-centric. The former principal enemy, the United States, quickly became Russia's principal friend. Other minor details were much less important. The ability of the Russian elite to perceive detail or to offer nuances was very low. The foreign policy of the early 1990s could be imagined as analogous to a narrow bridge, with one end in Moscow and the other in Washington. The establishment at the time believed that the receiving end was the desirable West itself, identical to the "Washington" concept. Far below the bridge was Europe. By the middle of

ARTEM V. MALGIN

the 1990s, Russia was taking pains to build a slope toward Western Europe, while Eastern Europe was still connected by a thin-planked footpath.

Paradoxically, though, what now seem to be "difficult matters," due to the peculiarities of the European politics of Russia, were at that time treated comparatively, perhaps excessively, as simple or commonplace. For instance, the common Russian-Polish declaration signed on 25 August 1993, during the visit of President Yeltsin to Warsaw, regarding potential Polish membership in NATO confirmed that it "would not contradict the interests of other countries, including Russia." That neutral attitude later was transformed into a rigidly negative one. But NATO heard the first signal, even if it was given by mistake.

In fact, just two or three years later, Moscow vehemently tried to oppose NATO expansion, though Russian reason and suggestion never affected or infringed on Polish sovereignty, in spite of the impression given by some modern experts. The Russian problems regarding NATO were caused by late reactions. Russia discussed the issue mainly with Washington. It did not bother to find ways of coordination with the European and Polish establishment, including military authorities, though support for joining the alliance was far from unanimous within military circles.

However, it should also be taken into consideration that Poland showed signs that the close relations with its eastern neighbor were weakening and that it was even beginning to mistrust the fairly reasonable idea of the multilateral guarantees for Central and Eastern European countries. Above all, the majority of the population considered joining NATO to be the shortest way to the West, shorter even than association with the EU.

By the early 2000s, the dynamics of Russian-Polish relations were in decline based on some minimally coordinated, though objectively parallel, processes of adapting to the changes happening in Europe and inside their own countries.

The major and most important issues inherited from the Soviet era had been solved. Business was steadily developing, regardless of the state of official contacts. The strategic energy supply and transit sectors relied on a mutually acceptable legal and economic framework. This framework was one that Russia has still failed to establish in its relations with Ukraine and Belarus. Polish membership in NATO became a sober background detail. Polish diplomatic circles and the political elite focused their gaze on the beckoning European horizon.

Relations with Moscow were developing along the old, not very promising route. The situation was well understood in both capitals, and officials tried to offer a way out. High-level contacts intensified, though, as it would later seem, the contacts lacked efficiency regarding long-term results. Eleven high-level meetings were organized between presidents Putin and Aleksander

Kwaśniewski from 2000 to 2005. The first and most important meeting was during the visit of President Kwaśniewski to Moscow on 10 July 2000. On 16 January 2002, Poland perceived a significant boost in its relationship with Russia when President Putin arrived in Warsaw, the first such official visit in more than nine years. These meetings served as focal points for developing contemporary treaty relations between Russia and Poland, based on more than four dozen interstate and interagency agreements. These agreements involved creating consultative mechanisms and reactivating the Intergovernmental Commission. During the Russian foreign minister's visit to Poland in June 2002, the Committee for the Russian-Polish Cooperation Strategy (also known as the Strategy Committee) was created and led by the two countries' foreign ministers.

In 2004, however, many people in Moscow considered Polish politicians' active support for the so-called "Orange Coalition" and President Kwaśniewski's mediation in Ukraine to be anti-Russian measures.

Paradoxically, even after this rough patch in relations, an exchange of visits took place at the highest level. But, in truth, they were memorial in nature. In January 2005, President Putin arrived in Poland to mark the sixtieth anniversary of the liberation of Auschwitz, and President Kwaśniewski, despite the strong anti-Russian sentiments that prevailed in the Polish political establishment and that had been crystallized in the mass media, came to Moscow in May to celebrate the sixtieth anniversary of Victory Day. These visits could not resolve the situation; indeed, they were accompanied by a hard-hitting media campaign.

The intensity increased on the Polish side as the presidential and parliamentary elections approached. Russian relations became a prominent element in the political campaign as many blunt, hurtful, and myopic statements were made, leaving President Kwaśniewski and the whole Polish "Lewica" (the Left) under heavy preelection fire, including criticism of the president's activities toward Russian industry (which may seem counterintuitive to Russian readers). People around the president were accused of illegal mediation on behalf of a major Russian oil company.

The climate of bilateral relations has drastically deteriorated since then. A peculiar symbol of this deterioration was the fact that there were very strange attacks on a Polish journalist and the children of Russian diplomats. Various issues related to foreign property began to emerge, and, most importantly, there came a change in publicity. Moscow withstood an obscenely long pause in the appointment of a new ambassador to Warsaw.

During the same time, an alarmist mood developed in Poland, which remains in part to this day, regarding energy relations with Russia. This tension arose out of difficult relations between Russia, Ukraine, and Belarus over the transportation of energy resources, termination of Russian oil deliveries to the Mažeikiai refinery in Lithuania due to an accident, and construction of the Nord Stream pipeline. However, no significant energy-related problems or failures actually occurred.

The culmination of this poor relationship, which dragged on for two years, was the temporary restriction on exports of meat products from Poland to Russia, begun on 10 November 2005, and restrictions on crop production that started on 14 November 2005. Obviously, under normal circumstances, based on a few specific cases, any problems Russian sanitary services identified regarding Polish products would have been resolved according to standard practice, without recourse to publicity or raising the issue to political significance. President Kaczyński, who had inherited the troubled relationship and the government coalition led by the Law and Justice (Prawo i Sprawiedliwość) Party, had neither the power nor the policies to correct them. The general deterioration in relations between Moscow and the West, much of which was due to different understandings of the situation in the former Soviet Union, was also superimposed on these bilateral issues. Another major irritant was the insistence by the Polish establishment on placing US missile defense facilities in Polish territory. However, it should be noted that the political leadership of both countries and foreign ministries, while not yet ready to improve relations, prevented them from slipping over a critical line. Relations were maintained between deputy ministers, certain foreign ministers, and security contacts through NATO.

It should be mentioned that, except for embargoed goods, Polish exports to Russia continued to grow. Simultaneously, the price of Russian hydrocarbons kept increasing, and, as a result, revenues showed promise, in contrast to the state of political dialogue. Paradoxically, the meat embargo led to intensified contacts between the countries, and the ban was lifted in January 2006.

The "sanitary" problem took on an entirely new political dimension exactly one year after it began. On 24 November 2006, the eve of the Russia-EU summit, Poland vetoed talks between Moscow and Brussels on a new agreement to replace the Partnership and Cooperation Agreement that was to expire in December 2007. I believe this decision by Warsaw made many realize the danger of unresolved or lingering problems in relations with individual European Union countries, even those that, like Poland, had just joined the union.

Despite the belief of the Russian Foreign Ministry that the meat embargo issue was purely technical and purely bilateral in nature, the EU leadership held different beliefs.

At the Russia-EU summit, which took place in May 2007, German chancellor Angela Merkel and European Commission president José Manuel Barroso voiced unequivocal support for Warsaw's position and confirmed that the meat embargo was considered a problem in relations between Russia and the EU. This unique solidarity finally convinced many people of the European identity of Poland, as well as the unsuitability of operating within the "inter-imperialist contradictions."

Breaking the deadlock over the meat embargo would not have been so quick, even in this case, if early parliamentary elections had not been held in Poland in October 2007. Prime Minister Jarosław Kaczyński's cabinet resigned and was replaced by a pragmatic coalition of the Civic Platform (Platforma Obywatelska) Party and the Polish People's Party (Polskie Stronnictwo Ludowe). Donald Tusk, leader of Civic Platform, won the premiership, and Waldemar Pawlak, representing the Polish People's Party, was appointed deputy prime minister.

The new government of Donald Tusk appeared to be a much smarter and more creative administration than its predecessor, in which the operative word was *rozliczenie*, which can be translated as "reckoning," that is, settling the score with history, political opponents, ideological opponents, their own organizations, neighbors, and so forth, but, in the end, with common sense.

Completely new ideas and new intonations were already evident in the prime minister's initial address to the parliament. It would have been extremely foolish of Russia not to notice them and to spoil relations with Polish farmers, whose party was the key to sustaining the new coalition.

By mutual agreement, all restrictions on the supply of Polish agricultural products to Russia were removed between December 2007 and January 2008.

On 7 December 2007, at a meeting of the NATO-Russia Council, diplomatic ministers discussed the state of relations and "expressed their mutual belief in the necessity and the possibility of normalization." This statement makes it possible to characterize the previous period as having been "abnormal."

In February 2008, a new chapter in Russian-Polish relations was opened by Donald Tusk's visit to Russia, the main objectives of which were to restore normal relations, to resume former or create new mechanisms for dialogue, to solve pending legal issues, and to return to a depoliticized format for difficult joint historical issues.

Despite the ever-repeated mantra that we have a complicated relationship, Russia and Poland rapidly developed better relations in the course of three years after Civic Platform came to power in Poland. This notion that complexity persists in the bilateral relationship confirms the slow growth in awareness exhibited by social consciousness and the mass media.

The positive trend in Russian-Polish relations was consolidated by the participation of Russian prime minister Vladimir Putin in memorial events at Westerplatte and in the meeting with his Polish counterpart in Sopot. The significance of this visit for promoting the resolution of historical issues between the two countries has already been noted. Other important elements addressed by the premiers included resolving navigational issues in the Kaliningrad Gulf (Wisła Lagoon/Gulf of Gdańsk) and reviewing the entire subject of economic relations.

After the September meeting, active Russian-Polish dialogue focused on regional cooperation and local cross-border mobility. Interaction between Moscow and Warsaw in this matter was so fruitful that it led to the preparation of an unprecedented joint statement to the European Commission calling for a change in the internal rules of the EU. On 6 April 2010, representatives from the two countries conveyed it to the European Commission. This document speaks of a very simplified way for residents of the Kaliningrad region to travel to bordering Polish territories up to a distance of fifty kilometers.

Generally speaking, it is apparent that Poland, being a member of the EU, showed solidarity with Russia and proposed that the European Commission amend the seemingly immutable Schengen rules. By the way, Poland, followed by Lithuania, began to gradually erode the rigor of the Schengen regime precisely due to such arrangements with their neighbors—Belarus and Ukraine. Poland is still trying to legalize another fair and worthwhile innovation for Russia—a "Polish card"—for its residents who do not have Polish citizenship. This card makes available certain visa and in-country facilities to those people who are historically associated with Poland and who fall into a category similar to Russian "compatriots."

The author repeatedly had to prove that, in the long term, we cannot be in a bad relationship because, for Poland, Russia is the second-largest foreign trade partner it has, after Germany. Warsaw, in Moscow's view, is the leading economic partner in Central and Eastern Europe and one of the leading economic partners in general. Poland is ranked seventh in the foreign trade of Russia. Yes, the crisis in 2009 reduced the volume of bilateral trade. But nothing tragic has happened. This reduction is in part due to falling energy prices that distorted the statistics. In 2009, trade revenues with the EU decreased 40 percent for these "technical" reasons. Improved relations between Warsaw and Minsk were also the reason for a slight change in the pattern and volume of Polish exports to Russia.

Russia and Poland are now moving into a new stage of economic relations that features an increasing role for more complex foreign economic cooperation. This type of cooperation is imperative because Russian products of comparable price and quality will increasingly replace relatively simple, though qualified Polish consumer imports. Polish producers are beginning to understand this situation. No less important for the Polish economy, which is better than almost any other in Europe experiencing the economic crisis, are foreign investments capable of supporting economic growth.

Freedom from political phobias opens the door to Russian money in the Polish economy. It is no accident that the prime ministers devoted much of their meeting on 7 April 2010 to matters of mutual investment, followed by an announcement about it at a press conference.

Another important aspect of bilateral relations involves energy. Here again, the real situation and various speculations about "Russian energy blackmail" vary widely. In terms of Russian oil purchases and transportation agreements in which the scheme of joint Russian-Polish pipelines is working smoothly, in contrast to efforts in Ukraine and Belarus, Poland is almost a model country in the Central and Eastern Europe region. Proof of this characterization was the agreement announced by the prime ministers for the procurement of natural gas through 2037 and for transportation through 2045.

The prospect of uniting electrical networks for more sustainable supplies in cross-border regions and the possibility of cooperation in the atomic energy sector began to be discussed in Gdańsk in September 2009, and discussions continued in Smolensk. In other words, in terms of bilateral relations, the making of new configurations in the energy system together with Russia is actually under way in the Baltic region.

The situation being what it is, Putin's announcement in Smolensk of the start of work on the Nord Stream pipeline's undersea branch looked like another logical step in creating Europe's united power complex, and it drew no fire on the part of his Polish counterpart.

It is worth noting the absolute public disorderliness of Polish businesses operating in Russia as a serious problem of political and economic relations. Efficient bilateral frameworks of business dialogue are missing. As often as not, Polish businesses in Russia prefer to operate "under false colors," that is, registering as being from Germany, Austria, or any other country than Poland. It would seem that, on the territory of Russia, as opposed to many other countries, Polish authorities have not managed to create an operative promotion system, a mechanism for securing their country's businesses, or stable relations with state and private counteragents in the economic sphere. The exception is in the traditional energy sector.

On the Russian side of business relations, a similar situation may be observed. The business arena is dominated by power brokers who are content with a minimal level of stability. Sensing the general political environment, they successfully attribute problems in their communications with Polish counterparts to a political agenda. The non-energy business on the Polish side is poorly organized and is secondary to the general line. Only one example can be given of an instance in which non-energy businesses proved to be a relevant force. This was when manufacturers, meat processors, and chain retailers suffering from the embargo on Polish meat made certain lobbying efforts to lift the restrictions.

A discreet business that has intentionally distanced itself from the general context of Russian-Polish interaction cannot play a role as a serious stabilizer in relations and, as a consequence, falls victim to the irregular and emotional nature of those relations.

Specific communication problems in Russian-Polish relations exist in both the political and foreign policy communities. Such problems seem especially apparent on the Russian side, because for Poles, whose middle generation speaks Russian for the most part, it is easier to quickly pick up the necessary informational scope about the Russian partner and enter into intermediate contacts than it is for Russians for whom information about present-day Poland in English, let alone in Russian, is either extremely scant, inadequate, or historically suspect.

For many representatives of the Russian establishment, Poland remains terra incognita. Paradoxically enough, those Russians who were shuttle traders in the early 1990s have somewhat adjusted their image of Poland in comparison with the times of developed socialism. Politicians and experts were deprived of this opportunity to see the new Poland, as they mostly visit the capital cities where global and European politics are centered. It was not often imagined that parts of the mosaic for the general European scene were set in Poland, too, on four specific occasions: initially, when Poland entered NATO; again, when it entered the EU; a third time, when Kwaśniewski visited Kiev; and finally, when Poland vetoed negotiations on the new EU agreement. Normally an expert, Moscow, unfortunately, was not yet used to this systematic approach to the Polish political process.

In Russia, experts on Poland, who are evidently fewer in number than specialists on Russia in Poland, having lost interest in Central and Eastern Europe, either turned out to be washed out of the profession entirely or at least were not mobilized to engage in foreign policy discussions. It is also worthy of note that the majority of professional specialists on Poland are of the older generation. To no less an extent this concerns the situation with specialists on Poland in the foreign service. They appeared to be scattered over different departments of the Ministry of Foreign Affairs. This is bad from the point of view that sometimes the concentration of intellect, as well as workers, in specific fields falls short. Yet, many of these specialists on Poland, having left for adjacent fields in post-Soviet, European, and integration studies, now become highly sought after due to Poland's more prominent profile in these areas. The same problem exists in getting the younger generation of students graduating from the Moscow State Institute of International Relations with Polish-language fluency to stay in the profession. But the depth of this trend is only a few years old at this point.

It should be optimistically noted that new frameworks for dialogue have been created since 2010, thus demonstrating substantial activity. One example is the Public Forum, whose co-chairs are Leonid V. Drachevsky, the former ambassador to Poland, and Krzysztof Zanussi, the acclaimed film director. Another example is the Forum of Regions, established on the initiative of the heads of the upper chambers of the two countries' parliaments. In the Federation Council, a separate group charged with maintaining contacts with Polish colleagues was singled out from the general Eastern European group. Dialogue and accord centers must become another pillar for public dialogue.

Russia and Poland in European and International Relations

As mentioned above, the two countries' relations are progressively being built up, not only in terms of bilateral issues but also in terms of the subjects of the European and international agendas involving Moscow and Warsaw. We turn our attention to three subjects with different effects, as well as different perspectives, in terms of their respective points of contact.

NATO at present is more like a background element for the development of Russian-Polish relations and not a source of current foreign policy dynamics. As Bogdan Klich, Poland's defense minister, wrote, "Poland considers NATO a unique forum for consultations and cooperation between Europe and America. The USA's membership in the Alliance is viewed by us as an absolutely necessary condition of the organization's power and resiliency, which provides key security warranties for its members. . . . Warsaw respectfully supports those initiatives that strengthen the USA's influence in Europe, and contribute to close cooperation between European and American allies on the continent." These words may be regarded as the essence of Poland's relationship to the North Atlantic Alliance. Unlike many less-than-tangible factors (such as the overall romanticism in the fight for independence) or factors losing their effect (such as Polish emigration), it is NATO that secures a transatlantic dimension for Polish politics. Consequently, it increases the country's weight in the international arena. It is important to understand Poland's somewhat stronger examples of solidarity and involvement in specific operations (e.g., Iraq and Afghanistan) than those afforded by older, larger European NATO countries. They have other ways of self-positioning in Euro-Atlantic relations.

In the meantime, Poland's solidarity with the United States, whose military and political establishment is, as a rule, a bearer of tougher and more aggressive plans in terms of NATO development than are its European colleagues, may be expressed in issues not irrelevant to Russia. This primarily concerns the eventual wave of alliance enlargement:

> Three rounds of NATO enlargement after the end of the Cold War are a serious proof of the Alliance's resiliency and attractiveness and its stabilizing role in Europe. . . . Due to NATO enlargement, the Euroatlantic space is now more quiet and safe than in previous decades. . . . Therefore, it is extremely

important to keep NATO's doors open for those countries that are willing and ready to join the organization. . . . Nobody should be surprised that Poland is still [as of mid-2009] a partisan of the Euroatlantic ambitions of both Ukraine and Georgia[,] and it believes that partnership with these countries is of importance to the Alliance.

Technically, it is a statement that helps maintain a prominent image for Poland in the alliance. Alongside that, it should be clear that the actual contents of this provision depend not only on realism or the lack thereof on the part of Polish authorities in each particular period but also on bilateral Russian-Polish relations.

On the applied level, partnership with the Polish side in terms of the NATO agenda looks quite realistic and far more feasible than partnership with Western European allies. This is clearly favored by geographical proximity and military compatibility. In our case, it is accounted for by a similar military mentality, traditions, a reduced language barrier, knowledge of the particularities of Soviet/Russian armed forces by the (progressively decreasing) officer corps, and largely identical arms and weapons.

The antiballistic missile (ABM) defense agenda for 2005–9 seriously complicated bilateral relations. The first negotiations for the possible deployment of units of an antiballistic missile defense system in Poland began in 2003; this issue used to be a regular agenda item in meetings of Polish and American officials. For Poland's side, these "conversations around possible negotiations" meant specifically obtaining information on the system concept, its operating development, and alternatives to participation. In early 2005, special commissions of inquiry into this issue under Poland's Ministry of National Defense and Ministry of Foreign Affairs were set up.

The ABM issue "was considered mainly in terms of a possible benefit from reinforcement of 'American military presence' in the country and strengthening of strategic relations between Warsaw and Washington."

Following the parliamentary election in September 2005, Kazimierz Marcinkiewicz's and, later on, Jarosław Kaczyński's new government undertook the obligation to "work on introducing Poland to the American system of antiballistic missile defense."

The discussion initiated in public showed the existence of different opinions on this matter. The critics noted that the presence of American ABMs on the country's territory enhanced the likelihood that Poland would become the target of a first attack. Thus, Poland would prove to be in danger because the bilateral agreement with the United States might also lead to a discussion of Poland's mandates as a NATO and EU member, not to mention the inevitable exacerbation of relations with Russia. It is clear that no benefit gained from relations with the United States would compensate for aggravating Poland's security status.

The main argument of most ABM system supporters is that this issue should be tackled not in view of external threats to Europe or the United States but in terms of Washington's role in security policy. It should be noted that, in the public discussion launched in the press, the American argument for ABMs was used only in passing, in the form of banalities. Poland did not accept this rationale, and it was not used by ABM opponents or supporters. Klich, the renowned Polish analyst in the field of security, has clearly noted that "the majority of supporters of Poland's involvement in the antiballistic missile system project unanimously point at Russia and its possible policy in the future."

The uncertainty and ambivalence of attitudes toward ABMs among the Polish political and ruling elite were manifested in the fact that Warsaw offered a fairly lengthy list of problems it wanted to resolve with the help of Washington in exchange for ABM installations. Apart from military needs, primarily for modernization of regular Polish armed forces and the strengthening of military cooperation, Poland also wanted to address with the Americans some traditional issues, such as eliminating the need for Polish citizens to obtain travel visas and obtaining US assistance in diversifying energy supplies.

Thus, given the barely estimated costs of rapprochement with Washington in terms of such a tricky issue, Warsaw decided to stay on the safe side.

It seems that those observing this discussion from the vantage point of Moscow have been omitting one aspect that could be regarded as positive from the perspective of Poland's European conventionality. Serious debates about an ABM system demonstrated that public opinion toward the United States was changing. According to many experts, the proposal for the ABM project, made in 2002–3, "would meet objections only on the part of a few social groups and some radical political groupings." The ABM agenda paradoxically demonstrated that Poland's European identity recognition was speeding up while romantic Atlanticism was receding. To a considerable degree, this shift occurred due to the influx of funds from various EU structural foundations, agricultural producers' support of general agricultural policy, the large labor migration, and students' and professors' mobility in EU countries.

The nature of the completion (or delaying) of the development of Polish-American relations in terms of the ABM agenda may be estimated differently. On the one hand, Poland demonstrated a significant level of Atlantic loyalty, which would not be forgotten by Washington, regardless of the administration in power. On the other hand, Warsaw, by virtue of prevailing trends in Washington, did not cross the line beyond which differences with the less pro-Atlantic-oriented EU and NATO countries could appear. Yet, Warsaw's readiness to present political opposition to Washington would also be remembered in "moderate" capitals. Paradoxically enough, in the context of the ABM agenda, Poland and Russia started a dialogue on subjects that normally were discussed either with nuclear countries or with NATO's "heavyweight countries."

As far as the author, not being a specialist in the field of military and strategic issues, can judge, Russian officials exposed the presence of a substantial circle of strong experts in these topics. This "exposed resource" will hopefully contribute to better contacts between Warsaw and Moscow in multipartite strategic cooperation.

"Eastern Policy," Russia, and Poland Cooperation in Terms of the EU Agenda

The last few years of the century's first decade have expressly demonstrated that Russia, in its relations with Poland, cannot ignore the European Union context. At the same time, Poland acts more and more insistently and to some purpose as a force having a significant political and economic effect in the region of the "new" Eastern Europe, including the former Soviet European countries. Moreover, according to the conventionalization of internal policy, Warsaw has managed to translate its vision of the "Eastern policy" to the level of the EU in general and to the capital cities of the union's "older" members. It is not by chance that Warsaw became a zealous supporter of the European Union's Eastern policy. The idea had been distilled by the early 1970s in Polish émigré circles, its authors being bright political writers and public men—Juliusz Mieroszewski and Jerzy Giedroyc.

As Sławomir Dębski, a renowned Polish international relations historian, notes, the concept of the Eastern policy is part of "the elite circle of great ideas that changed the fates of people. It contributed to the de-imperialization of Polish thinking on Eastern Europe, abolishing the temptations of retaliation." At the time of its appearance, the concept of an Eastern policy was to a considerable extent an element of the battle of ideas in émigré circles, and, in the intelligentsia milieu of the People's Republic of Poland, "it was solely a concept of the political writer, an intellectual provocation with regard to those who still ignored reality, believing in the 'return to Kresy.'"

In simplified terms, which means more popular interpretations, the concept of an Eastern policy was to a large extent based on the understanding that Poland, having resigned from historical ambitions of sovereignty, was building up equal relations with its neighbors, which helped to balance relations with Russia and even secure itself from some threatening situations. The question of Russia's place in the Eastern policy is always crucial and disputable. There is no consensus of opinion in Poland (or the EU) as to whether Russia is an organic part of it or, rather, some negative point of reference.

It would seem that the goals of the Eastern policy had been achieved in a natural way already by the 1990s, when, as historical developments willed,

Ukraine, Lithuania, and Belarus gained independence (in writings on the Eastern policy concept, they traditionally were abbreviated as ULB) and established quite conventional relations with Poland.

Again, I will take the liberty of a concise quotation from Dębski:

> In the course of time, Mieroszewski's and Giedroyc's conceptions ceased to be a ready-made recipe for Polish policy in relation to Eastern European countries, but they still inspired thinking on its long-term objectives. Under the influence of both EU and NATO membership, they took the form of a political doctrine, which was the basis of policy and activities of subsequent governments and presidents. The doctrine stipulates that sustainable security in Europe will be ensured as a result of the harmonization of public and economic development on the whole continent. In other words, we will reach this goal when all Eastern European countries establish a democratic order arising from public aspirations and when all countries become members of integration institutions encompassing the whole continent.

Clearly, the Eastern policy in postsocialist Poland did not have such a liberal democratic interpretation. Many public forces, more often than not having influence (fortunately, not predominant) on government agencies, understood it to be a renewed Prometheism, that is, a return to the theory and practice of relations with Ukraine and Belorussia popular in the 1920s and early 1930s and based on the maximum extension of Polish influence, for the primary purpose of diminishing Russian influence.

"Compromise" variants of these interpretations are popular, when, voluntarily or not, today's European understanding of the Eastern policy is mixed with historical sentiments or deeply rooted myths. As a rule, the emotional component of such an approach is manifested in politically tense periods.

Paradoxically enough, the presence of such different currents in Poland's Eastern policy aligns it with Russia's policy in relation to former Soviet European countries. Both in retrospect and within present-day political discourse in Russia, we can observe a wide variety of viewpoints. There is a "neodemocratic" aspiration to "get rid of the burden" of union republics, which recur in the "accounting" approach to external policy, as well as in plainly imperial aspirations. Proposals of institutional cooperation frameworks for such countries as Belarus and Ukraine oriented toward Russia are middle of the road. The "larger" Commonwealth of Independent States (CIS) can also be related to them, as well as the narrower formats of the Common Free Market Zone, Customs Union, and Common State.

In proposing such schemes, Moscow is openly supported by the post-Soviet multifaceted resource, because, except for Common State, more than two members are implied in all cases, but it counts mainly on its own forces.

Poland, due to its smaller potential, highlights the key points a little differently. Following the active policy of bilateral contact development in the

1990s, when Poland gained immense political, business, and cultural capital in Ukraine and Belarus, Warsaw realized it would be short of its own resources for maintaining dynamic relations. Poland, not yet an EU member, was trying to westernize its Eastern policy and was ready to its share ideas and experience with Brussels in exchange for EU resources.

Poland's first (and ultimately unsuccessful) attempt to develop Eastern policies for expanding the EU was a document generated by the Polish Ministry of Foreign Affairs. The ministry publicized it in December 2002 as containing proposals concerning "new Eastern neighbors." The policy focused on three countries—Ukraine, Belarus, and Moldova—and contained provisions relating to Russia. Those provisions were clearly more muted, and long-term relations with Moscow were supposed to be less significant than those with countries that might consider entering the EU. In Russia, the efforts of their Polish counterparts from the foreign service were traditionally viewed negatively, as in, "we don't need mediators in relations with the EU." At that point, Warsaw's mediation could not be considered the strongest tool of communication with Brussels. Germany was more likely the stimulus of European neighborhood policy on the EU level. Yet, Moscow did not talk of these topics with Berlin either, until 2008–9, even with all the friendliness of the countries' bilateral relations.

European neighborhood policy in Russia on the official level was perceived neutrally or negatively, whereas, in expert circles, it caused concern by virtue of the fact that the schemes proposed by Moscow were stalled. Above all, this matter concerned the Ukrainian trajectory. The EU had an attractive idea: an eventual membership of neighbors in the EU—a prospering integration alliance that would stimulate post-Soviet countries to choose Europe as their prime associate. In a number of capital cities, most notably in Kiev, the "European choice" was mixed with the "Atlantic choice," too. The belief of many in Moscow was that "aspirations of new independent states for NATO reflects distrust in Russia, as well as doubts in its prospects as a stable and successful state. This gives rise to Russia's countermistrust in candidate countries. Aspirations in the same countries for EU membership reflect the increase of Brussels's economic control over them and the ebbing of Russia's influence in these countries, which has its own economic, cultural, and psychological dimension."

Indeed, in spite of all representations, in many cases quite sincere, specific geopolitical competition in the zone of the "common neighborhood" of both Russia and the EU is one of the "Eastern" motifs: will Russia or Europe attract more neutral countries? "Eastern policy" is perceived by many as a tool of this particular geopolitical competition.

According to the Polish analyst Konrad Szymański, "Despite more and more wide-scale programs of cooperation with the European Union and tumid political plans of neighborhood policy, it is clearly seen that because of Russia's policy in the region, the Eastern part of the EU neighborhood is unstable in terms of not only reliability of democracy, but also political affiliation."

Poland's Eastern policy, as well as the EU's, is, in general, usually caught in a position between understanding Russia as a privileged EU partner and preventing it from gaining an excessive number of privileges, so that it will not obstruct the European prospects of Ukraine, Belarus, and Moldova. In consideration of Belarus's political autocracy in the 1999–2009 period, the relatively small foreign policy benefit and lack of prospects for the government in Chişinău to make a European choice under Pres. Vladimir Voronin, and the evanescence of Transcaucasian prospects, Poland's Eastern policy has in fact become Ukraine's foreign policy. An involuntary and surprising return to the 1918–20s scheme occurred. The Polish scholar Marek A. Cichocki makes the case that "what surprises is the absence of new and fresh strategic impulses in the view of 'Eastern policy,' which contradicts common views on Poland's having special competencies in this issue. . . . Our 'Eastern policy' constantly centers around old schemes and images."

In Russia, the general public also noticed the Polish accent in the EU's Eastern policy, namely, in the course of the "Orange Revolution" in Ukraine, and, by virtue of its predominantly negative perception (without going into detail as to the reason why), it began to be negatively perceived, much as other bright manifestations of Polish activities in the post-Soviet direction began to be perceived negatively. Despite this negative perception of Polish efforts, the general public often did not understand the driving forces behind these actions.

I am convinced that Kwaśniewski's Ukrainian mission can only be compared with Kaczyński's mission to Georgia on purely external grounds.

Similar to each other, and derived from the common root of the late socialist elite, Ukrainian president Leonid Kuchma's and Kwaśniewski's groups had many interests in common, including economic ones, not visible from Moscow but essential for Kiev and Warsaw. In this respect, the mission of Kwaśniewski, who was concerned with stability and changes in Ukraine, was indeed intermediary, not at all a mission of the "Orange messiah." The attempt by another president to repeat the feat during the Georgian events appeared in the guise of farce. It is not by chance that Polish authorities and Polish society virtually split in relation to this issue. This is always the case when actions are driven solely by emotions, disconnected from pragmatic interests or knowledge of the case.

Following Tusk's rise to power, attentive observers noticed that the "Eastern dimension" returned to Poland's foreign policy agenda, too, but it became far more Westernized and balanced. "Particular attention will be paid to relations with Ukraine and Russia, as well as to the situation in Belarus," the prime minister noted in an address upon his appointment to office. Regarding the latter situation, Tusk noted that "convincing all political circles to place bets on democracy will be the objective of Polish policy." The broad and compromiselike nature of this statement is indicative of Warsaw's intention to make a departure from the prospectless orientation solely toward the Belarusian opposition.

Acceptance of the Polish-Swedish proposal, the "Eastern Partnership," in 2008 as the European Union's official initiative became the brightest success of Poland's Eastern policy. The Eastern Partnership became the central political element of the updated European neighborhood policy.

The partnership initiative was the bearer of Warsaw's Eastern priorities, which have become standard fare on the national menu of foreign policy: "A proposal for a deeper integration with the EU must concern all Eastern partners. In the first stage [of integration], it could be used by Ukraine." A reference to Russia in the context of a somewhat clouded Moscow-Warsaw relationship was made in passing and, to a large extent, rather vaguely: "Russia, too, might be covered by projects funded within the framework of the European Neighborhood and Partnership Instrument (ENPI)."

It is obvious that, in case of further implementation of the "Eastern dimension" in exclusively Polish, as well as in European, policy, Poland's government will encounter a higher dynamic of factors independent of Warsaw. This equally concerns all three post-Soviet "sisters" from Eastern Europe, not to mention the Transcaucasian countries. For example, in Ukraine, only events such as severe economic crisis, manifestations of historical nationalism by Pres. Viktor Yushchenko on leaving office, and the coming of a new leader, Viktor Yanukovych, who is unpopular in Warsaw, became those "surprises" that made Poland's political establishment start anew in understanding Eastern policy.

I think it is important for Polish diplomacy to achieve a breakthrough in the Russian direction in particular, which will be a guarantee of success for the whole "Eastern dimension" and a success in the eyes of EU countries. It is important to develop cooperation on European subjects, whether it be the energy sector, visas, general political issues, or others, in particular because of Poland's presidency of the European Union in 2011. Moscow and Warsaw, most probably, must "run through" the whole agenda in advance, in order not to solve problems hastily and extemporaneously.

Obviously, Poland's future presidency will be, more than any other, concentrated on topics dealing with the post-Soviet space. In this respect, it is important for us to begin thinking right now about how to coadapt and bring into focus such dimensions of European policy as the Russia-EU partnership and the "Eastern Partnership."

The number of questions and tasks of Russian-European policy to be posed and resolved in regard to contacts with Poland is quite large. If we think seriously about these questions, and then work toward achieving answers, we will logically come to an understanding that one of the most important and dynamic members of the European system has become Russia's asset.

I will allow myself to quote from the article published in *Nezavisimaya Gazeta* five years ago: "Not only the old greats France, Germany, and Italy should be Russia's active partners in the European policy." The EU has expanded, so the scope of our national counteragents should also be expanded. In Russia's relations with the European Union, forty million people in Poland can play the role of such a "great." This argument becomes increasingly widespread in Russia's foreign policy community.

14

CONTINUITY AND CHANGE

THE MUTUAL PERCEPTIONS OF POLES AND RUSSIANS

Andrzej Grajewski (Poland)

Doctorate in political science, head of the Foreign Department of the weekly *Gość Niedzielny*, member of the Polish-Russian Group on Difficult Matters since 2008.

Nikolai I. Bukharin (Russia)

Leading researcher at the Institute of Economy of the Russian Academy of Sciences.

ANDRZEJ GRAJEWSKI

THE MUTUAL PERCEPTIONS OF POLES AND RUSSIANS

The Burden of Communism

One of the chief factors distinguishing the sociopolitical reality in Russia from that of Poland was the attitude toward coming to terms with the communist system, that is, taking appropriate action or refusing to deal with it. In Poland, the process consisted of the following important stages: the rehabilitation of persons subjected to repressions in the People's Republic of Poland (Polska Rzeczpospolita Ludowa, or PRL) for having sought independent statehood, the transfer to new state institutions of the archives of the former security agencies and the opening of the documents therein, and the introduction of a mandatory examination of the past of public officials to determine whether they had cooperated with the secret political police.

It turned out that, in the process of coming to terms with the past, the rehabilitation of persons repressed for political reasons aroused the least resistance in both Poland and Russia. In July 1991, the Sejm adopted, practically without opposition, a law that permitted the invalidation of sentences passed against persons repressed in the PRL for activity in support of independent statehood, and it created the possibility of compensation for any sustained wrongs. A similar law in Russia did not arouse controversy either and was adopted by the Supreme Soviet in October 1991. The prosecution of Stalinist crimes was initiated in Poland in 1991. That was the result of changes introduced in the functioning of the Commission for the Investigation of Nazi Crimes in Poland, which since 1945 (originally as the Commission for the Investigation of German Crimes in Poland) had been tasked with the prosecution of Nazi crimes. In its new form, the institution was renamed the Commission for the Investigation of Crimes against the Polish Nation and also conducted investigations into crimes committed in the years 1945–56.

Problems with Archives

The opening of the archives of the communist security agencies and the conducting of lustration proved considerably more complicated. The records of the totalitarian state's secret police aroused high emotions and political quarrels after 1989—as, indeed, they had during earlier key junctures in the country's history. This was because whoever controlled them possessed not only knowledge about the past but also powerful documentary weapons for the political infighting at the time. In the early 1990s, the secret police archives in the former German Democratic Republic, or GDR (subsequently, the Federal Republic of Germany, or FRG), and Czechoslovakia were transferred to independent institutions. Those entities were tasked with providing access to documents produced by the security apparatus of the communist state. Procedures were also put in place for the lustration of public officials. Later, similar solutions were introduced in the Baltic States, Hungary, and Romania. Attempts to come to terms with the legacy of the totalitarian state were abandoned in Poland and the post-Soviet space in the early 1990s. This move stemmed from the dominant conviction of the political elite, best reflected by Aleksander Kwaśniewski's 1995 election slogan: "Let us choose the future." That vision was underpinned both by the fears of certain politicians that they might be brought to account for participation in the totalitarian system and by the belief that it was of utmost importance for Poland to muster its forces for fast social and economic modernization, whereas the past would always be divisive.

A comprehensive proposal for the utilization of records assembled in the archives of the Polish security agencies was only put forward in the act on the Institute of National Remembrance (INR). It was intended to give citizens access to the files on them that had been compiled in the past by the security organs of the communist state. The act, prepared by Solidarity Electoral Action and the Freedom Union, was vetoed by President Kwaśniewski. He prepared his own draft law, which envisaged the establishment of a civic archive, accessible to a select group of scholars. The Sejm overturned the veto, but it took another year (i.e., until 2000) to elect Prof. Leon Kieres as the first president of the INR; in 2006, Kieres was replaced by Dr. Janusz Kurtyka.

The Commission for the Prosecution of Crimes against the Polish Nation is a key part of the INR; it is tasked with prosecuting perpetrators of Nazi and communist crimes. Importantly, the act on the INR introduced a definition of communist crimes into Polish jurisprudence. It covers all crimes committed between July 1944 and September 1989, which made it possible to prosecute and bring to justice former security officials and members of the judicial apparatus of the PRL. In 2006, the Vetting Office also became a part of the INR; it verifies the lustration statements of persons employed in professions of public trust and prepares a catalog in which information is disclosed about such persons and former security apparatus officials of the PRL.

The fates of the archives of the former communist security agencies have become a point of departure for discussions not only about history but also about the security of the respective countries that regained their sovereignty after 1989. It was underscored in public debates that the security agencies of the PRL, and similar such agencies in other countries of the Eastern bloc, were subordinated to their Soviet counterparts. In the mid-1980s, the latter began transferring from Eastern Europe to the Soviet Union the most important documents of the local civilian and military security agencies. No records of that operation have been preserved, so we may only assume that the successors to the first chief directorate of the KGB (i.e., the Foreign Intelligence Service) and the Chief Intelligence Directorate (GRU), still possess documents relating to the most important cases and the most valuable operatives, as well as information about the security staff of those countries. Just how effectively such assets can be used is illustrated by some remarkable business and political careers across Eastern Europe—particularly in the energy and banking sectors—of individuals employed in the past by local security agencies or having past contacts with the Soviet agencies.

A corresponding institution did not exist on the Russian side. This led to speculation that the authorities of the Russian Federation intentionally did not want to come to terms with the totalitarian system, which in turn meant that the anti-Soviet resentments in Poland were transferred to the sphere of current Polish-Russian relations. One of the leading Soviet dissidents, Vladimir Bukovsky, criticized Boris Yeltsin's failure to come to terms with communism:

> It was absolutely essential to neutralize the remaining parts of the totalitarian system, including the KGB with its tangled web of agents. . . . Most importantly, it was necessary to publicly discredit and expose the socialist regime, to push it off its pedestal, to demonstrate and prove its crimes, which would have been best done by way of an open trial or a public investigation, with the mass media receiving for publication the relevant documents from CPSU or KGB archives. In other words, it was necessary to do away with the old power structures and establish new ones.

Alas, no one in Russia attempted such a radical break with the previous system, which had been changed not by revolution but through transformation. No social force in Russia wanted to implement such a radical scenario. Let it be noted, however, that it was not more viable in Russia than in any other country of Eastern Europe. Everywhere, change took place gradually, and the forces of the old order long retained considerable political and economic positions.

Problems with Lustration

The vetting of public officials to determine their possible cooperation with the secret political police of the communist state proved to be one of the most difficult and controversial political processes in the Third Republic. Let me add that practically all public opinion polls conducted in Poland since the 1990s have shown majority support for the lustration of public officials and the disclosure of documents produced in the past by the security services of the communist state.

The first attempt to address the problem took the form of a Sejm resolution passed on 28 May 1992. It obligated the minister of internal affairs to reveal the names of members of parliament, senators, and state officials, from the voivodeship level up, who in the years from 1944 to 1990 had collaborated with the Polish Security Office (UB) or the Security Service (SB). Pursuant to the resolution, on 4 June 1982, Minister of Internal Affairs Antoni Macierewicz sent a document containing the names of two high-level state officials to the president, prime minister, the speakers of the Sejm and the Senate, the president of the Supreme Court, and the president of the Constitutional Tribunal. At the same time, the Council of Seniors of the Sejm received a list of sixty-four of its own members, as well as of senators and members of the government whose names had been discovered in Ministry of Internal Affairs archives. When Macierewicz presented the list of persons about whom information had been discovered in the records of the former UB and SB—possibly indicating their collaboration with these institutions—he did not categorically declare that such collaboration had taken place, but to the public the list came to be seen as the names of agents of the communist secret police. The debate over the way Macierewicz had fulfilled the vetting resolution triggered one of the most acute political crises in the history of the Third Republic, leading to the fall of Jan Olszewski's cabinet and permanently polarizing the Polish political scene. Many press articles and several books were published on the subject.

Another attempt to deal with the problem took place on 11 April 1997, when the parliament adopted an act on the disclosure of work or service in state security organs or collaboration with them in the years 1944–90 by persons holding public posts. The act stipulated that persons subject to lustration had to submit lustration statements concerning work and service for or covert cooperation with security agencies of the PRL. The ascertainment of such work, service, or cooperation was to be publicly disclosed. An admission of cooperation with the security organs did not involve sanctions under the law but the concealment of such cooperation, that is, the commission of the so-called "lustration lie," resulted in a ten-year ban on the fulfillment of public functions. The veracity of the lustration statements was to be checked by the official "spokesman for public interest," who represented public interest in lustration proceedings before one of the departments of the Court of Appeals in Warsaw.

In a judgment from 26 October 2005, the Constitutional Tribunal invalidated that model of lustration since it would have given everyone, including former secret collaborators of security agencies, access to the files about them compiled in the past by the secret police. That led to the initiation of work on a new lustration law. The act of 18 October 2006, on the disclosure of information on documents of state security organs from the years 1944–90 and the content of such documents—adopted with the votes of the ruling majority (Law and Justice, Self-Defense, League of Polish Families) and part of the opposition (Civic Platform)—changed the way lustration was conducted. The institution of Spokesman for the Public Interest was replaced by the INR Vetting Office. In doubtful cases, the content of the lustration statements was to be investigated by an independent court. The statements were to be compiled in a special register and published online in the INR public information bulletin. Under the law, some seven hundred thousand citizens were obliged to submit lustration statements. The act set off a stormy debate in the media. Some supporters of lustration, including Sen. Zbigniew Romaszewski and Senate Speaker Bogdan Borusewicz, protested against the provisions of the act. Pres. Lech Kaczyński also had certain doubts; he signed the act into law but initiated work on amending it.

The act, amended by President Kaczyński, did not enter into force since it was blocked by another ruling, dated 11 May 2007, from the Constitutional Tribunal. However, the lustration procedures were retained, along with the obligation to submit lustration statements, though the group of professions whose representatives had to submit the statement was altered. However, it was the lustration of members of the clergy—and not of public officials— that aroused the most animated discussions. The installation of Archbishop Stanisław Wielgus of Warsaw was called off on 7 January 2007, amid charges of his cooperation with the Security Service. Broad discussions also followed the publication of a book by Rev. Tadeusz Isakowicz-Zaleski on the infiltration by the secret police of the Kraków archdiocese.

A Decommunization That Never Happened

The legislation of the Russian Federation does not contain lustration provisions. That situation instilled in the Polish political elite and public opinion the conviction that the RF was largely a continuation of the communist state that had relied on security agencies and the influence of their agents. It is generally believed that that is the reason why Russia has not conducted a lustration, has not opened the archives of the communist security agencies, and has not removed Lenin's mummified body from the mausoleum in Red Square, even though that seemed likely in 1999. The only attempt to give redress to victims of the totalitarian system consisted of an act of 18 October 1991 on the rehabilitation of victims of political repression. The act, besides providing for material assistance to victims of repression, made it possible to prosecute members of the Cheka, GPU-OGPU, NKVD, and the Soviet Ministry of State Security (MGB), as well as prosecutors and judges who had participated in the organization of state terror. In practice, that category of crime has not been subject to prosecution in the Russian Federation. It is noteworthy that work on the act had already begun in Soviet times; in 1987, the Politburo set up a commission to investigate documents connected with Stalinist repressions. The commission conducted its investigations on the basis of documents stored in KGB archives. In 1990, the authorities started giving NKVD victims and their families access to certain documents connected with their cases. However, the perpetrators of the related crimes have not been prosecuted in the RF.

An attempt to delegalize the CPSU after the putsch in August 1991 was also unsuccessful. On 23 August 1991, Pres. Boris Yeltsin issued a decree delegalizing the Communist Party (CPSU) and ordering the seizure of its assets. The next day, Yeltsin signed a decree under which the archives of the KGB and the CPSU were to be transferred to the Russian Federation archives. A breakthrough seemed imminent, particularly since, on 24 August 1991, Mikhail Gorbachev had resigned as secretary-general of the CPSU. Alas, things turned out differently. On 30 November 1993, the Constitutional Tribunal of the RF issued its ruling on the delegalization of the CPSU. The court found most of the provisions of Yeltsin's decrees constitutional, but it also invalidated some of them. In particular, it upheld the ban on activity by the top party bodies but allowed the operation of local party cells. The CPSU assets acquired at the expense of the state were seized, though other property was not confiscated. Ultimately, the Communist Party—operating in Russia under the changed brand of "CPR"—retained its political and organizational power. The members of the State Committee for Martial Law, arrested in 1991, were not brought to justice, either. They started testifying before the Constitutional Tribunal in July 1991. A year later they were released, and the State Duma granted them amnesty in 1994. Yeltsin called the judgment a scandal. These setbacks had serious consequences. They put on hold efforts for a radical settling of accounts, especially since the dramatic social and political situation in Russia undercut Yeltsin's popularity and transferred Russians' sympathies to the resurrected postcommunist Left headed by Gennady Zyuganov.

A plan to grant general access to archive materials of the CPSU and the KGB also failed. Although Yeltsin established an international commission on 24 August 1991 to investigate the activity of the CPSU and the security agencies, granting it limited access to the central CPSU archive, its activity quickly ceased. In late 1991, the Center for the Preservation of Contemporary Documentation opened in Moscow in the former Central Committee building; it was to receive and declassify Communist Party archives. However, on 14 January 1992, President Yeltsin signed the regulation "On the Observance of State Secrets of the Russian Federation," which in practice restored the document confidentiality classifications used in the Soviet Union. In October 1991, the parliament established a commission tasked with transferring the CPSU and KGB archives to the state; it was led by Gen. Dmitry Volkogonov and made little headway.

The fate of party and security agency archives was determined in July 1993, when the parliament adopted an act on the Archive Collections of the Russian Federation. It explicitly determined that all documents relating to state security or foreign intelligence were subject to procedures laid down in acts on the security agencies. Documents could be declassified only after thirty years had elapsed since their creation, and that period could be further extended. The final decision on declassification was to be made by the Interministry Commission for the Protection of State Secrets, acting upon the advice of experts from the security agencies.

The most comprehensive attempt at a legal settling of accounts with the communist system in Russia was made by legislator Galina Starovoitova: at the Third Congress of the Democratic Russia Party, she unveiled a draft law on decommunization and lustration. The congress endorsed her proposal. In December 1992, the Supreme Council of the Russian Federation considered the draft law "On the Prohibition of the Fulfillment of Public Functions by Officials Responsible for Political Repressions." It envisaged a ten-year ban on the holding of public posts by CPSU apparatchiks from the level of secretaries of plant and territorial party branches and by former KGB officers and agents in certain sectors, the executive branch, mass media, security agencies, and higher education. The draft also envisaged a form of lustration to be administered by designated common courts. This draft was not adopted. In 1997, Starovoitova tried to submit a slightly modified version of the legislation to the State Duma but was again unsuccessful, as it was not adopted.

Addressing the Past

In order to clear the ground for dialogue with Russia, it is important to achieve a breakthrough on the outstanding historical issues that impact public opinion, stimulate negative stereotypes, and thus influence political attitudes. The most important political issues that need to be resolved within the realm of Polish-Soviet relations include compensation for Poles who were forced laborers in the Soviet Union and for victims of Stalinist repressions, the recognition of the Poles as a people subjected to repression, access to the 183 volumes of files from the Katyn investigation conducted by the Military Prosecutor's Office of the RF (so that Poland will be able to complete its own investigation into Katyn), and the legal qualification by the RF of the crime committed in Katyn, Kharkov, Starobelsk, and Mednoye as falling within the category of war crimes and crimes against humanity, which are not subject to the statute of limitations.

It is important that the settling of historical accounts should not focus exclusively on negative events. In particular, it would be desirable to honor those Russians who, in the period of Stalinist terror and repressions, demonstrated goodwill toward Poles. Poland should, similar to Israel and its "Righteous among the Nations" medal, establish its own "Righteous in the Inhuman Land" medal—to be awarded to those citizens of the former Soviet Union who in various ways assisted Poles incarcerated in camps and prisons or languishing in exile. Many Poles who experienced detention in Soviet camps recall Russians who helped them, sometimes at great risk to themselves. Thus, we would be able to honor Russians and members of other nationalities who made remarkable demonstrations of their humanity in extreme circumstances, as well as to highlight the distinction between ordinary Russians and *Homo sovieticus,* who ruthlessly enslaved their own people and bear responsibility for the crimes of the totalitarian regime. Moreover, we would be documenting the difference between the Soviet machine of terror, which also mercilessly struck at its own society, and the attitudes of ordinary Russians, who were often friendly toward Poles and willing to help. In the long term, an appropriate cultural policy that incorporated the effective promotion of Polish culture in Russia should allow for changes in many negative stereotypes— which in turn would yield political benefits. Director Andrzej Wajda's film *Katyn* has shown that even the most difficult Polish-Russian issues can be discussed truthfully, while also inducing the parties to reflect on the nature of communist totalitarianism, which victimized both Poles and Russians.

While caring for the final resting places of the Poles who died in Russia, we must be mindful of our own duty to ensure the proper condition of the cemeteries of Soviet soldiers who died while fighting on the territory of the Polish state. They contributed to the liberation of Poland from Nazi occupation. Care for such places is not only the obligation of the Polish state pursuant to a special agreement on the matter but also can be seen as an important gesture to ordinary Russian soldiers and their families, who today live somewhere in Russia and remember that their ancestors lost their lives liberating Poland from Nazi occupation. In this context, let me note how important it would be for the cause of Polish-Soviet reconciliation if the two great Christian churches—the Catholic and the Orthodox—took part in this historic dialogue, lending the matter of accounts-settling an essential moral dimension and enriching it with reflection on the significance of reconciliation and Christian forgiveness.

Policy regarding Historical Events

The tensions in Polish-Russian relations have also been a consequence of the policies pursued by the two states with regard to historical events. In both Poland and Russia, that sphere became an instrument of domestic and international policy, although its subject matter did not relate exclusively to Polish-Soviet relations. Initially, in Poland, the related endeavors were not institutionalized. They were launched by a group of historians, museologists, and political scientists affiliated within the Political Thought Center in Kraków. Their book, *Pamięć i odpowiedzialność* (Memory and responsibility), marked the first comprehensive exposition of the tenets of the new historical policy. In the introduction, the authors argue that the state has a duty to pursue an active and well-reasoned historical policy since "history is not only a subject of internal discussions but also of serious controversies between states and is often exploited in political battles over quite contemporary matters." A motto of sorts for these undertakings was Hannah Arendt's idea that the state is not only a community of well-organized and just endeavors but also a community of organized memory. Polish-Russian accounts-settling was not the only stimulus for these initiatives; Polish-German relations also played a part, as did the great debate concerning the crime committed against Jews who were inhabitants of Jedwabne on 10 July 1941. The latter was triggered by Jan T. Gross's book *Sąsiedzi* (Neighbors) and the results of the investigation concerning the crime, conducted by the INR. The debate continued after Gross published another book on the subject, titled *Strach* (Fear).

The "Jedwabne trauma" changed the Poles' self-perception of having been exclusively victims during World War II and forced them to reflect on situations in which Poles were evildoers. This self-confrontation also applied to Polish-Ukrainian relations—both in the context of the mass murders committed by Ukrainian fascists in Volhynia and eastern Galicia and regarding Polish crimes against Ukrainians living in Poland. Polish-German relations in the context of attempts to rewrite history and apportion blame for the suffering of the German population after World War II constitute a subject that transcends the scope of these deliberations. Particularly objectionable have been efforts to portray Germans as victims and Poles and Russians as perpetrators. This charge applies to new literature, films, and the *Visible Sign* exhibition commemorating the expulsion and flight of Germans from the eastern provinces of the former Reich. In another development, the German Union of Expellees sought to commemorate in Berlin its postwar fates, which in turn provoked a debate on the supposed responsibility of Poles for the hardships of the expelled Germans.

However, it was the establishment in 2004 of the long-awaited Museum of the Warsaw Uprising—at the initiative of the then-president of Poland, Lech Kaczyński—that had the greatest impact on the emergence of Poland's new historical policy. The facility turned out to be a resounding success, not only in museum terms but also as a factor that changed the timbre of the historic debate in Poland. It is noteworthy that the museum was not founded as a result of intentional state policy but as a local initiative, implemented at the grass-roots level, with an enormous input of civic work. The team that founded the museum managed to develop a formula that proved attractive to young people. Soon, the museum started addressing other issues pertaining to Poland's modern history. It was a time when history became an important political instrument and factor legitimizing the rule of a specific political group.

The Museum of the Warsaw Uprising was also significant in the context of Polish-Russian relations: while affirming that, in the military sense, the uprising was directed against the German occupiers, the museum also accentuated its role as an element meant to secure Poland's sovereignty and independence in the face of the advancing Red Army and the actions of so-called Lublin Poland, created by Stalin and subservient to his wishes. That evoked a Russian reaction. On 12 February 2005, the Information Department of the Russian Ministry of Foreign Affairs issued a statement, "Comments in the Polish media concerning the results and consequences of the conference of the Allied powers in the Crimea (Yalta)." According to the Russian Ministry of Foreign Affairs, Poles were rewriting the history of World War II and distorting the truth about the Yalta conference. Some analysts pointed out that the Russian statement had coincided with Poland's involvement in attempts to resolve the political crisis in Ukraine. At about the same time, Russia was preparing for the sixtieth anniversary of the end of World War II, marked in Moscow on 9 May 2005 as a great national holiday. That, in turn, coincided with a clear change of emphasis in the assessment of Stalin's role. State Duma Speaker Boris Grizlov called for "a new appraisal of Stalin's outstanding personality." School curricula underscored that Stalin had been a great leader, while glossing over the topic of Stalinist repression. In this context, discussion was revived on the Ribbentrop-Molotov Pact, and some Russian media (and also Foreign Minister Sergei Lavrov) presented a new political interpretation. Pres. Vladimir Putin displayed greater reserve on the matter: on 10 May 2005, during a press conference at the Kremlin following an EU-Russia summit, he recalled that the 1989 Congress of the People's Deputies of the USSR had denounced the Ribbentrop-Molotov Pact, proclaiming that "it was null and void and did not reflect the opinion of the Soviet people." Putin asked rhetorically, "What more do you want? Should we denounce it every year? We consider the matter closed and will not it raise it again. We've said it once—and that's enough."

ANDRZEJ GRAJEWSKI

President Putin put the finishing touches on that new historical policy in a speech delivered during the main ceremonies in Moscow on 5 May 2005. He highlighted the role of the German and Italian resistance movements but ignored the Poles who had fought against Hitler on all fronts of World War II, as well as shoulder to shoulder with the Red Army and within its ranks. Later that evening, Putin met with German chancellor Gerhard Schroeder. In an address on that occasion, the Russian leader underscored that "antifascists in Germany had been the first victims of the Nazi regime." He also made a symptomatic observation: "We know well that when our nations were building together, European civilization flourished." Alas, any Polish listener would have associated those words with the period of Poland's partitions. It would be hard not to agree at this point with Prof. Adam Daniel Rotfeld, who made the following comment on these developments: "We are witnessing a propaganda attempt at the heroization and instrumentalization of the past for the sake of building a new Russian identity."

Prof. Yuri Afanasyev was right when he noted that, during Putin's presidency, Russia had avoided a radical settling of accounts with the past and instead had committed itself to the reconciliation of its citizens with their own history, which was symbolized by the retention of the old Soviet national anthem, though with new lyrics. Within that vision, communism had brought Russia not only the annihilation of millions of its citizens, repression, and labor camps but also civilizational and economic advancement. During the same period, public opinion in Poland—including most of the political elite—agreed that communism in Eastern Europe, throughout its existence, had been based on force and fear. One of its pillars was the secret police, the role of which rose across Eastern Europe as the system declined. That fact largely determined the debate on accounts-settling in Poland and other East European countries. Such a broad, civic debate did not take place in Russia. It is noteworthy, however, that near the end of his second term, President Putin made a significant gesture toward the communities that had been victimized by the totalitarian regime. On 30 October 2007, he took part in ceremonies marking the Day of Remembrance of the Victims of Political Repressions and declared that Stalinist repressions had been a national tragedy. He added, however, that specific individuals were not to blame for the tragedy, which had been brought on by "an empty ideology" that was given precedence over human rights.

The Polish political elite, with the exception of the Democratic Left Alliance, took the position that a sovereign state had to deal with the burden of that legacy. The effort of settling accounts was made in countries that had decided to build their futures on clear and legible criteria. However, this stance was omitted in countries of the former Soviet Union, with the exception of the Baltic States and Ukraine. This was determined—especially in Russia—

by diverse internal factors. Perhaps the Russian leaders had decided that their society was not mature enough to attempt accounts-settling. That process would have entailed excessive social and political costs and thus would be possible only after a natural change in generations had taken place. Furthermore, it would have been difficult to eradicate by decree the mindset and system of values that had served as the basis of civic education for several generations. These factors are the objective reason for the differences in Poland's and Russia's approaches to the matter of coming to terms with the past. Simultaneously, let it be underscored that this is no "substitute topic," as opponents of accounts-settling seek to banalize the subject. In a historical perspective, one can imagine that future researchers will distinguish clear boundary lines between areas where a thorough coming to terms with the totalitarian past took place and those where such an effort was omitted—with all the systemic, social, and moral consequences of the fact. If one is to concur with Aleksander Smolar that historical policy is an expression of conscious endeavors by politicians to influence collective memory and identity, then the brief review here of the actions taken by the state authorities of Russia and Poland shows that the points of departure in either case consisted of both different interpretations of facts and totally different systems of values. This is likely to constitute a barrier that will continue to be extremely difficult to overcome.

ANDRZEJ GRAJEWSKI

NIKOLAI I. BUKHARIN

THE MUTUAL PERCEPTIONS OF POLES AND RUSSIANS

THE DIFFICULT PROCESSES of the transitional period in Russia and Poland have significantly altered the perceptions each has of the other, as well as of itself. The collapse of the Soviet Union meant a loss of the former national identity for residents of the Russian Federation. Therefore, the emergence of the new Russia in 1992 raised a question about the new identity of Russian society. On the one hand, today's Russia is a new state, while on the other, it is the successor to the thousand years of history of the Russian state that existed in various historical guises. In contrast to the Soviet period, today's new national identity of Russia has a greater number of sources. It is formed on the basis of the history of Kievan Rus, the Russian principalities, the Golden Horde, the Grand Duchy of Moscow, the Russian kingdom, the Russian Empire, and the Soviet Union. Different religions play an important role in shaping that identity, especially Orthodoxy, which has strong Byzantine roots, as well as Islam, Judaism, and Buddhism.

The Russian Orthodox Church (ROC) has claimed the role of the most important factor in the formation of a new identity, and, in the coming decades, this role will obviously increase. In the new historical conditions, the role of the ROC as the traditional religion of the state-forming peoples and their relationship with the government has been restored. The Church again performs the symbolic function of memory and culture for Russian society while it is in search of national identity. The hierarchs of the ROC put forward as the most important task of the Church the establishment of a moral and ideological base that could serve as a foundation for the nation's new identity. Ideological sources of the new Russian identity also come from the traditions of Westernism, Eurasianism, and Slavophilism.

As is well known, during the Russian Empire, Orthodoxy dramatically contrasted itself to Catholicism, which is closely linked with the Polish national origin. In the new Russia, this problem has lost much of its relevance, but the old tradition to some extent can influence the attitude of Russians to Poles and Poland.

An important role in the formation of a new Russian identity is played by the process of the de-Sovietization of society in the course of political and economic reforms. This process was controversial and extremely lengthy. On the one hand, the political and economic system of the country has changed. However, the movement toward a democratic constitutional state is slow. If the Russian Federation is already fairly advanced in the development of a market economy, democratization is quite a long historical process, as the country's democratic traditions are very weak and one cannot demand the immediate introduction of Western standards in this area. Lustration of the Russian elite has not been undertaken. Due to the fact that many of the Soviet elite were associated with the KGB, Boris Yeltsin and his entourage considered it was not worth aggravating the situation because it was difficult in the new Russia, and he refused to conduct a cleansing. As a result, de-Sovietization was inconsistent and left unfinished. The persistence of a postideological consciousness, a prolonged transition to modernization of the new Russia, and the global economic crisis make it difficult to return to this issue.

However, a dispute about a new national identity was quick to appear in post-Soviet Russia. The fight over it is still ongoing. In the early 1990s, the ideological political movement known as Democratic Russia urged a break with the past, both tsarist and communist, and the building of a new Russia from scratch based on the ideals of freedom and human rights. In connection with a post-Soviet ideological vacuum in the 1990s, the government of Boris Yeltsin tried to formulate an idea that would give the country a new identity and cement its people as one nation. However, the attempts to develop a Russian national idea failed.

In recent years, the country has continued the dispute between supporters of following the Russian way and those who favored the choice of developing a closer association with the European identity. That discussion has seen the communists recommend that the path to development would lead to the restoration of the Soviet Union, while the nationalists recommend the revival of the empire (including a tsar), suggesting an inevitable return to an authoritarian or totalitarian regime, which is incompatible with democracy and market economics. Only liberal-democratic intellectuals prefer the Western development path. The failure of the reforms of Russian democrats and the first wave of the global financial and economic crisis in the 2000s caused doubts among a portion of the population about the correctness of this route.

An important key to comprehending Russia's new role is also played by a dispute about what kind of state this country should be: a democracy, an empire, a superpower, or a great power. Communists and nationalists are for restoring the empire or superpower, while the ruling party, United Russia, aims to revive the country as a great power. With regard to the population, most are still nostalgic for imperial greatness and have a postimperial syndrome.

Polls show that 34 percent of Russians consistently supported the need for the revival of Russia's status as a superpower in 2003 and 37 percent felt that way at the end of 2008. The majority of citizens (53 percent) believed that only "modern economic development" could provide the country status as a major power. Up to half of Russians have continued to define themselves as Soviet citizens, that is, citizens of the empire. Russians insist on their peculiarity and uniqueness and are not eager to immediately become part of larger communities—European or global. Nevertheless, there have been clear trends of openness toward the outside world. An increasing number of Russians identify themselves with all of humanity.

Most analysts, both Russian and foreign, tend to believe that the new Russia will be restored as a great power, but in the medium term it will not be a superpower.

Russians have yet to truly realize that Russia is a country radically different from the Soviet Union, that its origin was not due to historical accident but to the objective course of events. It seems that the military-imperial way is a dead end. According to the democratic intellectuals, a great democratic European state, rather than an authoritarian military empire, is the only type of future that offers an optimistic outlook for Russia.

The foregoing suggests that the identity of modern Russia has a complex, eclectic nature. It is ambiguous and contradictory. Different political and social circles appeal to different historical traditions. At the same time, Russia lives by Russian and anti-Russian, Soviet and anti-Soviet, Western and anti-Western rules. The Russian national identity is not a "melting pot" (as is, for example, the identity of the United States), nor is it a "layer cake"; none of the layers of modern Russia is completely rejected. Most likely, it will remain as it is for many years.

The current government does not want to witness new contradictions and splits in Russian society. Therefore, it does not support calls for a clear definition of the nation. As for polls, one of them implies the following: Russia today is most often seen as a successor to the Soviet Union, through which continuity with the empire of the Romanovs is obtained. The pain of the collapse of empire in Russian society gradually recedes. The current uncertainty about Russian national identity affects and will negatively affect Russia's relations with Poland.

The new Russia is still a country that currently has not made serious progress and has little of which to be proud. Russia is not quite successful in its role as an energy power. The implementation of a new, larger project of modernization of the country has been delayed due to the global economic crisis. Therefore, the current government badly needs important historical traditions associated with the legacy of the Russian Empire and/or the Soviet Union.

As we have noted, an important part of national identity consists of historical memory. State, media, political and expert groups, education, and science are involved in its formation and preservation. In Russia, this memory, for quite clear reasons, is multifaceted, and its elements are in tension with each other.

In modern society, politics and history are closely linked. No matter what politicians and historians say, certain historical events and personalities, depending on the current situation, are present in the sociopolitical realm and are used for political purposes. The historical memory is a very extensive and plastic substance. It is always possible to extract historical events and personalities, characters and symbols from the common memory for the needs of the day. In countries experiencing a new milestone, often a normal process of historical research and reevaluation of the past are transformed into ideological campaigns of settling scores with the past.

It is no coincidence that, in recent years, the concept of "historical politics," when history is deliberately used in its current state for political purposes by various political entities and community groups, the politicization of history takes place. Historical politics has begun to occupy an increasingly prominent place in foreign policy in recent years. States increasingly push each other's historical claims, especially when relations are strained. These claims have a negative effect on mutual political relations, making them ideology driven.

The conscious use by the political class of one state of historical grievances caused by a neighboring state for internal and external purposes leads a neighboring state to look for events in the history of mutual relations to strike back at the opposite side. The desire to use some layers of the national memory of one state's own people against a neighbor fuels mutual animosity. The past in the hands of politicians often leads to confrontation rather than a deliverance from the negatives of the past and to cooperation among nations. And when politicians do not stop using such destructive activities, it is difficult to expect normal bilateral relations between neighbors.

Differences in assessments of national history are a reality, and, as such, it is pointless and damaging to paper over that fact. It is not sufficient to simply take the differences for granted; it is necessary to try to understand why the variations exists. In almost all of the diverse images of the past generated by national memory, one can see both people's desire to justify their own actions and a component of historical truth that one side understands implicitly but that is less noticeable to their neighbors. People will never erase from their historical memory what has been associated with loss. Under no circumstance should one try to turn specific features of national memory into a reason for interethnic enmity and interstate conflicts. Every nation should strive to see and understand the images of the past retained in memory by their neighbors and to understand the historical reality behind these images—not to accept, but rather to understand, and not to replace one's own truth of history with foreign truth, but to supplement and enrich it. As with any historical vision, it is unproductive and dangerous nowadays to divide nations into "victims" and "executioners," to assess the past in terms of the "historical guilt" of one over the other. The only way to overcome the growing divide between nations is a free, impartial, and civilized exchange of views on all controversial issues of our common history. In our opinion, the purpose of this exchange is not to eradicate differences but only to learn more about them and to try to understand another's point of view. The only conditions for a dialogue must be a general willingness by the participants to respect the other's point of view, no matter how "wrong" it may seem at first glance, and with a sincere interest in this point of view and a sincere desire to understand it.

The task of Russian and Polish historians is to defend historical truth. We should strive to approach history honestly, without hiding the sins and mistakes of the past. This effort requires access to archives, including departmental ones.

We should not forget that historical memory both separates Russians and Poles and unites them. A different understanding of history is often related to fundamental differences in historical experience and the national consciousness of Russians and Poles. These differences are especially noticeable when it comes to sensitive issues. In particular, Russians and Poles perceive events in their mutual relations in various ways.

Both Russians and Poles remember and interpret the history of the twentieth century in their own way, even though at first they lived in a single empire and later were in the same "socialist community." National memory, in its own way, redesigned and allowed for comprehension of the overall experience. Therefore, Russians and Poles each have their own twentieth century. It is senseless for Russians to ignore the Polish memory, pretending that it does not exist; it is not reasonable to deny its validity, indiscriminately declaring false the facts and interpretations that stand behind it. The Russians have a new way of understanding Poland and Poles, and so do the Poles with regard to Russia and Russians.

It is hardly necessary to offer a reminder that there are elements of a common historical memory for Russians and Poles. During World War II, the peoples of both countries suffered at the hands of the Nazi invaders. We should not forget about the blood jointly spilled in the struggle against Hitlerism or about the large-scale postwar cooperation. Millions of Soviet citizens and hundreds of thousands of Poles languished or died in Stalin's torture chambers and concentration camps or were subjected to deportation.

In the new Russia's historical memory, some of the historical traditions associated with the Russian Empire and related to Poland and the Poles have been revived. These elements of memory are beginning to appear in the modern consciousness of Russians through the historical events of the seventeenth and eighteenth centuries. There is particular interest in the period of the Russian "Time of Troubles" of the seventeenth century. A long-standing negative assessment of the Polish uprisings for national liberation from tsarism in 1794, 1830–31, and 1863–64, because they held an anti-Russian orientation, has partly returned. The history of Russian-Polish relations again starts to be perceived as a struggle for the existence of the Russian state and as competition between countries for influence in Eastern Europe.

At the end of 2004, a new national holiday in the Russian Federation was established—the Day of National Unity. It is celebrated on 4 November in memory of the "liberation of Moscow from Polish-Lithuanian invaders" in 1612, by troops of a militia led by Kuzma Minin and Dmitry Pozharsky. There were concerns in Poland that the holiday in Russia would lead to a rise in anti-Polish mood and strengthen a negative stereotype of Poles in the mass consciousness of Russians. However, the first and subsequent celebrations of the 4 November holiday showed that it has not turned into an anti-Polish campaign. A sociological survey conducted in October 2009 by the All-Russian Center for Public Opinion Research (VCIOM) shows that half of Russians (51 percent) did not know what kind of holiday was being celebrated in the country on 4 November. Only 16 percent of respondents were able to recall its correct name. We can assume that artificially assembled national and historical traditions (as opposed to Soviet historical traditions, e.g., 7 November), backed by new knowledge and experience, will gradually return.

Unfortunately, in both countries, textbooks and movies that popularize individual fragments of historical memory try to draw attention to confrontational episodes in Russian and Polish history. Russian textbooks currently interpret history from the perspective of the victorious countries, while Polish textbooks portray a number of periods in the history of Poland when it was a victim of Russia, then acting as invader and executioner. Poland in the nineteenth and twentieth centuries is invariably portrayed as a victim of Russia and Germany and sometimes even as a victim of the United States because of the "betrayal" at Yalta. In Russia, there are community groups willing to distort facts in the history of Soviet-Polish relations in order to present an image of the Poles as enemies.

In attempting to inculcate a feeling of national identity among Russian youth, historical films, such as *1612* (directed by Vladimir Khotinenko) and especially *Taras Bulba* (directed by Vladimir Bortko), created on political orders, began to feature a particular character type. Bortko described the Polish theme of the film: "As for the Poles, well, do not worry—let bygones be bygones. It's not a secret that they have their own point of view on events, and we have another. I'm glad we are not fighting today." In another interview, Bortko, while discussing the hostility of the Russians and Polish, explained the significance of his position in the following manner: "The Russians and the Poles are relatives—at least because they are Slavs. But we belong to different confessions, and this is very serious along the line Poland-Russia runs—the boundary between two worlds—the Eastern Orthodox and Western Catholic." Such an excessively expressive film would undoubtedly have an adverse impact on the attitude of Russian youth toward Poland and Poles.

However, the modern historical consciousness of Russians is not as intense as that of the Poles. The two nations have different historical experiences: the Poles in the late twentieth century had a more bitter view than did the Russians because of major historical grievances against the Russian Empire and Soviet Union arising over the last two centuries.

The peculiarity of the Russian historical consciousness consists of the fact that no state mechanism for reproducing this consciousness exists. The mass historical consciousness is concentrated on the major themes of Soviet history. The main historical events are the October Revolution, the Great Patriotic War, and space exploration. Sometimes even World War I is mentioned, but everything else escapes from that memory to the mythological space. The Soviet Union was a great superpower. The entire pantheon of the country's history is mythologically heroic.

Beginning in 2003, Russians identified Vladimir Putin as one of the ten most significant historical figures; by 2008, he was already in the top five. At the same time, Vladimir Lenin is fading, while Aleksandr Pushkin and Joseph Stalin are rising (in 1989, Stalin was not in the top ten, but, by 2008, he was among the top three).

In the collective consciousness, the image people held of their country was of a peaceful, gentle, patient sufferer, whose existence was exposed to a variety of internal dangers and external threats. On the whole, national history appears to be a regular endurance exercise, one of struggle, sacrifice, and resistance to the enemy. Salvation and transformation of the country into one of the most powerful nations on earth is possible only through a strong and purposeful government, uniting and guiding the amorphous and passive mass of the population.

Russians know relatively little of the history of Russian-Polish relations. In January 2005, a poll conducted by the Public Opinion Foundation showed that the majority of the population (54 percent) did not know anything about the Katyn crime—the mass execution of Polish prisoners of war in 1940; only 16 percent of respondents said that they knew about it, while 24 percent said they had heard something about it and 6 percent were unsure. When respondents were asked whether Vladimir Putin should offer an official apology for the offense, one-third (33 percent) said he should, 35 percent stated he should not, while 32 percent were undecided. Among those who believed that an apology was needed, based in general on their opinion that the Russians are historically responsible for the actions taken by the country in the past (11 percent of all respondents), 6 percent of all respondents said it was necessary, given the gravity of the crime and the benefits of an apology for the further development of Russian-Polish relations. To the question asked by the Levada Center in July 2009—"Did you know that, in September 1939, Red Army troops entered Poland, which fought against Nazi Germany and the occupied territories specified in the secret Molotov-Ribbentrop plan?"—16 percent of respondents answered "yes" while 61 percent answered "no."

In the collective historical memory of the Russians, the victory in the Great Patriotic War of 1941–45 holds the most prominent position. According to a survey conducted in July 2008, it was the Great Patriotic War that the Russians considered the most outstanding event of the last century. It is also recognized as the most tragic event in modern history. The victory in World War II is thus an important element of Russian identity. When it is questioned or even put under discussion, Russians feel offended.

The victory over Nazism is treated as a major legacy of Soviet times, and often the only positive one, so it becomes useful in the effort to consolidate Russian society. At the same time, it allows one to move the crimes of Stalin to the background.

On 27 January 2009, in the opening speech at a meeting of the Russian Organizing Committee of "Victory," which was working to commemorate the defeat of the Nazis, Russian president Dmitry Medvedev stressed that "the legacy of Victory is not just our memories, it's our history. This is a powerful moral resource of our state. The historical truth about the war, the lessons of the war, the link with the present are also of paramount importance." He spoke out against the distortion of the truth about the war, about the indisputable and decisive contribution the Red Army and the Soviet Union made to the defeat of Nazism and the liberation of Europe, and the subsequent influence of the victory on the development of world historical processes. A commission on countering attempts to falsify history to the detriment of Russian interests was established under the Russian Federation president in May 2009. Thanks to the victory of the Soviet Union and its allies in World War II, the genocide of the nations planned by the Nazis was prevented. Those nations have preserved their identity. In some countries, there are attempts to make anti-Russian sentiment a component of the national identity by demonizing the Soviet Union's role in the war.

Russians strongly oppose attempts to falsify the history of World War II, primarily efforts to distort the role of the Soviet Union in defeating Nazi Germany. Attempts to equate the Soviet Union and Nazi Germany are considered attempts to equate the victims and the executioners. In Russia, people find the attempts of certain politicians to "put the Nazi occupation and liberation mission of the Red Army in one row, blasphemous." Russia and Russians are very sensitive to cases of desecration, destruction, or transfer of monuments and graves of Soviet soldiers who died during the liberation of the Baltic countries and Central and Eastern Europe. Totalitarian symbols on these monuments are rejected by part of Polish society.

In February 2009, the head of the Ministry for Emergency Situations, Sergey Shoigu, proposed adopting a law that made it a crime to deny Soviet victory in World War II. Opponents of the proposal correctly noted that the evaluation of historical events may not be subject to criminal penalties. As a result, the United Russia Party refused to adopt any such law. However, in April 2009, Shoigu again proposed introducing criminal liability for misrepresentation and failure to recognize the history of the Soviet victory in World War II.

The Russian government elite has increasingly recognized the continuity of Soviet and Russian foreign policy. Therefore, it seems that a radical revision of estimates of Soviet foreign policy will not be coming very soon. This is especially true for the period just prior to World War II, during the war itself, or immediately after its end. This is evidenced by the debate about the causes and lessons of the war that unfolded in Russia in the summer and autumn of 2009. The defenders of Soviet policy in the period preceding the World War II, primarily referring to the Molotov-Ribbentrop Pact, dominated the discussion. The justification of Stalin's foreign policy mistakes was concealed behind this approach. A very controversial film about the causes of World War II, *Mystery of the Secret Protocols,* shown by the state television channel Vesti and supported by two government-related funds, Historical Memory and Historical Perspective, announced the second Rzeczpospolita to have been an ally of the Third Reich and that together the two were planning the division of the Soviet Union.

Prime Minister Putin, in an article published in *Gazeta Wyborcza* in connection with his visit to Poland and in a speech on 1 September 2009 at Westerplatte, said that Russia had long ago denounced the Molotov-Ribbentrop Pact (Putin himself called it immoral) and that he expected other countries' decision makers to recognize improper treaties made with the Nazis on the eve of World War II. The Russian prime minister called all attempts to appease the Nazis immoral and noted that it was the totality of these actions that led to the outbreak of World War II. Putin has managed to find a way to point out that moral condemnation of the Molotov-Ribbentrop Pact and the Katyn crime does not mean that the responsibility for them is assigned to present-day Russia.

Modern-day official Russia has opposed and will continue to oppose any attempts to impose responsibility for the outbreak of World War II on the Soviet Union, any interpretations of Nazism and communism as being equally evil, or any arguments that equate the German occupation with the liberation mission of the Soviet Union. Such estimates are offensive not only to veterans but to all Russians, especially those whose families suffered under Stalin's government. However, today's Russia also cannot accept all the sins of the Soviet past.

Russian democrats are opposed to the excessive mythologizing of World War II. They argue that "for the Soviet system, the war really ended in victory because it [had] been preserved and spread to Eastern Europe. And for the nations of our country, it's too cynical to talk about the victory. Such victory is more like a tragedy. After all, the saved system for half a century continued to torture and terrorize its own citizens." However, these statements are not currently finding support among the majority of Russian society.

The memory of World War II both unites and divides Russians and Poles. On the one hand, the Soviet Union and Poland were allies in the anti-Hitler coalition. On the other, the prewar Polish political elite lost twice to Nazi Germany, once in September 1939 and again in August 1944, when it lost the struggle for power in Poland to the leftist forces of the country, which supported the Soviet Union. The elite of "post-Solidarity" Poland has its historical roots in the prewar elite that was defeated. Therefore, the former opposition elite and historians oriented to it tend to believe that Poland lost World War II, and the country's liberation by the Red Army is now referred to as having been a new occupation.

Positive memories of the Soviet Union are deeply embedded in the historical consciousness of Russians. The Soviet Union existed for about seventy years, and it was—in a bipolar world—a period of maximum power of Russia. Therefore, the disintegration of the Soviet Union was and remains a profound historical trauma for Russians. In a message to the Federal Assembly of the Russian Federation in April 2005, Putin said that "the collapse of the Soviet Union was the greatest geopolitical catastrophe" of the twentieth century. Therefore, in the new Russia, the umbilical cord that connects it with the Soviet past cannot be completely cut. A number of "Soviet" elements became part of the new Russian identity. Not by accident, in 2008, during voting for the official "Name of Russia," Alexander Nevsky, Grand Duke and a saint of the Russian Orthodox Church, took first place, but the declared winners were Joseph Stalin and Vladimir Lenin.

However, in the end, from a sociological point of view, there are very few events that are understood as having value in Russia's historical memory of the Soviet period. According to a poll by the All-Russian Center for Public Opinion Research (VCIOM) in early 2007, respondents identified the exploits of the heroes of World War II, the space flight of Yuri Gagarin, and the launch of the Sputnik satellite as events of the Soviet period to be proud of even today.

In Russia, there is no such thing as a renunciation of Soviet history, as has happened in some former Soviet republics after they became independent states. In Russia, the history of the Soviet Union has been updated and is presented in accordance with the requirements of modern times. The revision of views about Soviet history is gradual.

In modern Russia, as a rule, memorials, monuments, and commemorative plaques associated with the Soviet period remain untouched. New and old symbols of the state often coexist on public buildings. But recently, society has begun to fight about these Soviet symbols. Discussions about Lenin's mausoleum and the burial of his body have become antagonistic. Representatives of local authorities are beginning to raise the issue of getting rid of the monuments of the previous epoch. However, as evidenced by the results of a survey by VCIOM in November 2008, the majority (65 percent) of Russians consider it feasible or even necessary to retain as part of their history the symbols of communism, particularly the names of streets and squares, monuments, pictures of the hammer and sickle, and so forth.

The Soviet Union was a totalitarian, excessively centralized state that limited various rights and freedoms, including the freedoms of the states that were part of the Soviet bloc. Soviet totalitarianism did not arise by accident or from scratch. It was based on centuries-old traditions of great-power monarchical, autocratic rule. After the Bolsheviks came to power, the protracted civil war contributed to the preservation of totalitarianism. It also emerged for other objective reasons, including the need for rapid modernization in the 1930s, undertaken using mass mobilization techniques. Therefore, it is not easy to overcome the legacy of totalitarianism.

Totalitarianism and Stalin's regime were concepts of the same order in the Soviet Union. The constituent parts of that regime were neglect of the human personality, state violence, and mass repression. The repression affected not only Soviet citizens and nations but also foreigners. Hundreds of thousands of Poles were among the victims.

In recent years, a campaign to glorify Stalin has been observed in certain circles of Russian society. He is represented as a great statesman, a modernizer, and an "effective manager" who gave a heroic identity to Soviet society, and his reputation is covered with a halo of glory, triumph, and pride for the country's achievements. Some of the conservatives associated with the ruling United Russia Party openly call for the use of Stalinist-type modernization, without its kinks and victims. For many ordinary citizens, frustrated by the not entirely successful attempt at democratic reconstruction of the country and the introduction of a market economy, Stalin's times seem like a model of "order in the state and efficiency in the economy." In addition, Stalin's mythology is closely linked with symbols of both great power and victory. More than half of Russians sympathized with Stalin in 2008. The current government, implicitly supporting the statist and leadership discourse with respect to Stalin's personality, does not transmit clear signals. It should be noted that President Medvedev said in his video blog on 30 October 2009 that "it is important to not allow, in the guise of restoring historical justice, the justifying of those who destroyed his people. No development of the country, none of her achievements [or] ambitions can be achieved by the cost of human suffering and loss."

Stalin and Stalinism are still in need of an objective historical assessment. Among democratic intellectuals in recent years, there is concern that Russia has intensified the hushing up and even justification of Stalin's crimes. Arseny Roginsky, chair of the human-rights organization Memorial, believes that the memory of Stalinism in Russia is the memory of the victims, for whom monuments are erected in various locations, not of the crimes of Stalin's regime. For a country that has experienced totalitarianism, the refusal to recognize and condemn the crimes of the past is dangerous and can lead to a repetition of the tragedy.

The debate in Russian society about the legacy of the Stalinist regime and its crimes has proceeded very sluggishly. Only democrats show specific activity.

In February 2009, the Political Committee of the Yabloko Party adopted a "program for overcoming Bolshevism, Stalinism, and nationalism in political practice and social consciousness." This program offers to give a "clear and unambiguous legal, political, and moral assessment of the violent seizure of power committed by the Bolsheviks in 1917–1918, the nature and value of the political regime created by them, and its follow-up," and to equate "the justification and denial of the mass repressions [and] action on the destruction of social groups and nations to a criminal offense."

The initiative by Yabloko was supported by the Right Cause Party, which in March 2009 stated that the introduction of criminal liability for the justification of extremism would strike a blow at Stalinism: "It is time once and for all to recognize [Stalin as] creator of the anti-humanism regime and to admit in front of the whole country and the whole world his guilt for the genocide of his people, to make an irreversible choice in favor of civilized development."

Memorial, also known as the International Human Rights Historical and Educational Charitable Society, plays an important role in preserving the memory of the victims of Soviet state terror, including Poles, in the history of repression. The group's chair, Roginsky, speaking at the Day of Remembrance of Victims of Political Repression on 30 October 2009, said that "'de-Stalinization' is the most urgent problem of modern Russia. I can't find anything as important. It is crucial to the construction of a normal future." In 2008–9, Memorial helped several Polish citizens achieve a judicial order of rehabilitation for relatives who had been executed by shooting in 1940.

However, the problem of a moral and political assessment of Stalin's crimes, and the guilt for those crimes, remains. It should be recalled that, in the late 1980s and early 1990s, when the opportunity presented itself to speak the truth about the terrible events of the past, the official Russian approach to the issue of guilt for Stalin's crimes against foreigners was formulated by Boris Yeltsin. In a joint statement at the signing by the presidents of Russia and Poland (Yeltsin and Lech Wałęsa) of the Treaty on Friendly and Good Neighborly Cooperation in the spring of 1992, it was mentioned in particular that the "parties recognize that the Stalinist regime has caused enormous suffering and caused irreparable damage to the nations of Russia and Poland." In an interview with Polish television on 17 October 1992, Yeltsin said, "Russia cannot accept responsibility for the Katyn crime. It was done by the Party, it was done by totalitarianism."

The current Russian government, and the historians and political scientists related to it, do not want Russia, as the successor, to a certain extent, of the totalitarian regime, constantly repenting for the crimes of the past regime. Despite the fact that the Soviet Union, in contrast to Germany, was a victorious power and the new Russia is the successor of that state, in June 2007, Putin said, "We cannot afford to impose a sense of guilt on us." The Russian elite shares the view that nations, as well as individuals, cannot live a full life with an inescapable sense of guilt. Therefore, any new versions of history should make this feeling go away. In 2009, the country's leaders, Medvedev and Putin, came out with a moral condemnation of certain aspects of Stalin's foreign policy and repression.

Russian society is reacting to the issue of the crimes of Stalin's regime in several ways—with condemnations of the crimes or denial. Some are calling for a "trial of communism." Others believe that today's Russia is a new state and does not bear guilt for the crimes of Stalin. Some external forces are still trying to impose on modern Russia a sense of historical guilt for the sins of Stalin's totalitarianism. The paradox is that, although the Soviet Union disappeared, russophobia outside of Russia grew larger in scale, amplified by the relative weakness of present-day Russia. According to the political analyst Gleb Pavlovsky, there are attempts to turn Russians into twenty-first-century Jews. According to the "imperial" weekly journal *Tomorrow,* "The continuing calls to repentance" for a criminal Soviet past "will automatically make us heirs" of the criminal regime, "which is very demoralizing to society." The piece also charged that there were calls for a new version of the postwar Nuremberg Tribunal.

It is probably right and proper to call for a broad public debate on this subject, in order to dot the "i" and cross the "t" in this matter and to find a just moral and political decision. It should be remembered that Soviet totalitarianism caused damage not only to Soviet citizens but also to the Poles and people of other nations.

So, for example, not only Poles but also Russians should be aware of the tragic pages in the history of Soviet-Polish relations. We cannot leave the victims of the Katyn crime to reside only in the memory of the Poles. It is also part of the memory of Russians. Along with official Polish representatives, Russian officials of comparable rank should participate in public events commemorating the Polish prisoners—victims of Stalinist repression—every year in April at the Katyn Memorial and the Memorial Complex at Mednoye.

Russian officials should take a clear position on attempts by certain Russian circles to revise the official Russian view of Katyn as a crime committed by the NKVD on the order of top Soviet leaders and to once again put the blame solely on the Nazis.

Russia, which has a historical problem in relations with its neighbors, should try to build a new relationship with them based on respect, kindness, tolerance, neighborliness, and cooperation in all spheres. Thus, sooner or later, the attitude toward Russia and the Russians will steadily get better.

In the 1990s, the interest of Russians in Poland and the Poles, though reduced, still remained significant. The Russian elite were interested in the Polish experience of transitioning to a market economy. As Sergey Stankevich, advisor to President Yeltsin, wrote, Poland was for Russia an object of imitation, an example of a "true reformist." Some Russian business leaders acquired their first professional experience dealing with Polish partners. At that time, tens of thousands of Russian "shuttle traders" were able to get acquainted with domestic Polish culture.

In the second half of the 1990s, the interest of Russians in Poles in Poland decreased sharply. After the establishment of direct contacts between Russia and the West, the "new Russia" become allergic to Eastern Europe and treated it like something of only secondary importance. As a reader of the website inoSMI commented there, "Poland, from a close country in the previous period, has become a country on the edge of consciousness, somewhere far away in the West."

The perception of Poles as friends has changed as a result of the unexpected realization that the Poles were enemies in the past, and Poles now refer to Russia with hostility. Russophobia in Poland has caused alienation of the Poles and Poland among some Russian intellectuals.

The Russians did develop a feeling of superiority over the Poles over the 1990 to 2010 period, since the beginning of the changes, but Poland is not and was not treated as a danger and threat. However, in recent years, Poland has seemed to guide the foreign policy interests of the United States, and Polish politicians and media in their approach to Russia are seen as projecting a double standard.

What is the image of a Pole in the minds of contemporary Russians? A survey conducted in October 2001 by the Public Opinion Foundation (POF) shows that Russians see similarities between the two nations in terms of racial and ethnic relations (Slavs, white), language, character (among the positive qualities that stand out are "sincerity," "kindness," "hardworking," "generous spirit," "simplicity," "hospitality," "peace loving," "naïvety"), a common history, one religion (Christianity), accommodation in Europe, and so forth. Russians and Poles differ from each other by language, religion (Russians are Orthodox; Poles, Catholic), traits of national character, culture and customs, and national traditions. As for the traits of national character, the Poles are characterized as having greater activity, entrepreneurial spirit, solidarity, and good organization. At the same time, Poles are referred to as tricky, secretive, and intolerant, unlike Russians. Some of the respondents believe that Poles have a different "approach to life" than Russians and that "they are closer to Western psychology" and so have "a more capitalistic way of thinking" and "more attraction to private property[;] they are more free." "Poles are closer to the West," they are "more civilized" than the Russians, more educated, "more cultured," and have a higher "culture of production." This poll seems to indicate that Russia is the one nation in Europe that understands the Poles better than the others.

Russians' characterizations of Poland, mainly inherited from the recent socialist decades, were revealed in a sociological survey conducted by the Public Opinion Foundation in August 2005. In it, Russians associated Poland with the television series *Four Tank-Men and a Dog,* the city of Kraków, sausage, and Moda Polska (meaning Polish fashion), which is a chain of shops. At the time of the survey, only 4 percent of Russians associated Poland with Solidarity.

According to the same survey, the people who came to mind when Russians thought of Poland were two popular singers, Anna German and Edyta Piecha (47 and 45 percent of respondents named them). Coming in well behind those performers were individuals directly related to culture and science: Barbara Brylska, Frédéric Chopin, and Mikołaj Kopernik (Nicolaus Copernicus) (altogether, these were named by 19 to 22 percent of respondents). Another 16 percent responded that they associated Poland with Pope John Paul II. Modern Polish political leaders, such as Wałęsa, Wojciech Jaruzelski, and Aleksander Kwaśniewski, are mentioned by Russians less frequently (8–14 percent).

If the opinion polls conducted in Russia at the beginning of the twenty-first century testify that Russians had few prejudices and antipathies toward Poles, then later surveys showed that the alienation of Russians with respect to Poles and Poland has slightly increased. A good attitude toward Poland during the Soviet era has carried over and slowed this process of alienation among Russians. This attitude is gradually changing, but it is not hostile. Sociological surveys conducted by POF from October 2001 to December 2006 showed that the number of respondents who believed that Poland was friendly toward Russia decreased from 57 to 30 percent. Accordingly, the number of Russians who believed that Poland was an unfriendly state had grown from 25 to 38 percent. On the question, "If you compare your attitude toward Poland in the past and now, which of these sentences most closely matches your view?" 40 percent of respondents said Russians have treated Poland well in the past and treat it well today, while only 10 percent of Russians believed their country treated Poland badly.

According to a sociological survey on the attitude of Russians toward different countries, conducted by VCIOM in April 2008, 2 percent of respondents considered Poland to be a friend of Russia, while 5 percent considered it to be an enemy. Sociological probing conducted in June 2009 by the Levada Center showed that 2 percent of Russians considered Poland to be a friend of Russia, and 10 percent considered it an enemy.

Case studies conducted by Russian and Polish sociologists from 1998 to 2002 show that negative stereotypes about Russia in Polish society are part of the European identity promoted by the ruling elites. In the minds of the Russians, Poles look like "squires" of aggressive Western policies, encroaching on Russia's interests. As a general rule, and this is conclusively shown by the results of the study, the ethnopolitical myths of each of the parties have little in common with reality.

The identity associated with the state remains significant for Russians, while the Polish one grows out of national and cultural traditions. The past dominates the present and leads to the fact that the Poles' national identity is in a state of mobilization, as if the threat to this identity exists to this day. However, this identity is manifested "softly," along with an openness to the outside world. Polish colleagues who participated in the study agreed that the Russian public mind is more open to ethnic and cultural variability; it looks more modern than the more hermetic identity of the Poles. However, after joining the EU, the Poles have overcome their hermetism.

Russians and Poles have different identities; they evaluate their past and see their future differently. However, these differing natures should not be an obstacle for developing neighborly relations between the countries. A constant dialogue between the societies and historians of Russia and Poland is necessary. Russian and, above all, Polish politicians have to decide whether to face an uneasy future that awaits us all in the coming years and whether to continue to highlight the historical memory of the events that divided us and now are sowing enmity and preventing the development of cooperation. In order to find a solution to or alleviate these problems whose sources lie in the difficult history of mutual relations, it is important to the path of understanding of Russians and Poles that the development of Russian-Polish relations be based on the principles of neighborliness and partnership.

15

HERITAGE IN ARCHIVES

DISPLACED COLLECTIONS AND ACCESS TO ARCHIVES

Władysław Stępniak (Poland)

General director of the State Archives, professor at the Institute of History and Archives, Mikołaj Kopernik University in Torun, member of the Polish-Russian Group on Difficult Matters since 2008.

Vladimir P. Kozlov (Russia)

Professor and member of the Russian Academy of Sciences.

WŁADYSŁAW STĘPNIAK

DISPLACED COLLECTIONS AND ACCESS TO ARCHIVES

THE SOVIET UNION established a framework for its relations with Poland after World War II with respect only to problems it considered important, while disregarding its partner's sovereignty with respect to resolving those problems. The list of issues regulated by international accords did not include the status of archive materials, even though changes under the border agreement of 16 August 1945, imposed on Poland, and the mass transfer of collections during World War II created a situation that demanded solutions through international law. That is why, after the Polish transformation of 1989, the problem of cultural property was assigned high priority. Since the Soviet side appeared receptive to Polish overtures in this area, on 25 May 1990, Foreign Minister Krzysztof Skubiszewski and Minister of Culture and Art Izabella Cywińska appointed the Polish members of the Polish-Soviet Commission on Archival Heritage, set up for the purpose of "addressing certain problems relating to cultural heritage, particularly the return . . . of [and restitution for] Polish cultural property. The Polish side will strive to recover national mementos and cultural property essential to Polish science and culture and possessing special symbolic significance for the Polish people." However, the commission never held any plenary sessions. The clear signs that the Soviet Union was disintegrating induced the Polish side to refrain from conducting such meetings, even though Moscow was sending encouraging signals that many problems could be resolved. Still, work conducted at that time led to the compilation of documentation related to archive materials that once were of Polish territorial provenance but had been held in the Soviet Union. In November 1989, the Polish Historical Society took a stand on the matter: it issued two memorandums concerning the return of Polish archive materials and access to such materials in Soviet collections.

The disintegration of the Soviet Union and Pres. Boris Yeltsin's decision to grant the Polish side access to the Katyn documentation invigorated contacts and cooperation between the state archives of the two countries. An agreement on cooperation between the Head Office of State Archives (HOSA) and the State Committee on Archives of the Government of the Russian Federation was signed on 27 April 1992. As for the issue of the return of cultural properties and access to Russian archives, the provisions contained in several points should be particularly noted: points 2 ("Search for documents on the history of the partner country and exchange of copies"), 4 ("Assistance to researchers in using collections and guarantee of access to finding aids"), and 6 ("Parties have agreed that archival documents constituting the property of the other side shall be returned to their rightful owner. The return of such materials shall take place in line with mutual arrangements").

In addition to signing that agreement, the parties signed a special protocol and a memorandum that detailed the form and scope of the mutual obligations. It was decided to establish a group of experts (three persons per side) to monitor any problems with cooperation. Point 2 of the memorandum was of historic significance: it provided for joint work on the publication of Katyn-related documents.

The Head Office of State Archives treated these provisions with all seriousness and took various steps to implement them. The Russian side, however, was not fulfilling its commitments concerning the return of cultural goods and archives. The Russians advised HOSA that matters relating to the return of collections could be settled only through diplomatic channels. As a result, the joint group of experts was not established and no actions envisioned under the agreement were implemented. Polish authorities repeatedly communicated with their Russian counterparts on these issues, as evidenced by several volumes of correspondence, diplomatic notes, and minutes of talks conducted by politicians (the presidents of Poland and the Russian Federation also became involved), diplomats, and HOSA representatives. On 13 January 1992, Lech Wałęsa wrote to Boris Yeltsin, "You, Mister President, and I are opening a new era in Poland's relations with Russia. I believe that the return to Poland of all our archival materials stored at the Special Archive would affirm the breakthrough taking place in our relations. Thus, I am asking you kindly to cause the return of these records to Poland." Wałęsa also asked Yeltsin to grant the Polish side access to archival materials concerning Polish prisoners of war. The letter opened the way for the disclosure of documents connected with Katyn but had no positive impact on the matter of restitution.

Still, a Polish military archival mission was allowed to begin its activity in Russia. Its greatest achievement consisted of bringing to Poland numerous copies of documents concerning Polish soldiers and repression against Poles in the Soviet Union during World War II. Yet, the Russians refused to budge on returning the collections. In 1994, Poland—aware that France had benefited from an agreement with Russia on the return of archival documents—started weighing the conclusion of a similar intergovernmental treaty. However, the Russian parliament put a freeze on all moves connected with returning the cultural property and archives: the MPs had decided that cultural property transferred to Russian territory in connection with World War II now constituted its property as *sui generis* substitute compensation for the destruction of Russian institutions and their cultural assets, including archival materials.

Under those circumstances, all diplomatic representations proved futile. This happened even though Rosarkhiv (the head board of the Russian state archives), in its contacts with the Polish side and opinions conveyed to the government Commission for the Restitution of Cultural Property, endorsed the request by the Polish archives to return archival materials displaced in connection with World War II. Russian officials insisted that Polish representation would be considered in line with the act of 5 February 1997, on cultural property transferred to the Soviet Union as a result of World War II and now stored in the territory of the Russian Federation. The act was subsequently amended.

The act was incompatible with international law—something that provoked criticism in other countries. President Yeltsin was also against its provisions and challenged it in the Constitutional Court of the Russian Federation. The court found the act unconstitutional in the part dealing with cultural property, including archival materials from the collections of allied states. Such items could not be treated as substitute compensation for assets lost by the Soviet Union during the war.

Despite an amendment introduced on 20 May 2000, in accordance with the Constitutional Court's ruling, the act still raised serious reservations among all the states that had been allies of the Soviet Union during World War II and had parts of their cultural property removed by the Red Army. Poland also took the position that there was no basis for adhering to Russian domestic law on matters regulated by international public law. Furthermore, it was noted that the provisions of the amended act obligated countries seeking the return of their cultural property to pay compensation to Russia for storage, conservation, and the processing of cultural property looted in the past and held for decades without the possibility of access.

Thus, in these circumstances, the most challenging problem in the cooperation between the Polish and Russian archives is the return of Polish archival materials that, due to historical developments, are today stored in Russian collections. Over the past three centuries, Poland's relations with Russia and, subsequently, with the Soviet Union were replete with situations that resulted in transfers and changes of ownership of archival materials. The partitions of Poland caused unprecedented fragmentation and transfers of the archival assets of a state that for centuries had been a European power. The period of the deprivation of independence involved numerous successive changes in ownership and location of materials that should be legitimately considered Polish national archival assets. It was only the restoration of independent Polish statehood after World War I that created conditions for ameliorating that state of affairs. With regard to Polish-Russian relations, the basis for the relevant solutions was provided by the Riga Peace Treaty of 18 March 1921.

Article 11 of the treaty, along with executive instructions that were an integral part of the pact, guaranteed that Poland would recover archival materials removed from it after 1 January 1771. The article also related to its territory within the new borders. Thus, the materials in question not only included items from the period of the First Republic but also those created during the partitions, including materials removed from the Kingdom of Poland between 1 August 1914 and 1 October 1915. Alas, the provisions of the treaty were never fully implemented.

After World War II, the Soviet Union returned various archival materials to Poland, though often with the exclusion of specific items, which resulted in the destruction of the integrity of many archival fonds. The Russian archivists involved did not adhere to the rule of respecting the integrity of archival fonds. They excluded from the materials being returned records that could in any way "harm" the Soviet Union or put an unfavorable light on the history of tsarist Russia—actions that Pyotr Voikov described as the "sterilization" of the archives.

After 1945, a considerable amount of archivalia was transferred to Poland. The Soviet Union returned these materials in several stages, though always on the basis of decisions made by its own institutions and often as "gifts." Poland also transferred archival materials to the Soviet Union. The first archivalia returned to Poland consisted of materials displaced in connection with World War II, including numerous records belonging to central institutions. Regrettably, they continued to be "sterilized." It is noteworthy that the materials returned to Poland included parts of the collections of the former Prussian archives in Wrocław and Szczecin and the Gdańsk archive (the property of the Free City of Gdańsk). However, many file units were extracted from additional records returned to Poland under the protocols of 4 October 1961 (sixty-six thousand file units) and 5 November 1963 (some seventy thousand file units).

One of the points of contention at present relates to the issue of succession to states not covered by relevant treaty provisions or those for whom the provisions have not been fulfilled. Another dispute concerns materials displaced in connection with historical events, mainly World Wars I and II.

It is notable that, in its actions on the international scene regarding the problem of archival succession and the eradication of consequences for their illegitimate displacement, Poland is guided by the principles that are also upheld by the officials in charge of the Russian archives. It is pivotal to recognize that archivalia belong to the territory in which they were created and that their accidental or illegal displacement has no effect on their ownership. The parties concur on this issue. In this connection, Poland also refers to numerous positions of the United Nations Education, Scientific, and Cultural Organization on the subject, including the proposal by the UNESCO director-general, who, on 28 August 1978, presented a report containing guidelines on the resolution of international disputes connected with archival materials. The concept of a common archival heritage is one of the courses of action advocated in these guidelines. Its use is advocated in situations when, due to territorial transfers between states, a fond or the assets of an archive containing records produced by administrative bodies, whose successors are two or more states, cannot be divided without detriment to their legal, administrative, or historical value. Thanks to the concept of common heritage, records of this type remain intact, constituting part of the archival holdings of one of the partners, while other partners enjoy the right of their unrestrained utilization. That UNESCO postulate, though not incorporated in the Vienna convention on the succession of states—which concerns state property, archives, and debts—is interesting and deserves to be applied in resolving international disputes over archivalia.

Displaced Collections

Poland has advanced claims concerning several groups of archivalia. All of them constitute fragments or larger components of fonds excluded from Soviet transfers of materials back to Poland after World Wars I and II. As a result, files belonging to the same fond, created by institutions or persons in Poland within its present borders, are dispersed across both Polish and Russian collections.

The first group consists of fragments of fonds created by local authorities and institutions within the territory of the Kingdom of Poland in the postpartition period. These are parts of 126 fonds from the years 1808–1915 (1918)—a total of twenty-two thousand file units removed from Warsaw in 1915. After the return to Poland of some files in the 1960s, these materials remained classified until the 1990s and were stored in the Asian part of the Russian Federation. After the collapse of the Soviet Union, they were declassified and incorporated into the holdings of the State Archive of the Russian Federation in Moscow.

Another group consists of fragments of fonds created by institutions and persons between the wars, within the present territory of Poland. Intelligence, police, and border guard records dominate, though the group also contains files of certain central authorities and social organizations and institutions. It further includes records of German institutions that operated in the western and northern territories before 1945. Poland has also asked for the return of these documents. In most cases they, too, constitute parts of fonds recovered by Poland after World War II.

The list of specified Polish claims also includes fragments of the holdings of the Russian State Historical Archives, among them several Brańsk, Drohiczyn, Mielnik, Supraśl, and Brześć court registers (fifteenth to eighteenth centuries). Some of them were stolen by the Germans during World War II, while others are fragments of registers that were stored at the Polish Central Archive of Historical Records. These, too, are files that were excluded from materials returned to Poland after World War II. The exclusions were not made for political reasons but because the Russian side had problems with their identification; the materials were later identified by Polish archivists.

No action has been taken to fulfill the provisions of Poland's peace treaty of 18 March 1921 with Russia and Ukraine concerning the transfer to Poland of archival materials belonging to central institutions established in Russia after the partitions to deal with matters related to the former Kingdom of Poland. Documents of this kind are stored at the Russian State Historical Archives in Saint Petersburg in the fonds of the Committee on the Kingdom of Poland (no. 1170, records from the years 1831–41, 97 file units), the Codification Commission of the Kingdom of Poland (no. 1254, records from the years 1813–68, 250 file units), and yet another Committee on the Kingdom of Poland (no. 1270, records from the years 1864–81, 1,605 file units). In this context, it is also essential to determine the status of the Ruthenian books of the Register of the Crown (Volhynia Register), kept at the Russian State Archive of Early Acts in Moscow. These books constitute an integral part of the Register of the Crown stored at the Central Archives of Historical Records in Warsaw.

Another Russian repository holding records of Polish territorial provenance is the Russian State Military History Archives. It has assembled several fonds of the Warsaw Military District (nos. 1858–64, 1867, 1872–74) comprising a substantial number of documents. For example, the fond of the Warsaw Military District court, which includes materials relating to the suppression of the Polish national independence movement in the years 1874–1914, numbers 53,594 file units, while the fond of the Warsaw Military District staff is composed of 5,952 file units from the years 1863–1916.

Various Polish institutions have asked the Head Office of State Archives for assistance in locating parts of their archival heritage; for example, nothing is known of the whereabouts of materials from the Drohiczyn Diocese Archive, requisitioned in October 1939 by Russian authorities.

This review of missing documents indicates that the numerous problems that hobbled our predecessors are still confounding us today. Are these problems truly so complicated that their resolution is impossible? Assuming that we take a professional approach, there is nothing to stop us from developing concrete solutions. In particular, the 1997 act of the State Duma should not prevent us from resolving the dispute over the originals of archival materials. That is because the most important issue from the Polish point of view is the return of documentation that, at historic critical junctures (at the time of its transfer to the territory of the present-day Russian Federation), was stored in the chanceries of the offices and institutions that created it and not in historical archives, that is, documentation that had not yet attained the status of cultural property. Thus, we are dealing with state property to which the act of the State Duma is not applicable. The documentation in question was the subject of a special publication in 2000 by the Head Office of State Archives. The materials in question had been removed from the territory of the Republic of Poland during World Wars I and II.

Insightful consideration is also due the issue of archivalia that in the past comprised the holdings of Polish historical archives and that were subsequently removed by invaders and are today in archival repositories in the Russian Federation. Originals from these sources should be returned to Poland.

As for other categories of materials mentioned here, it would be possible to take into account other courses of action than the transfer of originals from their present repositories. The most convenient formula would be based on the UNESCO concept of common archival heritage, which could be introduced in full or limited to the transfer of copies. However, the party receiving the copies should not have to bear the cost of the scientific processing of the originals or their preparation for reproduction. Claims of this sort have been made in contacts between the Russian and Polish state archives. However, the Russian position that archivalia with the territorial provenance of a partner country cannot be taken into account in the programming of research because materials created by domestic offices and institutions are given precedence casts doubt on the legitimacy and sense of their storage in the present depository.

Mutual Relations

These examples demonstrate that the changes of state borders resulting from World War II have had diverse consequences. As for archives, we can speak of a veritable earthquake, the impact of which has not been completely overcome. The State Archive of Królewiec (in German, Königsberg; in Russian, Kaliningrad) stands out against the background of those deep transformations. While archives that were located in other places and incorporated into other states still exist, in the case of the present-day state archive of the district of Kaliningrad we are dealing with a completely new institution.

Poland has transferred to successor states archival assets that had been collected by the archives in its former eastern territories, lost as a result of the war. Yet, it would be untrue to say that Poland, as with Lithuania, Belarus, and Ukraine, has obtained the assets of the former German archives in the western and northern territories acquired after the war. Polish archivists estimate that Poland has obtained only 30 to 60 percent of the historical assets of those territories. The rest, relocated deep into the German Reich at the end of World War II, are stored in German depositories, including the former Prussian Privy State Archive of the Prussian Cultural Heritage Foundation. That archive and the State Archive in Olsztyn received significant parts of the fonds of the former State Archive in Królewiec. The fragments of the former Królewiec archive today stored in Kaliningrad and Vilnius constitute only a small fraction of its former holdings. Thus, it is justified to say that the assets of the former State Archive in Królewiec have been divided between Poland and Germany.

In other words, we are dealing with an array of problems that deserve an extensive monograph. While Kurt Forstreuter's treatise brings to light the convoluted fates of the Królewiec archive after 1945, the status of the collection after World War II under international law remains open. In order to take up the issue, it is essential to address these two problems, with this chapter serving as a prologue to the formulation of proposals concerning future action.

The removal of the Królewiec collection by the Nazi authorities at the end of World War II suggests that they were not fully aware of the impending unconditional surrender of the Third Reich and unavoidable loss of East Prussia. The holdings of the Królewiec archive were dispersed to many localities, with the oldest part being transferred to what became the Federal Republic of Germany. The rest was stored, for the most part, in Poland's present Warminsko-Mazurskie voivodeship. Few records remained in Królewiec itself or to the east of it.

It is noteworthy that, in addition to archivalia evacuated from Królewiec into the former East Prussia, the State Archive in Olsztyn and the Central Archive of Historical Records in Warsaw also hold materials that Poland received from Germany after 1945, per regulations imposed by the victorious Allied powers on their vanquished foe. The archivalia from Królewiec had been evacuated to what would become the British occupation zone. In 1947, its authorities decided to transfer part of the collection of the State Archive in Królewiec to Poland, including the act of the district of Olsztyn (nineteenth century) and the so-called Folianten Ermland und Westpreussen. In the part of East Prussia acquired by Poland under the Potsdam Agreement (the change of state borders was subsequently affirmed by the Polish-German treaty of 14 November 1990), Polish authorities discovered archivalia from the State Archive in Królewiec. Today, they constitute an integral part of the collection of the State Archive in Olsztyn, an institution that is the successor to the former State Archive in Królewiec with regard to the part of East

Prussia (three-quarters of its total area) incorporated into Poland. These materials prominently include fonds of the province conservator of culture and art for East Prussia, of the Gąbin and Królewiec districts, and of Królewiec University. The State Archive in Olsztyn holds some twenty-eight hundred linear meters of post-Prussian archivalia. In addition to those mentioned above, these materials also include records produced by the chanceries of state, self-government, and community institutions, Evangelical (Lutheran) parishes, unions, associations, banks, and individuals from the period of the East Prussian province (nineteenth century and the years 1901–44).

During the campaign for return of archivalia in the years 1947–49, Poland advanced claims on the part of the Królewiec collection that had been removed to Germany, treating it, on the one hand, as partial compensation for the extreme damage to Polish archives perpetrated by German occupiers and, on the other, as a natural consequence of the change of state borders.

Poland considered itself entitled to the historical assets of the former State Archive in Królewiec because it had taken more than three-quarters of the territory of the former East Prussia, the history of which had been closely linked to Polish statehood. These links were seen as being closer than those with Germany or Russia. Still, Poland recognized the principle of territorial provenance of the archivalia in question and expressed a readiness to transfer to the Russian side those fonds stored at the State Archive in Olsztyn that had been created by the Prussian authorities within the area of the present district of Kaliningrad. The matter was discussed by the heads of the Polish and Russian archives, which led to the signing in Moscow of a special protocol on 6 November 1992. It stipulated that, in exchange for the Prussian records, Poland would receive from the Russian Federation pre-1945 records produced by German authorities in the eastern and northern parts of the German territory granted Poland by the Allied powers. In the document, the Russians also pledged to hand over the entire documentation of the Auschwitz concentration camp.

The time seems ripe to take up the matter again and bring the 1992 accord to fruition. Simultaneously, Poland and Russia should elaborate their positions concerning the remaining, larger part of the collection of the former State Archive in Królewiec, stored at present at the Prussian Cultural Heritage Foundation in Berlin. Both Poland and Russia have every right to seek those materials; in doing so, they might invoke the UNESCO concept of common archival heritage.

Access to Archives

The Polish scientific community attaches particular importance to access to source materials in the Russian archives. That is why the Head Office of State Archives has made every effort to ensure the best possible relations between the archive services of Poland and Russia. A new chapter in bilateral relations began in late 1990, when the parties signed a protocol for preparation of a draft agreement. It underlined the necessity for close cooperation between the archive services and the provision of broad access to source materials for researchers from both countries in accordance with the guidelines of the International Council on Archives for the purpose of casting light on the so-called "white spots" in historical research. In particular, the need for the reproduction of materials concerning the tragic fates of Polish soldiers after September 1939 was stressed. The agreement between the Head Office of the Polish Archives and the Committee on Archives of the Government of the Russian Federation was signed on 27 April 1992. In it, the parties underlined the need for the joint preparation of source publications on the history of relations between Poland and Russia and undertook a search for the relevant documents in their archives. Copies of the documents were to be exchanged on mutually advantageous terms. Scholars representing the other party were to have the same access to state archives as researchers of the host country.

Since then, a joint edition of sources on key events in the history of the two countries has become one of the most important areas of cooperation. To date, the parties have issued a four-volume source publication, *Katyń: Dokumenty zbrodni* (Katyn: Documents of a crime). The year 2004 saw the publication of *Krasnoarmeitsy v polskom plenu v 1919–1922 gg.: Sbornik dokumentov i materialov* (Red Army soldiers in Polish captivity in the years 1919–1922: Collection of documents and materials). The project continued with the publication in 2009 of a compilation of archival documents on the fates of Russian soldiers in Polish captivity. The Polish side met the requests of Rosarkhiv concerning the provision of access to sources and thus fulfilled all its obligations toward its Russian partners.

Regrettably, further projects could not be implemented—including a joint Polish-Ukrainian initiative to issue a multivolume publication devoted to the tragic events in Volhynia, the sixtieth anniversary of which was marked in 2003 (the parties managed to publish only the first work in the planned series, titled *Wołyń—Galicja Wschodnia 1943–1944: Przewodnik po polskich i ukraińskich źródłach archiwalnych* [Volhynia—Eastern Galicia 1943–1944: A guide to Polish and Ukrainian archival sources]), because Rosarkhiv informed the Head Office of State Archives that the Russian archives did not contain any source materials on the subject.

Further requests to the Russian side for it to conduct searches of its archives, including repositories of the diplomatic service and special services, for documents relating to other important historical events have met with a similar response. The documents sought include, for example, source materials concerning the death of Gen. Władysław Sikorski in Gibraltar. We were hoping that a joint publication on the subject would be possible.

The same fate awaited another initiative: a joint edition of sources on relations between the Polish People's Republic and the Soviet Union in the years 1945 to 1980. The Polish participants in the project were to include—along with the Head Office of State Archives—the Institute of Political Studies of the Polish Academy of Sciences. The requests by HOSA for access to sources illustrating the attitude of the Soviet Union to the Warsaw Uprising were similarly denied.

Another problem, crucial from the point of view of many people in Poland, is inadequate cooperation regarding the issuance of certificates concerning Soviet repression against Poles.

These issues confirm the existence in Russia of restrictions on access to archival materials for scholarly purposes. Considering the strong historical ties between the two countries, as well as the importance and quantity of the archivalia in Russian repositories concerning recent historical events in need of research, this situation is highly unfavorable. We want to change it. Poland and the Russian Federation, as member states of the Council of Europe, should adopt the council's relevant recommendations as the basis of their policies on access to archival documents. The latter prominently include the "Recommendation of the Committee of Ministers to Member States on a European Policy on Access to Archives" of 2000. One of the tenets of European policy on access to archivalia is the resolution of any related problems in accordance with the law and the traditions and needs of the member states. Thus, it is possible to close access to archival documents for predetermined periods of time. However, it would be against the spirit and letter of the recommendation to conceal the existence of such documents.

VLADIMIR P. KOZLOV

DISPLACED COLLECTIONS AND ACCESS TO ARCHIVES

THE HISTORY OF relations between Russia and Poland has always reminded me of a spindle that for many centuries has been spinning the thread of mutual suspicions, hatred, and revenge. It is extremely unpleasant and most undesirable to continue embroidering this patchwork and turning the coiled thread into a forever thickening skein. We need to lay to rest all the vile actions of both parties against each other and detach them from current policies. We need to stop listening to unprincipled politicians from both countries and try to preserve existing bridges of mutual understanding and build new spans between Russians and Poles, ones that are even stronger than before.

One of those bridges is cooperation in the sphere of archival collections involving the two countries. Archival work can be something positive and is a present reality, as well as a possible future development, despite the fact that Russia and Poland have faced numerous problems in this area.

In the postcommunist period, relations between Russian and Polish archivists remained varied but stable for many years. Polish historians and archivists will always be interested in Russian archives. The history of the two countries has been closely intertwined for centuries. In the twentieth century, Polish archives suffered considerable damage in the two world wars. Russian archivists value professional contacts with their Polish colleagues. When the sociable and vibrant Daria Nałęcz was put in charge of the Polish archival service, Polish archivists became more actively involved in Western European archival and information collaboration. Today, they have a considerable claim to being the leader in archive storage among Central and Eastern European countries, to a certain extent acting as a link in the chain between archivists of this region and Western European countries.

Stark evidence of this fact is the annual Skowronek Readings (Colloquia Jerzy Skowronek Dedicata) held in Poland, which is attended by foreign archivists. The popularity of the readings among archivists is confirmed by their regular attendance. In 2004, the readings had their tenth anniversary. Russian archivists have remarkably been attending the readings every year since the first sessions in 1994.

Harsh preelection remarks against Russia by several Polish politicians cooled relations between archivists of both countries. In essence, they ended up in a frozen state of affairs. The former distinctness and permanency of professional and friendly relations have been replaced by a cold air of expectancy, which is perpetuated by actual and alleged archival disputes.

One of those conflicts is the dividing of the Russian Empire's archival heritage and the moving of archives belonging to the Polish state and private organizations and citizens to Russia after World War II. This is not a new issue and is indeed, to a large extent nowadays, international in character. It is an international issue that has never lost its relevance, particularly in modern and recent history. The twentieth century did not eliminate this issue but exacerbated it by turning it into a global problem. It relates to the two world wars and breakup of empires, as a result of which colonialist countries generally refused to share cultural antiquities, principally archives, with their former colonies. The archives of France today may be used to study the history of Algeria, Tunisia, and Vietnam; the archives of England, the history of India; and the archives of Austria, the history of Hungary, and so forth. The world is not as fair as it seems, and numerous attempts to create an international legal framework to solve this issue face opposition and at best are limited to nonbinding declarations such as the Hague Convention of 1954, which remains unsigned even by many European countries.

In the late 1970s and early 1980s, the United Nations Education, Scientific, and Cultural Organization (UNESCO) and the International Council of Archives (ICA) attempted to find a partial solution to the problem of imperial archival heritage in relation to former colonies that had become independent states. Documents removed from colonies by colonialist countries would, if combined, fill archival shelves extending approximately seventy kilometers, and the goal was to preserve all of these materials on microfilm. This project (now being conducted in digital formats) has been slowly implemented for many years based on bilateral agreements. This solution seems fairly reasonable, though former colonies will undoubtedly be frustrated by its half-hearted measures. However, former colonialist countries, in particular Belgium, France, Portugal, Spain, and the United Kingdom, show a tendency to copy documents of their colonial administrations without returning the original documents to the countries of origin. In this regard, it is noteworthy that the collapse of the Soviet Union was not accompanied by any significant removal from former republics to Russia of archival documents created by the republic or even allied organizations.

The archival materials of the Russian Empire were divided between Soviet Russia and Poland according to the Treaty of Riga in 1921. Poland received original archival documents from the Russian archives in 1922–24. Comments are sometimes made that such a transfer was incomplete and that some documents were intentionally withdrawn (a kind of "sterilization").

The following may be said in response. While still preparing for the Riga Peace Treaty, Russian experts had doubts regarding the validity of transferring a number of documents to Poland. The questions primarily concerned archives of central government agencies of the Russian Empire dealing with affairs of the Kingdom of Poland, for instance, the Committee for the Kingdom of Poland's affairs. Further examples include documents of other central establishments of the Russian Empire that had their government organs in Poland, for instance, materials regarding the organization of the Warsaw military district governed by the imperial War Ministry. One cannot agree that, in this case, the principle of origin in dividing archival materials, which Polish archivists insist on using, is fairly relative and requires professional discussion in any case. Archives of local establishments of the Russian Empire's authorities, which were part of the vertical structures of such authorities, are more likely to be logically referred to as the heritage of the empire rather than that of some part having declared its independence. By the same token, Russian experts were opposed to returning to Poland the documents of the Wołyńska metrics (Metryki Ruskiej Wołyńskiej), which are also related to the history of other states. Regarding these and other, similar documents, the idea of joint archival heritage seems quite realistic and reasonable in the current conditions.

As for the deliberate "sterilization" of archives given to Poland under the Treaty of Riga of 1921, while I am by no means seeking to justify predecessors who prepared archival documents for Poland in the 1920s, it should be noted that it was done under conditions of civil war in Russia, when archives were "in disorder." Due to these reasons, certain documents could have been "withdrawn," which Polish archivists could now ascertain with the help of scientific and referencing tools created at Russian archives. Preparation of an exhaustive register could become the first step in discussing their legal status and determining the validity of the Peace Treaty of Riga of 1921 at the present time.

Therefore, dividing the archival heritage of the Russian Empire between modern Russia and modern Poland based on contemporary international practice seems even more complicated than in 1921. The idea of a common archival heritage in these conditions seems the most promising solution. First, it implies the creation of joint catalogs that would give a general idea of Russian historical documents in Polish archives and Polish historical documents in Russian archives and virtually "join" the divided parts of the archives of institutions that ended up in the two countries. A certain, though incomplete, example for creating such a catalog of Russian and Polish archives is already available; this foundation work was conducted by Russian and Polish archivists in an international archival project sponsored by the Council of Europe and titled "Preservation of Poland's Historical Memory." In the future, the countries could do a large-scale exchange of microfilmed archival documents and a series of cross-border documented publications based on the archival documents of both countries.

Access to a shared archival heritage (as well as other elements) should be open and equal. From the late 1980s to 2010, Russia has proven its openness on numerous occasions. Here is just one example. In the late 1980s, the Polish Ministry of Defense created a special archival and historical committee headed by the businesslike and vibrant Col. Jan Pięta. After the opening of the "Special Archives" containing numerous documents relating to the fate of Polish troops in 1940 and the events of August 1991, members of the committee, equipped with several copiers and sufficient funds, started large-scale reproduction of archival materials. Over time, this work was carried out with the National Archives of the Russian Federation and Central Archives of the Russian Defense Ministry, covering a wider range of prewar history on relations between the two countries. The work was successful, and thousands of pages of copied archival documents from Russian archives filled the shelves of the Polish military archives on the outskirts of Warsaw, subsequently allowing Polish military historians to establish their special periodical publications.

The situation with Polish archives transferred to Russia during and after World War II is a slightly different one.

The problem of cultural items from European countries transferred to Russia after World War II is particularly acute due to losses suffered by Russian archives in the twentieth century. The 1917 revolutions and the civil war resulted in the destruction of valuable documents, as well as the mass export from the country of personal archives and archives of official government institutions, mostly Russian embassies, consulates, trade missions, joint enterprises, and military units. Partial information on the location of such documents abroad (mostly personal archives) is currently accessible, while other materials are likely to be kept confidential by the state and private organizations of foreign states. It can be assumed that a significant number of exported documents that did not get to the Russian Foreign Historical Archive in Prague, established by the first wave of Russian emigrants (after World War II it was given to the Soviet Union by the Czechoslovakian government), have been irretrievably lost.

More severe damage was done to national archives during World War II as a result of military operations, the savage behavior of the occupiers, the removal of archives to Germany by special military divisions, losses owing to evacuation and reevacuation, and the destruction of archives to prevent their capture by the enemy. During and after World War II, Soviet authorities attempted to estimate the damage done to the country's archives. Primary inventory documents formed the basis for the preparation and publishing of a catalog of government and party archives lost during that period. It included 6,000 titles. If each archive had on average 100 or more files, then Russia lost more than 600,000 of its most valuable documents of prerevolutionary history in the first decades after the revolution. For instance, as a result of the bombing of Leningrad, the Russian State Historical Archive lost more than 6,000 files of the prerevolutionary management of state railways, the branch of the State Archives of the Tver region in Rzhev lost 117 files of the Kholmogory City Council, the state archives of the Voronezh region lost 351 files of the Voronezh vicegerent board, and so on.

The losses of Russian archives, partially a result of the first wave of emigration and of World War II, cannot be explained by *force majeure* circumstances, which are always a result of some insuperable force. They were the result of Nazi Germany's attack on the Soviet Union. In Russian public opinion, these losses have fueled and are fueling the idea of reparations for damages, including Russian ownership claims to archives brought to Russia from the European countries. It is difficult to refute this belief, particularly when it concerns countries that have suffered from Nazi aggression.

However, the process of repatriating archives started with Poland. In 1945, 1956, 1957, 1958, 1961, 1963, and 1967, at least one hundred archives with three hundred thousand files were returned to Poland by the Soviet Union.

By the beginning of 1992, the new Russian state had neither the experience nor the legal framework to resolve issues regarding archives moved to Russia. In the Soviet Union, solving such problems had required secret decrees of the Central Committee of the Communist Party of the Soviet Union (CPSU). The search for ways to return archives in this period was based on the return of French archives under a special international treaty. A similar procedure was proposed to the Netherlands and Poland. The former accepted that proposal, while Poland hesitated and returned to this issue in 1994, when the State Duma of the Russian Federation blocked the transfer of archival documents to France under the international treaty. The Duma demanded an internal mechanism be developed for addressing issues of displaced cultural items and passed a corresponding law in February 1997. This law is currently effective as per amendments by the Constitutional Court of the Russian Federation.

No other country has such a law. It may not be perfect, but it contains standards regarding displaced archives, in particular for countries and allies of the Soviet Union in World War II. Based on the law, Russia has successfully returned archives to Austria, Belgium, the Netherlands, Liechtenstein, and Luxembourg, with various arrangements for the reimbursement of expenses to Russia for their processing and storage, including the exchange of archival documents. After 1997, Russia expressed its willingness on many occasions to return to Poland the remaining archives displaced to Russia during World War II (as stated above, most Polish archives were returned in 1945–67) based on Russian laws. Russia was willing to receive either financial compensation for their storage or to exchange the materials for archives of White Russian emigrant files. According to records of negotiations between the archival services of Russia and Poland, it is clear that Polish archivists were willing to accept either of these options at various times. The country was probably lacking the political will to solve that issue with Russia, however. It still lacks the will. It is up to Poland today to initiate this process.

Over the course of many years, the defining and most challenging issue in the collaboration of Russian and Polish archivists was Katyn, which finally resulted in the joint work of preparing a multiple-volume, documented publication.

The history of this documented publication goes back to Soviet times, when a number of Soviet historians, primarily Natalia Lebedeva and Yuri N. Zorya, broke the archival and information silence and first found fragmented documents and then whole documents relating to the fate of Polish prisoners of war in the Soviet Union in 1939–40. The key documents, including the infamous ruling of the Politburo of the Central Committee of the All-Union Communist Party (Bolsheviks) on the execution of Polish prisoners of war, were missing for a long time, but those documents that were available were sufficient to confirm the tragedy and give a definite answer to the public, in particular to Poland, which insistently asked about the fate of more than twenty thousand of its compatriots. The CPSU leaders were aware of the results of our historians' archival research but delayed their disclosure upon realizing the scope of the negative effect it would have on the party's image.

However, the process was irreversible. First, there were rumors of what Zorya and Lebedeva had discovered, and then a series of publications of the documents gradually unveiled the fate of the Polish prisoners of war. On 27 April 1992, Roskomarkhiv (the Russian Archival Committee) and the General Directorate of Public Archives of the Republic of Poland signed a collaboration agreement. It did not directly mention the Katyn issue based on Russian archival documents, but it was tacitly present and eventually resulted in a special agreement, made on 11 June of the same year, under which the parties agreed "to prepare and publish in the original language and in full all documents regarding the history of the prisoners of war and interned Poles in camps in the former USSR from 1939 which had been stored in the Center of Historical and Documented Collections, State Archives of the Russian Federation, Russian State Military Archives, and the Center for Contemporary Documents." The agreement made provisions for the creation of task groups by each party and the large-scale copying of all relevant documents, funded by the General Directorate, which was to receive one copy of all documents.

The author of these lines was put in charge of the Russian task group, which slowly started developing a model for future document publication. A strong impulse for further work was the discovery of documents on the fate of Polish prisoners of war in the archives of the Russian president, stored in a sealed envelope. The discovery candidly exposed a procedure initiated for the annihilation of Poles and the subsequent concealment of this fact. The head of the Russian archives, Rudolf Pikhoya, was immediately sent to Poland to personally deliver certified copies of these documents to Polish president Lech Wałęsa.

It was a sensational event that almost became the topic of mainstream international news for several days. In early November, we were supposed to meet with a large delegation of Polish archivists headed by Prof. Marian Wojciechowski, director of the Polish Archive Service, who brought a letter of gratitude from the Polish president to Boris Yeltsin.

In his letter, besides expressing gratitude for the copies, Wałęsa stated, "Both you, Mr. President, and I want our relations to be based on a new candid foundation to fully liberate them from the burden of the past. Such are the relations the Polish people want with Russia. Therefore, I believe the next step in the new era of our relations should be the complete liberation from the weight of the past. We should be able to overcome it without impediment."

Talking about his mission, the Polish president further wrote, "I would like to ask you, Mr. President, to lend your assistance and support to the mission. I am referring to immediate access to all Russian archives, including the presidential archives and the KGB archives and providing Poland with copies of documents relating to issues listed in both attachments."

Poland was clearly not satisfied with the Katyn materials it had received and was interested in a wide range of issues relating to bilateral relations in the past. It was a normal position of being on the offense, something Russia had not encountered in a long time.

The next morning, after an official reading of Wałęsa's letter to Yeltsin at the Russian archives and its delivery to the Russian president at the Kremlin through Sergey Stankevich, our negotiations started. The results were recorded in special minutes, which, among other things, stated, "Regarding the publication of documents on the fate of Polish prisoners of war and internees in the USSR, the parties agreed that the publication should have several volumes (presumably three to five) and should fully divulge this issue. The parties have agreed that the publication should be research-based and archaeographically objective." The work was to be completed in five years and financed by Poland.

By January 1993, the Russian task group had the first draft concept for the future five-volume publication developed by Lebedeva. Over the course of the discussions, the team members naturally disagreed on some issues. One of the major points of disagreement was the reason for the harsh decision of the Politburo of the CPSU (b) Central Committee. Our colleagues from the Institute of Military History and the Institute of Slavonic and Balkan Studies tried to connect it with the fates of Red Army prisoners in Poland after the Soviet-Polish war of 1919–21 and suggested that the first volume should include the relevant documents concerning this event, which also resulted in discussions regarding the number of Red Army prisoners of war who had died in Poland. Moreover, the "narrow" approach to the problem caused some consternation. The head of the Military History Institute of the Russian Ministry of Defense wrote in this regard, "The research does not cover the fate of surviving Polish prisoners of war who have subsequently had a significant impact on Soviet-Polish relations. I'm talking about released Polish prisoners of war that became the foundation of the Anders Army, Polish Armed Forces, those who were instrumental in restoring liberated Poland. The need to expand the research subject is called for on account of the significant number of Poles interned during the disarmament of [Armia Krajowa] during the final stages of World War II. Their fate is no less dramatic."

Finally, by February, the Russian task group, amid heated discussions, came up with a concept for a future document publication. The publication was to consist of four volumes presenting documents in chronological order, under these titles: (1) Prisoners of the Undeclared War, (2) Massacre, (3) Fates of the Living, and (4) Katyn's Echo.

At the end of February 1993, the concept was discussed in Moscow. The Polish delegation was headed by Aleksander Gieysztor, a renowned Polish historian and an honorary member of the Soviet Academy of Sciences. The large Polish delegation also included the new director of the General Directorate of Polish Archives, Jerzy Skowronek. Skowronek, a genteel and kind person, understood as a historian that it was possible to explain your position to others but that it is never worth quarreling. He gave strong impetus for organizing the annual meetings of archivists of Central and Eastern Europe (Colloquia Jerzy Skowronek Dedicata), on the suggestion of the writer of this article (in 2004, they were terminated at Poland's request).

Discussions of the concept did not result in serious controversies. It is important to note that, during these meetings, Polish archivists demonstrated considerable professionalism, which further allowed them to avert the active involvement of certain politically driven Polish military historians in the project and start working directly with Russian archivists. The meeting of task groups regarding the first volume of the future publication took place 2–5 November 1993 in Warsaw, entirely within the framework of bilateral professional relations and in an atmosphere of efficiency, creativity, and mutual understanding, supported by the participation of Wojciech Materski, a professor at the University of Warsaw who has become one of the key figures in preparing the publication on the Polish side.

Actual work on the publication's preparation began at the end of 1993. Documents were selected and processed. Comments and a foreword by the Russian party were prepared. The driving force behind the project was Lebedeva, who, with her characteristic energy, has literally "driven" our archivists forward. Lebedeva received assistance from N. Petrosova, a quiet employee of the Russian archives, who carried out archaeographic processing of the documents. The work of the Russian group was "supervised" by the cultural attaché of the Republic of Poland in Russia, Henryk Kurowski, whose interest had such a strong impact on Russian and Polish archivists' collaboration that its effect has continued to be felt for a number of years since, manifesting itself in new projects.

The volumes published in subsequent years, dedicated to the fate of Polish prisoners of war, contained documented evidence of the earlier published facts and research. The publication has caused little in the way of sensation. Its academic nature, which I am personally not fully satisfied with, as it could have been better, has ruled out any speculations in principle. A book by Yuriy Mukhin that appeared after the publication of the first volume is just a pitiful attempt to rehabilitate one of Stalinism's crimes. In the book, the author tried to prove that the documents on the fate of Polish prisoners of war in the Russian archives were falsified, upon the orders of Boris Yeltsin, by a group of Russian archivists under the leadership of Pikhoya. Although political speculations regarding the tragedy will continue to crop up in Russia and Poland, they will inevitably clash with the four volumes of documents covering and commemorating those who were massacred and thus revealing the face of a new Russia. These volumes, of course, only show part of the truth about episodes of world history prior to and at the very beginning of World War II. The entire truth and the truth of these events is yet to be discovered and understood. This is the task of objective historians, not those biased by hatred of communism, honor for their country, political requests, or promises of good pay. Archivists have done their work.

The preparation by Russian and Polish archivists of the Katyn documents, now completed with the publication of the fourth volume, has become an important consolidating factor in the relations of archivists from the two countries. In April 2007, a small delegation of Russian historians and archivists participated in the presentation of this volume. The hall of the Polish Archives of Ancient Acts, which was housed in the palace of the Russian en-

VLADIMIR P. KOZLOV

voy to Poland during the time of the Russian Empire, was overcrowded with people (at least 150 people showed up for the event). Contrary to our apprehensions, the speeches of our Polish colleagues were essentially civil and humane. The crux of their speeches was that the completion of the four-volume publication had "put an end" to the painful division between the two nations. The Russian people suffered from Stalin's dictatorship much more than the Polish people. The format of the presentation was broadly consistent with diplomatic standards, but I feel that it was still a sensitive issue both for the audience and others. It was not laid bare simply because of the presence of the Russians who made the Katyn publication possible.

Returning to Wałęsa's letter of gratitude to Yeltsin, it is worth noting that the Russian party had to submit a belated counterrequest to Poland. Academic establishments and the Russian Foreign Ministry prepared a response from Boris Yeltsin in which Russia requested copies of archival documents regarding Polish policies toward the Soviet Union in the 1920s and 1930s.

This exchange of letters between the presidents did not yield any major results but had an overall positive significance for archivists in Russia and Poland. A diplomatic clash between the countries in the field of archives and history resulted in a special Russian delegation being sent to work with Polish archives. This may be the only case in which the Russian government has specially financed such a project. In a number of Polish state archives (we were politely refused access to the main departmental archives), we identified interesting documents, though not of primary importance and partially already known to the research community. We made a list of such documents on many pages and obtained copies of four thousand documents, including those referring to the history of the Soviet-Polish war of 1920–21 and materials on Soviet prisoners of war in Poland.

Polish archivists were interested in our proposal that we should prepare a joint publication of documents on the fate of Red Army prisoners of the Soviet-Polish war of 1920–21, providing documents from Polish archives and commenting on them. In 2002, they arranged a trip for the Russian authors of the publication to the city of Torun, next to which a camp for prisoners of war had been located.

This visit deserves special attention. The site of the camp is now a forest. Only barely visible mounds among the trees recall the mud huts and low wooden structures that used to be there in the 1910s and 1920s. Time has ruthlessly erased the traces of people forced to stay there. Local residents and even those advanced in years just shrug their shoulders in response to our questions about the camp. No memories of the camp are left. Not far from the camp, there is a cemetery in fairly decent condition, with white gravestones arranged in even rows marking the final resting places of prisoners of war, including those from World War I (the camp was established by Germans for

Russian and Polish prisoners of war). I pondered the imperfection of human memory preserved by the seemingly fragile but most durable method of documentation. The publication of documents helped reconstruct the everyday life and activities of our compatriots in the Polish camps so that a modern reader could sigh bitterly and lament the world's imperfection that so often causes the unnatural death of human beings.

The joint trans-border publication, which was based on documents from the archives of the two countries, was released in Russian in 2004. It has put an end to speculations regarding this unfriendly page in the history of the two countries in the twentieth century. It was accompanied by a similar joint publication by Russian and Polish archivists and historians about the fates of Polish prisoners of war in Russia during the first years of Soviet power, which was published five years later in Polish.

This is the current, albeit contradictory, situation as it stands. On the one hand, documented evidence has shed light upon three sensitive issues in Russian-Polish relations. Alas, it has not stemmed the flow of political speculations either in Russia or in Poland. But reasonable politicians have learned from these three publications facts about the past that can hardly be disposed of dishonestly. It marks the main road to understanding the complicated past relations in the two countries' joint research of archival heritage. On the other hand, purely archival issues are still acute. Some of these issues relating to the return of the remaining Polish archives displaced to Russia after World War II could find a solution in accordance with Russian law. Other issues regarding the archival heritage of the Russian Empire require professional study and complex legal analysis. All of this can be resolved. Archival relations between Russia and Poland need to "thaw," as they are now frozen where they stood in 2005. Political events of spring 2010, despite the tragedy at Smolensk, seem to give reason for hope.

. . . .

REPORTS ON SESSIONS OF THE GROUP ON DIFFICULT MATTERS

. . . .

Communiqué on the Meeting of the Co-Chairs of the Polish-Russian Group on Difficult Matters (Brussels, 1–2 February 2008)

On 1–2 February 2008, the co-chairs of the Polish-Russian Group on Difficult Matters stemming from the complicated history of Polish-Russian relations, Prof. A. D. Rotfeld, former minister of foreign affairs of the Republic of Poland, and Prof. A. V. Torkunov, rector of the Moscow State Institute of International Relations (MGIMO), held an informal meeting in Brussels.

The co-chairs agreed on the future rules of operation of the group in its new composition and ways of building on its achievements since it was established in 2002. The parties intend to review these achievements in the near future.

The co-chairs highlighted the importance of making maximum use of research into bilateral relations conducted outside the group by historians, as well as works by archive services and materials collected by other state institutions. They concurred on the need for broader distribution of existing joint publications and underlined the role of mass media in familiarizing public opinion in the two states with the positive effects of Polish-Russian cooperation on historical issues.

The co-chairs noted the importance of preserving symmetry in the Polish and Russian membership of the group. They emphasized the need for giving the group a primarily social and expert character, which was connected with the fact that the group included members who not only knew the history of bilateral relations but also were capable of collaborating on a foundation of similar views and values.

Since involving the Polish Roman Catholic Church and the Russian Orthodox Church would be an important element of building mutual understanding and confidence, the co-chairs intended to conduct consultations for the purpose of elaborating specific mechanisms and formulas to include the two churches in the Polish-Russian dialogue.

The co-chairs recognized the importance of stimulating—independent of official group meetings—the academic and social activity of group participants. The idea of a joint publication was under consideration.

A meeting of the group in its new composition is planned in Warsaw in May 2008.

PIOTR PASZKOWSKI, MFA PRESS SPOKESMAN

Communiqué on the Meeting of the Polish-Russian Group on Difficult Matters (Warsaw, 12–14 June 2008)

1. On 12–14 June 2008, Warsaw played host to the first session of the Polish-Russian Group on Difficult Matters meeting in its new composition (a list of the Polish and Russian group members is attached).

2. The group co-chairs, Prof. Adam D. Rotfeld and the academician Prof. Anatoly V. Torkunov, informed the group members on their contacts to date and preliminary decisions made during their meetings in Brussels (1–2 February 2008) and Moscow (19 May 2008).

3. The participants agreed on the need to build on the group's achievements since its establishment in 2002. Accordingly, it was recommended that a review be conducted of the work to date, particularly with a view to gaining access to and publishing previously unknown documents of significance to Polish-Russian relations. This also applied to joint Polish-Russian publications on recent history and to mutual access to archives. In this context the participants expressed support for the intensification of research and launching of work, the results of which would be made available to the public of both countries, under the auspices of the group.

4. In the course of discussions on the group's mandate and new tasks, the participants noted that, in recent years, the political and social relations between the two countries, as well as contacts between their scientific communities, had corresponded to the public's expectations in Poland and Russia. Group members welcomed the improving political climate, which created the conditions for addressing difficult and sensitive issues that remained as the legacy of history. They expressed the opinion that such matters should not be the subject of political games; these matters required courage and responsibility on the part of politicians and researchers in studying and resolving them. This applied, in particular, to a definitive clarification of all the circumstances of the Katyn crime and adoption of the relevant political decisions.

5. One of the group's key goals consisted of clearing the way for and removing obstacles to top-level decisions that would create a solid foundation for partner-like relations, based on truth and mutual respect.

6. The group did not have the task of replacing the competent institutions and state bodies established to promote the development of relations between the Republic of Poland and the Russian Federation. Instead, it intended to facilitate the resolution of problems rooted in the past that hindered mutual relations and the adoption of appropriate decisions.

7. The group members devoted much attention to the idea of a joint historical documentary publication aimed at presenting the Polish and Russian viewpoints on many crucial and controversial twentieth-century problems in the relations between the two peoples and states. The topic would be taken up at the group's next meeting.

8. The group participants welcomed the report by the co-chairs on their contacts with representatives of the Roman Catholic Church in Poland and the Russian Orthodox Church. The willingness indicated by the two churches to become actively involved in a social dialogue and rapprochement between the peoples of Poland and Russia would enhance the spiritual dimension in the shaping of a new type of relations.

9. The Group on Difficult Matters in Polish-Russian relations expressed its gratitude to the top representatives of the Polish state for their interest in its work, as demonstrated by the reception of the two co-chairs by Polish president Lech Kaczyński and their working meetings with Prime Minister Donald Tusk and Minister of Foreign Affairs Radosław Sikorski, who were briefed on the group's plans and the results of its work.

10. The group expressed appreciation to Prime Minister Donald Tusk for his suggestion that a scientific conference be organized in Poland on the seventieth anniversary of World War II and devoted to the origins and consequences of the war.

It was decided that the group's next meeting would take place in Moscow in autumn 2008.

Communiqué on the Meeting of the Polish-Russian Group on Difficult Matters (Moscow, 27–28 October 2008)

The second session of the Polish-Russian Group on Difficult Matters, convening in its new lineup, took place in Moscow 27–28 October 2008.

Opening the event, Russian foreign minister Sergei Lavrov appealed for the depoliticization of problems relating to the common history of the two nations. Group co-chairs Prof. Adam D. Rotfeld and academician Anatoly V. Torkunov presented a report on the progress of work since the previous meeting. The co-chairs also briefed journalists on the group's achievements to date and plans for the future.

The group members conducted an incisive debate on an earlier proposal for a joint publication and ultimately agreed on the final formula of the book devoted to difficult matters in Polish-Russian relations.

The publication would address issues pertaining to the interwar period, the genesis of World War II, the Katyn crime, and other topics relating to bilateral relations, including recent decades. A list of authors responsible for the respective chapters of the book was presented at the meeting.

The participants pledged to submit preliminary versions of their chapters by mid-April 2009.

The group members also endorsed a proposal for another publication connected with the approaching seventieth anniversary of World War II. The Moscow State Institute of International Relations (MGIMO) and the Polish Institute of International Affairs (PISM) assumed responsibility for preparing the publication.

The participants underlined the need for easier access to archive materials, which would allow faster work on the two publications. Minister Lavrov promised to facilitate access to the Foreign Policy Archive of the Russian Federation—something that was welcomed by those present.

Several members of the group noted that issues pertaining to archives could be settled through standard procedures, in line with international regulations.

The participants appealed to the leaders of the two countries to attach due significance to the clarification of all the circumstances of the Katyn crime perpetrated by Stalin's regime, which would permit its removal from the agenda of relations between the two societies and states. The group expressed readiness to consider possible ways of attaining that goal.

The Polish side expressed its appreciation to the Russian side for its hospitality and efficient organization.

In accordance with the rule on alternate venues, it was decided to convene the next session of the group in Poland, in mid-May 2009.

Final Communiqué on the Meeting of the Polish-Russian Group on Difficult Matters (Kraków, 28–29 May 2009)

On 28–29 May 2009, Kraków was the site of the third plenary session of the Polish-Russian Group on Difficult Matters.

1. The group co-chairs, Prof. Adam Daniel Rotfeld and academician Anatoly V. Torkunov, reviewed the group's work since its previous meeting in Moscow (27–28 October 2008). They also shared plans and expectations connected with the present stage of work on the joint publication dealing with difficult matters in Polish-Russian relations in the twentieth century.

2. The participants agreed on the final content and form of the joint publication, exchanged prepared texts, and decided that, during the next session, they would make the final decision on sending all the book chapters to publishers for preparation of the Polish and Russian editions of the book. It was decided to convey a summary of the future publication, agreed to by both parties, to the media and the public.

3. On the eve of the seventieth anniversary of the Katyn crime, debate focused on that tragedy, which had remained at the center of attention of public opinion. The group members were unanimous in supporting a proposal that public opinion in both countries should take joint steps to honor the victims of the Katyn crime and that the relevant efforts should be institutionalized. The co-chairs were authorized to draft concrete proposals addressed to the foreign ministers and leaders of the two states.

4. The group expressed support for the commemoration of prisoners of war and Polish and Russian victims of repression and for the appropriate maintenance of memorial sites in both countries.

5. The participants welcomed the information that the group co-chairs had met in Moscow on 24 April 2009 with Archbishop Hilarion, the metropolitan of Volokolamsk.

6. The participants expressed gratitude to Cardinal Stanisław Dziwisz, the metropolitan of Kraków, for his meeting with group members and words of support.

7. Appreciation was expressed for the readiness of senior hierarchs of the Russian Orthodox Church and the Roman Catholic Church in Poland to lend a spiritual and moral dimension to the process of overcoming difficulties on the path to deeper mutual understanding.

8. The group participants welcomed the constructive character and results of the international conference on the genesis of World War II (Warsaw, 26–27 May 2009). Members of the Group on Difficult Matters took active roles in the conference. The fruitful work during the conference of academics from Poland, Russia, Germany, and other countries constituted a tangible example of scholarly dialogue and the prevention of attempts to falsify history.

9. The participants thanked the mayor of Kraków, Prof. Jacek Majchrowski, for the hospitality extended to the group.

10. The parties agreed that, in accordance with the rule on alternate venues, the next session of the group would take place in Russia in autumn 2009.

Final Communiqué on the Session of the Polish-Russian Group on Difficult Matters (Moscow, 9 November 2009)

The latest session of the Polish-Russian Group on Difficult Matters took place in Moscow on 9 November 2009. The participants were welcomed by Russian deputy foreign minister A. Grushko.

The group's co-chairs briefly reviewed the activity since the previous meeting in Kraków (May 2009) and pointed to favorable changes in the historical dialogue between the Polish and Russian societies. In particular, they referred to the results of the visit to Poland by Russian prime minister V. Putin (1 September 2009) and the statement by Russian president D. Medvedev on his blog (30 October 2009), in which he underlined the necessity of "investigating the past, and overcoming indifference and the tendency to forget tragic pages of the past."

The co-chairs underlined the importance of the social and public dimension of the group's activity, including the publication by PISM and MGIMO of a joint book devoted to the genesis of World War II, inspired by the group's work. They also noted the publication of a special edition of the bimonthly foreign affairs journal *Vestnik MGIMO,* devoted to the seventieth anniversary of World War II, largely composed of texts by group members.

The co-chairs stressed the importance of the group's cooperation with other dialogue-oriented institutions, prominently including the Forum of Civic Dialogue and the Senate Poland-Russia Group.

The participants focused on finalizing works on the joint publication: they considered issues pertaining to historiography, relations between the two states during and immediately after World War II, and "historical policy." The debate was marked by mutual respect and professionalism.

The participants discussed concrete measures stemming from the statements of 1 September 2009 by the Polish and Russian premiers, including the establishment of Common History Centers.

Group members favored the creation of such historical-memorial centers, which would be nonstate and noncommercial institutions. The co-chairs expressed a readiness to present to their respective governments detailed proposals concerning the creation of the centers.

The participants discussed proposals concerning the organization in April 2010 of ceremonies commemorating the seventieth anniversary of the Katyn crime. The co-chairs will ask the Russian Orthodox Church and the Roman Catholic Church in Poland to jointly honor the victims of the Katyn crime and the other victims of Stalin's regime buried at Katyn.

The group members decided to hold their next session in Smolensk in April 2010, on the occasion of ceremonies to commemorate the crimes perpetrated at Katyn.

The participants agreed on the need to highlight the ninetieth anniversary of the Polish-Soviet war of 1920, including ceremonies at burial sites of war victims and prisoners of war who died in captivity. The participants further noted that it would be desirable, in connection with the tragic anniversary, to present a collection of documents connected with Soviet POWs and to consider the possibility of a historical conference commemorating the anniversary.

The participants commended the leadership of the Polish and Russian foreign ministries for their support, which enhanced the development of the group's activity.

The group's next session is planned in Warsaw in June 2010. Its agenda would include a presentation of the joint publication on difficult matters in Polish-Russian relations.

Final Communiqué on the Meeting of the Polish-Russian Group on Difficult Matters (Warsaw, 4 October 2010)

The Polish-Russian Group on Difficult Matters held its sixth plenary session in Warsaw on 4 October 2010.

Polish deputy foreign minister Henryk Litwin welcomed the participants on behalf of the foreign minister.

The group co-chairs, Prof. Adam D. Rotfeld and academician Anatoly V. Torkunov, reviewed the group's activity since its establishment in the spring of 2008. They particularly focused on events of the past year after the group's Moscow session (9 November 2009) and the co-chairs' meeting in Smolensk (7 April 2010) with the prime ministers of the two countries, Donald Tusk and Vladimir Putin.

The peoples of Poland and Russia were shocked by the tragic air crash in Smolensk on 10 April 2010 that claimed the lives of Polish president Lech Kaczyński and ninety-five other persons, including leading Polish politicians and other public figures, top commanders of the Polish Armed Forces, representatives of the cultural community, and members of the Katyn Families group.

The participants noted the significant contributions to the group's work made by the late deputy foreign minister, Andrzej Kremer, by Secretary of the Council for the Protection of Struggle and Martyrdom Sites Andrzej Przewoźnik, and Katyn Families Federation president Andrzej Sariusz-Skąpski—all of whom perished in the air disaster outside Smolensk.

The spontaneous expressions of deep, heartfelt sympathy extended to Poles by millions of Russians constituted yet another impulse in the process of rapprochement between the two nations.

The co-chairs ascertained that the conclusion of work on the joint publication *White Spots—Black Spots: Difficult Matters in Polish-Russian Relations, 1918–2008* concluded the first stage of the group's activity. The joint publication of the views of Polish and Russian historians, archivists, and researchers on key problems in Polish-Russian relations over the past ninety years marked the first joint attempt to systematize our knowledge about the past of Polish-Russian relations, and it presented to the public diverse positions on issues that had overshadowed mutual relations between Poland and Russia. It was agreed that the co-chairs would ask the ministers of education and higher schooling of the two countries to recommend that the joint publication be added to school libraries as a teaching aid for history teachers. The participants recognized the need for steps to encourage and prepare young scientists to conduct research into Polish-Russian relations.

The participants agreed on the need for further research and access to documents that were not well known to the public or had not yet been investigated. In this context, Polish members referred to the declaration of Foreign Minister Lavrov concerning easier access to Russian Foreign Ministry archives and postulated the gradual preparation of a multivolume collection of diplomatic documents pertaining to Polish-Russian relations during and after the war. Also raised was the matter of exchanging archive documents of particular importance to the national memory of Poles and Russians (the Polish participants mentioned in this context the Belweder Archive, which was of special interest to the Józef Piłsudski Museum currently being established). The Russian side suggested the organization of several scholarly meetings devoted to the ninetieth anniversary of the Riga Treaty, the 1941 Sikorski-Maisky Agreement, and the Polish Armed Forces in the Soviet Union during World War II.

The group welcomed the implementation of the decision by Russian president Dmitry Medvedev concerning systematic declassification and transfer of documents and materials on the Katyn crime to the Polish side.

It was pointed out in this connection that the progress and achievements of the Polish-Russian Group on Difficult Matters had attracted much interest in many countries and earned high praise.

The participants heard a report on the progress of work concerning the establishment under the auspices of the two culture ministers of centers for Polish-Russian dialogue and understanding. This constituted the implementation of a decision by the premiers of the countries, adopted in Sopot (1 September 2009) and confirmed in Smolensk (7 April 2010). In line with the recommendation of the two governments, group members—after the establishment of the centers in

Poland and Russia—could serve as an international consultative council on program issues. It was agreed that group members would become actively involved in research and other projects carried out by the Centers on Polish-Russian Dialogue and Understanding and by other institutions. The mandate of such institutions should include archival investigations and historical research, which could be sponsored by various government departments, including the ministries of science and higher education. Particular attention was devoted to Russia's cooperation with the European Union in the context of the Polish presidency of the EU in 2011. It was recommended that the principle of "changing geometry" be applied in the cooperation of different panels on different projects. The participants also discussed the initiative of tripartite meetings of scientists from Poland, Russia, and Germany.

As suggested by the chairs of the foreign affairs committees of the higher and lower chambers of the two parliaments, joint research into the fixed perceptions of Poles in Russia and Russians in Poland could constitute a new area of cooperation. The relevant materials could become the subject of a Polish-Russian conference, to be attended by scholars and parliamentarians from both countries.

The participants expressed appreciation to the Ecumenical Foundation "Tolerance" for awarding its 2010 medal, Merited for Tolerance, to the Polish-Russian Group on Difficult Matters.

The participants thanked Polish president Bronisław Komorowski for his high assessment of the group's work. Group members particularly appreciated the president's praise for their efforts and encouragement to seek rapprochement and understanding between the two nations.

The parties agreed that, in line with the rule regarding alternate venues, the group's next session would take place in Russia, in spring 2011 (the precise date would be determined through working contacts).

Communiqué on the Extraordinary Session of the Polish-Russian Group on Difficult Matters (Riga, 1 June 2011)

The Polish-Russian Group on Difficult Matters met on the eve of the international conference Poland, Russia, Europe: from War to Peace, held on the ninetieth anniversary of the Riga Peace Treaty. The participants assessed the group's activity during the six months since its previous session in Warsaw (4 October 2010) and considered its program of work and specific proposals for the immediate future.

1. The group co-chairs, Prof. Adam D. Rotfeld and academician Anatoly V. Torkunov, reported in detail on the reception of the joint book *White Spots— Black Spots: Difficult Matters in Polish-Russian Relations (1918–2008),* which had appeared in Polish and Russian, in Warsaw and Moscow, during the last quarter of 2010. Numerous press and scholarly reviews of the volume have appeared in Poland and Russia. The authors of these publications highlighted the pioneering character of the book and its importance in soothing emotions over historical

issues and in lending a substantive, constructive profile to the dialogue between scholars in both countries. The co-chairs briefed the group on their contacts and joint meetings with politicians and academics in Germany, France, Sweden, Denmark, Austria, and other countries. The participants welcomed plans for the co-chairs' meeting with representatives of the diplomatic corps and scientific circles of the Holy See.

2. The participants expressed concern over attempts to disrupt the dialogue and understanding between Poland and Russia. They noted the need for the further popularization of research and scientific work that enhanced links between the two countries.

3. Group members recommended the acceleration of work on an abridged, English-language edition of the book. It was decided to initiate contacts with foreign publishers, who would be offered the manuscript of the joint book after linguistic editing and unification of terminology by an English-language editor. The cost of the publication would be shared by both parties.

4. The participants advocated urgent preparation of a joint report on relations between the European Union and Russia. The report should be prepared before the conclusion of the Polish presidency of the EU. With that in mind, a panel would be appointed to compile a working draft of the report by the end of October 2011.

5. It was decided that parallel works would be initiated on a joint monograph devoted to Polish-Russian relations in the context of security and cooperation in Europe and the world. The chapters of the monograph would consist of "mirror-image" contributions by Polish and Russian authors.

6. The participants welcomed reports by plenipotentiaries of the culture ministers of Poland and Russia concerning the implementation of the two governments' decision to establish Centers for Polish-Russian Dialogue and Understanding, which were beginning activity in both countries. Decisions were still needed on the role, tasks, and composition of the joint International Council of the two centers, with the participation of Polish and Russian members of the group.

7. The participants welcomed the news that preparations were advanced for the First Polish-Russian Media Congress in Wrocław (23–24 June 2011). They listened with interest to a report by a representative of the Foreign Affairs Department of the Russian Orthodox Church concerning its dialogue with the Roman Catholic Church in Poland. The members of the Group on Difficult Matters opined that progress on a joint document by the Russian Orthodox Church and the Catholic Church in Poland would lend Polish-Russian relations a new, spiritual dimension. This dialogue had historic significance and was congruent with the group's goals and tasks; it was religious in character and autonomous.

8. The participants welcomed the Russian side's invitation to Saint Petersburg (7–8 December 2011) for the next session of the group.

Communiqué on the Meeting of the Polish-Russian Group on Difficult Matters (Saint Petersburg, 8 December 2011)

1. The co-chairs reported on the group's activity since its previous meeting, with particular focus on conferences and seminars connected with the group's area of interest, held in Rome and Paris in autumn 2011.

2. The participants devoted special attention to the report *Rethinking EU-Russia Relations,* prepared by group members and invited experts. A presentation of the report took place in Brussels on 25 November 2011. It was agreed that the report required additional editing work and the drafting of annexes on the following topics:

(a) relations between Russia and the EU in the sphere of the "common neighborhood";

(b) international cooperation in the Baltic area—with special reference to the district of Kaliningrad;

(c) Russia's cooperation with the EU in the area of the humanities, education, and science; it was decided that the Polish and Russian sides would exchange texts by the end of March 2012; unified texts would be prepared by mid-May 2012 and presented at the next session of the group.

All three annexes were to be analytical in character, contain specific recommendations, and not exceed fifteen to twenty typewritten pages. Within the next few days, each side would appoint persons responsible for organizational works relating to the three annexes.

3. The parties discussed in detail the English-language edition of the book *White Spots—Black Spots: Difficult Matters in Polish-Russian Relations (1918–2008).* The parties assured each other that the English translations of the texts of Polish and Russian authors were near completion and in the near future would be submitted for verification by English editors. Preparatory works on both sides were expected to be completed in the winter and spring of 2012—including the elaboration of the scientific-methodological apparatus and drafting of comments to the English edition. The Polish and Russian sides would conduct parallel negotiations with foreign publishers who had expressed initial interest in publishing the book. The parties expected that the book would appear by the end of 2012. The parties intended to limit the expenses connected with the book's publication while ensuring its maximum accessibility to English-speaking readers. The Polish and Russian sides would equally share the costs involved in the preparation and publication of the book.

4. The participants also considered the group's future work—including European security issues and the possibility of dialogue between Polish and Russian experts on this subject.

5. The parties discussed specific historical issues as topics for future work and ways of facilitating access to archives.

6. The Polish and Russian members of the group took part in a joint orga-

nizational meeting of the Polish and Russian Centers for Dialogue and Understanding and actively contributed to the discussion on the centers' plans of work in 2012.

7. The group members acquainted themselves with the possibilities of joint research work offered by the Saint Petersburg Russian State Historical Archive, which had hosted the meeting of the group and the two centers.

8. The next session of the Polish-Russian Group on Difficult Matters will be held in Poland on 31 May–1 June 2012.

Communiqué on the Session of the Polish-Russian Group on Difficult Matters (Warsaw, 31 May–1 June 2012)

The latest session of the Polish-Russian Group on Difficult Matters, in its new composition, met in Warsaw on 31 May–1 June 2012 (see enclosed list of participants). The meeting was also attended by top officials of the Polish and Russian Centers for Dialogue and Understanding.

The participants were welcomed by Polish foreign minister Radosław Sikorski, who lauded the group as an important instrument of bilateral dialogue. In another welcoming address, Russian ambassador to Poland Alexander Alexeyev noted the need for broader public access to the results of the group's work and to Polish-Russian dialogue in general.

The two co-chairs, Prof. Adam Daniel Rotfeld and academician Anatoly V. Torkunov, referred to changes in the group's composition and to issues relating to cooperation with the Centers for Polish-Russian Dialogue and Understanding. They took note of foreign ministry and public reactions in both countries to the group's work and touched on general questions relating to Polish-Russian links. The participants also adopted the final decision on the publication of the English edition of *White Spots—Black Spots: Difficult Matters in Polish-Russian Relations (1918–2008)*.

In line with the decisions of the working meeting in Kaliningrad (15 May 2012), group members heard proposals by experts concerning the structure of analytical documents devoted to the mechanisms of bilateral, integration-oriented cooperation in the area of the "common neighborhood" of Russia and the EU; Baltic issues, including local border traffic between Poland and Russia; the strategic culture of the two states; and confidence-building measures.

The participants also considered the mutual recognition of education diplomas and the preparation by the group of a letter on the subject addressed to the appropriate government institutions in Poland and Russia.

The issue of document collections was another topic on the agenda. The participants in the debate on the Polish side included Prof. Władysław Stępniak, director of the Head Office of State Archives, and Dr. Sławomir Dębski, director the Warsaw Center for Polish-Russian Dialogue and Understanding. Contributions on the Russian side were made by A. N. Artizov, head of the Russian State Archives (Rosarkhiv) and chair of the Supervisory Council of the Center for Dialogue and Understanding in Moscow; Ambassador P. V. Stegny, director of the Moscow Center; and Ambassador A. I. Kuznetsov, director of the History and Documentation Department of the Russian Ministry of Foreign Affairs.

The participants heard a briefing by Prof. Natalia S. Lebedeva on the search for additional documents concerning the Katyn crime and, in particular, the so-called Belarusian list of victims of the crime. The Polish Center for Dialogue and Understanding conveyed to the Russian side a list of Polish citizens whose names were believed to constitute part of the "Belarusian list."

Following a discussion on these and other subjects, the session participants agreed on a program of action for the next six months. In particular, they decided to:

1. Prepare the conception of a new three-volume publication of documents concerning Polish-Soviet relations in the years 1918–45 and, optionally, of a separate volume of documents concerning the years 1989–91.

2. Elaborate the structure and content of a new publication on Polish-Soviet relations in the years 1939–45. The book should cover several themes: the politico-conceptual tenets of the two sides, their diplomatic activities, and the relations between Polish and Soviet partisan units and between the Polish resistance and the Red Army.

3. The participants discussed the proposed preparation by the Warsaw Center for Dialogue and Understanding of a documentary research project on relations between the Red Army and the Polish Home Army and considered the possibility of Russian researchers becoming involved in the project.

4. Finalize the contract with the publisher of the English edition of the book *White Spots—Black Spots: Difficult Matters in Polish-Russian Relations (1918–2008)*; the group would become involved in broad distribution of the book.

5. The participants agreed to recommend the use of public television for promoting the idea of Polish-Russian dialogue and understanding.

The participants approved the initiative to have a seminar, Christianity in the Twentieth Century: Memory, Forgiveness, Reconciliation, which would be attended by scholars and prominent members of the clergy of the Roman Catholic Church in Poland and the Russian Orthodox Church. The meeting would take place at the invitation of the Higher Theological Seminary in Kraków. The date and list of participants would be agreed upon before the visit to Poland (in August 2012) of Kirill, patriarch of Moscow and All Russia.

During the Warsaw session, the participants also addressed the issue of cooperation and interdependence between the group and the Centers for Dialogue and Understanding; the heads of the centers—S. Dębski and P. Stegny—detailed the premises for work and cooperation between the two institutions. In particular, they focused on the possibility of stimulating youth exchanges and the implementation of joint research and cultural-educational projects. Group members postulated that the centers monitor all undertakings in both countries designed to advance Polish-Russian dialogue and understanding.

A Polish-Russian conference in October 2012 devoted to the period of Smuta [Time of troubles] and the shaping of Polish and Russian statehood in the seventeenth century would be the next joint undertaking of the centers and the group.

President of the Republic of Poland Bronisław Komorowski received the members of the group and heads of the centers at Belweder Palace in Warsaw. In recognition of the outstanding services of the academician Anatoly V. Torkunov in the development of Polish-Russian dialogue, President Komorowski decorated him with the Commander's Cross with Star of the Order of Merit of the Republic of Poland.

The next session of the Polish-Russian Group on Difficult Matters is scheduled for autumn 2012 (with Kaliningrad being considered as the venue).

Final Communiqué on the Results of the Tenth Session of the Polish-Russian Group on Difficult Matters (Moscow, 3 December 2012)

On 3 December 2012, Moscow hosted another meeting of the Polish-Russian Group on Difficult Matters. Also attending were members of the councils of the Centers for Dialogue and Understanding and representatives of the foreign affairs ministries of the two states.

The session was opened by Deputy Foreign Minister of the Russian Federation S. A. Riabkov, who noted the significance and model character of the Polish-Russian dialogue and the group's activity in the process of defusing tensions and establishing additional channels of cooperation between Russia and its neighbors. The deputy minister underlined the consistent support of the Russian Ministry of Foreign Affairs for the group's activity.

The group co-chairs reviewed its work and activities of group members since the previous meeting. They also presented their own analyses of the internal political situations in Russia and Poland and their impact on bilateral relations.

Particular attention was devoted to the visit to Poland by the patriarch of Moscow and All Russia and the Joint Message of the Russian Orthodox Church and the Roman Catholic Church in Poland to the faithful and peoples of the two states.

The meeting participants also addressed issues connected with the erection at Smolensk of a monument to the victims of the airplane crash of 10 April 2010 and transfer to Poland of the airliner wreckage, which was still in Russia. It was noted that the delay in resolving these issues was creating an unhealthy, emotion-charged atmosphere in bilateral relations.

The participants welcomed the conclusion of work on the English-language edition of a joint publication on difficult issues in Polish-Russian relations. The co-chairs stressed the importance of publicizing information about the book in the academic communities of anglophone countries. In particular, it was suggested that the book be presented at the International Studies Association convention in the United States, in April 2013.

The meeting approved the conception of the respective parts of a multivolume edition of documents on Polish-Soviet relations and appointed the editors of the respective volumes. It was decided to begin parallel work on four volumes covering the period 1918–45 and to consider the additional publication of volumes devoted to the postwar period. The elaboration of detailed guidelines for the first four volumes would begin in the near future, and these would be on the agenda of a working meeting of the editorial group in Warsaw, in January 2013.

The participants discussed in detail a historical-archival project concerning Polish-Soviet relations during World War II. The project is being implemented with the backing of the Centers for Dialogue and Understanding of the two states, as well as the Federal Archives Agency of Russia and Poland's Head Office of State Archives. The project is intended to yield a collection of documents pertaining to the mutual relations between partisan and underground groupings in the territories of Poland, Western Ukraine, Western Belarus, and Lithuania. The collection is designed to reflect the complexity of the political, social, and military situation in territories behind the front line.

In view of the forthcoming seventieth anniversary of the end of World War II, the parties also agreed to prepare a joint publication, in which—similarly to books issued earlier under the group's auspices—Polish and Russian authors would present their views on all aspects of Polish-Soviet relations in the years 1939–45, including relations between the Polish Home Army and the Red Army. The authors would base their work on new documents and the group's methodological experience in seeking compromise.

The group members discussed in detail the theses of two studies, scheduled for completion in spring 2013. One of the studies concerns Polish-Russian dialogue in the area of confidence-building measures and security, with reference to the possible contribution of our states to ensuring the stability of all Europe. The second study will contain a minute analysis of the possibility of legal and institutional harmonization of various multilateral frameworks of collaboration in the area of the "common neighborhood" of Russia and the European Union.

The two group co-chairs pledged to make every effort to bring about the speediest possible signing of an agreement on the mutual recognition of documents on education between Poland and Russia.

The directors of the Polish and Russian Centers for Dialogue and Understanding delivered detailed reports on the activity of the respective centers in 2012 and their plans for 2013. The group gave its full approval to the plans and also to a list of books selected for translation into Polish and Russian, as well as to the proposed methods of their distribution in Poland and Russia.

The participants noted the need for involving broad social circles—including the business community—in the activity of the group and the centers.

The parties agreed to present a project of the group's activities in specific fields of bilateral relations at the December session of the Committee for Polish-Russian Cooperation Strategy.

The next session of the group is to take place in spring 2013. The precise venue and date will be determined in due course.

Final Communiqué on the Results of the Eleventh Session of the Polish-Russian Group on Difficult Matters (Gdańsk, 7–8 June 2013)

On 7–8 June 2013, Gdańsk hosted the latest meeting of the Polish-Russian Group on Difficult Matters. Also attending were members of the International Council of the Centers for Dialogue and Understanding and representatives of the foreign ministries of the two states.

In their opening statements, the group co-chairs presented their analysis and assessment of the internal political processes in Poland and Russia and the impact thereof on the mutual relations between the two states. Progress has been achieved on many issues. In particular, this applies to Polish-Russian links in the spheres of economy and trade, as well as cooperation in the areas of culture and science.

The co-chairs also reported on the progress of work agreed upon at the group's Moscow session (3 December 2012) and suggested topics of possible joint projects connected with the upcoming anniversaries in 2014 and 2015 of great historical events, marked in both Poland and Russia. These include the one-hundredth anniversary of World War I, the seventieth anniversary of the Warsaw Uprising (1 August 2014), the anniversary of the liberation by the Red Army of the Auschwitz-Birkenau death camp (January 2015), and the anniversary of victory over the Third Reich in World War II (9 May 2015).

The participants received a detailed briefing on and assessment of the results of the Polish-Russian agreement on visa-free travel of Polish nationals to the district of Kaliningrad and of Russian nationals traveling within the extended free-movement zone in northeastern Poland, adjacent to the territory of the Russian Federation.

The group welcomed a report on the collaboration of the Polish and Russian archive services, presented by the directors of the relevant institutions.

The heads of Polish and Russian documentation and research projects briefed the participants on the methodology of works on a joint collection of documents titled *The Soviet Union and the Polish Political-Military Underground* and on the progress of work on a collection of documents connected with Polish-Soviet relations in the years 1918–45. In this context, the participants made note of issues evoking particular public interest, with special reference to unpublished documents relating to the Augustów Roundup in 1945 and the tragic events in Western Ukraine in 1943 (the Volhynia Massacre).

The participants also discussed bilateral cooperation in the sphere of education and matters relating to an agreement on mutual recognition of education documents—with reference to recommendations adopted by the Regions Forum in Nizhny Novgorod (May 2013).

Next, the directors of the Polish and Russian Centers for Dialogue and Understanding reported on their activities and suggested ways of harmonizing their work and developing collaboration with other organizations.

The group expressed its appreciation to Ambassador Pyotr Stegnyi, former director of the Moscow center, for his work in establishing the center and overseeing its initial stage of activity.

The participants also addressed issues that hinder the implementation of joint projects. In this context, the Polish side mentioned certain unresolved issues, including the delay in the return to Poland of the wreckage of the Tu-154 M airliner, which crashed at Smolensk on 10 April 2010, and in the erection of a monument to the crash victims.

The Polish and Russian members of the group recognized the highly positive significance of the progress achieved in relations between the leaders and faithful of the Roman Catholic Church in Poland and the Russian Orthodox Church. They underlined the special importance of the Joint Message of 17 August 2012, which offers hope for the implementation of the goals pursued by the authors of the document—the heads of the two churches.

Next, the mayor of Gdańsk briefed those present on the experiences of regional cooperation, with special reference to visa-free local border traffic by Polish and Russian nationals.

The group participants also met with the former Polish president and leader of Solidarity, Lech Wałęsa.

The group acquainted itself with the highly positive assessment of its work by the international political and scientific communities and intergovernmental organizations.

The group members ascertained that its work had proceeded in a businesslike and constructive atmosphere, in a spirit of mutual understanding that facilitates the eradication of ingrown prejudices and stereotypes, which undermine mutual confidence.

The next meeting of the group is to take place in Kaliningrad, in November 2013. The precise date will be determined in due course.

Communiqué on the Meeting of the Polish-Russian Group on Difficult Matters (Kaliningrad, 16 November 2013)

On 16 November 2013, Kaliningrad hosted another meeting of the Polish-Russian Group on Difficult Matters. The gathering was also attended by the heads of the Polish and Russian Centers for Dialogue and Understanding and representatives of the foreign ministries of the two countries.

The meeting of the group coincided with the work of the Second Polish-Russian Media Forum, which brought together more than one hundred experts and journalists. Group members had the opportunity to attend various public events and informal working meetings held in the framework of the forum. For this reason the group's formal meeting was shorter than usual.

Plenary sessions of the forum were attended by group representatives and members: Prof. Adam D. Rotfeld, academician Anatoly V. Torkunov, Dr. Sławomir Dębski, Prof. Andrei N. Artizov, Dr. Artem V. Malgin, Prof. Inessa S. Yazhborovskaya, and Prof. Gennady F. Matveev.

The main item on the group's agenda consisted of a report by the directors of the Polish and Russian Centers for Dialogue and Understanding on the activity of the two institutions in 2013 and their plans for 2014. The presentation by the directors, Yuri K. Bondarenko and Sławomir Dębski, was the subject of a highly animated and often critical discussion. The director of the Russian Center explained that many of the problems at issue were connected with the fact that the preceding year had been the first full year of the institution's activity under his leadership.

The participants highlighted the need for coordination of the two centers' activities, including implementation of joint projects designed to address key historical issues as well as current events. Group members called for broader involvement of young people in the activity of the two centers and greater participation by various social and business communities capable of supporting dialogue between Poland and Russia.

The group co-chairs informed the center directors of the need for closer reflection on issues addressed at group meetings and for their incorporation in the work plans of the two centers. The directors were advised to prepare and submit a plan of joint undertakings.

The one-hundredth anniversary of World War I, which had a fundamental impact on the fates of Poland and Russia, was prominently mentioned among the historical events requiring treatment by the group and the centers.

The group participants reviewed the progress of work on documentary publications devoted to Polish-Russian relations in the years 1943–45. Prof. Mikhail M. Narinsky briefed the gathering on the conclusions of a coordinating meeting of the editors of a multivolume publication of documents on Polish-Soviet relations, held before the group's session.

The heads of the Polish and Russian state archives—Prof. Władysław Stępniak (Poland) and Prof. Andrei N. Artizov (Russia)—provided detailed reports on the extent of archival work and issues pertaining to the commemoration of history.

Other meeting participants—Dr. Andrzej Towpik, Dr. Leszek Jesień, and Dr. Artem V. Malgin—underlined the need for accelerating ongoing work on studies devoted to security issues and integration initiatives in Europe.

Two new publications, issued under the auspices and with support of the group and the Centers for Dialogue and Understanding, were unveiled during the meeting of the group and the work of the media forum. They included the Russian edition of a collective work titled *The Forgotten Peace: Riga Peace Treaty of 1921* and a monograph by the eminent Polish studies expert and former group member, the late Nikolai I. Bukharin.

On November 16, following the group's meeting, the patriarch of Moscow and All Russia, Kirill, who was paying a pastoral visit to Kaliningrad at the time, met with the Polish co-chair, Prof. Adam D. Rotfeld. The patriarch, who consistently supports Polish-Russian dialogue, thanked the group—and especially the Polish co-chair—for their contribution to rapprochement between the two nations. During the meeting, the patriarch thus described the process of drafting the message of the Roman Catholic Church and the Russian Orthodox Church, signed on 17 August 2012 at the Royal Castle in Warsaw: "We proceeded from both directions toward our goal, with full understanding of the responsibility and full awareness that there was no other way. Regardless of the obstacles we encounter, nothing must be allowed to hinder our progress."

The Group on Difficult Matters expressed appreciation to the Emmanuel Kant Baltic Federal University for its assistance in preparing the group's session and the media forum.

The next meeting of the group will take place in Lublin in May–June 2014. The precise date will be determined in due course.

∙ ∙

THE LETTER OF THE CO-CHAIRS OF THE GROUP ON DIFFICULT MATTERS TO THE FOREIGN MINISTERS OF POLAND AND RUSSIA

∙ ∙

Moscow, 22 June 2009
Minister of Foreign Affairs of the Republic of Poland
Radosław Sikorski
Minister of Foreign Affairs of the Russian Federation
Sergei Lavrov

Excellencies,

As you are aware, on 28–29 May 2009, the group held in Kraków its third meeting, during which the participants agreed on the final formula and structure of the joint publication devoted to complex problems arising from their common history and exchanged the prepared texts. They also discussed and endorsed another joint publication prepared with the group's input, devoted to the genesis of World War II. The group members further reviewed issues connected with the involvement of the Russian Orthodox Church and the Roman Catholic Church in Poland in the bilateral social dialogue, with particular reference to historical issues. As usual, the group's work was conducted in a constructive and friendly atmosphere.

The participants noted on this occasion that, with regard to the Katyn crime, the group's work had attained the limits of its competency and that it could not ensure further progress without the appropriate support of the foreign ministers and leaders of the two states.

Mindful that the forthcoming seventieth anniversary of World War II and the anniversary of the Katyn tragedy might become an additional factor evoking negative emotions over historical issues and hindering the development of relations between our states, the group enjoined the co-chairs to draft concrete proposals concerning settlement of the Katyn crime question and to advise the foreign ministers and leaders of Poland and Russia of their content.

The participants unanimously supported recommending to the leaders of the two states that joint new measures be taken to commemorate the victims of Katyn and that free access to all documents connected with this matter be ensured.

The group's members believe it essential to give the relevant efforts of the parties a durable and institutional character so as to jointly and conclusively remove the issue of the Katyn crime from the agenda of bilateral relations.

Guided by the above motives and also opinions expressed during meetings, the co-chairs propose that consideration be given to the establishment in Russia (e.g., in Smolensk) and in Poland (in Warsaw) of two Polish-Russian centers concerned with preserving memory as well as documenting and conducting archival works.

The institutions thus established (e.g., Polish-Russian Houses of Common History) would also be concerned more broadly with issues relating to historical-memorial matters.

In particular, these institutions could fulfill the following functions:

- Commemorating the victims and passing moral-political judgment on the perpetrators of the crime
- Maintaining burial sites in proper condition, including those connected with the Katyn crime as well as other Polish and Russian burial sites on the territories of both states
- Countering attempts to falsify history by promoting historical research
- Conducting educational activity, primarily addressed to the young generation

The leaders of the two states might appoint the persons responsible for executing this decision.

The adoption of a joint decision by the governments of the two states and its public announcement during the visit to Poland by the prime minister of the Russian Federation, planned this autumn, would be an important step in improving and shaping a new type of mutual Polish-Russian relations. Such a decision would remove the significant obstacles that in recent years have had negative impact on Polish-Russian relations and are being exploited by certain circles to inflame unfriendly emotions.

The meetings of the co-chairs with high-ranking hierarchs of the Roman Catholic Church in Poland and with the patriarchate of the Russian Orthodox Church have convinced us that the Church in Poland and the Orthodox Church in Russia are prepared to actively engage in resolving this issue and, more broadly, in the process of rapprochement of the two nations.

Professor   Academician
Adam D. Rotfeld   Anatoly V. Torkunov

INDEX